THREE KINGDOMS

THREE KINGDOMS

A HISTORICAL NOVEL

ABRIDGED EDITION

Attributed to
LUO GUANZHONG

Translated from the Chinese with Afterword by
MOSS ROBERTS

Foreign Languages Press /
University of California Press
Beijing · Berkeley · Los Angeles · London

University of California Press
Berkeley and Los Angeles, California

University of California Press, Ltd.
London, England

© 1999 by
The Regents of the University of California

Unabridged edition published by
University of California Press
Berkeley and Los Angeles, California
University of California Press, Ltd.
London, England
and by
Foreign Languages Press
Beijing, People's Republic of China

©1991 by
The Regents of the University of California

Library of Congress Cataloging-in-Publication Data

Lo, Kuan-chung, ca. 1330–ca. 1400:
[San kuo chih yen i. English. Selections]
    Three kingdoms : a historical novel / attributed to Luo Guanzhong:
translated from the Chinese with afterword by Moss Roberts.—
Abridged ed.
        p.   cm.
    ISBN 0-520-21584-2 (alk. paper).—ISBN 0-520-21585-0 (pbk : alk.
    paper)
    1. China—History—Three Kingdoms, 220–265—Fiction.
I. Roberts, Moss, 1937-   . II. Title.
PL2690.S3E5325   1998
895.1'346—dc21

                                                                98-39516
                                                                CIP

Printed in the United States of America

08   07   06
9   8   7

The paper used in this publication is both acid-free and totally chlorine-free
(TCF). It meets the minimum requirements of ANSI/NISO Z39.48-1992
(R 1997) (*Permanence of Paper*). ∞

CONTENTS

PREFACE TO THE ABRIDGED EDITION

This abridged translation of *Three Kingdoms,* based on the University of California Press—Foreign Languages Press edition (Berkeley, 1991, Beijing, 1994), has been designed to serve students in courses on Asian history and literature as well as comparative literature. Where necessary the excerpts have been connected by bridging material written by the translator to ease the reader's transitions from one section of the novel to another and to preserve to the fullest extent possible the main lines of the narrative. Working closely with University of California Press editor Doug Arava, the translator has tried to strike an appropriate balance between the epic dimensions of the whole novel and the need of students and the reading public for a relatively convenient and manageable way to become acquainted with the work.

The extensive scholarly apparatus of the unabridged edition has been altered as follows: all footnotes to the text and to the Afterword have been removed, but the complete Afterword has been retained. Those who wish to know more of the novel's historical and literary context, or who wish to pursue particular problems of character, incident, or style, may benefit from consulting the unabridged edition. For convenience of reference to the unabridged edition chapter numbers and titles have been retained even for shortened chapters.

ACKNOWLEDGMENTS
TO THE
UNABRIDGED EDITION

A number of people have made this project possible and helped bring it to completion—first of all my teachers, whose devotion to the subject matters of sinology has inspired me and guided my studies. Among the most influential were the late P. A. Boodberg, who instructed me in ancient Chinese and the connections between language and history, and W. T. de Bary, whose instruction in Chinese thought has stood me in good stead as a translator. As a student, I also benefited from the devoted labor of many language lecturers at Columbia University and the University of California at Berkeley, who shared their learning without stint.

This project first took shape as an abridged *Three Kingdoms,* which Pantheon Books published in 1976 for use in college classes. That abridged version has its limitations and its mistakes, however, and I harbored the hope that some day the opportunity to translate the entire text would present itself. That opportunity came in 1982 when the late Luo Liang, deputy editor-in-chief at the Foreign Languages Press, proposed that I translate the whole novel for the Press. He and Israel Epstein arranged for me to spend the year 1983–84 at the FLP as a foreign expert. I arrived in Beijing and began work in September of 1983. At the FLP I enjoyed the friendship and benefited from the advice of a number of colleagues. I wish to thank the staff of the English section, in particular the senior staff, for the help and encouragement that made that first year of work so pleasantly memorable. I was also fortunate to have been awarded a National Endowment for the Arts fellowship for the translation.

In the middle stages of the project Xu Mingqiang, vice director at FLP, and his colleague Huang Youyi, deputy editor-in-chief, facilitated my work in many ways. I am particularly grateful that they arranged to have the late C. C. Yin (Ren Jiazhen) serve as the FLP's reader. Mr. Yin read the whole manuscript with painstaking care and his recommendations improved the translation considerably. I thank him for sharing his learning and experience with me. At the same time I benefited from the erudition of my life-long teacher, friend, and colleague C. N. Tay, now retired from New York University. Professor Tay served as my reader, and many of his suggestions have been incorporated into the translation.

During 1984 Brian George of the University of California Press visited the FLP and helped to prepare the way for joint FLP-University of California Press publication. I thank him for his interest in my work and his encouragement over the long years of this project. William McClung and James Clark of the University of California Press arranged the joint publication with the late Zhao Yihe of the FLP. Shortly thereafter, the University of California Press, the FLP, and I concluded that the Western reader would be best served by adding a full set of notes and an extended commentary on the text. This format was adopted, and the translation became eligible for support from the National Endowment for the Humanities; in 1985 and 1986 I was fortunate to hold a fifteen-month fellowship from the NEH that relieved me of half my teaching duties.

The translation owes much to the wisdom of John S. Service, whom the University of California Press engaged to serve as its reader when the manuscript was completed. His stylistic grace has refined many a phrase, and his pertinent and penetrating queries on both the text and the introduction were of great value to me. Having so demanding and knowledgeable a reader turned the arduous last years of the project into an energizing experience. I also wish to thank Deborah Rudolph for contributing her considerable sinological and proofreading skills. In the later stages of the project William McClung and Betsey Scheiner of the University of California Press were generous with their encouragement and good counsel, lightening my task and my spirits.

Another scholar I wish to thank is Robert Hegel, who read the first half of the manuscript for the University of California Press. I made use of a significant number of his suggestions. Chauncey S. Goodrich kindly read the introduction in draft and suggested useful changes; these too have been incorporated. I would like to thank as well my friend James Peck; although he did not work directly on the manuscript, his thoughtful comments have widened the view on many issues. Mr. Peck was the editor for the abridged version published by Pantheon, and his continued interest in the project has been encouraging.

The abovementioned, by giving so generously of their time and talent, have improved this project greatly. Errors and doubtful points surely remain, and for these I take full responsibility. A word of recognition is also due to C. H. Brewitt-Taylor, whose 1925 translation of *Three Kingdoms* I read long before gathering enough Chinese to confront the original.

To the students in my Chinese language and literature classes, my thanks for twenty years of challenge and excitement in what has been (at least for me) a learning experience; and to my colleagues in the East Asian Studies Program of Washington Square College, New York University, my appreciation for the years of sustaining companionship and critical interchange.

To my mother, Helen, who takes a loving interest in my work, my gratitude for years of support and encouragement. The translation is dedicated to my wife, Florence, who serves the poorer citizens of New York City as a Legal Services attorney in family law.

Moss Roberts—1991

FOREWORD
TO THE UNABRIDGED EDITION
John S. Service

In 1942, during China's war against Japan, I happened to be a solitary American traveling with a party of Chinese from Chengdu to Lanzhou and beyond. They were officials and engineers of the National Resources Commission, with a sprinkling of journalists. All were college graduates; many had advanced degrees from foreign study. We rode together intimately in a small bus, and our first main objective was Hanzhong in southern Shaanxi.

Almost from the start I noticed that my companions were having vigorous discussions that seemed to involve the old names of various towns that our road passed through. Changing place-names are one of the problems of Chinese history, and I paid little attention. About the third day the discussions could no longer be ignored. Our youngest member, the *Dagong bao* correspondent, excitedly announced that the walled town we were approaching was the site of Zhuge Liang's "Empty City Stratagem." The whole area we were passing through, it turned out, had been the scene of many hard-fought campaigns during the wars of the Three Kingdoms.

Years before, as a boy in China, I had heard vaguely of the famous novel. Travel in Sichuan in those days was by sedan chair. About once an hour the bearers would set us down while they regained strength at a tea shop. Sometimes, sitting at a small raised table at the rear, there would be a storyteller. To my queries, my patient father usually replied: "Probably something from *Three Kingdoms*." Also, we occasionally saw a snatch of Chinese opera. Again, it seemed to be "something from *Three Kingdoms*." But the tea shop rests were brief, and missionary families did not spend much time at the Chinese opera. Having read about King Arthur and his knights of the round table, I decided that *Three Kingdoms* must be something of the same: romantic myths of a misty never-never land of long ago. It was startling to find that for these men of modern China it was fact and history. Furthermore, these tales of martial valor and deepest loyalty had special relevance for them in that time of foreign aggression—with Chinese resistance being based on the actual area of Liu Bei's old kingdom of Shu.

Eventually, of course, I read *Three Kingdoms*. It was like donning a special pair of glasses. Our family's life while I was growing up in Sichuan had been dominated by the cataclysmic ebb and flow of local warlord politics (having the misfortune to be both rich and populous, Sichuan perhaps surpassed all other provinces as a "warlord *tianxia*"). Now the dramatic posturings and righteous manifestos, the unending intrigues and sudden changes of alliances, the forays and retreats and occasional battles, even the actual tactics used—all had a familiar ring. The whole cast of players, it seemed, had absorbed the stories and lessons of *Three Kingdoms* and could not forget them.

It was not only the warlords who found guidance and inspiration in *Three Kingdoms*. After the success of the communists' Long March, the Guomindang spent the years from 1934 to 1937 in largely fruitless efforts to obliterate all traces of the remnants left behind. It is recorded that the military leader of the old Eyuwan base area "was an avid reader, though not apparently of Marxist books. His favorite works included . . . *The Romance of the Three Kingdoms.* [This] he carried with him always, while fighting or marching, and he consulted it as a military manual between battles."

The Guomindang, too, was not immune. When Chiang Kai-shek commissioned Dai Li in 1932 to set up a military secret service, he is reported to have instructed Dai to look for an organizational ethos in the Chinese traditional novels. Thus Dai's organization adopted operational techniques from the KGB, the Gestapo, and eventually the FBI, but it was built as a sworn brotherhood devoted to benevolence and righteousness and held together by bonds of mutual loyalty and obligation—with a clear model in *Three Kingdoms*.

One could go on. But perhaps I have sufficiently made the

point that *Three Kingdoms* continues to have vitality in Chinese attitudes and behavior. That fact alone makes it important to us outsiders who seek to know and understand China.

There is another important reason, more general and non-utilitarian, why *Three Kingdoms* well merits a reading. For at least four hundred years it has continued to be a favorite of the world's largest public. The literate of China read and reread it; those who can not read learn it (perhaps even more intensely) from story-tellers and opera and word of mouth. It is, simply, a terrific story. Every element is there: drama and suspense, valor and cowardice, loyalty and betrayal, power and subtlety, chivalry and statecraft, the obligations of ruler and subject, conflicts in the basic ties of brotherhood and lineage. By any criterion, I suggest, it is an important piece of world literature.

We are fortunate, therefore, to have this new complete and, for the first time, annotated translation by Moss Roberts. Professor Roberts has admirably preserved the vigor and flavor of the Chinese text. His erudition and patience have produced a clarity of language and yet enable us to enjoy the subtleties and wordplays of the original. His translations of the poems, important in the story, are often inspired.

Though urging the reader on, I cannot promise that it will be an easy read. The story, admittedly, is long and complex. We are doubly fortunate, then, that Professor Roberts has complemented his excellent translation with background information and the translated notes and commentary by the editor of the traditional Chinese version of the novel. With the help of his research and the guidance of the Chinese commentary, the way is greatly eased. Few, I hope, will falter and thus fail fully to enjoy this absorbing, rewarding, and majestic novel.

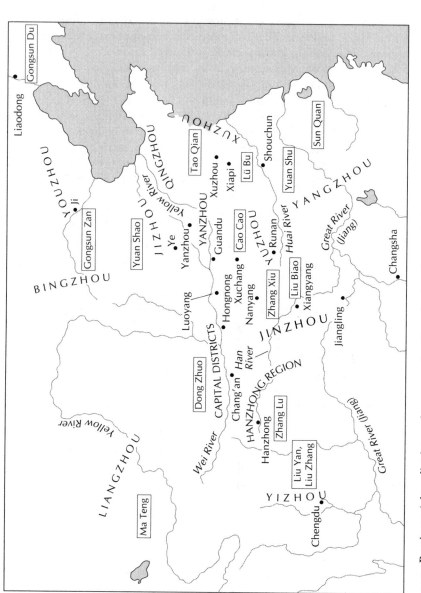

MAP. Provinces (*zhou*), districts and towns, and military leaders (names in boxes) at the end of the Han dynasty. SOURCE: Lin Chunfen, *Sanguo Shihua* (Beijing, rbd no. 1988)

THREE KINGDOMS

A Historical Novel

ABRIDGED EDITION

On and on the Great River rolls, racing east.
Of proud and gallant heroes its white-tops leave no trace,
As right and wrong, pride and fall turn all at once unreal.
Yet ever the green hills stay
To blaze in the west-waning day.

Fishers and woodsmen comb the river isles.
White-crowned, they've seen enough of spring and autumn tide
To make good company over the wine jar,
Where many a famed event
Provides their merriment.

From Ershiwu shi tanci

CHAPTER 1

Three Bold Spirits Plight Mutual Faith in the Peach Garden; Heroes and Champions Win First Honors Fighting the Yellow Scarves

Here begins our tale. The empire, long divided, must unite; long united, must divide. Thus it has ever been. In the closing years of the Zhou dynasty seven kingdoms warred among themselves until the kingdom of Qin prevailed and absorbed the other six. But Qin soon fell, and on its ruins two opposing kingdoms, Chu and Han, fought for mastery until the kingdom of Han prevailed and absorbed its rival, as Qin had done before. The Han court's rise to power began when the Supreme Ancestor slew a white serpent, inspiring an uprising that ended with Han's ruling a unified empire.

Two hundred years later, after Wang Mang's usurpation, Emperor Guang Wu restored the dynasty, and Han emperors ruled for another two hundred years down to the reign of Xian, after whom the realm split into three kingdoms. The cause of Han's fall may be traced to the reigns of Xian's two predecessors, Huan and Ling. Huan drove from office and persecuted officials of integrity and ability, giving all his trust to his eunuchs. After Ling succeeded Huan as emperor, Regent-Marshal Dou Wu and Imperial Guardian Chen Fan, joint sustainers of the throne, planned to execute the power-abusing eunuch Cao Jie and his cohorts. But the plot came to light, and Dou Wu and Chen Fan were themselves put to death. From then on, the Minions of the Palace knew no restraint.

On the fifteenth day of the fourth month of the second year of the reign Established Calm [Jian Ning A.D. 169], the Emperor arrived at the Great Hall of Benign Virtue for the full-moon ancestral rites. As he was about to seat himself, a strong wind began issuing out of a corner of the hall. From the same direction

3

a green serpent appeared, slid down off a beam, and coiled itself on the throne. The Emperor fainted and was rushed to his private chambers. The assembled officials fled. The next moment the serpent vanished, and a sudden thunderstorm broke. Rain laced with hailstones pelted down for half the night, wrecking countless buildings.

In the second month of the fourth year of Established Calm an earthquake struck Luoyang, the capital, and tidal waves swept coastal dwellers out to sea. In the first year of Radiant Harmony [Guang He, A.D. 178] hens were transformed into roosters. And on the first day of the sixth month a murky cloud more than one hundred spans in length floated into the Great Hall of Benign Virtue. The next month a secondary rainbow was observed in the Chamber of the Consorts. Finally, a part of the cliffs of the Yuan Mountains plunged to earth. All these evil portents, and more, appeared—too many to be dismissed as isolated signs.

Emperor Ling called on his officials to explain these disasters and omens. A court counselor, Cai Yong, argued bluntly that the secondary rainbow and the transformation of the hens were the result of interference in government by empresses and eunuchs. The Emperor merely read the report, sighed, and withdrew.

The eunuch Cao Jie observed this session unseen and informed his associates. They framed Cai Yong in another matter, and, dismissed from office, he retired to his village. After that a vicious gang of eunuchs known as the Ten Regular Attendants— Zhang Rang, Zhao Zhong, Feng Xu, Duan Gui, Cao Jie, Hou Lan, Jian Shuo, Cheng Kuang, Xia Yun, and Guo Sheng—took charge. Zhang Rang gained the confidence of the Emperor, who called him "Nuncle." Court administration became so corrupt that across the land men's thoughts turned to rebellion, and outlaws swarmed like hornets.

One rebel group, the Yellow Scarves, was organized by three brothers from the Julu district—Zhang Jue, Zhang Bao, and Zhang Liang. Zhang Jue had failed the official provincial-level examination and repaired to the hills where he gathered medicinal herbs. One day he met an ancient mystic, emerald-eyed and with a youthful face, gripping a staff of goosefoot wood. The old man summoned Zhang Jue into a cave where he placed in his hands a sacred book in three volumes. "Here is the *Essential*

Arts for the Millennium," he said. "Now that you have it, spread its teachings far and wide as Heaven's messenger for the salvation of our age. But think no seditious thoughts, or retribution will follow." Zhang Jue asked the old man's name, and he replied, "The Old Hermit From Mount Hua Summit—Zhuangzi, the Taoist sage." Then he changed into a puff of pure breeze and was gone.

Zhang Jue applied himself to the text day and night. By acquiring such arts as summoning the wind and invoking the rain, he became known as the Master of the Millennium. During the first month of the first year of the reign Central Stability [Zhong Ping, A.D. 184], a pestilence spread through the land. Styling himself Great and Worthy Teacher, Zhang Jue distributed charms and potions to the afflicted. He had more than five hundred followers, each of whom could write the charms and recite the spells. They traveled widely, and wherever they passed, new recruits joined until Zhang Jue had established thirty-six commands—ranging in size from six or seven thousand to over ten thousand—under thirty-six chieftains titled general or commander.

A seditious song began to circulate at this time:

> The pale sky is on the wane,
> Next, a yellow one shall reign;
> The calendar's rotation
> Spells fortune for the nation.

Jue ordered the words "new cycle" chalked on the front gate of every house, and soon the name Zhang Jue, Great and Worthy Teacher, was hailed throughout the eight provinces of the realm—Qingzhou, Youzhou, Xuzhou, Jizhou, Jingzhou, Yangzhou, Yanzhou, and Yuzhou. At this point Zhang Jue had his trusted follower Ma Yuanyi bribe the eunuch Feng Xu to work inside the court on behalf of the rebels. Then Zhang Jue made a proposal to his two brothers: "Popular support is the hardest thing to win. Today the people favor us. Why waste this chance to seize the realm for ourselves?"

Zhang Jue had yellow banners made ready, fixed the date for the uprising, and sent one of his followers, Tang Zhou, to inform the agent at court, the eunuch Feng Xu. Instead, Tang Zhou reported the imminent insurrection to the palace. The Emperor summoned Regent He Jin to arrest and behead Ma Yuanyi. This done, Feng Xu and his group were seized and jailed.

His plot exposed, Zhang Jue mustered his forces in great haste. Titling himself General of Heaven, his first brother General of the Earth, and his second brother General of Men, he addressed his massed followers: "Han's fated end is near. A new sage is due to appear. Let one and all obey Heaven and follow the true cause so that we may rejoice in the millennium."

From the four corners of the realm the common folk, nearly half a million strong, bound their heads with yellow scarves and followed Zhang Jue in rebellion, gathering such force that the government troops scattered on the rumor of their approach. Regent-Marshal He Jin appealed to the Emperor to order every district to defend itself and every warrior to render distinguished service in putting down the uprising. Meanwhile, the regent also gave three Imperial Corps commanders—Lu Zhi, Huangfu Song, and Zhu Jun—command of three elite field armies with orders to bring the rebels to justice.

As for Zhang Jue's army, it began advancing on Youzhou district. The governor, Liu Yan, was a native of Jingling county in Jiangxia and a descendant of Prince Gong of Lu of the imperial clan. Threatened by the approaching rebels, Liu Yan summoned Commandant Zou Jing for his estimate of the situation. "They are many," said Jing, "and we are few. The best course, Your Lordship, is to recruit an army quickly to deal with the enemy." The governor agreed and issued a call for volunteers loyal to the throne.

The call was posted in Zhuo county, where it drew the attention of a man of heroic mettle. This man, though no scholar, was gentle and generous by nature, taciturn and reserved. His one ambition was to cultivate the friendship of the boldest spirits of the empire. He stood seven and a half spans tall, with arms that reached below his knees. His ear lobes were elongated, his eyes widely set and able to see his own ears. His face was flawless as jade, and his lips like dabs of rouge.

This man was a descendant of Liu Sheng, Prince Jing of Zhongshan, a great-great-grandson of the fourth Han emperor, Jing. His name was Liu Bei; his style, Xuande. Generations before, during the reign of Emperor Wu, Liu Sheng's son, Zhen, was made lord of Zhuolu precinct, but the fief and title were later forfeited when Zhen was accused of making an unsatisfactory offering at the eighth-month libation in the Emperor's ancestral temple. Thus a branch of the Liu family came to settle in Zhuo county.

Xuande's grandfather was Liu Xiong; his father, Liu Hong. Local authorities had recommended Hong to the court for his filial devotion and personal integrity. He received appointment and actually held a minor office; but he died young. Orphaned, Xuande served his widowed mother with unstinting affection. However, they had been left so poor that he had to sell sandals and weave mats to live.

The family resided in a county hamlet called Two-Story Mulberry after a tree of some fifty spans just southeast of their home. Seen from afar, the mulberry rose tall and spread broadly like a carriage canopy. "An eminent man will come from this house," a fortuneteller once predicted. While playing beneath the tree with the boys in the hamlet, young Xuande often boasted, "When I'm the Son of Heaven, my chariot will have a canopy like this." Impressed by these words, his uncle Liu Yuanqi remarked, "This is no ordinary child." Yuanqi sympathized with the impoverished family and often helped out his nephew. At fifteen Xuande was sent away by his mother to study, and Zheng Xuan and Lu Zhi were among his teachers. He also formed a close friendship with Gongsun Zan.

Xuande was twenty-eight when Governor Liu issued his call for volunteers. Reading the notice in Zhuo that day, Xuande sighed heavily. "Why such long sighs?" someone behind him asked brusquely. "A real man should be serving his emperor in the hour of peril." Xuande turned and faced a man eight spans tall, with a blunt head like a panther's, huge round eyes, a swallow's heavy jowls, a tiger's whiskers, a thunderous voice, and a stance like a dashing horse. Half in fear, half in admiration, Xuande asked his name.

"The surname," the man replied, "is Zhang; given name, Fei; style, Yide. We've lived in this county for generations, farming our piece of land, selling wine, and slaughtering pigs. I seek to befriend men of bold spirit; when I saw you sighing and studying the recruitment call, I took the occasion to address you." "As a matter of fact," Xuande answered, "I am related to the imperial family. My surname is Liu; given name, Bei. Reading of the trouble the Yellow Scarves are stirring up, I had decided to help destroy the bandits and protect the people and was sighing for my inability to do so when you came by." "I have resources," said Zhang Fei, "that could be used to recruit in this area. Let's work together for the cause. What about it?"

Xuande was elated, and the two went to a tavern. As they drank, they watched a strapping fellow pushing a wheelbarrow stop to rest at the tavern entrance. "Some wine, and quickly—I'm off to the city to volunteer," the stranger said as he entered and took a seat. Xuande observed him: a man of enormous height, nine spans tall, with a two-foot-long beard flowing from his rich, ruddy cheeks. He had glistening lips, eyes sweeping sharply back like those of the crimson-faced phoenix, and brows like nestling silkworms. His stature was imposing, his bearing awesome. Xuande invited him to share their table and asked who he was.

"My surname is Guan," the man replied. "My given name is Yu; my style, Changsheng, was later changed to Yunchang. I am from Jieliang in Hedong, but I had to leave there after killing a local bully who was persecuting his neighbors and have been on the move these five or six years. As soon as I heard about the recruitment, I came to sign up." Xuande then told of his own ambitions, to Lord Guan's great satisfaction. Together the three left the tavern and went to Zhang Fei's farm to continue their discussion. "There's a peach garden behind my farm," said Zhang Fei. "The flowers are in full bloom. Tomorrow let us offer sacrifice there to Heaven and earth, and pledge to combine our strength and purpose as sworn brothers. Then we'll plan our course of action." Xuande and Lord Guan agreed with one voice: "So be it."

The next day the three men had a black bull, a white horse, and other offerings brought to the peach garden. Amid the smoke of incense they performed their ritual prostration and took their oath:

> We three, though of separate ancestry, join in brotherhood here, combining strength and purpose, to relieve the present crisis. We will perform our duty to the Emperor and protect the common folk of the land. We dare not hope to be together always but hereby vow to die the selfsame day. Let shining Heaven above and the

fruitful land below bear witness to our resolve. May Heaven and man scourge whosoever fails this vow.

So swearing, Xuande became the eldest brother; Lord Guan, the second; and Zhang Fei, the youngest. After the ceremonies they butchered the bull and spread forth a feast in the peach garden for the three hundred local youths they had recruited; and all drank to their heart's content.

The next day they collected weapons, but they wanted for horses. Two visitors whose servants were driving a herd of horses toward Zhang Fei's farm provided the solution. "This must mean that Heaven is with us," said Xuande as the three brothers went forth to greet the men, Zhang Shiping and Su Shuang, two wealthy traders from Zhongshan. Every year, they said, they went north to sell horses; but this year they had had to turn back because of the Yellow Scarves. Xuande invited them to the farm, where he set out wine and entertained them before revealing his intention to hunt down the rebels and protect the people. The visitors were delighted to support the cause by supplying the brothers with fifty fine mounts, five hundred ounces of gold and silver, and one thousand *jin* of wrought iron to manufacture weapons.

After bidding the traders a grateful farewell, Xuande had the finest smith forge for him a pair of matching double-edged swords; for Lord Guan a Green Dragon crescent-moon blade, also known as Frozen Glory, weighing eighty-two *jin,* and for Zhang Fei, an eighteen-span spear of tempered steel. He also ordered full body armor for each of them.

At the head of five hundred local youths, the brothers presented themselves to Commandant Zou Jing. Jing brought them to Liu Yan, governor of Youzhou, before whom the brothers gave account of themselves. When Xuande mentioned his royal surname, the governor was delighted and acknowledged him as a nephew.

Some days later it was reported that the Yellow Scarves chieftain Cheng Yuanzhi was advancing on Zhuo district with fifty thousand men. The governor had Commandant Zou Jing lead the brothers and their five hundred against the enemy. Eagerly, Xuande took his company to the base of Daxing Mountain where he encountered the rebels, who as always appeared with hair unbound and yellow scarves across their foreheads.

The two forces stood opposed. Xuande rode out, Lord Guan to his left, Zhang Fei to his right. Raising his whip, Xuande cried out, "Traitors to the Emperor, surrender now!" Enraged, Cheng Yuanzhi sent his subordinate commander Deng Mao into the field. Zhang Fei sped out, leveled his eighteen-span serpent-headed spear and jabbed his adversary through the chest. Seeing Deng Mao tumble dead from his horse, Yuanzhi cut toward Zhang Fei, slapping his mount and flourishing his blade. Lord Guan swung out his mighty sword and, giving his horse free rein, rushed the foe. Cheng Yuanzhi gulped with fright and, before he could defend himself, was sliced in two with a stroke of Lord Guan's weapon. A poet of later times praised the two warriors:

> Oh, what a day for gallantry unveiled!
> One man proved his lance and one his blade.
> In maiden trial their martial force was shown.
> A thrice-torn land will see them gain renown.

Their leaders slain, the rebels dropped their spears and fled. Xuande pursued, taking more prisoners than could be counted, and the brothers returned triumphant. Governor Liu Yan met them personally and rewarded their soldiers. The next day Liu Yan received an appeal from Governor Gong Jing to relieve the rebel-besieged city of Qingzhou. Xuande volunteered to go there, and Liu Yan ordered Zou Jing to join him and his brothers with five thousand men.

As the rescue force approached Qingzhou, the Yellow Scarves divided their army and tied up the government troops in a tangled struggle. Xuande's fewer numbers could not prevail, and he had to retreat some thirty *li* [ten miles] where he pitched camp. "They are too many for us. We can win only by surprising them," Xuande told his brothers. He had Lord Guan and Zhang Fei march off with one thousand men each and conceal themselves along both sides of a hill.

The following day Xuande and Zou Jing advanced noisily but drew back when the enemy gave battle. The rebel horde eagerly pursued, but as they passed the hill the gongs rang out in unison. From left and right, troops poured down as Xuande swung his soldiers around to resume combat. Squeezed between three forces, the rebels broke up and were driven to the very walls of Qingzhou where an armed populace led by Governor Gong Jing met them. After a period of slaughter the Scarves were routed and the siege of Qingzhou was lifted. In later times a poet praised Xuande:

> Seasoned plans and master moves; all's divinely done.
> To one mighty dragon two tigers can't compare.
> At his first trial what victories are won!
> Poor orphan boy? The realm is his to share.

After the governor had feasted the troops, Commandant Zou Jing wanted to return to Youzhou. But Xuande said, "We have word that Imperial Corps Commander Lu Zhi has been battling the rebel chief Zhang Jue at Guangzong. Lu Zhi was once my teacher, and I'd like to help him." So Zou Jing returned to Youzhou with his men, and Xuande headed for Guangzong, with his brothers and their five hundred men. They entered Lu Zhi's tent and, after the customary salutations, explained their purpose in coming.

Lu Zhi rejoiced at the arrival of this relief and took the brothers under his command. At this time Zhang Jue's one hundred and fifty thousand and Lu Zhi's fifty thousand were deadlocked at Guangzong. "We have them contained here," Lu Zhi said to Xuande, "but over in Yingchuan, Zhang Jue's two brothers, Zhang Liang and Zhang Bao, are holding out against our generals Huangfu Song and Zhu Jun. Let me add one thousand to your company. Then go and investigate the situation there and fix the time to sweep the rebels out." On Lu Zhi's order, Xuande rode through the night to Yingchuan.

Meanwhile, checked by Huangfu Song and Zhu Jun, the Yingchuan rebels had retreated to Changshe, where they hastily built a campsite near a field. "If they're by a field," General Huangfu Song said to Zhu Jun, "we should attack with fire." They ordered each soldier to lie in wait with unlit torches of straw. That night the wind rose. After the second watch the government soldiers burned the camp. Huangfu Song and Zhu Jun attacked the rebels' stockade as flames stretched skyward. Without saddling their horses or buckling their armor, the rebels fled panic-stricken in every direction. The slaughter continued until morning.

Zhang Liang and Zhang Bao were in full flight when their fire-decimated forces were intercepted by a contingent of men with red flags flying. The leader of this new unit flashed into sight— tall, narrow-eyed, with a long beard. This man's rank was cavalry commander. His surname was Cao; his given name, Cao; his style, Mengde. Cao Cao's father, Cao Song, was originally not a Cao but a Xiahou. However, as the adopted son of the eunuch Cao Teng he assumed the surname Cao. Cao Song was Cao Cao's natural father. In addition, Cao Cao had the childhood nickname Ah Man and another given name, Jili.

As a youth Cao had loved the hunt and delighted in song and dance. He was a boy with ingenious ideas for any situation, a regular storehouse of schemes and machinations. Once Cao's uncle, outraged by his nephew's wild antics, complained to Cao's father, who in turn reproached Cao. The next time the boy saw his uncle, he dropped to the ground and pretended to have a fit. The terrified uncle fetched the father, who rushed to his son's side only to find him perfectly sound. "Your uncle told me you'd had a fit," said Song. "Has it passed?" "Nothing of the sort ever happened," responded Cao. "My uncle accuses me of everything because I have lost favor with him." The father believed the son and thereafter ignored the uncle's complaints, leaving Cao free to indulge his whims.

At about that time a man called Qiao Xuan said to Cao, "The empire is near ruin and can be saved only by a man capable of dominating the age. You could be the one." On another occasion He Yu of Nanyang said of Cao Cao, "The house of Han is going to fail. Yet I feel certain this is the man to steady the realm." In Runan a man named Xu Shao, known for his insight into human character, refused to give Cao a reading. But pressed repeatedly, the man finally spoke: "You could be an able statesman in a time of peace or a treacherous villain in a time of chaos." This prediction pleased Cao immensely.

At twenty, Cao received his district's recommendation for filial devotion and personal integrity, and this led to his initial appointment to the palace. Later, he was given command of security in the northern half of the district where the capital, Luoyang, was located. On assuming office he had a dozen decorated cudgels placed at the four gates of the city. They were to be a sign that any violator of the laws, however high or mighty, would be punished. One night the uncle of the eunuch Jian Shuo was seen going through the streets carrying a broadsword. Cao, making his nightly rounds, apprehended him and had one of the bludgeons applied. Thereafter no one dared to break the laws, and Cao Cao's prestige increased. Later he was made magistrate of Dunqiu.

During the Yellow Scarves uprisings the court elevated Cao to the rank of cavalry commander, and it was in this capacity that he led five thousand mounted warriors and foot soldiers to the Yingchuan district. He encountered the routed troops of Zhang Liang and Zhang Bao and cut off their retreat. In the ensuing fray his men took ten thousand heads as well as flags, banners, gongs, drums, and horses in large numbers. Zhang Liang and Zhang Bao, however, managed to escape after a desperate struggle. Cao presented himself to Huangfu Song and Zhu Jun, the imperial field generals, and then went after the two rebel leaders.

*   *   *   *

Meanwhile Xuande and his brothers neared Yingchuan, hurrying toward the roar of battle and the glowing night horizon. They reached the scene only to find the rebels already scattered. Xuande presented himself to Huangfu Song and Zhu Jun and explained why Lu Zhi had sent him. "Zhang Jue's two brothers are done for by now," said Huangfu Song. "They'll be taking refuge with Jue at Guangzong. That's where you are needed." Xuande accepted the order and led his men back. En route they came upon some soldiers escorting a cage-cart holding none other than Lu Zhi as prisoner. Amazed to find under arrest the commander whom he so recently had been serving, Xuande dismounted and asked what was the matter. "I had Zhang Jue surrounded and nearly defeated," Lu Zhi explained, "when he prevented our victory by some kind of magic. The court sent the eunuch Zuo Feng from the Inner Bureau to investigate. He was only looking to get paid off, but I told him that with supplies exhausted we had nothing to spare for the imperial envoy. My refusal only angered him. He bore the grudge back to court and reported that I was weakening morale by keeping on the defensive and not engaging the enemy. The court sent Imperial Corps Commander Dong Zhuo to relieve me and return me to the capital to face charges."

Outraged by this treatment of Xuande's former teacher, Zhang Fei moved to cut down the guard and rescue the prisoner. But Xuande checked him. "The court will see to it that justice is done" he said. "Better not act rashly." They let the escort pass. "With Lu Zhi arrested and replaced," said Lord Guan, "we have nowhere to go but back to Zhuo district." Xuande agreed and began marching north. But on the next day they heard a great tumult beyond a hill. Xuande and his brothers climbed to high ground. A beaten Han army came into their view. Behind it, hill and dale swarmed with Yellow Scarves bearing banners that read "Heavenly Commander." "Zhang Jue himself!" cried Xuande. "Let's attack at once."

The three brothers swung their men into fighting position just as Zhang Jue was beating down the forces of Dong Zhuo, Lu Zhi's replacement as Imperial Corps commander. Carried by their momentum, the rebels drove hard until they ran up against the brothers. A murderous clash followed. Jue's men were thrown into confusion and had to retreat more than fifty *li*. The brothers rescued Dong Zhuo and saw him back to his camp. Zhuo inquired what offices they held but, upon learning that they were commoners without position, disdainfully refused to acknowledge their service. The three started to leave the camp with Zhang Fei grumbling, "Is that how the wretch treats us for risking our lives to save him? Then I'll have another kind of satisfaction!" Bent on revenge, Zhang Fei turned and stamped back toward Dong Zhuo's headquarters, a sword in his hand. It was a case where, indeed:

> Status is what counts and always has!
> Who needs to honor heroes without rank?
> Oh, let me have a Zhang Fei straight and true,
> Who'll pay out every ingrate what he's due.

Did Zhang Fei kill the Imperial Corps commander?
Read on.

CHAPTER 2

Zhang Fei Whips the Government Inspector; Imperial In-Law He Jin Plots Against the Eunuchs

Governor of Hedong Dong Zhuo (styled Zhongying), a native of Lintao in Longxi in the far northwest, was a man to whom arrogance came naturally. His rude treatment of Xuande had provoked Zhang Fei to turn back and seek satisfaction, but Xuande and Lord Guan warned their brother, "He holds the court's mandate. You cannot take the law into your own hands." "If we don't do away with the wretch," Fei retorted, "we'll be taking orders from him—the last thing I could stand. You two stay if you like. I'm leaving." "We three, sworn to live and die as one," said Xuande, "must not part. We'll go elsewhere." "We're all going, then?" responded Zhang Fei. "That's some consolation."

Riding all night, the three warriors reached the camp of Zhu Jun, the Imperial Corps commander, who welcomed them heartily and united their forces with his own. Together they advanced against the second rebel brother, Zhang Bao. (The third brother, Zhang Liang, was battling Cao Cao and Huangfu Song at Quyang at the time.) Zhang Bao had command of eighty or ninety thousand troops camped behind a mountain. Zhu Jun sent Xuande forward, and Zhang Bao dispatched his lieutenant Gao Sheng to taunt the government forces. Xuande waved Zhang Fei into combat, and he charged and ran Gao Sheng through after a few brief clashes. Sheng toppled from his horse as Xuande signaled his men to advance.

Zhang Bao, on horseback, unbound his hair and, sword in hand, began to work a magic formula. As throngs of Xuande's soldiers charged, a thunderstorm started to gather, and a black mist surrounded what seemed like an army of warriors in the sky. When the apparition plunged toward them, the men were thrown into confusion. Xuande hurried back to camp to report the defeat. "They were using shamanic tricks," said Zhu Jun. "Tomorrow we will slaughter a pig, a goat, and a dog and throw down on the rebels a mixture of the animals' blood, entrails, and excrement." Xuande placed Lord Guan and Zhang Fei, each with a thousand men, in ambush high on a slope of the hill, ready to hurl down the abominable preparation when Zhang Bao's troops passed.

The next day, with banners waving and drums rolling, Zhang Bao arrived in force. Xuande rode out to face him. As the soldiers prepared to engage in battle, Bao used his powers and a storm sprang up as before. Sand and stones went flying, and a murky mist packed with men and horses began to descend from the sky. Xuande wheeled and fled, drawing Bao in pursuit past the hill. At the given signal Lord Guan and Zhang Fei dumped their concoction over the enemy. In front of everyone's eyes, the storm died away, and the mist dissolved as paper men and straw horses tumbled from the sky every which way. Sand and stone lay still. Seeing his craft undone, Bao retreated quickly, but Lord Guan came forth on his left and Zhang Fei on his right, while Xuande and Zhu Jun raced up behind. Between these converging forces the rebels were crushed.

Xuande spotted Bao's "General of the Earth" banner some distance away and gave chase. Bao rode frantically for the brush, but Xuande shot an arrow through his left arm. The wounded rebel sought shelter in the city of Yang, to which Zhu Jun at once lay siege. Zhu Jun also sent for news of Huangfu Song's battle with Zhang Bao's brother, Liang, and received the following message:

> Huangfu Song won a great victory, and the court used him to replace the oft-defeated Dong Zhuo. Song arrived to find the chief rebel, Jue, dead, and Liang, who had taken over his command, locked in battle with our units. Song won seven battles in sucession; he killed Liang at Quyang. Then they opened up Jue's coffin, mutilated the corpse and impaled his head, which they later sent to the capital. The surviving rebels gave themselves up, and the court rewarded Song with the title of general of Chariots and Cavalry and appointed him protector of Jizhou. Song then petitioned the Emperor, stating that Lu Zhi's conduct was meritorious, not blame-worthy, and the court restored his former office. Cao Cao's service, too, was recognized, and he was awarded a fief at Jinan. When I left, they were about to return to the capital in triumph before assuming their new posts.

This was heartening news to Zhu Jun, and he pressed the siege harder. The rebels' position became critical. Finally, Zhang Bao was slain by Yan Zheng, one of his own commanders, who then surrendered with his leader's head. The battle won, Zhu Jun pacified several neighboring districts and reported to the throne.

*　　*　　*　　*

Meanwhile, three other rebel leaders—Zhao Hong, Han Zhong, and Sun Zhong—had gathered tens of thousands of followers to avenge their fallen master, Zhang Jue, by new acts of plunder and destruction. The court summoned Zhu Jun to punish them with his victorious units. Bearing the imperial command, Zhu Jun advanced on the rebel-held city of Wancheng. Zhao Hong sent Han Zhong to engage Zhu Jun's army. Zhu Jun ordered Xuande and his brothers to attack the southwest corner of the city wall. Han Zhong rushed to its defense with seasoned troops. Zhu Jun personally led two thousand hardened cavalrymen directly to the northeast corner. Fearful of losing the city, the rebels quickly withdrew from their southwest position. Xuande beset their rear, and the horde, badly defeated, fled into the city. Zhu Jun responded by dividing his force and surrounding Wancheng. The city was short of food, and Han Zhong offered to surrender. But Zhu Jun refused his offer.

Xuande argued for accepting: "Gao Zu, founder of the Han, won the empire because he knew how to invite surrender and how to receive it. Why refuse their offer, my lord?" "That was then," Zhu Jun replied. "Now is now. Before Han, the empire was convulsed with uprisings against Qin, and there was no established sovereign for the people to acknowledge. To welcome submission and reward allegiance was no doubt the way to attract adherents. But this land of ours enjoys unity today. It is only the Yellow Scarves who have resorted to arms. If we accept their surrender, how will we encourage loyal and decent men? If we allow those who pillage at will when they win to give themselves up when they lose, we give an incentive to subversion. A rather poor idea, I'd say."

"You are right," Xuande conceded, "to deny an appeal from these criminals. And yet, trapped like this in an iron grip, they can only fight to the last. Myriad single-minded men cannot be withstood, let alone desperadoes several times that number. We could pull back from the southeast and concentrate on the northwest. The rebels will flee the city; and having lost their taste for combat, they can be quickly captured." Zhu Jun acted on Xuande's suggestion, and the rebel Han Zhong, as expected, led his soldiers in headlong flight from Wancheng. Zhu Jun, joined by Xuande and his two brothers, attacked them in full force. Han Zhong was killed with an arrow shot. The survivors scattered. But as the government forces were mopping up, the battle took another turn. Zhao Hong and Sun Zhong arrived and engaged Jun, who retreated before this unexpected show of strength. The Yellow Scarves retook Wancheng.

Zhu Jun removed ten *li* and was preparing to counterattack when he saw a mass of soldiers coming from the east. At their head was a man of broad forehead and wide face, with a body powerful as a tiger's and a torso thick as a bear's. This man from Fuchun in the imperial district of Wu was surnamed Sun. His given name was Jian; his style Wentai; he was descended from the famous strategist Sunzi.

Years before, when Sun Jian was seventeen, he and his father watched a dozen pirates seize a merchant's goods and divide the spoils on the shore of the Qiantang River. Jian said to his father, "Let's take them prisoner." Sword bared, Jian leaped ashore and confronted the thieves, gesturing left and right as if signaling his followers. Fooled into thinking government troops were nearby, the thieves left their loot and fled, except for one whom Jian killed. This is how he made a name for himself in the region and was recommended for the post of commandant.

Some time after Sun Jian's appointment, one Xu Chang of Kuaiji revolted, titling himself the Sun Emperor and mobilizing tens of thousands of men. Jian and a district commanding officer recruited a thousand fighters and rallied the province's districts. Together they destroyed the rebels and killed Xu Chang and his son Shao. The imperial inspector of the province, Zang Min, reported Sun Jian's achievements to the Emperor, and Jian was promoted to deputy magistrate of Yandu, Xuyi, and Xiapi.

In response to the risings of the Yellow Scarves, Sun Jian gathered young men from his village, as well as many traders and experienced soldiers from the area of the Huai and Si rivers—some fifteen hundred in all—and went to aid the embattled Zhu Jun at Wancheng. Thus reinforced, Zhu Jun ordered Jian to attack the south gate and Xuande to attack the north. Zhu Jun himself lay siege on the west, giving the rebels a way out only on the east. Sun Jian was the first to gain the city wall, where he cut down twenty men and threw the rebels into confusion. Zhao Hong brandished his lance and made for Sun Jian, but Jian flung himself on his attacker, wrested away the lance, and ran him through. Then, taking Hong's horse, he charged the swarming rebels and slew many. Sun Zhong and his rebel force tried to break through the north gate, only to encounter Xuande, before whom Zhong fled in panic. Xuande felled him with a single arrow. Zhu Jun's main force then set upon the rebels from behind. Tens of thousands were beheaded, and untold numbers gave themselves up. Throughout the Nanyang area more than ten imperial districts were pacified.

Zhu Jun returned in triumph to the capital, where he was raised to the rank of general of Chariots and Cavalry and appointed governor of Henan. As governor, he reported to the throne the merits of Sun Jian and Xuande. Profiting from his connections, Jian obtained a post as an auxiliary district commanding officer and went at once to assume his new office. Only Xuande was left waiting many days, receiving no word of an appointment.

$$* \qquad * \qquad * \qquad *$$

Disheartened, the three brothers were walking in the capital when they came upon the carriage of the courtier Zhang Jun. Xuande presented himself and gave a brief account of his victories. Zhang Jun was surprised that the court had neglected such a man, and at his next audience with the Emperor said, "Sale of office and rank by the Ten Eunuchs is the fundamental cause of the recent uprisings. They have appointed only their own and punished only their enemies, and have thrown the realm into chaos in the process. For peace to prevail, it would behoove Your Majesty to execute the Ten, hang their severed heads outside the south gate of the capital, and proclaim to all the empire that hereafter merit will be well rewarded." The eunuchs counterattacked, accusing Zhang Jun of lese majesty. The Emperor resolved the dispute by ordering his guards to expel Zhang Jun from court.

The eunuchs continued discussing the matter: "This complaint," they agreed, "must have come from some deserving warriors who were passed over. It might be useful to have the central office review some of the lesser ones for appointment. We will have time enough to deal with them afterwards." And so Xuande was appointed judicial officer of Anxi county in the Zhongshan jurisdiction of Dingzhou imperial district, with orders to depart on a specified date. Xuande disbanded his troops and set out with his brothers and some two dozen followers. In Anxi he avoided all injury to the interests of the local people, and civic morality improved within a month. While in office Xuande shared bed and board with his brothers, and they stood beside him throughout long public sessions.

In a few months' time, however, the court decreed a purge of leading officials whose posts had been awarded in recognition of military service, a measure Xuande suspected would lead to his removal. Just then a district inspector came to Anxi, one of the counties under his jurisdiction. Xuande received the official outside the city with full honors. But the inspector remained mounted, reciprocating Xuande's salutation with a faint flick of his whip. Zhang Fei and Lord Guan seethed with resentment. At the posthouse the inspector seated himself upon a raised platform and faced south like an emperor holding court, while Xuande stood respectfully at the foot of the platform. After an extended wait the official spoke: "Tell me about your background, Officer Liu." "I am a descendant of Prince Jing of Zhongshan," replied Xuande. "I began campaigning against the Yellow Scarves in Zhuo county and have destroyed many of them, achieving some slight merit in over thirty engagements, some small, some large. As a result, I was appointed to this post."

"Isn't your claim of imperial ancestry a lie?" roared the inspector. "Like those phony reports of your 'achievements'? I have here in hand the court's decree purging such undeserving officials and corrupt officers as you." Xuande could only back away, humbly voicing his agreement. "Yes, sir. Yes, sir," he said and returned to the yamen to consult with another officer. "The inspector is creating a scene," the latter suggested, "only because he wants a bribe." "But I have never taken advantage of the people here," Xuande argued, "and have acquired nothing of value to give him." The following day the inspector sent for this county officer and pressured him into accusing Officer Liu of abusing the people. Every time Xuande tried to see the inspector to justify himself, guards turned him away.

After comforting himself with a few cups of wine, Zhang Fei rode by the posthouse. At the door he saw dozens of elderly folk weeping and wailing. When Zhang Fei asked the reason, they said, "The inspector is forcing the county officer to make statements that will enable him to get rid of our Lord Liu. We have come to plead for him but cannot get inside. The guards beat us back for our pains."

Zhang Fei's eyes widened with anger. Jaw set, he slid from his saddle and went straight to the posthouse, broke through the guard, and dashed to the rear. He saw the inspector holding formal session and the county officer, bound, on the ground. "Plague to the people," thundered Zhang Fei, "do you know me?" Before the inspector could open his mouth, Zhang Fei had him by the hair, dragged him to the front of the posthouse, and tied him to the hitching post. Then with some light switches stripped from a nearby willow, he whipped the inspector across the legs so soundly that a dozen of the switches split.

Xuande, having been kept from the inspector's presence, could not tell what was going on. Then he heard the commotion outside the posthouse and was told, "Commander Zhang Fei is beating the life out of somebody there." Xuande found out who the victim was and, aghast, went to demand an explanation of Zhang Fei. "This enemy of the people should be beaten to death," his brother said, "and the sooner the better." But the inspector pleaded, "Let me live, my good lord," and Xuande, a kindhearted sort when all was said and done, shouted to Zhang Fei to desist.

At this moment Lord Guan turned up. "Brother," he said, "your great service has been ill rewarded with this miserable post. Add to that this inspector's insults. Does a phoenix belong in a briar patch? Let's kill him, resign the office, and go home to plan for a better day." At these words Xuande took his seal and cord of office and hung them on the inspector's neck, saying, "For the harm you've caused the people we should have your life. However, we shall spare you. You may take these back, and I shall take my leave."

The inspector returned to Dingzhou and reported the incident to the governor, who in turn notified higher central and regional authorities in order to have the brothers arrested. But the wanted men found refuge in Daizhou with Liu Hui, who hid them in his home in consideration of Xuande's imperial lineage.

*   *   *   *

Meanwhile, at the court the Ten Eunuchs were using their great power to do away with anyone who went against them. Zhao Zhong and Zhang Rang demanded payment of gold and silk from all who had won distinction fighting the Yellow Scarves, and removed from office those who would not pay. In consequence, commanders Huangfu Song and Zhu Jun were deprived of office. The Emperor added the rank of general of Chariots and Cavalry to Zhao Zhong's other honors and awarded lordships to Zhang Rang and twelve others.

Administration worsened and the people grumbled. Ou Xing staged an uprising in Changsha. In Yuyang, Zhang Ju and Zhang Chun rebelled, Zhang Ju claiming to be emperor and Zhang Chun his marshal. The court was swamped with emergency appeals from every quarter of the land, but the Ten blithely filed them away and never informed the throne.

One day the Emperor and the Ten were feasting in the rear garden when Liu Tao, a court counselor, came before the sovereign and began weeping passionately. The Emperor requested an explanation, and Liu Tao replied, "With the empire in peril, how can Your Majesty continue feasting with these capons?" "Why, our nation is as peaceful as ever," the Emperor said. "What 'peril' do you have in mind?" "Bandits and rebels rise everywhere," responded Liu Tao, "plundering province and district—all because of the sale of office and the abuse of the people by the Ten Eunuchs, who have wronged and deceived Your Majesty. All upright men have fled your service. Disaster looms."

At this indictment, the Ten threw down their caps and prostrated themselves. "If Counselor Liu Tao cannot tolerate us," they cried, "we are done for. We beg only our lives and your permission to return to our farms. Everything we own will be donated to the army." Then they wept freely. The Emperor turned on the court counselor. "You," he said, "have your attendants. Should I not have mine?" He ordered the guards to march Liu Tao out and behead him. "I care not for my life," cried Tao, "but how my heart aches for the empire of Han—on the verge of extinction after four hundred years!" The guards had removed him and were about to execute him when a high official checked them with a shout: "Stay your hand until I make my plea!"

The assembly saw that it was Minister of the Interior Chen Dan, coming directly into the palace to place his objections before the Emperor. "What fault of Counselor Liu's deserves such punishment?" he asked. "He slanders our close attendants," said the Emperor, "and sullies our person." "These eunuchs whom you honor like parents," said the minister, "the people would eat alive if they could. They are raised to lordships without the least merit—to say nothing of the traitors among them like Feng Xu, who colluded with the Yellow Scarves. If Your Majesty will not consider this, the sacred shrines of the royal house could fall at any moment."

The Emperor said, "Feng Xu's role in the rebellion was never proven. As for the Ten Eunuchs, do you mean to tell me there isn't a single one who is loyal?" Chen Dan emphasized his protest by striking his head against the steps below the throne. The indignant Emperor had him dragged off and thrown into prison beside Liu Tao. That night the eunuchs had the two officials murdered. Then they forged an official decree making Sun Jian governor of Changsha with a commission to put down the rebellion of Ou Xing. Within fifty days Sun Jian reported victory and the Jiangxia region was secured.

A decree enfeoffed Sun Jian as lord of Wucheng and made Liu Yu protector of Youzhou. Liu Yu launched a campaign against Zhang Ju and Zhang Chun in Yuyang; and Liu Hui of Daizhou wrote the new protector recommending Xuande, whom he had sheltered. Liu Yu was delighted and appointed Xuande district commander. Xuande took the battle straight to the bandits' lair. In several days' hard fighting Xuande beat down the impetuous spirit of the rebels, who then turned upon Zhang Chun, their violent and autocratic leader. He was killed by one of his own chieftains, who brought Chun's head to the government authorities and surrendered with his soldiers. Zhang Ju, his position collapsing, hanged himself. Now Yuyang, too, was fully pacified.

Protector Liu Yu reported Xuande's great service to the court. Not only was he forgiven for having flogged the inspector, but he was promoted to deputy magistrate of Xiami and made judicial officer of Gaotang. Gongsun Zan added his praise of Xuande's former service; on his recommendation Xuande was made an auxiliary corps commanding officer and assigned to Pingyuan county as magistrate. At Pingyuan, Xuande had considerable resources and manpower at his disposal and was able to reestablish the atmosphere of former days. Liu Yu, for his great service in quelling the bandits, was made grand commandant.

*   *   *   *

In the fourth month of the sixth year of the Zhong Ping reign [A.D. 189], Emperor Ling fell gravely ill and called for Regent He Jin to make plans for the succession. He Jin was from a butcher's family and had attained his powerful position only through the influence of his younger sister, Lady He, a royal concubine who on giving birth to a son, Bian, had become Empress He. Emperor Ling had a second favorite, Beauty Wang. Lady Wang too bore a son, and Empress He out of jealousy poisoned her. The child, Xie, was raised in the palace of the Emperor's mother, Dong.

Queen Mother Dong was the wife of Liu Chang, lord of Jiedu precinct. Because Huan, the previous emperor, had had no male issue, Liu Chang's son was made heir apparent and became Emperor Ling upon the death of Huan. When Ling succeeded to the throne, his mother was taken into the palace and honored as queen mother. In the matter of Ling's heir apparent, Queen Mother Dong urged the Emperor to name Xie, son of the murdered concubine Wang, over Bian, son of Empress He. The Emperor himself was disposed to make this change as he was partial to Prince Xie.

As Emperor Ling's end drew near, the eunuch Jian Shuo advised him, "If it is Your Majesty's wish that Prince Xie, not Prince Bian, follow you on the throne, first get rid of Regent He Jin, Bian's uncle, to forestall countermeasures." Emperor Ling took his advice and commanded He Jin to appear. He Jin arrived at the palace gate but there was warned by the commanding officer, Pan Yin, not to enter because Jian Shuo meant to kill him. He Jin fled to his quarters and summoned the ministers and high officials to consider executing all the eunuchs. To this drastic step one man rose to object. "The influence of the eunuchs," he argued, "goes back to the reigns of emperors Chong and Zhi [A.D. 145–47]. Now they have overrun the court. How can we kill each and every one of them? If discovered, we will be killed and our clans exterminated. Pray consider this thoroughly."

Regent-Marshal He Jin regarded the man. It was Cao Cao, commandant for Military Standards. "What do you junior officers know of court matters?" said Jin, turning disdainfully to Cao. The problem was still under discussion when Commanding Officer Pan Yin brought the news of the Emperor's demise. "Jian Shuo and the eunuchs," he informed He Jin, "plan to keep the death secret. They have forged a decree summoning you to the palace and expect to have their way by eliminating you before declaring Prince Xie emperor." The group had not yet reached a decision when the court's messenger came commanding He Jin's immediate appearance to resolve all pending issues.

"Today before all else we must rectify the succession," cried Cao Cao. "Then we can take care of the traitors." "Who will join me," asked He Jin, "in supporting the legitimate heir, Prince Bian, and bringing the traitors to justice?" "Give me five thousand crack troops," one official spoke up, "and I will march into the palace, enthrone the rightful emperor, destroy the eunuchs, and purge the court, thus restoring peace in the land." He Jin eyed the speaker. It was Yuan Shao (styled Benchu), son of former Minister of the Interior Yuan Feng, nephew of Yuan Wei; at the time Shao was commander of the Capital Districts. He Jin, gratified by the offer, assigned five thousand of his Royal Guard to Yuan Shao's command.

Yuan Shao girded himself for battle. With He Jin in the lead, He Yu, Xun You, Zheng Tai, and some thirty other high officials filed into the palace. There before the coffin of Emperor Ling they placed He Jin's nephew, Prince Bian, on the throne as Ling's successor, Emperor Shao. When shouts of allegiance from the assembled officials died down, Yuan Shao entered the palace to arrest Jian Shuo. Jian Shuo fled to the royal garden and hid himself, but Guo Sheng, one of the Ten, found and killed him, and the Palace Guard, which Jian Shuo had commanded, all surrendered. Yuan Shao said to He Jin, "These eunuchs have organized their own gang. But today the tide runs with us. Let's kill every last one."

Zhang Rang and his group of Ten Eunuchs, realizing that their end was near, rushed to see the Empress He, sister of Regent-Marshal He Jin. "Jian Shuo and Jian Shuo alone," they assured her, "tried to kill your brother the regent. Not one of us was involved. But Yuan Shao has won the regent over and is bent on doing away with all of us. Have pity, Your Majesty." Empress He, whose son, Bian, had just been enthroned, said, "Have no fear. I shall protect you." She ordered He Jin before her and spoke to him privately: "You and I are humbly born and could not enjoy the wealth and status we have today except for Zhang Rang and the Ten. Jian Shuo has paid for his crime. Don't listen to those who want to kill them all." Thus admonished, He Jin came out and addressed the assembly: "Jian Shuo tried to murder me. Now he is dead, and his clan will be destroyed. There is no need to punish the rest." "If we don't root them out for good," objected Yuan Shao, "we will pay with our lives." "The decision is made," He Jin insisted. "Let no more be said." With that the assembly retired. The following day Empress He ordered He Jin to supervise the work of the Imperial Secretariat, which issues decrees, and the regent-marshal's associates were granted official positions.

Now the rival empress, Dong (mother of the late Emperor Ling and guardian of Prince Xie), summoned Zhang Rang of the Ten Eunuchs. "I was the one," she told him, "who first helped Empress He. Now her son reigns over all officialdom, inside and outside the court. Her power is great. What are we to do?" "Your Majesty," replied Rang, "control the courts from behind the scene; preside over administration; have the imperial son, Xie, enfeoffed as a prince; have high office conferred on your brother, the imperial uncle; see that he gets real military power; use us in important ways, and we can aim higher soon enough." Immensely pleased with this advice, Empress Dong held court the following day and issued a decree naming Xie as prince of Chenliu and Imperial Uncle Dong Chong as general of the Flying Cavalry. Zhang Rang and the eunuchs were again permitted to participate in court affairs.

Empress He, seeing her rival gather power, arranged a banquet in the palace for her. When the company was well warmed with wine, Empress He lifted her cup and kneeled respectfully as she addressed Empress Dong: "We two women should not concern ourselves with court affairs. In the founding reign of this dynasty Empress Lü wielded great power. But in the end her clan, one thousand strong, was extinguished. You and I should seclude ourselves in the palace and leave court business to the great ministers and elder statesmen. The ruling house will benefit. I hope you will give this your consideration."

To this challenge Empress Dong rose angrily. "Your jealousy drove you to poison Beauty Wang," she accused. "Now you have the temerity to say any damned thing you please because your son rules and your brother is in power. But without lifting a finger I can have the general of the Flying Cavalry cut off He Jin's head." "I spoke in good faith," responded Empress He hotly. "What gives you the right to lash out at me?" "A lot you know," retorted Empress Dong, "you offspring of butchers and wine merchants!" The two queens quarreled back and forth until Zhang Rang persuaded them to return to their chambers. That night Empress He summoned her brother and described to him the scene at the banquet.

Regent He Jin then met with the three elder lords (grand commandant, minister of the interior, minister of works). And the following morning, in accordance with their decision, a courtier petitioned the Emperor not to allow Empress Dong to remain in the palace, on the grounds that she was originally a provincial princess, but to return her to Hejian, her original fief, without delay. The He faction assigned escorts for the rival empress and detailed the Palace Guard to surround the home of Flying Cavalry General Dong Chong and demand his insignia. Chong knew he was trapped and cut his throat in a rear chamber. The household raised the cry of mourning and the cordon was lifted. The eunuchs Zhang Rang and Duan Gui, foiled by the destruction of Empress Dong's faction, proceeded to cultivate He Jin's brother Miao and his mother, Lady Wuyang. Plying them with gifts of gold and pearls, the eunuchs had them visit Empress He day and night and gloss their deeds with fine phrases. In this way the Ten Eunuchs regained the privilege of waiting on the Emperor.

In the sixth month He Jin had Empress Dong poisoned at the government relay station in Hejian. Her coffin was brought to the capital and buried in the tombs at Wen. On the pretext of illness, Regent He Jin was absent from the ceremonies. The commander of the Capital Districts, Yuan Shao, visited He Jin and told him, "Zhang Rang and Duan Gui are spreading the rumor that you poisoned Empress Dong in order to usurp the throne. Unless you eliminate the eunuchs this time, the consequences will be unspeakable. Early in the last reign Dou Wu tried to destroy them, but they discovered his plans and killed him instead. Today you and your brother have the finest commanders and officers in your service. If they are with you, events can be kept in control. Do not let a Heaven-sent opportunity slip your grasp." He Jin responded, "This is a matter that bears further consideration."

Meanwhile, some of He Jin's men were secretly reporting to Zhang Rang, who in turn informed He Miao, Jin's brother, and also bribed him richly. Miao then went before Empress He and said, "The regent, mainstay of the new Emperor, has been guilty of cruel and inhuman conduct. Killing seems to be his sole concern. He has been trying to do away with the Ten Eunuchs for no good reason. It is going to lead to chaos." The Empress agreed, and when He Jin later declared his intention to liquidate the gelded attendants, she replied, "Supervision of palace affairs by these officials of the women's quarters is a long-standing practice of the Han. With the late sovereign so recently departed, your desire to put the old ministers to death does not show proper respect for the ancestral temple of the ruling house."

He Jin, by nature an indecisive man, feebly muttered his agreement as he left his sister's presence. And to Yuan Shao's question, "How fares our cause?" he could only answer, "The queen mother does not concur. What can we do?" "Indeed," said Yuan Shao sharply, "let us summon the gallants of the realm, march into the capital, and wipe out these capons. Now is the critical moment. Forget the queen mother's disapproval!" "A superb idea," He Jin exclaimed and issued a call to various military stations for troops.

But Chen Lin, first secretary to He Jin, objected: "That's not going to work! You know the proverb, 'You can't catch a sparrow with your eyes shut.' Even trivial ends cannot be gained by self-deception; what of affairs of state? Now, General, you have the weight of the throne behind you and military authority in your hands. You can 'prance like a dragon and prowl like a tiger.' Whatever you wish is yours. You can execute the eunuchs as easily as you can burn a hair in a furnace. Act with lightning speed, with decision and expedition, and the whole world will go along. There's no need to call in outside forces and bring a mob of warriors down on the capital, each with his own ambitions. That is like handing someone a weapon pointed toward yourself! You will fail, and worse, you will create an upheaval." With a laugh, He Jin said, "This weak-kneed scholar understands nothing!" Another officer beside He Jin was laughing and applauding. "This really presents no problem," he said. "Why waste so much time discussing it?" The speaker was Cao Cao, and his advice was simple. Indeed:

> Wise counsel can undo the harm of vicious ministers
> When and if it is heeded.

What did Cao Cao say?
   Read on.

CHAPTER 3

In Wenming Garden, Dong Zhuo Denounces Ding Yuan; with Gold and Pearls, Li Su Plies Lü Bu

"Eunuchs," Cao Cao went on, "have been a plague since ancient times. But the founder of the Eastern Han, Emperor Guang Wu, granted them excessive power and favor and sowed the seeds of the crisis that is upon us today. The remedy is to eliminate the ringleaders. A single bailiff could do it. Why involve regional forces? Any attempt to execute the lot of them is bound to get out and likely to fail for that reason." Angered, He Jin shot back, "You have your own view of the matter, Mengde, I see." "He Jin will be the one to undo the empire!" Cao Cao muttered as he left the meeting. Having disposed of his opponent, He Jin dispatched messengers bearing secret decrees to various regional garrisons.

In chapter 3 Regent-Marshal He Jin, ignoring Cao Cao's advice for dealing with the eunuchs, summons outside forces to the capital to protect the throne. General Dong Zhuo answers the call, but upon arriving in Luoyang seizes power himself. Meanwhile the eunuchs murder He Jin, and those loyal to the minister retaliate by slaying the eunuchs en masse. Out of the strife Zhuo emerges victorious and makes allies of the counselor Li Ru and the warrior Lü Bu. In chapter 4 Zhuo deposes the child-emperor, Shao (Liu Bian), and enthrones He Jin's nephew Liu Xie, the prince of Chenliu. In A.D. 189, Liu Xie becomes Emperor Xian, the last Han emperor, while Dong Zhuo retains all real power.

CHAPTER 4

The Installation of the Chenliu Prince; Emperor Shao Is Deposed; A Plot against Traitor Dong; Cao Cao Presents a Jeweled Knife

On the first day of the ninth month the Emperor was invited to ascend the Hall of Praiseworthy Virtue before a grand convocation of civil and military officials. Dong Zhuo drew his sword and addressed them: "The Son of Heaven is too feeble in mind and in body to sustain his reign. I have a statement to make." At Zhuo's order Li Ru read it:

> Although the late Majestic Emperor Ling the Filial departed all too soon, there were high expectations in the land when the present Emperor assumed the throne. But Heaven did not endow him with the steady and serious character, the deportment and demeanor to command respect. His inattention and nonchalance during the mourning period exhibit his meagre virtue. All this has been detrimental to the throne itself. Queen Mother He has failed to give proper guidance, leaving government administration untended and disordered. The violent death of Queen Mother Dong has confused public opinion. The mainstays of our social order, the very bonds between Heaven and earth, have fallen slack.
>
> The prince of Chenliu is rich in sagely virtue and strictly devoted to proper rule. Throughout the mourning he was distraught with grief. His words were unfailingly apt, and all the world knows his excellent name. It is thus fitting and proper for him to receive the boundless patrimony of the Han as legitimate heir for all time. Thus: the sovereign is hereby deposed and reduced to prince of Hongnong. The queen mother will be relieved of all administrative duties. We enthrone the prince of Chenliu, in response to Heaven, in concurrence with men, and to satisfy the people's expectations.

When Li Ru had finished reading, Dong Zhuo sharply ordered the attendants to lead the Emperor down from the hall and to remove his seal and cord. They told him to face north and on bended knees declare his intention to serve and to obey. The queen mother was ordered to remove her royal costume and await instructions. Mother and son wept bitterly, and the assembly of officials moaned. But from below one official cried out indignantly, "Traitor Dong Zhuo. Dare you abuse Heaven itself? Then let my blood bear witness." He shook his pointed ivory tablet and attacked Dong Zhuo, at whose angry command the guards seized the man, Imperial Secretary Ding Guan. Dong Zhuo ordered him removed and beheaded. To the moment of his death his oaths streamed forth; neither his spirit nor his expression altered. In later times men still sighed for his sacrifice, as these lines attest:

> The traitor's plot to change a sovereign
> Would soon consign to dust the shrines of Han.

A courtful of courtiers helpless in Dong Zhuo's hand,
And no one but Ding Guan to take a stand!

Dong Zhuo invited the prince of Chenliu to ascend, and the assembly voiced its congratulations. Dong Zhuo ordered Queen Mother He and the former emperor, now prince of Hongnong, together with the imperial consort, Lady Tang, immured in the Palace of Eternal Peace. No access to them was permitted. Alas for the Emperor Shao, enthroned in the fourth month and deposed in the ninth.

The new Emperor, prince of Chenliu, Liu Xie (styled Bohe), second son of Emperor Ling, became known to history as Emperor Xian. He was nine years old, five years younger than his deposed brother. A new reign period, Beginning Peace (Chu Ping, A.D. 190–93), was proclaimed. Dong Zhuo became prime minister. But he did not as required use his personal name when saluting the sovereign nor comport himself reverently by scurrying in his presence, nor did he remove his boots and sword before the throne. The prestige and wealth he amassed raised him above all. Li Ru urged Dong Zhuo to broaden his support by elevating a few eminent men, Cai Yong in particular. Accordingly, Dong Zhuo summoned Cai Yong, but he refused to appear until threats of death to himself and his clan forced the scholar to present himself. Dong Zhuo was so pleased that he advanced Cai Yong three times within the month, finally making him privy counselor. Such was the kindness and generosity Cai Yong enjoyed.

*   *   *   *

Meanwhile the former Emperor Shao, his mother, and his consort—all imprisoned in the Palace of Eternal Peace—were allotted but meagre shares of food and clothing. Emperor Shao's tears were never dry. One day he happened to notice a pair of swallows flying in the courtyard and intoned these lines:

> Fresh vernal grasses tint the morning haze;
> Homing swallows lace the sky in pairs;
> The River Luo, a stretch of darker green—
> People cry in wonder at the scene.
> But out beyond the depths of yonder clouds

> Stand palaces and courts that once were ours.
> Who will stand for loyalty, take honor's part,
> And ease the heavy wrongs upon my heart?

A spy, who kept the deposed Emperor under constant surveillance, reported to Dong Zhuo the words he heard sung. "Well, if grievance is his theme, we have our excuse," said Dong Zhuo and commanded Li Ru to take ten armed men and murder the Emperor.

The Emperor, Empress He, and Consort Tang were in an upper story of the palace when Li Ru was announced. The Emperor panicked. Li Ru offered him a cup of poisoned wine. The Emperor wanted to know the occasion for the toast. "The prime minister drinks your health to greet the spring season," replied Li Ru. "If it is 'our health,'" said the queen mother, "you may drink first." "You won't drink it?" Li Ru said impatiently and ordered his men to show their knives and silken cords. "If the toast is refused, these will have to do," he added. Consort Tang fell to her knees and said, "Let this humble woman drink instead. Only, my lord, preserve the mother and the son." "And who are you to offer yourself in a prince's place?" snarled Li Ru, holding out the wine to the queen mother. "You drink first," he said. She cursed He Jin for having ruined the family by letting traitors into the capital. Li Ru pressed the cup on the Emperor. "Allow me to bid my mother good-bye," he said. Then he sang with deep feeling:

> Earth tops Heaven; sun and moon change place.
> Once I had a kingdom; now, a border town.
> Robbed of life; by subjects overthrown.
> All is lost; tears in vain flow on.

In turn the consort also sang:

> Majestic Heaven falls; mother earth sinks down.
> Given in marriage, I follow where he goes.
> Two different paths—life and death—here part.
> So swift the course, and sorrow-filled my heart.

After the song the two embraced and wept. "The prime minister awaits our report," said Li Ru cruelly. "You are delaying things. Who do you think is coming to save you?" At that, the queen mother cried, "The traitor Dong drives us to our doom. But Heaven will never sanction it. Your entire clan will perish for aiding this criminal." Li Ru laid hands on the queen mother and thrust her out of a window. Then he barked the order to strangle the consort and force the wine down Emperor Shao's throat. His work finished, Li Ru reported to Dong Zhuo, who ordered the three buried outside the city wall.

Dong Zhuo now began to indulge himself freely, debauching the imperial concubines and sleeping in the Emperor's bed. One day he took some troops to the city of Yang, a place outside Luoyang. It was the second month when the villagers, men and women, were celebrating the spring thanksgiving festival in honor of their local god. Dong Zhuo ordered his troops to surround the crowd and behead all the men. He seized the women and the goods that the people had with them and loaded everything onto his carts, tying to the sides the severed heads of more than one thousand. As the train reentered the capital Dong Zhuo announced that he was returning from a great victory over some bandits. The heads were burned at the city gate; the women and valuables were distributed among the army.

The commandant of the Exemplary Cavalry, Wu Fu (styled Deyu), indignant at Dong Zhuo's cruelties, put a vest of armor and a knife under his court dress in order to assassinate him. When Dong Zhuo entered the court, Wu Fu greeted him outside the ministerial chambers and then lunged at him with the knife. Dong Zhuo, a powerful man, caught Wu Fu with both hands, and Lü Bu stepped in at once and forced him to the ground. "Who is behind this treason?" cried Dong Zhuo. Wu Fu stared boldly and shouted: "You are not my sovereign. I am not your subject. What 'treason' are you talking about? Your crimes tower to Heaven, and the whole world longs to see you dead. My one regret is that I cannot have you pulled apart by horses—like any traitor—to satisfy the realm." In a fury Dong Zhuo had Wu Fu dragged out and carved up. The curses streamed from his lips till the moment of death. A verse of later times praised him:

> If you must tell of loyalty,
> Tell of Wu Fu's to the Han.
> His courage mounted to the skies
> When down below was none.

> He struck at Dong Zhuo in the court;
> His fame is with us still.
> Forever and ever he's won the name
> Of a man of iron will.

Thereafter armed guards constantly attended Dong Zhuo.

At this time Yuan Shao was governor of Bohai. Informed of Dong Zhuo's abuses, he wrote secretly to Minister of the Interior Wang Yun:

> This traitor wronged Heaven itself when he dethroned the Emperor, more than one can bear to say. Yet you have indulged his outrageous conduct as if you have heard nothing. Does this befit a subject who owes the dynasty his utmost loyalty? I am calling up and training soldiers to clear the royal house of villains, but I am not yet ready to act. If you share my views, be alert for any opportunity. I stand at your beck and call, awaiting your command.

———————————

Minister Wang Yun plots against Dong Zhuo with loyal courtiers, and Cao Cao tries to assassinate him. The attempt fails and Cao Cao flees the court. In the beginning of chapter 5, Cao Cao recruits an army in his home region and mobilizes the lords of the realm. They form a war confederacy, headed by Yuan Shao, to expel Dong Zhuo and save the dynasty.

CHAPTER 5

Cao Cao Rallies the Lords with a Forged Decree; The Three Brothers Engage Lü Bu in Battle

The war-ruler scanned the audience. Behind Gongsun Zan three extraordinary-looking strangers stood smiling grimly. Yuan Shao asked who they were. Gongsun Zan had Xuande step forward. "This is Liu Bei," he said, "magistrate at Pingyuan. We were fellow students and like brothers even then." "Not the one who helped break the Yellow Scarves?" asked Cao Cao. "The very one," answered Gongsun Zan. He told Xuande to salute Yuan Shao and Cao Cao and then proceeded to describe his protégé's origins and accomplishments. "Since he belongs to a branch of the imperial family," Yuan Shao concluded, "let him come forward and be seated." But Xuande modestly declined. "It is not your name or rank I salute," insisted Shao, "but your lineage." With that, Xuande took his place at the end of the line. Lord Guan and Zhang Fei posted themselves behind him, hands folded on their chests.

At this point a spy reported that Hua Xiong had brought his armored cavalry down from the pass, displaying Sun Jian's captured red headdress on the tip of a pole, and was at the camp's entrance mouthing taunts. "Who will go?" asked Yuan Shao. From behind Yuan Shu, Yu She, a commander known for bravery, stepped forward and volunteered. But Hua Xiong made short work of him. Alarm stirred the assembly. Governor Han Fu recommended his own champion commander, Pan Feng, and Yuan Shao urged him to the field. Pan Feng went forth with a huge axe, but the news came back swiftly of his death too at Hua Xiong's hands. The assembly began to panic. "It's a pity Yan Liang and Wen Chou, my own top generals, are not here," Yuan Shao said. "Either one could end our worries." At that, a voice from the back boomed, "I offer to present Hua Xiong's head to you personally."

The assembled lords turned to the speaker, a man over nine spans, with a great beard flowing from rich ruddy cheeks. His eyes were like those of the crimson-faced phoenix, his brows like nestling silkworms, his voice like a tolling bell. He fixed his eyes directly on the audience. "Who is this man?" demanded Shao. "Guan Yu, sworn brother of Xuande," answered Gongsun Zan. "His position?" asked Shao. "Mounted archer under Xuande," was the reply. At that, the war-ruler's brother, Yuan Shu, burst out, "Are you trying to insult us? A mere archer! Have we no more commanders? What nonsense! Get him out of here!" But Cao Cao checked Yuan Shu: "Pray, hold your temper. This man has made his boast. He can't be a coward. Now let him make it good. You'll have plenty of time to condemn him if he fails." "But to send out an archer!" Yuan Shao said. "Hua Xiong will laugh in his sleeve!" "He doesn't look like an ordinary soldier," Cao Cao replied. "How is Hua Xiong going to know?" Finally, Lord Guan spoke: "If I fail, my head is yours."

Cao Cao had a draft of wine heated for Lord Guan before he mounted. "Pour it," said the warrior, "and set it aside for me. I'll be back shortly." He leaped to his horse, gripped his weapon, and was gone. The assembly of lords heard the rolling of drums and the clamor of voices outside the pass, and it seemed as if the heavens would split open and the earth buckle, as if the hills were shaking and the mountains moving. The terror-struck assembly was about to make inquiry when the jingling of bridle bells announced Lord Guan's return. He entered the tent and tossed Hua Xiong's head, freshly severed, on the ground. His wine was still warm. A poet of later times sang Lord Guan's praises:

> His might sufficed to hold in place
>   the frames of sky and land.
> The painted war drums charged the air
>   at the chieftains' field command.
> The hero put the cup aside
>   to slake his combat lust:
> Before the wine had time to cool,
>   Hua Xiong lay in the dust.

Cao Cao was elated by Lord Guan's display of prowess. "My brother has taken Hua Xiong's head," cried Zhang Fei, stepping forward. "What are we waiting for? Let's break through the pass and take Dong Zhuo alive!" But Yuan Shu was enraged. "Even I," he bellowed, "a district governor, do not presume upon my position. How dare this magistrate's underling flaunt his powers before us! Drive the lot of them from our presence!" "The meritorious must be rewarded without regard to status," Cao Cao cautioned Yuan Shu. "Since you are so impressed with a mere magistrate," Shu retorted, "I announce my withdrawal." "Are we going to jeopardize our cause," Cao asked, "on account of a few words?" He ordered Gongsun Zan to take Xuande and his brothers back to camp. The assembly adjourned. Cao quietly sent meat and wine to cheer the three heroes. . . .

The lords again took counsel. "Lü Bu has no match," said Cao Cao. "Let us assemble the whole body of eighteen lords to form a sound plan. If we can capture him, Dong Zhuo will be easily defeated." As they conferred, Lü Bu returned to sound the challenge, and the eight lords answered it. Gongsun Zan thrust his spear into the air and took on Lü Bu, only to flee after a brief clash. Lü Bu gave Red Hare free rein and came pounding after Gongsun Zan. The horse's great speed and stamina brought him close behind. Lü Bu leveled his halberd, aiming for the center of Gongsun Zan's back.

To the side of the action stood a single warrior, his eyes rounding, his whiskers bristling. Holding high his eighteen-span snake-headed spear, he flew at Lü Bu, shouting mightily, "Stay! Bastard with three fathers! Know me for Zhang Fei of Yan!" Lü Bu veered from Gongsun Zan to confront the new challenger. Zhang Fei's fighting spirit flashed at this welcome chance. The two crossed and tangled more than fifty times. Lord Guan, seeing that neither could best the other, urged his horse forward and, flourishing his crescent-moon blade, Green Dragon, attacked from another side. The three horsemen formed a triangle. They fought another thirty bouts, but Lü Bu was unconquerable.

Then Xuande, clenching his matching swords, angled into the field on his tawny-maned horse, and the three brothers circled Lü Bu like the figured shade of a revolving lamp. The warriors of the eight lords stood transfixed. Soon Lü Bu could no longer fend off his enemies. Eyeing Xuande squarely, he feinted at him with the halberd. In dodging the thrust, Xuande opened a corner of the trap, and Lü Bu made good his escape, letting his weapon hang behind him, but the brothers would not let up. They gave chase, and the warriors who were witnessing the spectacle swept after them onto the field with a roar that shook the ground. Lü Bu's army broke and ran for the pass with the three brothers still leading the pursuit. A poet of later times described the contest thus:

> The house of Han approached its Heaven-destined end;
> Deep in the west its fiery sun had bent.
> Dong Zhuo deposed the rightful Emperor
> And filled the feeble prince with dreams of fear.
> So Cao Cao sent his writ to all the lords,
> Who summoned up ten thousand righteous swords,
> Elected Yuan Shao to their league's command,
> And swore to stay the house and calm the land.
> Dong Zhuo's man, Lü Bu, warrior without peer,

Far surpassed the champions of his sphere:
In armor clad, a dragon etched in scales,
His headpiece fledged with gallant pheasant tails,
His jagged jade belt scored with lion jaws,
A phoenix spread in flight; his surcoat soars.
His chafing charger stirred a fearsome wind,
In every eye his halberd's piercing glint.
No lord could face his call to brave the field:
Their hearts went faint, their senses reeled.
Then Zhang Fei made his way into the list,
His giant snake-head lance fast in his fist.
His beard stuck out, defiant strands of wire;
The circles of his eyes shot angry fire.
They fought their fill. The contest undecided,
Before his line Lord Guan no more abided:
His dragon blade as dazzling as fresh snow,
His war coat, parrot-hued, aswirl below.
His pounding horse aroused the dead to howl.
Blood would flow before his dreadful scowl.
With double swords Xuande now joins the fight.
The crafty owl will show his zeal and might.
The brothers circle Lü Bu round and round.
He fends, he blocks, too skillful to be downed.
The hue and cry set sky and land ajar;
The bloodlust sent a shudder through the stars.
His power spent, Lü Bu found an out
And rode for safety to his own redoubt,
His mighty weapon trailing at his back,
His gilded five-hued streamers all awrack.
Riding hard, he snapped his horse's rein,
Hurtling up to Tiger Trap again.

The brothers chased Lü Bu to the gateway to the pass. There they saw the blue silk command canopy fluttering above. "Dong Zhuo himself!" cried Zhang Fei. "Why bother with Lü Bu now? Let's get the chief traitor and root out the whole faction." The brothers started toward Dong Zhuo. Indeed:

"To catch a thief, you have to catch his chief."
But who, in fact, had the genius to do so?

In chapter 6 the three heroes' charge on the despot's army comes to naught. Dong Zhuo withdraws to the capital city of Luoyang. After plundering that city and murdering its elite, he abducts the puppet emperor and

*cruelly forces the entire population of Luoyang to march west to Chang'an,
the ruined capital of the Former Han. Luoyang is destroyed; the year is
190. In the wreckage of the city, Sun Jian, a confederate lord from the
Southland, finds the imperial seal and secretly takes it back to his kingdom. The confederacy that Cao Cao and Yuan Shao organized against
Dong Zhuo breaks apart.*

*In chapter 7, while Dong Zhuo holds the emperor in Chang'an, fur-
ther conflicts break out: Yuan Shao and Gongsun Zan fight in the north,
Sun Jian and Liu Biao (governor of Jingzhou) war in the south. Sun
Jian is killed, and his son Sun Ce replaces him as leader of the Southland. During this time Liu Xuande meets Zhao Zilong, who will be a
lifelong comrade.*

CHAPTER 8

*Wang Yun Shrewdly Sets
a Double Snare; Dong Zhuo Starts
a Brawl at Phoenix Pavilion*

In Chang'an, Dong Zhuo learned of Sun Jian's death and said,
"I am well rid of a mortal enemy. But how old is his first son?"
"Seventeen," someone said. This answer persuaded Dong Zhuo
he need not fear the south.

Dong Zhuo's behavior became more arbitrary and arrogant
than ever. He had himself addressed as Honorary Father and in
his public appearances usurped the regalia of the Emperor. He
appointed his brother, Min, general of the left and lord of Hu,
and his nephew, Huang, privy counselor with overall command
of the Palace Guard. All members of the Dong clan—whether
young or old—were honored with titles. Preceptor Dong put a
quarter of a million people to hard labor building a large structure, called Mei, two hundred and fifty *li* from Chang'an. The
walls, which enclosed palaces and granaries, were modeled in

height and thickness after those of the capital. Twenty years' supply of grain was placed in store. From among the commoners Dong Zhuo chose eight hundred beauties to adorn the palace rooms, where gold and jade, colored silks and rare pearls were hoarded. The Dong family lived amidst this wealth and splendor while Dong Zhuo himself traveled to the capital once or twice a month. Each time he left or returned to Chang'an all ranking court officials saw him off or greeted him outside the city's northwest gate, the Heng. Usually, Dong Zhuo set up tents on the way side to feast these high officials.

On one such occasion, with all of officialdom present, several hundred enemy troops from the north who had voluntarily surrendered were brought in. Then and there Dong Zhuo ordered his guards to mutilate them: some had their limbs lopped off; some, their eyes gouged out; some, their tongues cut; some were boiled in vats. The howls of the victims shook the officials so that they could not hold their chopsticks. But Dong Zhuo kept drinking, chatting, and laughing away, utterly unperturbed, as was his wont.

Another day Dong Zhuo convened the officials in front of the ceremonial platform. The assembly was seated in two long rows according to rank. As the wine was going round, Lü Bu stepped over to Dong Zhuo and whispered a few words. "So that's how it is!" said Dong Zhuo, smiling, and he had Lü Bu haul out the minister of public works, Zhang Wen. The other officials paled. Moments later Zhang Wen's head was carried in on a red platter. Dong Zhuo laughed at the terrified assembly, saying, "Nothing to fear, my lords. My son, Fengxian [Lü Bu], came upon a letter Yuan Shu had written to Zhang Wen. The two were conspiring against me; but no one here was implicated, so don't worry." "Of course not, of course not," the officials chimed in obsequiously. With that the banquet ended.

Minister of the Interior Wang Yun returned home despondent over the day's events. Late that night, strolling in his garden under a high moon, he stopped by a rose trellis and gazed at the sky. His eyes filled with tears. In the silence he heard moans and sighs near the Peony Pavilion. Stealing over, he discovered the singing girl, Diaochan, a child he had taken in and trained in the arts of dance and song. She was now sixteen and possessed unearthly beauty and skill. Wang Yun regarded her as his own daughter.

After listening a good while, Wang Yun called her to him. "Wretched girl, is there someone you pine for?" he asked sharply. Diaochan dropped to her knees and replied, "Would this humble maid dare?" "Then why," Wang Yun continued, "are you sighing here deep into the night?" "Allow me to open my innermost thoughts to you," the girl replied. "Keep nothing back," Wang Yun said. "Tell me the whole truth." "My lord," Diaochan began, "I am obliged to you for your unstinting care, for having me instructed in the arts of music and dancing, and for treating me with the utmost kindness and generosity. No sacrifice on my part could repay even one ten-thousandth of what I owe you. Recently you have been looking terribly sad, as if burdened by some great affair of state, but how could I inquire into such matters? This evening again I saw you pacing uneasily, and it brought a sigh to my lips. I never thought my lord would take notice. But if there is any way I can serve you, I would welcome death ten thousand times before declining." At these words Wang Yun struck the ground with his walking stick and cried out, "It never occurred to me that you could be the one to save the Han! Come with me to the gallery of murals." Diaochan followed Wang Yun to the room. Impatiently he dismissed the waiting maids and servants and conducted Diaochan to a seat. Then he touched his head and hands to the floor in front of her. At once Diaochan prostrated herself in astonishment. "My lord," she said, "what is the meaning of this?"

"Have pity," Wang Yun pleaded, weeping openly, "on those who live under the Han!" "I can only repeat what I have just said," the girl replied. "Ten thousand deaths would not deter me from doing whatever it is you wish me to do." "The common folk," Wang Yun went on, still kneeling, "are in dire peril. The sovereign and his officials are balanced on the edge of disaster. You may be the only one who can save us. Here is how matters stand: the traitor Dong Zhuo is preparing to seize the throne, and our civil and military officials have no means to prevent him. Now then, Dong Zhuo has an adopted son, Lü Bu, a man of extraordinary courage and might, but, like his stepfather, a slave to his passions. I would like to catch them in a double snare by first promising you in marriage to Lü Bu and then offering you to Dong Zhuo, thus putting you in a perfect position to turn them against one another. Drive Lü Bu to kill Dong Zhuo, and you will have eliminated a great evil, stabilized the dynastic shrines, and restored our ruling house. It lies in your power. But are you willing?" "I have already agreed to serve," said Diaochan. "I am eager to be presented to them. Leave all the rest to me." "If this gets out," Wang Yun cautioned her, "my house will be destroyed." "Have no fear, my lord," she said. "If I cannot live up to my duty, may I die by ten thousand cuts." Wang Yun saluted her in gratitude.

The next day Wang Yun had a smith fashion a golden headpiece studded with priceless pearls from his family's treasure chest. When the helmet was finished, he sent a man to present it secretly to Lü Bu. Delighted with the gift, Lü Bu came to Wang Yun's home to express his appreciation. The minister received him outside the main gate and ushered him into his private apartment, where he prepared a feast of choice delicacies. Then Wang Yun led Lü Bu to the seat of honor. "I am merely one of the prime minister's generals," the guest said, "but you are a great minister. I am not worthy of such courtesy." "In this day and age," Wang Yun replied, "the world has no heroes save you, General. It is not your office but your great ability to which I pay homage." These words gave Lü Bu immense pleasure. Wang Yun toasted him with solicitous hospitality, never ceasing to extol the virtue of Imperial Preceptor Dong Zhuo and General Lü Bu. Lü Bu laughed broadly and imbibed freely.

Wang Yun dismissed the attendants, keeping a few serving girls to pour the wine. Both men were well warmed when Yun called for his "daughter." Two maids led out Diaochan, dressed most alluringly. Lü Bu, startled, asked who she was. "My daughter, Diaochan," was the reply. "You have favored me, General, with more kindness than I could possibly deserve, as if we were closely related. That's why I would like to present her to you." He ordered Diaochan to offer a cup to Lü Bu. As she held out the wine with both hands a subtle interest crept into their glances. Wang Yun, feigning intoxication, said, "My child, invite the general to drink deeply. He is the mainstay of our household."

Lü Bu offered Diaochan a seat, but she feigned a move to withdraw. "The general is my closest friend," Wang Yun admonished her, "there is no reason not to sit with him." Diaochan seated herself beside Yun. Lü Bu's eyes never left her. A few more cups and Wang Yun said, "I would like to offer my daughter to you—if you would be willing to have her as your concubine." Lü Bu rose to express his appreciation: "For that I would be bound to you in loyalty even as a horse or a dog." "Then," said Yun, "we will select an auspicious day to deliver her." Lü Bu's delight knew no bounds. His glance clung to her, and she reciprocated with her own suggestive signs. The party came to an end. "I would have asked you to stay the night," said Wang Yun, "but was afraid the imperial preceptor would become suspicious." Lü Bu saluted his host repeatedly and departed.

Several days later at court, choosing a time when Lü Bu was out of sight, Wang Yun knelt before Dong Zhuo, hands touching the floor, and said, "Would the imperial preceptor deign to dine at my humble home?" "The invitation from the minister of the interior is accepted with pleasure," was the response. Wang Yun expressed his thanks and returned home.

Delicacies of land and sea furnished Wang Yun's feast. The setting was placed at the center of the main hall. Exquisitely embroidered cloths were spread over the ground, and drapes hung inside and outside the dining chamber.

Toward noon Dong Zhuo arrived by carriage. Dressed in court attire, bowing and tendering his respects, Wang Yun received his guest as he descended. One hundred halberdiers escorted him into the room and ranged themselves at either side. At the dais Wang Yun prostrated himself again. Dong Zhuo ordered his men to help his host to a seat beside him. "Imperial Preceptor," Wang Yun said, "your magnificent virtue towers above us. The greatest sages of antiquity—Preceptor Yi Yin and Regent Zhougong—cannot approach you in virtue." These words pleased Zhuo enormously. The wine was served and the entertainment began. Wang Yun continued to shower his guest with gracious compliments.

The day waned. The wine warmed them well. Wang Yun invited Dong Zhuo to his private apartment. Zhuo dismissed his guard. Yun proffered a goblet and congratulated the preceptor. "Since my youth," said Wang Yun, "I have been studying the patterns of the heavens. The signs I see at night say that the Han has completed its allotted span. The whole realm is moved by your achievements and virtue. The wish of Heaven and the hopes of men would be well fulfilled if you followed the example of the ancient worthies Shun and Yu, who accepted their sovereigns' abdication on the strength of their own merit."

"That," Dong Zhuo exclaimed, "is more than I dare hope for." Wang Yun continued, "Since earliest times those who would govern rightly have taken action against those who govern ill, and those without virtue have yielded power to those with virtue. In the present circumstances there would not be the slightest question of your exceeding your proper place." Dong Zhuo smiled and said, "If the Mandate of Heaven should actually settle upon me, you would be honored as a founder of the house." Wang Yun bowed deeply to show his gratitude.

In the chamber decorated candles were lit. Only the serving maids stayed behind, tendering wine and food. "Our regular musicians," Wang Yun said, "are too ordinary for such an occasion as this. But there happens to be a performer here whom I beg leave to have appear before you." "A wonderful and ingenious thought!" exclaimed Dong Zhuo. Wang Yun ordered the curtain lowered and outside it, encircled by an ensemble of pipe and reed, Diaochan began her dance. Admiration of her art is expressed in this lyric:

> Like Flying-Swallow of Zhaoyang Palace,
> The swan-sprite turns in an opened palm—
> Is she fresh from Dongting's vernal lake?
> Her graceful step keeps the Liangzhou air:
> As the tender scent a flowering branch exhales
> Fills the paneled room with springtime warmth.

Another poem describes her performance:

> To the quickening beat the swallow now takes wing,
> Reaching the gorgeous room still trailing mist:
> Those black brows caused the rover's heart to ache,
> Those looks have pierced the souls of all who sued.
> No elmseed coin could buy those golden smiles;
> No gem or jewel need gild her willow waist.
> Now done and screened again, she glances to discover
> Who next will play the goddess's royal lover.

Dong Zhuo ordered the dancer to approach him. Diaochan entered from behind the curtain, making profound salutations. Dong Zhuo took in the expressive beauty of her face and asked, "Who is this girl?" "The songstress Diaochan," answered Wang Yun. "Then she can sing as well?" Dong Zhuo inquired. Wang Yun had Diaochan take up the sandalwood blocks and tap the rhythm as she sang. This poem describes the moment well:

> Her parting lips were like the cherry bud.
> Across two rows of jade an air of spring flowed forth.
> But her clove-sweet tongue proved a steely sword
> That put to death a base, betraying lord.

Dong Zhuo could not stop marveling at her voice. Wang Yun ordered Diaochan to serve more wine. Dong Zhuo lifted his cup and asked, "How many springs have you passed?" "Your servant is just sixteen," she replied. "You must have come from a land of fairies," Dong Zhuo said. At that moment Wang Yun rose from his mat and declared, "I would like to present this girl to the imperial preceptor, if it would be agreeable." "I would be at a loss to repay such a boon," Dong Zhuo responded. "To serve the imperial preceptor would be splendid luck for her," Wang Yun added. Again Dong Zhuo voiced his thanks. Wang Yun immediately ordered a felt-lined closed carriage to carry Diaochan ahead to the prime minister's residence. Then Dong Zhuo rose and bade his host goodbye. Wang Yun escorted his guest home before taking his leave.

Wang Yun was halfway home again when he saw two lines of red lanterns on the road ahead; in their light stood Lü Bu, armed and mounted. Lü Bu reined in and reached over, taking hold of Yun's upper garment. "You promised Diaochan to me," he snarled. "Now you give her to the imperial preceptor. What kind of game are you trying to play?" "This is not the place to talk," Wang Yun responded. "Come to my house. Please." Lü Bu accompanied Wang Yun home. They dismounted and went to the private apartment. After the amenities Wang Yun asked, "What grounds do you have for such an accusation, General?" "It was reported to me," Lü Bu answered, "that you delivered Diaochan to the prime minister's residence in a felt-lined closed carriage. What is the meaning of this?"

"Then you really do not know! Yesterday," Wang Yun explained, "the preceptor said to me at court, 'There is something I wish to discuss. I will visit you tomorrow.' So I prepared a small banquet. As we were dining, he said, 'I understand you have a daughter, Diaochan, whom you have promised to my son, Fengxian. Lest the agreement seem less than official, I have come especially to confirm it and to meet your daughter as well.' I could hardly disobey, so I led her out to pay her respects to her future father-in-law. The preceptor said, 'Today is an auspicious day. I shall take Diaochan back with me for my son.' A moment's reflection, General, and you will realize that I could hardly refuse the preceptor's personal request." "Then you must forgive me, Your Honor," Lü Bu said. "I was mistaken and will come another time to apologize properly." "My daughter," Wang Yun added, "has a sizable trousseau. I will deliver it as soon as she joins you at your residence." The general thanked the minister and left.

The next day Lü Bu made inquiries at Dong Zhuo's residence but was unable to learn anything. He went directly into the ministerial quarters and questioned the serving maids. "Last night," they informed him, "the imperial preceptor had a new girl with him. They have not yet arisen." Lü Bu felt great anger swell within him. He stole close to the outside of Dong Zhuo's bedroom and peered in. Diaochan was combing her hair by the window. Suddenly she saw a reflection in the pool outside, that of a huge man with a headpiece that caught his hair in a knot. Assuming it was Lü Bu, she puckered her brows, feigning sorrow and dabbing at her eyes with a filmy scarf. Lü Bu observed her a good while before moving away. Moments later he reentered the main hall where Dong Zhuo was seated.

Dong Zhuo saw Lü Bu come in and asked, "Is everything all right outside?" "No problems," answered Lü Bu and stood in attendance beside the preceptor. Dong Zhuo was eating. Lü Bu glanced around. He spotted a young woman moving back and forth behind a damask curtain, peeking out now and then and letting a corner of her face show. Her eyes bespoke her affection. Lü Bu knew her to be Diaochan, and the soul within him fluttered. Dong Zhuo noticed Lü Bu's distraction and, pricked by jealousy and suspicion, said, "If there is nothing else, you may go." Sullenly, Lü Bu left.

Enthralled by Diaochan's charms, Dong Zhuo let official business lapse for more than a month. Once he fell ill, and Diaochan stayed up every night catering to his needs and wishes. On one occasion Lü Bu entered the private apartments to see him. Dong Zhuo was sleeping. Behind the bed Diaochan tilted her shoulders toward Lü Bu and pointed first to her heart and then to Dong Zhuo. Her cheeks were moist. Lü Bu felt his own heart crumble within him. Dong Zhuo opened his eyes and slowly focused on Lü Bu, who was staring at the rear of the bed. Dong Zhuo swung around and spied Diaochan behind him. "Have you been flirting with my favorite concubine?" he screamed and ordered Lü Bu thrust from the room. "Never enter here again!" he shouted.

Rage and hatred struck deep in Lü Bu. On the way home he met Li Ru and told him what had happened in the bedroom. Li Ru rushed to see Dong Zhuo. "Imperial Preceptor," he pleaded, "if you hope to make the realm your own, there's no point in blaming Lü Bu for so trifling an offense. Our cause is lost if he turns against us." "What shall I do?" asked Dong Zhuo. "Summon him tomorrow morning," Li Ru counseled, "and honor him with presents of gold and silk. Mollify him with gentle phrases. There should be no further problems." Dong Zhuo agreed and the next day had Lü Bu called before him. "Yesterday," Dong Zhuo began, "I was unwell and not at all myself. I said the wrong thing and did you injury. Do not hold it against me." Dong Zhuo conferred on his general a bounty of ten catties of gold and twenty rolls of silk. Lü Bu thanked him and went home. But from then on, though his body remained with Dong Zhuo, his mind dwelled on Diaochan.

After Dong Zhuo got over his illness, he held court once again. Lü Bu, armed as always, attended him. One day he saw the preceptor in conference with Emperor Xian and slipped away to Dong Zhuo's residence. He tied his horse at the front entrance and went into the rear chambers, halberd in hand, where he found Diaochan. "Wait for me," she said, "in the back garden by the Phoenix Pavilion." Lü Bu went where he was told and stood by the curved railing that surrounded the little belvedere. After a long while he saw her coming, parting the flowers and brushing aside the willows—truly, to any mortal eye, a celestial being from the Palace on the Moon. Weeping, she joined him and said,

"Though I am not his real daughter, Minister Wang Yun treats me as his own flesh and blood. The moment he presented me to you, my lifelong prayers were answered. I can't believe that the preceptor's conscience could permit him to stain my purity, so that I now despair of life itself. I have borne my shame and prolonged my worthless existence only for the chance to say good-bye to you. Our fortunate meeting today answers my wish. But never again, disgraced as I am now, could I serve a hero such as you. I shall die before your eyes to show my earnest heart." With that, she grasped the curved railing and started into the lotus pool.

Lü Bu lunged forward and caught her. Through his tears he said, "I have long known your real feelings, but alas, we could never speak." Diaochan reached out and clutched Lü Bu's clothing. "Since I can never be your wife in this world," she said, "I want to arrange to meet you in the next." "If I cannot have you as my wife in this world," answered Lü Bu, "then I am no hero worthy of the name." "I count my days as years. Pity me, my lord, and save me," the girl implored. "I had to slip away or else the old villain would suspect something," Lü Bu said. "Now I must go back." Diaochan would not let go of him. "If you are so afraid of the 'old villain,'" she cried, "then I will never see the light of day again, for I am lost." Lü Bu stood still. "Give me time to think," he said finally, as he took his halberd and turned to leave. "Oh, General!" cried Diaochan, "even in the seclusion of my boudoir your name resounded like thunder. I thought you the foremost man of the age and never imagined another could subjugate you." Her tears rained down. Shame covered Lü Bu's face as he leaned on his halberd, listening. Then he turned and embraced Diaochan, comforting her with tender words. The pair clung together fondly.

Dong Zhuo, who was still at court, began to wonder where Lü Bu had gone. He bid the Emperor a hasty good-bye and returned home in his carriage. Seeing Lü Bu's horse tied at his front gate, he questioned the gateman and was told that the general was in the rear chamber. Dong Zhuo dismissed his servants roughly and went looking for Lü Bu. Not finding him in the rear chamber, he called for Diaochan. She too was not to be found. "She is in the back garden viewing the blossoms," the maidservants told him. Dong Zhuo rushed there and saw the amorous pair tête-à-tête at the Phoenix Pavilion. The halberd had been set aside. Dong Zhuo's anger flared and he let out a dreadful shout. Lü Bu spotted him, panicked, and fled. Dong Zhuo picked up the great halberd and gave chase. Lü Bu was swift. Dong Zhuo, too fat to catch up, heaved the weapon. Lü Bu knocked it aside. Dong Zhuo retrieved it and continued running, but Lü Bu was already out of range. Dong Zhuo dashed out the garden gate, collided head on with another man running in, and fell to the ground. Indeed:

> His fury mounted to the sky,
> But his heavy frame sprawled upon the ground.

Who had knocked him down?
    Read on.

CHAPTER 9

Lü Bu Kills the Tyrant for Wang Yun; Li Jue Invades the Capital on Jia Xu's Advice

The man who plowed into Dong Zhuo was none other than his most trusted adviser, Li Ru. Horrified, Li Ru scrambled to help Dong Zhuo into the library, where the preceptor sat down and composed himself. "Whatever brought you here?" gasped Dong Zhuo. "I came in through the main gate," Li Ru replied. "They told me you'd charged off into the rear garden looking for Lü Bu. I rushed over too, and saw him bounding away, crying, 'The preceptor's after me!' So I headed into the garden to try and smooth things over, but I have only offended Your Worship and made things worse. I deserve to die." "Oh, to be rid of that scoundrel!" Dong Zhuo said fiercely. "He was flirting with my darling. I'll have his head for it." "That would be most unwise, Your

Worship," Li Ru responded. "In ancient times at the famous banquet where all guests were told to tear the tassels from their hats, King Zhuang of Chu overlooked an amorous gesture toward his queen from Jiang Xiong, the very man who later saved the king from Qin soldiers. Now, this Diaochan is just another woman; but Lü Bu is a fierce and trusted general. Give her to him now, and he will risk life and limb to requite your generosity. I entreat you, consider it carefully." After absorbing this advice, Dong Zhuo said, "You have a point. I shall think it over." Li Ru thanked him and left.

Dong Zhuo returned to his private apartments and asked Diaochan, "Are you having an affair with Lü Bu?" Diaochan burst into tears before replying, "I was enjoying the flowers in the back garden when he accosted me. I was frightened and tried to slip away. He said, 'I am the imperial preceptor's son. You don't have to avoid *me*.' Then he chased me with that halberd of his over to the Phoenix Pavilion. I could see he meant no good. What if he forced himself on me? I tried to throw myself into the pool, but the brute wrapped his arms around me. My life was hanging there in the balance when you came—just in time to save me."

"I have made a decision," Dong Zhuo declared. "I am going to give you into Lü Bu's service. What do you think of that?" Panicked, Diaochan pleaded through tears: "Having had the honor of serving Your Worship, I could not bear the shame of being handed down to an underling." She took hold of a sword hanging against the wall and pressed it to her throat. Dong Zhuo snatched it away and embraced her. "I spoke in jest," he said. Diaochan collapsed in his arms. "I know this is Li Ru's doing," she murmured as she hid her face and sobbed. "He and Lü Bu are fast friends and must have worked this out between them without giving the slightest consideration to the dignity of the imperial preceptor or to my own life. Oh, I could eat him alive!" "I will never give you up," said Dong Zhuo, comforting her. "Though I enjoy the favor of your attention," Diaochan went on, "I don't think I should remain here too long. Lü Bu will find a way to ruin me." "Tomorrow," said Dong Zhuo, "you and I shall repair to the new palace at Mei and take our pleasure there together. Try not to worry." Diaochan mastered her fears and thanked Dong Zhuo.

The following day Li Ru appeared before Dong Zhuo and said, "Today is an auspicious day for presenting Diaochan to Lü Bu." "Lü Bu and I," Dong Zhuo replied, "are father and son. It would be unseemly for me to present her to him. Despite his offense, however, I will take no action against him. Convey my wishes and speak gently to comfort him." "Preceptor," Li Ru urged, "you should not let a woman beguile you." Dong Zhuo's expression turned ugly. "Would you care," he asked, "to give your wife to Lü Bu? Let us hear no more of this, or the sword will speak for me." Li Ru left Dong Zhuo's presence and, raising his eyes to Heaven, sighed, "We are all doomed, and at a woman's hands." A reader of later times was moved to write this verse:

> Wang Yun staked the empire's fate
>   on a gentle maiden's charm.
> Spear and shield were set aside,
>   no soldier came to harm.
> In the fray at Tiger Pass
>   three heroes fought in vain.
> Instead the victory song was sung
>   at Phoenix Pavilion.

That same day Dong Zhuo prepared to return to Mei. The whole assembly of officials came to see him off. From her carriage Diaochan picked out Lü Bu in the throng, staring at her. She covered her face as if weeping. The carriage began to move. Lü Bu led his horse to a knoll and watched the dust rising behind the wheels. A sigh of remorse escaped from his lips. "Why are you staring into the distance and sighing?" someone asked from behind. "Why aren't you with the preceptor?" It was Minister of the Interior Wang Yun.

After they had exchanged greetings, Wang Yun said, "A slight indisposition has kept me indoors the past few days, that's why we haven't seen each other, but I felt I had to get myself out for the preceptor's departure. And now I have the added pleasure of meeting you. Forgive my question, General, but is something the matter?" "Your daughter, that's all," was the reply. "You mean, he's kept her all this time?" Wang Yun asked, affecting surprise. "That old villain made her his favorite long ago," answered Lü Bu. "I don't believe it!" Wang Yun exclaimed. Lü Bu then related what had happened to Diaochan as Wang Yun looked skyward and stamped his feet. Finally he spoke: "It amazes me that the preceptor could do such a beastly thing." He took Lü Bu's hand and said, "Why don't we discuss this further at my home?"

Lü Bu returned with Wang Yun, who ushered him into a private room. Given wine and treated cordially, Lü Bu narrated in full his confrontation with Dong Zhuo at the pavilion. "Then the preceptor has violated my daughter!" responded Wang Yun, "and snatched your wife. We stand shamed and mocked before the world. He is not mocked—only you and I. I am nothing but a useless old man, and I suppose I will have to swallow the insult. What a pity, though, for you, General—for a hero, head and shoulders above them all, to suffer such disgrace!"

Lü Bu's anger could have lifted him to the heavens. He struck the table and roared. "I should never have said what I did," Wang Yun said immediately. "Please compose yourself." "The villain's life will clear my name," Lü Bu shouted. "Do not say so, General," Wang Yun admonished, hastily touching Lü Bu's mouth. "I'm afraid I shall be implicated." "As a man of honor standing before Heaven and earth," Lü Bu went on, "I will not be his underling forever." "A man with your abilities," Wang Yun agreed, "should not be subject to the authority of someone like Preceptor Dong." "I would love to be rid of the old villain," confided Lü Bu, "but history would brand me an unfilial son." Smiling faintly, Wang Yun said, "You are a Lü. He is a Dong. Where was his fatherly feeling when he threw that halberd?" Lü Bu's temper flared again. "I nearly overlooked that!" he cried. "Thank you for reminding me."

As his suggestions took hold, Wang Yun continued working on Lü Bu: "Your service to the Han will secure your reputation for loyalty, and historians will preserve your good name for posterity. But support for Dong Zhuo is disloyal and will earn you an eternity of condemnation." Lü Bu shifted off his seat and bowed to the ground to show his respect. "My mind is made up," said Lü Bu. "Do not doubt it." "But failure means disaster," Wang Yun cautioned. With his knife Bu pricked blood from his arm to seal his pledge. In response Wang Yun dropped to his knees and said, "Your gracious favor enables the temple services of the Han to continue. But you must disclose nothing. A plan of action will be ready in due time, and you will be informed." Lü Bu assented and took his leave.

Next, Wang Yun summoned Shisun Rui, a supervisor in the Secretariat, and Huang Wan, commander of the Capital Districts, to try to work out a plan. "The Emperor," Rui began, "has recently recovered from an illness. Send a smooth talker to the new palace in Mei requesting Dong Zhuo's presence in the capital. At the same time have the Emperor secretly authorize Lü Bu to place an ambush at the court gates. Escort Dong Zhuo in and kill him there. That's the best way." "Who will take the message?" asked Huang Wan. "Cavalry Commander Li Su," suggested Rui, "comes from Lü Bu's own district. He has resented Dong Zhuo ever since he was passed over for promotion, but Dong Zhuo is unlikely to suspect him." "A good choice," said Wang Yun.

Wang Yun presented the plan to Lü Bu, who said, "Li Su! He talked me into killing Ding Yuan! He'll go all right, or I'll have his head." Li Su was secretly brought in, and Lü Bu confronted him: "Once you convinced me to kill my benefactor and stepfather Ding Yuan and go over to Dong Zhuo. Now he has wronged the Emperor and caused the people to suffer. His foul crimes have roused the indignation of men and gods alike. We want you to carry the Emperor's edict to Mei, commanding Dong Zhuo to appear at court, where soldiers in hiding will be ready to kill him. We must work for the house of Han as loyal subjects. Do we have your consent?" "I, too," replied Li Su, "have longed to be rid of him, but I despaired of finding allies. If *you*, General, are so minded, then Heaven itself favors our cause. I am with you, heart and soul." He broke an arrow to confirm his oath. "If your mission succeeds," said Wang Yun, "a handsome commission awaits you."

Li Su and a dozen riders went to Mei the following day. The arrival of the imperial edict was announced, and Dong Zhuo received the bearer. Li Su paid his respects. "What edict from the Emperor?" asked Dong Zhuo. "His Majesty," began Li Su, "has recovered from his illness and desires to call together the full assembly in the Weiyang Hall. This edict was issued in connection with a decision to yield the throne to the preceptor." "What is Wang Yun's view?" asked Dong Zhuo. "The minister of the interior," Li Su replied, "has already arranged for the construction of a platform for the ceremony of abdication. Only your presence is awaited, my lord." Delighted, Dong Zhuo said, "Last night I dreamed that a dragon was encircling me; today these auspicious tidings arrive. My time has come. I must not miss it." Dong Zhuo ordered four trusted generals—Li Jue, Guo Si, Zhang Ji, and Fan Chou—to guard Mei with three thousand men from his Flying Bear Corps. Then he made ready to return to Chang'an. "When I am emperor," he said, turning to Li Su, "you will bear the gilded mace as chief of the Capital Guard." Li Su gave thanks, speaking as a subject addressing his sovereign.

Dong Zhuo went to take leave of his mother, a woman more than ninety years old. "Where are you going, son?" she asked. "I am going to accept the succession from the Han," he replied. "Shortly you will be made Queen Mother." "These few days," she said, "I have been feeling unsteady, and my heart won't quiet down. Could it be an ill omen?" "Mother," Dong Zhuo answered, "you are going to be Mother of the Realm. That's what these little premonitions mean." He took his leave. Before departing, he told Diaochan, "When I am emperor, you will be made Precious Consort." Diaochan, who realized he was falling into the trap, feigned great pleasure and expressed profound gratitude.

Surrounded by his adherents, Dong Zhuo ascended his carriage and set out for Chang'an. He had traveled less than thirty *li* when a wheel broke. Dong Zhuo switched to horseback. After another ten *li* the horse began snorting wildly and snapped its reins. Dong Zhuo said to Li Su, "First the wheel, now the horse—what do these signs mean?" "Simply," Li Su answered smoothly, "that the preceptor will be replacing the Han, discarding the old for the new, and should soon be riding in the imperial carriage with its jewels and golden gear!" Dong Zhuo found this answer delightful and convincing.

The next day the journey continued. A fierce storm sprang up, and a dark mist spread over the heavens. "What does this signify?" Dong Zhuo asked. "When you ascend the dragon throne," answered Li Su, "there will be red streaks of light through purple mists demonstrating the heavenly power of Your Majesty." Dong Zhuo's doubts were again satisfied by this interpretation.

Dong Zhuo's carriage reached the capital gate. The assembly

of officials welcomed him. Only Li Ru had absented himself for reasons of health. Dong Zhuo entered his official residence, followed by Lü Bu, who extended his congratulations. "I shall be ascending the imperial throne," Dong Zhuo said, "and you will become the head of all military forces." Lü Bu thanked his patron and spent the night outside his sleeping quarters. That night a dozen boys were singing in the outskirts of the city, and the wind carried their melancholy voices into the bed chamber:

> A thousand *li* of green, green grass
> Beyond the tenth day, one can't last.

"What is the meaning of the rhyme?" asked Zhuo. "It only means," Li Su replied, "that the house of Liu will fall, and the house of Dong will rise."

At dawn the following day Dong Zhuo arrayed his honor guard. As his sedan chair reached court, he was surprised to see a Taoist priest in a dark gown and white headdress, holding a long staff. Tied to the top was a strip of cloth about ten feet long with the word "mouth" written on either end. "What is this priest trying to say?" asked Dong Zhuo. "He is deranged," Li Su replied and had him chased away.

Dong Zhuo went into the main court area. The assembled officials, splendid in their formal robes and caps, greeted him from the sides. Sword in hand, Li Su followed the carriage. They came to a side gate on the north. Only twenty of Dong Zhuo's charioteers were let through. Further ahead at the entrance to the main hall Dong Zhuo could see a group with drawn swords standing around Wang Yun. Perturbed, Dong Zhuo asked, "What is the meaning of these swords?" Li Su made no reply as he helped push the carriage straight on in.

"The traitor is here!" shouted Wang Yun. "Where are my men?" On either side a hundred weapons appeared. Halberd and lance were thrust against Dong Zhuo, but his armor prevented injury. Then, wounded in the arm, he fell from the carriage. "Where is my son?" he screamed. Lü Bu stepped out from behind the carriage. "Here is the edict to punish the traitor!" he cried and cut Dong Zhuo's throat with his halberd. Li Su severed the head and held it aloft. Lü Bu produced the edict, shouting, "This is the Emperor's writ. Only the traitor Dong Zhuo is to answer for his crime." Officers and men hailed the Emperor. Dong Zhuo's fate moved someone to write these lines:

> Success would have placed him on the throne itself;
> Failing that, he meant to have an easy life of wealth.
> What he forgot is that the gods ordain a path so strict:
> His palace newly done, his enterprise lay wrecked.

At once Lü Bu said, "Li Ru abetted Dong Zhuo in all his brutal crimes. Who will seize him?" Li Su volunteered to go. Suddenly there was a commotion at the gate. Li Ru's household servants had already tied him up and brought him in. Wang Yun ordered Li Ru executed in the marketplace. Dong Zhuo's corpse was displayed on the main thoroughfare. There was so much fat in his body that the guards lit a fire in his navel; as it burned, grease from the corpse ran over the ground. Passing commoners knocked Dong Zhuo's severed head with their fists and trampled his body. Wang Yun ordered Lü Bu, Huangfu Song, and Li Su to march fifty thousand men to the new palace complex at Mei and take custody of all property and residents.

Meanwhile the four generals Dong Zhuo left in charge of Mei—Li Jue, Guo Si, Zhang Ji, and Fan Chou—hearing that their master was dead and that Lü Bu was on his way, led their Flying Bears west to Liangzhou by rapid night marches. At Mei, Lü Bu first took Diaochan into his charge, while Huangfu Song freed the sons and daughters of the good Chang'an families. All members of Dong Zhuo's family, including his aged mother, were put to death. The heads of Dong Zhuo's brother Min and his nephew Huang were publicly displayed. The entire wealth of the new complex was confiscated: several hundred thousand taels of gold, millions of silver coins, fine sheer silks, pearls, precious implements, grain stores—a vast treasure. When the results were reported back to Wang Yun, he feasted the troops and held a grand celebration at the Office of the Secretariat.

The festivities were interrupted by a report that someone had kneeled and wept beside Dong Zhuo's body. "Everyone cheered his execution. Who dares mourn?" Wang Yun said angrily and ordered the man arrested. Brought before the astonished officials was none other than Privy Counselor Cai Yong. Wang Yun denounced the offender: "For what reason do you, a subject of the Han, mourn a traitor whose death benefits the dynasty, instead of joining our celebration?" Cai Yong acknowledged his offense: "Despite my meagre abilities," he said, "I can tell right from wrong and would never honor Dong Zhuo instead of the Han. Yet I could not help shedding a tear out of gratitude for the favor he has shown me. I know I should not have done it. I only pray that if my face is branded and my feet cut off, I may nonetheless be permitted to continue my work on the history of the Han as a form of atonement. I seek no other mercy."

The court officials, who esteemed Cai Yong's ability, pleaded for him strenuously. Imperial Guardian Ma Midi also urged Wang Yun privately, "It would be a boon to let so unique a talent complete the history. Moreover, his filial devotion is widely respected. If you condemn him without due consideration, we may forfeit people's confidence." "Centuries ago," responded Wang Yun, "Emperor Wu spared Sima Qian and let him write his history, with the result that we have a slanderous account whose ill effects are felt to this day. At a time when our destiny is uncertain and court administration faltering, how can we permit a toady like Cai Yong to wield the pen by the side of a junior emperor? He will defame us." To these words the imperial guardian made no reply; but privately he told officials, "May Wang Yun leave no posterity. Able men of character are the mainstay of the ruling house, institutions its legal basis. Destroy the mainstay, discard the basis, and the Han cannot long endure." Wang Yun rejected Ma Midi's appeal and had Cai Yong taken to prison and strangled. The news moved many scholars to tears. Later, many held that Cai Yong was wrong to mourn Dong Zhuo but that Wang Yun went too far when he had him killed. A poet voiced these feelings:

> Power was Dong Zhuo's means to tyranny;
> And Cai Yong's death, his own ignominy.
> Kongming lay low in Longzhong and every hero weighed
> Would he waste his talents on a renegade?

The loyalists' victory is short-lived, as the four generals whom Dong Zhuo stationed at his home palace instigate a rebellion and march on Chang'an. They defeat Lü Bu in battle, execute Wang Yun, and install themselves

as *"protectors" of Emperor Xian. In chapters 9 to 19, warfare and treachery are the only constants. Various would-be protectors of the young emperor rise and fall, each as tyrannical as the last. Alliances are made
and broken. Regional centers form: Yuan Shao establishes himself north
of the Yellow River; the Sun clan builds an independent kingdom called
the Southland (Wu or Jiangnan) below the Yangzi River. But there is no
center: "The deer is loose," the emperor has no home and no stable court
in a secure capital. Many of the warring nobles consider the Han dynasty to be weak and waning, and only a few, such as Liu Xuande, remain loyal. Some dream of ascending the throne themselves; Yuan Shu
obtains the imperial seal and declares himself emperor but is cut down
in battle.*

*Cao Cao, who has emerged as the dominant warlord in the east, now
assumes the role of protector of the emperor. He makes a new capital in
Xuchang and divides his main rivals, Liu Xuande and Lü Bu, who
once had a clear if uneasy understanding. Lü Bu sustains heavy losses
and defeats, and finds comfort in heavy drinking and the overly cautious advice dispensed by his wife, Lady Yan, and his concubine Dianchan. But his comfort is ephemeral. Cao Cao, allying with Liu Xuande,
conquers and kills Lü Bu. Dianchan is not heard from again.*

CHAPTER 20

Cao Cao Leads the Royal Hunt near the Capital; Dong Cheng Receives a Mandate in the Palace

Lü Bu's wives and daughters were transported to the capital. The
imperial army was feasted; then all units decamped and the army
marched back to the capital. As they passed through Xuzhou (the
province Lü Bu had taken over from Xuande), the people lined
the road, burning incense and appealing to Cao Cao to restore
Xuande as protector. But Cao Cao said, "Protector Liu has ren-

dered great service. Let him first come before the Emperor for his enfeoffment." The common folk touched their heads to the ground in appreciation. Meanwhile, Cao Cao appointed General of Cavalry and Chariots Che Zhou provisional protector of Xuzhou. Back in Xuchang, Cao Cao rewarded all who had joined his campaign and assigned Xuande comfortable quarters near his ministerial residence.

The next day Emperor Xian held court. Cao Cao hailed Xuande's feats of arms and presented him. Attired in court apparel, Xuande paid homage at the base of the steps to the throne. The Emperor then instructed him to ascend. "Tell me of your lineage," the Emperor said. "I can trace my ancestry through Prince Jing of Zhongshan," Xuande replied, "back to his father, Jing, the fourth emperor. My grandfather was Liu Xiong, my father Liu Hong." Emperor Xian ordered the director of the Imperial Clan to recite from the clan registry.

"Emperor Jing had fourteen sons," the official intoned, "the seventh of whom was Prince Jing of Zhongshan, Liu Sheng by name. Sheng begat Zhen, precinct master of Lu; Zhen begat Ang, lord of Pei; Ang begat Lu, lord of Zhang; Lu begat Lian, lord of Yishui; Lian begat Ying, lord of Qinyang; Ying begat Jian, lord of Anguo; Jian begat Ai, lord of Guangling; Ai begat Xian, lord of Jiaoshui; Xian begat Shu, lord of Zuyi; Shu begat Yi, lord of Qiyang; Yi begat Bi, lord of Yuanze; Bi begat Da, lord of Ying-chuan; Da begat Buyi, lord of Fengling; Buyi begat Hui, lord of Jichuan; Hui begat Xiong, prefect of Fan, a county of Dongjun; Xiong begat Hong, who held no office; Xuande is the son of Hong."

The Emperor checked the order of the lineage and found that Xuande was indeed an imperial uncle. Elated, Emperor Xian summoned him to an adjoining room, where they enacted the formalities befitting uncle and nephew. The Emperor mused, "Cao Cao abuses his authority to the point that state affairs are out of our control. But now we may have a remedy in this heroic uncle of mine." He made Xuande general of the Left and precinct master of Yi. After a grand banquet to mark the occasion, Xuande thanked the sovereign for his generosity and left the court. He was known thereafter as Imperial Uncle Liu.

Returning to his quarters, Cao Cao was confronted by his advisers. "You have nothing to gain, Your Excellency," Xun Wen-ruo argued, "from this new relationship between Liu Bei and the Emperor." "Although he has been recognized as an imperial uncle," Cao Cao replied, "I still command him by imperial decree. He is thus doubly bound. Don't forget: so long as he's here in Xuchang, we have him well in hand—however near the Emperor he may be. There's nothing to fear. What really worries me is that Yang Biao, our grand commandant, is a member of Yuan Shu's clan and could do us great harm if he decided to work for the Yuan brothers. I want him eliminated at once." Accordingly, Cao Cao had Yang Biao incarcerated for alleged connivance with Yuan Shu. Man Chong was assigned to the case.

At this time Kong Rong, governor of Beihai, was in the capital; he protested to Cao, "Yang Biao comes from a family that has exhibited the purest virtue for four generations. You can't prosecute him for his ties to the Yuans." "It is His Majesty's wish," Cao Cao replied. "Suppose," Kong Rong retorted, "that at the beginning of the Zhou dynasty the child emperor Cheng had had Duke Shao killed. Who would believe a protestation of innocence from the regent, the Duke of Zhou?" On the strength of this argument Cao Cao released Yang Biao and sent him home to his village. But when Court Counselor Zhao Yan, indignant at Cao Cao's high-handed rule, accused the prime minister of lese majesty in arbitrarily arresting high ministers, Cao Cao arrested Zhao Yan and had him killed. The whole court trembled at this demonstration of Cao's temper.

Cheng Yu advised Cao Cao, "Sir, your prestige increases day by day. Perhaps the time is ripe for preparing to ascend the throne yourself?" "The court," Cao Cao replied, "has too many loyal ministers for us to move imprudently. I plan to invite the Emperor to a grand hunt. We'll see what the reaction is then."

Prime horses, pedigreed hunting hawks, and champion hounds were selected; the bows and arrows were made ready. Cao Cao assembled his soldiers outside the city and then entered the palace to invite the Emperor to lead the hunt. "This appears somewhat unorthodox," the sovereign commented. "The kings and emperors of ancient times," Cao explained, "held four grand hunts yearly, riding forth from the capital each season to show the world their prowess. Now with the empire in commotion, a hunt should provide an ideal occasion for us to demonstrate our skill at arms." Unable to refuse, the Emperor mounted his easy-gaited horse and, armed with jeweled bow and gold-tipped arrows, led the procession out of the city.

Liu Xuande, Lord Guan, and Zhang Fei, bows and blades at the ready, breastplates under their dress, led several dozen horsemen in the cavalcade. On a rich chestnut horse, a "flying spark," Cao Cao rode at the head of one hundred thousand men. Arriving at Xutian, they fanned out and enclosed the field in a ring of some two hundred *li*. Cao Cao kept his horse parallel to the Emperor's, never more than a head apart. His trusted commanders and officers massed behind him. The regular imperial officials, civil and military, trailed in the rear, none daring to draw close.

As the Emperor galloped toward the field, Xuande saluted him from the roadside. "I look forward to admiring the imperial uncle's marksmanship today," the Emperor said. As if receiving a command, Xuande took to his horse. That moment a hare sprang from the bushes. Xuande felled it with one shot from his bow. The Emperor complimented him and rode on. The procession turned and was crossing a low hill when a stag charged from the wood. The Emperor shot three arrows but missed. "Try for it, my lord," the Emperor cried to Cao Cao. Impudently, Cao asked for the Emperor's jeweled bow and gold-tipped arrows. Drawing the bow to the full, he released an arrow that pierced the deer's back; the animal toppled in the grass.

The crowd of ministers and generals, seeing the royal arrow, assumed that the Emperor had scored the hit and surged forward to congratulate him, crying, "Long life to the Emperor!" But it was Cao Cao, guiding his horse ahead of the Son of Heaven, who acknowledged the cheers. All who saw it blanched. Behind Xuande, Lord Guan seethed. Brows arching, eyes glaring, he raised his sword and rode forward to cut Cao Cao down. A sharp look with a motion of the head from Xuande changed his mind, and he reined in.

Xuande bowed to Cao Cao and congratulated him: "Your Excellency shoots with more than human skill. Few in this age can equal you." "It was the largess of the Emperor, really," Cao replied, laughing as he rode his horse round to express his compliments to the sovereign. But instead of returning the jeweled bow, he simply hung it at his side. When the hunt was over, the multitude feasted in Xutian. Afterward the Emperor led the procession back to the capital, and it dispersed.

Later Lord Guan asked Xuande, "Why did you stop me? I could have rid the dynasty of a traitor at whose hands the Emperor suffers personally." "'If you aim for the mouse,'" Xuande warned, "'don't bring down the house!' Cao Cao was at the Emperor's side, and his lieutenants were thick around him. Dear brother, had you accidentally injured the Emperor in a moment of foolish wrath, we would be the ones accused of the very crimes you denounce." "Spared today—a plague tomorrow," Lord Guan retorted. "Say no more," said Xuande. "We cannot speak freely."

*　　*　　*　　*

Inside the palace the Emperor spoke tearfully to his consort Empress Fu: "Since I first assumed the throne, treacherous pretenders have multiplied. First we suffered the disaster of Dong Zhuo, followed immediately by the sedition of generals Li Jue and Guo Si. We have faced griefs unknown to most. Then came Cao Cao, whom we thought a loyal servant of the dynasty, never dreaming he would usurp the government and abuse his authority by arbitrary exercise of fear and favor. I wince to see him. Today in the hunting field he impudently acknowledged the cheers meant for his sovereign. Before long there will be a usurpation, and you and I shall not die natural deaths." Empress Fu replied, "In this court full of lords and peers—not a one of whom but eats and lives at the pleasure of the Han—is there none to assist the dynasty in distress?"

As the Empress was speaking, her father, Fu Wan, entered. "Your Majesties," he said, "do not despair. I have the man who can remove the scourge of the royal house." The Emperor wiped his tears as he replied, "Then you too can see how imperious Cao Cao is?" "Who could have missed the incident at the deer hunt?" Fu Wan responded. "But the whole court consists of either his clansmen or his followers. Except for the imperial in-laws, who will demonstrate loyalty by bringing the traitor to justice? I don't have the power to do it, but why can't we turn to Dong Cheng, brother of the imperial concubine, general of Cavalry and Chariots?" "He has stepped into the breach more than once," the Emperor agreed. "Have him summoned."

"All Your Majesty's attendants," Fu Wan went on, "are Cao Cao's confidants. If they find out, the consequences will be serious." "What can we do?" the Emperor asked. "I have an idea," Fu Wan responded. "Fashion a garment and obtain a jade girdle, both of which you can privately bestow on Dong Cheng. Sew a secret decree into the girdle lining. When he reaches home and discovers the decree, he will devote himself to devising a strategy, and not even the spirits will know." The Emperor approved and Fu Wan withdrew.

Emperior Xian prepared to write the mandate. He bit his finger, transcribed his words in blood, and instructed the Empress to sew the text into the purple embroidered lining of the girdle. The Emperor then slipped on the brocade robe he had had made, tied the girdle, and ordered a palace officer to command Dong Cheng's appearance. The formalities of audience concluded, the Emperor spoke: "Last night the Empress and I were recalling the loyal service you tendered us when we fled from Chang'an across the River Ba, and decided to send for you to express our gratitude." Dong Cheng touched his head to the ground and disclaimed the honor.

The Emperor guided Dong Cheng to the ancestral temple and then into the Gallery of Meritorious Officials, in whose honor the Emperor burned incense before walking on with Dong Cheng to admire the portraits. "Tell me," the Emperor said, stopping before a portrait of the Supreme Ancestor, "where did the founder of the Han commence his career, and how did he create the heritage we enjoy?" "You mock me," Dong Cheng responded, astonished. "How could I forget the deeds of our sacred ancestor? He began as a precinct master in Sishang. From there he went on to slay the white serpent with his three-span sword, marking the rising against the Qin dynasty. Traversing the land, he annihilated Qin in three years and Chu in five. Thus he took possession of the empire and established this enduring patrimony."

"So splendid, so heroic the forefather," sighed the Emperor, "so fainthearted and feeble the progeny. One can't help sighing." As he spoke, he directed Dong Cheng's attention to the portraits of the two officials on either side of the Supreme Ancestor. "Is this not Zhang Liang," he went on, "lord of Liu? And this, Xiao He, lord of Cuo?" "Indeed," replied Dong Cheng, "the Supreme Ancestor relied greatly on them in founding the dynasty." The Emperor observed that no one was near and whispered, "So should you, uncle, stand by us." "I have no merit," Dong Cheng answered, "to serve as they served." "We remember well," the Emperor continued, "your service at the western capital, for which no reward could suffice." Then, pointing to his garments, he added, "Won't you wear this robe of mine and tie it with this girdle so that you will always seem to be by my side?"

Dong Cheng touched his forehead to the ground. The Emperor undid the robe and girdle, whispering, "Examine these carefully when you get home. Do not fail me." Perceiving the Emperor's intention, Dong Cheng put on the garment and, taking leave, quit the gallery.

Informed of this audience, Cao Cao intercepted Dong Cheng outside the palace gate. Where could he hide? Alarmed but helpless, he stood at the roadside and offered a ritual greeting. "What is the imperial in-law here for?" asked Cao. "The Emperor summoned me to present this brocade robe and jade girdle," replied Dong Cheng. "For what reason were you so honored?" Cao Cao asked again. "In recognition of my service at the western capital," was the answer. "Show me the girdle," Cao demanded. Believing the girdle to contain a secret decree concerning the prime minister, Dong Cheng demurred until Cao Cao barked to his attendants, "Strip it off him!"

Cao Cao examined the girdle closely. "A beautiful belt," he said. "Now take off the robe." Dong Cheng dared not refuse. Cao Cao held the garment up to the sun and scrutinized it. Then he slipped it on, tied the girdle and turned to his men, saying, "Fits me well, doesn't it?" "Perfectly," was the reply. "Would the imperial in-law," Cao Cao suggested, "consider turning these over to me as a gift?" "What the sovereign bestows of his generosity," Dong Cheng protested, "may never be given away. Let me have others fashioned to present to you." "These clothes," Cao Cao snapped, "must be connected with some intrigue." "How could one dare!" Dong Cheng gasped. "If Your Excellency insists, of course I shall leave them with you." "Sire," Cao Cao reassured him, "would I seize what the sovereign vouchsafes? Bear with my facetiousness." He returned the garment and the girdle to Dong Cheng, who took his leave and went home.

Alone in his library that night, Dong Cheng went over the robe inch by inch. Finding nothing, he mused, "When the Son of Heaven instructed me to examine these clothes, he must have had something in mind. But there's no sign of anything. Why?" He inspected the girdle: white jade tesserae wrought into a miniature dragon snaking through a floral design; the underside was lined with purple brocade. The stitching was flawless. Nothing was visible. He placed the girdle on his desk and puzzled over it until he grew drowsy.

Dong Cheng was on the verge of falling asleep, his head on the desk, when a spark from the lamp's smoldering snuff flew onto the material and burned through the lining. He brushed it out, but the spark had already eaten away a bit of the brocade, revealing the white silk and traces of blood. He slit open the girdle: there was the decree, bloodscript in the Emperor's hand:

> We believe that in the human order the bond of father and son is foremost, and that in the social order the obligation between sovereign and servant is paramount. Of late the treasonous Cao Cao, abusing his authority, insulting and degrading his sovereign, has connived with his cohorts to the detriment of our dynasty's rule. Instructions, rewards, land grants, and punishments now fall outside the imperial jurisdiction. Day and night we brood on this, dreading the peril to the realm. General, you are a prominent public servant and our nearest relative. Think of the obstacles and hardships the Supreme Ancestor faced when he founded this dynasty: forge a union of stouthearted men, stalwarts of unimpaired integrity and unimpeachable loyalty; exterminate this perfidious faction and restore the security of our holy shrines for our ancestors' sake. I have cut my finger and shed this blood to compose this decree confided to you. Remain vigilant. Do not fail our hopes. Decree of the third month, spring, Jian An 4 [A.D. 199].

Dong Cheng read the edict through his tears. He could not sleep that night and in the morning returned to the library to reread the document. But no concrete plan occurred to him. Finally he fell asleep against his desk pondering the means to get rid of Cao Cao.

The courtier Wang Zifu arrived. Recognizing his master's intimate friend, the gateman did not stop him, and he went straight into the library. Wang Zifu saw Dong Cheng dozing at his desk, a silk scroll under his sleeve. The imperial "we" was barely visible on it. Becoming curious, Wang Zifu quietly took up the document. After reading it, he stowed it in his own sleeve. "Imperial In-law Dong," he cried, "are you not ashamed? How carefree to be sleeping so!" Dong Cheng came to immediately. Missing the decree, he felt his senses swim and his limbs fail. "You plan to murder the prime minister, then?" Zifu demanded. "I shall have to denounce you." "Brother," Dong Cheng wept, "if that is your intention, the house of Han expires."

"I was simply playing a part," Wang Zifu reassured Dong Cheng. "Our clan has enjoyed the fruits of service to the Han for many generations. Far from failing in loyalty, I mean to lend my all to the task of destroying the traitor." "The dynasty is fortunate indeed if you are so minded," Dong Cheng responded. "Let us retire, then," Wang Zifu suggested, "and draw up a loyalist pledge to do our duty to the Emperor whatever the risk to ourselves and our clans."

In great excitement Dong Cheng fetched a length of white silk and wrote his name at the head. Wang Zifu added his, saying, "My trusted friend General Wu Zilan should make cause with us." "Within the court," Dong Cheng said, "only Changshui Commandant Chong Ji and Court Counselor Wu Shi are trusted friends who will join us." At that moment a servant announced the two officials. "Thus Heaven aids us!" Dong Cheng exclaimed and sent Wang Zifu behind a screen to observe while he received the two in his library. After tea Chong Ji said, "The incident at the hunt must have infuriated you." "Yes," replied Dong Cheng, "but what could I do?" "I'd vow to do away with the traitor," Wu Shi added, "but I despair of finding allies." "To rid the dynasty of evil," Chong Ji said, "I would die without regret."

At these words, Wang Zifu emerged from behind the screen and cried, "So! The two of you would assassinate the prime minister! I mean to turn you in, and the imperial in-law will corroborate my charge." "A loyal subject does not fear death!" Chong Ji shot back angrily. "I'd rather be a ghost of the Han than a traitor's lackey like you!" Dong Cheng smiled. "We staged this to test you both. Wang Zifu did not speak in earnest," he explained as he drew the edict from his sleeve and showed it to them. The two men wept copiously as they read. Dong Cheng then asked for their signatures. "Will you gentlemen stay here a while," Wang Zifu said, "while I see if Wu Zilan will join us?" He returned shortly with the general, who added his name. Dong Cheng invited the four to dine in a rear chamber.

The unexpected arrival of Ma Teng, governor of Xiliang, was announced. "Say I am not well and cannot receive him," Dong Cheng instructed the gateman. But when this answer was brought, Ma Teng shouted angrily, "I saw him only yesterday at the Donghua Gate in a new robe and girdle. Why is he giving me excuses? I have important business. He must let me in." After hearing the gateman's report, Dong Cheng excused himself and received his latest guest.

"I am on my way home after an audience with His Majesty," Ma Teng said, "and have come to take leave. Why refuse to see me?" "I had a sudden illness," Dong Cheng said, "and failed my duty as a host. Forgive the offense." "You look in the pink of health to me," Ma Teng remarked. Dong Cheng could not bring himself to speak. Flicking his sleeves, Ma Teng rose to leave. "And no one to save the dynasty!" he said with a sigh. Dong Cheng caught his words and held him back, saying, "What do you mean, 'no one to save the dynasty'?" "I am still fuming over the incident at the deer hunt," Ma Teng said. "Even you, it seems, the closest relative of the ruling house, are sunk in dissipation and give no thought to punishing the traitor. How could you be one to relieve the dynasty's distress?"

Wary of deception, Dong Cheng feigned surprise and said, "His Excellency Cao Cao is a high minister, the mainstay of the court. How can you say such a thing?" Enraged, Ma Teng cried, "You still believe that traitor is a decent man?" "There are eyes and ears everywhere," Dong Cheng cautioned. "You must lower your voice." "Those who crave life above all," Ma Teng retorted, "are unfit to discuss serious matters." He rose to leave. Convinced of Ma Teng's loyalty, Dong Cheng said at last, "Restrain yourself a moment, my lord. I have something to show you." He drew the governor into his chamber and handed him the imperial edict.

As he read, Ma Teng's hair stood on end; he bit his lips until blood covered his mouth. "If you plan to act," he said, "my Xi-liang troops will help." Then Dong Cheng led the governor to meet the other supporters of the indictment against the prime minister. At Dong Cheng's request, Ma Teng affixed his signature, confirming his oath with a swallow of wine and some drops of blood. "What we swear here we will never disavow," he said, and pointing to the five men, he added, "If five more will join us, our cause will succeed." "Loyal and stalwart men," Dong Cheng warned, "are all too few. If we take in the wrong ones, we will only ruin ourselves." Ma Teng asked to see the register of current office holders. Coming to the names of the house of Liu, he clapped his hands and cried, "Here is the man we must talk to!" The group asked who. Calmly and deliberately, Ma Teng spoke the name. Indeed:

> Because an in-law received the Emperor's call,
> An imperial kinsman came to the dynasty's aid.

Whom did Ma Teng name?
Read on.

CHAPTER 21

*Cao Cao Warms Wine and Rates
the Heroes of the Realm; Lord Guan
Takes Xuzhou by Stratagem
and Beheads Che Zhou*

"Whom do you recommend?" Dong Cheng had asked Ma Teng. "I see here the name of Liu Xuande, protector of Yuzhou. Why not try him?" was the reply. "True, he's the Emperor's uncle," Dong Cheng said thoughtfully, "but he is too close to Cao. He can't get involved in this." "I saw what happened on the hunting field," Ma Teng responded, "when Cao Cao accepted the public accolade meant for the Emperor. Lord Guan was right behind Xuande and would have struck Cao Cao down had not Xuande stopped him with an angry glance. Xuande is more than willing to organize against Cao, but he feels thwarted, unequal to Cao's many guards. Try to enlist his help—I know he will respond eagerly." The group dispersed with Wu Shi cautioning, "Let's not be too hasty. This requires careful consideration."

The next night Dong Cheng pocketed the imperial decree and paid a quiet call on Xuande. Flanked by his brothers, Xuande received him in a small chamber. After host and guest were seated, Xuande said, "Only a most serious occasion would bring the imperial in-law in the dead of night." "I couldn't risk coming by day," Dong Cheng replied. "Cao would have suspected something." Xuande called for wine, and Dong Cheng went on, "The other day at the hunt Lord Guan seemed set to kill Cao Cao, but you motioned him off. Why?" Taken by surprise, Xuande parried the question, asking, "How do you know that?" "No one else noticed," Dong Cheng said, "but I did." Unable to maintain his pose of indifference, Xuande answered, "My brother, outraged by Cao's insolent ambition, acted impulsively."

Dong Cheng hid his face and wept. "If only the vassals at court compared with Lord Guan," he cried, "the peace of the land would be assured." Wondering if Cao Cao had sent the imperial brother-in-law to sound him out, Xuande said, "With His Excellency Cao Cao in power, is not the peace of the land already well assured?" Dong Cheng's face stiffened as he rose. "It is only because you are the Emperor's uncle that I opened my heart and soul to you. Why have you played me false?" he asked. "Lest *you* play *me* false, Imperial Brother-in-law," Xuande admitted at last, "I had to test you." Dong Cheng then produced the secret edict. Dismay and indignation welled up in Xuande as he read the Emperor's sacred words.

Next, Dong Cheng handed him the loyalists' pledge bearing six signatures: Dong Cheng, general of Cavalry and Chariots; Wang Zifu, an official in the Ministry of Works; Chong Ji, commandant of the Changshui command; Wu Shi, court counselor; Wu Zilan, General of Manifest Trust; and Ma Teng, governor of Xiliang. "Since the Emperor has charged you with the task of punishing the traitor," Xuande said, "I commit myself to the cause and offer my fullest devotion." Dong Cheng thanked him, and Xuande placed his name and title, general of the Left, on the silk roll. "There are three more we should approach," Dong Cheng said. "If they join, we will have ten righteous men confronting the traitor." But Xuande warned Dong Cheng to act with the utmost caution and secrecy. The two men continued talking until the fifth watch; then they parted.

To avoid arousing Cao Cao's suspicions, Xuande took to his back garden, planting and tending vegetables, keeping his purposes hidden. Lord Guan and Zhang Fei asked, "Brother, why have you lost interest in the great issues of the realm and given yourself to a commoner's toil?" "This is something you might not appreciate," responded Xuande, and his brothers did not ask again.

One day when Lord Guan and Zhang Fei were away and Xuande was watering his plants, two of Cao's generals, Xu Chu and Zhang Liao, led a score of men into the garden. "His Excellency," they announced, "requests that Your Lordship come at once." Alarmed, Xuande asked, "An emergency?" "I don't know," Xu Chu answered. "I was told to request your presence." Xuande could only follow the two men to Cao Cao's residence.

A smiling Cao Cao greeted Xuande. "That's quite a project you have under way at home," he said in a tone that turned Xuande's face pale as dust. Taking Xuande's hand, Cao led him to his own garden. "You have taken up a most difficult occupation in horticulture," Cao continued. "Just to while away the time," Xuande answered, relieved. "There is nothing else to occupy me."

"I was admiring the plums on the branch," Cao remarked. "The new green ones called to mind last year's campaign against Zhang Xiu, when we ran short of water on the march. How parched the men were! Then something occurred to me. 'There's a plum grove ahead,' I cried and pretended to locate it with my whip. When the troops heard me, their mouths watered and their thirst was gone. Seeing these plums now, I can't help enjoying the sight, and having some wine just heated, I decided to invite Your Lordship for a drink at this little pavilion." Regaining possession of himself, Xuande went along with Cao Cao. Delicacies had already been set out: a plate piled with new green plums and a jar brimming with warmed wine. Sitting opposite one another, the two men drank freely and enjoyed themselves without constraint.

The wine had enlivened their spirits when dark clouds appeared and overspread the heavens: a flash storm was threatening. An attendant pointed to what seemed like a distant dragon suspended on the horizon. The two men leaned against the balcony and watched it. Cao turned to Xuande and asked, "Does my lord understand the dragon's multiform manifestations?" "Not in great detail," Xuande replied. "The dragon," Cao continued, "can enlarge and diminish itself, surge aloft or lie beneath the surface of the water. Enlarged, it creates clouds and spews mist. Diminished, it can veil its scaly form from view. Aloft, it prances triumphant in the upper realm of space. Under the surface, it lurks among the surging breakers. Now in the fullness of spring it mounts the season, like men who would fulfill an ambition to dominate the length and breadth of the land. In this respect the dragon can well be compared to the heroes of the age. You yourself have traveled widely and surely must be familiar with the great heroes of our time. Please try to point them out for me."

"How can these eyes of mine sight heroes?" Xuande said. "Set your modesty aside," Cao urged. "Thanks to Your Excellency's gracious benefaction," Xuande responded, "I have succeeded in serving the dynasty. But as for the heroes of the realm, such things are more than I would know of." "Even if you do not know any personally," Cao Cao persisted, "you should at least have heard of some." "Yuan Shu of Huainan?" Xuande ventured. "His warriors are first rate, his provisions abundant. Would he be one?" "Dry bones," Cao laughed, "rattling in the grave. Sooner or later I will have him." "Yuan Shao, then," Xuande suggested. "For four generations the Yuans have held highest office, and many officials served under them. Shao has a firm grip on Jizhou, where he is supported by capable men. Would you count him?" "His expression is fierce enough," Cao said. "But his courage is thin. He enjoys conniving but lacks decision. He plays for high stakes but begrudges personal sacrifice, spots a minor gain and risks his life. No hero he!"

Xuande asked, "And how would you rate Liu Biao, a paragon whose reputation stretches across the realm?" "Liu Biao?" Cao answered. "A name without substance, and no hero either." "There is Sun Ce," Xuande suggested. "The leader of the Southland is in his prime." "Sun Ce," Cao replied, "stands on his father's reputation. He's no hero." "Liu Zhang, then," Xuande said, "perhaps he could be considered." "Though connected to the royal house," Cao Cao said, "he is nothing but a watchdog by the gate and hardly deserves the name of hero." "Then," Xuande continued "what about Zhang Xiu, Zhang Lu, Han Sui, and the other warlords?" Cao Cao clapped his hands and laughed. "Petty mediocrities," he said, "beneath our notice." "Truly," said Xuande, "I can think of no one else."

"Now," Cao Cao went on, "what defines a hero is this: a determination to conquer, a mine of marvelous schemes, an ability to encompass the realm, and the will to make it his." "Who merits such a description?" Xuande asked. Cao pointed first to Xuande, then to himself. "The heroes of the present day," he said, "number but two—you, my lord, and myself." Xuande gulped in panic. Before he realized it, his chopsticks had slipped to the ground. Then the storm came on. A peal of thunder gave him the chance to bend down casually and retrieve them. "See what a clap of thunder has made me do?" he remarked. "A great man afraid of thunder?" Cao asked. "Confucius himself became agitated in thunderstorms," Xuande reminded him. "How could I not fear them?" In this way he succeeded in glossing over the cause of his anxiety. Later a poet left these lines in admiration:

> Xuande sheltered in the tiger's lair:
> Cao betrayed two names that made him quake.
> He seizes on the thunder as the cause—
> A perfect ploy negotiates the pause.

The rain stopped. Two men burst into the garden. Swords in hand, they dashed to the pavilion, shoving aside the guards. There before Cao's eyes stood Lord Guan and Zhang Fei! The two warriors, after returning from archery practice, were told that Xu Chu and Zhang Liao had escorted Xuande to see Cao Cao. Anxious for their elder brother's safety, the two had rushed to the prime minister's residence and pushed their way into the rear garden, only to find Cao Cao and Xuande calmly drinking together. Lord Guan and Zhang Fei stood still, hands resting on their weapons. Cao asked the reason for the visit, and Lord Guan replied, "We heard Your Excellency was carousing with our brother and have come to present a sword dance for your amusement." "Not another Hongmen, I hope," Cao said, smiling. "We hardly need a repeat of that performance." Xuande smiled too. "Two more cups," ordered Cao, "to take the edge off these would-be Fan Kuais!" But the brothers respectfully declined and the party broke up. Xuande bid Cao Cao good-bye and returned to his quarters.

"We thought it was the end," Lord Guan said. Xuande told them how he had dropped his chopsticks, and his brothers asked what that meant. "I work in the garden," Xuande explained, "to show Cao Cao I have no ambition. But he caught me off guard by calling me a hero, and the chopsticks slipped from my hand. I told him it was the thunder to put him off the track." The brothers marveled at Xuande's quickness.

The following day found Xuande a guest of Cao's once again. While they were together, Man Chong reported that Yuan Shao had defeated Gongson Zan. Xuande, anxious about his longtime friend, asked for details.

Man Chong replied, "Zan could not cope with Yuan Shao in the field, so he walled in his position, built a hundred-span tower above it called Yijing Tower, and laid in three hundred thousand measures of grain. His soldiers, however, kept passing in and out of the fortified area, and some were caught outside. Zan's followers wanted to rescue them, but Zan said, 'Rescue one, and others who will have to fight will be looking for help instead of fighting to the death.' Zan's denial of help only prompted many of his men to surrender to Yuan Shao. Isolated now, Zan sent to the capital for help. Unfortunately, Shao captured his messenger. Next, Zan tried to get Zhang Yan to cooperate inside of Shao's camp by setting a fire as a signal. Again, Shao intercepted the letter and used the information to draw Zan into an ambush. Zan lost more than half his men before retreating into the city. Shao then tunneled under the Yijing Tower and set it ablaze. Trapped, Zan killed his wife and children and hanged himself. The rest of his family was consumed in the flames.

"Consequently, Yuan Shao is now vastly strengthened by the new forces he has acquired. Meanwhile, Yuan Shu, Shao's brother, lives a dissipated life, scorning the needs of his army and his people—many of whom have already turned against him. Shu has proposed transferring to Yuan Shao the imperial title he usurped, and Shao for his part wants the royal seal more than anything. Shu has promised to deliver it personally and is now moving from south of the Huai to north of the Yellow River. If the Yuan brothers overcome their former enmity and join forces, we may not be able to handle them. I beg Your Excellency to deal with this emergency."

Xuande grieved for the loss of Gongsun Zan, who had once so kindly recommended him. And where, he worried, could his dear friend General Zhao Zilong be? The time had come, Xuande calculated, to make his break with Cao Cao. Xuande stood up and faced the prime minister. "For Yuan Shu to join his brother, Shao," Xuande declared, "he will have to pass through Xuzhou. Grant me an army to attack him en route, and I will capture Yuan Shu." Cao Cao smiled and said, "Shall we submit your proposal to the Emperor? We can take action after that."

The following day, after formal request to the Emperor, Cao Cao gave Xuande command of fifty thousand men and sent two generals, Zhu Ling and Lu Zhao, to accompany him. The Emperor was distraught as Xuande begged his leave, and wept in parting with his uncle. Back at his quarters, Xuande spent the night preparing weapons and gear; then he took his general's seal and set out. Dong Cheng rushed to the wayside pavilion ten *li* beyond the city to see him off. "You must bear with this," Xuande said to him. "I will find a way to fulfill the decree." "Take care and remain loyal to the Emperor's purpose," Dong Cheng pleaded. The two men parted. Lord Guan and Zhang Fei, riding beside Xuande, asked, "Brother, what made you so eager to fight this battle?" "Here I am a caged bird, a trapped fish," Xuande replied. "With this move I gain the sea, the lofty space, free of cage or net." He told his brothers to have Zhu Ling and Lu Zhao hurry the troops along.

Cao Cao's advisers, Guo Jia and Cheng Yu, who had just returned to the capital from checking the treasury and granary, opposed Cao Cao's decision to send Xuande to Xuzhou. "How could you give him a military command?" they asked. "I wanted to cut off Yuan Shu," Cao explained, "that's all." "When Xuande was protector of Yuzhou," Cheng Yu said, "we urged you to kill him. You ignored the advice. Now by giving him troops you have let the dragon into the sea, the tiger into the hills. You can never again dominate him." "Even if you could not bring yourself to kill him," Guo Jia added, "what was the point of letting him leave? The ancients warned that 'endless difficulties ensue when you let the enemy escape.' I hope Your Excellency will consider what we say." Persuaded by this advice, Cao Cao sent Xu Chu ahead with five hundred men to bring Xuande back. Xu Chu took up his orders and left.

The small force sent in pursuit of Xuande is met with polite but irresistible rejection and returns empty-handed. Liu Xuande goes on to defeat the upstart would-be emperor Yuan Shu, and the imperial seal that confers royal legitimacy is secretly conveyed to Cao Cao. In chapters 22 to 24, Cao Cao rebuilds central power. Working behind the facade of protector to Emperor Xian, Cao Cao becomes a virtual shogun of the Han dynasty. Among his rivals only Liu Xuande can challenge his power, for though he is militarily weak, Liu Xuande has Emperor Xian's decree authorizing him to save the Han from Cao Cao. Tragically, a disaffected servant informs on the palace conspiracy. Dong Cheng, Wang Zifu, and the others are executed and their families slaughtered. Even the emperor's favorite and very pregnant wife, Dong Cheng's sister, is taken from the weeping emperor's embrace and strangled. Only Ma Teng, away on business, escapes the bloodbath.

Meanwhile Liu Xuande forms a defensive alliance with Yuan Shao, hegemon of the north. Cao Cao aims to destroy Yuan Shao, for if he can control the provinces to his rear, those north of the Yellow River, he can then take on his foes to the west and to the south. Cao Cao's first move is to attack Lui Xuande. In the fighting Cao Cao captures Lord Guan, Xuande's second brother. Cheng Yu advises Cao Cao how to deal with Lord Guan.

CHAPTER 25

Trapped on a Hill, Lord Guan Sets Three Conditions; At Baima, Cao Cao Breaks the Heavy Siege

Cheng Yu's plan was this: "Lord Guan can stand off a myriad of men. To take him we need a stratagem. Now suppose we send some of the soldiers we've just captured back to Xiapi posing as escapees but remaining in covert contact with us. Next, we draw Lord Guan out to battle, feign defeat, and lure him to a pre-arranged point while crack troops cut off his way back. Then you can begin to negotiate with him." Cao Cao approved and put Cheng Yu's plan into action by sending a few score of Xuzhou troops to Xiapi to surrender. Lord Guan took the men back in good faith.

The next day Xiahou Dun spearheaded Cao Cao's attack. With five thousand in his command he tried to provoke Lord Guan to battle, but it was in vain. Finally, he sent a man to the base of the city wall to denounce Lord Guan personally. And Lord Guan, incensed, rode forth with three thousand. The two warriors clashed, but after ten bouts Dun wheeled and fled. As Lord Guan pursued, Dun fought and ran in turn until he had drawn his man some twenty *li* from the city. Fearing that Cao's army might seize Xiapi, Lord Guan turned back—only to hear the peal of bombards. To his left, Xu Huang; to his right, Xu Chu. Their squadrons checked his retreat. Lord Guan moved to force a path. Ambushers concentrated their crossbow shots from two sides, and bolts whizzed down like locusts. Lord Guan could not pass. He pulled his men back, but Xu Huang and Xu Chu were ready for him. With a supreme effort Lord Guan pushed them back, making a valiant last attempt to fight his way through to Xiapi, but Xiahou Dun barred the way. The battle raged into the night. Finding no way home, Lord Guan struggled to a hilltop with his followers. There he rested.

Cao Cao's men clustered around the base of the hill, sealing all avenues of escape. In the distance Lord Guan could see flames rising from the city. (In fact, the false defectors sent by Cao Cao had quietly opened the gates, and Cao, after battling his way into Xiapi, had told his men to set some harmless fires to weaken Lord Guan's will.) Distraught at the sight, Lord Guan charged down the hill again and again throughout the night, only to be driven back by volleys of arrows. At dawn he marshaled his men for a breakthrough when he saw a single rider—as if from nowhere—racing toward him. He recognized Zhang Liao.

"You come as an adversary, I presume," Lord Guan called to him as he approached. "No," Liao replied. "I come in respect of our long-standing friendship." The envoy threw down his sword and dismounted. The formalities concluded, the two men sat together at the summit. "You must have come to win me over," Lord Guan began. "Not so," Zhang Liao responded. "Brother, you once saved my life. How could I not try to return the favor?" "Then you come to lend us aid!" Lord Guan exclaimed. "Not that, either," Zhang Liao said. "Then why have you come?" Lord Guan asked. "Xuande's survival is in doubt," Zhang Liao went on, "as is Zhang Fei's. Last night Lord Cao took Xiapi, without injury to soldier or civilian. A special detail guards Xuande's family for their safety and peace of mind. I come first of all to tell you this."

"You will not succeed in influencing me," Lord Guan said angrily. "Bad as things look, death means no more to me than a welcome homecoming. You'd better leave at once. I will be riding down to do battle." Zhang Liao laughed loudly. "Brother," he said, "do you want to be the laughingstock of the empire?" "I shall die," Lord Guan said, "devoted to my duty. I don't think the world will take it as a joke." "Dying here," Zhang Liao said, "you commit three offenses." "Well then," Lord Guan replied, "what are they?"

"In the beginning," Zhang Liao said, "when you, brother, and Protector Liu bound yourselves in fraternal allegiance, you swore to share life or death. Now your brother has been defeated, and you are about to die in combat. If Xuande survives and seeks your aid in vain, won't you have betrayed your oath? That is your first offense. Protector Liu's immediate family was placed in your care. If you die now, his two wives will have no one to defend them, and you will have betrayed his trust. That is your second offense.

And third, not only is your martial skill incomparable, you are learned in the classics and the histories. You joined with the protector to uphold the house of Han. If you lapse in your determination and achieve a fool's valor instead by vainly rushing to certain death, how have you fulfilled your 'duty'? This is the statement, brother, I felt obliged to make."

Lord Guan pondered. "Well," he said at last, "you have explained the three offenses. What would you have me do?" "Lord Cao's troops," Zhang Liao replied, "are on four sides. If you refuse to submit, you will die. To die in vain avails nothing. It makes more sense to submit, for now, while you seek news of the protector. When you learn where he is, you may go to him immediately. That way you will ensure the safety of the two ladies, you will remain true to the peach garden oath, and you will preserve your own most useful life. These, brother, are the advantages for you to weigh." "Brother," Lord Guan replied, "you speak of three advantages. I have three conditions. If His Excellency agrees, I will lay down my arms at once. If not, I am content to die with the three offenses upon my head." "His Excellency is magnanimous and accomodating and has always shown forebearance. I beg to hear your conditions," answered Zhang Liao.

"First," Lord Guan said, "the imperial uncle, Liu Xuande, and I have sworn to uphold the house of Han. I shall surrender to the Emperor, not to Cao Cao. Second, I request for my two sisters-in-law the consideration befitting an imperial uncle's wives. No one, however high his station, is to approach their gate. And third, the moment we learn of Imperial Uncle Liu's whereabouts, no matter how far away he may be, I shall depart forthwith. Denied any of these conditions, I shall not surrender. Please return to Cao Cao with my terms."

Zhang Liao communicated Lord Guan's terms to Cao Cao. Told of Lord Guan's insistence on yielding to the Emperor and not to the prime minister, Cao Cao laughed and said, "I am the prime minister of the Han. The Han and I are one. This then may be granted." To the second condition, protection of the women, Cao Cao responded, "To the income of the imperial uncle I will add a like amount, thus doubling it. As for prohibiting outsiders from entering the residence of Xuande's wives, that is the rule of any decent house and a matter of course here." But at Lord Guan's third condition, rejoining Xuande if he was located, Cao Cao demurred. "In that case," he said, "I would be feeding him for nothing. It is difficult to grant." Zhang Liao asked Cao Cao, "Have you forgotten Yurang's saying? Liu Xuande treats Lord Guan with generosity and consideration—no more. If Your Excellency extends a greater largess to bind his love, need we fear his leaving us?" "Apt words," Cao replied. "I agree to his three conditions."

Zhang Liao returned to the hilltop and announced Cao Cao's acceptance. "Nevertheless," Lord Guan said, "I shall have to request that His Excellency withdraw temporarily so that, before formally surrendering, I may reenter the city and inform my two sisters of the arrangements." Zhang Liao carried this new request back to Cao Cao, who ordered the army to remove thirty *li*. Xun Wenruo opposed it, saying, "It could be a trap." But Cao Cao answered, "Lord Guan's word is his bond. He would never break faith." The pullback was implemented.

Escorted by his own soldiers, Lord Guan entered Xiapi. He found public order undisturbed. At Xuande's residence Lady Gan and Lady Mi received him eagerly. Lord Guan saluted them from below the stair. "The distress you have suffered," he said, "is my fault." "Where is the imperial uncle?" they asked. "I do not know," Lord Guan replied. "What are we to do now, brother-in-law?" they asked. "When I left the city," he replied, "I fought as hard as I could but was trapped on a hill. Cao Cao sent Zhang Liao to talk me into surrendering, and I agreed—but on three conditions, which Cao Cao has already accepted. Then, at my request, he withdrew his troops, enabling me to enter the city and consult you two first."

"What are the three conditions?" the ladies asked. Lord Guan recounted the terms of his agreement with Cao Cao. Lady Gan said, "Yesterday, when Cao's army entered the city, we thought we were doomed. To our surprise we have enjoyed security. Not a single soldier has dared come through our gate. Brother-in-law, since you have already given your word, why bother asking us? But I do fear Cao Cao will prevent you from finding the imperial uncle." "Rest assured, sisters," he said. "I will handle that in my own way." "Brother," they said, "make all these decisions yourself. It is not necessary to consult us womenfolk."

Lord Guan took his leave and rode to Cao Cao's camp with a few dozen horsemen. Cao greeted him before the entrance as Lord Guan dismounted and made obeisance. Cao rushed forward to reciprocate. "As the general of a defeated army," Lord Guan began, "I am obliged by your mercy in sparing me." "Having long esteemed your loyalty and sense of honor," Cao responded, "I am favored today with a meeting which fulfills a lifelong desire." Lord Guan said, "Zhang Liao has conveyed to you on my behalf the three conditions of my surrender. I am honored by your consent and trust there will be no retraction." "My word, once given, is honored," was Cao's reply. "Should I learn of the imperial uncle's whereabouts," Lord Guan went on, "I must go to join him, whatever the dangers or obstacles. In that event, I may not have time even to take formal leave, so I humbly beg your pardon against that time." "If Liu Xuande still lives," Cao Cao said, "you are free to join him. But he may have perished unnoticed in the confusion of battle. For the time being you might as well content yourself while we gather more information." Lord Guan expressed his respectful appreciation. Cao Cao held a banquet in his honor.

The following day Cao Cao began withdrawing the imperial army from the newly conquered Xiapi for the march back to the capital. Lord Guan prepared for the journey, provided the carriage guard, and bade his sisters-in-law ascend. En route he rode alongside in attendance.

They broke their trip at a hostel, where Cao Cao, aiming to disrupt the proprieties between lord and liege man, assigned Lord Guan and his sisters-in-law to a single chamber. But Lord Guan never entered the chamber; he remained at attention outside the door, holding a candle that burned through the night until dawn. His eyes showed no trace of fatigue. Cao Cao's respect for him grew. In the capital Cao Cao provided official quarters for Lord Guan and Xuande's wives. Lord Guan had the dwelling divided into two compounds. At the inner gate he posted ten elderly guards. He occupied the outer compound himself.

Cao Cao conducted Lord Guan into the presence of the Emperor, who conferred on him the title adjutant general. Lord Guan gave thanks for the sovereign's grace and returned to his quarters. The next day Cao Cao held a grand banquet, assembling his entire corps of advisers and officers and treating Lord Guan as an honored guest. Cao invited him to take the seat of honor and presented him with brocade silks as well as gold and silver utensils—all of which Lord Guan gave over to his sisters-in-law for safekeeping. Cao Cao showed unusual generosity, giving him small banquets every third day, large ones every fifth. Ten handsome women were given to Lord Guan, but he sent them on to serve his two sisters-in-law. Every three days he would appear at their door to perform the proper formalities and inquire about their condition. They in turn would ask for news of the imperial uncle. Only when the ladies had excused him would he retire. Learning of this high courtesy, Cao Cao inwardly honored Lord Guan more than ever.

One day Cao Cao noticed that Lord Guan's green embroidered combat garb was badly worn. He had the warrior's measure taken and presented him with battle dress of the rarest brocade. Lord Guan accepted it, but he wore it underneath the old one. Cao Cao teased him for being frugal, and Lord Guan said, "It is not frugality. The old dress was a gift from Imperial Uncle Liu. I feel near him when I wear it. I could never forget my elder brother's gift on account of Your Excellency's new one. That is why I wear it underneath." "Truly, a man of honor," Cao Cao exclaimed. But inwardly he was troubled.

One day a message was brought to Lord Guan: "The ladies have collapsed in tears. No one knows why. Pray go to their chamber soon." Lord Guan, formally attired, kneeled before their door and asked the cause of their distress. "Last night," Lady Gan began, "I dreamed the imperial uncle was trapped in a pit. I woke and told Lady Mi, and we believe he is now in the netherworld. That is why we have lost our composure." "Dreams of the night bear no credence," Lord Guan responded. "This is from excessive worry. Please do not let such matters vex you."

At this time Cao Cao invited Lord Guan to a banquet. Lord Guan took leave of his sisters and came before Cao Cao, who asked the reason for his sorrowful look. "My sisters-in-law," Lord Guan replied, "yearn for my elder brother and cry so pitifully that I grieve despite myself." Cao Cao smiled and tried to console him, urging him to drink. Lord Guan became intoxicated and, stroking his beard, said, "I have lived in vain, having neglected my responsibility to the imperial house and my duty to my elder brother." "Have you ever counted the hairs in your beard?" Cao asked. "There are several hundred," Lord Guan replied. "In autumn I lose a few. In winter I wrap it in a black silk sack so the hairs don't break." Cao Cao had a gorgeous silk sack made to protect Lord Guan's beard.

Early the next morning they were received by the Emperor, who asked the purpose of the sack that hung on Lord Guan's chest. "As my beard is rather long," Lord Guan informed the sovereign, "the prime minister bestowed this sack on me to keep it safe." At the Emperor's request he unfurled it in the royal sanctum, and it reached below his stomach. The Emperor called him the Man of the Magnificent Beard—and so he was known thereafter.

One day after a banquet Cao Cao was escorting Lord Guan from the ministerial residence when he noticed that his mount was emaciated. "Why is your horse so skinny?" Cao inquired. "My worthless carcass has grown heavy," Lord Guan replied. "The horse is worn out from bearing me." Cao had his aides bring in a horse. Its color was like fiery coal, its stature magnificent. Pointing to it, Cao asked, "Do you recognize this horse?" "Isn't it Red Hare," Lord Guan answered, "the horse Lü Bu once rode?" Cao Cao nodded and presented the mount, completely equipped, to Lord Guan, who bowed repeatedly and declared his gratitude. Piqued, Cao Cao asked, "I have sent you beautiful women, gold, rolls of silk, one after the other, and never did you condescend to bow. Now for this horse you keep bowing and bowing. Do you value a beast above humans?" "I admire this horse," Lord Guan said. "It can cover a thousand *li* in a single day. It is a gift that will enable me to reach my brother in a single day should his whereabouts become known." Cao Cao swallowed his astonishment and regretted the gift. Later a poet wrote:

> Upon a realm divided shines this hero's fame;
> Staying by his sisters, he kept his honor clean.
> The cunning chancellor showed false courtesy,
> Little knowing Guan would never bend the knee.

Cao Cao asked Zhang Liao, "Why is Lord Guan so determined to leave us when I have treated him with the greatest generosity?" "Let me look into it," Zhang Liao replied. The next day he visited Lord Guan. After greetings were exchanged, Zhang Liao said, "Since I recommended you to the prime minister, has anyone been favored over you?" "I am deeply grateful," Lord Guan answered, "for the prime minister's generosity. But though my body is here, my heart is still with the imperial uncle. He never leaves my thoughts." "I believe your attitude is incorrect," Zhang Liao said. "In this world a real man must be able to establish correct priorities. Xuande could not have treated you better than His Excellency has. Why are you bent on leaving?" "I know only too well," Lord Guan continued, "how lavishly Lord Cao honors me. But I have received Xuande's favor. We are sworn to die for each other. Bound by that oath, I cannot remain here. Nonetheless, before I leave, I am determined to perform some act of merit to requite Lord Cao's kindness." "And if Xuande is no longer alive?" Zhang Liao asked. "I am bound to follow him to the world below." Seeing Lord Guan immune to persuasion, Zhang Liao took his leave and went to report the results of his conversation to Cao Cao. "To follow one's lord, always true to the first oath," the prime minister said with a sigh, "that is the meaning of loyalty in this world." Then Xun Wenruo added, "He said he would not leave until he had done us a major service. If we deny him the opportunity to do so, it will be difficult for him to go." Cao Cao indicated his approval.

*   *   *   *

Meanwhile, having joined Yuan Shao, Liu Xuande was in a state of constant fretfulness. "What troubles you?" Yuan Shao asked him. "Not a shred of news of my two brothers," Xuande answered. "My family is in the traitor Cao's hands. I have neither served the Han nor kept my loved ones from harm. How can I help grieving?" "I have long wanted," Yuan Shao said, "to move against the capital. The spring thaw has arrived—the ideal time for marshaling the army." The two men discussed strategies for defeating Cao Cao. But Tian Feng objected. "Last time," he said, "when Cao attacked Xuzhou and left the capital undefended, you did not respond to the opportunity. Now Xuzhou has fallen, and Cao's troops are keen. He is formidable now. Shouldn't we hold fast here until some weakness shows itself in Cao's army?" "Give me time to think it over," Yuan Shao said.

Yuan Shao asked Xuande's view of Tian Feng's conservative tactics. "Cao Cao," Xuande said, "is a traitor to the sovereign. If Your Lordship fails to bring him to justice, I fear that in the eyes of the world you will forfeit our claim on the great principle of allegiance." "Your position is well taken," Yuan Shao replied and ordered the mobilization. To Tian Feng's repeated protests he said angrily, "Those like you, addicted to civil procedures, despise the military side of things. Do you want us to renege on our allegiance to the Han?" Tian Feng bowed low and knocked his head on the ground. "Ignore my words," he cried, "and you will march into disaster." Yuan Shao wanted Tian Feng executed, but agreed to have him simply incarcerated after Xuande's strenuous appeals.

Tian Feng's fate prompted Ju Shou to gather his clan, distribute his property among them, and say farewell. "I am off to war," he explained. "If we win, there will be no limit to my wealth and influence. If we lose, not even my life can be saved." Tearfully, his people saw him off.

Yuan Shao sent General Yan Liang in the lead; his first target, Baima. Ju Shou protested: "Yan Liang, though brave and spirited, is too narrow to assume command alone." "He is my best general," Yuan Shao replied. "The likes of you cannot take his measure." Yuan Shao's army advanced to Liyang. Liu Yan, governor of Dongjun, reported the invasion to the capital, and Cao Cao called his advisers into conference to work out tactics. Lord Guan went to see the prime minister. "I understand Your Excellency is calling up the army," he said. "I volunteer for the vanguard." "I don't think I should trouble you, General," Cao Cao replied. "But sooner or later we will require your services, and I shall come to you then." Lord Guan withdrew.

Cao Cao had command of a force of one hundred and fifty thousand divided into three armies. As they marched, bulletins from Liu Yan kept arriving. Cao Cao took one army of fifty thousand to Baima and pitched camp there with the hills to his back. In the distance he could see Yan Liang's one hundred thousand deployed over the open fields and the flats near the river. Uneasily Cao said to Song Xian, formerly in Lü Bu's service, "You are known as one of Lü Bu's fiercest fighters. I want you to go against Yan Liang." As ordered, Song Xian galloped out in front of his line, spear couched for combat. Yan Liang, sword leveled, horse poised, waited beneath the bannered entrance to his formation. When he spotted Song Xian, a roar burst from his throat, and he raced forth. The clash was brief. A hand rose, a sword struck, and Song Xian fell. "What a warrior!" Cao Cao exclaimed in consternation.

Wei Xu volunteered to avenge his comrade, and Cao Cao sent him out. Lance set, Wei Xu galloped to the front where he loudly cursed Yan Liang. Liang wasted no words. On the first exchange he cleaved Wei Xu's forehead. "Who have we left to oppose him?" Cao asked. In response Xu Huang took the field and fought twenty bouts with Yan Liang, only to be driven back to his line. Cao's commanders began to tremble. Cao recalled the army, and Yan Liang withdrew also.

The spectacle of his fallen generals left Cao Cao depressed. Cheng Yu said to him, "I can suggest a match for Yan Liang— Lord Guan." "I fear that if he scores such a victory," Cao replied, "he will leave." "If Xuande lives," Cheng Yu said, "he must be with Yuan Shao. If Lord Guan destroys Yuan Shao's troops, Shao is sure to turn against Xuande and kill him. With Xuande dead, where can Lord Guan turn?" Satisfied, Cao Cao sent for Lord Guan to request his help. Lord Guan went first to bid his sisters-in-law farewell. "This is your chance," they said, "to get news of the imperial uncle." Lord Guan accepted the call.

Armed with his blade Green Dragon, mounted on Red Hare, and accompanied by a handful of men in train, Lord Guan rode to Cao Cao at Baima. Cao described to him the exploits and ferocity of Yan Liang and asked his opinion. "Let me have a look at him," Lord Guan said. Cao ordered wine for the warrior. While drinking, they were told that Yan Liang was issuing his challenge. Cao Cao led Lord Guan to a hilltop to observe. They sat together, ringed by the chief commanders, and Cao pointed to the foot of the hill, where Yan Liang's forces had camped. Their banners and standards were fresh and brilliant, and their spears stood tall like a stand of trees, impressive in their strict array. "How strong and valiant, this army from north of the river!" Cao Cao exclaimed. "Mud hens and clay dogs to me!" was Lord Guan's response. Cao Cao pointed again. "Under the command canopy," he said, "with the brocade robe and gold-trimmed armor, armed with a sword, erect on his horse—that's Yan Liang." Lord Guan glanced over the scene. "His head is ours for the asking," he said. "Do not underrate him," Cao Cao warned. "With as little merit as I have," Lord Guan answered, "I beg permission to present his head to Your Excellency. I will seize it from under their very noses!" "We do not make sport in the army," Zhang Liao commented. "Take care."

With a thrust Lord Guan mounted. Pointing his blade to the ground, he raced downhill, his phoenix eyes round and fixed, his silkworm eyebrows bristling. He dashed into the enemy line. The northern army parted like a wake as Lord Guan charged straight for Yan Liang, who was still under his canopy. Before Liang could identify the figure crashing toward him, the speed of Red Hare had already brought them face-to-face. Yan Liang was too slow, and with a stroke of the blade Lord Guan pierced him. Before the stunned enemy Lord Guan dismounted and cut off the head, strapped it to the neck of his horse, remounted, and sped away, sword raised in warning. All the while it seemed as if Lord Guan were moving across an empty plain. The men and leaders of the northern force were thrown into tumult, routed without having fought. Cao's troops seized their chance and struck, taking a toll in lives beyond numbering. The booty in weapons and horses was enormous.

Lord Guan reascended the hill to the acclaim of Cao's generals, and placed the head before the prime minister, who said, "General, this is more than any mortal could do!" "Not worth mentioning," Lord Guan replied. "My brother Zhang Fei could snatch the head of the chief general of an army ten times that size." Cao Cao turned in astonishment to his aides, saying, "Hereafter, should we encounter Zhang Fei, we must not risk engaging him!" And he had them write down the warning under their lapels.

*   *   *   *

Yan Liang's defeated force fled homeward. Meeting Yuan Shao on the way, the soldiers described all that had happened. Yuan Shao asked in amazement who the warrior could be. "It must have been Lord Guan, Liu Xuande's younger brother," Ju Shou answered. Angrily, Yuan Shao turned to Xuande and said, "Your brother has killed my beloved commander. I am certain you were involved. What am I keeping you for?" He had the axemen take Xuande to be executed. Indeed:

> Moments ago an honored guest;
> Now a prisoner awaiting death.

Would Xuande meet his doom?
　　Read on.

————————

Liu Xuande easily placates Yuan Shao. Meanwhile, Cao Cao cleverly defeats Yuan Shao's army. Lord Guan learns of Xuande's whereabouts, and determined to rejoin him, seeks a way to safely leave the capital. Zhang Liao, at Cao Cao's urging, pays a visit.

CHAPTER 26

Yuan Shao Loses a Battle and Another General; Lord Guan Returns His Official Seal

Zhang Liao found his friend sitting, depressed. "I hear you had news of your brother on the last campaign," Zhang Liao said, "and come especially to congratulate you." "My former lord may be alive," Lord Guan replied, "but I have yet to see him. There is no cause for rejoicing." Zhang Liao asked, "How does your relation with me differ from that between you and Xuande?" "You and I," Lord Guan replied, "are just friends. Xuande and I are friends to begin with, brothers in the second place, and, finally, lord and vassal. The relationships are not comparable." "Xuande is with Yuan Shao," Zhang Liao continued. "Are you going to join him?" "I must stand by my pledge," Lord Guan replied. "Please convey my best wishes to the prime minister." Zhang Liao reported the conversation to Cao Cao, who said, "I have a way to detain him."

Lord Guan was mulling over the situation when an old friend was announced. But it turned out to be someone Lord Guan did not recognize. "Who are you, sir?" he asked. "Actually," the man replied, "I am in the service of Yuan Shao—Chen Zhen of Nanyang." Astounded, Lord Guan dismissed his attendants and said, "What have you come for, sir?" The man handed him the letter from Liu Xuande. It read in part:

> In the peach garden you and I once swore to share a single fate. Why have you swerved from that course, severing the bond of grace and allegiance? If you seek recognition for your deeds or aspire to wealth and status, I will gladly offer up my head to make your accomplishment complete. Who can write all he wishes to say? Unto death I will abide by your instruction.

Lord Guan wept bitterly reading Xuande's words. "Would I not have sought out my brother," he cried, "had I known where to seek him? Would I break our original covenant for the sake of wealth and status?" "Xuande's anxiety to see you is most keen," the messenger said. "If you remain true to the oath, you should go to him as soon as possible." "In this life," Lord Guan said, "man stands between Heaven and earth. He who fails to finish as he starts is no man of honor. I came to Cao Cao open and aboveboard and can leave him no other way. I shall compose a letter for you to carry to my brother. This will give me time to take leave of Cao and bring my sisters-in-law to Xuande." "What if Cao Cao refuses?" the messenger asked. "I am content to die rather than remain here," Lord Guan declared. "Then draft it quickly," the messenger said, "for Lord Liu despairs." Lord Guan sent the following reply:

> In my humble view, honor brooks no reservation, nor does loyalty respect death. In my youth I came to know the classics and to appreciate something of our traditions and code of honor. When I reflect on the fraternal devotion and sacrifice of such ancient models as Yangjue Ai and Zuo Botao, I cannot help sighing over and over through my tears. At Xiapi, which you assigned me to guard, we had no stores and no reinforcements. My own wish was to fight to the death, but with the heavy responsibility of my two

sisters-in-law, could I sacrifice myself and thus abandon those entrusted to me? So I assumed a temporary obligation in hopes of rejoining you later. Only recently at Runan did I first receive reliable information about you. Now I shall go at once in person to bid Lord Cao good-bye. I will then deliver the two ladies to you. May the gods and man scourge me if I harbor any undutiful intent. I open my bosom to you, but pen and silk cannot convey my loyalty, my sincerity. Humbly awaiting the time when I can bow before you, I offer this for your examination.

The messenger took the letter. After informing the ladies of what he had done, Lord Guan went to the ministerial residence. But Cao Cao knew why he was coming and had a sign saying "Absent" hung at his gate. Lord Guan left, perturbed. He next ordered his original followers to prepare the carriages and horses for departure at a moment's notice. Finally he instructed the members of his household to leave all gifts from Cao—even the least trifle—in place. Nothing was to be taken away.

The following day Lord Guan went to the prime minister's residence. The same sign greeted him. He returned several more times but never succeeded in seeing Cao Cao. Lord Guan then sought out Zhang Liao at his home, but he would not appear, pleading ill health. Realizing that the prime minister would not formally let him leave and yet resolved to do so, Lord Guan wrote this farewell message:

In my youth I undertook to serve the imperial uncle, vowing to share with him both life and death. Radiant Heaven and fertile earth bore witness to the oath. When I lost my command at Xiapi, I received your gracious consent to my three demands. Now I have discovered that my first liege is in the army of Yuan Shao. Our covenant is ever in my thoughts; to betray it is unthinkable. Despite the great favor you have bestowed on me of late, this original bond must be honored. I hereby deliver this letter to announce my departure, presuming to hope that you may consider it. For whatever benefaction I may yet remain in your debt, kindly defer the accounting until some future day.

Transcribed and sealed, the letter was taken to the prime minister's residence.

Lord Guan locked away all valuables received during his stay and left his seal of office, lord of Hanshou precinct, hanging in the hall. Next he had his sisters-in-law mount the carriage readied for them. Astride Red Hare, the sword Green Dragon in hand, and ringed by his original followers, Lord Guan, with menacing eye and leveled blade, pushed straight out of the north city gate, past the objecting gate warden. Lord Guan then dropped back to deal with any pursuers as the retinue hastened along the highroad.

Cao Cao was still considering his next move when Lord Guan's letter was brought to him. Stunned, Cao said, "So he has left!" Next, the warden of the north gate reported: "Lord Guan burst out of the gate. One carriage and some twenty riders are heading north." Lord Guan's house staff also reported, "He locked up all Your Lordship's gifts; the ten ladies-in-waiting are in a separate room. His seal of office was left hanging in the hall. He took none of the servants assigned to him, only his followers from former days and some personal belongings. They left by the north gate." Cao Cao's entire council was shocked. But one general stood boldly forth and said, "Give me three thousand horsemen and I will deliver him alive!" It was Cai Yang. Indeed:

> Lord Guan exchanged the dragon's lair
> For a pack of wolves in hot pursuit.

Would Cao Cao send Cai Yang to seize Lord Guan?
Read on.

CHAPTER 27

The Man of the Magnificent Beard Rides Alone a Thousand Li; The Lord of Hanshou Slays Six Generals and Breaches Five Passes

Lord Guan had two friends in Cao Cao's camp, Zhang Liao and Xu Huang. Moreover, he was generally respected by the other generals, with one exception—Cai Yang. But Cai Yang's offer to bring him back drew an angry rebuke from Cao Cao: "Lord Guan is a man of highest honor, for his loyalty to his lord and for leaving as aboveboard as he came. All of you would do well to emulate him." "Your Excellency," Cheng Yu declared, "you treated that fellow with the utmost generosity, yet he departed without taking leave. That scrap of nonsense he wrote insolently sullies your prestige—a great offense. If you permit him to give his allegiance to Yuan Shao, you lend your enemy new strength. Pursue and dispatch him, and spare yourself future troubles." "At the beginning," Cao said, "I granted his demands. Can I break my own promises? He acts for his own lord. Let him go!"

Turning to Zhang Liao, Cao continued, "Lord Guan locked away his valuables and left his seal. Rich bribes seem not to move him, nor do dignities and emoluments deflect his purpose. We cannot esteem such men too highly. He must still be within range. We might as well make one last effort to cultivate him. Ride ahead and beg him to stop until I can escort him off properly—provide some money for the journey and a battle dress—so he will remember me in future times." Zhang Liao raced off, followed by Cao Cao and a few dozen riders.

Lord Guan, on Red Hare, could not normally have been overtaken. But he was keeping to the rear to guard the carriage. Hearing a shout, he turned. Zhang Liao was pounding toward him. Lord Guan ordered the carriage guard to press on while he reined in and, hand on sword, said, "I trust you are not coming in pursuit?" "I am not," Zhang Liao replied. "The prime minister, in consideration of the long road ahead of you, wishes to see you off personally and has sent me to request that you delay for a few moments. I have no other intent." "Even if he comes in force," Lord Guan replied, "I will do battle to the death." He poised his horse on a bridge, surveying their approach. Cao Cao himself, surrounded by a small contingent, was racing up, trailed by Xu Chu, Xu Huang, Yu Jin, and Li Dian. Before the bridge Cao Cao told his commanders to rein in and spread out. Seeing they carried no weapons, Lord Guan became easier.

"Why do you go in such haste?" Cao Cao asked. Remaining mounted, Lord Guan bent forward to show respect and replied, "It is as I petitioned on arriving: now that my original lord is north of the river, I must not delay. Time after time I presented myself at your quarters but never succeeded in seeing you, so in all humility I wrote to announce my departure, stored away your valuable gifts, and hung up my seal for return to Your Excellency, who, I am confident, will not forget what we agreed to." "I seek the trust of all the world," Cao Cao said. "Would I renege on my word? I was only concerned that you might run short on your journey, General, and so I have made a point of coming to see you off with something for your expenses." At this point one of Cao Cao's commanders extended toward Lord Guan a plate heaped with gold.

"Time and again," Lord Guan said, "I have benefited from your considerable bounty, of which much yet remains. Reserve this treasure to reward your officers." "This trifling recompense for your magnificent services," Cao Cao responded, "is but one ten-thousandth of what I owe you. Why decline it?" "My paltry efforts," Lord Guan answered, "are not worth the mention." "You are the model of the honorable man," Cao Cao exclaimed. "I only regret that destiny deprives me of the opportunity to keep you. This damask robe is an expression of my good will." One of Cao Cao's captains dismounted, carried the robe to Lord Guan, and offered it up to him with two hands. Cautiously, Lord Guan leaned down, lifted the garment on the tip of his sword, and draped it over his body. "I am indebted," he said, "for Your Excellency's gift. Another day we may meet again." Turning, Lord Guan rode off the bridge and headed north.

"Insolent barbarian!" Xu Chu cried. "Why not seize him?" "He was outnumbered, more than ten to one," Cao Cao replied. "He had to be on his guard. I gave my word. Do not pursue him." Cao Cao led his men back to the capital, but the loss of Lord Guan weighed on him.

Lord Guan leaves Cao Cao's domain, escorting Liu Xuande's two wives. On his way Lord Guan kills six pass guards who try to stop him. Upon reaching Yuan Shao's territory, Lord Guan learns that Xuande has left Shao's faction-ridden court and fled to Runan. Accompanied by Liu Xuande's man Sun Qian, Lord Guan journeys on to Runan. Along the way, a reformed bandit, Zhou Cang, begs to be taken into Lord Guan's service.

CHAPTER 28

Lord Guan Slays Cai Yang, Dispelling His Brothers' Doubts; Liege and Liege Men Unite Again at Gucheng

Lord Guan and Zhou Cang proceeded in the direction of Runan. As they neared a city in the hills, a local resident told them, "This is Gucheng. Some months back a general named Zhang Fei rode in with a few dozen horsemen, threw out the county officer, and established himself. He recruited troops, purchased horses, gathered fodder, and stored grain. Now he has a few thousand men, and no one dares oppose him in this area." "This is the first I've heard about my younger brother since the debacle at Xuzhou," Lord Guan cried joyfully. "Who would have thought he'd turn up here!" Sun Qian was sent into the city to talk with Zhang Fei and arrange for him to come and receive his two sisters-in-law.

After fleeing Xuzhou, Zhang Fei had lain low in the Mang-Dang Hills for more than a month. Once, coming into the open in hopes of getting word of Liu Xuande, he had chanced upon Gucheng and entered the town to borrow grain. The county officer refused him, however; so Zhang Fei drove him off, took his seal, and occupied the city. Thus things stood when Sun Qian arrived.

After the formal greeting Sun Qian said to Zhang Fei, "Xuande left Yuan Shao and went to Runan. Lord Guan is here from the capital with Lady Gan and Lady Mi and requests that you receive them." Zhang Fei made no response. Arming himself, he mounted and led one thousand men out of the north gate. Lord Guan saw his brother approaching and, excitedly handing his sword to Zhou Cang, raced forward. Moments later he was confronting Zhang Fei's steady, menacing gaze and bristling tiger whiskers. With a thundering shout Zhang Fei brandished his spear. Lord Guan, aghast, dodged the taunting thrusts and cried, "What does this mean, worthy brother? Can you have forgotten our pact in the peach garden?"

Zhang Fei shouted, "You have the face to confront me after dishonoring yourself!" "Have I dishonored myself?" Lord Guan demanded. "You betrayed our elder brother," Zhang Fei cried, "by submitting to Cao Cao and accepting rank and title under him. Now it looks as if you've come back to trick me. Let's settle things here once and for all." "Can you actually not know?" Lord Guan continued. "How can I explain myself? You see our two sisters. Question them yourself, worthy brother."

Raising their screen, the ladies spoke: "Third Brother, what is the reason for this?" "Sisters," Zhang Fei replied, "watch me dispatch a faithless man before I escort you into the city." "Second brother did not know where you were," Lady Gan pleaded, "so we lodged temporarily with Cao Cao. Then we learned that eldest brother was in Runan. Second brother has borne great hardship attempting to bring us to him. Do not misjudge him!" "Second brother's sojourn in the capital," Lady Mi added, "was beyond his control." "Be deceived no longer, sisters," Zhang Fei went on. "A loyal vassal prefers death to disgrace. What self-respecting man serves two masters?"

"Worthy brother," Lord Guan pleaded, "you do me wrong." Sun Qian interjected, "Lord Guan has been looking for you. That's why he is here." "You too speak like a fool," Zhang Fei snapped. "Don't tell me of his good intentions. He's here to capture me." "Wouldn't I have needed an army?" Lord Guan asked. "And what is that?" Zhang Fei cried, pointing at an armed cohort approaching in a haze of dust: Cao Cao's troops, the windblown banners proclaimed. "Still trying to keep up the act?" Zhang Fei shouted, moving toward Lord Guan with his eighteen-span snake-headed spear. "Brother," Lord Guan protested, "hold on. Let me kill their leader to show my true feelings." "If you have 'true feelings,'" Zhang Fei said, "get him before the third drum roll." Lord Guan agreed.

Cai Yang, in the lead, galloped toward Lord Guan. "You killed my nephew Qin Qi," he shouted, "yet expect to escape me here? I have the prime minister's warrant to take you prisoner." Lord Guan did not trouble to respond. He lifted his blade and aimed his blow. Zhang Fei himself sounded the drum. Before the first roll had ended, Cai Yang's head was tumbling on the ground in the wake of Lord Guan's stroke.

Cai Yang's cohort fled. Lord Guan captured the flag-bearer and demanded an explanation. "Cai Yang was furious over his nephew's death," the soldier said, "and wanted to cross the river to attack you. The prime minister would not allow it and sent him instead to Runan to destroy Liu Pi. We ran into you by accident." Lord Guan had the soldier tell his story to Zhang Fei, who questioned him carefully concerning Lord Guan's conduct in the capital. The soldier's answers confirmed Lord Guan's account, and so Zhang Fei's faith in his brother was restored.

At this moment a report came from the city that a dozen unfamiliar horsemen were riding hard toward the south gate. Zhang Fei rode to the scene and found a small contingent with light bows and short arrows. They dismounted at once when Zhang Fei appeared. Recognizing Mi Zhu and Mi Fang, Zhang Fei also jumped down and welcomed them. "After the rout at Xuzhou," Mi Zhu said, "my brother and I fled to our native place. We inquired high and low and finally heard that Lord Guan had submitted to Cao Cao and that Lord Liu—and Jian Yong too— were with Yuan Shao. We had no idea you were here, General. Yesterday a group of travelers told us that a General Zhang, whom they described briefly, was occupying Gucheng. We thought it must be you and came to find you. How fortunate that we have met!" Zhang Fei replied, "Lord Guan and Sun Qian have just brought my sisters-in-law. Eldest brother too has been located." Overjoyed at the reunion, the brothers Mi presented themselves to Lord Guan and then to the two ladies. Zhang Fei led his sisters to his headquarters in the city. At their description of their ordeals Zhang Fei wept and bowed deeply to Lord Guan. The brothers Mi were profoundly moved as well. Later Zhang Fei recounted his own adventures at a grand feast.

*   *   *   *

The following day Zhang Fei was for going at once to Runan to see Xuande. "Not yet, brother," Lord Guan said. "Better stay and guard the ladies while Sun Qian and I seek news of our brother." Zhang Fei consented. Lightly attended, Lord Guan and Sun rode to Runan, where Liu Pi and Gong Du informed them, "The imperial uncle remained here only a few days; then he went back to Yuan Shao to see if he could work things out since we simply had too few troops here." Lord Guan looked downcast. "Do not lose heart," Sun Qian said. "One more hard ride will take us to him, and we can all go back to Gucheng together."

The two returned and told Zhang Fei what they had found out. Once again they had to persuade him to stay behind. "This city," they said, "is our only retreat. We can't afford to lose it. Qian and I will bring our elder brother here. Please stay to defend it." "Brother," Zhang Fei argued, "you have killed Yuan Shao's finest generals. How can you go there?" "It's all right," Lord Guan assured him. "When I get there, I'll do whatever's called for." Then he asked Zhou Cang, "How many troops does the rebel Pei Yuan-shao have on Sleeping Ox Hill?" "Four or five hundred," was the reply. "I'll take a short cut to my elder brother," Lord Guan said. "You go to the hill, assemble the men, and meet me on the main road." Zhou Cang left to carry out the order.

Lord Guan and Sun Qian headed north of the Yellow River with two dozen followers. At the boundary Sun Qian advised, "Let's not rush in. You stay here while I talk to the imperial uncle." Sun Qian rode on, and Lord Guan headed for a nearby farm to spend the night. He was met by an old man who steadied himself on a cane. After an exchange of courtesies Lord Guan gave an account of himself. "I too am surnamed Guan," the old man said. "My given name is Ding. I am most gratified by this unexpected meeting with one I have long admired." He called out his sons, and they welcomed Lord Guan and his men warmly.

Meanwhile, Sun Qian had entered Yuan Shao's base, Jizhou city, capital of Jizhou province, and described the multiple reunion to Xuande. Xuande called in Jian Yong, an advisor, and the three considered ways and means of escape. "My lord," Jian Yong suggested, "when you see Yuan Shao tomorrow, tell him you want to go to Jingzhou to convince Liu Biao to join our struggle against Cao Cao. That will be your excuse for leaving." "Ingenious!" Xuande exclaimed. "But can you come too?" "I have my own plan for escape," Jian Yong replied.

The next day Xuande said to Yuan Shao, "Liu Biao keeps guard over the nine districts of Jingzhou and Xiangyang. He has keen soldiers and ample grain. We should cooperate in a joint attack on Cao Cao." "I have tried to arrange it," Yuan Shao responded, "but he is unwilling." "Liu Biao is my clansman," Xuande said. "If I go to him now, I know he will not turn us down." "Liu Biao could be worth far more to us than that Liu Pi," Yuan Shao said and approved Xuande's mission. He then added, "There's been a report that Guan has left Cao Cao and wants to come here. If he does, I mean to avenge Yan Liang and Wen Chou." "My lord," Xuande replied, "once you desired his service, so I summoned him. Now you want to kill him? Those two generals were but stags. Guan is a tiger. You've traded two stags for a tiger; how have you been wronged?" Yuan Shao smiled and said, "A jest, a jest! Indeed I do prize the man. Have him sent for at once." "Sun Qian will take care of it," Xuande said. Yuan Shao was content.

After Xuande had set out for Jingzhou, Jian Yong came before Yuan Shao. "Liu Bei," he said, "is unlikely to return. I think I should accompany him—to help him work on Liu Biao and also to keep an eye on him." Persuaded by this argument, Yuan Shao directed Jian Yong to go with Xuande. The adviser Guo Tu cautioned Yuan Shao, however, "Liu Xuande has just returned after failing to win Liu Pi to our side. Now you are sending him and Jian Yong to Jingzhou. I can tell you, they will never come back." "You are too mistrustful," Yuan Shao replied. "Jian Yong is experienced and knowledgeable." Guo Tu left in despair.

Sun Qian was sent ahead to join Lord Guan. Xuande and Jian Yong took their leave and rode to the border, where Sun Qian picked them up and took them to Guan Ding's farm. Lord Guan was waiting at the entrance. He bowed low, then took his brother by both hands, unable to master his tears. Guan Ding led out his two sons to pay their respects, and Lord Guan introduced the father to Xuande. "This man is named Guan too," he said, "and these are his sons, Guan Ning, a student of letters, and Guan Ping, the junior, a student of martial arts." Guan Ding said, "I wish my second son could enter General Guan's service. I wonder if it would be possible." "How old is he?" Xuande asked. "Eighteen," the father replied. "Since you have been so generous," Xuande said, "and since my brother has no son, your son may become his. What do you say?" Guan Ding was delighted and had Guan

Ping honor Lord Guan as his father and address Xuande as uncle. Then, fearful of pursuit, Xuande quickly organized their departure. Guan Ping followed Lord Guan, and Guan Ding escorted them a good stretch before returning to his farm.

Xuande, Lord Guan, and their party headed for Sleeping Ox
Hill to join Zhou Cang, whom Lord Guan had sent to rally his
five hundred followers. But Zhou Cang rode up with only a few
score of men, many badly wounded. "Before I reached the hill,"
Zhou Cang said, "a lone rider had killed Pei Yuanshao and all
the men had surrendered. He took over our fortress. I could persuade only these few to join us; the rest were too afraid. I tried
to put up a fight, but that warrior overpowered me. I took three
wounds. I was just on my way to inform you, master." "What did
he look like?" Xuande asked. "Do you know his name?" "He was
formidable!" Zhou Cang answered. "His name I don't know."
Lord Guan and Xuande headed for the hill, and Zhou Cang
hurled curses at his conqueror from the bottom of the slope. The
warrior emerged, fully armored, a spear in his fist. He rode downhill like the wind with his newly acquired followers. Xuande
pointed with his whip. "It's Zhao Zilong!" he cried.

The warrior leaped from the saddle and prostrated himself
by the roadside. It was Zhao Zilong indeed. Xuande and Lord
Guan dismounted and asked him how he came to be here. "I rejoined Gongsun Zan after leaving Your Lordship," Zhao Zilong
began, "but Zan was too headstrong to accept good advice. Yuan
Shao defeated him, and he burned himself to death. Yuan Shao
made many offers to me, but he couldn't seem to make good use
of those serving him, either. So I stayed away. I went to join you
in Xuzhou but heard that you had lost it and that Lord Guan
had gone over to Cao Cao. When I learned Your Lordship was
with Yuan Shao, I often thought of coming to you but doubted
Shao would accept me now. I was still at loose ends, roaming the
realm, when I passed by here and Pei Yuanshao tried to steal my
horse. After I killed him, I decided to settle here. Next I heard
that Zhang Fei was in Gucheng, so I decided to join him if it was
true. What a miracle, meeting Your Lordship like this!"

Xuande excitedly recounted for Zhao Zilong the recent events,
and Lord Guan filled it in with his story. "Since our first meet-

ing," Xuande said, "I have hoped you would remain with us. I too rejoice in this reunion." Zhao Zilong replied, "I have covered this land in search of a lord to serve, and have not found your like. To follow you now satisfies my lifelong aspiration. Though my heart's blood stain the ground in your service, I shall never regret my choice." He destroyed his fortifications on Sleeping Ox Hill and led the men into Gucheng with Xuande.

Zhang Fei, Mi Zhu, and Mi Fang welcomed the party. Amid ritual bows and salutes they exchanged their stories. Xuande sighed over and over as the two ladies described Lord Guan's trials. Then they slaughtered an ox and a horse, gave thanks to Heaven and earth, and feasted their men. Reunited with his brothers, Xuande rejoiced at having his commanders and advisers back uninjured and Zhao Zilong added to his service. Lord Guan too was delighted beyond measure with his newly adopted son, Guan Ping, as well as with Zhou Cang. For several days they all caroused exuberantly. Later a poet left these lines:

> Like severed limbs, three brothers torn apart:
> Doubtful news, scant word, a fading into silence.
> But when the liege and liege men renewed their brother-tie,
> Tiger winds joined dragon clouds, masters of the sky.

At this time Xuande, Lord Guan, Zhang Fei, Zhao Zilong, Sun Qian, Jian Yong, Mi Zhu, Mi Fang, Guan Ping, and Zhou Cang commanded an army of some four or five thousand, including infantry and cavalry. Xuande proposed leaving Gucheng to protect Runan, and, as luck would have it, Liu Pi and Gong Du sent an envoy requesting their aid. Thus Xuande and his followers set out, recruiting men and buying horses along the way and planning for their campaign.

*   *   *   *

When Yuan Shao realized Xuande would not return, he wanted to attack him. But Guo Tu said, "Xuande need not concern you. Cao Cao is a more formidable opponent. He must be eliminated. And Liu Biao, even though he holds the province of Jingzhou, will never become a power. On the other hand, Sun Ce dominates the land below the Great River, the Southland, an area that includes six districts. His counselors and commanders are numerous. Ally with him to attack Cao!" Yuan Shao accepted his advice and sent Chen Zhen to represent him. Indeed:

> Having lost Xuande, hero of the north,
> Yuan Shao sought a champion from the south.

What happened next?
   Read on.

Chapter 29 turns to events in the Southland, where, following the death of his brother Sun Ce, Sun Quan has built a southern kingdom. One of the Southland's advisers is Lu Su, who advocates alliance with Liu Xuande against Cao Cao. Sun Quan's chief general, Zhou Yu, shares Lu Su's view. However, Liu Xuande, after the vicissitudes of war, allies himself not with Sun Quan but with Liu Biao, a distant kinsman and protector of Jingzhou.

   In chapters 30 to 33 Cao Cao attacks the northern domains of Yuan Shao, who dies of illness from battle. Yuan Shao's two sons destroy each other in a power struggle, and Cao Cao is the ultimate victor. With the north secure, Cao Cao pursues his main objective: to seize the central province of Jingzhou in order to establish his rule over the south.

CHAPTER 34

Lady Cai Eavesdrops on a Private Talk; Imperial Uncle Liu Vaults the River Tan on Horseback

Once again Cao Cao assembled his council to discuss a southern campaign against Liu Biao. Xun You was opposed. "Our main force," he argued, "is not yet ready for mobilization after the northern campaigns. If we wait half a year to recover our strength and nourish our mettle, Liu Biao and Sun Quan too will fall at the first roll of our drums." Cao Cao accepted this advice and assigned the soldiers to settle and reclaim wasteland until the next call to arms.

*   *   *   *

Since Liu Xuande's arrival in Jingzhou, Liu Biao had treated him with kindness and generosity. One day as guests were gathering for a banquet, there was a report that the generals who had previously submitted, Zhang Wu and Chen Sun, were pillaging in Jiangxia and organizing an insurrection. Liu Biao said in alarm, "So, they have rebelled again. This may be serious." "Do not trouble yourself, elder brother," Xuande said. "Let me go and punish them." Delighted, Liu Biao gave Xuande a force of thirty thousand.

A day later Xuande was in Jiangxia. The insurgents met him in the field. Xuande, Lord Guan, Zhang Fei, and Zhao Zilong rode to the front of their position. Ahead they could see Zhang Wu astride a magnificent horse. "An extraordinary animal!" Xuande exclaimed. At that moment Zhao Zilong braced his spear and rushed the enemy line. Zhang Wu raced to meet him. After three passages-at-arms the rebel, pierced through, dropped from his horse. In one motion Zhao Zilong seized the unguided animal's reins and pulled it back to his own line. The other rebel charged out to retake the horse. But Zhang Fei, shouting lustily, plunged into the fray and stabbed the pursuer. With both leaders slain, the rebel host broke and dispersed. Xuande pacified the remnants, restored order in the several counties of Jiangxia, and returned to the capital of Jingzhou. Liu Biao received him outside the walls and led him into the city.

At a banquet to celebrate the victory Liu Biao, warmed with wine, said to Xuande, "If this is an example of your valor and skill, our Jingzhou will be safe. But we still face constant raids by the Southern Viets, and Zhang Lu to the west and Sun Quan are an ever-present danger." "Elder brother," Xuande answered, "I have three commanders who are more than equal to such enemies. Let Zhang Fei cover the Southern Viet border, send Lord Guan to Guzi to restrain Zhang Lu, and have Zhao Zilong hold Three Rivers against Sun Quan. What will remain to worry about?"

Liu Biao was ready to adopt Xuande's recommendation, but

there was opposition from Cai Mao, brother of Lady Cai, Liu Biao's wife. Cai Mao said to his sister, "If Xuande sends his three generals to those strategic points and remains in the capital himself, there's bound to be trouble." Accordingly, Lady Cai spoke to Liu Biao that night: "I've heard that a number of our people have entered into liaison with Xuande. You can't afford not to take precautions. It does us no good to let him stay in the capital. Why not send him elsewhere?" Liu Biao answered, "Xuande is a humane and benevolent man." "Others," Lady Cai responded, "may not be so well-meaning as you." Liu Biao pondered her words but did not reply.

The next day outside the city wall Liu Biao noticed Xuande's magnificent horse. Someone told him it had been captured from the Jiangxia rebels. Liu Biao expressed such admiration that Xuande presented the animal to him. Liu Biao was delighted and rode back to the city. Kuai Yue found out the horse was a gift from Xuande and said to Liu Biao, "My late brother, Kuai Liang, an expert judge of horses, taught me something about them. Notice the little grooves or tear tracks under the eyes and the white spots on the side of his forehead. They call such horses 'marked'; they bring their masters bad luck. Zhang Wu fell in battle because of that horse, and you, my lord, must not ride it."

Impressed by this warning, Liu Biao told Xuande the following day, "I am deeply grateful for the horse you so generously gave me, but, worthy brother, you go off to war from time to time and will need it yourself. With all respect I return the gift." Xuande rose to thank him. Liu Biao went on, "Worthy brother, you have been here so long that your military skills are wasted. We have a prosperous county over in Xinye. What about establishing your command there?" Xuande agreed.

The next day Xuande took formal leave of Liu Biao and led his force toward Xinye. As he was exiting the city gate, a man stepped before him, made a lengthy salutation, and said, "My lord, you should not ride that horse." It was Yi Ji (Jibo) of Shanyang, an adviser to Liu Biao. Xuande dismounted hurriedly. "Yesterday," Yi Ji explained, "I heard Kuai Yue say to my master, 'This horse has a marked head; it will bring its master ill fortune.' That's the reason he returned it. Do not ride it any more." "I am deeply grateful," Xuande replied, "for your concern. But all men have their appointed time; that's something no horse can change." To this wisdom Yi Ji deferred, and afterward he kept in frequent touch with Xuande.

Liu Xuande's arrival at Xinye was a boon to soldier and civilian alike, for he completely reformed the political administration. In the spring of the twelfth year of Jian An (A.D. 207) Xuande's wife, Lady Gan, bore him a son, Liu Shan. On the night of the birth a white crane alighted on the *yamen*, sang some forty notes, and flew into the west. During parturition an unknown fragrance filled the room. Once Lady Gan had dreamed that she swallowed the stars of the Northern Dipper and conceived as a result—hence the child's milkname, Ah Dou, or Precious Dipper.

*   *   *   *

Previously, when Cao Cao was campaigning in the north, Xuande had returned to the capital of Jingzhou to persuade Liu Biao to take action. "All Cao's forces are engaged," Xuande argued. "His capital stands vulnerable. With a surprise attack we can assume control of the dynasty." But Liu Biao replied, "I am content with the nine districts of Jingzhou. What would I do with more?" Xuande fell silent. Liu Biao invited him to his private apartments for wine. Becoming mellow, Liu Biao sighed deeply, and Xuande asked why. "There is something on my mind," Liu Biao answered, "that is difficult to speak of. . . . " Xuande had started to inquire further when Lady Cai emerged from behind a screen. Liu Biao lowered his head and said no more. Shortly afterward they adjourned, and Xuande rode back to Xinye.

*   *   *   *

Winter came, and Cao Cao returned triumphant from his campaigns. Xuande despaired over Liu Biao's refusal to adopt his proposal. Unexpectedly, Liu Biao sent for him, and Xuande went with the envoy. The ceremonies of greeting concluded, Liu Biao conducted Xuande to a banquet. "We have had word," Liu Biao told him, "that Cao Cao is back in Xuchang with his forces, strengthening his position daily. Surely he covets this land. Now I regret ignoring your excellent advice. We lost a perfect opportunity to attack." "The empire," Xuande responded, "is breaking apart. Armed clashes occur every day. Do you think 'opportunity' no longer exists? If you can make the most of it in the future, then 'regret' is premature." Liu Biao responded, "What you say makes sense."

They drank more and grew warmer. Suddenly Liu Biao began weeping profusely. Xuande asked what was the matter. "Something is on my mind," was the reply. "I tried to broach it that last time we were drinking but circumstances made it awkward." "What is the problem, elder brother?" Xuande asked. "If I can be of use, death itself could not daunt me." "I first married Lady Chen," Liu Biao began, "who bore my first son, Qi—a worthy enough lad, but too weak and timid to keep affairs of state on a steady course. My second marriage was to Lady Cai. She bore my younger son, Zong, a bright and perceptive boy. If I set aside the elder to make the younger my heir, I will be going against tradition and law, but if I leave the elder as my heir, what do I do about the Cai clan? They control the military and will stage a coup. This is my dilemma."

Xuande responded, "From most ancient times removing the elder and confirming the younger has led to disaster. If you are worried about the extent of the Cai clan's power, try paring it down a bit at a time. But on no account should you confirm the younger because you dote on him." Liu Biao fell silent.

Lady Cai had been suspicious of Xuande from the start and eavesdropped on his conversations with Liu Biao whenever she could. On this occasion she was listening behind a screen and bitterly resented what she heard. Xuande himself realized that he had said more than he ought and rose to excuse himself. Doing so, he noticed the extra weight around his middle. Suddenly he found tears welling in his eyes. When Xuande resumed his place, Liu Biao asked what was distressing him. "I used to spend all my time in the saddle," Xuande replied with a deep sigh. "Now it has been so long since I have been riding that I am growing thick around the waist. Time is passing me by. My years come on but my task languishes, and it grieves me."

Liu Biao responded, "They say, worthy brother, that in the capital you and Cao Cao once judged the heroes of the age over hot plum wine. Cao would acknowledge none of the renowned men whom you proposed, saying, 'Of heroes, this world has but two—you and me!' If Cao with all his power and influence did not rate himself above you, why are you so concerned that your task is not being accomplished?" Under the effect of the wine Xuande said more than he meant to when he replied, "If I had a real base, these tedious types would no longer vex me." Liu Biao made no response. Xuande realized his mistake. Alleging intoxication, he rose and went back to the guesthouse. Many years later a poet wrote of Xuande:

> Lord Cao named the rivals that he owned:
> "Inspector, you're the second of the realm!"
> But Xuande felt his sinews going slack—
> How could he keep the world of Han intact?

Liu Biao made no reply, but Xuande's last comment had perturbed him deeply. He retired to the company of Lady Cai, who said to him, "I overheard Xuande just now. How contemptuous he is! It's easy enough to see he means to have our province. Unless he is eliminated now, there will be great trouble." Liu Biao, however, simply shook his head and kept silent. Lady Cai secretly summoned Commander Cai Mao, and they discussed the matter. "I could go to Xuande's lodging and kill him," Cai Mao suggested. "We would report it to His Lordship afterward." Lady Cai agreed, and Cai Mao called up soldiers for the purpose that night.

Meanwhile, Xuande was sitting in his quarters in the candlelight. He was about to retire, a little after the third watch, when someone knocked on his door and came in. It was Yi Ji, the man who had warned him about the marked horse. He had learned of the plot to kill Xuande and had come to inform him. He described Cai Mao's scheme and urged Xuande to get away immediately. "How can I leave before saying a proper farewell to Liu Biao?" Xuande asked. "If you wait for that, Cai Mao will get you, I know." Xuande therefore bade Yi Ji a grateful good-bye, summoned his followers, and rode off before daybreak. By the time Cai Mao had reached the guesthouse with his soldiers, Xuande was back in Xinye. Vexed that Xuande had eluded him, Cai Mao inscribed a poem on the wall of Xuande's room and then reported to Liu Biao, "Xuande intends to rebel. He wrote a seditious poem on his wall and then departed without bidding you good-bye." Liu Biao, unwilling to believe this tale, went to Xuande's room, where he found the following:

> So many years in hard adversity,
> Staring back at the same old hills and streams—
> In a pond no dragon's meant to lie;
> He'll ride the thunder to the sky!

The verse enraged Liu Biao; he drew his sword and swore, "I'll kill the faithless ingrate!" But he reconsidered almost at once. "In all our time together," Liu Biao mused, "I have never known him to compose poetry. Some outsider may well be trying to estrange us." Liu Biao walked slowly back into Xuande's room and scratched out the poem with the point of his sword; then he threw down the weapon and mounted his horse. "My men are all in readiness," Cai Mao said. "We should go straight to Xinye and arrest Xuande." "Don't be so impetuous," Liu Biao replied. "It will take careful planning."

Unable to provoke his lord to act, Cai Mao planned privately with Lady Cai to hold a grand feast in Xiangyang for all the officials and to use the occasion to kill Xuande. The next day Cai Mao petitioned Liu Biao: "Let us have a gathering of officials at Xiangyang to show our satisfaction over the excellent harvests of recent years. Would Your Lordship be willing to make the trip?" "My breathing ailment has been acting up of late," Liu Biao replied. "My two sons may serve in my stead." "I am afraid," Cai Mao responded, "they are too young to do justice to the ceremony." "Then invite Xuande to officiate," Liu Biao suggested. Secretly delighted that his plan was working, Cai Mao sent a messenger to Xinye to request Xuande's presence in Xiangyang.

Xuande had fled back to Xinye well aware of the danger his careless comments had placed him in. He kept his own counsel, however, until the unexpected invitation arrived. "My lord," Sun Qian said to him, "you came home so distracted, I feared something had happened in Jingzhou. Now this invitation. . . . We must consider it carefully." Xuande then confided to his companions the events of the preceding day. "Elder brother," Lord Guan said, "you are being overly suspicious if you think you misspoke. Liu Biao is not holding it against you. Why should you believe a stranger like Yi Ji? But if you refuse to go to nearby Xiang-yang, you will arouse Liu Biao's suspicions." "I agree," Xuande said, but Zhang Fei objected. "There's no such thing as a good banquet or a good conference," he asserted flatly. "Better not go!" Zhao Zilong said, "I will take three hundred men to escort you and prevent anything from happening." "That would be best," Xuande decided.

Cai Mao received Xuande and Zhao Zilong outside of Xiang-yang and showed himself both modest and attentive. Following Cai Mao were Liu Qi and Liu Zong, Liu Biao's two sons, leading a delegation of officers and officials. They greeted Xuande, who felt somewhat reassured by the presence of the sons. He was taken to the guesthouse, and Zhao Zilong set up the guard. Fully armed, he never left Xuande's side.

Liu Qi said to Xuande, "My father suffers from a breathing ailment. It is difficult for him to move. He especially wanted you, uncle, to receive the guests and give sympathetic encouragement to the officials who guard and govern our districts." "For myself," Xuande replied, "I would never dare undertake it. But since my elder brother commands it, I dare not decline." The next day it was reported that official personnel from the forty-two counties of Jingzhou had arrived for the celebration.

Before the ceremonies, Cai Mao conferred with Kuai Yue. "Xuande," he said, "is a hero of our age, and shrewd as an owl. If he remains with us, it means trouble. But today we have the chance to get him out of the way." "Don't you think," Kuai Yue replied, "that would risk our losing popular support?" "I already have Protector Liu's secret instruction on this," Cai Mao replied. "In that case," Kuai Yue answered, "let's get ready." Cai Mao said, "The east gate leads to Xian Hill. My brother Cai He is guarding that road. Cai Zhong is outside the south gate, and Cai Xun by the north gate. There's no point in covering the west: that direction is cut off by the rapids of the River Tan. Even if Xuande had tens of thousands of men with him, he still couldn't get through." "What about Zhao Zilong? He never leaves Xuande's side," Kuai Yue asked. "I have five hundred men hidden in the city," Cai Mao replied. "Have Wen Ping and Wang Wei host a dinner for the military commanders in one of the outer rooms," Kuai Yue proposed, "and get Zhao Zilong to attend. That's when we'll do it." Cai Mao approved the plan. That day oxen and horses were slaughtered for the feast.

Xuande, riding the marked horse, arrived at the Xiangyang *yamen,* where attendants hitched his mount in a rear courtyard. The officials assembled in the main hall. Xuande took the host's seat with Liu Biao's sons on either side, and the guests were placed according to rank. Zhao Zilong, armed with a sword, stood beside Xuande. As arranged, Wen Ping and Wang Wei invited Zilong to the commanders' feast. Zilong declined at first, but Xuande told him to go. Meanwhile, Cai Mao had sealed the place as tight as an iron barrel and sent Xuande's three hundred guards to their quarters. He was waiting only for the company to mellow with drink before giving the signal to strike.

During the third round of wine Yi Ji raised his cup and approached Xuande. With a meaningful look in his eye, Yi Ji murmured, "Excuse yourself!" Xuande took the hint and went at once to the privy. Yi Ji drained his cup and rushed to the back courtyard. Catching up with Xuande, he whispered, "Cai Mao plans to kill you. Outside the wall, all routes to the east, the south, and the north are patrolled. The only way out is west. Get away at once." In high alarm Xuande untied his horse, pulled it through the courtyard gate, and vaulted into the saddle. Without giving a second thought to his escort, he fled by the western gate of Xiangyang. To the challenge of the gatekeepers he made no reply. He laid on the whip and dashed off. The guards could not check him, but they reported his flight at once, and Cai Mao pursued with five hundred men.

Xuande had traveled only a *li* or two when a river loomed before him several rods broad, its waves whipping. It was the Tan, a spur of the Xiang; Xuande rode to the bank. Seeing he could not get across, he turned back only to see dust clouds in the distance, west of the city: his pursuers would soon arrive. Thinking his time had come, he turned again to the river. Cai Mao's troops were already close behind. At his wit's end, he charged into the racing current. After a few paces the horse lost its footing. As they began to sink, Xuande's surcoat became soaked. Belaboring the horse, he shouted, "A jinxed horse, indeed! Today you have brought me misfortune." But the horse reared and, making thirty spans with every thrust, gained the opposite shore. Xuande emerged from the wild water as if from cloud and mist. This ballad by Su Dongpo in the old style sings of Xuande crossing the Tan:

> Late one spring day official service took me by the Tan:
> The sun was low; the blossoms newly down.
> I stopped the carriage and paced the bank, gazing across;
> Shreds of catkin, stirred by the wind, caught the sun.
> I saw in them the dying fire of Double Suns,
> That time dragon battled dragon and tiger, tiger.
> At Xiangyang the guests of honor reveled,
> While Xuande, marked for death, made his escape.
> Out the western gate he rode,
> Reaching the rushing mistbound Tan
> Moments ahead of an angry cavalry—
> The rider's shout urged the *dilu* in.
> The pounding hooves break up the glassy waves,
> Under a golden whip flailed like Heaven's wind.
> Behind, to hear the clamor of a thousand cavalry!
> Amid the waves, to see those dragons rear:
> The noble hero who would rule the west,
> Borne (by some design) upon the dragon-steed.
> And eastward race the currents of the Tan;
> The dragon-steed, its master—whither gone?
> By river's edge, heartsore, to sigh, to sigh. . . .
> The last rays touch the hills, deserted, void.
> Was it more than dream—that age of kingdoms three?
> More than idle traces in our memory?

Looking back across the Tan, Xuande saw Cai Mao on the far bank. "My lord," Cai Mao shouted over, "why have you fled our feast?" "We were never enemies," Xuande answered back, "why do you want to kill me?" "I never meant to," Cai Mao responded. "You give too much credence, my lord, to others." But Xuande had noticed Cai Mao reaching for his bow and arrow, so he headed his horse southwest and rode off. "Sheer providence!" Cai Mao said to his followers. At that moment he saw Zhao Zilong and his three hundred fighters racing toward him. Indeed:

> The river-vaulting steed had saved its master.
> Would the oncoming tiger take revenge on Cai Mao?

What was Cai Mao's fate?
  Read on.

CHAPTER 35

Xuande Encounters a Recluse in Nanzhang; Shan Fu Finds a Hero-Lord in Xinye

Cai Mao was turning back to the city of Xiangyang as Zhao Zilong hastened toward him with the three hundred guards. Earlier, during the banquet arranged for the military commanders, Zilong had noticed the movement of the host's cavalry and went to check on Xuande. Unable to find Xuande in the main hall, he went to the guesthouse. There he was told that Cai Mao and a party of troops had ridden west. Zhao Zilong, spear in hand, hastened after him. Now meeting up with Cai Mao he demanded, "Where is my lord?" "Lord Liu," Cai Mao replied, "left the banquet. We do not know where he is."

Circumspect by nature, Zhao Zilong did nothing rash. He rode on to the river and stared across its swift flow. Where could his lord have gone? He confronted Cai Mao again. "Lord Liu was your guest," he said. "Why were you chasing him?" "We have officials from the forty-two counties of Jingzhou's nine districts meeting here," Cai Mao answered. "As senior commander I am responsible for the security of them all." "Where have you driven my lord?" Zhao Zilong pressed him. "I was told," Cai Mao said evenly, "that Lord Liu had left unattended through the west gate. I went to look but could not find him." Alarmed but uncertain, Zhao Zilong returned to the edge of the river. He spotted a watery trail on the opposite shore and mused, "Could he have made it over on the horse?"

An extensive search turned up no trace of Xuande. Cai Mao returned to the city, and Zhao Zilong pressed the gate guards for information. They confirmed that Xuande had left by the west gate at a gallop. Zhao Zilong decided it was too dangerous to reenter the city and led his men back to Xinye.

*   *   *   *

Having vaulted the Tan, Xuande was dazed with excitement. "I couldn't have spanned that broad a stretch," he thought, "except by Heaven's will." He rode on toward Nanzhang by a winding path. In the setting sun he saw an ox drawing closer. On its back a cowherd blew on a flute. "Oh, for such a life!" Xuande said with a sigh. He held his horse and watched the lad bring the beast to a halt. The cowherd stopped piping and scrutinized Xuande. "You must be General Liu Xuande," he said, "who destroyed the Yellow Scarves!" Startled, Xuande replied, "How does a lad from this out-of-the-way village come to know my name?"

The youth replied, "Not from my own knowledge, of course. But when guests come and I attend my master, I often hear talk of Liu Xuande—over six spans tall, arms reaching past his knees, eyes that can almost see behind him—one of the heroes of the age! The description fits, so I think you must be the man." "And who is your master?" Xuande asked. "He has a double surname, Sima," the youth replied. "His given name is Hui, his style De-cao. He comes from Yingchuan and answers to the Taoist name of Still Water." Xuande inquired about the master's companions, and the boy answered, "His closest friends are Pang Degong and Pang Tong, uncle and nephew, from Xiangyang. Pang Degong is styled Shanmin; he's ten years older than my master. Pang Tong is styled Shiyuan; he is five years younger than my master. One day Pang Tong came by while my master was picking mulberry leaves, and they spent the whole day talking without tiring. My master has the greatest affection for Pang Tong and regards him as a younger brother." "And where is your master now?" Xuande inquired. Gesturing toward the woods, the lad said, "The farm is over there." Xuande finally acknowledged his identity and asked to be taken to Master Still Water.

The cowherd guided Xuande some two *li* to a farmstead, where they dismounted. Entering through the central gate, they heard a lute being played. Xuande listened attentively to the exquisite sounds and asked the boy to wait before announcing him. The notes stopped, however, and the lute was struck no more. A man came out, smiling as he said, "The harmonies of the lute were somber yet distinct. Suddenly, through the melody a proud, assertive tone surged up. Some noble hero must have come to listen unobtrusively." "This is my master," the lad said to Xuande.

Xuande remarked that he had the configuration of a pine tree, the bone structure of a crane. His physique and his aura were utterly extraordinary. Flustered, Xuande came forward to offer a greeting. His war coat was still soaking.

"My good lord," Still Water said, "today it was your blessing to be spared calamity." Xuande was struck speechless. Still Water invited him into his thatched cottage, where they sat as host and guest. Xuande saw written scrolls heaped on the shelves; pine and bamboo flourished outside the window. The lute lay on a stone frame. The atmosphere was pure and euphoric. "What brings you here, my lord?" Still Water asked. "I happened to be passing through," Xuande replied, "and thanks to the boy's assistance I now have the satisfaction of being able to pay homage to your venerable self."

Still Water smiled and said, "There is nothing to conceal or evade. You seek refuge, surely." This comment led Xuande to recount the details of his escape. "I knew. The look on your face bespoke the circumstances," the recluse said, and went on to ask, "I have long been acquainted with your great name, illustrious sir. But why has fortune frowned on you?" "The road ordained for me," Xuande conceded, "has not been smooth. That's why I am where I am." "There may be a different reason," Still Water continued. "It seems to me, General, that you have not found the right men to assist you." Xuande replied, "I know that I myself am not particularly capable. But among my civil officials I have Sun Qian, Mi Zhu, and Jian Yong; and among my military officers Lord Guan, Zhang Fei, and Zhao Zilong. The unstinting loyalty of these men sustains me, and I rely on their support." "Each of the warriors, it is true," Still Water responded, "is a match for ten thousand. The pity is that you have no one to make good use of them. As for your civil officials, they are no more than pasty-faced bookworms, not of a caliber to unravel the complexities of the age and see our poor generation through these troubled times."

"Actually," Xuande confessed, "I have been anxious to find a worthy man who has absented himself from the world of men. But, alas, I have yet to encounter him." Still Water replied, "You can't have forgotten Confucius' words: 'Even in a hamlet of ten households one is sure to find loyalty and good faith.' Do not despair of finding the man you seek." "I am dull and unobservant," Xuande said, "and would be grateful for your guidance." Still Water asked him, "Have you heard the jingle going around the Xiangyang area?

> In nine years' time things start to waste;
> In thirteen years there isn't a trace.
> Heaven sends things where they're due;
> The mudbound dragon mounts the blue.

The song originates from the early years of Jian An. In the eighth year the death of Governor Liu Biao's first wife gave rise to domestic turmoil. 'Things start to waste' refers to this. As for 'there isn't a trace,' Liu Biao will shortly pass away himself, and his officials and officers will scatter to the four winds. 'Heaven sends things where they're due' and 'The mudbound dragon mounts the blue' find their echo in you, General."

Xuande was alarmed. "How dare I?" he protested. "Now," Still Water replied, "the most extraordinary talents of the empire are gathered here. You should seek them out." "Where?" Xuande asked eagerly. "Where are these extraordinary talents? And who are they?" "Sleeping Dragon, Young Phoenix," Still Water answered. "With either of them you could settle our unsettled realm." "But who are they?" Xuande asked again. Rubbing his palms, Still Water laughed out loud. "Good! Good!" he said. "Good! Good! But it grows late. You should stay the night. We can discuss it further tomorrow." So saying, he ordered his young attendant to see to the needs of man and horse.

After his dinner, Xuande was taken to a room adjoining the thatched cottage. He lay down but could not sleep for thinking of Still Water's words. The night wore on. He heard a man knock and enter his host's room. "Yuanzhi!" Still Water said, "what brings you?" Xuande sat up in bed, attentive. He heard the visitor say, "I have long heard that Liu Biao treats both the virtuous and the wicked as they deserve, and so I made a point of presenting myself to him. But I found his reputation false. He favored the virtuous all right, but he couldn't use them in government. And though he recognized the wicked for what they were, he couldn't get rid of them. So I took my leave by letter and came here." Still Water replied, "You have the ability to be a king's right-hand man and should be more selective about whom you serve. What's the use of lowering yourself to go before Liu Biao—especially now when we have a heroic contender and enterprising champion right here with us? You have only failed to spot him!" "What you say makes sense," the visitor answered. Listening with elation, Xuande surmised that the visitor must be Sleeping Dragon or Young Phoenix. But much as he wanted to show himself, he was reluctant to appear undignified and so waited until daybreak before going to see Still Water.

"Who came last night?" Xuande asked Still Water. "A friend of mine," was the reply. Xuande expressed his desire to meet him. "He seeks," Still Water explained, "to commit himself to an enlightened ruler and has already gone elsewhere." Xuande asked his name, but Still Water only smiled, saying, "Good, good. Good, good." "Sleeping Dragon, Young Phoenix—who are these men?" Xuande pressed him. But Still Water kept smiling as he repeated, "Good, good. Good, good." Xuande then appealed to the recluse to leave the hills and join him in upholding the house of Han. But Still Water demurred. "Carefree recluses like me," he said, "are not fit to serve the world. There are men ten times my superior to aid you; you should take yourself to them."

While Xuande and Still Water were speaking, they heard noise and commotion outside. A commander had ridden up with several hundred men. Xuande rushed out and was delighted to find Zhao Zilong. Dismounting, Zilong said, "Last night I went back to Xiangyang, but you were not there, so I tracked you here. My lord, you are needed at Xinye. Fighting could break out there anytime." Bidding Still Water good-bye, Xuande rode off with Zhao Zilong. En route they met Lord Guan and Zhang Fei. It was a joyful reunion. Xuande astonished everyone by describing how he had crossed the Tan.

Xuande reached Xinye county and took counsel with his advisers. Sun Qian said, "Before anything else, Liu Biao must be informed of the recent events." Xuande thus sent Sun Qian with a letter to the governor. Liu Biao called Sun Qian before him and said, "I invited Xuande to preside over the provincial assembly in Xiangyang. What made him depart so unceremoniously?" Sun Qian handed him Xuande's letter detailing Cai Mao's attempt on his life and his escape over the Tan. The governor was outraged. He summoned Cai Mao, castigated him for threatening Xuande, and ordered him beheaded. Even Lady Cai's tearful pleas for mercy failed to temper the governor's wrath. But when Sun Qian argued, "If you kill Cai Mao, Imperial Uncle Liu will not be safe here," Liu Biao decided to release Cai Mao after further reproof. He also sent his older son, Liu Qi, back with Sun Qian to extend his personal apologies to Xuande.

At Xinye, Xuande received Liu Qi and prepared a banquet in his honor. As the wine mellowed them, Liu Qi began to weep. Xuande asked the reason. "Since she became my stepmother," the youth began, "Lady Cai has been intent on eliminating me—and I have no way to escape her. I would be most grateful for your advice, uncle." Xuande urged him to remain circumspect and scrupulously filial, and assured him no calamity would ensue. The next day Liu Qi bid Xuande a tearful farewell. Escorting the youth past the city wall, Xuande pointed to his own horse and said, "If not for him, I would have been a man of the netherworld." "It was not the horse, uncle," Liu Qi responded, "rather your great good fortune." Thus they parted. Liu Qi was inconsolable.

Back in Xinye, Xuande rode through the market and saw a man in a linen scarf and plain cloth robe, black belt and black footgear, crooning as he approached Xuande:

> Heaven and earth are topsy and turvy, O!
> The "fire" is growing cold.
> A stately hall is coming down, O!
> It's hard for one beam to hold.
> But away in the valleys are worthy men, O!
> Who long for a lord to whom to repair.
> And though that lord is seeking the men, O!
> Of me he is all unaware!

Xuande heard the song and thought, "This must be one of the men Still Water spoke of—Sleeping Dragon or Young Phoenix." He got down and addressed the singer, inviting him into the county office. Xuande asked his name. "My surname is Shan, given name Fu; I am from Yingchuan," was the answer. "I have always thought Your Lordship hospitable to worthy men and have been hoping to enter your service. But rather than approach you too directly, I decided to catch your attention by singing in the marketplace."

Delighted, Xuande treated Shan Fu as a guest of honor. "Could I have another look at your horse?" Shan Fu said. Xuande had it led unsaddled before the building. "Isn't he the *dilu*, the marked horse?" he inquired. "He may have phenomenal powers, but he will bring his master misfortune. Do not ride him." "But he has discharged his sign," Xuande said, and he related his crossing of the Tan. "Indeed," Shan Fu said, "that time the animal saved its master instead of ruining him. But in the end the horse will ruin a master—though I have a scheme for avoiding it." "I would like to hear it," Xuande said.

"If you have an enemy," Shan Fu continued, "give him the horse as a gift. Wait until its curse is spent upon that man, and then you can ride it without incident." Xuande turned color. "Sir!" he cried. "You come to me for the first time, and instead of advising me to be just and fair would have me harm another for my own gain. Excuse me if I decline to hear such advice." With a smile Shan Fu apologized. "Everyone," he explained, "holds Your Lordship to be humane and virtuous. But how could I simply accept the common view? I've used this idea to test you, that's all." Xuande's expression relaxed, and he too rose to apologize. "What humanity or virtue have I to benefit others?" he asked, adding, "It is for you, good master, to show me." "When I arrived here," Shan Fu said, "I heard people in Xinye singing, 'Since Imperial Uncle Liu took Xinye in his care, / The people roundabout have enough and to spare!' This shows how Your Lordship's humane virtue has benefited the populace." After this, Xuande appointed Shan Fu director general and had him reorganize and train the army.

*   *   *   *

Cao Cao, since returning to the capital, had been determined to take Jingzhou, Liu Biao's province. For this purpose he assigned Cao Ren, Li Dian, and the recently surrendered generals Lü Kuang and Lü Xiang to assemble thirty thousand soldiers in the city of Fan. In Fan, Cao's generals, probing strengths and weaknesses, threatened the capital of Jingzhou, Xiangyang. The Lü brothers petitioned Cao Ren: "Xuande is now stationed at Xinye. He recruits troops and purchases horses, accumulates fodder and stores grain. His ambitions are not petty. You had better prepare your moves against him in good time. We two, since submitting to the prime minister, have achieved nothing. Grant us five thousand crack troops, and we will present Xuande's head to Your Excellency." Cao Ren agreed with pleasure, and the two generals marched their unit to Xinye to commence hostilities.

Spies rushed word to Xuande, who consulted Shan Fu. "They must not enter our territory," he advised. "Send Lord Guan with a company to meet their center from the left; Zhang Fei, to the right to meet their rear; and you, my lord, together with Zhao Zilong, will receive their vanguard. This way the enemy can be defeated." Xuande adopted Shan Fu's plan. He dispatched his two brothers to intercept Cao Ren's force; then, joined by Shan Fu and Zhao Zilong, he led two thousand men beyond his defense barrier to meet the attack.

Xuande had hardly advanced a few *li* when, lo, he saw dust rising behind the hills. Lü Kuang and Lü Xiang were drawing near. The two sides secured their flanks. Xuande emerged mounted from his bannered entrance and shouted out, "Who dares breach our boundary?" Lü Kuang rode forward to reply. "I am General Lü Kuang," he cried. "I bear the prime minister's mandate to seize you." With fierce determination Xuande ordered Zhao Zilong into battle. The two warriors closed in combat, and before many passages Zhao Zilong had unhorsed his man with a fatal spear thrust. Xuande motioned his forces to charge.

Unable to hold his ground, Lü Xiang drew back and fled; but Lord Guan's company attacked the retreating unit. After a short period of clash and slaughter, the bulk of Lü Xiang's unit was wiped out. He managed to flee, but he had hardly made ten *li* when another force blocked his path. The leader hoisted his lance and shouted, "Meet Zhang Fei!" He took Lü Xiang at spearpoint, thrust him through, and overturned him under his horse. The rest of the enemy scattered. The units of the three brothers now combined and gave chase, capturing a great number. Afterward, Xuande withdrew to Xinye, where he feasted Shan Fu and rewarded the three contingents.

The report of the battle appalled Cao Ren. Li Dian said to him, "Our generals were killed because they took the enemy too lightly. All we can do now is hold our forces in place while we petition the prime minister for enough soldiers to wipe them out.

That's the best strategy." "Not at all," Cao Ren countered. "In a single clash we have lost two commanders and a good number of men to boot. Reprisal must be swift. For a 'bowshot' of a place like Xinye, should we be troubling the prime minster?" Li Dian warned, "Xuande is a champion warrior. Do not underrate him." "Losing your nerve?" Cao Ren asked pointedly. "The rules of war," Li Dian retorted, "tell us that if you 'know the other side and know your own, then in a hundred battles, a hundred victories.' It's not that I'm losing my nerve but that victory is uncertain." "Perhaps it's your loyalty that's uncertain," Cao Ren shot back irritably. "I am going to take Xuande alive!" "If you go," Li Dian said, "I will guard Fan." "If you refuse to go with me," Cao Ren said with finality, "your disloyalty is certain!" Li Dian had no alternative. Together they mustered twenty-five thousand, crossed the River Yu, and made for Xinye. Indeed:

> Lieutenants dishonored, corpses carted home;
> The general raises troops again to take revenge.

Which side would prevail?
  Read on.

CHAPTER 36

Xuande Surprises the Town of Fan;
Shan Fu Recommends Zhuge Liang

That night Cao Ren struck out across the River Yu in full force, determined to trample Xinye flat. Meanwhile, back in Xinye after the victory, Shan Fu warned Xuande, "Cao Ren is stationed at Fan. He knows the fate of his two commanders and is sure to attack in full force." Xuande asked him the best defense. "If Cao Ren comes," Shan Fu replied, "Fan will be vulnerable to capture." Asked for specific tactics, Shan Fu whispered certain things, to the delight of Xuande, who proceeded to make the suggested preparations.

Soon the outposts reported the attack Shan Fu had predicted. Xuande, following his adviser's counsel, put his forces into the field against Cao Ren. The opposed ranks were drawn up. Zhao Zilong issued the challenge to the enemy commanders. Cao Ren ordered Li Dian forth from the line to begin combat. Zhao Zilong and Li Dian crossed weapons several times. Li Dian saw he was no match for Zhao Zilong and wheeled back to his line. Zhao Zilong charged after him but was stopped by sustained volleys of arrows from both enemy wings. The two combatants returned to their camps.

Li Dian said to Cao Ren, "They have a crack company, one to be reckoned with. We would do better to return to Fan." "You!" Cao Ren hissed. "Even before the battle you were undermining morale. And we should have your head for that half-hearted performance in the field." Only the strenuous appeals of the asssembled commanders prevented Cao Ren from executing Li Dian. Cao Ren took over command of the vanguard and assigned Li Dian to the rear. The next day he advanced with the beating of drums, and deployed before Xinye. He sent a messenger to Xuande to ask if he recognized the formation he was using.

Shan Fu surveyed the enemy from an elevation and told Xuande: "They are using the formation called 'Eight Gates to Impregnable Positions.' The first gate is Desist; the second, Survive; the third, Injure; the fourth, Confound; the fifth, Exhibit; the sixth, Perish; the seventh, Surprise; and the eighth, Liberate. If you can enter through Survive, Exhibit, or Liberate, things will go in your favor. If you take Injure, Surprise, or Desist, you will suffer casualties. If you take Confound or Perish, you are doomed. These 'gates,' or points of articulation between units, are deployed perfectly, and yet the central mainstay or axis is missing. Surprise them at Survive from the southeast corner, move due west and out at Exhibit, and their ranks will be dislocated."

Xuande ordered his men to defend both ends of their advanced position and commanded Zhao Zilong to take five hundred men and do as Shan Fu had advised. Spear high, Zhao Zilong cut his way in, his horse leaping and thrusting, his men howling and yelling. Cao Ren retreated north. Instead of pursuing, Zhao Zilong burst through the west gate and swung round to the southeast again, throwing Cao Ren's forces into disarray. Xuande signaled his men to redouble their blows upon the foe, and Cao Ren fled the field in utter defeat. Shan Fu called off the action and recalled his contingents.

Cao Ren, who was beginning to see the merit of Li Dian's caution, said to him, "Someone very, very capable is in Xuande's army. My formations were completely destroyed." "While we are here," Li Dian responded, "I am worried about Fan." "Tonight then," Cao Ren said, "we'll raid their camp. If we succeed, we can take the next step. If not, we return to Fan." "It won't work," Li Dian said. "Xuande is sure to be ready for that." "How can we wage war without taking chances?" Cao Ren cried in exasperation. Ignoring Li Dian's advice, he took command of the vanguard, had Li Dian reinforce him, and marched to Xuande's camp that same night. It was the second watch.

Xuande and Shan Fu had been discussing the course of the battle when the seasonal northeast wind that visits the area began blowing up. "Cao Ren should strike tonight," Shan Fu predicted, "but we will be ready." Quietly he put his defense in place. By the second watch Cao Ren's men were nearing Xuande's camp. They found it surrounded by flames. The enclosing palisade had been set afire. "They were waiting for us!" Cao Ren thought. At once he ordered a retreat, but Zhao Zilong struck before the retreat could be effected. Cao Ren fled north to the river where he searched for boats; another contingent, led by Zhang Fei, confronted him. After hard fighting with Li Dian protecting him, Cao Ren managed to ferry himself across the river; most of his men drowned. He returned to Fan and called at the gate, but a barrage of drumming greeted him. A general came forward and shouted, "I took Fan long ago!" Cao Ren's brigade looked in awe at the general. It was Lord Guan. Cao Ren fled in fright, losing more men to Lord Guan's pursuing warriors, until he had made his way back to the capital, Xuchang. On the way, however, Cao Ren had discovered the identity of Xuande's new military adviser.

Xuande's victory was complete. Entering Fan, he was welcomed by Liu Mi of Changsha, the prefect of the county. Like Xuande, Liu Mi was an imperial kinsman. After the populace had been reassured, Liu Mi invited Xuande to his home and feasted with him. There Xuande noticed a pleasing youth with dignified deportment standing to the side. He asked the host who it was. "A nephew, Kou Feng," Liu Mi replied, "son of Kou, lord of Luo. He became our ward when his parents died." Xuande took a great liking to the lad and wished to adopt him. Liu Mi eagerly agreed. He had Kou Feng honor Xuande as his father and had the youth's name changed to Liu Feng. Xuande brought Liu Feng back from the feast and bid him honor Lord Guan and Zhang Fei as uncles. But Lord Guan said, "Elder brother, you already have a son of your own. What use do you have for another's? It will lead to trouble." "If I treat him as my son," Xuande insisted, "he will serve me as his father. What trouble can there be?" This answer left Lord Guan sulking. Xuande turned to the problems of tactics. On Shan Fu's advice he returned to Xinye, ordering Zhao Zilong to guard Fan with a force of one thousand.

*   *   *   *

In the capital Cao Ren and Li Dian prostrated themselves tearfully before Prime Minister Cao Cao and confessed their failure. "A soldier must take the fortunes of war in his stride," Cao Cao said. "But I wonder who drafted the plans for Liu Bei." Cao Ren mentioned the name he had heard on the way home. "Shan Fu?" Cao Cao asked. "Who is he?" Cheng Yu smiled and answered, "That's not his real name. In his youth he was an expert swordsman. Then, sometime toward the end of Emperor Ling's reign, he killed a man to avenge an injustice—and became a disguised fugitive. When he was finally apprehended, he refused to identify himself. The officers paraded him through the market area tied up on a cart. They beat the drums to collect a crowd, hoping someone would name him. But even those who did recognize the man would not speak up. Soon his comrades quietly freed him. He fled again, changed his name, and resolved to lead a scholar's life. He has paid his respects to all the well-known teachers and masters in our area and has studied with Sima Hui too. His real name is Xu Shu, and he's originally from Yingchuan. His style is Yuanzhi. Shan Fu is an assumed name."

Cao Cao asked Cheng Yu, "How does Shan Fu's ability compare with yours?" "Ten times greater," was the reply. "It is most unfortunate," Cao Cao said, "that Xuande is winning the loyalty of worthy and capable men. His wings are fully formed. What can we do?" "Although Shan Fu is with the other side," Cheng Yu said, "if Your Excellency is determined to have him serve you, there is an easy way to do it." "How can we win him over?" Cao Cao asked. "He is devoted to his mother," Cheng Yu replied, "his father having died when he was young. She is all he has. His brother Kang is also dead, so there is no one else to look after her. If you can entice his mother here and induce her to write Shan Fu to join her, he cannot refuse." Cao Cao was delighted with Cheng Yu's advice.

Shan Fu's mother, Madame Xu, was brought to the capital and treated royally. Cao Cao said to her, "They say your excellent son, Yuanzhi, is actually one of the extraordinary talents of the empire. Now he is in Xinye assisting the disobedient subject Liu Bei in his revolt against the court. For so precious a jewel to fall in the muck is truly regrettable. We would prevail upon you to write and call him back to the capital. I will guarantee him before the Emperor, who will reward him amply." Cao Cao ordered writing instruments brought.

"What manner of man is Liu Bei?" the matron asked. "A low-class sort, once based in Xiaopei," Cao Cao replied. "He makes preposterous claims to being an imperial uncle and is utterly without credibility or righteous commitment. He is a perfect example of 'a noble man on the outside, a base man within.'" Madame Xu reacted sharply to this indictment. "You!" she cried harshly. "What fraud and fabrication! I have long known Xuande to be a descendant of Prince Jing of Zhongshan, the great-great-grandson of Emperor Jing the Filial. Xuande is a man who humbles himself before men of ability and treats others with self-effacing respect. And he is renowned for his humanity. Why, callow youths and grey old men, herdsmen and wood-gatherers all know his name. He is one of the true heroes of our age. And if my son serves him, then he has found himself the right master. As for you, though you claim the name of prime minister to the Han, you are in reality a traitor who perversely takes Xuande to be the 'disobedient subject,' and would have my son forsake the light and elect the dark. Where is your shame?"

With that, Madame Xu struck Cao Cao with an inkstone. In a

fury Cao Cao ordered armed guards to march the matron out and behead her. But Cheng Yu intervened. "The woman," he said, "antagonized you in order to die. If you kill her, you will earn yourself a vicious name even as you confirm her virtue; and once she is dead, Shan Fu will commit himself to assisting Liu Bei avenge his mother. But if you detain her, the son's body will be in one place, his heart in another. That way, even if he remains with Liu Bei, he will not give his utmost. Furthermore, if we keep the woman alive, I think I can induce Shan Fu to come here and serve Your Excellency." Cao Cao concurred and spared the woman.

Madame Xu was held in custody and cared for. Cheng Yu visited her regularly and, pretending he had once sealed a pact of brotherhood with her son, attended her solicitously, as if she were his own mother. Cheng Yu honored her with gifts, always including a personal note, and the matron would answer in her own hand. Having coaxed these samples of her script out of her, Cheng Yu proceeded to imitate it. He then forged a letter and had a henchman carry it to Xinye. A guard brought the messenger to Shan Fu, who, knowing there was a letter from his mother, immediately received him. The messenger said, "I am a house servant. Your mother sent me with this." The letter read:

> The recent death of your younger brother has left me with no other kin save you. In the midst of my sorrow and isolation, I never dreamed His Excellency Cao would lure me to the capital to denounce your betrayal and to put me in chains. My life has been spared only through Cheng Yu. If you surrender, I will be saved. When you read this, do not forget the hardships your mother endured to raise you. Come with all speed to fulfill your duty as a filial son. Afterward, we will bide our time until we can go home and tend our garden. That way we will avoid calamity. My life hangs by a thread. You are my sole hope of salvation. Need I implore further?

Tears flooded Shan Fu's eyes as he read the letter. He went to Xuande to acknowledge his identity and explain his intentions. "At the beginning," Shan Fu said, "I went to Governor Liu Biao, impressed by his reputation for welcoming men of learning. But in advising him, I soon discovered how unfit he was. I took my leave by letter, went to the farm of Still Water, and told him all that had happened. He took me to task for not recognizing my true lord, and then urged me to serve you. I put on that mad show in the market to attract Your Lordship's interest. I was favored by your gracious invitation and given grave responsibilities. But what am I to do now that my mother has been tricked and taken by Cao and threatened with harm? She has written herself summoning me, and I cannot fail her. It is not that I am loath to toil for Your Lordship to repay your confidence in me, but with my dear mother in his hands I would not be able to give your cause my best. Permit me therefore to announce my departure. Surely we shall find a way to meet again."

Xuande cried out at these words, but then he said, "Mother and son are nature's nearest kin. You need not give further thought to me. I can wait until you have been reunited with your mother for another opportunity to profit from your instruction." Shan Fu prostrated himself in gratitude and begged permission to leave. Xuande prevailed upon him not to leave at once but to remain the night for a final farewell dinner.

Sun Qian took Xuande aside and said, "This extraordinary genius is thoroughly familiar by now with our military situation. If you let him go, they will use him at the highest level, and we will suffer for it. Try your utmost, my lord, to get him to stay—then Cao Cao will execute his mother, and to avenge her Shan Fu will fight all the more fiercely against Cao Cao." But Xuande replied, "That I cannot do. It would be inhumane to let them kill the mother so that we can use the son. It would be unjust and dishonorable to hold him against his will and keep mother and son apart. I would rather die first." Xuande's firmness moved all who heard of it.

Xuande invited Shan Fu to drink. But Shan Fu said, "Knowing my mother is imprisoned, I could not swallow the most precious potion, the most exquisite liquor." "When you said you were leaving," Xuande declared, "I felt as if I were losing my very hands. The rarest delicacies will seem tasteless to me." The two men faced one another and wept, then they sat down to await the dawn. Xuande's commanders had already arranged the farewell banquet outside the walls of Xinye. Afterward, Xuande and Shan Fu rode out of the city side by side. Reaching a pavilion, they dismounted and prepared to part. Xuande, proposing a last toast, said, "My meagre lot, my paltry destiny keep us from remaining together. I hope you will serve your new master well and gain recognition for your merits."

Weeping freely, Shan Fu said, "Despite my insignificant talent and superficial knowledge, Your Lordship charged me with the gravest responsibilities. Now on my mother's account I have to leave, though our task remains incomplete. But no matter how Cao Cao pressures me, I will not propose a single strategy for him to my dying day." "Once you have gone, master," Xuande said, "I intend to withdraw to the mountain forest." "When I laid plans with Your Lordship for the royal cause," Shan Fu went on, "my meagre intelligence was all I had to count on. But now, because of my mother, I cannot think clearly. Even were I to remain, I would be of no use. My lord would do well to seek elsewhere some high-minded worthy to support and assist you in your great enterprise. You must not lose heart like this."

"Not one of the worthy men of our age," Xuande said, "surpasses you." "How can my useless, commonplace qualities deserve such high praise?" Shan Fu asked. Then, on the verge of parting, Shan Fu turned to the commanders and said, "It is my earnest wish that you all continue to serve our lord well. Leave behind a record of worthy deeds and shun my example of failing to finish what I have begun." The commanders grieved.

Xuande could not bring himself to say good-bye and saw him off one stage farther, then another stage. "You should not take the trouble to escort me so far," Shan Fu said. "Here I bid you farewell." Xuande took Shan Fu's hand. "Now we part," Xuande said, "to go to different worlds. Who knows when we may meet again?" Xuande's tears fell like rain. Shan Fu, too, wept as he parted from his lord. Xuande poised his horse at the forest's edge, watching Shan Fu and his attendants race into the woods. "Gone!" Xuande cried. "What will become of me now?" Through blurry eyes he gazed into the distance, but a clump of trees blocked his line of vision. "I want those trees cut down," he shouted, "so I can see Shan Fu once again!"

At that very moment Shan Fu reappeared, whipping his horse to a gallop. "He's coming back! Can he have changed his mind?" Xuande cried and eagerly rode out to meet him. "Good sir," Xuande addressed him, "can it be that you are not leaving after all?" Shan Fu reined in and said, "My emotions were so conflicted, I forgot one thing. There is an extraordinary scholar in this area, in Longzhong, barely twenty *li* from Xiangyang. Your Lordship should seek him out." "Dare I trouble you to request that he come to see me?" Xuande inquired. "It would not be appropriate to send for him," Shan Fu replied. "Go to him in person, my lord. If you gain his services, it will be like the Zhou dynasty's winning Lü Wang, or the Han's winning Zhang Liang."

Xuande asked Shan Fu, "Compared to yours, sir, what are his talents like?" "To compare him to someone like me," Shan Fu answered, "would be like comparing the fabled unicorn to a dray, a peafowl to a crow. He is in the habit of likening himself to Guan Zhong and Yue Yi—but he surpasses them in my view, for he is perhaps the one man in the empire who can plot the interaction of the heavens and the earth." "I would hear his name," Xuande said. "He is from Yangdu in Langye," Shan Fu replied, "and bears the double surname Zhuge. His given name is Liang; his style, Kongming. He is a descendant of Zhuge Feng, former commander of the Capital Districts. His father, Zhuge Gui (styled Zigong), was a governor's deputy in Taishan district. Zhuge Gui died young, leaving Liang in the care of his younger brother Xuan. Zhuge Xuan, Liang's uncle, was a long-standing friend of Liu Biao, protector of Jingzhou. That is why they made their home in Xiangyang, under Liu Biao's protection. After Zhuge Xuan died, Liang and his younger brother Jun worked on the family's farm in Nanyang. Liang enjoyed chanting the Liangfu elegies. Where they lived there was a stretch of hills known as Sleeping Dragon Ridge; he took the sobriquet Master Sleeping Dragon from that. His talents are indeed transcendent. Your Lordship, ignore his low estate and visit him—the sooner the better, for if he is willing to assist you, you need have no fear for the stability of the empire."

Xuande said to Shan Fu, "Master Still Water once said to me, 'If either Sleeping Dragon or Young Phoenix will help you, you can reestablish order in the realm.' Could the man you speak of be one of the two?" "Young Phoenix," Shan Fu replied, "is Pang Tong of Xiangyang. Sleeping Dragon is none other than Zhuge Liang—Kongming." In his excitement Xuande leaped up and cried, "Now I know what Still Water meant. These great men are before my very eyes. But for you, I should have remained blind to them." A later poet left these lines commemorating the moment Shan Fu recommended Zhuge Liang:

> To part for aye made Xuande sore with grief.
> At road's fork they stopped; in each emotions deep.
> A word is dropped, like thunder's boom in spring,
> Rousing the dragon sleeping in Nanyang.

Having imparted Kongming's name, Shan Fu once again took leave. Xuande, now awakened to the meaning of Still Water's words, led his men back to Xinye to prepare gifts to take to Kongming in Nanyang.

On the road, Shan Fu was moved by his lord's love and his unwillingness to say good-bye, but he began to wonder if Kongming would actually be willing to leave the hills and help guide Xuande's course. Before going to Cao Cao, therefore, Shan Fu rode straight to the young recluse in his thatched hut. Kongming asked his purpose in coming. "My wish," Shan Fu said, "was to serve Protector Liu, but Cao Cao seized my mother, and she has written summoning me. What choice do I have? I'm on my way to her now. Just before leaving, I recommended you to Xuande; he should be coming to pay his respects. I hope you will not deny him, but will put at his disposal those great abilities you have always shown. It would be a blessing for us all."

Kongming was annoyed. "And you mean to make *me* the victim of this sacrifice?" he said, and with a flick of his sleeves retired. Shan Fu retreated in embarrassment and resumed his journey. Indeed:

> Out of love for his lord, Shan Fu appealed to a friend;
> Out of love for his mother, he was homeward bound again.

What would the outcome be?
Read on.

CHAPTER 37

Still Water Recommends Another
Noted Scholar; Liu Xuande Pays
Three Visits to Zhuge Liang

Riding at breakneck speed, Shan Fu reached the capital. Informed of his arrival, Cao Cao had Xun Wenruo, Cheng Yu, and
other advisers greet him at the city gate. From there Shan Fu went
to the ministerial residence and paid his respects to Cao Cao. Cao
Cao said to him, "How could so noble and enlightened a scholar
as you, sir, lower himself to serve Liu Bei?" "In my youth," Shan
Fu responded, "I fled my village and drifted through all sorts of
places. Chance brought me to Xinye, where I formed a strong
friendship with Xuande. But since my mother is here now in your
care, I feel overcome with shame and gratitude." "Now that you
are here," the prime minister said, "you will be able to tend and
care for your honorable mother at dawn and at dusk as ritual pre-
scribes. And I, too, perhaps may benefit from your superior learning." Shan Fu expressed his thanks and withdrew to his mother's
chamber.

Shan Fu prostrated himself tearfully before his mother. "What
brings *you* here?" she exclaimed in amazement. "I was in the service of Liu Xuande," he explained, "when your letter came. I
rushed here at once." Mother Xu exploded in fury, swearing as
she struck the table. "You disgraceful son," she shouted, "flitting
hither and thither for so many years. I thought you were finally
making progress with your studies. Now you've ended up worse
than you started out. As a scholar, you should be aware that loyalty and filial devotion may conflict. How could you have failed
to see Cao Cao for what he is—a traitor who has abused and ruined his sovereign—while Liu Xuande is widely known for humanity and righteousness? Moreover, he is a scion of the royal
house. You had found yourself a proper master, but trusting a
forged scrap of paper, which you never bothered to verify, you

left the light for the dark and have earned yourself a name beneath contempt. Oh, you utter fool! With what kind of self-respect am I supposed to welcome you, now that you have shamed
the spirit of your ancestors and uselessly wasted your own life?"

During his mother's tirade Shan Fu cowered on the ground,
hands clasped over his head, not daring to look up. Suddenly,
she turned and vanished behind a screen. Moments later a
house servant appeared and called out, "The lady has hanged
herself from the beams!" Beside himself, Shan Fu rushed to her,
but her breath had ceased. Later someone wrote "In Praise of
Mother Xu":

> Mother Xu's integrity
> Will savor for eternity.
> She kept her honor free of stain,
> A credit to her family's name.
> A model lesson for her son,
> No grief or hardship would she shun.
> An aura like a sacred hill,
> Allegiance sprung from depth of will.
> For Xuande, words of approbation,
> For Cao Cao, utter condemnation.
> Boiling oil or scalding water,
> Knife or axe could not deter her.
> Then, lest Shan Fu shame his forebears,
> She joined the ranks of martyred mothers.
> In life, her proper designation;
> In death, her proper destination.
> Mother Xu's integrity
> Will savor for eternity.

Seeing his mother dead, Shan Fu lay broken on the ground.
Much time passed before he recovered. Cao Cao sent him ritual
gifts of condolence and personally attended the sacrificial ceremonies. The coffin was interred in the high ground south of the
capital. Shan Fu fulfilled the mourning and guarded the grave
site. Everything that Cao Cao proffered he declined.

At this time Cao Cao was considering a southern expedition.
But Xun Wenruo warned, "Winter is no time for that. After the
spring thaw we can make an all-out attack." Cao Cao agreed. He
then diverted water from the River Zhang to make a lake for naval

training for the attack on the south. The lake was called the Pool of the Dark Tortoise.

*   *   *   *

As Liu Xuande was preparing gifts for his visit to Kongming in Longzhong, the arrival was announced of an unusual-looking Taoist with a tall hat and broad sash. "Why, this must be Kongming himself!" Xuande said and attired himself formally to welcome him. It turned out, however, to be Still Water. Delighted, Xuande took him into his private quarters and led him to the seat of honor. Xuande said, "Since leaving your saintly presence, I have been beset by military concerns and thus failed to pay a courtesy call. Now I am honored by this visit, which gratifies my deeply felt longing and admiration." "I had heard," Still Water replied, "that Shan Fu was here and came especially to see him." "He went to the capital," Xuande explained, "in response to an appeal from his mother, whom Cao Cao had jailed."

"So he fell for the ruse!" Still Water said. "Mother Xu is known for her absolute integrity. Even if Cao imprisoned her, she would never agree to call for her son. The letter has got to be a forgery. By not going he could have saved her; his going dooms her." Agitated, Xuande asked for an explanation. "She lives according to the highest ethic," Still Water said, "and would be ashamed for her son." "As he was leaving," Xuande said, "he recommended Zhuge Kongming of Nanyang. What do you know about him?" "If Shan Fu had to leave, he had to leave," Still Water replied. "But why did he have to drag Kongming into this to sweat out his heart's blood?" "What do you mean by that, good master?" Xuande asked.

Still Water said, "Kongming befriended Shan Fu and three others: Cui Zhouping of Boling, Shi Guangyuan of Yingchuan, and Meng Gongwei of Runan. These five dedicated themselves to esoteric rituals of spiritual refinement. Kongming, however, was the only one who contemplated the doctrine in its entirety. Once while sitting embracing his knees and chanting invocations he remarked to his four friends: 'In official service any of you might advance to inspector or governor.' But when they asked what ambitions he had, he only smiled. He was wont to liken himself to

Guan Zhong and Yue Yi. His ability is beyond measuring." "I wonder," Xuande commented, "why the Yingchuan area has produced so many great men." "Long ago," Still Water replied, "Yin Kui, a skilled observer of the constellations, remarked that with so many stars congregated in its part of the sky, the district was sure to have many worthy men."

Lord Guan, who had been listening to this conversation, interjected, "To my knowledge Guan Zhong and Yue Yi were outstanding figures of the Spring and Autumn and Warring States periods, men whose merit overarched the realm. Is it not presumptuous for Kongming to compare himself to them?" "To my mind," Still Water replied smiling, "he might rather be compared to Jiang Ziya, who helped found the eight-hundred-year Zhou dynasty, or Zhang Liang, whose advice was responsible for the Han's four hundred years of glory." This praise left all hearers astonished. Still Water then took his leave, declining Xuande's invitation to stay. But on reaching the gate, he gazed upward and laughed aloud, "Sleeping Dragon has found his lord but not his time. A pity!" So saying, he was gone like a breeze. "Truly a recluse of great worth," Xuande said with a sigh.

The next day Xuande, Lord Guan, and Zhang Fei went to Longzhong. On the hills men were carrying mattocks to their acres, singing:

> The sky's a curving vault of blue,
> The level earth a chessboard,
> Where men their black and white divide,
> Disgrace or glory to decide.
> For the winners, peace and comfort,
> For the losers, tiring toil.
> In Nanyang someone lies secluded,
> Securely sleeping. Stay abed!

Xuande reined in and asked who had composed the song. "Why, Master Sleeping Dragon," was the reply. "Where does he live?" Xuande asked. A farmer answered, "A short way south runs a high ridge called Sleeping Dragon Ridge. In front is a thin wood where you'll find the little thatched lodge that he's made his refuge." Xuande thanked the man and rode on. Soon the ridge came into view. It was a soothing scene of extraordinary peace, as depicted in this old-style ballad:

West of Xiangyang county twenty *li,*
A rising ridge leans over a flowing stream.
The twisting, turning ridge bears heavy clouds;
The frothing, churning stream is liquid jade.
Caught between the rocks, this dragon winds;
Shadowed by the pines, this phoenix hides.
A wattle gate half-screens a thatched retreat:
Undisturbed, the recluse rests within.
The bamboo forms a veil of green outside,
Where year-round hedgerows exhale flowery scents.
Learned works are piled around his bed;
No common men have come before his seat.
Now and then a gibbon taps to offer fruit;
A crane, his gateguard, attends his nightly chants.
A brocade sack contains the precious lute;
The seven-star sword is hung upon the wall.
In this refined seclusion the master waits
And works his acres in his leisure hour,
Until spring thunder starts him from his dream
To calm the kingdom with one impassioned cry.

Xuande arrived at the farmstead and knocked at the brush-wood gate. A lad answered the door and asked his name. "General of the Left under the Han," Xuande declared, "Lord of Yicheng Precinct, Protector of Yuzhou, Imperial Uncle Liu Bei comes to pay his respects to your master." "Too many names to remember," said the youth. "Just say Liu Bei is paying a call," Xuande urged him. "My master," the lad said, "went out for a bit earlier this morning." "Where to?" Xuande asked. "His movements are uncertain; I don't know where he has gone," was the reply. "When will he be back?" Xuande asked. "I don't know that, either," the lad said. "It could be three to five days or ten or more."

Xuande was greatly disappointed. Zhang Fei said, "Since we have failed to see him, let's go home and have done with it!" Xuande was for waiting a little longer, but Lord Guan also said, "We might as well be off. We can send someone later to inquire." Xuande finally agreed and told the lad, "When your master returns, will you say that Liu Bei came to call?"

The brothers remounted and rode off. Several *li* later they reined in and looked back on the scenic figurations of Longzhong. Now the hills seemed more elegant than lofty, the streams more sparkling than deep, the land more smooth than spacious, the woods more lush than large, with gibbons and cranes join-ing in play, pine and bamboo blending their green. Xuande could not take his eyes away. Suddenly a man appeared, his coun-tenance imposing, his bearing stately yet simple. A scarf was wound casually around his head; a plain black gown covered his frame. With a staff of goosefoot wood he trod down a hillside path.

"This must be Master Sleeping Dragon," Xuande said eagerly as he dismounted and made a gesture of respectful greeting. "Could you be Sleeping Dragon, master?" he asked. "Your name, General?" the man responded. "Liu Bei," he answered. "I am not Kongming," the man went on, "but a friend of his, Cui Zhouping of Boling." "Your name has been long known to me," Xuande said. "This is a meeting ordained by fortune. I would like to benefit from your instruction if you could find the time. . . . "

The two men sat on some rocks in the woods; Lord Guan and Zhang Fei stood to either side. Cui Zhouping began, "For what reason, General, do you wish to see Kongming?" "There is such disorder in the empire," Xuande replied. "The four quarters are as unsettled as the clouds. I would seek of Kongming the strat-egy to secure and stabilize the government and the country." "My lord," Cui Zhouping responded with a smile, "you are bent on bringing the disorder of our day to an end? However benevolent your intentions, since ancient times periods of discord and civil order have come and gone quite unpredictably. When the Su-preme Ancestor of the dynasty slew the white serpent and em-barked on the rising that destroyed the despotic Qin, that in-terval, which led to the founding of the Han, was a time of transition from discord to civil order. Two hundred years of peace and prosperity followed. Then, in the time of the Emperors Ai and Ping, Wang Mang usurped the throne and brought us again from order to disorder. But the first emperor of the Later Han, Guang Wu, revived the dynasty and, righting its foundations, brought us out of discord and back to civil order.

"Now after another two hundred years, during which the pop-ulation has enjoyed peace and contentment, we find sword and shield around us. This only shows that we are moving again into a period of disorder, and one which cannot be quickly ended. For Kongming to try to reverse the course of events or mitigate what fortune has in store would be, I am afraid, a futile expense of mind and body. It is said, 'Adapt to Heaven and enjoy ease; oppose it and toil in vain.' It is also said, 'None can deduct from the reckoning, or force what is fated.'"

"There is great insight in your words," Xuande conceded. "But I, a Liu, scion of the Han, committed to maintain the dynasty's rule, may not leave the task to fate or reckoning." "A mountain rustic like myself," Cui Zhouping responded, "is hardly fit to discuss the affairs of empire. You honored me with your profound question, and I expressed myself rashly." "You have favored me with your insight and instruction," Xuande said, "but I would know where Kongming has gone." "I, too, was hoping to pay a call on him," Cui Zhouping replied, "so I could not tell you where he is." "Would you be interested, master," Xuande inquired, "in coming back with me to our humble county seat?" "My uncultured nature," Cui Zhouping replied, "has grown too fond of leisure's freedoms to give thought to success and fame. But there will be occasion for us to meet again." With that, the man left after making a deep bow. "We have failed to find Kongming," Zhang Fei said, "and bumped into that rotten pedant instead. Too much idle talk!" "That is how men in seclusion express themselves," Xuande admonished him.

A few days after returning to Xinye, Xuande made inquiries and was told that Kongming had come back from his rambles. Xuande ordered the horses readied for another visit. "Do you have to go yourself for that village bumpkin?" Zhang Fei demanded. "Have him summoned." "It looks," Xuande said sharply, "as if you do not know what the sage Mencius meant when he said, 'Trying to meet a worthy man in the wrong way is as bad as closing the door on an invited guest.' Kongming is one of the greatest men of our time, and yet you expect me to send out a summons?" And so a second time, attended by his brothers, Xuande went to Sleeping Dragon Ridge.

It was the dead of winter, severely cold. Dense, somber clouds covered the sky. The brothers rode into a cutting northern wind. A heavy snow made the mountains gleam like arrowheads of white jade and gave the woods a silvery sheen. "The air is bitter," Zhang Fei said, "and the ground frozen solid. A bad time even for military operations, and yet you think we should be going this distance to meet someone of no use to us at all? Let's go back and get out of the storm." "I am determined," Xuande replied, "to show Kongming my earnest intentions. If you can't stand it, brother, go on back yourself." "If death doesn't frighten me," Zhang Fei retorted, "why should the cold? I just hate to see my elder brother waste his energy." "Then stop complaining," Xuande said, "and follow me." As they approached the thatched cottage, they were surprised to hear someone singing in a roadside wineshop:

> No deeds, no fame achieved at manhood's prime:
> Shall he ever find his lord or meet his time?
> Remember when Jiang Ziya,
> The old sage of the Eastern Sea, quit his hazel wood
> And followed Zhou's first king, Wen, as servant and
>   as kinsman?
> When, uncalled, eight hundred lords converged,
> And a white fish flew into King Wu's boat
> As he forded at Meng
> To battle the Shang at Grazing Field,
> Where he shed a tide of blood
> That bore off sword and shield,
> As, fierce and majestic, an eagle on the wing,
> He towered above
> King Wu's martial vassals?
> And when
> The tippler from Gaoyang (as he liked to call himself),
> Li Yiji, came and made a common bow
> To the "Big Nose Governor" in those dark hours
> And spoke such startling truths of reign and rule
> That the king-to-be dismissed his footwashers
> And feasted Li Yiji, honoring his splendid spirit?
> The surrender of the east soon followed:
> Seventy-two cities and towns.
> What man has followed in those footsteps?
> Such were the deeds of Jiang Ziya and Li Yiji,
> Heroes unsurpassed unto this very day.

As soon as this song was finished, another man tapped the table and began to sing:

> Han's first king took the realm by sword;
> The house he founded lasted twenty score.
> With Huan and Ling, Han's fire-virtue waned.
> And evil men the chancelorship profaned.

> They saw a serpent coiled beside the throne;
> A rainbow in the consort-quarters shone.
> Ant-like, outlaws gathered everywhere;
> Villains rose like raptors in the air.
> We pound our hands and keen, but all in vain;
> Our sorrows take us to the village inn.
> Leading lives of simple decency,
> Who needs a name that lasts eternally?

Their songs sung, the two men clapped and laughed aloud. Convinced that Sleeping Dragon was within, Xuande dismounted and entered the wineshop. The singers were leaning over a table drinking. One had a light complexion and a long beard, the other a fresh, ageless look. Xuande saluted them and asked, "Which of you is Master Sleeping Dragon?" "Who are you, sir?" the long-bearded one responded. "And what have you to do with him?" "I am Liu Bei," was the reply, "and I need the master's skill to aid my cause and succor our age." "I am not the man you seek," the long-bearded man replied, "nor is he. But we are friends of his. I am Shi Guangyuan of Yingchuan, and this is Meng Gong-wei of Runan." "Noble names long known to me," Xuande exclaimed with delight. "I am favored by this fortunate encounter, and I have extra horses if you gentlemen would be willing to accompany me to Sleeping Dragon's farm." "Country idlers like us," Shi Guangyuan replied, "have no knowledge of the weighty matters that concern you. Do not waste time on the likes of us, sir, but resume your search yourself."

Xuande bade the drinkers good-bye and rode toward Sleeping Dragon Ridge. He dismounted at Kongming's farm and, finding the youth at the gate, asked, "Is your master in today?" "In the house reading," was the reply. Excitedly, Xuande followed the lad. Coming to the inner gate, they stopped before a couplet on the wall that read: "Only through austerity and quiescence can one's purpose shine forth; only through concentration and self-control can one's distant goal be reached." As Xuande was studying the words, he heard someone singing inside. Standing attentively by the door of the thatched house, he peered in and saw a young man with his arms about his knees, chanting:

> The phoenix winging on the air
> Will choose no tree

Except the *wu*.
The scholar keeping to his lair
Will have no lord
Except the true.
Oh, let me till these furrowed fields,
By this sweet home
That I call mine.
In books and song I place my dreams
And wait the time
The fates assign.

When the singer stopped, Xuande entered and extended his courtesies. "I have long held you in admiration," Xuande began, "but wanted occasion to express it personally. The other day, thanks to Shan Fu's suggestion, I came to pay my respects at this retreat of yours. Unable to meet you, however, I went home disappointed. Now I come a second time, undaunted by the storm. This glimpse of your learned countenance is an untold blessing."

Flustered by this speech, the young man returned the greeting and then replied, "General, you must be Liu Xuande and, I believe, wish to see my elder brother." "Master," Xuande said in astonishment, "then you are not Sleeping Dragon, either?" "No, I am his younger brother, Zhuge Jun. There are three of us brothers. The oldest, Zhuge Jin, is in the Southland advising Sun Quan. Kongming is the second brother." "Is the Sleeping Dragon at home?" Xuande inquired. "Yesterday," Zhuge Jun replied, "he was invited by Cui Zhouping to go on a jaunt." "Do you know where?" Xuande asked. "They might have gone rowing down some lake or river," Zhuge Jun answered. "Or to visit some Buddhist or Taoist on his hilltop retreat. Or to look for friends in the villages. Or they might have simply decided to entertain themselves with lutes and chess in some cavern den. My brother comes and goes quite unpredictably, and I have no idea where he might be."

"How meagre my lot!" Xuande exclaimed. "Twice now have I missed this excellent man!" "Sit awhile," Zhuge Jun suggested. "Let me offer you tea." But Zhang Fei broke in, "The master is not here. Let's get going!" "Why go back," Xuande answered him, "without having spoken to anyone?" With that, Xuande turned to Zhuge Jun and said, "Your esteemed brother is known for his mastery of military arts. They say he applies himself to the sub-

ject daily. Can you tell me more about this?" When Zhuge Jun
said he knew nothing about it, Zhang Fei spoke again. "Look at
that storm," he said. "Better be starting back." But Xuande told
him sharply to be quiet. "Since my brother is not here," Zhuge
Jun said, "I should not detain you officers. He will return your
courteous call at a future time." "I would not want him to have
to travel," Xuande replied. "I expect to be coming again in a few
days. Could I trouble you, though, for a brush and paper? As an
expression of the earnestness of my wish, I shall leave your elder
brother a letter." The writing instruments were brought.

Xuande thawed the frozen hairs of the brush with his breath
and unrolled the writing paper. His letter read:

> A longtime admirer of your honored name, I, Liu Bei, have come
> twice to present myself, only to leave again without having met
> you—a keen disappointment. I am humbly mindful that as a re-
> mote kinsman of the court, I have enjoyed prestige and rank far
> beyond my merits. When my thoughts turn to the rude displace-
> ment at court—our laws and customs crumbling and swept aside
> while countless contenders subvert the state and vicious factions
> abuse the sovereign—my heart breaks, my gall is rent. Whatever
> sincerity I may offer to the cause of delivering the Han is wasted
> for want of strategy.
>
> I admire your humane compassion, your sense of loyalty and
> honor. If in your greatness of spirit you would unfold your mighty
> talents, talents comparable to those of Jiang Ziya, and apply your
> grand strategy in the manner of Zhang Liang, then the empire
> and the sacred shrines of the royal house would be doubly blessed.
> I am forwarding this to convey my intention, after further cere-
> monial purification, to pay homage yet again to your honored
> presence, respectfully offering my poor, simple sincerity and en-
> treating your discerning consideration.

Xuande handed the letter to Zhuge Jun, bade him good-bye, and
left. Zhuge Jun accompanied him past the gate, listening to his
earnest reiterations. Finally they parted.

Xuande was starting homeward when he saw the lad beyond
the fence waving and shouting, "The old master is coming!"
Ahead, past a small bridge, a man in winter headdress and fox
furs was riding a donkey through the descending snow. He was
followed by a youth in simple black carrying a gourd of wine.
Turning onto the bridge, the rider sang:

> Nightlong, north winds chill,
> Myriad-leagued, dusky clouds expand.
> Capering snow through an infinite sky
> Transforms the never-changing land.
> He looks into the ether's vastitude:
> Are jade dragons at war up there,
> Strewing their scales every which way,
> And filling up the hollow sphere?
> Alone,
> Sighing for the plum trees' battered blooms.

Certain that Sleeping Dragon was coming, Xuande leaped from the saddle to extend his greetings. "It must be hard for you, master," he said, "to brave this bitter cold. I have long been awaiting you." The startled rider climbed off his beast and returned the salutation. Then Zhuge Jun came up and said, "This is not Sleeping Dragon; it is his father-in-law, Huang Chengyan."

"I happened to hear you chanting just now," Xuande said. "It sounded so elevated and poignant." "I was reading the 'Liangfu Elegies' in my son-in-law's home," the man replied. "I had that stanza in mind as I crossed the bridge; the plum blossoms near the fence moved me to sing. I never imagined an honored guest might hear me." "Have you seen your esteemed son-in-law?" Xuande asked. "Actually, I am coming to see him," was the reply. With that, Xuande took his leave, remounted, and headed home. The wind and snow grew fiercer. Giving a last look back over Sleeping Dragon Ridge, Xuande felt overwhelmed by sadness and uncertainty. As a poet of later times wrote,

> That stormy day he sought the sage in vain,
> And sore at heart, he started home again.
> The creek bridge, frozen; the land, sheer ice
> His trembling horse has many *li* to cross.
> Pear-petal flakes descending from the skies,
> Antic willow puffs darting at his eyes,
> He turns and halts to view the scene behind:
> Banked with snow, the silvered ridges shine.

Back in Xinye time crept by until it was again spring. Xuande ordered the diviners to cast for a propitious time to visit Kongming. After three days' abstinence from meat and wine, Xuande bathed, smeared himself with ritual oils, changed his clothes, and went back to Sleeping Dragon Ridge. His two brothers expressed intense displeasure and protested. Indeed:

> The worthiest has yet to bend the hero's will;
> Servility could shake his fighters' confidence.

What would Xuande say to them?
Read on.

CHAPTER 38

Kongming Determines the Realm's Division and Charts a Course; Sun Quan Leads a Naval Attack and Exacts Revenge

Despite his two fruitless visits, Liu Xuande resolved to pay another call on Kongming. "Twice, brother," Lord Guan said, "you have respectfully presented yourself. Such courtesy is indulgence. It seems to me that Kongming has a false reputation and no real learning. That is why he avoids receiving you. Why are you so captivated by this man?" "You fail to understand," Xuande replied. "Long ago Prince Huan of the state of Qi tried five times before he succeeded in seeing the recluse of Dongguo, Guan Zhong. Getting to see the wise and worthy Kongming may well demand even more of us."

"Dear brother," Zhang Fei declared, "I think you overrate this village bumpkin. What makes him so wise and worthy? Spare yourself the trip. If he refuses to come, it will only take a bit of rope to bring him here!" "I suppose," Xuande said with a scowl, "you've never heard of King Wen, founder of the Zhou, presenting himself to Jiang Ziya. If King Wen could show a wise man such respect, what excuses your utter discourtesy? This time you may stay here. Lord Guan and I will go on together." "Since my elder brothers are going," Zhang Fei replied, "I cannot stay behind." "Let us have nothing unsociable out of you, then," Xuande warned. Zhang Fei agreed.

The brothers and their attendants rode toward Longzhong. Half a *li* from the hermitage they dismounted as a sign of respect. Approaching on foot, they met Zhuge Jun. Xuande hastily extended a greeting and asked, "Is your honored brother at the farm?" "He came home last night," was the reply, "and today, General, you may see him." With that, Zhuge Jun sauntered away. "We're in luck this time," Xuande said. "We will see the master." "What a rude fellow!" Zhang Fei exclaimed. "What would it have cost him to walk us to the farm? Why did he make off just like that?" "He must have something to attend to," Xuande remarked. "Don't be unreasonable."

The three went to the front gate and knocked. A youth received them. "May I trouble you, young acolyte," Xuande said, "to report that Liu Bei has come especially to pay his respects to the master?" "The master is at home today," the lad replied, "however, he is napping in the cottage and has not yet awakened." "In that case, do not announce us for now," Xuande said. He ordered his brothers to wait near the door, and slowly entered the cottage himself. He saw the master lying on a couch and assumed a humble posture as he stood below. A while passed; the master continued sleeping.

Growing impatient, Lord Guan and Zhang Fei came into the chamber and found Xuande standing in attendance as before. Zhang Fei said angrily to Lord Guan, "The insolence! Our brother standing in attendance, while he pretends to sleep peacefully on! Let me go out and torch the rear. We'll see whether that gets him up or not!" Lord Guan calmed his junior, and Xuande ordered both outside to resume their watch. When Xuande looked into the chamber again, the master was turning over and seemed about to wake, but then he rolled back toward the wall, sleeping soundly once again. The lad came in and tried to announce the visitor, but Xuande persuaded him not to disturb Kongming. After another hour or so Kongming finally rose and chanted a song:

> From this great dream who would waken first?
> All along I've known the part to play:

To sleep in springtime, and to ask no more,
Though outside, longer, longer grow the days.

"Any callers from the outside world?" Kongming asked, turning to the lad. "Imperial Uncle Liu," he replied, "has been waiting here for some time." Kongming stood up. "You should have told me sooner! I need time to change my clothes," he said and hurried to his private quarters. It was another while before he reappeared, clothes and cap correct, and greeted his guest.

To Xuande, Kongming appeared singularly tall, with a face like gleaming jade and a plaited silken band around his head. Cloaked in crane down, he had the buoyant air of a spiritual transcendent. Xuande prostrated himself and said, "I, Liu Bei, a foolish fellow from Zhuo district, a distant scion of the house of Han, have long felt your mighty name thunder in my ears. Twice before I have presented myself and, failing to gain audience, finally set my worthless name to a letter. I have never learned whether it was brought to your discerning attention." "A simple rustic of Nanyang," Kongming replied, "negligent and indolent by nature, I am indebted to you, General, for the pains you have taken to travel our way. I have been remiss." After further civilities they seated themselves as host and guest, and tea was served.

The conversation continued. "I could see in your letter," Kongming began, "a compassionate concern for the people and the dynasty. But I fear that you are mistaken in seeking the help of one so young and so limited in ability." "I don't think Sima Hui and Shan Fu would have praised you so highly without good reason," Xuande responded, adding, "I only hope that you will overlook my crudeness, my lack of status, and vouchsafe your edifying instruction." Kongming answered, "Sima Hui and Shan Fu are two of the noblest scholars of the age. I am but a common tiller of the soil. What right have I to speak of the empire? These gentlemen have made a preposterous recommendation. What good can it do, General, to pick the dull and useless stone but pass up the precious jewel?" "How can a man with the ability to shape the times waste himself among the groves and springs?" Xuande continued. "I beg you to consider the living souls of this land and for their sake enlighten me, free me of ignorance and folly." "I would like to know your aspirations, General," Kongming said with a smile.

Xuande dismissed everyone present, shifted his mat closer to Kongming's, and declared, "The house of Han teeters on ruin. Unscrupulous subjects have stolen the mandate of rule. Failing to recognize my limitations, I have tried to promote the great principle of true allegiance throughout the empire; but my superficial knowledge and inadequate methods have so far kept me from achieving anything. If you, master, would relieve my ignorance and keep our cause alive, the blessing would be truly ten-thousandfold."

"Since the time of Dong Zhuo's sedition," Kongming began, "powerful and aggressive figures have come into their own. Cao Cao could overcome Yuan Shao, though his strength was initially inferior, thanks to wise planning and favorable occasion. Now Cao has an army of one million and uses his hold on the Emperor to make the feudal barons do his bidding. There is no way you can cross spearpoints with him. As for Sun Quan, he has a firm grip on the Southland and represents the third generation of his family's power there. The terrain deters invaders and the people are devoted to him. Hence, the south may serve as a supporting ally, but it is not a strategic objective.

"Now consider the central province, Jingzhou. To the north it commands the Han and Mian rivers; to the south it draws wealth from Nanhai; eastward it communicates with the Southland districts; westward it offers access to the districts of the Riverlands— Ba and Shu. Jingzhou—that's the place to fight for! Only a fitting ruler can hold it. And Jingzhou seems to be the very place that Heaven wants to give you, General, if you have the ambition for it.

"Yizhou in the west, strategically located, is an inaccessible frontier province whose fertile wildlands extend thousands of *li*— a kingdom rightly called Heaven's Cornucopia. The first emperor of the Han consummated his imperial enterprise by basing himself there. The present provincial protector, Liu Zhang, is benighted and feeble, and even though the people are well-off and the realm is thriving, he does not know how to care for either. Yizhou's men of insight and capability are yearning for enlightened rule.

"Now, General, you are known across the land as a trustworthy and righteous scion of the Han, one who keeps noble warriors in hand and thirsts for men of merit. If you sit astride these two provinces, Jing and Yi, guard well their strategic points, come to terms with the Rong tribes on the west, placate the Yi and the Viets to the south, form a diplomatic alliance with Sun Quan, and conduct a program of reform in your own territory—then you may wait for the right moment when one of your top generals will be able to drive north to Luoyang by way of Wancheng while you yourself mount an offensive from the Riverlands through the Qinchuan region. And won't the good common folk 'basket food and jug wine' to welcome you, my general! Thus can your great endeavor be brought to fulfillment and the house of Han revived. This is how I would shape strategy for you, General. It remains for you to consider it."

Kongming hung a map and continued: "These are the fifty-four counties of the west. To establish your hegemony, let Cao Cao in the north have the advantage of timely circumstance; let Sun Quan in the south have his geographical advantages; you, my general, will have the allegiance of men. First, take Jingzhou and make it your home base. Then move into the Riverlands and build your third of the triangle of power. Eventually, the northern heartland will become your objective."

Rising from his mat and joining his hands in respectful gratitude, Xuande said, "Master, you have opened the thicket that barred my view and have made me feel as if clouds and mists have parted and I have gained blue sky. The only thing is, Liu Biao of Jingzhou and Liu Zhang of the Riverlands are both, like myself, imperial kinsmen. How could I bear to seize what is theirs?" "Every night," Kongming replied, "I study the configurations of the heavens. Liu Biao will not be long among the living. And Liu Zhang has no ambition worthy of the name. In time he will transfer his allegiance to you." Xuande pressed his head to the ground to show his respect.

By this single interview Kongming, who had never left his thatched cottage, demonstrated his foreknowledge of the tripodal balance of power—truly an incomparable man in any generation! A poet of later times has recorded his admiration:

> Governor Liu, cast adrift, alone,
> By fortune found Nanyang's Sleeping Dragon.
> He sought to know the shape of things to be;
> Smiling, the master mapped his strategy.

Xuande humbly petitioned Kongming: "Though my name be inconsiderable, my virtue meagre, I beg you not to spurn me as a vulgar man of little worth. Come out from these hills to lend us your aid, and I will listen obediently to your enlightening instruction." Kongming replied, "Here I have long been content, with my plow and mattock, and hesitate to respond to the demands of the world. Forgive me if I am unable to accept such service." Xuande began to weep. "If you remain here," he said, "what of the living souls of this land?" Xuande's tears wet the sleeves of his war gown and soaked his lapel. Kongming, moved by the sincerity of his intent, said, "If you will have me, then, General, I shall serve you like a hound or horse."

Elated by Kongming's answer, Xuande called in Lord Guan and Zhang Fei. They offered the gifts Xuande had prepared, but Kongming adamantly declined until Xuande assured him, "Think of this not as a formal petition to a man of great worth, but simply as a humble expression of personal feeling." At last Kongming received the gifts. Xuande and his brothers stayed at the farm overnight. The next day Kongming told Zhuge Jun, who had come back, "I am accepting the kind generosity of Imperial Uncle Liu, who has favored me with three calls. I am obliged to go. Remain at your labors and do not let our acres go fallow. When my work is done, I shall return to resume my life of seclusion." A wistful poem, written in later times, goes:

> About to soar, he felt himself drawn back;
> His task complete, he'll think of this farewell.
> Only for the monarch, who pleaded and pleaded again:
> The "falling star," the "autumn winds"—the "last campaign."

There is another ballad in the old style:

> Han's founding king drew his snow-white sword
> And slew the silver serpent in the Mang-Dang Hills;
> He quelled Qin, smote Chu, and claimed Xianyang.
> Ten score passed; the line would have expired,
> But mighty Guang Wu revived its fortunes in Luoyang;

The throne remained secure till Huan and Ling:
Court rule broke down; Xiandi was moved to Xu.
Bold spirits now arose at every turn:
Cao Cao seized power; the times were in his favor;
In the south, the Sun clan rose and ruled.
Lost and sorely tried, Xuande roamed the realm;
Off in Xinye, he took to heart the people's woes.
Nanyang's Sleeping Dragon dreamed great dreams;
In his mind deep strategies took form.
If Shan Fu had not spoken Kongming's name,
Could Xuande's triple quest have ever been?
So Kongming at an age of three times nine
Packed his books and lute and quit his fields.
"Take Jingzhou first and then take the west!"
Here was a plan to alter destiny.
Across the realm his words created storms.
Juggling stars that held men's fate, he smiled.
Dragons ramped, tigers stalked, sky and land stood calmed;
Time itself can never waste his name.

After bidding Zhuge Jun good-bye, Xuande returned to Xinye with his brothers and Kongming. Xuande treated Kongming as his mentor. They ate together and slept together and spent the days analyzing events in the empire. Kongming observed: "Cao Cao has built the Pool of the Dark Tortoise to train his fighters for naval warfare. That means he intends to invade the south. We ought to send agents south to find out what is happening." And it was done.

*   *   *   *

After the death of Sun Ce, Sun Quan had consolidated his hold on the Southland and extended the patrimony founded by his late father and brother. He brought into his government scholars of merit, and established a guesthouse in Kuaiji in Wuxian, commissioning Gu Yong and Zhang Hong to receive worthy guests from all regions. Over the years the following scholars came by mutual recommendation: Kan Ze (Derun) of Kuaiji; Yan Jun (Mancai) of Pengcheng; Xue Zong (Jingwen) of Pei county; Cheng Bing (Deshu) of Ruyang; Zhu Huan (Xiumu) and Lu Ji (Gongji) of Wujun; Zhang Wen (Huishu) of Wu; Luo Tong (Gongxu) of Wushang; Wu Can (Kongxiu) of Wucheng. These men received generous and courteous treatment in the Southland. A number of important military leaders came too: Lü Meng (Ziming) of Runan; Lu Xun (Boyan) of Wujun; Xu Sheng (Wenxiang) of Langye; Pan Zhang (Wengui) of Dongjun; Ding Feng (Chengyuan) of Lujiang. Sun Quan's civil and military officials worked in close cooperation, and the Southland gained a reputation as a land that fostered talent.

In the seventh year of Jian An [A.D. 202], Cao Cao, having vanquished Yuan Shao, ordered his representative to the Southland to demand that Sun Quan send a son to the capital to serve the Emperor. Sun Quan could not decide whether or not to comply. His mother, Lady Wu, summoned Zhang Zhao and Zhou Yu. Zhang Zhao advised, "Cao Cao's attempt to get one of our lord's sons in his court is a traditional device for keeping the feudal barons under control. If we do not comply, he could raise an army and subjugate the Southland."

Zhou Yu, however, argued, "General Sun has inherited the task his father and brother began. He has brought together the population of the six districts. His army is elite, his grain supplies ample. His officers and men are responsive to command. Why should we send hostages to anyone? Once we do, it will lead to an alliance with Cao Cao, and whenever he calls on us, we will have to go. Rather than become subject to his authority, I think it best to send no hostage but to observe how things develop and prepare a sound defense." "Zhou Yu is correct," Lady Wu decided. Sun Quan, in deference to his mother, cordially dismissed Cao Cao's representative and refused to send a son. After that Cao Cao was determined to subdue the Southland, but disturbances in the north gave him no respite for a southern campaign.

In the eleventh month of the following year Sun Quan attacked Huang Zu. They fought on the Great River, and Huang Zu's forces were demolished. But Sun Quan's commander, Ling Cao, racing ahead on a skiff into Xiakou, was shot down by Gan Ning, Huang Zu's commander. The slain man's son, Ling Tong, a lad of fifteen, took a desperate chance and recovered his father's body. Seeing that the situation was unfavorable, Sun Quan brought his forces back to the Southland.

*   *   *   *

Sun Quan's younger brother, Sun Yi, governor of Danyang, was an inflexible, hard-drinking man whose excesses had been known to drive him to beat his men. The district military inspector, Gui Lan, and the assistant governor, Dai Yuan, had long desired to murder Governor Sun Yi. Together with one of the governor's attendants, Bian Hong, the two officials decided to conspire against him.

Sun Yi had prepared a grand banquet on the occasion of a gathering of the generals and county prefects in the capital town of Danyang. On the day of the feast Sun Yi's wife, Lady Xu, a beautiful and intelligent woman, skilled at divination, cast a hexagram in the *Book of Changes* signifying dire misfortune. She urged her husband not to attend the reception, but he ignored her pleas and joined the festivities. Afterward, as the guests were dispersing, Bian Hong, armed with a knife, followed Sun Yi out the gate and cut him down.

The principal conspirators, Gui Lan and Dai Yuan, then charged their fellow plotter, Bian Hong, with the crime, and he was publicly beheaded. The murderers proceeded to plunder the governor's household, seizing his property and female attendants. Gui Lan found himself attracted to Sun Yi's wife and said to her, "I have avenged your husband's death, and you will have to live with me or die." "With my husband dead so recently," Lady Xu said, "I cannot bear to serve another yet. Would it be asking too much to wait until the last day of the month? Then, after I make the offerings and remove my mourning robes, we can solemnize the relationship." Gui Lan agreed.

Lady Xu summoned two of the late governor's confidants, Sun Gao and Fu Ying. Tearfully she appealed to them: "My husband often spoke of your loyalty and honor. Those two villains, Gui Lan and Dai Yuan, murdered my husband, then blamed Bian Hong and punished him for it, all the while helping themselves to our property and servants. Gui Lan even tried to possess me. I pretended consent to allay his suspicions. Now if you two could get word to Sun Quan and devise a plan to take care of the villains, my husband's death would be avenged and my honor redeemed; I would be eternally grateful." With that, Lady Xu flung herself to the ground.

Tears stood in the men's eyes. "We two," they said, "have ever been grateful for the late governor's generosity. We did not follow him in death only because we were trying to avenge him. What you command is ours to perform." And they sent secret messages to Sun Quan.

On the day appointed for the ceremony Lady Xu concealed her husband's two commanders behind the curtains in an inner chamber and commenced the sacrificial ritual in the main hall. That done, she removed her mourning attire, bathed and perfumed herself, and dressed seductively. She spoke to everyone with artful ease and gracious self-possession. Gui Lan was elated when informed of her behavior.

That night Lady Xu invited Gui Lan to her quarters, where she had prepared a feast. After he had drunk deeply, she led him to the inner chamber. Intoxicated as he was, the delighted guest went in. "Commanders, come forth!" Lady Xu cried out. Gui Lan had no time to defend himself. The two armed men leaped into view. Fu Ying felled Gui Lan with a single stroke of his blade, Sun Gao followed up with another cut, and Gui Lan lay dead. Lady Xu then sent Dai Yuan an invitation to the banquet; he too was killed when he arrived at the hall. All the followers and family members of the two slain murderers were executed. Lady Xu resumed her mourning attire and sacrificed the heads of her enemies before the altar of her dear lord, Sun Yi.

Before long Sun Quan himself arrived in Danyang with a party of soldiers. Since the two criminals had already been dispatched by Lady Xu, Sun Quan appointed Sun Gao and Fu Ying garrison commanders, put them in charge of Danyang, and took the widow, his sister-in-law, home with him that he might care for her for the rest of her life. The Southland celebrated Lady Xu's strength of character. A later poet wrote:

> So able and so chaste—in this world all too rare!
> The widow lured two villains into her cunning snare.
> Vassals base chose treachery, vassals loyal chose death;
> To this Southland heroine does any man compare?

Now all the rebels in the Southland had come under Sun Quan's control. And he had more than seven thousand war-boats on the Great River. At Sun Quan's behest Zhou Yu became supreme commander of the Southland's land and sea forces.

In winter, the tenth month of Jian An 12, Sun Quan's mother, Lady Wu, fell gravely ill. She called for Zhang Zhao and Zhou Yu and said to them, "Though originally a woman of Wu, I lost my parents when young and, following my younger brother, Wu Jing, settled among the Viets. Later I married Sun Jian and bore him four sons. At the birth of Ce, my eldest, I dreamed that the moon was coming into my body. When Quan, my second, was born, I dreamed that the sun had entered me. The diviners said, 'Such dreams portend great rank for your sons.' Alas, the eldest died too young, and now our patrimony passes to the second son. If I can count on you two gentlemen to concert your efforts to support him, I shall not die in vain."

Lady Wu then spoke her final charge to Sun Quan: "I want you to serve Zhang Zhao and Zhou Yu as if they were your teachers, without lapse or negligence. Remember, my younger sister was given in marriage with me to your father. She is your mother as well. Serve her as you would have served me. Care for your younger sister, too, and marry her well." With these words she passed away. Sun Quan wailed in grief. He duly fulfilled the ceremonies of mourning and interment.

In the spring of the following year, Sun Quan raised the question of attacking Huang Zu. Zhang Zhao counseled caution: "We are still in the first year of the mourning period. It is not the time for military action." But Zhou Yu countered, "Avenging a humiliation brooks no waiting period." Sun Quan was brooding over the matter when District Commander Lü Meng was announced. "I was guarding Dragon's Gorge," he said, "when Gan Ning, one of Huang Zu's lieutenants, unexpectedly surrendered. Gan Ning's style is Xingba, and he comes from Linjiang in Bajun. On close questioning I found him to be a man of considerable learning, quite vigorous, and something of an 'honorable adventurer.' It seems he once led a gang of desperadoes who were active all over the region. Gan Ning always carried a brass bell at his waist. The sound of it put people to flight. He earned the nickname Bandit of the Colored Sails because he used Riverlands imported silk in his sails. Eventually he came to regret his earlier excesses, changed his ways, and entered the service of Liu Biao.

"Soon enough Gan Ning realized that Liu Biao would accomplish nothing, and he now desires to join us. At Xiakou, how-

ever, Huang Zu detained him. The last time we defeated Huang
Zu he retook Xiakou only by the efforts of Gan Ning. Even then
Huang Zu treated him most stingily. The chief of guards, Su Fei,
tried several times to recommend Gan Ning to Huang Zu, but
Huang Zu always answered, 'Ning is a criminal who has preyed
upon the people all along the river. I can't give him an important
position.' So Gan Ning's resentment burned hotter and hotter.

"At this point Su Fei invited Gan Ning to dine at his home and
said to him, 'Lord Liu Biao has refused you a fitting appointment
despite my recommendations. The years are passing and life is
short. It's time to plan ahead. I am going to set you up as a magistrate in Zhu county. You can look for a new lord from there.'

"And that, my lord," Lü Meng concluded, "is how Gan Ning
came to surrender to us. At first he was fearful that his having
rescued Huang Zu and killed Ling Cao would be held against
him, but I assured him that Your Lordship thirsted for worthy
men and would never bear him a grudge, especially since he had
acted out of loyalty. He has crossed the river with his men to present himself to you. I beg to know your will."

Sun Quan was jubilant. "This defection ensures Huang Zu's
defeat," he said and had Gan Ning brought before him. After Gan
Ning's formal salutations, Sun Quan told him, "Your coming wins
our good will. There can be no thinking of old grudges. Be assured of that. We only hope you will show us the way to destroy
Huang Zu." To this Gan Ning responded, "The sacred Han
throne is in imminent danger. Cao Cao's ministry is bound to
end in a usurpation, and Jingzhou is the place he will fight for.
Its protector, Liu Biao, makes no provision for the future, and
his two sons are clumsy mediocrities who could never keep what
he has built up. My lord, make his territory yours—before Cao
Cao makes it his. First, Huang Zu must be captured. He is old
and apathetic, absorbed in profit and gain. He infringes upon
the interests of his officials and exacts much from the populace. This has led to widespread disaffection. His military equipment is in disrepair; his army has no discipline. He will fall if
you attack. And then—sound the drum and march west. Hold
the Chu pass and aim for the Riverlands. Your hegemony can be
achieved." "Precious advice," Sun Quan responded.

Sun Quan had made Zhou Yu supreme commander of all land

and naval forces. He now made Lü Meng leader of the vanguard of the front unit and Dong Xi and Gan Ning, deputy commanders. Sun Quan himself took charge of the main army, which numbered one hundred thousand. Thus the expedition against Huang Zu began.

Huang Zu summoned his counselors as spies and scouts reported these developments back to Jiangxia. He appointed Su Fei his chief general, assigned Chen Jiu and Deng Long to the vanguard, and mobilized the entire district. The two van leaders led a squad of war-boats and blocked the passage near Miankou. Each boat held a thousand archers and crossbowmen. Heavy ropes linked the craft to steady them. When they sighted the Southlanders, the defenders rolled their drums and let fly volleys of arrows, driving the invaders back several *li*.

Gan Ning said to Dong Xi, "Having come this far, we can't turn back." They put five thousand crack troops on one hundred small craft; each carried twenty rowers and thirty men in armor. Steel swords in hand, braving the oncoming bolts, the sailors of the south drove toward the long junks. Drawing alongside, they severed the heavy ropes, causing the junks to drift away from each other. Gan Ning leaped onto the main ship and cut down Deng Long. Chen Jiu abandoned his ship.

Lü Meng sprang at once into a small boat, rowed directly into the enemy fleet, and set the junks afire. Chen Jiu struggled ashore, but Lü Meng, heedless of all risk, raced ahead of him and felled him with one stroke through the chest. By the time Su Fei arrived at the bank to assist, the Southlanders had already gained the shore in overpowering force. Huang Zu was routed. Su Fei took to his heels but was captured handily by Pan Zhang and brought to Sun Quan's ship. Sun Quan had him caged pending the capture of Huang Zu so that he could execute the two together. He then hastened on to Xiakou in full force. Indeed:

> Slighted by Liu Biao, the Bandit of the Colored Sails
> Blasted apart the war-junks of Huang Zu.

Huang Zu's fate hung in the balance.
Read on.

CHAPTER 39

Jingzhou's Heir Pleads Three Times for Advice; The Director General Makes His Debut at Bowang

The attack Sun Quan delivered against Xiakou had wiped out Huang Zu's whole force. Huang Zu abandoned Jiangxia and fled west toward Jingzhou. Anticipating his line of flight, Gan Ning had posted an ambush outside the eastern gate of Jiangxia. When the defeated commander hurried through with a few dozen mounted followers, he found Gan Ning's men massed across the way, shouting in unison. From horseback Huang Zu said to Gan Ning, "I always did right by you in the old days. Why do you threaten me now?" Scowling, Gan Ning replied, "All I ever got for my service was the title River Bandit. Do you have anything else to say?" Denied mercy, Huang Zu wheeled about and galloped off. Gan Ning pursued him.

A fresh commotion signaled the arrival of another Southland commander, Cheng Pu. Gan Ning suspected Cheng Pu had come to take credit for the capture of Huang Zu, so he drew his bow, felled Huang Zu, and severed his head. He subsequently rejoined Cheng Pu, and the combined force rode back to Sun Quan. Gan Ning presented the enemy commander's head, and Sun Quan stored it in a wooden box until he could return to the Southland and offer it at his father's altar. The leader of the Southland rewarded his army handsomely and elevated Gan Ning to district commander. Then he had to decide whether to hold the city captured from Huang Zu.

"Jiangxia is too far from our bases to defend," Zhang Zhao argued. "Pull the men back. Liu Biao will attack us the moment he hears of Huang Zu's fate. Let him come. His overextended troops will soon yield to our well-rested soldiers, and then we can carry our counterattack as far as Jingzhou's capital and capture it." Sun Quan approved Zhang Zhao's advice and withdrew all units to the south.

Meanwhile, Su Fei was in the prisoner's cage. He appealed through someone for Gan Ning's help. "Su Fei did not even have to mention it," Gan Ning told the emissary. "I could never forget how he helped me." The Southland forces returned and Sun Quan ordered Su Fei executed so that his head could be placed with Huang Zu's on Sun Jian's altar.

Gan Ning came before Sun Quan to plead for his former patron: "Without Su Fei, I'd be a pile of bones underground and never would have come to serve under you, General. His offense, I grant, is capital. But in view of his past kindness to me, I beg to redeem him with the office and rank you have so generously granted." "For your sake only," Sun Quan said, "I pardon him—but what if he escapes?" "He would be too grateful to do that," Gan Ning assured him. "But if he does, I will answer for it with my head." Thus Su Fei was spared, and Huang Zu's head alone was offered at the sacrificial altar.

After the ritual, a feast was held to congratulate the civil and military officials. As the wine was circulating one man rose, uttered a cry, and went for Gan Ning with drawn sword. Gan Ning used a chair to parry the attack. Sun Quan recognized the assailant as Ling Tong. Gan Ning had shot and killed his father, Ling Cao, while still in the service of Huang Zu at Jiangxia. Now Ling Tong wanted revenge. Intervening, Sun Quan said, "When Gan Ning killed your father, he was bound to another lord. He was doing what he had to do. Now that we are all in the same family, old grudges must be forgotten—for my sake." "Blood debts must be paid!" Ling Tong shouted, pressing his forehead to the ground in front of Sun Quan, who, along with the officials present, tried to talk Ling Tong round. But the young warrior kept staring angrily at Gan Ning. Sun Quan made a quick decision to reassign Gan Ning to Xiakou with five thousand men and one hundred war-junks. Gan Ning thanked him and left. At the same time Sun Quan appointed Ling Tong District Commander, Filial and Heroic, an offer the indignant son reluctantly accepted.

The defense of the Southland was now begun in earnest, with

a great boatbuilding campaign and the deployment of troops along the banks of the Great River. Sun Quan assigned his brother, Sun Jing, to guard Wujun while he positioned the main army at Chaisang. Zhou Yu directed maneuvers on the Poyang Lakes daily, preparing his marines for the next invasion of Jingzhou.

*   *   *   *

The spies that Xuande had sent south now returned to Xinye with the following intelligence: "The southerners have struck. Huang Zu is dead. They're digging in at Chaisang." Xuande was discussing the new developments with Kongming when he was summoned by Liu Biao. Kongming said, "Since the Southland has routed Huang Zu, Liu Biao will want to see you to help plan his revenge. I'll go along to weigh the possibilities and advise you accordingly." Xuande agreed. He left Xinye in Lord Guan's hands and, joined by Kongming, went to the capital of the province. Zhang Fei and five hundred men escorted him.

As they rode, Xuande asked Kongming, "What should I say to Liu Biao?" "First of all," Kongming advised, "you must apologize for the incident at Xiangyang when you fled the banquet. Then, if he orders you to undertake a punitive expedition against the Southland, decline—no matter what he says. Tell him you need time to go back to Xinye and get your forces into condition." Xuande approved. In Jingzhou the two men settled into a government guesthouse while Zhang Fei stood guard outside the city.

Liu Biao received Xuande and Kongming. The necessary formalities performed, Xuande expressed regret for his offense. "I am well aware, worthy brother," Liu Biao said, "of the mortal danger you were in. I was fully prepared to behead Cai Mao then and there to satisfy you but was induced by many appeals to forgive him. Will my worthy brother kindly not take offense?" "It was not really General Cai's doing," Xuande replied. "I assume the plot was hatched by his subordinates."

"Now that we have lost Jiangxia," the protector of Jingzhou continued, "and Huang Zu has met his death, I have called you here to take part in planning our retaliation." "Huang Zu was a violent sort," Xuande responded, "quite incapable of using men. That's how he brought on this catastrophe. Now if we mobilize and march south, Cao Cao could strike from the north. What then?" "The years weigh on me," Liu Biao said. "My ailments multiply. I cannot cope with the affairs of this province. Worthy brother, if you come to assist me, you will become ruler of Jingzhou after I pass away." "Elder brother," Xuande cried out, "do not say that nor imagine that I would presume to undertake such a responsibility."

At this point Kongming eyed Xuande, who continued, "We must allow more time to devise a sound strategy." Xuande excused himself and returned to his lodgings. "My lord," Kongming said to him, "Liu Biao was ready to put the province in your hands. Why did you decline?" "The Protector," Xuande replied, "has treated me with consummate consideration and etiquette. To exploit his moment of peril by seizing his estate is the last thing I could bring myself to do." "What a kindhearted lord," Kongming said with a sigh.

While this discussion was going on, Liu Qi, the eldest son of Liu Biao, entered and tearfully importuned Xuande and Kongming. "My stepmother will suffer my existence no longer," he said. "I may be killed at any moment. Rescue me, uncle, for pity's sake." "This is a family matter, nephew," Xuande replied. "You cannot come to me with it." Xuande turned to Kongming, who was smiling faintly. "Yes," he said, "this is a family matter, with which I would not presume to acquaint myself." Afterward Xuande escorted the lad out and whispered to him, "Tomorrow I shall have Kongming return your call. Make sure to say thus and so . . . " Xuande proposed a ruse to obtain Kongming's advice, adding, "He should have some ingenious suggestions for you." Liu Qi thanked Xuande and left.

The next day Xuande put off all obligations, claiming a stomach ailment, and persuaded Kongming to repay Liu Qi's call alone. Liu Qi received Kongming in his private apartment. When they had finished tea, Liu Qi said, "My stepmother has no use for me. Master, favor me with a word to relieve my plight." "I am here as a guest," Kongming replied. "If people found out I had meddled for no good reason in a conflict among kinfolk, it could do us great harm." So saying, Kongming rose to leave. Liu Qi appealed to him: "You have honored me with your presence here. I must see you off with more ceremony than this." He led Kongming into another chamber and served him wine. "My step-mother," he reiterated, "has no use for me. I implore you to speak the word that can save me." "I may not give counsel in such matters," was the reply. Again Kongming asked to leave. "Master," Liu Qi went on, "if you will not speak, then there is nothing more to say. But must you leave so precipitately?"

Kongming returned to his place. "I have an ancient text," Liu Qi said, "that I would like you to examine." He guided his guest up to a small attic. "Where is the book?" Kongming asked. Bowing tearfully, Liu Qi said, "My stepmother has no use for me. My death is imminent. Do you mean to be so cruel as to deny me a single word of help?" Kongming rose angrily and tried to leave, only to find that the ladder they had ascended was gone. "I need a sound plan," Liu Qi appealed. "Your fear of discovery makes you reluctant to speak. Well, here we are, alone between Heaven and earth. Your voice can reach no ear but mine—therefore, bestow your wisdom." "'Strangers never meddle among kin,' as the saying goes," Kongming replied. "I cannot give counsel." "If you are so resolved," Liu Qi said, "my life cannot be preserved. Let me end it before your eyes." With those words he drew his sword.

Kongming moved to restrain him, saying, "There is a way. You must remember the ancient story of the brothers Shensheng and Chong Er? The former stayed home and lost his life; the latter went into exile and saved himself. Now, with Huang Zu's defeat, Jiangxia stands unguarded. Why not petition your father for a company of men to hold Jiangxia? That might save you." Liu Qi thanked Kongming profusely and had the ladder replaced. Kongming returned to Xuande and informed him of the disposition of Liu Qi's problem. Xuande was delighted.

Liu Qi's petition for a defense force put Liu Biao in a dilemma. For advice he turned to Xuande. "Jiangxia is a crucial location," Xuande said. "You cannot have just anybody guarding it. Your son is the right man. And while your son takes care of the southeast, let me handle the northwest." "I'm told," Liu Biao said, "that Cao Cao has built an artificial lake to train his forces for a southern expedition. We must be prepared." "We already know this," Xuande replied. "Do not be anxious, brother." Xuande returned to his base at Xinye, and Liu Biao assigned Liu Qi three thousand men to secure Jiangxia.

*   *   *   *

It was at this time that Cao Cao terminated the duties of the three elder lords and attached their functions to his own office. He made Mao Jie and Cui Yan his staff supervisors, and Sima Yi his chief of the Bureau of Documents. Sima Yi (Zhongda) came from Wen county in Henei district. He was the grandson of Sima Juan, governor of Yingchuan; the son of Sima Fang, governor of the western capital district Jingzhao; and younger brother of Sima Lang, chief of the advisory staff. Having thus brought his civil staff up to full strength, Cao Cao held discussions with his generals on the southern campaign against Jingzhou. Xiahou Dun proposed: "We have been informed that Liu Bei has been steadily developing his fighting force in Xinye. We should plan to attack him before he becomes a serious problem." Cao Cao directed Xiahou Dun to take command of a hundred-thousand-man force, and Yu Jin, Li Dian, Xiahou Lan, and Han Hao to serve as his deputy generals. Their orders were to march to Bowang and keep Xinye under close watch.

The adviser Xun Wenruo objected, however: "Xuande is one of the greatest heroes of our time and, with Kongming as his director general, is not to be recklessly confronted." "Xuande is a mouse that won't escape me," Xiahou Dun retorted. Then Shan Fu spoke: "General, do not underestimate Xuande. He is a tiger to whom Zhuge Liang gives wings." "Who is Zhuge Liang?" Cao Cao interjected. "His style is Kongming," Shan Fu replied, "his Taoist sobriquet, Master Sleeping Dragon. He is one of the rarest talents of the age. He can plot the motions of sky and land and design plans of divine perfection. On no account should you belittle him." "And how does he compare with you?" Cao Cao asked. "No comparison," Shan Fu said. "I am a firefly; he, the full-risen moon." "How absurd!" Xiahou Dun cried. "He's a straw reed to me. I fear him not. If in a single engagement I fail to capture Xuande and take this Kongming alive, the prime minister is welcome to my head." "Well then," Cao Cao replied, "send us an early report of victory and dispel our qualms." Filled with energetic determination, Xuahou Dun took his leave and commenced the operation.

*   *   *   *

Xuande's ritual acknowledgment of Kongming as his teacher caused his two brothers no little consternation. "Kongming is so young," they said to him, "what knowledge or ability could he have? Brother, you have obliged him beyond all reason—before even putting him to the test." But Xuande closed the matter by saying, "He is to me as water to the fish. Say no more, brothers." Rebuffed, Lord Guan and Zhang Fei silently withdrew.

One day someone presented Xuande with a yak's tail, and he wound it into a headdress. When Kongming saw it, he said severely, "My illustrious lord must be forgetting his aspirations if this is all he has to devote himself to." Xuande tossed the yak's tail away and apologized. "I was only killing time, trying to forget my troubles," he said. "In your judgment," Kongming continued, "how do you and Cao Cao compare?" "I fall short," Xuande answered. "Your soldiers," Kongming went on, "number in the thousands. How would you deal with Cao's army if it appeared?" "That very question has been consuming me," Xuande admitted, "but I have not found a good answer." "You had better recruit a militia as quickly as possible," Kongming urged. "I will train them myself." On this advice Xuande called for volunteers. Three thousand men of Xinye joined the army, and Kongming instructed them intensively in field tactics.

Word of Cao Cao's approaching invasion force of one hundred thousand reached Xinye. Zhang Fei said to Lord Guan, "We'll have Kongming deal with it, and that will be that." When Xuande summoned his brothers to counsel, Zhang Fei said, "How about sending the one you call 'water'?" "For brains," Xuande retorted, "I have Kongming; for courage, you two. Don't bandy responsibilities!" The brothers left, and Xuande called Kongming to him. "My main concern," Kongming said, "is that Zhang Fei and Lord Guan obey my orders. If you wish to have me as your military executive, empower me with your sword and seal." Accordingly, Xuande turned these articles over to Kongming, who then assembled the commanders. "We might as well go along, too," Zhang Fei said to Lord Guan, "if only to see how he runs things."

Before the commanders Kongming issued his orders: "Left of Bowang are the Yu Hills; to the right, the forest of An—two good places for concealing men and horses. Lord Guan, you hide in the hills with a thousand fighters and let the enemy pass unopposed. Their equipment and food supplies will be in the rear. The moment you see fire on the southern side, unleash your men and burn the enemy's grain and fodder. Zhang Fei, you hide in the ravines behind the forest. When you see fire, head for the old supply depot at Bowang and burn it. I want Liu Feng and Guan Ping to take five hundred men with combustible materials and wait on either side of the area behind the slope of Bowang itself. At the first watch, when the enemy troops will be arriving, set fires." Kongming also ordered Zhao Zilong recalled from the town of Fan to lead the forward army, but with specific instructions to feign defeat. He concluded: "Our lord should lead one contingent as a rear support. All must act according to the plan without the slightest deviation."

Lord Guan's reaction was sharp. "So," he said, "we are all to go forth and engage the enemy. And when will we have the opportunity of reviewing your own role as director general?" "My role is simply to stay and guard our base," was Kongming's reply. Zhang Fei guffawed. "We all go to the slaughter," he cried, "while you sit home, perfectly content and comfortable!" "I have the sword and seal," Kongming said. "Whoever violates my orders will die." "Brothers," Xuande said, "have you forgotten? 'Plans evolved within the tent decide victories a thousand *li* away.' You must obey his orders." Smiling coldly, Zhang Fei left. "We shall see," Lord Guan said, "whether his ideas work. There will be time enough to confront him if they don't." With that, he followed Zhang Fei out. The commanders, uncertain about Kongming's strategy, remained doubtful but followed their orders.

Kongming said to Xuande, "My lord, station your troops at the foot of Bowang Hill. Tomorrow evening when the enemy arrives, abandon camp. At the fire signal, turn back upon them. I shall hold Xinye with Mi Zhu, Mi Fang, and five hundred guards." Kongming then ordered Sun Qian and Jian Yong to prepare the victory feast and ready the honor rolls. Now complete, Kongming's orchestration had even Xuande perplexed.

*   *   *   *

Cao Cao's commanders, Xiahou Dun and Yu Jin, neared Bowang. They assigned half their troops to the front, half to guard the grain wagons. It was autumn. Strong winds began to blow. As the soldiers rushed ahead, their leaders noticed dust flying in the distance. Xiahou Dun drew up his forces and asked his guide to describe their position. "Ahead lie the slopes of Bowang," was the reply, "behind, the mouth of the River Luo."

Xiahou Dun had Yu Jin and Li Dian call a general halt while he rode in front of the line to scan the horizon. A force of cavalry was approaching them. Laughing loudly, Xiahou Dun said to his commanders, "Before the prime minister himself Shan Fu extolled Kongming as a divine strategist. Now look how he uses his troops! Sending such puny forces in the van is like sending sheep and dogs against tigers and panthers. I told His Excellency I would take Xuande and Kongming alive, and I shall make good my claim." So saying, he charged forward.

Zhao Zilong rode forth, and Xiahou Dun reviled him: "You and your men follow Xuande like lost souls chasing a ghost." Zilong gave his horse its head, and the two warriors closed. After several passages Zhao Zilong retreated, and Xiahou Dun chased him twenty *li*. Zilong turned and fought, then retreated again.

Cao's commander, Han Hao, raced up and warned Xiahou Dun that he was being drawn into an ambush, but he received a contemptuous answer: "Let them set a ten-sided ambush. I still have nothing to fear!" He pressed on to the slope. Thereupon, Xuande ordered his bombards to pound the enemy as he joined the battle. Engaging the new opponent, Xiahou Dun said derisively to Han Hao, "Is this the ambush you warned me about? I shall not halt again until we reach Xinye." And he moved forward, driving Xuande and Zhao Zilong in full retreat before him.

The sky was darkening. Thick clouds stretched across it. There was no moon. It had been gusty all day, and now the night winds were rising. Xiahou Dun was intent on the kill. His commanders, Yu Jin and Li Dian, reached a narrow point where dry reeds crowded the road on both sides. Li Dian said to Yu Jin, "'Despise your enemy and you will lose.' To the south the roads narrow, and the hills and river hem us in. The foliage is dense and tangled. What if they use fire?" "Of course!" Yu Jin exclaimed. "I'll go and warn the general-in-command. You go and halt the rear at once." But Li Dian could not arrest the forward momentum

of the army. Yu Jin dashed ahead. "Stop the march!" he cried to
Xiahou Dun. "They could use fire on these tight roads. The hills
and the river have us hemmed in, and the undergrowth crowds
us." How real the danger was now dawned on Xiahou Dun, but
by the time he turned back to stop the advance, he caught the
sound of fire hissing and rising in crescendo as arms of flame
reached up through the dry reeds hugging the road. In moments
the blaze, whipped by the wind, roared on all sides of them. Panic
ensued. Cao Cao's soldiers trampled one another, adding to the
incalculable losses. Zhao Zilong then returned to take a further
toll on the enemy. Xiahou Dun, braving heat and smoke, broke
through the walls of fire and fled.

Li Dian, who had been watching this disastrous turn of events,
raced for Bowang. But another contingent, illuminated in the
fires, barred his way; at its head was Lord Guan. After a spell of
confused and desperate fighting, Li Dian managed to escape; and
Yu Jin too, seeing the wagons consumed in the flames, fled for
his life. Xiahou Lan and Han Hao tried to save the grain and fodder; but Zhang Fei intercepted them, made short work of Xiahou Lan, and sent Han Hao into headlong flight. The slaughter
went on until dawn. Corpses littered the land, and the blood ran
in rivers. This poem commemorates the victory:

> With fire he broke the battle at Bowang,
> All smiles and small talk, giving each his cue.
> Striking fear deep into Cao Cao's soul,
> Thus Kongming scored a coup at his debut.

Xiahou Dun rounded up the survivors and returned to Xuchang.

Kongming recalled all units. Lord Guan and Zhang Fei said
to one another, "He is a true hero, a champion!" The brothers
had ridden only a short distance when they saw Mi Zhu and Mi
Fang leading a party of soldiers. In their midst was a small carriage. A man, perfectly poised, sat inside. Lord Guan and Zhang
Fei dismounted and bowed low before the carriage in acknowledgment of the director general's ability. Moments later Xuande,
Zhao Zilong, Liu Feng, Guan Ping, and others arrived. The men
regrouped into their companies, and the captured spoils were
shared among officers and men. Afterward all marched back to

Xinye. Along the road the townspeople prostrated themselves before the victors, exclaiming, "We are saved thanks to Lord Liu, who has won the service of an able man."

Back in the county seat, Kongming said to Xuande, "Xiahou Dun has beat a retreat, but Cao Cao himself will return in force." "What are we to do?" Xuande asked. "I think I know how to hold him off," Kongming replied. Indeed:

> After the victory neither man nor mount may rest:
> A perfect strategy is needed to avoid the next attack.

What was Kongming's plan?
Read on.

CHAPTER 40

Lady Cai Proposes Ceding Jingzhou to Cao Cao; Zhuge Liang Burns Cao's Men in Xinye

Xuande asked Kongming how to counter Cao Cao, and Kongming said, "We cannot stay in a small town like Xinye. The latest news is that Liu Biao may be dying. The time has come to establish ourselves in Jingzhou and put ourselves in position to throw Cao Cao back." "It sounds sensible," Xuande said, "but I will not conspire against the man who has hosted us so kindly." "If you fail to take the province now," Kongming warned emphatically, "you will soon regret it." "I would rather die than do this dishonorable deed," Xuande responded. "This matter is going to come up again," Kongming said.

*   *   *   *

Xiahou Dun returned to Xuchang and presented himself in bonds before the prime minister. Touching his head to the ground, the defeated general offered to atone with his life for the losses at Bowang. But Cao Cao undid the ropes. "I fell afoul of Zhuge Liang's treacherous scheme," Xiahou Dun explained. Cao Cao said, "How could a man who has waged war all his life forget to guard against fire on those narrow pathways?" "Li Dian and Yu Jin tried to warn me," Xiahou Dun admitted, "but I did not heed them." Cao Cao rewarded the two commanders.

"Xuande grows bolder," Xiahou Dun warned. "Action must be taken now." "Yes, Liu Bei and Sun Quan are our first concern," Cao Cao replied. "The others are not worth worrying about. The time has come to make the south submit." So saying, he ordered the mobilization of half a million soldiers into five equal contingents: the first, led by Cao Ren and Cao Hong; the second, by Zhang Liao and Zhang He; the third, by Xiahou Yuan and Xiahou Dun; the fourth, by Yu Jin and Li Dian; the fifth, by Cao Cao himself and his staff commanders. The expedition was scheduled to set out in the seventh month of Jian An 13 [A.D. 208].

Imperial Mentor Kong Rong opposed the expedition. "Liu Bei and Liu Biao," he argued, "are members of the imperial clan; imperial sanction is required before taking military action against them. Sun Quan has a powerful hold on the six districts of the Southland, and the Great River affords his territory a formidable natural defense. It is not an easy place to capture. Putting an army into the field without the justification such an enterprise must have will cost Your Excellency the confidence of the realm." Cao Cao responded angrily, "Liu Bei, Liu Biao, and Sun Quan have disobeyed imperial decrees. Their chastisement is both necessary and proper." With that, he dismissed Kong Rong harshly and ordered any further protest punished by execution.

Kong Rong left Cao Cao's residence, lifted his eyes to Heaven, and sighed as he said, "How can the most inhumane of men succeed in war against the most humane of men? The former cannot win." A household retainer of Imperial Censor Chi Lü overheard the remark and reported it to his master. The censor, whom Kong Rong held in disdain, deeply resented the scholar and gladly called the matter to Cao Cao's attention. "Day after day," Chi Lü added, "Kong Rong belittles you and slanders you. Moreover, he was friendly with Mi Heng. Mi Heng praised him as a second Confucius, and Kong Rong returned the compliment, calling Mi Heng another Yan Hui, Confucius's most treasured disciple. That time Mi Heng stripped himself at the drum concert and shamed you so—Kong Rong put him up to it." Shaking with fury, the prime minister ordered security officers to arrest the imperial mentor.

At the time Kong Rong's two young sons were at home playing chess. Their attendants said, "They've taken your father to be executed. Get away at once." "When the nest falls," the boys replied, "the eggs will break." Moments later the security officers swept in, seized all members of the household, including the two boys, and put them to death.

Soon after, the imperial mentor's corpse was publicly displayed. Zhi Xi of Jingzhao kneeled over the body and wept. Cao Cao would have had him killed too, but Xun Wenruo dissuaded him, saying, "I have been told that Zhi Xi often warned Kong Rong that his obstinacy would ruin him. His mourning is no more than a token of his personal loyalty. I would spare him." Xun Wenruo's words carried weight, and Cao Cao took no action against Zhi Xi. Zhi Xi arranged a suitable burial for Kong Rong and his sons. A later verse sang the imperial mentor's praises:

> When Kong Rong Beihai district ruled,
> His mighty spirit spanned the sky.
> His house was always filled with guests;
> Their cups were always filled with wine.
> By rhetoric he held his age in awe;
> His wit put kings and dukes to shame.
> Historians call him loyal and true
> In annals that preserve his rightful name.

After the execution of Kong Rong, Cao Cao ordered the five armies to commence their southern expedition. Xun Wenruo alone remained to protect the capital.

*   *   *   *

In Jingzhou, Liu Biao's illness had worsened. He called for Xuande, intending to entrust him with the care of his sons. Xuande, attended by his brothers, came before the protector. "My condition is incurable, worthy brother," Liu Biao began. "Before I die, I intend to place my sons in your charge. They are not fit to succeed me. After my death you should assume control of

Jingzhou yourself." Xuande bowed and wept. "I shall give my utmost support to my nephews," he said. "I have no higher ambition." As the two kinsmen spoke, the approach of Cao Cao's armies was reported. Xuande took his leave and hastened back to Xinye. Liu Biao, severely shaken, decided that his rule should pass to his eldest son, Liu Qi, whom he placed in Xuande's protection. Lady Cai, infuriated at the decision, had the inner gates sealed and the outer gates guarded by her men, Cai Mao and Zhang Yun.

Liu Qi had already positioned himself at Jiangxia when he learned that his father was near death. He hurried back to Jingzhou, only to find Cai Mao barring his entrance. "Young master," Cai Mao declared, "you were commissioned by your father to defend Jiangxia and have no authority to abandon your duties. What if the Southland soldiers strike? Your appearance here could only annoy the protector and aggravate his condition, which would be most unfilial. You should return at once." Liu Qi stood helplessly outside the gates; after a spell of lamentation he returned sadly to Jiangxia.

Liu Biao continued to fail. At last, despairing of his heir's arrival, he groaned loudly and passed away in the eighth month of Jian An 13 on the forty-fifth day of the chronological cycle. A poet of later times lamented the fate of Liu Biao:

> The Yuans held the Yellow River north,
> And Liu Biao the middle Yangzi.
> Till women's rule dragged their houses down,
> And without a trace they were gone.

With the provincial protector dead, Lady Cai, Cai Mao, and Zhang Yun forged a will appointing Liu Zong heir. Then they commenced mourning and announced the funeral. Liu Zong, a shrewd lad though only fourteen, said to the assembled advisers: "My father has departed this world. My elder brother, Qi, is presently in Jiangxia. And my uncle, Liu Xuande, is in Xinye. You have chosen me to succeed my father, but they may well challenge my succession by force of arms. How are we to justify ourselves?"

Before anyone could reply, Li Gui, a military adviser, stepped forward and said, "Our young master speaks good sense. We must dispatch a letter to Jiangxia announcing the mourning and inviting the elder son to govern us. At the same time we should have Liu Xuande share the administrative duties. In that way we will be able to withstand Cao Cao to the north and repel Sun Quan to the south. This plan provides for all contingencies."

Cai Mao turned on the speaker. "Do you dare to subvert the late protector's will?" he demanded sharply. But Li Gui stood firm and denounced Cai Mao: "After conspiring with your cohorts, you published a false will and then instated the junior son and deposed the senior. We will soon see the nine districts of our province fall into enemy hands. If our late lord's ghost be present, let him punish this crime." Cai Mao angrily ordered the officer removed and beheaded. Li Gui's curses ended only with his life.

Cai Mao set up Liu Zong as ruler of Jingzhou, and key members of the Cai clan assumed control of the province's military. He ordered Deng Yi, secretary to the protector, and Liu Xian, assistant protector; to guard the capital. Lady Cai and her son, Liu Zong, stationed themselves at Xiangyang to check any move by Liu Qi or Liu Xuande. Then, without informing Liu Qi or Xuande, Cai Mao had Liu Biao interred in the hills south of the River Han, east of Xiangyang.

Lady Cai and Liu Zong had hardly settled into Xiangyang when they discovered they were directly in the line of Cao Cao's march. Panicked, Liu Zong called Kuai Yue and Cai Mao for counsel. One of their staff supervisors, Fu Xuan, said to Liu Zong, "Cao Cao is not the only danger. Neither your elder brother in Jiangxia nor Xuande in Xinye has been informed of the funeral. If they move against us, Jingzhou could be lost. I have a plan, however, that will make our people as secure as Mount Tai and save your own rank and office as well." "What do you have in mind?" Liu Zong asked. "I advise you to offer the province to Cao Cao," Fu Xuan said. "He will surely treat you generously, my lord."

"What!" Liu Zong exclaimed. "Do you expect me simply to surrender the patrimony I have only now made mine?" Kuai Yue broke in: "Fu Xuan is right. The choice between rebellion and submission has to be made in broad perspective. The disparity between the strong and the weak cannot be overcome. Cao Cao has undertaken his expeditions north and south in the name of the imperial court. By resisting him, my lord, you win no name for obedience. Moreover, you are newly instated. Your hold on the territory is not firm. Problems abroad give us no peace, and problems at home are beginning to brew. Our people quail at the news of Cao's advance before a single battle has been fought. How can we make a stand with frightened men?" "My lord," Liu Zong conceded, "there is merit in your arguments, and I would be ruled by them, but to turn my late father's estate over to a stranger is bound to make me the mockery of the realm."

At this point someone strode boldly into the chamber and declared: "Fu Xuan and Kuai Yue have advised you well. You must act accordingly." All eyes turned to Wang Can (Zhongxuan), a man from Gaoping in Shanyang. Wang Can had a frail appearance and was short of stature. In his youth he had been received by the famed imperial courtier, Cai Yong. On that occasion, Cai Yong did Wang Can the honor of rising eagerly to greet him, even though he had many distinguished guests to meet. This gesture caused Cai Yong's startled retainers to ask him, "Why does the master single out this lad for such honor?" "Wang Can has extraordinary gifts," Cai Yong replied, "far beyond any I may have." Wang Can was widely informed and had a prodigious memory. He once recited the entire text of a roadside inscription after a single viewing. Another time he reconstructed perfectly a complex chess game after it had been played. He was also skilled in arithmetic, and he surpassed his contemporaries in rhetoric and poetry. At the age of seventeen he was advanced by the Emperor to attendant in the Inner Bureau, but he did not assume the post. Some time after that, to avoid the civil wars in the northeast, he came to Jingzhou, where Liu Biao had received him as an honored guest.

Now Wang Can asked Liu Zong, "How do you compare with Cao Cao, my lord?" "There is no comparison," he replied. "Cao Cao," Wang Can continued, "has a powerful army, brave commanders, and a staff of able tacticians. He captured Lü Bu at Xiapi; put Yuan Shao to flight at Guandu; chased Liu Xuande to Longyou; defeated the Wuhuan in the White Wolf Hills; and no man can count the others he has beheaded, eliminated, and swept aside, or the cities he has taken. If he comes in force, we cannot hold him off. Follow the proposal of Fu Xuan and Kuai Yue or suffer the consequences." "Excellent advice," Liu Zong answered, "but I shall have to inform my mother." At these words Lady Cai appeared from behind a screen and said, "That will not be necessary, since these three have agreed that you should tender the province to Cao Cao."

Having chosen his course, Liu Zong secretly sent his letter of surrender. The bearer, Song Zhong, was received in the city of Wancheng and richly rewarded by the prime minister. Cao Cao instructed Song Zhong to have Liu Zong welcome him in front of the city gate of Jingzhou; in return he would confirm Liu Zong's rule for all time.

Song Zhong was on his way back to Jingzhou with Cao Cao's answer when, nearing a river, he spied a party of soldiers under Lord Guan's command. Song Zhong tried to slip away but was called to a halt. Initially he evaded Lord Guan's questions, but persistent interrogation eventually forced him to disclose the nature of his mission. Astonished, Lord Guan took his prisoner back to Xuande, who wept at the story Song Zhong told.

"Under the circumstances," Zhang Fei said, "we have to behead the courier, take Xiangyang, do away with the Cai clan and Liu Zong, and go to war with Cao Cao." "Enough," Xuande retorted, "I will keep my own counsel on this." He then turned to Song Zhong and demanded, "If you knew of these moves, why didn't you inform me at once? I could have your life, but what good would it do? Get out!" Reiterating humble thanks for this reprieve, Song Zhong scurried off.

At this moment of deep dilemma for Xuande, Liu Qi's envoy, Yi Ji, arrived. Xuande was grateful to Yi Ji for having saved his life at the banquet, so he descended the steps, welcomed him personally, and thanked him profusely. "My master, Liu Qi," the envoy began, "was in Jiangxia when he learned of his father's death. Lady Cai and Cai Mao did not announce the funeral and colluded to establish Liu Zong. My master has verified this. Thinking Your Lordship might not have heard, my master sent me to convey his expression of grief and to request that Your Lordship march to Xiangyang with your finest troops and make the Cais answer for their crime."

Xuande read Liu Qi's letter. "Your information about Liu Zong's usurpation is correct," he said to Yi Ji, "but do you know that they have offered the province to Cao Cao?" "Who told you that, my lord?" Yi Ji asked, aghast. Xuande then described the capture of Liu Zong's messenger. "In that case," Yi Ji said, "hasten to Xiangyang on the pretext of attending mourning ceremonies for Liu Biao. Lure Liu Zong out to receive you, seize him, and wipe out his clique, and Jingzhou will be yours, my lord." "Good advice," Kongming remarked. But Xuande began to sob. "In his last hours," he said, "my elder brother entrusted his son to me. How could I face him in the netherworld if I laid hands on the other son and his estate?" "If you won't do it," Kongming said, "how do you propose to fight off Cao Cao when his troops are even now at Wancheng?" "We shall retreat to Fan," Xuande answered.

The advance of Cao Cao's army to Bowang was announced. Xuande sent Liu Qi's envoy back to Jiangxia with instructions to prepare for battle. He then sat down with Kongming to discuss tactics. "Put your mind at ease," Kongming said. "Last time we burned out half of Xiahou Dun's army at Bowang. This time we'll make another trap for him. But Xinye is no place for us now. We must hasten to Fan." Proclamations of the impending move were posted at the four gates of Xinye. The text read:

> Without regard to age or sex, let all those willing to follow us proceed directly to Fan for temporary refuge. Do not endanger yourselves by remaining.

Sun Qian arranged to move the populace across the river, and Mi Zhu escorted the families of the officials to Fan. At the same time Kongming assembled the body of commanders. His first instruction was to Lord Guan: "Hide a thousand men at the upper end of the White River and provide each one with bags of sand to dam the waters. Tomorrow, after the third watch, the moment you hear men and horses downstream, pull the bags out of the river and flood the enemy. Then hurry down to reinforce us."

Next, Kongming instructed Zhang Fei: "Hide a thousand men at the Boling crossing, where the river runs slow. If Cao's men are in danger of drowning, that's where they'll try to escape. I want you to join the battle at that point of vantage."

He then gave orders to Zhao Zilong: "Divide three thousand men into four contingents. Take one yourself and hide outside the eastern gate to Xinye. Have the other three contingents cover the remaining gates. Before you leave the city, place plenty of sulphur and saltpeter on the house roofs. When Cao enters, his soldiers will want to rest in the people's homes. Tomorrow evening the wind should be strong. The moment it starts blowing, have the men covering the three other gates shoot flaming arrows into the town. As the fire peaks, let those three contingents raise a great commotion—but leave the east gate open for the enemy to exit through. When they come through, attack from behind. Then catch up with Lord Guan and Zhang Fei and bring your three thousand, along with their men, over to Fan."

Finally, Kongming instructed Mi Fang and Liu Feng: "Station two thousand on Magpie Tail Hill, thirty *li* from Xinye: one thousand under blue flags, one thousand under red. When Cao's army comes up, have the red group flee left, the blue group right. This will confuse their leaders and prevent pursuit. Next, deploy an ambush and fall on the foe as soon as you see flames over Xinye. After you're finished, come to the upper end of the river and help us out." All parts of their plan now in place, Kongming and Xuande climbed to an observation point to await reports of victory.

*   *   *   *

In the lead of Cao Cao's army was the hundred-thousand-man force commanded jointly by Cao Ren and Cao Hong. Its three-thousand-man shock force fitted out in iron armor and under the command of Xu Chu was sweeping toward Xinye. Around midday Xu Chu reached the slopes of Magpie Tail and saw soldiers massed under blue and red flags. As he advanced, Liu Feng and Mi Fang began their prearranged maneuvers. Xu Chu called a brief halt. "There must be an ambush ahead," he said. "We'll hold here." He then hastened back to inform Cao Ren, who was leading the main force. "It's only a decoy," Cao Ren said to him. "There's no ambush there. Press on. We will follow."

Xu Chu returned to his forward position and resumed the advance. The contingent reached a small wood and stopped. The place looked deserted. The sun had set. As Xu Chu prepared to move forward again, the hilltops seemed to speak with the blaring of horns and the beating of drums. Xu Chu looked up into a field of flags and banners surrounding two umbrellas, one over Xuande, the other over Kongming. They were seated face-to-face enjoying something to drink. Maddened, Xu Chu sought a way up, but his ascent was prevented by the stone and wooden missiles that came pelting down. As thunderous shouts from behind the hill rang in the air, Xu Chu struggled to get his forces into action, but the light of day had already left the sky.

When Cao Ren's main force arrived, he ordered Xinye occupied in order to shelter and rest the horses. He reached the walls, had all four gates flung wide, and entered the evacuated city unchallenged. "As you see," Cao Hong remarked, "having neither strength nor strategy to oppose us, they have scurried off, followed by the entire population." Spent and famished, the invaders settled into whatever lodgings were at hand and began preparing their meals. Cao Ren and Cao Hong entered the *yamen,* there to enjoy the respite from war.

After the first watch strong winds blew up. Guards at the gates reported minor fires, but Cao Ren dismissed the danger, saying, "Take it easy. They must have been caused by our army's cooks." But more reports kept coming in, followed by the news that three of the city's gates were on fire. Frantically, Cao Ren ordered his commanders to mount, but the whole city was already ablaze. Flames covered the ground and reached into the sky—a conflagration that dwarfed the one that had foiled Xiahou Dun at Bowang. As a later poet wrote,

> The evil genius of the northern plain
> Marched his legions to the River Han.
> Within Xinye's walls he felt the wind god's wrath,
> And down from blazing Heaven the fire god ran.

Cao Ren led his men through the smoke and fire, dashing for any avenue of escape. Someone called out that the east gate was not burning, and everyone bolted for it in a mad rush that left many trampled to death. Cao Ren had barely made it out of the burning city when he heard voices roaring behind him. Zhao Zilong was charging up. In the melee the beaten invaders—too demoralized to fight—fled for their lives. Then Mi Fang hit them hard, inflicting more casualties. Cao Ren continued his flight. Again he was attacked, this time by Liu Feng. By the fourth watch the bulk of his force had been crushed. The remnant reached the edge of the White River, thankful that the water was low enough to cross. Men and horses waded in and drank their fill amid great clamor and neighing.

Upstream Lord Guan had dammed the current. At dusk he had seen the flames over Xinye. Now at the fourth watch he heard the men and horses downstream and ordered his troops to pull the sandbags from the river. The pent-up water burst forth, drowning men and mounts in its powerful surge. In order to cross, Cao Ren led the survivors to Boling, where the current was slower, only to be confronted by another party of soldiers. Suddenly their shouts filled the night, and before him stood Zhang Fei. "Cao, you bastard, I'll have your life!" he cried to the astonished enemy. Indeed:

> In the city Cao Ren witnessed the belching flames;
> At the river a new menace confronted him.

Would Cao Ren survive?
Read on.

CHAPTER 41

Liu Xuande Leads His Flock over the River; Zhao Zilong Rescues Master Liu Single-handedly

As Lord Guan released the torrents of the White River upstream, Zhang Fei joined the battle downstream, intercepting Cao Ren with a powerful offensive. Zhang Fei and Xu Chu suddenly came face-to-face, but Xu Chu had lost his taste for combat; he fled. Zhang Fei caught up with Xuande and Kongming, and all together they marched upriver to the boats that Liu Feng and Mi

Fang had waiting to take them to Fan. After the crossing Kongming ordered the ships and rafts burned.

Cao Ren collected the battered remnants of his troops and stationed them in Xinye, sending Cao Hong to Cao Cao with a full
report. "Zhuge, the bumpkin! How dare he!" Cao Cao raged. He
then mobilized his entire force and blanketed the region around
Xinye. He ordered the hills scoured, the White River blocked,
and his host divided into eight field armies. His objective was to
take Fan in a concerted attack.

"My lord," Liu Ye said, "you have barely arrived at Xiangyang
and must win the affections of the people before all else. Liu Bei
has moved the entire population of Xinye over to Fan; a direct
attack would wreak havoc on both counties. I suggest sending an
envoy to offer Liu Bei the opportunity to submit. If he refuses,
we will have made plain our wish to spare the people. If he accepts, Jingzhou will be ours without a fight." Cao Cao approved
and asked whom to send. "Shan Fu is close to Liu Bei. Why not
send him?" Liu Ye suggested. "What if he does not return?" Cao
Cao countered. "And make himself a laughingstock?" Liu Ye responded. "Have no fear of it, my lord."

On this advice Cao Cao summoned Shan Fu and said, "My original thought was to crush Fan. But I hesitate to put the common
people through such suffering. If you can convince Liu Bei to
surrender, I shall forgive his offenses and grant him rank. If he
clings to his delusions, soldier and civilian alike will perish, and
not a stone will be left unscathed. I know you for a loyal and honorable man. That is why I delegate you. I trust you will not fail
me." Shan Fu set out.

Liu Xuande and Kongming received Shan Fu at Fan, and the
three shared memories of former times. Then Shan Fu said, "Cao
Cao sent me to call for your surrender, my lord. But it is only a
pretext for winning popular approval. He has formed eight
armies and filled in the bed of the river for his advance. I fear this
city cannot be defended. You must find a way to leave as soon as
possible." Xuande wanted Shan Fu to stay, but the former adviser
said, "I would be universally scorned. Be assured, my mother's

death burns fresh in my heart. Though I stay with Cao in body, I am sworn never to devise a stratagem for him. With Sleeping Dragon's help you need not despair. I must go back. Please forgive me." Xuande did not press the matter. Shan Fu reported that Xuande had no intention of submitting, and Cao Cao began the southern campaign in a great show of anger that very day.

Xuande turned to Kongming, who said, "We have to leave at once. We can take Xiangyang and rest there temporarily." "These common folk have stayed by us so long," Xuande said, "are we to abandon them now?" "Send round word," Kongming said, "that those who wish to may follow you." He sent Lord Guan to the river to prepare the boats, and ordered Sun Qian and Jian Yong to issue the following proclamation: "Cao Cao's army is approaching. Our city cannot hold out. Those who wish to will have to follow us across the river." The people of Fan as well as those of Xinye shouted out in unison, "We will go with Lord Liu—even if we must die."

That same day, amid cries and tears, the exodus began. Bracing up elders, taking the young in hand, leading sons and daughters, the human tide traversed the water like great waves rolling on and on. Unabating cries rang out from the shores. On his boat surveying the scene, Xuande was profoundly shaken. "If I have made these good people suffer this for my sake, what will be left to live for?" He attempted to throw himself into the river but was restrained by those around him. Sorrow pierced all who heard his words. After reaching the south shore, Xuande looked back to those still waiting anxiously and tearfully to cross. He had Lord Guan urge the boatmen to greater efforts. Then at last he mounted.

Xuande led the mass march to the east gate of Xiangyang. He found the top of the wall crowded with banners, the moat below thick with sharp staves and barbed branches. Xuande reined in and shouted, "Liu Zong, worthy nephew, I seek but the succor of these people. Open the gates for us—and quickly!" But Liu Zong was afraid to show himself. Cai Mao and Zhang Yun raced to the tower and urged the archers to unleash their volleys on the human throng outside the wall. Staring upward, the people voiced their appeal. One commander inside the town raced to the tower with several hundred guards and bellowed, "Cai Mao!

Zhang Yun! Traitors to the Han! How dare you reject Governor Liu, a man of humane character who comes seeking refuge for the people in his care!"

Who was this man, eight spans tall, with a face swarthy as dark dates? It was Wei Yan (Wenchang) of Yiyang. Then and there Wei Yan cut down the gate guards with broad sweeps of his sword, threw open the gates and let down the drawbridge. "Imperial Uncle Liu," he shouted, "lead your men into the city and let us slay these tyrants together." Without hesitation Zhang Fei started forward, but Xuande checked him. "Don't create panic," he warned.

Wei Yan was doing his utmost to induce Xuande to enter the city, when another soldier rode forth and denounced him: "Wei Yan, common footslogger! Will you incite sedition? It's I, General Wen Ping!" Outraged, Wei Yan raised his spear and rode forth to engage his challenger. The men of both sides then fell upon one another at the base of the city wall in a wild mutual slaughter that made the ground shake. "I have brought the people the harm I meant to spare them," Xuande said. "We shall not enter Xiangyang!" "Jiangling is another strategically located town," Kongming said. "Let's take it and settle in." "My idea, exactly," Xuande responded. And with that he turned the throng away from Xiangyang and on toward Jiangling. In the commotion many people from Xiangyang slipped out and joined Liu Xuande.

Meanwhile, the fight between Wei Yan and Wen Ping continued. By afternoon Wei Yan's force had been decimated. He finally rode from the field, hoping to locate Xuande but ended up taking refuge with Han Xuan, governor of Changsha.

More than one hundred thousand soldiers and commoners, thousands of carts and carriages, and innumerable carriers and bearers came together in the procession. When they came upon Liu Biao's grave, Xuande led his commanders in ritual worship. In a trembling voice he declared, "Elder brother, I, wanting in virtue and lacking in talent, have failed to fulfill the heavy charge you laid on me. This shameful offense is mine alone and does not touch these good people. Brother, let your splendid spirit descend and save the people of Jingzhou." Xuande's voice conveyed such sad intensity that neither soldier nor civilian could contain his emotions.

A scout reported: "Cao Cao's main force is camped at Fan. They're gathering boats and rafts to cross over here today." "We can defend ourselves from Jiangling," the commanders assured Xuande, "but with such a multitude on our hands we're barely covering ten *li* a day. Who knows when we will make Jiangling? And how could we engage Cao's army if it found us now? Wouldn't it be expedient to leave the people behind for now and go on ahead ourselves?" Xuande replied with deep feeling, "The human factor is the key to any undertaking. How can we abandon those who have committed themselves to us?" These words became known, and all were deeply moved. Much later a poet left these lines commemorating the desperate flight across the waters:

> In mortal straits, good of heart, he kept his flock from harm;
> Riverborne, the tearful leader won his army's love.
> And still today men mark the site with solemn piety;
> And older folks keep Lord Liu in cherished memory.

Xuande advanced slowly in the midst of his multitude. "They will overtake us soon," Kongming warned. "Dispatch Lord Guan to Jiangxia. Have him ask young Liu Qi for boats to meet us at Jiangling." Accordingly, Xuande put this request in a letter, which Lord Guan and Sun Qian, guarded by five hundred riders, carried to Liu Qi. Xuande had Zhang Fei watch the rear, Zhao Zilong protect the members of his family, and the remaining leaders take care of the commoners. On they marched. In the course of one day they covered little more than ten *li*.

*   *   *   *

From Fan, Cao Cao sent a messenger across the river to summon Liu Zong. Liu Zong was afraid to appear before the prime minister, and so Cai Mao and Zhang Yun asked permission to go in his stead. Wang Wei secretly urged Liu Zong, "You, General, have surrendered, and Xuande is gone. Cao Cao's guard will be down. Why not organize your men, place them strategically, and surprise Cao Cao? Once he is captured, you will command the empire's respect and a general call to arms in your name would bring peace to the whole of the northern heartland. Such an opportunity rarely arises. Don't miss it!" Liu Zong took this proposal to Cai Mao, who berated Wang Wei and said, "How absurd! What do you know of the Mandate of Heaven?" To this, Wang Wei retorted, "Traitor! What I wouldn't give to devour you alive!" At this point Kuai Yue intervened to prevent Cai Mao from killing Wang Wei.

Cai Mao and Zhang Yun traveled to Fan and presented themselves in a most ingratiating manner before Cao Cao. "Tell me," the prime minister asked, "what are Jingzhou's resources in men, horses, cash, and grain?" "Fifty thousand horse soldiers," Cai Mao replied, "one hundred and fifty thousand foot soldiers, eighty thousand marines. Most of the coin and grain is in Jiangling; the rest is stored in various places—a year's supply." "How about the war-boats?" Cao Cao continued. "And who are the naval commanders?" "All told," Cai Mao answered, "seven thousand boats. Myself and Zhang Yun here are in command."

Then and there Cao Cao conferred on Cai Mao the title of Lord Who Controls the South and named him superintendent of the Naval Forces, and he made Zhang Yun Lord Who Upholds Obedience and lieutenant superintendent of the Naval Forces. Delighted with their new positions, the two men expressed respectful gratitude. The prime minister said, "I shall report to the Emperor Liu Biao's death and his son's submission, so that the proper heir may rule Jingzhou permanently." The two commanders withdrew, highly pleased with the outcome of their interview.

Xun You said to Cao Cao, "Why did you grant such exalted titles to those craven toadies? And why make them naval superintendents into the bargain?" "Do you think I don't know them for what they are?" Cao Cao replied. "Don't forget, we have an army of northerners unused to naval warfare. Those two can be of help at the moment. When we have accomplished what we want, they will be dealt with as they deserve!"

Cai Mao and Zhang Yun returned to Jingzhou and appeared before Liu Zong. "Cao Cao," they said, "has assured us that he will recommend your permanent control of Jingzhou to the Emperor." Liu Zong was delighted. The next day he and his mother, Lady Cai, prepared the seal of office and the tally of command and crossed the river to welcome Cao Cao and do him the honor of presenting the instruments of government personally.

Cao Cao offered words of comfort to the young prince. Then, to prepare his entrance, he directed the generals of the expeditionary army to station troops by the walls of Xiangyang. Cai Mao and Zhang Yun ordered the residents to welcome the prime minister with burning incense. Again, Cao Cao spoke kind and reassuring words to one and all. He entered the city and seated himself in the governmental hall. First, he summoned Kuai Yue and said to him, "Acquiring your services means more to me than the whole province." He made Kuai Yue governor of Jiangling and lord of Fan. Next, he made Fu Xuan and Wang Can honorary lords, and Liu Zong imperial inspector of Qingzhou, with orders to report to his post forthwith. Startled, Liu Zong declined, saying, "I have no wish to become governor of another province, only to remain on my parents' native soil." Cao Cao replied, "Qingzhou is close to the capital. I am making you an official attached to the court lest you come to harm here." Cao Cao overcame Liu Zong's objections, and the youth set off for Qingzhou, as required, with Lady Cai. They were accompanied only by the former general Wang Wei. The other members of Liu Zong's court returned after seeing him to the river.

Cao Cao called Yu Jin aside and said, "Take a few riders; overtake Liu Zong and his mother, and do away with them. That should prevent further trouble." Yu Jin soon overtook the little party. "I bear the prime minister's command," he declared. "Prepare to die!" Lady Cai cradled the boy and cried bitterly as Yu Jin's men set to work. Wang Wei put up a fierce struggle but was finally slain. Lady Cai and Liu Zong were subsequently killed swiftly. Yu Jin reported the success of his mission to Cao Cao, who rewarded him richly. Cao Cao also searched for Kongming's family in Longzhong, but on Kongming's instructions they had long since moved to Three Rivers—to Cao Cao's great frustration.

After Cao Cao had Xiangyang under his control, Xun You counseled him, "Jiangling, with its ample supplies of money and grain, is one of the keys to the province. Xuande will be well positioned if he gets hold of that town." "The thought has never left my mind," Cao Cao said and ordered that one of his generals in Xiangyang be selected to spearhead a move to Jiangling.

The planning session, however, was not attended by Wen Ping, and Cao Cao demanded to know the reason. When Wen Ping finally appeared, Cao Cao asked him, "Why are you late?" "A loyal subject who has failed to protect his master's lands cannot show his face," Wen Ping said and began to sob and weep. "A loyal follower and true," Cao Cao said. He promoted Wen Ping to governor of Jiangxia, granted him the title of honorary lord, and ordered him to lead the expedition to Jiangling.

At this moment spies reported: "Liu Bei is accompanied by a multitude of common folk. They're only three hundred *li* from here and moving at barely ten *li* a day." Cao Cao ordered five thousand crack horsemen to overtake Liu Bei within one day. The force set out that night, followed closely by Cao Cao's main army.

* * * *

Xuande was now at the head of more than a hundred thousand common folk and three thousand cavalry, all struggling to reach Jiangling. Zhao Zilong had charge of Xuande's two wives and young son. Zhang Fei was defending the rear. "We have heard nothing of Lord Guan," Kongming said, "since we sent him to Jiangxia. I wonder what came of his mission." "Perhaps we could trouble you to go there yourself," Xuande responded. "Liu Qi will never forget the good advice you once gave him, and if he sees you in person, we should get what we want." Kongming agreed and, joined by Liu Feng and five hundred men, set out for Jiangxia in quest of aid.

Liu Xuande pressed on. With him were Jian Yong, Mi Zhu, and Mi Fang. Suddenly a violent gale scooped up the dust in front of the horses and sent it skyward, blotting out the sun. "What does this signify?" Xuande asked in alarm. Jian Yong, who had some insight into the laws of yin and yang that govern all, took augury and said uneasily, "Great ill fortune should strike tonight, my lord. Abandon these people with all speed and be gone." "They have followed from as far as Xinye," Xuande replied. "I cannot abandon them." "If you continue like this, disaster is imminent." "What lies ahead?" Xuande asked. "Dangyang county," his attendants answered, "site of Scenic Mountain." Xuande ordered camp pitched at the mountain.

Autumn was passing into winter. Chill winds pierced the marchers' bones. As the day darkened, wailing voices filled the wilderness. By the fourth watch, the dead of night, the encamped multitude began to hear them—out of the northwest—the shouts of men that shook the ground as they came. Xuande leaped to his horse and led two thousand of his own crack troops to meet them. But Cao Cao's force had the advantage of numbers. Opposition was impossible. Xuande was fighting for his life. At just this juncture of mortal extremity Zhang Fei arrived with a body of men and cut a route for Xuande, enabling him to escape eastward. Wen Ping challenged Xuande, but Xuande denounced him: "Faithless traitor! To dare to stand before men!" Wen Ping, his face suffused with shame, turned away and headed northeast.

Zhang Fei stayed beside Xuande. They fought as they fled. By dawn the hue and cry of war had receded. For the first time Xuande rested his horse. Only a hundred riders remained with him. He had become hopelessly separated from the mass of his followers, from Mi Zhu, Mi Fang, Jian Yong, and Zhao Zilong, and also from his family. "One hundred thousand living souls," he lamented, "have borne these woes for remaining with us. Of the fate of our commanders and of my family we know nothing. Even a man of clay or wood would have to grieve."

In this moment of despair Xuande saw Mi Fang, his face pierced through with arrows, stumble toward him, crying, "Zhao Zilong has defected to Cao!" "So old a friend would not betray me," Xuande said heatedly. "He sees our position is hopeless," Zhang Fei said, "our strength spent, and probably expects wealth and rank from Cao Cao." "He has stayed with us through our worst tribulations," Xuande answered. "He has a will of iron; wealth and rank would not move him." "I saw him heading northwest," Mi Fang said. "I will find him," Zhang Fei said. "And when I do, this spear will do the rest." "Mistrust him not!" Xuande cautioned. "You should remember how our second brother, whom you likewise suspected, made short work of Cao's generals Yan Liang and Wen Chou. Zhao Zilong must have good reason for his absence. I cannot believe he has abandoned us."

Zhang Fei would not be reasoned with. He took twenty horsemen to Steepslope Bridge. A wood to the east gave him an idea: "If I cut some branches, tie them to the horses' tails, and trot the beasts back and forth in the wood, the dust they raise will suggest numbers that should deter the enemy's approach." Having thus instructed his men, Zhang Fei, spear ready, mount poised, rode onto the bridge and scoured the west for any sign of Zhao Zilong.

During Cao Cao's raid Zhao Zilong had attacked the enemy at the fourth watch and continued battling until daybreak. But he had become separated from Xuande's family and was unable to find them again. He thought: "Lord Liu placed his two wives, Lady Gan and Lady Mi, in my care, along with his child, Master Ah Dou. Having lost them in the fighting, I cannot show myself before my lord again. The least I can do is die in battle trying to locate his loved ones." With only thirty or forty riders behind him, Zhao Zilong charged into the tangle of fighters.

The common people of two counties, Xinye and Fan, shook Heaven and earth with their wails as they fled the scene of battle. Beyond all numbering, pierced by arrows, lanced by spears, they abandoned their young. Zhao Zilong, in search of his charges, came upon Jian Yong lying in the brush. "Have you seen our mistresses?" Zilong asked. "They abandoned their carriages," Jian Yong answered, "and fled on foot with Ah Dou. I was rounding a hill, racing after them, when one of Cao's captains stabbed me. I fell, and he took my horse. I could not move, much less fight." Zilong gave him the mount of one of his followers. He also detailed two men to help Jian Yong get to Xuande and report that he meant to seek high and low for Xuande's wives and son, or die on the field.

Zhao Zilong was galloping toward Steepslope Bridge when a soldier hailed him. "Where to, General Zhao?" "Who are you?" Zhao Zilong countered, reining up. "I was escorting our lord's wives," the man replied, "when an arrow knocked me down." Zilong asked for details. "Just now," the soldier said, "I saw Lady Gan, disheveled and barefoot, fleeing south with a group of women, commoners." At once Zhao Zilong turned away and raced south. He passed hundreds of civilians, men and women, helping each other make their way. "Is Lady Gan among you?" Zilong cried. To the rear of the crowd Lady Gan spotted Zilong and called out. Zilong dismounted and planted his spear in the ground. "Letting you slip from my sight was a dreadful crime," he said tearfully. "Where are Lady Mi and the young master?" "When Cao's troops chased us," Lady Gan said, "we quit the escort and fell in with these refugees. Another troop attacked us. We scattered, and I was separated from them. Somehow I escaped alive."

At that instant a fresh outcry announced another troop charging the crowd. Zhao Zilong flourished his spear and remounted to observe. In front of him was Mi Zhu, a prisoner in bonds. Just behind him, at the head of a thousand men, was Chunyu Dao, Cao Ren's corps commander, waving his sword. He had captured Mi Zhu and was going to claim his reward. With a short, sharp cry Zilong, spear leveled, went straight for Chunyu Dao. Chunyu Dao, unable to counter, was lanced and thrust under his horse. Zhao Zilong then rescued Mi Zhu and made off with two horses. He sat Lady Gan on one and, cutting a bloody swath, brought her to Steepslope Bridge.

Zhang Fei, poised on the bridge with leveled sword, confronted him. "Zhao Zilong!" he called at the top of his voice, "explain why you betrayed our brother!" "I couldn't find our mistresses or the young master," Zilong answered, "so I dropped back. What do you mean by 'betrayed'?" "If Jian Yong had not already vouched for you, you would not pass!" Zhang Fei said. "Where is our lord?" Zilong asked. "Ahead, not far," Zhang Fei replied. Zhao Zilong turned to Mi Zhu and said, "Go on with Lady Gan. I'm going back to look for Lady Mi and the young master." He took a few riders and left.

Along the way Zilong saw a captain with an iron spear in his hand and a sword strapped to his back. Behind him a dozen horsemen advanced at a gallop. Without wasting words, Zilong challenged the leader and dropped him in a single engagement. The dozen riders fled. The slain man was Xiahou En, Cao Cao's personal attendant and sword bearer.

Now, Cao Cao had two swords of exceptional value. One was called Heaven's Prop, the other Black Pommel. Cao wore the first himself, Xiahou En the second. Its blade could slice through iron as if it were mud, and its point was dagger sharp. Before he crossed Zhao Zilong, Xiahou En had let himself become separated from Cao Cao, for he never doubted his skill. Intent only on what he and his men could plunder, Xiahou En had little expected to lose his life, let alone the treasured weapon. Zhao Zilong, examining the sword, saw the words "Black Pommel" engraved in gold on the handle and realized the value of the weapon. He thrust it into his belt, raised his spear, and resumed his assault on the enemy ranks. Looking back, he could no longer see his riders behind him.

Undaunted, Zilong continued searching for Lady Mi, questioning any civilian he passed. Finally, someone pointed ahead, saying, "The mistress has the child. Her left leg is wounded, and she can't walk. She's sitting there in a crevice in the wall." Zhao Zilong hastened to the spot and found a dwelling with an earthen wall that had been damaged by fire. Lady Mi was sitting at the base, near a dry well, weeping. Zilong dismounted and pressed his palms and head to the ground.

"With you here, General," Lady Mi said, "I know Ah Dou will live. I pray you, pity the father who, after half a lifetime of being tossed hither and roaming thither, has nothing in this world but this scrap of blood and bone. Guard him well, General, that he may see his father once again—and that I may die without regret." "My negligence is responsible for the ordeals you have suffered," Zhao Zilong said. "Say no more, but take this horse. I intend to fight on, on foot and bring you safely through the enemy's lines." "I will not have it that way," Lady Mi responded. "You must keep the horse. You are the child's only protection. My wounds are heavy, and my death is of no moment. I pray, General, take the child on ahead, and quickly. Do not delay for my sake." "I hear pursuers," Zhao Zilong said. "Mount the horse." "No," she said. "Do not lose two lives." She held Ah Dou out to Zhao Zilong and added, "His life is in your hands." Steadfastly, she refused his offers. The enemy was closing in. Their shouts were everywhere. Zilong's tone grew more anxious. "My lady, what will you do when they come?" Without answering again, Lady Mi set Ah Dou on the ground, turned, and threw herself into the well. A poet of later times honored her sacrifice in these lines:

> The embattled captain had to have his steed;
> On foot he could not save the little prince.
> Her death preserved the Liu dynastic line:
> For bold decision mark this heroine.

To prevent the enemy from taking his mistress's corpse, Zhao Zilong pushed over the earthen wall, burying the well. He then loosened his armor straps, lowered his breastplate, and placed Ah Dou against his bosom. Hefting his spear, Zilong remounted.

By this time one of Cao Hong's corps commanders, Yan Ming, had brought up a body of foot soldiers. Wielding a two-edged sword with three prongs, he set on Zhao Zilong. After a brief clash Zilong ran him through. He dispersed Yan Ming's squad, killing several, and broke open a path. But another unit—commanded by a general—arrived and blocked Zilong. Their standard bore the words, large and clear, "Zhang He of Hejian." Without a word, Zilong raised his spear and joined battle. After more than ten passes Zilong had to break off the contest. He fled, and Zhang He gave chase.

Zhao Zilong applied the whip, but unfortunately his horse went crashing into a ditch, and Zhang He approached for the kill. Suddenly, a beam of reddish light formed an arc from the ditch, and the horse, as if treading on thin air, leaped out of the hole. The rescue of the prince is described in this verse of later times:

> The cornered dragon bathed in red took wing
> And cleaved the enemy lines by Steepslope Bridge.
> In two score years and two the babe will reign;
> Zhao's superhuman might thus earned his fame.

Zhang He fell back at the miraculous sight.

Zhao Zilong was in full flight when he heard two voices behind him: "Halt, Zhao Zilong!" Two more commanders before him, displaying weapons, blocked his way. Bringing up the rear were Ma Yan and Zhang Yi; blocking the way in front were Jiao Chu and Zhang Nan: all four had served Yuan Shao before surrendering to Cao Cao. Zhao Zilong fought them mightily. Cao Cao's men came trooping up. Zilong drew the sword Black Pommel and began slashing wildly. Wherever he struck, the blade cut through the armor, drawing blood. In this manner he slowly drove back the swarm of commanders and got through the encirclement.

From his vantage on Scenic Mountain, Cao Cao observed the general whom none could best and asked his attendants who it was. Cao Hong sped down the hill to find out, shouting: "Let the fighter speak his name!" "Zhao Zilong of Changshan!" was the instant reply. Cao Hong relayed the news to Cao Cao, who said, "There's a tiger-warrior for you! Try and get him here alive." He sent swift riders to inform various stations: "If Zhao Zilong comes your way, deliver him to the prime minister alive. No potshots!" And so, Zhao Zilong was able to get away. Was this too not the result of Ah Dou's good fortune?

After cutting through the encircling troops, the baby prince still on his breast, Zhao Zilong downed two standards and captured three spears. The sum total of noted captains speared or slashed by Zilong amounted to more than fifty. His exploits are remembered in these lines written long after the events:

> In bloodsoaked battle gown and armor bloody red,
> He faced down every foe at Dangyang town.
> Of all who ever fought to keep a king from harm,
> Who excels Zhao Zilong, hero of Changshan?

Zhao Zilong, his surcoat drenched in blood, had brought Ah Dou safely away from the main battleground when two armed companies intercepted him by the foot of the slope. They were led by two brothers, Zhong Jin and Zhong Shen, corps commanders under Xiahou Dun. Zhong Jin was wielding a giant axe; Zhong Shen, a figured halberd. "Dismount and submit, Zhao Zilong!" they shouted. Here was an instance, indeed,

> Of facing the waves in the dragon's pool
> Moments after escaping from the tiger's lair.

Would Zhao Zilong manage to get free?
Read on.

CHAPTER 42

Zhang Fei Makes an Uproar at Steepslope Bridge; Xuande, Defeated, Flees to the Han River Ford

Zhao Zilong worked his spear against the two attackers. Zhong Jin came on first, swinging a giant battle-axe. The riders tangled. Zilong downed his man neatly and rode on. Zhong Shen gave chase, halberd in hand, drawing close enough for his horse to touch the tail of Zilong's mount. The reflection of his halberd flashed in the back of Zilong's armor. Suddenly Zilong pulled up short and lurched around, confronting his pursuer: to the left, Zilong's spear checked the halberd; to the right, he swung Black Pommel, cutting through Zhong Shen's helmet and cleaving his skull in two. Shen's escort quickly vanished.

Riding unhindered, Zilong headed for Steepslope Bridge. Suddenly he felt the ground trembling behind him. Wen Ping was leading a company in pursuit. Man and mount spent, Zilong reached the bridge and saw Zhang Fei upon it, lance raised, horse steady. Zilong hailed him by his style: "I need help, Yide!" "Hurry across!" Zhang Fei said. "Leave the pursuers to me!" Zilong guided his horse over the bridge and rode another twenty *li*. Finally he found Xuande resting under a tree, surrounded by a group of men. Zilong dismounted and placed his head and hands to the ground. Lord and vassal wept.

Still breathing hard, Zilong said, "Ten thousand deaths could not redeem my offense. Lady Mi was wounded so badly that she refused my horse and threw herself down a well. I could do nothing but knock over an earthen wall to cover her body. Then, holding the young master on my chest, I broke through the enemy's lines, and by the favor Heaven bestows on you, my lord, I survived. A moment ago the young master was crying. But he's stopped moving now, and I fear . . . " Zilong untied his armor and looked inside. The infant was asleep. "Safe and sound," he announced happily. "Fortune smiles." He handed Ah Dou carefully to Xuande, who flung him to the ground the instant he received him. "For the sake of a suckling like you," Xuande cried, "I risked losing a great commander!" Zilong swept the child off the ground and prostrated himself, saying through his tears, "If I cut my heart out here, I could not repay your kindness to me." A poet of later times described the scene:

> The tigers sprang from Cao Cao's fighting line;
> Safe on Zilong's breast the little dragon curled.
> How did the liege requite his liege man's love?
> Down before the horse, Xuande his own son hurled!

Wen Ping, meanwhile, had tracked Zilong to the bridge. There he found Zhang Fei, tiger-whiskers upcurled, eyes two rings of fury, snake-lance in hand. Mounted and poised, Zhang Fei looked out from the bridge. Wen Ping spotted dust rising out of the adjacent copse to the east. Suspecting an ambush, he reined in. Soon Cao Cao's leading generals joined him—Cao Ren, Li Dian, Xiahou Dun, Xiahou Yuan, Yue Jin, Zhang Liao, Zhang He, Xu Chu, and others. Cao's commanders contemplated Zhang Fei's menacing glare and leveled lance. And, too, they remembered Kongming's clever traps. They dug in west of the bridge, therefore, and posted a man back to Cao Cao. News of the standoff decided Cao Cao to hurry to the scene.

Zhang Fei's probing eye made out Cao Cao's blue silk umbrella in the distance, his feathered battle-axe and fringed banner. "So he came to see for himself," Zhang Fei thought. He called out: "I am Zhang Fei of Yan! Have you a man who'll fight it out to the death?" The power of Zhang Fei's voice unnerved Cao Cao's men. Cao Cao ordered the command umbrella removed. Turning to his attendants, he said, "Once Lord Guan told me that Zhang Fei had taken the head of a chief general before the eyes of his own legions as easily as removing an object from a sack. Today we have crossed his path and must take care." As Cao Cao spoke, Zhang Fei widened his eyes and shouted again: "Here he stands! Zhang Fei of Yan, who'll fight to the death any man that dares!" But Cao Cao, daunted by the warrior's indomitable spirit, was content to draw back.

Zhang Fei watched the rear lines of Cao Cao's army shuffling about. He lifted his spear and bellowed: "What's it to be? Don't want to fight? Don't want to leave?" The mighty voice still commanded the air when Xiahou Jie, right beside Cao Cao, collapsed and fell from his saddle, panic-stricken. Cao Cao turned and rode back, followed by his commanders. Indeed, what suckling babe can bear the peal of thunder; what injured woodsman can stand the roar of tigers and leopards? At that moment Cao Cao's soldiers threw down their spears and helmets and trampled one another as they fled—a tide of men, an avalanche of horses. Later a poet expressed his awe:

> Zhang Fei's war blood rose at Steepslope Bridge:
> Spear leveled, horse poised, eyes round-fixed.
> With a single thunderous cry that shook the ground,
> Alone he turned Cao's mighty host around.

Zhang Fei's awesome presence had terrified Cao Cao. Dashing west, he let his cap and hairpin drop, and his hair streamed out behind him. Zhang Liao and Xu Chu overtook him and seized his horse's bridle. Cao Cao had lost control. "Do not panic, Your Excellency," Zhang Liao said. "Is one Zhang Fei so fearsome? Turn the army round again and fight. Liu Bei can be taken!" At these words Cao Cao got hold of himself and sent Zhang Liao and Xu Chu back to the bridge to find out what they could.

Zhang Fei dared not pursue Cao Cao's withdrawing army. He summoned his original retinue of twenty riders, had them remove the branches from their horses' tails, and ordered them to pull down the bridge. He then reported back to Xuande. Xuande said, "Your bravery, brother, is beyond question, but not your tactics." Zhang Fei began to protest. "Cao Cao is a man of many schemes," Xuande continued. "You should have let the bridge stand. Now he's sure to be back." "If a single shout sent him reeling several *li*," Zhang Fei argued, "he won't be back for more." "Had you let it stand," Xuande explained, "fear of ambush would have continued to deter him from attacking. Now that it's down, he'll know we were afraid, having no troops around. His million-man host could ford the Han and the Great River simply by filling them in! How could razing one bridge stop him?" With that,

Xuande set out at once on the side roads, moving diagonally toward Mianyang by way of Hanjin.

Zhang Liao and Xu Chu examined the bridge and reported back to Cao Cao: "Zhang Fei destroyed it and left." "So he was afraid," Cao Cao said and decided to cross the river that same night. He ordered ten thousand men to set up three floating spans. "This could be one of Zhuge Liang's tricks," Li Dian warned. "Do not be reckless." "Zhang Fei's a foolhardy warrior. He knows no tricks," Cao Cao retorted and commanded his men to advance swiftly.

Approaching Hanjin, Xuande saw dust rising in the air behind him. Drumbeats filled the air, and war cries shook the ground. "The Great River lies ahead," he said, "the enemy behind. What can we do?" He ordered Zhao Zilong to prepare a defense.

Cao Cao instructed his men: "Liu Bei's a fish in our pot, a tiger in our trap. If we don't take him, here and now, we'll be letting the fish back into the sea, setting the tiger free in the hills. Press forward and spare no effort." With renewed vigor Cao's men started off one by one to get their man. But suddenly they heard a burst of drumming as a body of men and riders dashed forth from behind a hill. "We've been waiting for you a long time," the leader called out. It was Lord Guan, sitting astride Red Hare and gripping his Green Dragon. He had borrowed ten thousand men from Liu Qi in Jiangxia. Hearing of the great battles at Dangyang and Steepslope Bridge, he had come to intercept Cao Cao's band of pursuers. The moment Cao Cao sighted Lord Guan, he cried in despair, "Another of Zhuge Liang's traps!" and called a swift retreat.

Lord Guan chased Cao Cao's army for many *li* before he rode back to see Xuande safely to Hanjin, where boats had been readied. Lord Guan bade Xuande and Lady Gan seat themselves in one of them and had Ah Dou placed securely inside. He asked, "Why don't I see my other sister-in-law?" Xuande told him of Lady Mi's death in Dangyang. "Had you let me kill Cao Cao on the hunting field at Xuchang," Lord Guan said with emphasis, "you might have spared yourself these woes." "I had to consider how such an act could injure us," Xuande replied.

War drums from the southern shore intruded on their conversation. Boats were swarming across, sails to the wind. On the lead craft Xuande saw a man in white battle gown and silvery armor standing on the prow. "Uncle," he called out, "have you been well since we parted? I fear I have failed to serve you as a nephew should." It was Liu Qi. He boarded Xuande's boat and, tearfully prostrating himself, said, "I heard Cao Cao was closing in, uncle, so I have come to relieve you." Xuande was overjoyed. He merged the forces and continued his journey by water.

Xuande was describing the recent events for Liu Qi when a line of war-boats, stretching across the water from the southwest, came smartly up, borne by a full wind. "All my Jiangxia forces are here," Liu Qi said anxiously. "These must be Southland ships coming to cut us off—if they're not Cao Cao's! What are we to do?" Xuande surveyed the approaching craft. Seated in the front was Kongming, robed like a Taoist hermit with a band round his head. Behind him stood Sun Qian. Xuande excitedly hailed Kongming and asked how he had managed to turn up here. "As soon as I reached Jiangxia," Kongming explained, "I sent Lord Guan by land to meet you at Hanjin. I expected that Cao Cao would chase you, and that you, my lord, would cut over to take Hanjin rather than go on to Jiangling. That's why I had Master Qi here reinforce you. Then I went to collect the soldiers at Xiakou and lead them here."

Xuande could not have been more delighted. With all his forces reunited, he started planning to defeat Cao Cao. Kongming said, "Xiakou enjoys natural defenses and has ample cash and grain. It can be held indefinitely. I advise you, my lord, to station yourself there. Let Master Qi return to Jiangxia, work his navy into fighting condition, and prepare his weapons. We can hold Cao Cao off by thus placing our forces in pincer formation. For us to return to Jiangxia together would leave us isolated." "Wise counsel," Liu Qi said. "However, uncle, I thought I would invite you to stop at Jiangxia first and put your forces in shape. After that there'll be time enough for you to proceed to Xiakou." "My worthy nephew has a point," Xuande said and, after dispatching Lord Guan to Xiakou with five thousand men, he headed for Jiangxia with Kongming and Liu Qi.

*   *   *   *

Lord Guan's intervening land force had deterred Cao Cao from pursuing Xuande. Fearing an ambush, Cao Cao marched directly to Jiangling lest Xuande, traveling by water, take it before him.

In Jiangling the provincial secretary Deng Yi and the assistant inspector Liu Xian had already learned that Liu Zong had surrendered Xiangyang to Cao Cao. Unable to offer any defense against Cao Cao, the two officials led their armed forces out past the walls of the capital and submitted to the prime minister. Cao Cao entered the city and, after calming the populace, freed Han Song, who had been jailed by Liu Biao, and put him in charge of protocols. Other officials were given fiefs and handsome gifts.

Cao Cao said to his generals, "Xuande has fled to Jiangxia. If he forms an alliance with Sun Quan, our problems will multiply. What is the best way to defeat him?" "Now that we are in the field on a grand scale," Xun You advised, "send a messenger to the Southland summoning Sun Quan to join you in Jiangxia for a hunting party—with Xuande as the quarry! Offer Sun Quan half of Jingzhou to seal your amity. He will be too frightened, too confused not to submit. Our cause will thrive." Cao Cao approved this advice and sent an envoy south. At the same time he called up a force of eight hundred and thirty thousand—infantry, cavalry, and marines—which he rumored numbered a full million. Cao Cao's host advanced by land and sea. The cavalry rode along the Great River parallel to the long line of war-boats stretching westward back as far as Jiangling and the gorges, and eastward as far as Qichun and Huangzhou. The encampments extended for three hundred *li*.

*   *   *   *

In the Southland Sun Quan, stationed at Chaisang, heard that Cao Cao had accepted Liu Zong's submission and was marching on Jiangling double time. He therefore assembled his counselors to discuss the defense of the Southland. Lu Su said, "Jingzhou adjoins our territory. Rivers and mountains protect it. Its people are prosperous. If we can seize and hold the province, we will acquire the resources to establish our rule over the empire. I propose that you send me to Jiangxia to offer your official condolences on the occasion of Liu Biao's death. I believe I can persuade the newly defeated Liu Bei to encourage Liu Biao's commanders to make common cause with us against Cao Cao. Liu Bei's cooperation would provide a firm basis for our grand strategy." Sun Quan adopted the proposal and dispatched Lu Su to Jiangxia with mourning gifts.

*   *   *   *

At Jiangxia, Xuande, Kongming, and Liu Qi were conferring. "Cao Cao is too powerful. We cannot oppose him," Kongming said. "The best we can do is turn to Sun Quan for support. If the south keeps Cao Cao at bay to the north, we can pluck advantage from between them—and why not?" "The Southland is well endowed with worthy men," Xuande said. "They are bound to have their own long-range plans and have little need of us." With a smile Kongming responded, "Cao leads a million-man host. He's perched like a tiger on the Great River and the Han. You can be sure the south will be sending someone to find out about his strengths and weaknesses. And when he comes, I'll take a little sail south down the river. Trust my three inches of limber tongue to induce the south and the north to devour each other. If the southern armies are prevailing, we'll join them, settle Cao, and retake Jingzhou. If the northern armies are prevailing, we will have the possibility of taking the Southland itself!" "A profound estimation of the situation," Xuande said. "But how do we get a Southlander to come here?"

That very moment Lu Su was announced. He had arrived by boat bearing Sun Quan's condolences for the death of Liu Biao. "Our plans will carry," Kongming said with a smile. Turning to Liu Qi, he asked, "When Sun Ce died, was anyone sent to the services?" "There was deep enmity between our houses," Liu Qi replied, "for we had slain his father, Sun Jian. Exchanging ceremonial embassies would have been unthinkable." "Then," Kongming said, "Lu Su comes for no obsequies, but to sound out the military situation." Turning to Xuande he went on, "My lord, if Lu Su questions you concerning Cao's movements, simply plead ignorance. If he persists, send him to me." His analysis completed, Kongming had Lu Su escorted into the city.

After accepting the ritual gifts for the bereaved, Liu Qi bade Lu Su present himself to Xuande. After the formal introduction

Xuande invited the envoy to a private chamber, where wine was served. "Long has the imperial uncle's great name been known to me," Lu Su began, "though I have never had occasion to pay the man himself due homage. Our fortunate meeting today now satisfies that wish. They say you have joined battle with Cao Cao. I presume, therefore, that you know something about his strengths and vulnerabilities, and I venture to ask the approximate number of his forces." "Our own numbers," Xuande replied, "are insignificant, our generals few. No sooner do we hear of his approach than we make off. So, actually, I am unable to answer your question." "But I'm told," Lu Su pressed, "Zhuge Kongming twice succeeded in burning out Cao Cao and that Cao Cao twice lost his nerve. Your answer is difficult to accept." "If you must know the details," Xuande replied, "you will have to put your questions to Kongming himself." "Where would I find him?" Lu Su asked. "A meeting is what I desire." Xuande bade Kongming come forth and meet Lu Su.

The introduction concluded, Lu Su spoke: "Your talents and your virtue have ever been the objects of my esteem. But I have not had the honor of being presented to you. Now that fortune has made it possible, I would learn your view of the present state of affairs." Kongming replied, "I am well informed of Cao Cao's cunning devices. But, alas, our strength falls far short of his, and we have been avoiding engagement." "Will the imperial uncle be remaining here, then?" Lu Su asked. "Lord Liu," Kongming answered, "has an old friend, Wu Ju, governor of Changwu, south of Jingzhou, in northern Jiaozhou. He will entrust himself to his care." "Wu Ju hasn't enough grain or men to protect himself, let alone someone else," Lu Su said. "It will do for now, until we can make other plans," was Kongming's reply.

"General Sun Quan," Lu Su said earnestly, "holds the six districts of the Southland firmly in his hands. His soldiers are keen, his grain abundant. And because he shows the utmost courtesy to men of worth, heroes from all along the Great River have joined his cause. What could better serve your interest than to send a man you trust to the south for the purpose of forging an alliance with us to plan the conquest of the realm?" "Lord Liu and General Sun," Kongming said, "had no ties in the past. Your lord would turn a deaf ear to us, I fear. And we have no one to send." "Your own elder brother," Lu Su responded, "presently serving the Southland as an adviser, looks forward daily to seeing you. I myself have nothing to contribute. But I beg to go with you, sir, to see General Sun, so that we can confer on the future of the empire."

Finally, Xuande intervened. "Kongming is my mentor," he said. "I cannot spare him, even for a brief time. He may not go." Xuande feigned resistance to Lu Su's repeated appeals until Kongming said, "Matters are urgent. If you will authorize it, there's no harm in seeing what might come of a visit down there." At these words Xuande granted permission. Lu Su bade Xuande and Liu Qi good-bye and, together with Kongming, boarded his boat for the sail to Chaisang. Indeed:

> Because Kongming traveled south,
> Cao Cao's armies would taste sudden defeat.

The following chapter tells what Kongming meant to do.
  Read on.

CHAPTER 43

Kongming Debates the Southern Officials; Lu Su Rejects the Consensus

Lu Su and Kongming bade Xuande and Liu Qi good-bye and sailed for Chaisang. On board they reviewed the situation. "When you see General Sun, sir," Lu Su emphasized, "be sure to avoid mentioning how large and well-commanded Cao Cao's army is." "There is no need, Su, to keep reminding me of this," responded Kongming. "I will make my own replies to him." When their boat docked, Lu Su invited Kongming to rest at the guesthouse while he went ahead to see Sun Quan.

Sun Quan was already in council with his officers and officials. Informed of Lu Su's return, Quan summoned him and asked, "What did you learn in Jiangxia about the state of Cao Cao's forces?" "I have a general idea," replied Su, "but I will need time to report in full, sire." Quan showed him Cao Cao's summons and said, "Cao Cao had this delivered yesterday. I have sent the envoy back while we debate our response." Cao's note said:

> Under a recent imperial mandate, I have authority to act against state criminals. Our banners tilted southward; Liu Zong bound his hands in submission. The populace of Jingzhou, sensing the direction of events, has transferred its allegiance to us. We have one million hardy warriors and a thousand able generals. We propose that you join us, General, in a hunting expedition to Jiangxia in order to strike the decisive blow against Liu. Then, sharing the territory between us, we may seal an everlasting amity. Please do not hesitate but favor us with a speedy reply.

After he had read the document, Lu Su said to Sun Quan, "What is your most honored view, my lord?" "A decision has yet to be reached," he responded. The adviser Zhang Zhao joined the discussion, saying, "Commanding a host of one million, cloaked in the Emperor's authority, Cao Cao has campaigned the length and breadth of the land. To resist is to rebel. Moreover, your major advantage was the Great River—until Cao Cao took Jingzhou. Now we share the river's strategic benefits with him. Really, there is no opposing him, and in my poor estimation we would do better with the total security which submission will afford." "Zhang Zhao's views," the counselors declared in unison, "conform to the wishes of Heaven itself." But Sun Quan pondered in silence. "Have no doubts, my lord," Zhang Zhao continued. "If we submit to Cao, the people of the region will be protected and the six districts of the Southland preserved." Sun Quan lowered his head and said nothing.

A moment later Sun Quan rose to go to the privy. Lu Su followed. Aware that Su did not share the views of Zhang Zhao, Quan turned to him and asked, "But what is your mind on this?" "The majority's view, General, will be your ruin," Su replied. "They can submit to Cao, but you cannot." "What are you saying?"

Quan asked. "For someone like me," Su went on, "submission means being sent home to my clan, my village. Eventually I'll regain high office. But what have you to go home to? A minor estate? A single carriage? A single mount? A handful of followers? And what of your claim to royalty? Your advisers all consider only themselves. You must not heed them. It is time to make a master plan for yourself."

At these words Sun Quan sighed. "Their counsel fails my hopes," he said. "But the point you make—the master plan—accords well with my thinking. You come to me by Heaven's favor. Cao Cao, however, has Yuan Shao's legions as well as the troops of Jingzhou. He seems impossible to resist." "I have brought back with me," Su went on, "Zhuge Jin's younger brother, Liang. Put your questions to him, my lord, and he will explain how things stand." "Master Sleeping Dragon is here?" exclaimed Quan. "Resting in the guesthouse," answered Lu Su. "It's too late to see him today," Quan said. "Tomorrow I shall gather my civil and military officers so he can get acquainted with the eminent men of the south before we proceed to formal discussion." Lu Su went to arrange things accordingly.

The following day Lu Su came for Kongming. Again he warned the guest not to mention the size of Cao Cao's army. "Let me respond as I see fit," Kongming said with a smile. "Nothing shall go amiss, I assure you." Lu Su conducted Kongming to the headquarters of General Sun, where he was introduced to Zhang Zhao, Gu Yong, and some twenty other officials and officers of the first rank. As they sat erect in full dress, with their high formal caps and broad belts, Kongming was presented to each in turn. The formalities concluded, Kongming was shown to the guest's seat.

From Kongming's air of self-assurance and dignified, confident carriage, Zhang Zhao and the others understood that he had come to exert his powers of persuasion. Zhao initiated the discussion with a provocative comment: "I, the least of the Southland's scholars, have been hearing for some time how you, ensconced in Longzhong, have compared yourself to the great ministers of antiquity, Guan Zhong and Yue Yi. Have you actually made such claims?" "There could be some slight basis for the comparison," was Kongming's reply. "I have also heard that Liu

Xuande, protector of Yuzhou, solicited you three times at that thatched hut and, considering himself fortunate to get you—'a fish finding water' was how he put it—expected to roll up Jingzhou in the palm of his hand. Now that the province belongs to Cao Cao, we await your explanation."

Aware that Zhang Zhao was Sun Quan's foremost adviser—the man he had to confound or else lose all hope of convincing Quan himself—Kongming replied, "In my view that province on the River Han could have been taken as easily as one turns one's palm. But my master, Lord Liu, precisely because he conducts himself humanely and honorably, could never bear to steal a kinsman's estate and refused to do so. The adolescent Liu Zong, the victim of insidious counsel, secretly surrendered himself, giving Cao Cao a free hand in the region. My master, however, with forces stationed at Jiangxia, has promising prospects of his own, not to be lightly dismissed."

"Then your words and deeds do not agree," said Zhang Zhao. "For the men with whom you are wont to compare yourself helped their lords win fame and power. The patriarch Huan dominated the feudal lords and kept the realm together during Guan Zhong's tenure as minister; and Yue Yi helped the feeble state of Yan subdue the seventy cities of mighty Qi. Those two had the talent to set the empire to rights. But you, sir, have dwelled in a thatched hut, delighting yourself with the breeze and moon, profoundly absorbed in meditation. After you entered Lord Liu's service, we expected you to promote the welfare of the living souls of the realm and to root out and destroy treason and sedition.

"Before Lord Liu obtained your services, he was already a force to be reckoned with wherever he went, seizing this or that walled town. Now that he has you, people are saying that the ferocious tiger has grown wings and that we will witness the restoration of the Han and the elimination of the Caos. Old servants of the court and recluses of the mountains and forests have begun rubbing their eyes in expectation, imagining that the sky will clear, that the sun and moon will shine again. They hope to see the salvation of the people and the deliverance of the empire in their time.

"One can only wonder why, then, after you had committed

yourself to him, Lord Liu scurried for safety the moment Cao Cao stepped into the field, abandoning his obligations to Liu Biao for the security of the people of Jingzhou, and failing to sustain Liu Zong in the defense of his land. And what followed? Lord Liu quit Xinye, fled Fan, lost Dangyang, and bolted to Xiakou for refuge. But no one will have him! The fact is that Lord Liu was better off before you came. How does that measure up to what Guan Zhong and Yue Yi did for their lords? Kindly forgive my simple frankness."

Kongming broke into laughter. "The great roc ranges thousands of miles," he said. "Can the common fowl appreciate its ambition? When a man is gravely ill, he must be fed weak gruel and medicated with mild tonics until his internal state is readjusted and balanced and his condition gradually stabilizes. Only then can meat be added to his diet and powerful drugs be used to cure him. Thus is the root of the disease eradicated and the man's health restored. If you do not wait until breath and pulse are calm and steady but precipitately use powerful drugs and rich food, the attempt to cure the patient is sure to fail.

"When Lord Liu suffered defeat at Runan, he threw himself on Liu Biao's mercy. He had less than a thousand men and no generals at all, except for Lord Guan, Zhang Fei, and Zhao Zilong. He was like a man wasted by disease. Xinye, a small town off in the hills, with few people and scant grain, was no more than a temporary refuge, hardly a place to hold permanently. And yet, despite our poor weapons, weak city walls, untrained forces, and day-to-day shortages of grain, we burned Cao out at Bowang, flooded him out at the White River, and put his leading generals, Xiahou Dun and Cao Ren, in a state of panic and dismay. I am not sure that Guan Zhong and Yue Yi surpassed us in warfare.

"As for Liu Zong's surrender to Cao Cao, the truth is that Lord Liu knew nothing about it. Nor could he bear to exploit the treason of the Cais to steal a kinsman's estate—such is his great humanity and devotion to honor. In the case of the Dangyang defeat, Lord Liu had several hundred thousand subjects, including the elderly and many young people, who were determined to follow him. Could he leave them to their fate? He was moving a mere ten *li* each day but never thought of racing ahead to capture Jiangling. He was content to suffer defeat with his people if he had to—another instance of his profound humanity and sense of honor.

"The few cannot oppose the many, and a warrior learns to endure his reverses. The founder of the Han, Gao Zu, was defeated over and over by Xiang Yu, but the final victory at Gaixia was the result of Han Xin's good counsel, was it not? The same Han Xin who, in his long history of service to Gao Zu, had compiled no impressive record of victories! For the grand strategy of the dynasty, the security of our sacred altars, truly there is a master planner, one utterly different from the boasting rhetoricians whose empty reputations overawe people, who have no peer in armchair debate and standing discussions, of whom not even one in a hundred has any idea how to confront a crisis or cope with its rapid development. What a farce to amuse the world!"

To this oration Zhang Zhao had no reply, but another rose to the challenge. "Cao Cao has in place one million men and a roster of a thousand commanding officers. He can prance like a dragon while they glare down on us like tigers who could swallow Jiangxia with ease. What then?" Kongming eyed the speaker narrowly. It was Yu Fan. "Cao Cao did indeed bring into his fold the swarming hosts of Yuan Shao," Kongming replied. "And he stole the ill-organized soldiers of Liu Biao. But even his million are not that much to worry about!" With an icy smile Yu Fan countered: "Your forces were ruined at Dangyang. Your plans came to naught at Xiakou. You're desperate for any scrap of support and yet would boastfully deceive us by saying, 'Don't worry.'"

"And how," Kongming responded, "was Lord Liu to hold off a million murderous men with a few thousand troops dedicated to humanity and honor? We retired to Xiakou to bide our time. In the Southland the men are well trained and grain is plentiful. The Great River is your natural defense. And yet, giving no thought to the disgrace or to the mockery it would incur, you would have your lord crook his knee and submit to a traitor! By your standards it's not Lord Liu who fears the villain Cao!"

To this speech Yu Fan made no reply. But Bu Zhi rose to challenge Kongming, saying, "Are you not playing the part of those seductive diplomats of ancient times, Zhang Yi and Su Qin, striving to prevail upon our country to serve your ends?" Kongming turned his gaze to the speaker; then he responded: "You take those two for mere rhetoricians, forgetting their distinguished achievements. Su Qin held the highest office in six different kingdoms, while Zhang Yi twice served as chief minister to the state of Qin. Both men gave counsel that enlightened and strengthened their ruler, and are hardly to be put in a category with those who cringe before the mighty, victimize the weak, and cower before the sword. You gentlemen, hearing Cao Cao's empty threats, urged surrender with craven dispatch. Are you the ones to mock Zhang Yi and Su Qin?" Bu Zhi fell silent.

"What is your view of Cao Cao the man?" another asked. Kongming eyed the questioner, Xue Zong. "A traitor to the Han," he replied. "Is there any doubt?" "You are in error, sir," Xue Zong went on. "The mandate of the Han has devolved from sovereign to sovereign down to this day; now the dynasty's Heaven-ordained period draws to its close. Already Cao Cao possesses two-thirds of the empire, and all men tender him allegiance. Lord Liu, however, refuses to recognize the season of history, and in forcing the issue will fail as surely as an egg dashed against a rock."

Kongming answered harshly: "So, then, you mean to deny both king and father? In man's short life between Heaven and earth, loyalty and filial devotion are the foundation of personal integrity. Since, sir, you are a subject of the Han, when you see a man who disavows his duty as a subject, you are pledged to help destroy him—for such is a true subject's obligation. Cao Cao, far from honoring his debt to the Han for sustaining his forebears in office, bears within him a seditious usurper's heart, to the indignation of all. In tendering him allegiance on grounds of 'Heaven-ordained numbers,' you deny both king and father and render yourself unfit to speak in the company of men." Xue Zong was too humiliated to reply.

Another from the council picked up the argument. "Though Cao Cao enjoins the nobles through coercion of the Emperor, yet he is himself a descendant of the Supreme Ancestor's prime minister, Cao Shen. Lord Liu claims descent from Prince Jing of Zhongshan, but that has never actually been verified. As far as anyone can tell, he is a mere mat-weaver, a sandal merchant, hardly a worthy contender with Cao Cao." Kongming regarded this speaker, Lu Ji. A smile crossing his face, he asked, "Didn't you once steal an orange at one of Yuan Shu's banquets? I'd like

you to sit still while I tell you something. If Cao Cao is the descendant of the great minister Cao Shen, then the Caos have been
the subjects of the Han from that day to this. For him to mo-
nopolize power and recklessly wield it, deceiving and abusing the
sovereign, is more than negation of the emperor, it is nullifi-
cation of his own sacred ancestor. This makes Cao Cao more than
a seditious subject; it makes him a traitorous son. Lord Liu has
the dignity of an imperial scion. He is a man to whom the present Emperor has granted recognized status in accordance with
the official genealogy. How can you say there is no verification?
Consider further that the Supreme Ancestor, who began his career as a precinct magistrate, in the end took possession of the
empire. And what is there to be ashamed of in mat-weaving or
selling sandals? Your puerile point of view makes you an unworthy participant in the discussions of distinguished scholars." Lu
Ji was confounded.

Suddenly, another man rose and spoke: "Kongming's rhetoric is bereft of reason. His distorted judgments are not worth consideration. I beg to inquire, what classics have you mastered?"
Kongming turned to the speaker, Yan Jun, and said, "How can
the text-bound pedant revive our nation or further our cause?
And what of the ancient sages—Yi Yin, who tilled the soil in Shen,
or Jiang Ziya, who fished the River Wei? What of men like Zhang
Liang and Chen Ping, Zheng Yu and Geng Yan? These worthies
sustained their kings in time of peril. What canons did they master? Do you really think they simply spent their days confined between the pen and the inkstone like schoolmen arguing over texts,
flourishing words, wielding brushes?" Deflated by Kongming's denunciation, Yan Jun lowered his head and made no reply.

Yet another protested loudly: "You, sir, are certainly given to
exaggeration. I am not so sure that there is any real learning in
you, that you won't end up as the butt of scholars' ridicule." The
speaker was Cheng Deshu of Runan. Kongming answered the
man so: "There are scholars of noble character and scholars with
petty interests. The former are loyal to their sovereign and devoted to his government; they preserve their integrity and detest
renegades—for they are intent on making their influence felt in
their time and making their names known to later ages. But the
latter bend their efforts to polishing rhymes, knowing no skill but

that of trivial composition. Authors of grandiose odes in their youth, by old age they've digested the classics. In one sitting a thousand words may flow from their pens, but inside of them not a single useful idea is to be found. Take the scholar Yang Xiong who made a great reputation in his time only to disgrace himself by serving Wang Mang—for which he jumped to his death from the upper story of a building. He is an example of the petty scholar. Let him produce a ten-thousand-word rhapsody every day. What value does it have?" Cheng Deshu, like the others, was too confounded to reply. The assembly was unnerved at Kongming's exhibition of mastery in debate.

Two others, Zhang Wen and Luo Tong, were about to raise their objections when someone entered the chambers and cried, "Kongming is one of the rarest talents of our age. Belaboring these issues is hardly the way to show due respect to our guest. With Cao Cao, backed by a huge army, looking hungrily across our borders, what's the point of sterile polemics? We should be considering instead how to drive the enemy back." The assembly turned to see Huang Gai (Gongfu), a man from Lingling, presently serving as a commissariat officer in Dongwu.

"With your permission," Huang Gai said to Kongming. "Sometimes one carries the day by holding one's peace. Save your invaluable opinions for our lord rather than continuing this debate." "These gentlemen," said Kongming, "are unaware of the exigencies of our age, and their objections had to be answered." With that, Huang Gai and Lu Su took Kongming to see Sun Quan. At the entrance to the government hall they encountered Zhuge Jin, Kongming's elder brother, and saluted him. "Worthy brother," said Jin, "since you are in the Southland, why haven't you come to see me?" "For one in the service of Lord Liu," Kongming replied, "it is only fitting that public concerns take precedence over private ones. As long as these require my attention, I must beg your forgiveness." "Worthy brother," said Zhuge Jin, "come over and catch up on things after you have seen the lord of the Southland."

After Jin had departed, Lu Su said, "What I cautioned you about before—let there be no slip." Kongming nodded. As they reached the official chambers, Sun Quan himself appeared and descended the stair to welcome them, offering his highest regards. After the exchange of salutations he showed Kongming to a seat. Quan's officials stood in attendance, civil officials in one row, military in another. Lu Su watched as Kongming conveyed Liu Xuande's good wishes. Kongming stole a glance at Sun Quan. Jade green eyes and a purplish beard—an imposing presence. "His appearance is extraordinary," Kongming mused. "A man to be incited, not won over by argument. But I must wait for him to question me."

After the presentation of tea Sun Quan spoke: "Lu Su has told me of your great abilities. Now that we have the good fortune to meet you, I make bold to seek the benefit of your teaching." "One unfit and unlearned as I," Kongming responded, "could never do justice to your enlightened questions." "Recently," Sun Quan went on, "you assisted Lord Liu on strategic decisions in the war with Cao Cao. This must have given you profound knowledge of the enemy's military position."

"Lord Liu," answered Kongming, "is hardly in a position to resist Cao Cao. His forces are paltry, his generals all too few; on top of this, Xinye is a small town without grain supplies." "But how large a force does Cao have?" Sun Quan asked. "Mounted, foot, and naval, all told, over one million troops," replied Kongming. "This has to be a trick!" exclaimed Sun Quan. "No trick," Kongming went on. "He had the Qingzhou army of two hundred thousand when he took charge of Yanzhou. When he vanquished Yuan Shao, he added another five or six hundred thousand to that. Recently he recruited another three or four hundred thousand from the north-central plains. And now he has gained two or three hundred thousand more from the conquest of Jingzhou. It adds up to no less than one and a half million. I said 'one million' for fear of scaring off your warriors."

Stunned, Lu Su paled and tried to catch Kongming's eye. But Kongming pretended not to notice. "And how many military commanders?" Sun Quan asked. "He has competent, inventive advisers and hardened, seasoned leaders—over a thousand or two, easily," Kongming stated. "Now that he has conquered Jingzhou," Quan pressed, "has he greater ambitions?" "At the moment," replied Kongming, "he is making his way down the Great River, leaving a trail of camps in preparation for naval action. What other territory could his ambition lead him to, if not the

Southland?" "If he means to swallow and assimilate us," said Quan, posing his question, "must we fight or not? I crave your judgment on this." "I do have an opinion," Kongming conceded, "but I am afraid you would be reluctant to accept it." "I would know your esteemed view," was Quan's reply.

At this invitation Kongming began to speak: "When the realm was in turmoil, you formed a state in the south and Lord Liu rallied his hosts below the River Han in order to contest the empire with Cao Cao. Now Cao has freed himself of his greatest difficulties and has stabilized his position to a certain degree. This fresh triumph in Jingzhou has made him feared throughout the land, and whatever heroes would oppose him lack the base for waging war. That is why Lord Liu made good his removal to this region. I would urge you to weigh your strength and address the problem. If you can lead the forces of the south in contention with the north for mastery of the area, then break with Cao Cao at once. Otherwise, why follow your advisers' judgment, lay down your arms, face north, and submit to his rule."

Before Sun Quan could respond, Kongming continued: "General, you have let it be known that you incline toward submission, but I know how torn you are. The situation is precarious. Act before disaster strikes." "If all you say is true," Sun Quan said, "why hasn't Lord Liu submitted?" "Tian Heng," answered Kongming, "the stalwart loyalist of Qi, held fast to his honor and refused to disgrace himself. A scion of the royal house, renowned in his time, looked up to by men of learning everywhere, how could Lord Liu do less? His failures are ordained and not of his own making. He will not be humiliated."

His composure breaking, Sun Quan swept his robes about him and retired to his private apartments. The assembly dispersed, snickering. Lu Su berated Kongming: "What was the point of saying such things? My sovereign's temper is too liberal, fortunately, to censure you directly. But what you said has demeaned him." Kongming tilted his head and laughed. "Why is he so excitable?" he said. "I have my own plan for destroying Cao Cao. But he did not ask, so I did not mention it." "If you actually have a sound strategy," said Lu Su, "I will ask my lord to seek your instruction." "To me," Kongming rejoined, "Cao's host is like a million ants waiting to be pulverized with one swipe of the hand!" At these words Lu Su went to the rear chamber to talk to Sun Quan.

Quan's anger had not subsided, and he said pointedly to Lu Su, "His insolence is insufferable!" "I rebuked him for it," Lu Su responded, "but he only said that you were too 'excitable,' and that he was reluctant—on his own initiative—to broach the subject of Cao Cao's destruction. Why not solicit his plan, my lord?" Sun Quan's consternation passed, and his tone softened. "So he had a strategy all along. That's why he incited me. I was not thinking clearly at the moment and nearly spoiled everything." So saying, Sun Quan reappeared in the hall together with Lu Su and invited Kongming to resume discussions. Quan received Kongming with an apology: "Just now I recklessly sullied your high name. Kindly overlook the offense." Kongming conveyed his regrets too: "It was I who spoke offensively, and I beg your forgiveness for it." Sun Quan bade Kongming join him in his private apartments, where he had wine set out.

After several rounds Sun Quan began: "Cao Cao's lifelong enemies were Lü Bu, Liu Biao, Yuan Shao, Yuan Shu, Lord Liu, and myself. The first four heroes are no more. Lord Liu and I remain. I cannot give the Southland into another's control, not even to preserve it. That is certain. And none save Lord Liu can oppose Cao Cao. But after his recent defeats how can he continue to hold firm in adversity?" "Lord Liu's defeats notwithstanding," Kongming began, "Lord Guan commands ten thousand elite troops, and Liu Qi's fighters from Jiangxia number no less. Cao Cao's host is exhausted, having come so far. In their recent pursuit of Lord Liu, their light cavalry was covering three hundred *li* a day— clearly a case of 'a spent arrow unable to pierce fine silk.' Consider too that the northerners are unused to naval warfare and that the officers and men from Jingzhou follow Cao by coercion, not by choice. General, if you can unite hand and heart with Lord Liu, the destruction of Cao's army and his return to the north can be guaranteed. Then with the strengthening of the Southland and Jingzhou, a tripodal balance of power will come into being in the empire. The means to shape the outcome are in your hands today. It is for you to use them."

Sun Quan was exhilarated. "Hearing you, master, is like breaking out of a thicket and into a clearing. My mind is made up. I have no further doubts. Discussion of joint action to wipe out Cao Cao shall begin this very day." With these words Sun Quan commanded Lu Su to inform all officials of his intentions and escort Kongming to the guesthouse.

When Zhang Zhao heard the news, he said to the counselors, "We have fallen into Kongming's trap." He rushed to Sun Quan and said: "We have heard, my lord, that you mean to meet Cao Cao on the battlefield. How do you think you compare to Yuan Shao, whom Cao conquered with a roll of the drums when his own forces were still relatively weak? Do you think you can oppose him today when he has one million in his command? Listen to Kongming and undertake this ridiculous mobilization, and you will be carrying kindling to put out the fire."

Sun Quan lowered his head and said nothing. Another adviser, Gu Yong, added his arguments: "Because he suffered defeat at Cao Cao's hands, Liu Bei wants to use our forces to drive him back. Why should we serve his ends? I pray you will heed Zhang Zhao's advice." Sun Quan pondered and lapsed into indecision. Zhang Zhao and his party left, and Lu Su reentered to plead further: "Zhang Zhao and his faction oppose the mobilization and favor submission because they fear for the safety of themselves and their families. I beg my lord to ignore such self-interested calculations." Sun Quan continued to ponder his dilemma. "If you delay, my lord," Lu Su said, "you will be ruined by them." "Retire for now, my good vassal," Quan said, "and let me reflect." Lu Su withdrew. The military officers were divided, but the civil officials all advocated submission. All sorts of conflicting opinions were expressed.

Sun Quan retired, his mind deeply divided. He was unable to eat or sleep. His mother, Lady Wu offered a sympathetic ear. "Cao Cao is camped on the river," he said to her, "intent on subduing our land. I have put the question to our civil and military advisers. Some would capitulate, some would wage war. If we risk battle, I fear our fewer numbers will not be able to stand against their greater. If we risk submission, I fear Cao Cao will not accommodate us. I waver, therefore, unable to act resolutely." "Have you forgotten my elder sister's dying words?" his mother asked. This question woke Sun Quan from his quandary. Indeed:

Because Sun Quan remembered his mother's last words,
Zhou Yu would do great deeds of war.

What had she said?
Read on.

CHAPTER 44

Kongming Cunningly Moves
Zhou Yu to Anger; Sun Quan Decides
on a Plan to Defeat Cao Cao

To solve her nephew's dilemma Lady Wu said, "My late sister
passed on to us your brother's dying words: 'Consult Zhang Zhao
on domestic difficulties, Zhou Yu on external ones.' Isn't Zhou
Yu's counsel wanted now?" Pleased with Lady Wu's suggestion,
Sun Quan sent a messenger to the Poyang Lakes where Zhou Yu
was directing naval exercises, inviting him to join in the discussions. But even before the messenger left, Cao Cao's arrival at
the River Han had compelled Zhou Yu to go to Chaisang for a
military conference. There Lu Su was the first to meet Zhou Yu
and brief his close friend. "No need to worry," Zhou Yu reassured
Lu Su, "I think I know what we have to do. But you must get Kongming here for a meeting right away." Lu Su rode off to find him.

As Zhou Yu settled into his lodgings, a delegation of four was
announced: Zhang Zhao, Gu Yong, Zhang Hong, and Bu Zhi.
Zhou Yu showed them in, and the five men seated themselves.
The amenities concluded, Zhang Zhao began: "Commander, do
you know the trouble the Southland is in?" "I have not been informed," was his reply. "Cao Cao has one million men on the
River Han. Yesterday he summoned our lord to join his 'hunting party' at Jiangxia. Though he means to swallow us up, he has
made no overt move. We are advocating submission to spare the
Southland a debacle; we never expected that Lu Su would bring

back Liu Bei's military director, Zhuge Liang. Liang has his own scores to settle and will make sure to stir our lord with his all-too-convincing points, while Lu Su clings stubbornly to his illusions, refusing to recognize reality. We turn to you, Commander, to make the final decision." "Do you have a consensus, gentlemen?" asked Zhou Yu. "We have conferred and we concur," Gu Yong responded. "Such has been my own wish for some time," Zhou Yu said. "I beg you all to return to your quarters. Early tomorrow I am to present myself before our lord, when the debate will be settled accordingly." Zhang Zhao and his delegation excused themselves and left.

Soon Cheng Pu, Huang Gai, and Han Dang, representing the military faction, came to see Zhou Yu. After he had received them and greetings had been exchanged, Cheng Pu began: "Have you heard, Commander, that soon the Southland must lose its independence and be annexed to another power?" "I have not been so informed," was the reply. "We have followed General Sun," Cheng Pu went on, "in the founding of this domain through hundreds of battles, great and small. Thus we have come into possession of the towns and cities of our six districts. What shame we would suffer, what regret, if our lord should heed the advocates of surrender. But we who choose death before disgrace count on you to convince him to muster the troops—a cause to which we dedicate our all." "Is there consensus among you, Generals?" asked Zhou Yu. Huang Gai rose and, striking his palm to his forehead, said hotly, "This shall roll before I submit." The group echoed his oath. "To decide the issue by combat," said Zhou Yu, "is precisely what I desire. How could I acquiesce in surrender? I beg you, Generals, return. After I meet with our lord, the debate will be settled accordingly." Cheng Pu and his party took their leave.

Soon afterward a party of civil officials led by Zhuge Jin and Lü Fan was welcomed in. Greetings exchanged, Zhuge Jin began: "My younger brother Liang has come downriver to tell us that Lord Liu seeks our cooperation in operations against Cao Cao. Our civil and military officials remain locked in debate. Since my own brother is Lord Liu's representative, I have stood aside, biding my time until you would arrive to settle the question." "What is your own assessment?" Zhou Yu asked him. "Surrender means cheap security," replied Jin. "War puts all at risk." "I have some ideas of my own," Zhou Yu responded with a smile. "Join us tomorrow in the council hall, where we shall settle things."

As Zhuge Jin and his party withdrew, another group, this led by Lü Meng and Gan Ning, was announced. Zhou Yu invited them in and they expressed their views. Some insisted on surrender, some were determined to fight. They argued back and forth until Zhou Yu said, "This is enough discussion for now. Join us tomorrow in the council hall, where we shall settle things." Long after the group had departed, a cynical smile remained on Zhou Yu's face.

That evening Lu Su brought Kongming to pay his respects. Zhou Yu came from the central gate to escort them inside. After the formalities they seated themselves as host and guest. Lu Su began with a question to Zhou Yu: "Cao Cao has launched an offensive against the Southland, and between the two courses, war or peace, our lord cannot decide. In this matter he is yours entirely. I would inquire what your own view is." "Cao Cao acts in the name of the Son of Heaven, the Emperor himself," said Zhou Yu. "His host cannot be driven back. His power has grown to the point where it would be futile to risk engagement. If we fight, defeat is certain. If we surrender, security is cheaply bought. I have made my decision. Tomorrow before our lord I shall advocate sending a representative to convey our submission."

Lu Su was appalled. "But this is most misguided!" he responded. "The estate we have founded now spans three generations. How can we abandon it to strangers on the spur of the moment? The last words of Lord Sun's brother, Sun Ce, charged us to entrust external matters to you. What will befall us if you follow the counsel of cowards now, at the very moment we must rely on you—as if you were the great Mount Tai itself—to preserve the house of Sun?" To this appeal Zhou Yu replied: "The living souls in the six districts of the Southland are more than can be numbered. If we bring upon them the disasters of war, they will lay their grievance to us. That is why I have decided to sue for peace." "How wrong that would be!" cried Lu Su. "With a general of your mettle and the sure defensibility of the land, Cao is far from assured of fulfilling his ambitions." The two men argued round and round while Kongming looked on, detached, smiling with sangfroid.

"What makes you smile so disdainfully?" Zhou Yu asked him. "Your antagonist Lu Su, of course, who refuses to recognize the exigencies of the occasion," said Kongming. Lu Su snapped back, "Now you're mocking me for 'refusing to recognize the exigencies of the occasion'?" Kongming replied, "Zhou Yu advocates submission. It seems perfectly reasonable." "Any scholar who recognizes realities—and Kongming is surely one—must be of the same mind," said Zhou Yu. "You too argue this way?" Lu Su asked Kongming. "Cao Cao is a master of warfare," Kongming explained, "whom none in the empire dares engage. Those who did—Lü Bu, Yuan Shao, Yuan Shu, and Liu Biao—have been annihilated. And no such men remain in the empire—save Lord Liu, who has refused to 'recognize the exigencies of the occasion' and struggles with Cao for mastery. But Lord Liu stands alone in Jiangxia, his very survival in question. The general's plan to submit to Cao ensures his family's safety and protects his wealth and status. What if the sacred throne of the house of Sun is transferred to another house? Why, ascribe it to the Mandate of Heaven. What do we need these things for?" Lu Su was moved to wrath. "You would see our sovereign crook his knee and endure disgrace before a treasonous rogue?" he exclaimed.

Kongming went on: "I have thought of another possibility that might well save the ritual gifts of sheep and wine as we transfer our lands and render up the seals of state. You would not even need to cross the river yourself, but merely to send a solitary representative to escort two persons to the river. If Cao Cao can get hold of these two, his million-man host will discard their armor, furl their banners, and retire from the field." Zhou Yu spoke: "And with what two persons do you propose to effect this reversal?" "The Southland's parting with these two," Kongming continued, "may be likened to an oak shedding a leaf, a granary diminished by a grain of millet. Yet if he gets them, Cao Cao will depart content." Again Zhou Yu asked, "Well, what two persons?"

"When I was in residence at Longzhong," Kongming continued, "I heard that Cao was building a new tower on the banks of the Zhang. It is called the Bronze Bird Tower—an absolutely magnificent edifice, and elegant. He has searched far and wide for

beautiful women to fill its chambers. Cao Cao, who is basically
inclined to wantonness, has known for some time that the Southland patriarch Qiao has two daughters, beauties whose faces
would make fish forget to swim or birds to fly, abash the very blossoms and outshine the moon. He has vowed: 'First, I'll sweep the
realm and calm it and build an empire; next, I'll possess the
Southland's two daughters Qiao and install them in the Bronze
Bird Tower so that I may have pleasure in my later years and die
without regret.' Cao Cao may lead his million-fold host to men-
ace the Southland, but in reality he comes for the sake of these
two women. General, why not seek out the patriarch Qiao, pro-
cure his girls with a thousand pieces of gold, and dispatch someone to deliver them to Cao? Once he has them, he will be content and return to the capital. Long ago Fan Li of Yue succeeded
with a similar plan when he presented the beauty Xi Shi to the
king of Wu. Why not act at once?"

"Can you verify Cao's desire to possess these two women?"
asked Zhou Yu. "He once commissioned his son, Zhi (styled Zi-
jian), a writer of great genius, to compose a rhapsody. The result
was the 'Bronze Bird Tower Rhapsody.' Its theme is the fitness of
his house for sovereignty and his vow to wive the daughters Qiao."
"Can you recall it?" Zhou Yu asked. "Infatuated with its gorgeous
language, I committed it to memory," Kongming replied. "May
I request a recitation?" said Zhou Yu. Then and there Kongming
recited:

> A pleasant promenade beside His Majesty:
> They mount the tiered tower, delight their spirits,
> And view the teeming richness of the realm,
> The sphere his sagely virtue rules.
> These gates he built pierce the mid-sky;
> The double pylons float to the crystalline.
> Splendid viewing rooms sit suspended there,
> Linked chambers seem to hang above the western wall.
> They peer down on the ever-flowing Zhang,
> Whose gardens give promise of teeming glory
> Aloft on either side, twin towers—
> Left, Jade Dragon; right, Golden Phoenix—
> To hold his brides, the Southland daughters Qiao,
> With whom he will take his pleasure, morning, evening.
> Look down on the royal city's spacious elegance;
> Behold the shimmering tints of distant clouds.

Rejoice in the confluence of many talents;
Auspicious dreams of aid will be fulfilled.
Look up! The gentle solemnity of spring;
And hear! the lovelorn cries of every bird.
May these proud towers stand till Heaven's end.
Our house has gained a twin fulfillment.
Our benevolent influence spreads across the realm,
Winning universal homage for our capital.
Even the splendor of Huan and Wu, ancient hegemons,
Pales beside his sagely grace and wisdom.
Most blessed! Most marvelous!
His generous favor, extending far and wide.
Lend the sovereign house your aid
That unto the four corners peace may reign.
Our king is on a scale with Heaven and earth,
Radiant as the light of sun or moon,
Ever honored as the ultimate principle,
Immortal as the sky's sovereign star.
Driving the dragon banners round the royal circuit,
Guiding the phoenix chariot round the realm:
His clement influence bathes the kingdom's corners;
Prize offerings to him heap high—the people prosper.
May these towers stand firm for all time,
For pleasure never failing and without end.

When Kongming's performance was done, Zhou Yu started violently from his seat and pointed north. "Old traitor! Rogue!" he cried. "You abuse us past endurance." Kongming rose too, swift to check him. "Remember when the khan, chief of the Xiongnu, encroached on our border," he said, "and the Emperor of Han granted him a princess to forge amity through kinship? Can we not now spare two female commoners?" "There is something you are not aware of," Zhou Yu replied. "The elder daughter of the patriarch Qiao was the first wife of the late general Sun Ce. The younger is my own wife." "Truly, I did not know," said Kongming, feigning astonishment. "I have said something unforgivable and offended you most gravely. A thousand pardons!" "Cao, old traitor," Zhou Yu went on, "you and I cannot share footing on this earth. So I swear." "The situation calls for careful consideration," Kongming cautioned, "lest our actions entail regret." But Zhou Yu continued, "I had our late lord Sun Ce's solemn trust and could never crook the knee to Cao. I only meant to test you. When I left the Poyang Lakes I resolved to take up arms against the north. The executioner's axe upon my neck could not alter my resolve. I hope for your stout aid, Kongming, that together we may smite the traitor Cao." "If you would accept my humble efforts, I would toil unsparingly, like a dog or a horse, entirely at your service." "Tomorrow," Zhou Yu responded, "I will present myself to our lord to debate the mustering of the troops." With that, Kongming and Lu Su bid Zhou Yu good-bye and left.

On the morning of the next day Sun Quan ascended the assembly hall: to his left, some thirty civil officials led by Zhang Zhao and Gu Yong; to his right, thirty or more military officials led by Cheng Pu and Huang Gai. The caps and robes of the officials rustled against each other, and the swords and pendants of the officers jostled and clanked. All stood at attention in their respective lines. Moments later Zhou Yu appeared.

After formal salutations and a few kind words from Sun Quan, Zhou Yu said, "I have been told that Cao Cao has marched south, stationed his forces along the River Han, and sent us a letter. I wonder, my lord, what your own honorable wishes might be?" Sun Quan passed the letter to Zhou Yu, who read it and smiled. "The old traitor," he said, "must imagine we have no men worthy of the name in the Southland, to approach us so insolently!" "What is your own view?" Quan asked. "Have you discussed the matter thoroughly with your officers and officials, my lord?" responded Zhou Yu. "For days on end," replied Quan. "Some advocate submission, some war. Because I have not yet reached a final decision, I appeal to you to resolve it once and for all." "Who are those urging submission?" asked Zhou Yu. "Zhang Zhao and his party," said Sun Quan. Turning to Zhang Zhao, Zhou Yu said, "I beg to hear your reasons."

"Cao Cao controls the Emperor," Zhao began, "and his campaigns across the land enjoy the sanction of the court. His recent victory in Jingzhou makes his power all the more formidable. The Great River was the Southland's only hope of blocking him. But now he has thousands of light attack craft and war-boats; a combined advance by land and sea could never be stopped. It is better to submit for now and live to plan another day."

"The twisted reasoning of a pedant!" cried Zhou Yu. "Now, in the third succession since the founding of the Southland, how could we bear to throw it all away overnight?" "So then," Quan said to Zhou Yu, "what is your grand strategy to be based on?"

Zhou Yu replied: "Posing as prime minister of the Han, Cao Cao is in reality a traitor to the dynasty. But you, General, true heir to your father and your brother, have possession of this territory. Your martial skill is godlike, your troops are keen, and your grain stores are ample. Now is the time to make your might felt the length and breadth of the empire and eliminate a cruel and violent enemy for the sake of the ruling house. How can we submit! Furthermore, by coming here, Cao has broken the most sacred rules of military science. While the north is still untamed and while Ma Teng and Han Sui threaten his rear, he is losing time on this campaign. That's the first rule broken. With troops unused to naval warfare, Cao has put away his saddles and steeds and taken to boats to contest for this land of mariners. That's the second rule broken. Now the height of winter is upon us, and his horses want for hay. That's the third rule broken. He has driven his northerners far afield to unfamiliar rivers and lakes, into a strange clime where disease is rife. That is the fourth rule broken. However numerous his men, they will be defeated. This is the moment to make Cao Cao your captive. I appeal to you: grant me between fifty and a hundred thousand crack troops to place at Xiakou, and I will destroy the invaders for you."

Eyes flashing, Sun Quan stood up. "Long, too long," he cried, "has the traitor sought to remove the Han and establish his own house. Four of those he had to fear—Yuan Shao, Yuan Shu, Lü Bu, and Liu Biao—are gone. I alone remain. One of us—the old traitor or I—must fall. That is my oath. Good vassal, your voice for war meets my own thoughts. You must have come to me by Heaven's grace." "I am resolved upon the bloody course and shrink from no extremity. Yet I fear, General, that you remain undecided," Zhou Yu responded. Sun Quan drew his sword and sheared off a corner of the table at which he received the petitions of his ministers. "Any officer or official who advocates submission will be dealt with so!" he declared and, handing the sword to Zhou Yu, honored him as first field marshal. Cheng Pu was made second field marshal, and Lu Su consulting commander.

In giving his sword, Sun Quan had empowered Zhou Yu to

execute any officer or official who disobeyed. Zhou Yu accepted the weapon and addressed the assembly: "I am authorized to lead you in battle to destroy Cao Cao. Tomorrow all commanders and subordinate officers are to assemble at my headquarters on the riverbank to receive further orders. Anyone who delays or interferes with our mission will be punished in accordance with the Seven Prohibitions and the Fifty-four Capital Offenses." With these words, Zhou Yu took leave of Sun Quan and left the building. The officials adjourned without further comment.

Back at his quarters Zhou Yu summoned Kongming. "Now that the debate is settled," Zhou Yu began, "what would you consider a sound plan for defeating Cao Cao?" "General Sun's resolve is weak. We cannot make any decision," Kongming answered. "What do you mean, 'his resolve is weak'?" responded Zhou Yu. "The sheer size of Cao Cao's army still intimidates him," Kongming went on. "He wonders if the few can withstand the many. Before our cause can succeed, General, you will have to reassure him by making an analysis of the enemy's numerical strength." "Your judgment, master, is correct," said Zhou Yu, and he went back to see Sun Quan.

"Only a matter of some importance," said Sun Quan, "would bring you back so late at night." "My lord," replied Zhou Yu, "are you still in doubt about beginning the expedition tomorrow?" "My only concern," said Sun Quan "is the numerical imbalance between our forces." With a smile Zhou Yu reassured him: "I have come to set your mind at ease on precisely this point, my lord. Your fears and uncertainties arise from mention in Cao's letter of his million-man land and sea force. And you have taken his claim at face value. Let us lay out the facts: Cao Cao is leading no more than one hundred and fifty or sixty thousand northern troops, who are almost entirely exhausted. The soldiers he took over from Yuan Shao number some seventy or eighty thousand, the greater part of whom have little trust in their new leader and consequently little commitment. You hardly need fear one long-wearied army and another with no fixed purpose, whatever their numbers. Fifty thousand men are all I need to break them. Let Your Lordship worry no further." Sun Quan placed his hand gently on Zhou Yu's shoulder and said, "You have allayed my fears. Zhang Zhao has no sense and has deeply disappointed me. Only you and Lu Su share my view. You two and Cheng Pu should pick your forces at once and advance. I will reinforce you with more soldiers and plenty of supplies. If your vanguard runs into diffi-culties, come back to me at once, and I will meet the traitor Cao in combat personally. My doubts are dispelled."

Zhou Yu expressed his gratitude and left, observing inwardly, "Kongming divined my lord's state of mind before I did! In strat-egy, too, he excels me. In the long run such brilliance bodes dan-ger to our land; we would be well rid of him now." That night Zhou Yu sent for Lu Su and confided his thoughts to him. Lu Su responded, "Never! To kill a valuable ally before Cao Cao falls would be self-defeating." "The man is an asset to Liu Xuande, not to us," retorted Zhou Yu. "He will cause the Southland trou-ble." "Zhuge Jin is his elder brother," said Lu Su. "Wouldn't it be wonderful if Jin could induce Kongming to come over to the Southland?" Zhou Yu approved the suggestion.

As dawn broke the following morning, Zhou Yu entered his riverside headquarters and ascended the commander's seat in the main tent of the central army. Left and right stood swords-men and axemen. Officials and officers crowded below to hear his instructions. But Cheng Pu, the second marshal, was resent-ful at having to serve under Zhou Yu, who was his junior in age and now his superior in rank. Cheng Pu excused himself on grounds of illness and sent his eldest son, Cheng Zi, in his place.

Zhou Yu issued his commands to the assembly: "The king's law favors no man: let each of you good men perform his duty. Cao Cao's tyranny exceeds even Dong Zhuo's: he holds the Em-peror prisoner in Xuchang; and now his ruthless army stands poised at our borders. Today by our sovereign's authority I mean to bring him to justice. I call on you to give your all to this ac-tion. Wherever you march, the population is not to be disturbed. Rewards and punishments will follow the strictest standards."

Having delivered the charge, Zhou Yu dispatched the van-guard, Han Dang and Huang Gai, to take command of the naval force and proceed to Three Rivers, there to establish camp and await further orders. The second brigade was led by Jiang Qin and Zhou Tai; the third, by Ling Tong and Pan Zhang; the fourth, by Taishi Ci and Lü Meng; and the fifth, by Lu Xun and Dong Xi. The first marshal further assigned Lü Fan and Zhu Zhi to fa-

cilitate and supervise land and sea operations of all units and assure their strict coordination. When these assignments had been
made, the various commanders put their boats and armaments
in order and set out.

Cheng Zi reported to his father that Zhou Yu's measures were
the model of military procedure. Cheng Pu, greatly impressed,
said, "I mistook Zhou Yu for a coward, a man unworthy to lead.
But if he can do this, he is a true general, and I must not show
disrespect." He then presented himself at Zhou Yu's headquarters and apologized for his conduct. Zhou Yu accepted his apology graciously.

The next day Zhou Yu said to Zhuge Jin, "Your brother has
the talent to be a king's minister. It is beneath him to serve Liu
Xuande. His fortunate arrival in the Southland offers the occasion for persuading him to stay, if I might trouble you to undertake the mission. Our lord would then have a valued adviser and
you would be reunited with your brother. What could be more
desirable? Be so kind as to pay him a little visit." "I have accomplished nothing, I regret to say, since coming to the Southland,
but I shall do all that I can to carry out the field marshal's command." So saying, Jin rode directly to see Kongming. Receiving
him at the guesthouse, Zhuge Liang prostrated himself tearfully,
and the two brothers gave vent to their deep love for one another.

"Dear brother," Zhuge Jin began, sobbing, "surely you remember the tale of Bo Yi and Shu Qi?" "Hmm," thought Kongming, "Zhou Yu must have sent him to win me over." He answered, "You mean the worthy sages of antiquity?" "Though they
died of hunger at the foot of Mount Shouyang, the two brothers
stayed together," Zhuge Jin continued. "You and I came from the
same womb, suckled at one breast. But now we serve different
lords and lead divergent lives. Reflecting on the character of Bo
Yi and Shu Qi, can you help feeling a pang of shame?" "What
you speak of, brother," Kongming replied, "pertains to the realm
of sentiment. What I must preserve is in the realm of honor. You
and I are men of the Han. Imperial Uncle Liu is a scion of the
royal house. If you could leave the Southland and join me in serving the imperial uncle, then you would have no 'pang of shame'
as a true subject of the Han, and we, as brothers, would be reunited. In this way, neither the principle of sentiment nor of

honor would be impaired. I venture to inquire how you view this proposal." "I came to ply him," thought Zhuge Jin, "and end up being plied." He had no answer to make, so he rose and took his leave.

Zhuge Jin returned to Zhou Yu and related all that Kongming had said. "How do you feel about it?" asked Zhou Yu. "I have received General Sun Quan's grace and generosity. I could never leave him." "Good sir," responded Zhou Yu, "if you will serve our lord with loyal heart, there is no need to say more. I think I know the way to make Kongming give in." Indeed:

> When wits are matched, it's best if they agree;
> But when talents clash, it's hard for them to yield.

Would Zhou Yu outwit his rival yet?
Read on.

CHAPTER 45

Cao Cao Suffers Casualties at Three Rivers; Jiang Gan Springs a Trap at the Congregation of Heroes

Zhuge Jin recounted his conversation with Kongming. As Zhou Yu listened, his hostility deepened, and he made up his mind that he would have to dispose of Kongming.

The following day, after reviewing his commanders, Zhou Yu went to take leave of Sun Quan. "You proceed," said Quan, "I will bring up the rear with another force." Zhou Yu withdrew and, together with Cheng Pu and Lu Su, commenced the expedition. He also invited Kongming, who accepted eagerly. With the four on board, the ship hoisted sail and began tacking toward Xia-kou. Some fifty *li* from Three Rivers the convoy halted. Zhou Yu, commanding the center, established his headquarters and ordered a ring of camps built along the shore around the Western Hills. Kongming betook himself to a little boat of his own.

His arrangements completed, Zhou Yu called Kongming to his tent. After the formalities, Zhou Yu said, "In an earlier campaign Cao had far fewer troops than Yuan Shao; but he won all the same by following Xu You's advice and cutting off Shao's food supply at Wuchao. Now Cao has eight hundred and thirty thousand men to our fifty or sixty thousand. How can we resist? Only by cutting off his supplies. According to information I have already gathered, everything is stored at Iron Pile Mountain. Since you have lived on the River Han and are familiar with the terrain, I wonder if I could prevail upon you, together with Lord Guan, Zhang Fei, and Zhao Zilong—as well as the thousand men that I will give you—to go at once to the mountain and sever their supply line. This would be in the interest of both our lords. I hope you will accept." Kongming mused: "He is scheming to murder me because I will not agree to leave Lord Liu. Rather than look foolish, I'll go along and figure out later what to do." And so, to Zhou Yu's satisfaction, Kongming accepted the assignment enthusiastically.

After Kongming had left, Lu Su said privately to Zhou Yu, "What's behind this sending Kongming to steal their grain?" "Killing Kongming would only invite ridicule," Zhou Yu explained. "Let Cao Cao be the one to save us future trouble." Lu Su then went to Kongming to find out what he knew. But Kongming, betraying no anxiety, was gathering his forces for roll call, preparing to set out. The kindhearted Lu Su said pointedly, "What chance does this mission have, good sir?" With a smile Kongming replied, "I have mastered the fine points of every form of warfare, naval, foot, horse, and chariot. I fear no failure—unlike Southland leaders like you, sir, or Zhou Yu, who have only one specialty." "What do you mean?" answered Lu Su. Kongming replied: "Isn't there a children's rhyme going around the south, 'To ambush a trail or hold a pass, Lu Su's the man to trust;/For marine war, Commander Zhou Yu's a must'? So it seems that you're not good for more than a roadside ambush or guarding a pass and that Zhou Yu can fight on water but not on land."

Lu Su reported this conversation to Zhou Yu, who exclaimed angrily, "So he thinks I can't fight on land! Fine. Let him stay here.

I'll raid Cao's supplies myself with ten thousand men." Lu Su carried this new development back to Kongming, who smiled as he said, "All Zhou Yu really wanted was for Cao Cao to kill me. So I teased him with that remark. He is touchy, though. This is a critical moment. My only wish is for Lord Sun and Lord Liu to work together, for then we may succeed. Plotting against one another will undo our cause. The traitor Cao has plenty of tricks. In his career as a general he's made a specialty of severing enemy supply lines; his own storage is sure to be well prepared for raids: if Zhou Yu goes they'll only capture him. What is called for now is a decisive engagement on the river to blunt the enemy's mettle while we try to work out a plan for their defeat. It's up to you to explain this to Zhou Yu in a reasonable way."

As Lu Su recounted Kongming's words that night, Zhou Yu shook his head and stamped his feet, crying, "He is ten times my better. If we don't destroy him now, he will destroy this land of ours." "At this critical time," Lu Su argued, "I hope you will consider the Southland above all. There will be time enough for such schemes after Cao Cao is defeated." Zhou Yu had to agree.

*   *   *   *

Liu Xuande charged Liu Qi with the defense of Jiangxia, while he and his commanders moved ahead to Xiakou. In the distance they saw flags and banners shadowing the river's southern shore, and row upon row of spears. Surmising that the Southland had already mobilized, Xuande shifted all the Jiangxia troops across the Great River and east to Fankou. He then addressed his followers: "We have had no word from Kongming since he went south, and no one knows how things stand. Who will find out for us and report back?" Mi Zhu volunteered, and Xuande, having provided him with sheep, wine, and other gifts, instructed him to go to the Southland and learn what he could while pretending to feast the southern troops.

Mi Zhu piloted a small boat downriver and arrived in front of Zhou Yu's camp. After being received, Mi Zhu prostrated himself, conveyed Xuande's respects, and presented the articles he had brought. Zhou Yu accepted the gifts and called a banquet to welcome Mi Zhu. "Kongming has been here too long," Mi Zhu declared. "I would like to bring him back with me." "But he is consulting with us on the campaign against Cao Cao," said Zhou Yu, "he can't simply leave. I, for my part, desire to see Lord Liu in order to confer with him. But, alas, I am personally directing the army and cannot leave the scene. How gratifying it would be, though, if Lord Liu would consider traveling here to visit me." Mi Zhu assented and returned to Xuande.

Lu Su said to Zhou Yu, "Why do you want to see Xuande?" "He's the craftiest owl on earth," responded Zhou Yu. "I must be rid of him. This is my chance to lure him here and kill him, and save our house future grief." Lu Su argued over and over against such measures—to no avail. Zhou Yu issued a secret order: "If Xuande comes, I want fifty armed men hidden behind the wall curtains. I'll throw a cup to the ground as the signal to strike."

Mi Zhu returned to Xuande and relayed Zhou Yu's invitation. Xuande called for a swift boat and set out. Lord Guan objected: "Zhou Yu is a schemer; moreover, we have no letter from Kongming. I see treachery in this. Let's think it over some more." "But they are our allies in the struggle against Cao Cao," said Xuande. "Not to go when they call violates the spirit of the alliance. Constant mutual suspicion will ruin our cause." "If you insist on going, brother," said Lord Guan, "I shall join you." "And I too," added Zhang Fei. "No. Let Lord Guan accompany me," Xuande replied. "You and Zhao Zilong can guard the camp, and Jian Yong can guard Exian. I will return soon."

Xuande and Lord Guan boarded a light craft and, with a small guard of some twenty men, sped downriver to the Southland. Xuande viewed the cutters and war-boats of his ally, their flags and armored men, their orderly array, with mounting excitement. His arrival was swiftly reported to Zhou Yu, who asked, "With how many boats?" "Just one," he was informed, "and about twenty men." "His life is mine," said Zhou Yu, smiling. He deployed his men and went forth to greet his guest. Xuande, with Lord Guan and his guards, followed his host to the main tent. Salutations exchanged, Zhou Yu saw Xuande to the seat of honor. "General," Xuande protested, "you are renowned throughout the empire. I am a man of no talent. Do not trouble so much over ceremony." They partook of a banquet as host and guest.

At the riverside Kongming discovered that Xuande and Zhou Yu were having a meeting. Anxiously entering the main tent to see what was afoot, he noted a murderous look in Zhou Yu's eye and the armed guards behind the wall curtains. "What am I to do about this?" he said to himself in alarm. He turned and observed Xuande chatting and laughing, completely at ease, while Lord Guan stood behind him, hand on his sword. "He is safe," Kongming thought and left to return to the river.

Host and guest had savored several rounds of wine when Zhou Yu stood up, cup in hand. Observing Lord Guan, hand on sword, Yu inquired who he was. "My younger brother, Guan Yunchang," replied Xuande. "Not the one who cut down generals Yan Liang and Wen Chou?" Zhou Yu asked nervously. "The same," Xuande answered. Zhou Yu, alarmed, broke into a sweat. He poured a cup for Lord Guan and drank with him. Moments later Lu Su came in. "Where's Kongming?" Xuande asked him. "Could you bring him here?" "There'll be time enough for meeting when Cao Cao is defeated," said Zhou Yu, closing the subject. Lord Guan eyed Xuande, who sensed his brother's intent and rose. "I shall bid you farewell for now," Xuande told Zhou Yu, "but I will return expressly to celebrate with you the defeat of Cao Cao." Zhou Yu made no effort to detain his guest and escorted him out the main gate.

Xuande and Lord Guan reached the edge of the river, where they found Kongming in his boat. Xuande was elated. "My lord," said Kongming, "you were in more danger than you knew!" Aghast, Xuande said, "No!" "He would have killed you, but for Lord Guan," Kongming remarked. Xuande, only then realizing the actual situation in the Southland, begged Kongming to return with him to Fankou. But Kongming said, "Here in the tiger's mouth I am as secure as Mount Tai. What you have to do is prepare your forces for action. On the twentieth day, first of the cycle, of the eleventh month, send Zhao Zilong in a small boat to wait for me at the south shore. There must be no slip-up." Xuande asked what he was planning, but Kongming simply replied, "Look for a southeast wind. That's when I'll come back." Xuande wanted to know more, but Kongming hurried him aboard and returned to his own boat.

Xuande, Lord Guan, and their followers had sailed but a few *li* when they saw fifty or sixty boats speeding downriver toward them; in the lead was General Zhang Fei, spear at the ready. Fearing some mishap to Xuande, he had come to back up Lord Guan. And so the three brothers returned to their camp together.

*   *   *   *

Zhou Yu, having seen Xuande off, returned to camp. Lu Su asked, "You lured Xuande here. Why didn't you strike?" "Lord Guan is the fiercest of generals. He never leaves Xuande's side. If I had acted, he would have slain me," Zhou Yu explained. Lu Su was astounded at the awe Lord Guan had inspired.

At that moment an emissary from Cao Cao arrived, bearing an envelope with the words "The prime minister of the Han authorizes Field Marshal Zhou to open this." Zhou Yu angrily tore the envelope, unopened, into pieces and threw them to the ground. He then ordered the bearer put to death. "Two kingdoms at war don't kill each other's envoys," Lu Su urged. "I do so to show my confidence in our strength," answered Zhou Yu. The envoy was executed, and his head was given to his attendants to carry back to Cao Cao. Zhou Yu then commanded Gan Ning to lead the van, Han Dang to lead the left wing, and Jiang Qin to lead the right, reserving for himself the task of relief and reinforcement. The next day they breakfasted at the fourth watch and sailed out at the fifth, drums and battle cries heralding their advance.

*   *   *   *

The news that Zhou Yu had destroyed his letter and beheaded his messenger infuriated Cao Cao. At once he organized a vanguard led by Cai Mao, Zhang Yun, and other Jingzhou commanders who had submitted to him. Cao Cao himself took command of the rear and supervised the transfer of the fleet to Three Rivers. Soon he saw the approaching war-boats of the southerners spread across the length and breadth of the river. Their lead general, seated in the prow of one boat, shouted out, "Gan Ning comes! Who dares oppose?" Cai Mao sent his younger brother, Xun, to meet him. The two boats drew near. Gan Ning steadied his bow and toppled Xun with one shot. Gan Ning pressed ahead, his archers massing their bolts; Cao Cao's forces reeled before the assault. Following up, Jiang Qin sailed from the right and Han Dang from the left, straight into the center of the northerners' position. Most of Cao's soldiers, coming from the provinces of Qing and Xu, were unused to naval warfare and lost their balance on the rolling ships. This gave the southerners—now augmented by Zhou Yu's force—control of the waterway. Thousands of Cao Cao's men fell by bombard or arrow in a battle that lasted from midmorning to early afternoon. But despite his advantage, Zhou Yu, still wary of Cao Cao's greater numbers, beat the gong recalling his boats.

After his defeated troops had returned, Cao Cao appeared in his land headquarters and directed the reordering of his forces. He rebuked Cai Mao and Zhang Yun: "The troops of the Southland, though few, have defeated us—because you lack commitment." Cai Mao protested, "We were defeated because the Jingzhou sailors have been off their training and because the Qingzhou and Xuzhou troops have no experience in naval warfare. The thing to do now is to establish a naval camp, placing the Qingzhou and Xuzhou troops inside, the Jingzhou troops outside, and train them every day until they are fit for combat." To this Cao replied, "You are already the chief naval commander and can perform your duties at your discretion. There's no need to petition me."

Cai Mao and Zhang Yun undertook the training of a navy. Along the river they set up a row of twenty-four water lanes for communication; the larger boats formed the outer rim, enclosing the smaller like a city wall. At night the torches lit up the sky and river, while on land the camps, which stretched for three hundred *li*, sent up smoke and fire day and night.

*   *   *   *

The triumphant Zhou Yu had returned to camp, rewarded his troops, and sent news of the victory to Sun Quan. After nightfall Zhou Yu surveyed the scene from a height: the glow in the west reached the horizon. "The fires and torches of the northern army," his aides said. Shocked, Zhou Yu decided to investigate Cao's naval encampment himself the following day. He ordered a two-tiered boat outfitted with drums and other instruments. Accompanied by his ablest commanders, all armed with longbows or crossbows, he boarded and set out.

The craft threaded its way upriver. When it reached the edge of Cao Cao's camp, Zhou Yu dropped anchor. The drums and gongs sounded, and Zhou Yu observed how the camp responded. "They have mastered the finest points of naval warfare," he exclaimed. "Who's in general command?" "Cai Mao and Zhang Yun," his assistants reported. "Longtime residents of the Southland, they're skilled in naval tactics," Zhou Yu mused. "I'll have to put them out of the way before I can defeat Cao." At that moment Cao Cao was informed of the spy ship's presence and ordered it captured. Zhou Yu saw Cao Cao's signal flags in motion and had the anchor raised; the oarsmen had pulled the two-tiered vessel more than ten *li* into open water by the time Cao Cao's boats came forth. Finding the Southland vessel out of range, the captains returned and reported to Cao Cao.

Cao Cao conferred with his commanders. "Yesterday," he said, "we lost a battle and our momentum. Now they've sailed in again, close enough to spy on our camp. How can we defeat them?" As he spoke, one man stepped forward and said, "Zhou Yu and I have been close since childhood when we were students together. Let me try my powers of persuasion on him and see if I can get him to surrender." Cao Cao turned a grateful eye on the man. It was Jiang Gan (Ziyi) of Jiujiang, a member of his council. "You are on good terms with Zhou Yu?" Cao Cao asked. "Your troubles are over, Your Excellency," said Jiang Gan. "When I go south, I shall not fail." "What will you need?" asked Cao. "A page to accompany me, two servants to row me across." Cao Cao, immensely pleased, regaled Jiang Gan with wine and saw him off. The envoy, dressed in hempen scarf and plain weave robe, sped downriver, straight to Zhou Yu's camp. His arrival was announced—"An old friend comes to pay a call"—just when Zhou Yu was in conference. Delighted by the news, he turned to his commanders and said, "The 'persuader' has come." Then he told each of them what to do, and they left to perform their duties.

Zhou Yu adjusted his cap and garb and, surrounded by several hundred in brocade clothes and decorated hats, came forth. Jiang Gan approached boldly and alone, save for his one young attendant who was dressed in plain black. Zhou Yu received him with low bows. "You have been well since we parted, I trust," said the visitor. "My friend, you have taken great trouble, coming so far to serve as Cao Cao's spokesman," Zhou Yu responded. Taken aback, Jiang Gan said, "We have been apart so long, I came especially to reminisce. How could you suspect me of such a thing?" With a smile Zhou Yu answered, "My ear may not be so fine as the great musician Shi Kuang's, but I can discern good music and good intentions too." "Dear friend," Jiang Gan replied, "if this is how you treat an old friend, I must beg my leave." Still smiling, Zhou Yu took Jiang Gan by the arm and said, "I was afraid, brother, that you were working for Cao, that's all. If you have no such purpose, there is no need to rush. Please stay." And so the two of them went into the tent. After the ritual greetings they seated themselves, and Zhou Yu summoned the notables of the south to meet his friend.

Chief officials and generals in formal dress and subordinate officers and commanders clad in silvered armor entered shortly in two columns. Zhou Yu had each dignitary introduced to Jiang Gan and seated in one of two rows to the side. A great feast was spread and victory music performed. Wine came too, round after round. Zhou Yu addressed the assembly: "Here is one of my schoolmates, a close friend. Although he has come from north of the river, he is not serving as a spokesman of Cao Cao's cause. Set your minds at ease on that score." He then removed the sword at his side and handed it to Taishi Ci, saying, "Wear the sword and supervise the banquet. We will speak of friendship today and nothing else. If anyone so much as mentions the hostilities between Cao Cao and the lord of the Southland, take off his head!" Taishi Ci acknowledged the order and sat at the feast, his hand resting on the sword. Terror-stricken, Jiang Gan said little.

"Since taking command of the army," Zhou Yu declared, "I have drunk no wine. But today, in the company of an old friend, with no lack of trust, let us have our fill and then some." With that, he laughed loudly and drank deeply. The toasts came thick and fast. When they had grown flushed and mellow, Zhou Yu took Jiang Gan by the hand, and the two friends strolled outside the tent. To the left and right of them stood soldiers in complete outfit, armed with dagger and halberd. "Formidable, are they not?" Zhou Yu asked. "Ferocious as bears, fierce as tigers," Jiang Gan agreed. Then Zhou Yu led his guest around behind the headquarters where hills of grain and fodder were stored. "Enough for any eventuality, don't you think?" Zhou Yu asked his guest.

"'Crack troops and full bins.' Your high reputation is not for nothing," Jiang Gan agreed again.

Feigning intoxication, Zhou Yu laughed heartily. "To think we were once students together!" he said. "Who would have foreseen a day like today?" "Brother," said Jiang Gan, "with your supreme abilities, such accomplishment is only too fitting." Gripping Jiang Gan's hand, Zhou Yu said, "As a man of honor all my life and one having the good fortune to serve a lord who appreciates me, I am as obligated to that honored bond between liege and liege man as I am by my kinsmen's love. What I say, he does. What I propose, he approves. His misfortunes and his blessings are mine as much as his. Were the great rhetoricians of old— Su Qin, Zhang Yi, Lu Jia, Li Yiji—were they to walk the earth again, delivering speeches like cascading streams and wielding their tongues like sharp swords, they could not move me!" Having spoken, Zhou Yu burst into laughter. Jiang Gan's face was ashen. Zhou Yu led his guest back into the tent, and the general carousing resumed. Zhou Yu pointed to his commanders and said, "These are the flower of the Southland. And this gathering today shall be known as the Congregation of the Heroes." The company kept on drinking until it was time to light the lamps. Then Zhou Yu rose and performed a sword dance, singing:

> In this life a man must make his name:
> A good name is a comfort all life long.
> A lifelong comfort: Oh, let me feel the wine,
> And flushed with wine, I'll sing my wildest song.

When he finished, the whole table laughed gaily. As the night advanced, Jiang Gan prepared to take his leave. "The wine was too much for me," he said. Zhou Yu dismissed the guests, and the commanders departed. "We have not shared a couch for many a year, my friend," Zhou Yu said. "Tonight we share a bed foot-to-foot." Again feigning intoxication, he led Jiang Gan arm in arm into his bedchamber and there collapsed, sprawling into bed fully dressed and vomiting copiously. How could Jiang Gan sleep? He lay on his pillow, listening. The drum sounded the second watch. Lifting his head, he saw the wasted candle still giving light. Zhou Yu was snoring heavily. On the table Jiang Gan noticed a sheaf of documents. He rose and stealthily looked through them: among the correspondence was a letter from Cao Cao's two naval commanders, Cai Mao and Zhang Yun. He peeked at the contents:

> We surrendered to Cao by dint of circumstance, not for wealth or rank. We have tricked the northern army by enclosing it inside the large ships. The moment we have the chance, we will deliver the traitor Cao's head to you. Someone will come with further information. Have no doubts. Herein our respectful reply.

Jiang Gan said to himself, "So Cai Mao and Zhang Yun are in league with the Southland!" and stowed the letter in his clothes. He was going to look at some of the other papers, but Zhou Yu turned over in bed. Jiang Gan extinguished the lamp and lay down. Zhou Yu began to mumble, "My friend, wait a few days and you'll see the head of that traitor Cao!" Jiang Gan managed a reply. Again Zhou Yu said, "Do stay a while . . . you'll see Cao Cao's head . . . " Jiang Gan tried to question him but saw that he had fallen fast asleep.

Jiang Gan lay on the bed. The fourth watch was near. He heard someone come into the tent and call out, "Is the marshal awake yet?" Zhou Yu, giving the appearance of a man startled from his dreams, asked the man, "Who is this sleeping on my bed?" "Marshal," was the reply, "you invited Jiang Gan to share your bed. Can you have forgotten?" In a repentant tone, Zhou Yu said, "I never allow myself to get drunk. I was not myself yesterday. I don't remember if I said anything." "Someone came from the north," said the man. "Lower your voice!" said Zhou Yu urgently. He then called Jiang Gan, but Gan feigned sleep. Zhou Yu slipped out of the tent. Gan listened intently. Outside someone was saying, "Zhang Yun and Cai Mao said, 'We are not able to take quick action . . . '" The remainder was spoken too low for Jiang Gan to make out.

Moments later Zhou Yu reentered the tent and called his friend again. Jiang Gan continued the pretense by pulling the blanket over his head and making no response. Zhou Yu took off his clothes and lay down. Jiang Gan thought, "Zhou Yu is a shrewd man. He is sure to kill me in the morning when he discovers the letter is gone." Jiang Gan rested until the fifth watch, then rose and called Zhou Yu. No answer. He put on his hood and slipped out of the tent, called his young companion and headed for the main gate. "Where to, sir?" the guard asked. "I'm afraid I have been keeping the field marshal from his work, so I am saying good-bye for now." The guard made no attempt to stop them.

Jiang Gan boarded his boat and sped back to see Cao Cao. "How did it go?" the prime minister asked. Jiang Gan said, "Zhou Yu is too high-minded to be swayed by speeches." Angrily Cao replied, "The mission failed. And we end up looking like fools!" "Though I could not persuade him to join us, I did manage to find out something of interest for Your Excellency. Would you ask the attendants to go out?" So saying, Jiang Gan produced the stolen letter and related point by point all that had happened in the bedchamber. "That's how the villains repay my kindness!" roared Cao Cao and summoned Cai Mao and Zhang Yun to his quarters at once. "I want you two to begin the attack," Cao Cao said to them. "The training is still unfinished. It would be risky," they replied. "And when the training is completed, will my head be delivered to Zhou Yu?" said Cao. Cai Mao and Zhang Yun could make no sense of this and were too confused to respond. Cao Cao called for his armed guards to put them to death. But the moment the two heads were brought in, Cao Cao realized he had been tricked. A poet of later times left these lines:

> Cao Cao, a master of intrigue,
> Fell for Zhou Yu's cunning ruse.
> Cai and Zhang betrayed their lord
> And fell to Cao Cao's bloody sword.

Cao Cao's commanders wanted to know the reason for the executions. But Cao Cao was unable to admit his mistake. "They flouted military rules; therefore, I had them killed," he said. The stunned commanders groaned and sighed. Cao Cao chose Mao Jie and Yu Jin to serve as the new chief naval commanders.

Meanwhile, spies reported the executions to Zhou Yu. "I feared those two the most," he said with satisfaction. "With them out of the way, I have no problems." "Commander," said Lu Su, "if you can wage war this well, we will have nothing to worry about. Cao will be beaten." "My guess is that none of our commanders knows what happened," said Zhou Yu, "except for Kongming, who knows more than I do. I doubt if even this plan fooled him. Try to sound him out for me. Find out if he knew. And tell me right away." Indeed:

> His success in dividing his rivals would not be complete
> Until he knew what the stony-eyed observer on the side was thinking.

Once again Lu Su went to see Kongming for Zhou Yu. Could he keep the alliance from breaking up?
Read on.

CHAPTER 46

Kongming Borrows Cao Cao's Arrows through a Ruse; Huang Gai Is Flogged Following a Secret Plan

Zhou Yu sent Lu Su to find out if Kongming had detected the subterfuge. Kongming welcomed Lu Su aboard his little boat, and the two men sat face-to-face. "Every day I am taken up with military concerns and miss your advice," Lu Su began. "Rather, I am the tardy one, having yet to convey my felicitations to the chief commander," answered Kongming. "What felicitations?" asked Lu Su. "Why," replied Kongming, "for that very matter about which he sent you here to see if I knew." The color left Lu Su's face. "But how did you know, master?" he asked. Kongming went on: "The trick was good enough to take in Jiang Gan. Cao Cao, though hoodwinked for the present, will realize what happened quickly enough—he just won't admit the mistake. But with those naval commanders dead, the Southland has no major worry, so congratulations are certainly in order. I hear that Cao Cao has replaced them with Mao Jie and Yu Jin. One way or another, those two will do in their navy!"

Lu Su, unable to respond sensibly, temporized as best he could before he rose to leave. "I trust you will say nothing about this in front of Zhou Yu," Kongming urged Lu Su, "lest he again be moved to do me harm." Lu Su agreed but finally divulged the truth when he saw the field marshal. Astounded, Zhou Yu said, "The man must die. I am determined." "If you kill him," Lu Su argued, "Cao Cao will have the last laugh." "I will have justification," answered Zhou Yu. "And he will not feel wronged." "How will you do it?" asked Lu Su. "No more questions now. You'll see soon enough," Zhou Yu replied.

The next day Zhou Yu gathered his generals together and summoned Kongming, who came eagerly. At the assembly Zhou Yu asked him, "When we engage Cao Cao in battle on the river routes, what should be the weapon of choice?" "On the Great River, bow and arrow," Kongming replied. "My view precisely, sir," Zhou Yu said. "But we happen to be short of arrows. Dare I trouble you, sir, to undertake the production of one hundred thousand arrows to use against the enemy? Please favor us with your cooperation in this official matter." "Whatever task the chief commander assigns, I shall strive to complete," replied Kongming. "But may I ask by what time you will require them?" "Can you finish in ten days?" asked Zhou Yu. "Cao's army is due at any moment," said Kongming. "If we must wait ten days, it will spoil everything." "How many days do you estimate you need, sir?" said Zhou Yu. "With all respect, I will deliver the arrows in three days," Kongming answered. "There is no room for levity in the army," Zhou Yu snapped. "Dare I trifle with the chief commander?" countered Kongming. "I beg to submit my pledge under martial law: if I fail to finish in three days' time, I will gladly suffer the maximum punishment."

Elated, Zhou Yu had his administrative officer publicly accept the document. He then offered Kongming wine, saying, "You will be well rewarded when your mission is accomplished." "It's too late to begin today," said Kongming. "Production begins tomorrow. On the third day send five hundred men to the river for the arrows." After a few more cups, he left. Lu Su said to Zhou Yu, "This man has to be deceiving us." "He is delivering himself into our hands!" replied Zhou Yu. "We did not force him. Now that he has publicly undertaken this task in writing, he couldn't escape if he sprouted wings. Just have the artisans delay delivery of whatever he needs. He will miss the appointed time; and when we fix his punishment, what defense will he be able to make? Now go to him again and bring me back news."

Lu Su went to see Kongming. "Didn't I tell you not to say anything?" Kongming began. "He is determined to kill me. I never dreamed you would expose me. And now today he actually pulled this trick on me! How am I supposed to produce one hundred thousand arrows in three days? You have to save me!" "You brought this on yourself," said Lu Su. "How can I save you?" "You must lend me twenty vessels," Kongming went on, "with a crew of thirty on each. Lined up on either side of each vessel I want a thousand bundles of straw wrapped in black cloth. I have good use for them. I'm sure we can have the arrows on the third day. But if you tell Zhou Yu this time, my plan will fail." Lu Su agreed, though he had no idea what Kongming was up to, and reported back to Zhou Yu without mentioning the boats: "Kongming doesn't seem to need bamboo, feathers, glue, or other materials. He seems to have something else in mind." Puzzled, Zhou Yu said, "Let's see what he has to say after three days have gone by."

Lu Su quietly placed at Kongming's disposal all he had requested. But neither on the first day nor on the second did Kongming make any move. On the third day at the fourth watch he secretly sent for Lu Su. "Why have you called me here?" Su asked. "Why else? To go with me to fetch the arrows," Kongming replied. "From where?" inquired Lu Su. "Ask no questions," said Kongming. "Let's go; you'll see." He ordered the boats linked by long ropes and set out for the north shore.

That night tremendous fogs spread across the heavens, and the river mists were so thick that even face-to-face people could not see each other. Kongming urged his boats on into the deep fog. The rhapsody "Heavy Mists Mantling the Yangzi" describes it well:

Vast the river! Wide and farflung! West, it laps the mountains Mang and E. South, it grips the southern shires. North, it girdles the nine rivers, gathers their waters, and carries them into the sea, its surging waves rolling through eternity.

Its depths hold monsters and strange forms: the Lord of the Dragons, the Sea Thing, the river goddesses, the Ocean Mother, ten-thousand-span whales, and the nine-headed centipede. This redoubt of gods and spirits, heroes fight to hold.

At times the forces of yin and yang that govern nature fail, and day and darkness seem as one, turning the vast space into a fearful monochrome. Everywhere the fog, stock-still. Not even a cartload can be spotted. But the sound of gong or drum carries far.

At first, a visible gloom, time for the wise leopard of the southern hills to seclude itself. Gradually darkness fills the expanse. Does it want the North Sea leviathan itself to lose its way? At last it reaches the very sky and mantles the all-upbearing earth. Grey gloomy vastness. A shoreless ocean. Whales hurtle on the waves. Dragons plunge and spew mist.

It is like the end of early rains, when the cold of latent spring takes hold: everywhere, vague, watery desert and darkness that flows and spreads. East, it blankets the shore of Chaisang. South, it blocks the hills of Xiakou. A thousand warjunks, swallowed between the river's rocky steeps, while a single fishing boat boldly bobs on the swells.

In so deep a fog, the deep-domed heavens have gone dark. The countenance of dawn is dull: the day becomes a murky twilight; the reddish hills, aquamarine jade. Great Yu, who first controlled the floods, could not with all his wisdom sound its depths. Even clear-eyed Li Lou could not use his measures, despite his keen vision.

Let the water god calm these waves. Let the god of elements put away his art. Let the sea creatures and those of land and air be gone. For now the magic isle of Penglai is cut off, and the gates of the polar stars are shrouded.

The roiling, restless fog is like the chaos before a storm, swirling streaks resembling wintry clouds. Serpents lurking there can spread its pestilence, and evil spirits can havoc wreak, sending pain and woe to the world of men, and the storms of wind and sand that plague the border wastes. Common souls meeting it fall dead. Great men observe it and despair. Are we returning to the primal state that preceded form itself—to undivided Heaven and earth?

By the fifth watch Kongming's little convoy was nearing Cao Cao's river base. The vessels advanced in single file, their prows pointed west. The crews began to roar and pound their drums. Lu Su was alarmed. "What if they make a sally?" he asked. Kongming smiled and replied, "I'd be very surprised if Cao Cao plunged into this fog. Let's pour the wine and enjoy ourselves. We'll go back when the fog lifts."

As the clamor reached Cao Cao's camp, the new naval advisers Mao Jie and Yu Jin sent reports at once. Cao Cao issued an order: "The fog has made the river invisible. This sudden arrival of enemy forces must mean an ambush. I want absolutely no reckless movements. Let the archers and crossbowmen, however, fire upon the enemy at random." He also sent a man to his land headquarters calling for Zhang Liao and Xu Huang to rush an extra three thousand crossbowmen to the shore. By the time Cao's order reached Mao Jie and Yu Jin, their men had already begun shooting for fear the southerners would penetrate their camp. Soon, once the marksmen from the land camp had joined the battle, ten thousand men were concentrating their shots toward the river. The shafts came down like rain.

Kongming ordered the boats to reverse direction and press closer to shore to receive the arrows while the crews continued drumming and shouting. When the sun climbed, dispersing the fog, Kongming ordered the boats to hurry homeward. The straw bundles bristled with arrow shafts, for which Kongming had each crew shout in unison: "Thanks to the prime minister for the arrows!" By the time this was reported to Cao Cao, the light craft, borne on swift currents, were twenty *li* downriver, beyond overtaking. Cao Cao was left with the agony of having played the fool.

Kongming said to Lu Su, "Each boat has some five or six thousand arrows. So without costing the Southland the slightest effort, we have gained over one hundred thousand arrows, which tomorrow we can return to Cao's troops—a decided convenience to us!" "Master, you are indeed supernatural," Lu Su said. "How did you know there would be such a fog today?" "A military commander is a mediocrity," Kongming explained, "unless he is versed in the patterns of the heavens, recognizes the advantages of the terrain, knows the interaction of prognostic signs, understands the changes in weather, examines the maps of deployment, and is clear about the balance of forces. Three days ago I calculated today's fog. That's why I took a chance on the three-day limit. Zhou Yu gave me ten days to finish the job, but neither materials nor workmen. He plainly meant to kill me for laxity. But my fate is linked to Heaven. How could Zhou Yu have succeeded?" Respectfully, Lu Su acknowledged Kongming's superior powers.

When the boats reached shore, five hundred men sent by Zhou Yu had already arrived to transport the arrows. Kongming directed them to take the arrows—upward of one hundred thousand of them—from the boats and to deliver them to the chief commander's tent. Meanwhile, Lu Su explained in detail to Zhou Yu how Kongming had acquired them. Zhou Yu was astounded. Then, with a long sigh of mingled admiration and despair, he said, "Kongming's godlike machinations and magical powers of reckoning are utterly beyond me!" A poet of later times left these lines in admiration:

> That day the river-shrouding fogs
> Melted all distance in a watery blur.
> Like driving rain or locusts Cao's arrows came:
> Kongming had humbled the Southland commander.

Kongming entered the camp. Zhou Yu came out of his tent and greeted him with cordial praise: "Master, we must defer to your superhuman powers of reckoning." "A petty subterfuge of common cunning," Kongming replied, "not worth your compliments." Zhou Yu invited Kongming into his tent to drink. "Yesterday," Zhou Yu said, "Lord Sun urged us to advance. But I still lack that unexpected stroke that wins the battle. I appeal to you for instruction." "I am a run-of-the-mill mediocrity," replied Kongming. "What kind of unique stratagem could I offer you?" "Yesterday I surveyed Cao's naval stations," Zhou Yu continued. "They are the epitome of strict order, all according to the book, invulnerable to any routine attack. I have one idea, but it may not be workable. Master, could you help me to decide?"

"Refrain from speaking for a moment, Chief Commander," Kongming said. "We'll write on our palms to see whether we agree or not." Zhou Yu was delighted to oblige. He called for brush and ink, and, after writing on his own masked hand, passed the brush to Kongming, who wrote on his own. Then the two men shifted closer to one another, opened their hands, and laughed. The same word was on each: fire. "Since our views coincide," said Zhou Yu, "my doubts are resolved. Protect our secret." "This is our common cause," answered Kongming. "Disclosure is unthinkable. My guess is that even though Cao Cao has twice fallen victim to my fires, he will not be prepared for this. It may be your ultimate weapon, Chief Commander." After drinking they parted. None of the commanders knew of their plan.

*   *   *   *

Cao Cao had lost a hundred and fifty or sixty thousand arrows with nothing to show for it, and a surly temper ruled his mind. Xun You put forward a plan: "With Zhou Yu and Zhuge Liang framing strategy for the Southland, there is little hope of defeating them in a quick strike. Rather, send a man to the Southland claiming to surrender, one who can serve as our spy in their camp. Then we will have a chance." "I was thinking much the same thing," said Cao. "Whom would you choose for the mission?" "We've executed Cai Mao. His clansmen are all in the army: Cai Zhong and Cai He are now lieutenant commanders. Bind those two to you, Your Excellency, with suitable favors and then send them to declare their submission to the Southland. They will not be suspected." Cao Cao agreed.

That night the prime minister secretly called the two into his tent and gave them their instructions: "I want you to take a few soldiers south and pretend to surrender. Send covert reports of all you observe. When your mission is done, you will be enfeoffed and amply rewarded. Do not waver in your loyalties." "Our families are in Jingzhou," they replied. "How could our loyalties be divided? Rest assured, Your Excellency. We will secure the heads of Zhou Yu and Zhuge Liang and place them before you." Cao Cao paid them handsomely. The next day Cai Zhong and Cai He sailed south in several boats, accompanied by five hundred men and headed for the southern shore on a favorable wind.

Zhou Yu was working on preparations for his attack when it was reported that the ships approaching from the north shore were bringing two defectors, kinsmen of Cai Mao's, Cai He and Cai Zhong. Zhou Yu summoned them into his presence, and the two men prostrated themselves, weeping as they spoke: "Cao Cao has murdered our elder brother, an innocent man. We want to avenge him. So we have come to surrender in the hope that you will grant us a place. We want to serve in the front line." Delighted, Zhou Yu rewarded them handsomely and ordered them to join Gan Ning in the vanguard. The two men gave their respectful thanks, believing their plan had worked.

Zhou Yu, however, secretly instructed Gan Ning: "This is a false surrender. They have not brought their families. Cao Cao has sent them here to spy. I want to give him a taste of his own medicine by giving them certain information to send back. Be as solicitous of them as possible, but on your guard. The day we march, we will sacrifice them to our banners. Take the strictest precautions against any slip-up." Gan Ning left with his orders.

Lu Su said to the chief commander, "The surrender of Cai Zhong and Cai He is undoubtedly a pretense. We should not accept it." Zhou Yu rebuked him: "They have come to avenge their brother whom Cao Cao murdered. What 'pretense' are you talking about? If you are so full of suspicions, how are we going to open our arms to the talents of the realm?" Silently, Lu Su withdrew and went to inform Kongming, who smiled but said nothing. "What are you smiling at?" Lu Su demanded. "At your failure to detect Zhou Yu's plan. Spies cannot cross the river so easily. Cao Cao sent them to defect so that he could probe our situation. Zhou Yu is fighting fire with fire and wants them to transmit certain information. 'There is no end of deception in warfare'—Zhou Yu's plan exemplifies the adage." And so Lu Su left enlightened.

*   *   *   *

One night Zhou Yu was sitting in his tent when Huang Gai stole in. "You must have a fine plan to show me, coming in the night like this." said Zhou Yu. "The enemy is too numerous," said Huang Gai, "for us to maintain this standoff long. Why don't we attack with fire?" "Who told you to offer this plan?" Zhou Yu asked. "No one," he replied. "It's my own idea." "Well, it's exactly what I mean to do," said Zhou Yu. "That's why I'm keeping those two false defectors: to convey false information to Cao's camp. But I need a man to play the same game for us." "I am willing to do it," Huang Gai answered. "What credibility will you have," said Zhou Yu, "if you show no sign of having suffered?" "To requite the favor and generosity that the house of Sun has bestowed on me," Huang Gai answered, "I would freely and willingly strew my innards on the ground." Bowing low, Zhou Yu thanked him, saying, "If you are willing to carry out this trick of being flogged to win the enemy's confidence, it will be a manifold blessing to the Southland." "Even if I die, I will die content," was Huang Gai's reply. He took leave of Zhou Yu and departed.

The next day Zhou Yu sounded the drums, convening a general assembly of his commanders outside his tent. Kongming too was in attendance. Zhou Yu began: "Cao Cao's million-strong horde, deployed along a three-hundred-*li* stretch of land and shore, will not be defeated in a single day. I am ordering the commanders to take three months' rations and prepare to defend our line." Huang Gai came forward, interrupting him. "Never mind three months'—thirty months' rations won't do the job," he said. "If we can beat them this month, then let's do it. If not, what choice have we but to go along with Zhang Zhao's advice, throw down our weapons, face north, and sue for peace?"

Zhou Yu exploded in fury. "I bear our lord's mandate," he cried, "to lead our troops to destroy Cao Cao. The next man to advocate surrender dies! Now at the very moment of confrontation between the two armies, how dare you weaken our morale? If I spare you, how will I hold my men?" Roughly, he barked orders to his guards to remove Huang Gai, execute him, and report back when done. Huang Gai turned to denounce him: "My service to Lord Sun's father, General Sun Jian, has taken me the length and breadth of the Southland through three successive reigns. Where do the likes of you come from?" Zhou Yu ordered immediate execution.

Gan Ning rushed forward and made an appeal: "Huang Gai is one of the Southland's elder leaders. I beg you to be lenient." "What are you trying to do, destroy the rules of the army?" Zhou Yu shouted back and barked orders to his guards to drive Gan Ning from the assembly with their clubs. At this point the entire assembly got on their knees, attempting to intercede: "No doubt Huang Gai deserves to die for his offense, but that would not be in the interests of the army. Let the chief commander be lenient and simply make note of his act for the present time. There will be time enough to dispose of him after we have beaten Cao Cao." Zhou Yu would not relent, but in the face of the strenuous protests of his commanders, he said, "If not for my consideration for your views, he would lose his head. But I shall spare him for now." Then, turning to his attendants, he added, "Throw him to the ground. One hundred strokes across the back should teach him a proper lesson." The commanders renewed their appeals for Huang Gai, but Zhou Yu overturned his table, silenced them with a gesture, and ordered the whipping carried out.

Huang Gai was stripped and forced facedown to the ground. After fifty blows of the rod the officers once again appealed for mercy. Zhou Yu jumped to his feet and, pointing at Huang Gai, said, "You have dared to show your disrespect! The other fifty will be held in reserve. Any further insults will be doubly punished." Still muttering angrily, he reentered his tent. The officers helped Huang Gai to his feet. His skin was broken everywhere and his oozing flesh was crossed with welts. Returning to his camp, he fainted several times. All who came to express their sympathy wept freely. Among the callers was Lu Su.

Afterward Lu Su went to Kongming's boat. "Zhou Yu made Huang Gai pay for it today," Lu Su said. "As his subordinates, we couldn't plead too hard and incur Zhou Yu's displeasure. But you, sir, are a guest. Why did you stand by so apparently unconcerned?" Kongming smiled and answered, "Don't mock me, Lu Su." "Since crossing the river together," Lu Su protested, "when have I mocked you? Do not say such things!" "Don't tell me, my friend," Kongming went on, "you didn't know today's beating was all a trick. What would be the point of having me oppose it?" These words awakened Lu Su to the meaning of what had happened. "Without the 'battered-body trick,'" Kongming remarked, "how could Cao Cao be taken in? Zhou Yu will be sending Huang Gai over to 'defect,' so he wants Cai Zhong and Cai He to report today's events to Cao Cao. But it is imperative that Zhou Yu not know that I know. Tell him simply that I too resented the beating."

After leaving Kongming, Lu Su went to Zhou Yu, and the two men conferred privately. "Why did you condemn Huang Gai so bitterly today?" Lu Su asked. "Did the commanders resent it?" responded Zhou Yu. "Most of them were disturbed," answered Lu Su. "And Kongming?" Zhou Yu asked. "He too expressed unhappiness at your extreme intolerance," replied Lu Su. "This time around I have deceived him," said Zhou Yu. "What?" Lu Su asked. "The beating was a ruse," Zhou Yu explained. "I wanted Huang Gai to feign defection, and his body had to be badly bruised to make it convincing. While Huang Gai is in their camp, we will attack with fire; victory will be ours." Lu Su marveled to himself at Kongming's insight but dared not breathe a word.

*   *   *   *

Huang Gai lay in his tent. All the commanders came to sympathize. Gai moaned but did not speak. When the military counselor Kan Ze arrived to pay his respects, Huang Gai dismissed his attendants. "I can't believe you have made an enemy of the chief commander," Kan Ze said. "I haven't," Huang Gai replied. "Then your punishment must be a trick to win the enemy's confidence," Kan Ze said. "How did you know?" asked Huang Gai. "I was watching Zhou Yu's every move," Kan Ze responded, "and guessed the truth pretty much." "The house of Sun has been my benefactor under three masters," said Huang Gai. "I proposed this plan for destroying Cao because of my appreciation, and I submitted to this beating willingly. But there is no one in the army I could trust to help me, except for you, who have a loyal and honorable mind and the courage to serve our lord without question." "Do you mean," Kan Ze said, "that you want me to deliver the letter of surrender?" "That is my wish. Are you willing?" Huang Gai asked. Eagerly, Kan Ze accepted. Indeed:

> A brave general requites his lord without a thought for his own
>   safety;
> A counselor serves his land with the selfsame devotion.

What would Kan Ze say next?
Read on.

CHAPTER 47

Kan Ze's Secret Letter Offering a Sham Surrender; Pang Tong's Shrewd Plan for Connecting the Boats

Kan Ze (Derun) came from Shanyin county in Kuaiji district. His family was poor, but he was a devoted student and performed menial chores in exchange for the loan of books. Kan Ze could grasp a text in one reading and was eloquent in argument. Even as a youth he had the courage of his convictions. When Sun Quan summoned Kan Ze to serve as a consultant, Huang Gai, impressed by his ability as well as his mettle, befriended him; and this is how Huang Gai came to choose Kan Ze to present his sham appeal to Cao Cao.

Kan Ze responded eagerly to Huang Gai's proposition: "The man of honor will decay and vanish like a plant unless he can make his mark in this world. Since your life is pledged to requite your lord, can I begrudge my own worthless self?" Huang Gai rolled down from his bed and prostrated himself in gratitude. "This matter brooks no delay," Kan Ze said. "Let's start at once." "The letter is written," Huang Gai said and handed it over.

Disguised as a fisherman, Kan Ze guided a small craft to the north shore that very night under a winter sky filled with stars. At the third watch he reached Cao's camp. The river patrol who captured him reported to Cao Cao. "A spy for sure," Cao said. "Only a fisherman," said the guard, "but he claims to be Kan Ze, consultant to Sun Quan, with something confidential to present to you." Cao Cao had Kan Ze brought before him. In Cao's tent, lit by flaming candles, Kan Ze could see Cao Cao sitting rigidly at his desk. "If you are an adviser to Sun Quan," Cao said, "what brings you here?"

"People say," Kan Ze began, "that Your Excellency yearns for men of ability. But your question belies your reputation. Oh, Huang Gai, you have miscalculated once again!" "I am about to go to war with Sun Quan," Cao Cao said. "and you come stealing over here! How can I not ask?" "On Zhou Yu's orders," Kan Ze went on, "Huang Gai, who has served three rulers of the house of Sun, was brutally and gratuitously beaten today in front of all the generals. Outraged and vengeful, he wants to defect and has placed his case in my hands, for he and I are as close as flesh and blood. I have come directly to present his secret letter. I wish to know if Your Excellency is willing to take him in." "Where is the letter?" Cao asked. Kan Ze passed it up to the prime minister. Cao slit the envelope and read the letter beneath the burning candles. It said in essence:

As a beneficiary of the Suns' generous favor, I should never waver in my loyalty. But it is evident to all that the soldiers of the six southern districts have no chance whatsoever of stopping the north's million-fold host. All the southern generals and officials, even the most obtuse, recognize the impossibility of it—except for that rascal Zhou Yu, who, out of shallow willfulness and an exaggerated sense of his own ability, seems determined to "smash a rock with an egg." He has, moreover, assigned rewards and punishments without reason so that the blameless suffer and the deserving are ignored. And I, humiliated without cause after long years of service to the house of Sun, feel heartfelt hatred. Believing that Your Excellency handles all situations with true sincerity and welcomes men of ability with true humility, I have decided to lead my men in surrender to you, both to establish my merit and to erase my shame. Provisions and equipment will be offered in accompanying ships. Weeping bitter blood, I speak bent to the ground. Never doubt me!

Seated there, Cao Cao read the letter over and over. Suddenly he struck the table and, eyes widening in anger, cried, "It's the old trick of being flogged to win the enemy's confidence! Huang Gai had you carry a letter of sham surrender, fishing for advantage in the confusion. You dare trifle with me, do you?" He ordered Kan Ze removed and executed. But Kan Ze's expression did not alter as the guards hustled him off. He simply looked to the sky and laughed. Cao Cao had him dragged back and said viciously, "I have seen through your scheme. What are you laughing at?" "Not at you," replied Kan Ze, "but at Huang Gai for thinking he knows men." "Meaning?" asked Cao. "Kill me and be done with it," said Ze. "Why bother with questions?" "From my youngest days," said Cao, "I have studied manuals of warfare and am well acquainted with the ways and means of deception. This trick of yours might have fooled someone else, but not me." "Where do you find trickery in this letter?" Kan Ze responded. "I'll tell you so that you may die content," Cao said. "If this surrender were genuine, the letter would specify a time. Can you talk your way out of that?" Kan Ze laughed out loud again. "What a shame! And all that bragging about your knowledge of manuals. You'd better take your forces home as soon as you can, for if you fight, Zhou Yu will capture you. Know-nothing! More's the pity that I should die at your hands." "Why 'know-nothing'?" Cao demanded. "Because you know nothing of strategy or principles," answered Kan

Ze. "All right, then," said Cao, "point out my errors." "You mistreat the worthy—why should I say it?" said Ze. "Let me die and be done." "If you talk sense," said Cao, "of course I will show you due respect." Kan Ze continued, "You must know the adage, 'There's no set time for betraying one's lord.' Were Huang Gai to set a time and then at the crucial moment find himself unable to act while the other side was already making its move, why, the whole thing would be exposed. One can only wait for the convenient moment. How can such a thing be arranged ahead of time? If you don't understand even this basic principle and are determined to kill a well-meaning friend, that is indeed the height of ignorance."

On hearing this speech, Cao Cao relaxed his expression, came down from his seat, and apologized to Kan Ze, saying, "To be sure, I have been blind, and I have offended your dignity, too. But do not hold it against me." "Huang Gai and I," said Ze, "are coming over to your side with full hearts, like infants turning to their parents. There is no deception in this." Delighted, Cao Cao said, "If the two of you can achieve real merit, you will be rewarded far above all others." "It is not for rank or emolument that we come," answered Ze. "We are doing what Heaven ordains and men approve." Cao poured wine to entertain him.

In a little while someone entered the tent and whispered to Cao, who said, "Bring me the letter." The man presented a secret missive, which seemed to give Cao great satisfaction. Kan Ze said to himself, "This must be Cai Zhong and Cai He's report on the beating of Huang Gai. Cao looks pleased because this verifies that my surrender is genuine." "I will trouble you, sir," Cao Cao said to Kan Ze, "to return south to complete the arrangements with Huang Gai. Let me know when he will be coming, and my men will help him." "I cannot go south now that I have left," Kan Ze said. "I beg Your Excellency to send another trusted man." "If I do," Cao said, "our plans will be discovered." Kan Ze held back until at long last he said, "Then I must return here swiftly."

Refusing Cao Cao's parting offer of gold and silk, Kan Ze sailed back to the Southland, where he saw Huang Gai and related the details of his mission. "If not for your clever replies," Huang Gai said, "I would have suffered for naught." "I am going to Gan

Ning's camp to find out what Cai Zhong and Cai He have been up to," Kan Ze said. "A good idea," replied Huang Gai.

Kan Ze was received at Gan Ning's camp. "Yesterday, General," Ze said, "you were humiliated by Zhou Yu for trying to save Huang Gai. I am outraged at the injustice done you." Ning smiled and made no reply. At that moment Cai Zhong and Cai He entered. Ze eyed Ning, who caught his meaning and said, "Zhou Yu is all too confident of his own abilities and takes us for granted. I have been humiliated, disgraced before the notables of the south." So saying, he clenched his teeth, slammed the table, and shouted. Kan Ze then spoke softly into Gan Ning's ear. Ning lowered his head but only uttered a few sighs. Cai He and Cai Zhong, sensing their discontent, asked pointedly, "General, what vexes you? And you, good sir, what injustice have you suffered?" "How could you know the bitterness in our hearts?" Kan Ze said. "Could it be that you wish to turn from Sun Quan to Cao Cao?" asked Cai He. Kan Ze paled. Gan Ning drew his sword and stood up. "We are discovered!" he cried. "We must kill them lest they betray us." The two Cais said urgently, "Fear us not, gentlemen. We have something to confess."

"Out with it," said Gan Ning. "Cao Cao sent us as false defectors," said Cai He. "If you gentlemen are minded to give allegiance to the rightful ruler, we can arrange it." "Is what you say true?" asked Gan Ning. In unison the two Cais replied, "How could we falsify something like this?" Feigning pleasure, Gan Ning said, "Then Heaven sends this opportunity." "The disgrace that you and Huang Gai suffered has already been reported to the prime minister," the two Cais assured them. Kan Ze said, "I have already delivered to His Excellency a letter of surrender from Huang Gai. I have come to Gan Ning today to ask him to join us." "When a man of action meets a wise lord," said Gan Ning, "he should put himself wholeheartedly at his disposal." After these words the four men drank together and spoke in tones of deepest confidentiality. The two Cais informed Cao Cao at once of these developments, adding in their letter, "Gan Ning will be working with us from within." Kan Ze penned a separate letter, to be sent by secret courier, informing Cao Cao that "Huang Gai desires to come and awaits the opportunity. Look for a boat with a blue-green jack at the prow. That will be him."

*   *   *   *

Meanwhile, Cao Cao, having received the two letters, had yet to reach a decision. He summoned his advisers. "Gan Ning of the Southland," Cao began, "disgraced by Zhou Yu, has decided to collaborate with us. Huang Gai, condemned by Zhou Yu, has sent Kan Ze to negotiate his surrender. I remain dubious about both. Can anyone here get into Zhou Yu's camp and find out what's going on?" Jiang Gan proposed, "I still feel a sting of shame for the failure of my last visit to Sun Quan. I'd like to try again now, whatever the risk, in order to bring some solid information back to Your Excellency." Delighted, Cao Cao had Jiang Gan provided with a boat. Jiang Gan reached the camp on the river's southern shore and sent someone to announce him. Zhou Yu was overjoyed. "This man will bring me success again," he said. Zhou Yu also told Lu Su: "Now I want to see Pang Tong . . . "

Pang Tong (Shiyuan), originally from Xiangyang, had earlier come south to escape the disorders in the north, and Lu Su had recommended him to Zhou Yu. Though Pang Tong had not yet presented himself, Zhou Yu, through Lu Su, had solicited Pang Tong's advice on how to defeat Cao Cao. "You must use fire," Pang Tong had privately told Lu Su. "But on the river if one boat burns, the others will scatter unless someone can convince Cao to connect up his ships—you know, the 'boat-connecting scheme.' That's the only way it will work." Impressed with this advice, Zhou Yu had told Lu Su, "Only Pang Tong can get that done for us." "Cao Cao is too cunning," said Lu Su. "He won't succeed."

So things stood, with Zhou Yu brooding over the possibilities, when the announcement of Jiang Gan's arrival roused the chief commander to action. He ordered Pang Tong to carry out his plan. Remaining in his tent, Zhou Yu had his men receive the guest. Jiang Gan, uneasy because Zhou Yu had not met him personally, ordered his boat tied up at an out-of-the-way spot before appearing.

"Why have you deceived me so dreadfully?" Zhou Yu, looking wrathful, said to Jiang Gan. Jiang Gan smiled. "I was just thinking," he said. "You and I are brothers from way back. I have come to reveal something of particular import. Why do you speak of deception?" "You want to talk me into surrendering," said Zhou

Yu, "or else the ocean has dried up and the mountains have melted. Last time, mindful of our long-standing friendship, I invited you to drink with me and share my couch. But you stole a personal letter, left without saying good-bye, and betrayed me. Cao put Cai Mao and Zhang Yun to death and thereby ruined my plans. Now you come again, but what for? You certainly don't mean me well. Were it not for our old friendship, I'd have you cut in two! I was going to send you back, but we expect to attack the traitor Cao in a day or two. And I can't keep you here, either, or my plans will get out." Zhou Yu ordered his aides: "Escort Jiang Gan to the Western Hills retreat to rest," adding, "after Cao's defeat we'll send you home."

Jiang Gan tried to speak, but Zhou Yu had already walked away. The aides provided Jiang Gan with a horse to ride to the retreat, where two soldiers attended him. Inside, Gan found himself too depressed to sleep or eat. Stars filled the sky; dew covered the ground. Alone he stepped outside and behind the dwelling. Somewhere someone was reading aloud. He walked on and saw by the cliffside several thatched huts, lit from within. Jiang Gan went over and peeked into one: a man sat alone, sword hanging in front of the lamp, intoning the military classics of Sunzi and Wu Qi. "He must be someone extraordinary," thought Jiang Gan. And he knocked on the door, seeking an interview.

An unusual-looking man came out and met Jiang Gan. Gan asked his name, and he replied, "Pang Tong." "Not Master Young Phoenix!" exclaimed Jiang Gan. "The same," he said. "Your great name has long been known to me," Jiang Gan went on. "But what has brought you to this remote spot?" "Zhou Yu has the greatest confidence in his own ability," replied Pang Tong, "but he is too intolerant, so I have hidden myself here. Who are you, sir?" "Jiang Gan," he replied. Pang Tong invited him into his dwelling, where they sat and spoke freely. "A man of your talents," Jiang Gan said, "could prosper wherever he went. If you would consider serving Cao Cao, I could arrange it." "I have wanted to leave the Southland for a long, long time," Pang Tong said. "If you are willing to arrange the introduction, I will make the trip now. If I delay, Zhou Yu will hear of it and I will be killed."

And so Pang Tong left the hill that same night with Jiang Gan. They reached the shore and found the boat that had brought

Jiang Gan south. Swift rowers brought them to the north shore. At Cao's camp Jiang Gan came before Cao first and related the events of the past days. Cao Cao, hearing of Master Young Phoenix's arrival, came out of his tent to escort him in personally. When they had seated themselves as host and guest, Cao Cao said, "Zhou Yu is immature. Overconfident of his abilities, he oppresses his followers and rejects sound strategy. Your great name has long been familiar to me, and we welcome your gracious regard. May I hope that you will not deny us advice and instruction?"

Pang Tong replied, "People have always said that Your Excellency's use of military forces sets the standard. But I would like to look over the features of your deployment for myself." Cao called for horses and invited his guest to review his land bases. From an elevation they viewed the scene below. Pang Tong said, "Backed up against woody hills, easy signaling from front to rear, exits and entries, labyrinthine passages—if the ancient masters of the art of war, Sunzi, Wu Qi, Sima Rangju, were reborn they could not surpass it." "You should not overpraise me, master," said Cao, "I still look to you for improvement."

Next, they reviewed the naval stations. There were twenty-four openings facing south, and in each the attack boats and warships were laid out like a city wall, within which clustered the smaller craft. For passage there were channels, and everything proceeded in good order. Smiling delightedly, Pang Tong said to Cao Cao, "Excellency, if your use of forces is like this, your reputation has not preceded you for naught!" So saying, Pang Tong pointed across the river and cried, "Zhou Yu, Zhou Yu, the day of your doom is fixed!"

Immensely pleased, Cao returned to camp and invited Pang Tong into his tent to share his wine and talk of military machinations. Pang Tong spoke with profundity and eloquence. Cao Cao felt his admiration and respect deepen, and treated his guest with solicitous hospitality. Feigning intoxication, Pang Tong said, "You have good medical services for the troops, no doubt?" "Of what use would that be?" Cao asked. "There is much illness among the sailors," responded Pang Tong, "and good physicians are needed to cure them."

The truth was that at this time Cao's men, unable to adjust to the southern clime, had been seized with nausea and vomiting, and many had died. Cao Cao was preoccupied with the problem and was naturally receptive to Pang Tong's remark. "Your Excellency," Pang Tong went on, "your methods for training a navy are superb—only, unfortunately, something is missing." Cao Cao importuned him until Pang Tong replied, "There is a way to free the sailors of their ailments, to make them steady and capable of success." Cao Cao was delighted and eager to learn.

"On the Great River the tide swells and recedes," Pang Tong continued, "and the wind and the waves never subside. These northern troops, unaccustomed to shipboard, suffer from the pitching and rolling. This is the cause of their ailment. Reorganize your small and large vessels: marshal them in groups of thirty or fifty and make them fast with iron hoops, stem to stem and stern to stern. Then, if wide planks are laid so that horses as well as men can cross from ship to ship, however rough the waves or steep the swells, what will you have to fear?"

Cao Cao quit his seat to express his deep gratitude: "But for your sound advice, master, I could never destroy Sun Quan." "My uninformed views," responded Pang Tong, "are for Your Excellency to use as he sees fit." Cao Cao issued an immediate order for all blacksmiths in the army to manufacture hoops and large nails to bind the boats. The news cheered the men. In the words of a later poet,

> In Red Cliffs' bitter trial, they fought with fire:
> Fire's the perfect weapon, all agreed.
> But it was Pang Tong's boat-connecting scheme
> That let Zhou Yu accomplish his great deed.

Pang Tong turned to Cao Cao and added, "In my view, most of the great families of the south have deep grievances against Zhou Yu. Let me use my limber little tongue to persuade them on Your Excellency's behalf to join our side. If Zhou Yu can be isolated, he will be yours. And once Zhou Yu is defeated, Liu Bei will have nowhere to turn." "Master," replied Cao Cao, "if you can indeed accomplish so much, I will personally petition the Emperor to honor you as one of the three elder lords." "I do not care for wealth and status," Pang Tong answered. "My one concern is the common people. When you cross the river, Your Excellency, spare them, I pray you." "I act for Heaven," said Cao, "to promote the rightful way of government. How could I bear to do anything cruel?"

Pang Tong next requested a letter to ensure the safety of his own clan. "Where are the members of your family, now?" Cao asked. "They're all near the river," Tong answered. "Your letter will ensure their safety." Cao Cao ordered an official document for which Pang Tong thanked him, saying, "After I go, advance quickly. Waste no time, lest Zhou Yu realize what is up." Cao Cao agreed.

Pang Tong departed. He had reached the riverbank and was about to embark, when he spied someone on shore wearing a Taoist priest's gown and a hat of bamboo. With one hand the Taoist grabbed Pang Tong and said, "Your audacity is remarkable! Huang Gai works the 'battered-body scheme,' Kan Ze delivers the letter announcing Huang Gai's sham defection, and now you submit the plan for linking the boats—your only concern being that the flames might not consume everything! Such insidious mischief may be enough to take in Cao Cao, but it won't work on me." This accusation terrified Pang Tong, who felt as if his heart and soul would flee his body. Indeed:

> Can the southeast ever prevail in victory
> When the northwest holds men of genius, too?

Who challenged Pang Tong?
  Read on.

CHAPTER 48

Feasting on the Great River, Cao Cao
Sings an Ode; Linking Its Boats,
the North Prepares for War

Astounded by the stranger's whispered words, Pang Tong turned and found himself looking at his old friend Xu Shu [Shan Fu].

Tong became calm at once and, sure of their privacy, said, "If you reveal my plan, the inhabitants of the Southland's eighty-one counties will suffer disaster." "And what of the lives and fate of the eighty-three legions over here?" Xu Shu asked with a grin. "You don't mean to give me away?" Pang Tong pleaded. "I will always be grateful for Imperial Uncle Liu's kindness, and I intend to repay it. Cao Cao sent my mother to her death; I promised then I would never frame strategy for him. Of course I am not going to expose your very effective plan. The problem is, I am here with Cao Cao's army, and when they are destroyed, the jewel won't be distinguished from the rock. How do I avoid disaster? Suggest some device to save me, and I will sew up my lips and remove myself." Smiling, Pang Tong said, "Someone as shrewd and far-seeing as you should have no difficulty." "I crave your guidance," Xu Shu insisted, and so Pang Tong whispered a few vital words into his ear and received his heartfelt thanks. Thus Pang Tong left his friend and sailed back to the Southland.

That night Xu Shu secretly had a close companion spread rumors through Cao's camps. The following day the rumors were on everyone's lips. Soon informants reported to Cao Cao: "The whole army is talking about Han Sui and Ma Teng, saying they have rebelled and are on their way from Xiliang to seize the capital." Alarmed, Cao Cao summoned his advisers. "My greatest concern when I undertook this expedition," he said, "was the danger from the west, Han Sui and Ma Teng. Whether the current rumors are true or not, we must take measures."

Xu Shu came forward with a proposal: "I have the honor of being in Your Excellency's employ, but to my dismay have not in any way justified your confidence. I wish to request three thousand soldiers to take at once to San Pass to seal this key point of access against invasion from the west. In the event of an emergency, I will report immediately." Delighted, Cao said, "With you at the pass, I need not worry. Take command of the troops already there. I will give you three thousand more, mounted men and foot soldiers, and Zang Ba to lead the vanguard. Leave without delay." Xu Shu bid Cao Cao good-bye and set out with Zang Ba. Thus Pang Tong saved Xu Shu's life. A poet of later times wrote:

Cao's southern march—every day a trial,
As rumors spread of fresh calamity.
Pang Tong counseled Xu Shu what to do:
Once let off the hook, the fish swims free.

After dispatching Xu Shu to the north, Cao Cao's mind was easier. He rode to the riverbank to review the army camps and the naval stations. Boarding one of the larger ships, he planted in its center a banner marked "Supreme Commander." To his left and right the naval stations stretched along the river; aboard the ship a thousand crossbowmen lay in wait. Cao Cao stood on the deck. It was the thirteenth year of Jian An, the fifteenth day of the eleventh month [December 10, A.D. 208]. The weather was clear and bright, the wind calm, the waves still. Cao Cao ordered a feast and entertainment for the commanders that evening. The complexion of the heavens reflected the advancing night as the moon climbed over the eastern mountains and beamed down, turning night to day. The Great River lay slack, like a bolt of white silk unrolled.

Aboard ship, Cao Cao was surrounded by several hundred attendants in damask coats and embroidered jackets. They all shouldered lances and each man held a halberd. The officers and officials were seated in order. Cao Cao took in the picturesque Southern Screen Hills. To the east he could see the boundary marked by Chaisang. To the west he contemplated the course of the Great River before it reached Xiakou. To the south he looked out on Mount Fan; and to the north he peered into the Black Forest of Wulin. Wherever he turned, the view stretched into infinity, gladdening his heart. He spoke to the assembly: "We have raised this loyalist force to purge evil and dispel threats to the ruling family, for I have sworn to scour the realm, to calm the empire by my sure sword. The Southland alone remains outside our sphere. Today I possess a million heroic fighters. And with you to apply our commands, need we fear for our success? When we have received the submission of the Southland and the empire is at peace, we shall share with you the enjoyments of wealth and station to celebrate the Great Millennium." The audience rose as one to give their leader thanks: "May the song of victory soon be on your lips! May we live by Your Excellency's favor all of our days."

Cao Cao was gratified and ordered the wine sent round. The night of drinking wore on, and Cao Cao was well in his cups when he pointed south and said, "Zhou Yu! Lu Su! How little you know the appointments of Heaven. These defectors to our cause will be your ruin. You see, Heaven itself lends us aid." "Say no more, Your Excellency," Xun You warned, "lest the wrong people hear." Cao laughed and said, "Every man here—whether attendants or companions of our table—is in our deepest trust. Let us be free with one another." He turned toward Xiakou and, pointing again, said, "Liu Bei! Zhuge Liang! You have failed to measure your antlike strength in attempting to shake Mount Tai. What folly!" To his generals he said, "Now I am fifty-four. If we take the Southland, I shall have my humble wish. Long ago I befriended the patriarch Qiao, knowing that his two daughters were the beauties of the empire. To think that Sun Ce and Zhou Yu would take them to wife before me! Recently I built the Bronze Bird Tower on the River Zhang. If I win the Southland, I will take these women to wife and install them in the tower to pleasure me in my advanced years. And all my wishes will be satisfied!" With that he burst into laughter. The Tang dynasty poet Du Mu wrote these lines:

> Half-rusted, broken in the sand, this halberd,
> Scraped and cleaned, calls up an era past.
> Had that east wind not done Zhou Yu a turn,
> Two Qiaos in spring would have gone to the tower.

Cao Cao was still laughing and talking when they all heard a raven cawing as it flew southward. "Why does the raven cry in the night?" Cao asked. Those around him replied, "It supposes the brilliance of the moon to be the dawn. That is why it has left its tree and cries." Cao laughed again. Already drunk, he set his spear in the prow of the boat and offered wine to the river. Then he quaffed three full goblets and, leveling his spear, said to his commanders, "Here is the weapon that broke the Yellow Scarves, took Lü Bu, eliminated Yuan Shu, subdued Yuan Shao, penetrated beyond the northern frontier, and conquered the east as far as Liaodong. In the length and breadth of this land no man has withstood me. My ambitions have always been those of a man of action, a leader among men. And now the scene before us fills my soul with profound passion. I shall perform a song, and you must join me." Cao Cao recited:

> Here before us, wine and song!
> For man does not live long.
> Like daybreak dew,
> His days are swiftly gone.
> Sanguine-souled we have to be!
> Though painful memory haunts us yet.
> Thoughts and sorrows naught allays,
> Save the cup Du Kang first set.
> "Deep the hue of the scholar's robe;
> Deeper, the longing of my heart."
> For all of you, my dearest lords,
> I voice again this ancient part.
> Nibbling on the duckweed,
> "Loo! Loo!" the lowing deer.
> At our feast sit honored guests
> For string and reed to cheer.
> The moon on high beckons bright,
> But no man's ever stayed it.
> Heart's care rises from within,
> And nothing can deny it.
> Take our thanks for all your pains;
> Your presence does us honor.
> Reunited on this feasting day,
> We well old loves remember.
> The moon is bright, the stars are few,
> The magpie black as raven.
> It southbound circles thrice a tree
> That offers him no haven.
> The mountaintop no height eschews;
> The sea eschews no deep.
> And the Duke of Zhou spat out his meal
> An empire's trust to keep.

As Cao Cao finished, the assembly took up the singing amid general enjoyment, until someone stepped forward and said, "Great armies stand opposed. Our officers and men are ready for action. Why does Your Excellency utter ominous words at such a time?"

Cao Cao turned to the speaker, imperial inspector of Yangzhou, Liu Fu (Yuanying) from Xiang in the fief of Pei, Cao Cao's home district. Liu Fu had started his career at Hefei where he established the provincial seat of government. He collected those who had fled or scattered, established schools, expanded the "soldier-tiller" acreage, and revived orderly administration. During his long service to Cao Cao he had many accomplishments to his credit.

On this occasion Cao Cao leveled his spear and asked, "And what do you find 'ominous' about my words?" Liu Fu replied, "You sang,

> The moon is bright, the stars are few,
> The magpie black as raven.
> It southbound circles thrice a tree
> That offers him no haven.

These are ominous words." "You dare to wreck our delight and enthusiasm!" Cao cried angrily. With a single heave of his spear Cao Cao pierced Liu Fu through, killing him. The assembly was aghast. The banquet was dismissed. The following day, sobered and wracked with remorse, Cao Cao wept as he told Liu Xi, the son who had come to claim the body, "Yesterday while drunk I did your father a terrible injustice, for which I can never atone. He shall be interred with the highest honors, those reserved for the three elder lords." Cao Cao sent soldiers to escort the coffin for burial in Liu Fu's native district.

*   *   *   *

The next day the new naval commanders, Mao Jie and Yu Jin, informed Cao Cao: "The large and small boats have been joined together. All flags and weapons are in order. Everything is at Your Excellency's disposal. We await your command to launch the attack." Cao Cao took up his position on a large ship in the center of the fleet and called his commanders together for their instructions. Naval and land forces were divided into units under flags of five colors: yellow for the naval center, commanded by Mao Jie and Yu Jin; red for the forward, under Zhang He; black for the rear, under Lü Qian; green for the left, under Wen Ping; white for the right, under Lü Tong. The forward cavalry and infantry unit, under Xu Huang, flew a red flag; the rear, under Li Dian, a black flag; the left, under Yue Jin, a green flag; the right, under Xiahou Yuan, a white flag. Serving as reinforcement for naval and land forces were Xiahou Dun and Cao Hong. Protecting communications and overseeing the battle were Xu Chu and Zhang Liao. The remainder of Cao Cao's brave commanders returned to their respective squads.

When these arrangements were complete, three rounds of drumbeats thundered through the naval camp; Cao Cao's navy steered through the station gates and onto the river. The wind gusted sharply out of the northwest. The ships let out their sails, beating upon wave and billow yet steady as if on flat ground. On board the northerners, bounding and vaulting to display their courage, thrust their spears and plied their swords. The various units maintained ranks under the discipline of signal flags. Some fifty small craft patrolled the great floating war camp, monitoring its progress. Cao Cao stood in the command tower and surveyed the exercise, immensely pleased, thinking he had found the secret of certain victory. He ordered sails dropped, and all ships returned to the camps in good order.

Cao Cao proceeded to his tent and said to his advisers, "Divine decree has come to our aid in the form of Young Phoenix's ingenious plan. With iron bonds linking the ships, we can actually cross the river as if we were walking on land." To this Cheng Yu replied, "Though the linked ships are level and stable, if the enemy attacks with fire it will be hard to escape. This we must be prepared for." Cao Cao laughed loudly. "Despite your provident view," he said, "there are still things you do not know." "Cheng Yu's point is well taken," Xun You added. "Why is Your Excellency making fun of him?" "Any attack with fire," Cao explained, "must rely on the force of the wind. Now at winter's depth, there are only north winds and west winds—how could there be a south wind or an east wind? Our position is northwest; their troops are all on the southern shore. If they use fire, they will only burn out their own troops. What have we to fear? If it were the season for a late autumn warm spell, I would have taken precautions long ago." The commanders bowed respectfully. "Your Excellency's insight," they said, "is more than we can match." Cao turned to his commanders and added, "The men from Qing, Xu, Yan, and Dai lack naval experience. If not for this expedient, how could they negotiate the treacherous Great River?" Just then two commanders rose and said, "Though we are from the north, we have some skill at sailing. To prove it, we volunteer to take twenty patrol craft direct to Xiakou, seize their flags and drums, and return."

Cao Cao eyed the two: Jiao Chu and Zhang Nan, formerly under Yuan Shao's command. "You men," said Cao, "born and raised in the north, may find shipboard hard to take. The southern soldiers, accustomed to moving by water, have honed their sailing skills. If I were you, I would not trifle with my life." "If we fail," the two replied, "we are content to accept what martial law decrees." "The larger boats have already been made fast," said Cao. "There are only small ones free. They hold twenty men each. Too few, perhaps, to engage the enemy." Jiao Chu said, "If we were to use the large ships, we would not impress the enemy. Let us have twenty small ones: ten for me and ten for Zhang Nan. Before the day is out, we will hit their camp and return with their standard and a general's head." Cao Cao said, "Then I shall give you twenty boats and five hundred crack troops, experts with long spears and crossbows. Tomorrow morning the flotilla will make a show of force from the main camp, and Wen Ping will escort you back with thirty patrol boats." Gratified and eager for battle, Jiao Chu and Zhang Nan withdrew.

Early the next day at the fourth watch the men were fed; by the end of the fifth they were ready, and drums and gongs sounded in the naval camp. The main fleet emerged and fanned out on the water, their blue and red flags forming a pattern above the Great River. Jiao Chu and Zhang Nan led their twenty scouting craft through the camp and onto the river. Then they raced south.

During the night the beating of drums and the din of battle preparation had reached the southern shore, where the defenders watched Cao Cao's navy maneuvering in the distance. The Southland's intelligence brought word to Zhou Yu. He went to a hilltop to observe, but the force had already pulled back. The next day the same sounds from the north rent the sky. The southern warriors climbed quickly to a viewing place, from where they saw the twenty small boats moving south, breasting the waves. The news was sped to Zhou Yu, who called for volunteers. Han Dang and Zhou Tai stepped forward. Well pleased by their offer, Zhou Yu ordered a strict vigil at all camps as Han Dang and Zhou

Tai led their five-boat squadrons from the left and the right out onto the river.

Now Cao's volunteers, Jiao Chu and Zhang Nan, were relying on little more than raw nerve. As their swift-oared boats approached the southern craft, Han Dang, wearing a breastplate, stood on the prow of his boat, a long spear in hand. Jiao Chu arrived first and ordered his archers to shoot, but Han Dang defended himself with his shield. Next, Jiao Chu crossed spears with Han Dang, but Dang slew him with a single thrust. Then Zhang Nan came forth, shouting, and Zhou Tai darted out from the side. Zhang Nan stood at the prow, his spear leveled. Arrows flew in volleys and counter-volleys. Plying his shield with one arm, his sword with the other hand, Zhou Tai leaped onto Zhang Nan's approaching boat and handily cut him down. Zhang Nan's body sank in the river, as Zhou Tai slashed wildly at his crew. The other attackers rowed swiftly back to the north shore. Han Dang and Zhou Tai gave chase but were checked in the middle of the river by Wen Ping. The boats of both sides took battle formation and set about the slaughter.

Zhou Yu and his commanders stood on the hilltop surveying the fighting craft and warships deployed along the river's northern shore. The flags and emblems were in perfect order. The southerners watched as Cao's commander Wen Ping met the furious attack of Han Dang and Zhou Tai, then fell back, reversed course, and fled. The two southern commanders gave swift chase, but Zhou Yu feared they might sail too far into the enemy's strength; and so he raised the white flag summoning them to return while the gongs were struck.

Han Dang and Zhou Tai swung their boats around and rowed south. From his hilltop Zhou Yu watched Cao's warships across the river crowding into the camp. Turning to his commanders, Zhou Yu said, "Their ships are as dense as reeds. And Cao Cao is a man of many schemes. What plan do we have for defeating them?" Before anyone could answer, they saw the tall pole in the center of the enemy camp snap in the wind and its yellow flag drift into the river. With a hearty laugh Zhou Yu said, "Not a good sign for them!" Then erratic winds blew up and whipped the waves against the shore. Caught by a gust, a corner of Zhou Yu's own flag brushed his face. Suddenly a dreadful thought came to Zhou Yu. With a loud cry he fell over backwards, blood foaming up in his mouth. The commanders rushed to his assistance, but their leader had lost consciousness. Indeed:

> One moment laughter, the next a cry of pain;
> What hope did the south have in its battle with the north?

What happened to Zhou Yu? Would he survive?
Read on.

CHAPTER 49

On Seven Star Altar Kongming Supplicates the Wind; At Three Rivers Zhou Yu Unleashes the Fire

After Zhou Yu had been carried to his tent, the southern commanders came inquiring about his condition. Agitatedly they said to one another, "A million-strong host, set to pounce and devour us, holds the north shore. With our chief commander stricken, how can we cope with Cao Cao's army?" They sent a report to Sun Quan and called for a physician to treat Zhou Yu.

The turn of events caused Lu Su great anxiety. He went to Kongming, who asked, "What is your view?" "A blessing for Cao, a catastrophe for us," was Lu Su's reply. Kongming smiled and said, "Such an illness even I could cure!" "What a boon that would be!" Lu Su responded, and the two men went to see Zhou Yu. Lu Su, entering the tent first, found the chief commander on his back, bedclothes pulled over his head. "Commander, how is your condition?" Su inquired. "My insides feel unsettled and tender, and the fits return from time to time," he answered. "What medicines have you been taking?" Lu Su wanted to know. "I reject everything, can't keep the medicine down," was his reply. "I have just seen Kongming," Lu Su said. "He says he can cure you, Commander. He's outside now. Should we trouble him to try his remedy?" Zhou Yu ordered Kongming admitted and had himself propped up to a sitting position on the bed.

"It is many days since we last met, my lord," Kongming began. "But I never imagined that your precious health was failing." "A man may have good luck when the day begins, bad luck when it ends. Who can tell beforehand?" Zhou Yu replied. "And the winds and the clouds above come when least expected," Kongming said, smiling. "You never can tell." At these words Zhou Yu lost his color and moaned. "Commander," Kongming continued, "do you seem to feel vexation gathering inside you?" Zhou Yu nodded. "You must take a cooling tonic to dispel it," Kongming advised. "I have," was Zhou Yu's reply, "to no effect." "You must first regulate the vital ethers," Kongming explained. "When the vital ethers are flowing smoothly and in the proper direction, then in a matter of moments your good health will naturally be restored." Zhou Yu, sensing that Kongming must know his unspoken thought, tested him by saying, "What medicine would you recommend to get the vital ethers flowing in the proper direction?" "I have a prescription to facilitate this," said Kongming, smiling still. "I shall benefit from your advice," said Zhou Yu. Kongming called for writing brush and paper and, waving away the attendants, wrote sixteen words for Zhou Yu's eyes alone:

> To break Cao's back
> With fire we attack.
> Everything is set, save
> The east wind we lack!

Kongming handed the note to Zhou Yu, saying, "This is the source of the chief commander's illness." Zhou Yu was astounded and thought, "Truly beyond all belief. He realized my problem at once. I'll simply have to tell him the truth." And so with a chuckle he said, "Master, since you already know the cause of my suffering, what medicine shall we use to cure it? The situation is moving swiftly to a crisis, and I look for your timely advice." To this appeal Kongming answered, "Though I myself have no talent, I once came upon an extraordinary man who handed on to me occult texts for reading the numerology of the heavens. Their method can be used to call forth the winds and rains. If the chief commander wants a southeast wind, erect a platform on the Southern Screen Hills, call it the Altar of the Seven Stars. It should be nine spans high, three-tiered, surrounded by one hundred and twenty flag bearers. On the platform I will work certain charms to borrow three days and three nights of southeast wind to assist you in your operations. What do you say?" "Never mind three days and three nights," Zhou Yu cried, "with one night's gales our endeavor can be consummated! But time is of the essence. Let there be no delay." "On the twentieth day of the eleventh month, the first day of the cycle, we will supplicate the wind," Kongming said. "By the twenty-second day, third of the cycle, the winds will have died away." Elated, Zhou Yu sprang to his feet. He ordered five hundred hardy soldiers to begin work on the altar, and he dispatched one hundred and twenty guards to hold the flags and await further instructions. Kongming then took his leave.

Accompanied by Lu Su, Kongming rode to the Southern Screen Hills to take the lay of the land. He commanded the soldiers to build the altar of the ruddy earth of the southeast. It was a structure of some two hundred and forty spans all around, with three three-span tiers. On the lowest tier were twenty-eight flags representing the twenty-eight zodiacal mansions. Along the eastern face were seven blue-green flags for the eastern mansions— Horn, Neck, Root, Room, Heart, Tail, Basket—arrayed in the shape of the Sky-blue Dragon. Along the northern face were seven black flags for the northern mansions—Southern Dipper, Ox, Girl, Void, Rooftop, Dwelling, Wall—laid out in the form of the Dark Tortoise. On the western side flew seven white flags for the western mansions—Straddling Legs, Bonds, Stomach, Bridge, Net, Turtle, Triaster—in the menacing crouch of the White Tiger. On the southern side flew seven red flags for the southern mansions—Well, Ghost, Willow, Star, Drawn Bow, Wings, Axle—making the outline of the Vermilion Bird.

The second tier was encompassed by sixty-four yellow flags, one for each set of oracular lines in the Book of Changes, divided into eight groups of eight. On the top tier stood four men, hair tightly bound and heads capped, wearing black robes of thin silk, wide sashes emblematic of the phoenix, vermilion shoes, and squared kilts. At front left, one man held up a long pole fledged at the tip with chicken feathers to catch any sign of the wind. At front right, another held up a long pole with the banner of the Seven Stars fastened to the top to show the direction of the wind. At the left rear, a man stood respectfully holding a prized sword; at the right rear, a man held a cresset. On the outside, the platform was surrounded by twenty-four men holding, severally, emblemed flags, ceremonial canopies, large halberds, long dagger-axes, ritual gold battle-axes, white yak-tail banners, vermilion pennants, and black standards.

On the twentieth of the eleventh month, an auspicious day, Kongming performed the required ablutions, fasted, and assumed the sacred vestments of a priest of the Tao. Barefoot, hair flowing behind, he came to the front of the altar and instructed Lu Su: "Return now and help Zhou Yu with the deployment. Blame me not if my prayer draws no response." After Lu Su's departure Kongming instructed the guards: "No one here is to leave his position without authorization. The men are forbidden to engage in conversation or to make any irregular remarks or react as if anything were out of the ordinary. Whoever disobeys will be executed." The men acknowledged the order. Having surveyed all stations, Kongming ascended with deliberate steps, lit incense, and poured water into a vessel. Staring into the heavens he uttered a silent incantation, after which he descended and entered his tent for a brief respite, allowing the soldiers to eat in shifts. That day Kongming ascended and descended three times, but of a southeast wind no sign was seen.

*　　*　　*　　*

Cheng Pu, Lu Su, and other military leaders joined Zhou Yu in his tent, where they waited to start the offensive the moment a southeast wind arose. Zhou Yu also reported developments to Sun Quan, who was to direct the reinforcement. Huang Gai had already prepared twenty fireboats, whose prows were studded with nails. Each boat was packed with reeds and kindling soaked in fish oil and covered with an inflammable compound of sulfur and saltpeter. The materials were wrapped with black oilcloth. At the boats' prows, notched banners of the Green Dragon of the East; to the stern, light craft. Before the chief commander's tent Huang Gai and his men awaited the order to move. Gan Ning and Kan Ze kept Cai He and Cai Zhong snug and secure in their water camp and plied them with wine day after day, never permitting a single northern soldier on shore. The Southland guards made sure that not an iota of information got through to them. Everyone was watching for the command tent's signal.

Zhou Yu was with his advisers when a liaison man reported: "Lord Sun Quan's boats are moored eighty-five *li* away, ready for the chief commander's word." Zhou Yu sent Lu Su to inform all commanders, officers, and men under him: "Keep your craft, weapons, and rigging in readiness. Once the order comes down, the slightest delay will be punished with the severity of martial law." The troops prepared themselves, rubbing their hands in anticipation of battle. That day everyone watched the sky intently as evening drew on, but the heavens held clear and no wind stirred. Zhou Yu turned to Lu Su and said, "How absurd are Kongming's claims! There can be no east wind in the dead of winter." "I can't believe Kongming would make absurd claims," replied Lu Su. Toward the third watch they heard, as if from nowhere, the sound of wind. The banners and pennons began to loll to and fro, and when Zhou Yu came out to look, the fringes of the flags were actually fluttering to the northwest. Within moments a stiff gale was coming up out of the southeast.

In consternation Zhou Yu said, "This man has snatched some method from the creative force of Heaven and earth, some unfathomable technic from the world of departed spirits. Why allow him to remain among us and cause trouble, when his elimination would save such great grief?" Zhou Yu immediately called two military commanders, Ding Feng and Xu Sheng, into his presence and told them: "Take a hundred men each—Xu Sheng on the river, Ding Feng on the shore—and go to the Altar of the Seven Stars in the Southern Screen Hills. Take Kongming's head—no questions asked—and bring it to me for your reward." The two commanders left to carry out their assignment. Xu Sheng embarked with one hundred swordsmen working the oars; Ding Feng rode to his destination with one hundred archers astride battle mounts. Both companies moved against the rising southeast wind. In the words of a poet of later times,

Sleeping Dragon stood on Seven Star Altar,
As all night eastern winds roiled the Jiang.
Had Kongming not devised his artifice,
Could Zhou Yu have played the strategist?

Ding Feng's land force arrived first. He saw the flag bearers on the altar, standing into the wind. Ding Feng dismounted, drew his sword and climbed the platform. Kongming was not there. Distressed, he asked a guard, who said, "He stepped down just moments ago." As Ding Feng descended the platform, Xu Sheng was arriving by water, and the two men met at the shore. A soldier reported to them: "Last night a light craft stopped at that shallow stretch ahead of us. I saw Kongming, his hair all unbound, get into it a short while ago. Then the boat sailed upriver."

Ding Feng and Xu Sheng gave chase by land and on the water. Xu Sheng ordered his sails raised in an attempt to catch the wind. The boat was not too far ahead. Xu Sheng stood in the bow and hailed Kongming across the water: "Do not depart, Director. The chief commander sends his invitation." And there was Kongming, standing in the stern of his boat, laughing. "Tell the commander for me," he shouted, "to use his forces well. I am returning to Xiakou for now, but the time will come for us to meet again." "Stay a moment," Xu Sheng pleaded, "I have something urgent to say." Kongming replied, "I realized long ago that the chief commander could never abide me. I've been expecting him to try to kill me and arranged some time ago for Zhao Zilong to meet me here. You had best turn back."

Xu Sheng saw that Kongming's boat had no sail, so he pressed ahead despite the risk. As he pulled nearer, Zhao Zilong drew his bow and rose from the stern. "I am Zhao Zilong of Changshan," he cried, "sent to receive the director general. How dare you pursue us? A single arrow would serve to cut you down and signal the end to our two houses' amity. Instead, let me give you a demonstration of marksmanship." Zilong fitted an arrow and shot away Xu Sheng's sail cord, causing the sheet to drop into the water and the boat to veer sideways. Zilong then ordered his own sail raised and rode the strong wind west. His boat, hardly touching the water, could not be overtaken. From the shore Ding Feng called Xu Sheng back: "Kongming is a wizard of matchless ingenuity, and Zilong a warrior of peerless courage. Remember his performance at Steepslope in Dangyang? There's nothing we can do but return and make our report." And so the two men presented themselves to Zhou Yu and described how Kongming had escaped. The astonished Zhou Yu cried in despair, "How weary I am of his endless schemes!" "Why not wait until after Cao Cao has been defeated before taking further measures against him?" Lu Su suggested.

This met with Zhou Yu's approval. He called together his commanders to receive their orders. First he told Gan Ning: "Take Cai Zhong and the surrendered soldiers along the southern shore. Fly only the flag of the northern troops. Capture the area around the Black Forest, directly opposite Cao Cao's grain depot. Penetrate his camp, then signal with fire. Leave Cai He here, outside my tent. I have a particular use for him." Next, he called Taishi Ci and instructed him: "Take three thousand men to the Huangzhou boundary to intercept Cao's reinforcement from Hefei. Attack immediately and signal us by fire. Look for the red flag: it will mean that Lord Sun Quan is coming to your aid." Gan Ning and Taishi Ci had to travel farthest, and so they went off first.

The third to receive orders was Lü Meng, who was told to take three thousand men to the Black Forest to back up Gan Ning and to burn down Cao's fortifications. Ling Tong, fourth, was ordered to cut off all traffic from Yiling and then shift to the Black Forest area with his three thousand men when he saw flames shooting skyward. Zhou Yu gave Dong Xi, fifth, three thousand troops for a direct assault on Hanyang; he was also told to attack Cao's camp from the River Han on seeing white flags. Zhou Yu told Pan Zhang, sixth, to take three thousand men under white flags to Hanyang and there to support Dong Xi. The six marine squads departed to perform their separate missions.

Following these assignments, Zhou Yu ordered Huang Gai to ready the fireboats and speed word to Cao that he would surrender that very night. At the same time he directed four squads of warships to cover Huang Gai from the rear: the first under Han Dang; the second, Zhou Tai; the third, Jiang Qin; the fourth, Chen Wu. Each unit included three hundred warships and was preceded by twenty fireboats.

Zhou Yu and Cheng Pu oversaw the preparations from the deck of a large attack boat while Xu Sheng and Ding Feng stood guard on either side. Lu Su, Kan Ze, and a few advisers were the only ones left to hold the camp. Cheng Pu was deeply impressed by the order and logic of Zhou Yu's disposition of forces. At this point an envoy from Sun Quan appeared with military credentials, saying that Lord Sun had sent Lu Xun with the vanguard to attack the area around Jichun and Huangzhou with Sun Quan himself in support. In addition, Zhou Yu sent men to the Western Hills to release fire rockets and to the Southern Screen Hills to raise signal flags. All preparations now in order, they waited for dusk.

*   *   *   *

In Xiakou, Liu Xuande eagerly awaited Kongming's return. He spotted a squad of boats arriving, but it turned out to be Liu Qi coming for news. Xuande invited him to the observation tower and said, "The southeast wind has been blowing for some time. Zilong went to meet Kongming, but so far no sign. I'm very worried." A petty officer pointed toward the harbor at Fankou and said, "There's a single sail coming in on the wind. It has to be the director general." Xuande and Liu Qi climbed down to meet the boat, and moments later Kongming and Zilong came ashore. Xuande was elated.

After formal greetings Kongming said, "Let us put all else aside for now. Are the land and marine forces we called up before I left now ready?" "Ready long ago," Xuande said, "and awaiting your deployment." Kongming, Xuande, and Liu Qi seated themselves in the main tent, and Kongming began assigning battle stations. First he said to Zilong, "Take three thousand men across the river and seize the trails and bypaths in the Black Forest. Where the trees and reeds are thickest, place your men in ambush. Tonight after the fourth watch Cao Cao is sure to flee that way. When they pass, use your torches. You may not get them all, but you'll get half." "The Black Forest has two roads," said Zilong, "one to Jiangling, the other to Xiangyang. Which one will he use?" "Jiangling is unsafe," replied Kongming. "He'll head for Xiangyang and then repair to Xuchang with his main force." Zilong departed with his assignment.

Next Kongming summoned Zhang Fei: "Yide," he said, "you take three thousand across the river, cut off the road to Yiling, and set your ambush at Gourd Valley. Cao Cao wouldn't dare flee by South Yiling, only by North Yiling. After tomorrow's rain passes, they will set their pots in the earth to prepare a meal. The moment you see smoke, start fires on the hillside. I doubt that you will capture Cao Cao, but your accomplishment should be considerable." Zhang Fei left with his assignment. Then Kongming instructed Mi Zhu, Mi Fang, and Liu Feng to cover the river by boat and capture the defeated troops and their weapons. They too left to carry out their orders.

Kongming rose and said to Liu Qi, "The area in sight of Wuchang is absolutely vital. Please go back there with your own men and deploy them at all points up and down the shore. Some fugitives from Cao's defeat are bound to come, and you should be there to seize them—but do not risk leaving the city walls without good reason." So instructed, Liu Qi took leave of Xuande and Kongming. Then the director general turned to Xuande. "My lord," he said, "station your men at Fankou, find yourself a high vantage point, then sit back and watch Zhou Yu do great deeds tonight!"

All the while, Lord Guan had been waiting at the side, but Kongming spared him not even a glance. Unable to endure it further, Lord Guan cried out, "I, Guan, have followed in elder brother's wake through long years of war, and have never been left behind. Today we close with a great enemy, but the director has given me no assignment. What does this mean?" Kongming smiled. "Do not take offense, Yunchang," he said. "My intention was to trouble you to hold an absolutely crucial pass, but—forgive me—something held me back, and I was reluctant to ask." "What 'held you back'?" Lord Guan replied. "I want an explanation here and now."

"Once," Kongming went on, "Cao Cao treated you most generously, and you are bound somehow to repay him. When his host is defeated, Cao will take the road to Huarong. If we ordered you there, I was certain, you would let him pass. That is what held me back." "How mistrustful of you!" Lord Guan responded. "True, Cao Cao treated me well. But did I not repay him when I beheaded Yuan Shao's general, Yan Liang, and put to death General Wen Chou? And again when I broke the siege at Baima? Do you think I'd let him go today?" "But if you should, then what?" Kongming said, pressing the point. "Let military law be applied to my misdeed!" said Lord Guan. "Well and good," Kongming answered. "Now put it in writing." Lord Guan executed the document, saying, "And if Cao Cao does not take that route?" "I give you a formal commitment that he will!" Kongming answered, to Lord Guan's complete satisfaction, and then added, "But why don't you pile up dry brambles around the trails and hills by Huarong? At the right time, set them afire. The smoke should draw Cao Cao that way."

"Smoke would make Cao Cao think there's an ambush," Lord Guan protested. "It would keep him away." "Have you forgotten," Kongming responded, "the tactic of 'letting weak points look weak and strong points look strong'? Cao may be an able strategist, but this should fool him. The smoke will make him think we are trying to create an impression of strength where we are weak and thus draw him to this route. But I must remind you again, General, to refrain from showing him any mercy." Lord Guan accepted this assignment and taking his son Ping, Zhou Cang, and five hundred practiced swordsmen, headed for Huarong Pass to set up the ambush.

When Lord Guan had left, Xuande said to Kongming, "His sense of honor is very strong. If Cao Cao actually takes that route, I am afraid my brother will let him pass in the end." "Last night I surveyed the constellations," Kongming replied. "The traitor's doom is not written there. And to leave a good turn for Lord Guan to do is a rather nice touch, after all." "Master," Xuande said, "your superhuman calculations are more than any man could match." Kongming and Xuande then set out for Fankou to observe Zhou Yu's assault, leaving Sun Qian and Jian Yong to guard Xiakou.

*　　*　　*　　*

Cao Cao and his advisers were in the main tent awaiting news of Huang Gai's defection. That day the southeast wind blew strong. Cheng Yu went in and said, "We should be taking measures against this wind." But Cao Cao smiled and replied, "The winter's yin phase is spent; the yang now begins its cycle. A south-

east wind is quite normal. There is nothing to be alarmed about."
At that moment soldiers reported the arrival of a small craft from
the south bringing a secret letter from Huang Gai. Cao Cao immediately had the bearer shown into his presence. The letter said
in part:

> Zhou Yu has held me under tight surveillance, and so I have had
> no means to get away. Now we have a new grain shipment from
> the Poyang Lakes. Zhou Yu has put me on patrol, and opportu-
> nity presents itself. I will find a way to cut down one of our emi-
> nent commanders and present his head with my submission.
> Tonight at the second watch, look for a boat with the Green
> Dragon jack—that will be the shipment.

Delighted, Cao Cao and his generals went to the great ship to
watch for Huang Gai.

It was almost night. In the Southland Zhou Yu ordered Cai
He brought before him, bound, and thrown to the ground. "I
have committed no crime," Cai He cried. "Who do you think you
are," said Zhou Yu, "pretending to come over to our side? Today
we lack the ritual articles suitable for sacrifice to the flags. Your
head will have to serve instead." Cai He, unable to deny the
charge, shouted, "Your own Kan Ze and Gan Ning were in on
it!" "As arranged," answered Zhou Yu. To what avail were Cai He's
regrets now? Zhou Yu ordered him brought to the riverbank beneath the black standard, where they offered libations and
burned paper. Cai He was beheaded, and his blood was poured
in sacrifice to the flag. After that, the ships set sail.

Huang Gai was in the third fire vessel, wearing a breastplate
and holding a sharp sword; on his banner, four large characters:
"Vanguard Huang Gai." Riding the favoring wind, he set his sights
for the Red Cliffs. By now the gale was in full motion. Waves and
whitecaps surged tumultuously. Cao Cao scanned the river and
watched the rising moon. Its reflections flickered over the waters, turning the river into myriad golden serpents rolling and
sporting in the waves. Cao faced the wind and smiled, thinking
he would achieve his ambition. Suddenly a soldier pointed out:
"The river is serried with sails from the south bank riding in on
the wind!" As Cao strained his eyes from the height, the report
came: "They fly the Green Dragon jack; among them, a giant ban-

ner, 'Vanguard Huang Gai.'" Cao Cao smiled. "Huang Gai's defection is Heavensent." But Cheng Yu studied the approaching boats and warned, "It's a ruse. Don't let them near our camp." "How do you know?" asked Cao. "If they held grain," Cheng Yu answered, "they would be low and steady in the water. But the boats coming on are so light, they are practically skimming the surface. Besides—with the force of this southeast wind, could you evade a trap?"

Then the truth dawned on Cao Cao, and he called for a volunteer to stop the oncoming boats. "I have experience as a mariner," said Wen Ping. "Let me go." He leaped into a small craft and went forth, followed, at a signal from his hand, by a dozen patrol boats. Standing in the prow of his ship, Wen Ping shouted: "By the prime minister's authority, the ships from the south are to approach no farther but to anchor in midriver!" Wen Ping's warriors cried out in unison: "Lower your sails!" These words were hanging in the air when an arrow sang, and Wen Ping, struck in the left arm, toppled over in his boat. There was commotion on board, and the squad raced back to the naval station.

The ships from the south were now only two *li* from Cao's fleet. At the signal from Huang Gai's sword, the first line of onrushing ships was torched. The fire sped by the might of the wind, and the boats homed in like arrows in flight. Soon smoke and flame screened off the sky. Twenty fiery boats rammed into the naval station. All at once Cao's ships caught fire and, locked in place by their chains, could not escape. Catapults sounded from across the river as the burning ships converged. The face of the water where the three rivers joined could scarcely be seen as the flames chased the wind in piercing currents of red that seemed to rise to the heavens and pass through the earth.

Cao Cao looked back to his shoreside camps; several fires had already broken out. Huang Gai sprang into a small boat and, followed by a few men, braved smoke and fire to find Cao Cao. Desperate, Cao Cao was about to jump back on shore, but Zhang Liao steered a small cutter toward Cao and helped him down from the large ship, already on fire. Zhang, with some dozen men protecting Cao Cao, raced for a landing point. Huang Gai had spotted someone in a scarlet battle gown lowering himself into a boat and, surmising it was Cao Cao, made for him. "Go no far-

ther, traitor!" he cried, sword in hand. "Huang Gai has come!"
A series of angry cries broke from Cao Cao's throat. Zhang Liao
hefted his bow and fitted an arrow, squinting as Huang Gai drew
nearer. Then he let fly. The wind was roaring. Huang Gai, in the
center of the firestorm, could not hear the twang of the bow-
string. The arrow struck him in the armpit, and he fell into the
water. Indeed:

> When fatal fire reached its height, he met his fate in water;
> When wounds from wooden clubs had healed, he fell to a metal
> arrow.

Would Huang Gai survive the victory he had made possible?
Read on.

CHAPTER 50

Kongming Foresees the Outcome at Huarong; Lord Guan Releases, and Obligates, Cao Cao

After his shot had knocked Huang Gai into the water, Zhang Liao
brought Cao Cao safely ashore, where they found horses and fled.
Cao's army was in utter disorder.

The southern commander Han Dang, steering through smoke
and fire, attacked the naval station. Suddenly a soldier reported:
"Someone hanging onto the rudder is calling you." Han Dang,
straining, heard his name: "Dang, save me!" Recognizing Huang
Gai's voice, Han Dang had him pulled aboard. He saw the
wound and yanked the shaft out with his teeth, but the arrowhead remained in Huang Gai's flesh. He then removed Gai's
soaked garments, dug the metal head out with his sword, and
bound Gai's arm with a strip of his flag. Wrapping his own battle gown around Huang Gai, Han Dang sent him back to the main

camp for treatment. Huang Gai was used to the water, so he managed to survive the experience even though it was midwinter and he wore armor.

That day fires rolled across the river like waves, and the cries of men shook the earth. On the left, boat squads led by Han Dang and Jiang Qin attacked from the west of the Red Cliffs; to the right, Zhou Tai and Chen Wu guided in their craft from the east; in the center, Zhou Yu, Cheng Pu, Xu Sheng, and Ding Feng arrived in force. Their fighters spared not what the fires had spared, and the fires lent the fighters added strength. Such indeed was the naval battle at Three Rivers and the bloody trial of war at Red Cliffs. On Cao Cao's side, those who fell to spear or arrow, or burned to death or drowned were beyond numbering. A poet later wrote:

> Wei and Wu waged war to rule the roost;
> The northland's towered ships—to smoke reduced.
> Spreading flames illumined cloud and sea:
> Cao Cao went down; 'twas Zhou Yu's victory.

Another verse reads:

> High hills, a tiny moon, waters vague and vast—
> Look back and grieve: what haste to carve the land!
> The Southland had no wish for Cao's imperium;
> And the wind had a mind to save its high command.

While the naval war raged, on land Gan Ning ordered Cai Zhong to bring him deep into Cao's camp. Then he struck Zhong a single blow, and he fell dead from his horse. Gan Ning began setting fires at once. Southland commander Lü Meng, seeing flames above Cao Cao's central camp, set his fires in response. Pan Zhang and Dong Xi did the same, and their troops made a great uproar, pounding their drums on all sides.

Cao Cao and Zhang Liao had little more than one hundred horsemen. Fleeing through the burning wood, they could see no place free of fire. When Mao Jie rescued Wen Ping, another dozen riders caught up with them. Cao Cao demanded that they find an escape route. Pointing to the Black Forest, Zhang Liao said, "That's the only area that seems free and clear," so Cao Cao dashed straight for the Black Forest. A troop of soldiers overtook him as their leader shouted, "Cao Cao! Stand, traitor!" Lü Meng's ensign appeared in the fiery glare.

Letting Zhang Liao deal with Lü Meng, Cao pushed on, only to be confronted by a fresh company charging out of a valley, bearing torches. A shout: "Ling Tong is here!" Cao Cao felt his nerve fail, his courage crack. Suddenly a band of soldiers veered toward him. Again, a shout: "Your Excellency, fear not, it's Xu Huang!" A rough skirmish followed. Cao Cao managed to flee some distance north before he encountered another company stationed on a slope ahead. Xu Huang rode over and found Ma Yan and Zhang Kai, two of Cao's commanders, formerly under Yuan Shao, with their force of three thousand northerners arrayed on the hill. They had seen the night sky full of flames and had hesitated to move. Now they were perfectly positioned to receive Cao Cao. He sent the two commanders ahead with one thousand men to clear a path and reserved two thousand as his personal guard.

Fortified by this fresh body of men, Cao's mind was easier. Ma Yan and Zhang Kai rode swiftly on, but within ten *li* voices rent the air, and another band of soldiers materialized. Their commander cried, "Know me for Gan Ning of the Southland!" Ma Yan tried to engage him, but Ning cut him down with one stroke. Zhang Kai raised his spear and offered combat. Whooping, Ning struck again with his sword, and Zhang Kai fell dead. Soldiers in the rear raced to inform Cao Cao.

Cao had been counting on support from troops in Hefei, unaware that Sun Quan already controlled all routes to the east. Assured of victory by the conflagration on the river, Sun Quan had Lu Xun signal Taishi Ci with fire. The moment he saw it, Taishi Ci joined Lu Xun and raced toward Cao, forcing him to flee toward Yiling; on the way Cao met up with Zhang He, whom he ordered to guard the rear.

Cao Cao whipped his horse into a dead run. At the fifth watch he looked back: the great fire had receded into the distance, and he felt steadier. "Where are we?" he asked. "West of the Black Forest," his attendants said, "and north of Yidu." Cao looked at the tangled woods and steep hills. He raised his head and laughed without stopping. "What does Your Excellency laugh so hard at?" the commanders asked. "At nothing. Nothing but the folly of

Zhou Yu and the shallowness of Kongming. If I had been in their place, I would have laid an ambush right here. I, Cao Cao, would've been done for." Even as he spoke, drums thundered from both sides and flames shot upward. Cao nearly fell from his horse. A band of soldiers appeared. Then, a shout: "Zhao Zilong, here! On orders from the director general! And waiting a long time too!" Cao had Xu Huang and Zhang He engage Zilong together, while he turned into the smoke and flame and fled. Zilong made no attempt to pursue, intent only on capturing the flags. Again, Cao Cao made good his escape.

The night sky was beginning to grey. Dark clouds spread out above. The southeast wind had not let up. Suddenly torrential rains came down, soaking everyone. Cao Cao braved the downpour and pressed on. His men were wan with hunger. Cao ordered food seized from nearby villages and some embers gathered for cooking fires. Before they could start, a company of men arrived at the rear. Cao Cao despaired, but it was only Li Dian and Xu Chu guarding the prime minister's advisers. Delighted, Cao Cao ordered his men to continue advancing. "What's the area just ahead?" he asked. "On one side is the South Yiling road; on the other, the North Yiling road," he was told. "Which one runs to Nanjun's seat, Jiangling?" "The easiest way," the soldiers said, "is to take the southern road through Gourd Crossing." Cao ordered them to take it and soon they reached the crossing.

Cao's men, famished, could barely march on. The horses, too, were fatigued, and most of them had fallen. Cao called a brief halt. Some horses carried cauldrons; others, grain seized in the villages. Near a hillside they found a dry spot, set their pots in the earth, and began cooking. They fed on horseflesh; then they stripped and hung their clothes in the breeze to dry. The mounts were unsaddled, left to roam free and graze. Cao Cao sat in a sparse wood, threw back his head, and laughed loudly. His officials said, "The last time Your Excellency laughed at Zhou Yu and Kongming, it brought Zhao Zilong down on us, and we lost plenty of men and mounts. What are you laughing at now?" "At Kongming and Zhou Yu, whose knowledge and planning is in the end rather deficient," he replied. "Had I been in command, I would have set an ambush right here to meet our exhausted troops with their well-rested ones. Even if we had escaped with our lives, we'd have been mauled. But they did not see that far. And that's why I am laughing." At that moment shouts rang out, ahead and behind.

Terrified, Cao Cao flung aside his armor and mounted. But most of his soldiers, with smoke and fire closing in, had no time to get to their horses. Before them an enemy troop had control of the pass through the hills. Their commander, Zhang Fei of Yan, spear leveled, poised on his mount, bellowed at Cao, "Where goes the traitor?" Officers and men quaked at the sight of Zhang Fei, but Xu Chu mounted bareback and made ready to fight, and Zhang Liao and Xu Huang converged on Zhang Fei. Then the horsemen on both sides jammed together in close action. Cao broke free first. Others followed. Zhang Fei pursued hotly. Cao fled in a meandering pattern, slowly leaving the enemy behind.

Cao Cao observed that most of his commanders bore wounds. One soldier respectfully asked, "There are two roads ahead; which one does Your Excellency think we should take?" "Which is shorter?" Cao asked in response. "The main road is fairly flat, but more than fifty *li* longer. The trail toward Huarong is fifty *li* shorter, but narrow and treacherous and hard-going." Cao Cao ordered some men to climb a hill and survey the roads. "Smoke is rising from several places along the trail," one reported back. "But there seems to be no activity on the main road." Cao Cao ordered the front ranks on to the Huarong Trail. "Those smoke signals mean soldiers," the commanders protested. "Why go down there?" "Don't you know what the military texts say?" Cao said. "'A show of force is best where you are weak; where strong, feign weakness.' Kongming is a man of tricks. He purposely sent his men to some nooks in the hills to set fires to deter us from going that way, while placing his ambush on the main road. That's my judgment. I won't fall into this trap!" "Your ingenious calculations are beyond compare," the commanders agreed and directed their troops toward the Huarong Trail.

By now the men were staggering from hunger. The horses could barely move. Some men had burns; others bore wounds from spear or arrow. On they plodded with walking sticks, dragging themselves painfully along, their clothing and armor drenched. No one had escaped unscathed, and weapons and standards were carried in no semblance of good order. Few mounts had had gear since the rout north of Yiling, when saddles and bridles had been cast aside. It was midwinter, and the cold was severe. Who can fairly describe their sufferings?

Cao Cao saw the front line come to a halt and asked why. The report came back: "The hills ahead are rarely crossed; the paths are too narrow, and the horses have bogged down in the ditches after the morning's rains." In an exasperated tone Cao Cao said, "Are you telling me that an army that forges through mountains and bridges rivers can't get through a little mud?" Then he sent down the command: "Let the old, the weak, and the wounded follow as best they can; the able-bodied are to carry earth, wood, grass, and reeds to fill in the road. The march must resume, and whoever disobeys dies." As ordered, the soldiers dismounted and cut trees and bamboo by the roadside to rebuild the road. Cao Cao, fearing pursuit, had Zhang Liao, Xu Chu, and Xu Huang lead a hundred riders with swords bared to cut down slackers.

At Cao Cao's order the troops, starved and exhausted, trudged ahead, trampling over the bodies of the many who had fallen. The dead were beyond numbering, and the sound of howls and cries on the trail did not cease. Angrily, Cao said, "Fate rules life and death. What are all these cries for? I'll behead the next to cry." One third of the men fell behind; another third lay in the ditches; one third stayed with Cao Cao. They passed a treacherous slope. The road began to flatten out. Looking behind, Cao saw that he was left with a mere three hundred mounted followers, not a one with clothing and armor intact. Cao urged them forward. The commanders said, "The horses are spent; they need a short rest." "Push on. There'll be time for that in Jiangling," Cao answered.

They rode another *li* or two. Cao Cao raised his whip and laughed again. "Why is Your Excellency laughing?" the commanders asked. "Everyone thinks Zhou Yu and Kongming are such shrewd tacticians," he replied. "But as I see it, neither is especially capable. If they had set an ambush here we could only have surrendered quietly." That moment a bombard echoed. Five hundred expert swordsmen flanked the road. At their head, raising his blade Green Dragon, sitting astride Red Hare, the great general Lord Guan Yunchang checked Cao's advance. Cao's men felt their souls desert them, their courage die. They looked at one another helplessly.

"It is the last battle, then," said Cao, "and we must fight it." But the commanders replied, "Even if the men will fight, their horses lack the strength. We cannot fight again." "Lord Guan," said Cheng Yu, "is known to disdain the high and mighty but to bear with the humble. He gives the strong short shrift but never persecutes the weak. He knows clearly the difference between obligation and enmity, and he has ever demonstrated good faith and honor. In times past, Your Excellency showed him great kindness; now, on your personal appeal to him, we might be spared."

Cao Cao approved and guided his horse forward. Bowing, he addressed Lord Guan: "You have been well, I trust, General, since we parted?" Lord Guan bowed in return and said, "I bear orders from the director general and have been awaiting Your Excellency for some time." "My army is defeated and my situation critical," Cao Cao said. "At this point I have no way out. But I trust, General, you will give due weight to our old friendship." "Though I benefited from your ample kindness," Lord Guan replied, "I fulfilled the debt when I destroyed two enemy generals and relieved the siege at Baima. In the present situation I cannot set aside public duty for personal considerations."

"You still recall, do you not," Cao went on, "how you slew my commanders at five passes when you left my service? A man worthy of the name gives the greatest weight to good faith and honor. With your profound understanding of the Spring and Autumn Annals, you must be familiar with the story of the apprentice Yugongzhisi who pursued his archery instructor, Zizhuoruzi, only to release him, unwilling to use the man's own teachings to destroy him." And Lord Guan, whose sense of honor was solid as a mountain, could not put Cao Cao's many obliging kindnesses or the thought of the slain commanders from his mind. Moved, despite himself, at the sight of Cao's men distracted and on the verge of tears, Lord Guan softened. He swung away his mount and said to his soldiers, "Spread out on all sides," clearly signaling his intent to make way. When Cao Cao saw Lord Guan turn aside, he and his commanders bolted past, and when Lord Guan came back, they were gone.

Lord Guan gave a powerful shout. Cao's soldiers dismounted,

prostrated themselves, and wept. Lord Guan's sense of pity seemed to grow on him, and he hesitated. Then Zhang Liao came racing up, and Lord Guan was reminded of their old friendship. With a long sigh, he let all the remaining troops pass. A poet of later times has written:

> Cao Cao fled along the Huarong Trail,
> But Lord Guan barred his passage hardily.
> Then, weighing obligation once incurred,
> He slipped the lock and let the dragon free.

Cao Cao rode on to the mouth of the gorge. Looking back, he saw all of twenty-seven riders behind him.

It was dark when he neared Jiangling. Masses of torches lit up the area, and a cluster of troops blocked his path. "This is the end," Cao Cao cried in fear. But he was relieved to find a patrol under Cao Ren, who greeted him saying, "I knew of the defeat but chose to keep to my post so that I could meet you on your return." "I might never have seen you again," Cao Cao said and gathered everyone into Jiangling for the night.

Soon Zhang Liao rode up and told Cao Cao of Lord Guan's kindness. Cao Cao checked his commanders and lieutenants. Many were wounded. Cao ordered them all to rest. Cao Ren set forth wine to dispel Cao Cao's sorrow, and his advisers joined him. Suddenly Cao Cao lifted his head and cried out in grief. His advisers said, "Your Excellency, when you escaped the tiger's den you showed neither fear nor anxiety. Yet now that we are safe inside these walls, the men fed, the horses provisioned, the time come to reorganize ourselves for counterattack, you cry out in grief. Why?" "I mourn for Guo Jia. He could have prevented this dreadful defeat," Cao said. He beat his breast and howled: "I grieve for you, Guo Jia. Oh, what a loss, what a loss!" His advisers remained quiet, shamed.

The next day Cao Cao told Cao Ren, "I am going back to the capital briefly to replenish my forces for the counterattack. Keep guard here over Jiangling. I have a plan to leave with you, but you must keep it sealed—except in emergency. Should you have to use it, the Southland will never succeed with its designs on Jiangling." "Who will guard Hefei and Xiangyang?" asked Cao Ren. "Jingzhou is in your hands," Cao replied. "And I've tapped

Xiahou Dun to hold Xiangyang. The most critical point is Hefei. Zhang Liao will be in charge there, assisted by Yue Jin and Li Dian. The moment something arises, inform me." His arrangements completed, Cao Cao rode back to Xuchang, the capital, taking with him the remainder of his army as well as those originally under Liu Biao's administration who had subsequently submitted to him. Cao Ren sent Cao Hong to defend Yiling and Jiangling against Zhou Yu.

*   *   *   *

Before Lord Guan brought his men home, the other commanders assigned by Kongming had already returned to Xiakou with their booty of horses, grain, money, and equipment. Only Lord Guan came back empty-handed, having taken neither man nor mount. Kongming was in the midst of congratulating Xuande when Lord Guan's return was reported. Kongming rushed forth from his place, bearing the cup of congratulation, to greet him. "It is time to rejoice, General," he said, "in your epoch-making achievement—ridding the empire of a monstrous evil. I really should have made the effort to receive you on the road." Lord Guan was silent. "General," Kongming continued, "can it be that you are displeased because we did not come far enough to meet you?" He turned to his attendants and added, "Why did you not report his approach before he arrived?"

"I come only to request capital punishment," Lord Guan said. "You do not mean to tell me that Cao Cao did not take the Huarong Trail?" Kongming asked. "He did, in fact, come that way," Lord Guan answered. "But I was so inept, he got away from me." "What commanders and soldiers have you captured, then?" Kongming went on. "None," came the reply. "That means," said Kongming, "that you purposely released him, mindful of his past generosity. Nonetheless, since you made a formal commitment, we have no choice but to enforce it under martial law." Kongming shouted for the guards to execute him. Indeed:

> Lord Guan risked his life to thank a benefactor;
> And men forever after held his name in honor.

Cao Cao had escaped his doom; would Lord Guan?
Read on.

CHAPTER 51

Cao Ren Battles the Southland Troops; Kongming Spoils Zhou Yu's Victory

Kongming was about to execute Lord Guan, but Xuande intervened, saying, "When my brothers and I pledged mutual faith, we swore to live and die—as one. Now Yunchang has broken the law, but I haven't the heart to go against our former covenant. I hope you will suspend the rule this time and simply record his fault, allowing him to redeem his offense by future merit." With that, Kongming pardoned Lord Guan.

*　　*　　*　　*

Zhou Yu recalled his forces, reviewed his commanders' accomplishments, and reported them to Sun Quan. He also sent all surrendered northerners back across the river. After feasting and rewarding his southern troops, Zhou Yu mounted an attack on Nanjun.

His first echelon camped at the edge of the river, in five sites from van to rear. Zhou Yu occupied the central site. He was in the midst of conferring on the tactics of the campaign when a report came in: "Liu Xuande has sent Sun Qian to congratulate the chief commander." Invited into Zhou Yu's presence, Sun Qian performed the ritual salute and said, "My lord, Liu Xuande, has commanded me to convey his respectful gratitude for your magnanimity, and to tender these poor courtesies." "Where is Xuande?" Zhou Yu asked. "As far as I know," Sun Qian replied, "he has moved his troops into position at the mouth of the You River." Startled, Zhou Yu asked, "Is Kongming there too?" "He is with Lord Liu," Sun Qian answered. "Then please return; I shall go there myself, later, to express my gratitude."

Zhou Yu accepted the gifts and sent Sun Qian back ahead of him. Lu Su asked Zhou Yu, "Whatever made you lose your composure just now, Commander?" "If Xuande is at the River You," Zhou Yu answered, "it means he plans to take Nanjun! We are the ones who expended so many men and horses, who consumed so much coin and grain—and now Nanjun is ours for the plucking. But if they harbor such ruthless ambition as to snatch our prize, they'll have to reckon with the fact that I am still around." "What strategy could force them back?" Lu Su wanted to know. "I'm going to talk with Xuande myself. If all goes well, fine. If not, I'll not wait for him to take Nanjun; I'll finish him off first!" "I should go with you," said Lu Su. With three thousand light cavalry the two men headed for Xuande's camp on the You River.

When Sun Qian told Xuande that the Southland commander was on his way, Xuande asked Kongming, "What is he coming for?" Kongming smiled. "Hardly for trivial courtesies," he said. "He is coming for Nanjun." "If he comes with troops, what do we do?" Xuande asked. Kongming suggested certain replies for Xuande to make to Zhou Yu, and then ordered the warships arrayed on the river and the land forces along the shore.

The arrival of Zhou Yu and Lu Su and their battalion was announced. Kongming had Zhao Zilong take a few riders and greet them. Zhou Yu observed uneasily the strength and vigor of Xuande's military position. Soon he was taken to the main tent where he was well received by Xuande and Kongming. When the formalities were done with, a banquet was spread. Xuande raised his wine cup to thank Zhou Yu for his part in the difficult campaign. After several rounds, Zhou Yu began, "Lord Liu, are we to understand that in moving your forces here, you intend to take Nanjun?" "I had heard, Commander," Xuande replied, "that you wished to take it, and so I have come to lend my assistance. If you do not take it, of course, I shall." Zhou Yu smiled. "We in the Southland have long wished to assimilate the area around the Great River and the Han," he said. "Now Nanjun is within our grasp. How could we not take it?"

"The outcome of any engagement is hard to foretell," Xuande said. "Before returning north, Cao Cao assigned Cao Ren to defend Nanjun and other neighboring points. He is sure to have left some surprises for us, not to speak of Cao Ren's unchallengeable bravery. My only concern is whether you will be able to capture the city, Commander." "In the event that we fail," Zhou Yu answered, "you are welcome to try." To this, Xuande replied, "Lu Su and Kongming are here as witnesses. Do not go back on your word, Commander." Lu Su hemmed and hawed without answering, but Zhou Yu said, "When a man worthy of the name gives his word, there is no going back." "Your position, Commander, is certainly fair-minded," Kongming commented. "Let Lord Sun Quan go to take Nanjun first. If he does not subdue it, my Lord Liu will try. What objection can there be to that?"

After Lu Su and Zhou Yu had departed, Xuande asked Kongming, "All the same, those replies you had me make seem unjustified now that I think it over. I am isolated and destitute, without a place to set my feet. I sought Nanjun as an expedient refuge. If Zhou Yu takes the city for the Southland, where am I supposed to go?" Kongming laughed heartily. "Remember, my lord," he said, "when I tried to get you to take Jingzhou? How you ignored me? But today you yearn for it!" "Then it was Liu Biao's land," Xuande replied. "I could not bear to take it. Now that it is Cao Cao's, I'd be justified." "Never mind fretting and worrying, my lord," said Kongming. "Let Zhou Yu do a bit of the fighting now, and I will have you sitting in power within Nanjun's walls soon enough." "And how will you manage that?" asked Xuande. Kongming whispered a few phrases that dispelled Xuande's anxiety. He consequently held his troops in tight check at the mouth of the River You.

———————

Nanjun, key to Jingzhou province, is besieged by Sun Quan's forces, but Cao Cao's general deceives and defeats the attackers, giving Liu Xuande a chance to seize the prize that both north and south have let slip. Under Kongming's direction, Liu Xuande consolidates his power in Jingzhou.

CHAPTER 52

Zhuge Liang Temporizes with Lu Su;
Zhao Zilong Captures Guiyang

After Kongming captured Nanjun and Xiangyang, Zhou Yu passed out from exasperation, rupturing his wound. When he came to himself, his commanders tried to soothe him, but Zhou Yu said, "Nothing less than the life of Zhuge Bumpkin will quell my discontent. Cheng Pu can help me retake Nanjun for the Southland." At this point Lu Su entered, and Zhou Yu said, "I am going to assemble an army to recover our cities and have it out with Xuande and Kongming. Will you help me?" "Nothing doing," replied Lu Su. "With our struggle against Cao Cao undecided and with Lord Sun's advance on Hefei stalled, we become easy prey for Cao Cao if we turn on one other. Our whole position will crumble. What's more, Liu Xuande was once Cao Cao's good friend. If we push him into tendering his cities to Cao Cao and the two of them unite against us—then what?" "It is insufferable," cried Zhou Yu. "Our strategy, our casualties, our costs in coin and grain—and for what? A ready victory for them!" "Bear with it, my friend," Lu Su urged. "I shall go and reason with Xuande myself. If I fail to make him see things our way, there will be time enough for hostilities." Zhou Yu's commanders welcomed this idea.

Lightly attended, Lu Su headed for Nanjun. He came to the city gate and shouted up to be admitted. When Zhao Zilong came out, Lu Su said, "I have something to say to Liu Xuande." Zilong replied, "Lord Liu and the director general are over in Gong'an." Lu Su turned and headed there. At Gong'an he found the flags and banners in brilliant array and the appearance of the army magnificent. To himself he admitted boundless admiration for Kongming. The visitor's arrival was reported. Kongming ordered the city gate opened wide and ushered Lu Su into the yamen. Formal greetings completed, they seated themselves as host and guest.

After tea had been served, Lu Su began: "Lord Sun Quan and his chief commander, Zhou Yu, have sent me to communicate their emphatic view to the imperial uncle. When we first undertook this campaign, Cao Cao had command of a million men and threatened to descend on the Southland. His real objective, however, was the imperial uncle, whom by fortune's grace the Southland saved in a massive campaign that drove back the northerners. Jingzhou's nine imperial districts should now properly become part of the Southland. But the imperial uncle has used a subterfuge to seize and hold the area, handily reaping a benefit for which the Southland has vainly expended its coin, grain, and men. I doubt that this is consonant with accepted principles."

"My friend," Kongming said, "on what grounds does a high-minded and enlightened scholar like yourself make such statements? It is commonly agreed that 'things belong to their owners.' Jingzhou's nine districts are not the Southland's territory, but rather the estate of Liu Biao, and Lord Liu, as everyone knows, is his younger brother. Though Liu Biao himself is dead, his son is still alive. For an uncle to support a nephew in taking Jingzhou—what can there be to object to?" "If in fact the patriarchal son were holding the territory," Lu Su conceded, "I might understand. But he is in Jiangxia; he is obviously not here."

"Would you care to see him?" asked Kongming. He motioned to his attendants, and before Lu Su's very eyes, steadied by two supporters, Liu Qi came out from behind a screen and spoke to Lu Su: "My ill health prevents me from performing the proper courtesies; please forgive my offense." Lu Su swallowed his amazement and kept silent for some time. Then he said, "And if the patriarch's son were to die . . . " "He lives from day to day," Kongming replied. "Should he die, there will be something to negotiate." "When he dies," said Lu Su, "the territory reverts to the Southland." "I think your position is correct," Kongming said finally. A banquet was then prepared in Lu Su's honour.

Lu Su bore the news to his own camp that night. Zhou Yu said, "Liu Qi is in the prime of youth and unlikely to die. When will we ever get Jingzhou back?" "Chief Commander," Lu Su replied, "rest assured that the responsibility is mine alone. I will see to it that Jingzhou is restored to the Southland." "You have something up your sleeve?" Zhou Yu asked. Lu Su replied: "Anyone could see how dissipated in vice and luxury Liu Qi is. Disease has penetrated his vitals. His face looks feeble and wasted. His breathing is troubled, and he spits blood. The man cannot live beyond six months. At that time I shall go to claim Jingzhou, and Liu Bei should have no excuses whatsoever to put me off."

Lu Su's assurances gave Zhou Yu little comfort. But an unexpected messenger from Sun Quan resolved the matter. "Lord Sun," he announced, "has surrounded Hefei. Unable to subdue it after many battles, he now orders the chief commander to shift his forces over there." Zhou Yu had no choice. He withdrew to Chaisang to allow his wound time to heal and sent Cheng Pu in command of a naval force to serve Sun Quan. Liu Xuande, overjoyed with the acquisition of the key cities of Gong'an, Nanjun, and Xiangyang, began considering how they could be held permanently.

––––––––––––––

Sun Quan, outwitted and outraged, claims Jingzhou as his rightful spoils of war. When Liu Qi, titular governor of the province dies, Sun Quan sends Lu Su again to demand the return of Jingzhou.

CHAPTER 54

State Mother Wu Meets
the Bridegroom in a Temple;
Imperial Uncle Liu Takes His Bride
to the Wedding Chamber

Xuande and Kongming greeted Lu Su outside the city walls and ushered him into the government buildings. After the reception Lu Su said, "My lord, Sun Quan, learning of your honored nephew's passing, offers these trifling gifts and sends me to participate in the obsequies. Chief Commander Zhou Yu, moreover, conveys his sincerest respects to Imperial Uncle Liu and Master Zhuge Liang." Xuande and Kongming, rising, expressed thanks for the Southland's gracious sentiments and accepted the gifts. They then set wine before their guest, who continued, "On my previous visit Imperial Uncle Liu said that the province of Jingzhou would be restored to the Southland in the event of Liu Qi's death. Now that the young master has died, we expect its return as a matter of course. Would you inform us when the province can be transferred?" "Enjoy your wine, and we will discuss it," replied Xuande.

Lu Su steeled himself, and after swallowing several cups of wine, he again attempted to broach the subject. Before Xuande could reply, Kongming interrupted. "You're being quite unreasonable," he said with a stern expression, "if I have to speak plainly. The Supreme Ancestor slew the white serpent and rebelled against the Qin to found this great dynasty, which has enjoyed unbroken sovereignty to this very day. Now in these evil times treacherous contenders arise everywhere. Each one seizes a corner of the realm for himself, while the world waits for the rule of Heaven to be restored—under the rightful sovereign. Lord Liu Xuande is descended from Prince Jing of Zhongshan, of the progeny of Emperor Jing the Filial. And he is an uncle of the reigning Emperor. Is he not eligible to be enfeoffed as a feudal lord? All the more so when he is the younger brother of the late Liu Biao! Where do you find impropriety in a younger brother succeeding to an elder's estate? Your lord, son of a minor officer from Qiantang, has rendered no meritorious service to the Han court. At the present time, depending on sheer military power, he has possession of the six districts and eighty-one townships of the Southland. Yet his greed is not satisfied. He wants to devour more Han territory. In a realm ruled by the Liu family, my lord, a Liu himself, has no rightful share, while yours, a Sun, actually means to wrest this land from him. Don't forget that in the battle at Red Cliffs my lord bore the brunt of the fighting, and his commanders risked their lives in the field. Do you mean to tell us that the victory was due to the strength of the south alone? If I hadn't been able to borrow the force of the southeast winds, what strategy would Zhou Yu have used? Had the south fallen, not only would the ladies Qiao have been moved to the Bronze Bird Tower, even the safety of your own family could not have been guaranteed. The reason Lord Liu did not answer you just now is that he regards you as a high-minded gentleman who may be expected to understand such things on his own. How could you be so undiscerning?"

During this tirade Lu Su sat silent. At long last he commented, "There is some truth, I'm afraid, in what you say. The thing is, it puts me in a most difficult position." "How is that?" Kongming asked. "When the imperial uncle was in straits in Dangyang," Lu Su answered, "it was I who took Kongming to meet my lord. Later when Zhou Yu wanted to march on Jingzhou, I was the one who stopped him. When you told me you would return Jingzhou after Liu Qi died, once again I committed myself and guaranteed your word. If you do not honor your promise today, what kind of answer would you have me take to my lord, who, as much as Zhou Yu, can well be expected to resent the injury? If I must die for the failure of my mission, so be it. My only fear is that if the southerners are incited to arms, the imperial uncle will not be able to enjoy possession of Jingzhou and—all for naught—will end up the object of ridicule."

To this Kongming replied, "Cao Cao commands a million-man host and acts in the name of the Emperor, yet he causes us no concern. Do you expect us to fear a little boy like Zhou Yu? If it's a bit of face you're afraid of losing, I can have Lord Liu give it to you in writing that we are borrowing the province as our temporary base, and that once Lord Liu has completed his arrangements for taking another, he will return Jingzhou to the Southland. What do you think of that?" "What place do you expect to take over?" Lu Su wanted to know. "The north," Kongming replied, "is too unsettled for us to have hopes there. But the western province of the Riverlands, Yizhou, has in Liu Zhang a governor both foolish and weak. That's where Lord Liu is setting his sights. If we succeed, we will return Jingzhou."

Lu Su had to accept this arrangement. Xuande personally wrote out the document and affixed his seal. And Zhuge Kongming affixed his own, saying, "Since I am in the service of the imperial uncle, it hardly suffices for me to act as guarantor. May we trouble you, sir, to sign as well? I think it will look better when you see Lord Sun again." "I doubt," replied Lu Su, "that a man of humanity and honor like the imperial uncle would betray his commitment." With that, he added his seal and gathered up the document.

The banquet ended, Lu Su bade his hosts good-bye. Xuande and Kongming escorted him to the water's edge. Kongming left him with this parting admonition: "When you see Lord Sun, speak well of us—and do not get any strange ideas. If our document is not accepted, we'll show a different face and your eighty-one townships will be lost. Both sides need good relations or the traitor Cao will make fools of us all." Lu Su made his good-byes and climbed into his boat.

He traveled first to Chaisang to see Zhou Yu. "Well, how did you make out with our claim to Jingzhou?" Zhou Yu asked. "I have the document right here," Lu Su replied, handing it to Zhou Yu. Zhou Yu stamped his foot and cried, "So he's fooled you again! In name he borrows the province; in reality he's reneged. They say they'll give it back when they take the Riverlands. And when will that be? In ten years? Does that mean they'll keep Jingzhou for ten years? A document like this—what use is it? And you actually countersigned it! You will be implicated if they don't return it. Should our lord take offense, then what?" Zhou Yu's words left Lu Su numb. After a time he said, "I don't think Xuande will sell me out." "Oh, what a sincere soul you are," Zhou

Yu exclaimed. "Liu Bei is a crafty old owl, and Zhuge Liang a sly and wily sort. They don't think the way you do." "Then what shall we do?" asked Lu Su. "You are my benefactor," Zhou Yu answered, "and I shall always remember your kindness in sharing your grain with us. How could I let you suffer? Just relax and sit tight for a few days, until our spies bring word from the north. I have something else in mind." But Lu Su's agitation did not subside.

Several days later spies reported that Jingzhou city—that is, Gong'an—was all decked out with ceremonial flags, that a new burial site was being constructed outside the wall, and that the whole army was in mourning. Surprised by the news, Zhou Yu asked, "Who has died?" "Liu Xuande's wife, Lady Gan," was the reply. "They are arranging the funeral and the interment now." Turning to Lu Su, Zhou Yu said, "I have a plan that will deliver Liu Bei and Jingzhou into our hands with no effort at all." "What is that?" asked Lu Su. "If Liu Bei's wife is dead, he'll need another. Our lord has a younger sister, a tough, brave woman with a retinue of several hundred females who normally carry swords and who have chambers filled full of weapons. She is a woman to outman any man. I am going to propose to our lord that he send a go-between to Jingzhou and convince Liu Bei to marry into the family. When he bites the bait and comes to Nanxu, he'll find himself held prisoner instead of getting married. Then we'll demand Jingzhou in exchange for his release. After they hand over the territory, I'll have further plans. You need not be involved in any way." Lu Su expressed his gratitude.

Zhou Yu drafted his proposal and put Lu Su on a fast boat for Nanxu. There Su told Sun Quan the result of his mission to Jingzhou and showed him the agreement with Xuande and Kongming. "What a fool you were!" exclaimed Sun Quan. "What good is an agreement like this?" "Chief Commander Zhou sends this proposal," responded Lu Su, handing him the letter, "with which he says we can recover Jingzhou." Sun Quan read it through and nodded, secretly pleased, and began asking himself whom to send as the go-between. The name that sprang to mind was Lü Fan.

Sun Quan summoned Lü Fan and said to him, "Recently we have had news of the passing of Liu Xuande's wife. I desire to invite him to marry into my family by taking my younger sister to wife. Bound thus in lasting kinship, we can join wholeheartedly in the struggle to defeat Cao Cao and uphold the house of Han. You are my choice for go-between. I count on you to present our case in Jingzhou." Lü Fan accepted the assignment, readied a boat, and, lightly attended, set out.

*   *   *   *

Liu Xuande was sorely distressed by the loss of Lady Gan. One day while speaking with Kongming, he was informed of the arrival of Lü Fan from the Southland. Kongming smiled. "Zhou Yu's up to something; he's still after Jingzhou," he said. "I'll just step behind this screen and listen in. Go along with anything he says, my lord, and when he is resting up in the guesthouse, we can talk further."

Xuande invited Lü Fan to enter. Formalities completed, they took their places. After tea had been served, Xuande asked, "Well, what have you come to tell us?" "Imperial Uncle, I heard recently," Lü Fan began, "that Lady Gan's demise has left you a widower. Now, I have the perfect match for you, and even at the risk of arousing your mistrust have come to arrange it. May I ask your own wishes in this matter?" "To lose a wife in one's middle age is a great misfortune," replied Xuande. "I could not bear to talk about marriage, with my late wife still warm in her grave." "A man without a spouse," said Lü Fan, "is a house without a beam. One cannot abandon this fundamental relationship in mid-life. My lord has a younger sister, a woman both beautiful and worthy, who can 'serve you with dustpan and broom.' If the two houses of Sun and Liu ally through matrimony as the ancient states of Qin and Jin once did, the traitor Cao will never again dream of confronting the south. Such a union would benefit both families and both states. Please do not mistrust us, Imperial Uncle. The only thing is, the queen mother, Lady Wu, dotes on her youngest and is loath to send her away. We must request that the imperial uncle come to the Southland instead."

To this proposal Xuande replied, "Has Lord Sun been informed of this?" "Would I dare speak to you on my own without first presenting the idea to Lord Sun?" Lü Fan replied. "I am already fifty," said Xuande. "My temples are streaked with white. Lord Sun's sister is but a young woman, barely nubile. I wonder if she's the right mate for me." "Although still a girl," Lü Fan answered, "Lord Sun's sister has more strength of will than a man. She has often said, 'I will marry only a true hero.' Imperial Uncle, you are known in the four corners of the realm. This is the ideal match of 'the comely lass and the goodly man.' Why raise questions because of disparity in age?" "Remain with us a while," Xuande said, "and I will sleep on it."

That day a banquet was laid out, and Lü Fan was received in the guesthouse. In the evening Xuande consulted Kongming, who said, "I already know what he's here for, and I have divined great good fortune and prosperity from the Book of Changes. So, my lord, you may give your assent. But first have Sun Qian return with Lü Fan to confirm the agreement with Lord Sun face-to-face. Then we can select an auspicious day for the marriage." "Zhou Yu plans to murder me," responded Xuande. "How can I walk lightly into this trap?" Kongming gave a hearty laugh and said, "I doubt if he can outwit me. I have a little 'plan' of my own to make sure Zhou Yu gets nowhere while you make Sun Quan's sister your wife without the slightest risk to Jingzhou." Kongming's boast left Xuande bewildered.

At Kongming's behest Sun Qian accompanied Lü Fan south and presented himself before Sun Quan for the purpose of sealing the marriage alliance. "It is my desire," Sun Quan began, "to welcome Xuande here as my sister's groom. In this we are utterly sincere." Sun Qian bowed down and expressed thanks. He then returned to Jingzhou and declared to Xuande, "The lord of the Southland expectantly awaits Your Lordship's arrival that you may join his family through marriage." Xuande remained hesitant to go. Kongming said to him, "I have settled upon three stratagems, but only Zilong can carry them out." He called Zhao Zilong and whispered a few confidential words: "I leave our lord in your care when you enter the Southland. Take these three brocade sacks. Each contains a useful scheme. Use them in the correct order." Zhao Zilong secreted the sacks on his person. Kongming had already sent an envoy ahead with gifts; everything was ready.

It was the fourteenth year of Jian An [A.D. 209], winter, the tenth month. Xuande, together with Zhao Zilong and Sun Qian, selected ten swift vessels and five hundred followers to accompany them to Nanxu. All affairs in Jingzhou were left in Kong-ming's hands.

Xuande was unable to compose himself. As they reached Nanxu and his boat came along shore, Zilong said, "It is time to read the first of the director general's stratagems." He opened the first brocade sack and read the enclosed instructions, then gave certain orders to the five hundred warriors, who left to carry out their assignments. After that, Zilong suggested Xuande pay his respects to State Elder Qiao, the father of the two eminent ladies Qiao, who resided in Nanxu. Xuande got ready sheep and wine, went to the home of the respected elder, and explained the nature of his visit. His guard of five hundred, gaily clad in red, covered Nanxu, purchasing various articles and spreading the news that there would be a new son-in-law in the house of Sun. Soon everyone in the city knew of the affair. Learning of Xuande's arrival, Sun Quan had Lü Fan entertain him and pro-vide for his comfort in the guesthouse.

State Elder Qiao, after receiving Xuande, went at once to of-fer his congratulations to the state mother, Lady Wu. "And what would be the occasion?" she asked. "Your beloved daughter has been promised to Liu Xuande. He has already arrived," he said. "Are you trying to fool me?" the state mother said in surprise. "No one told me!" She called for Sun Quan so that she could question him. At this time a man she had sent into town to learn what he could reported back: "The rumor is true. The prospec-tive son-in-law is presently resting in the guesthouse, and five hun-dred of his soldiers are all over town buying up pigs and sheep and fruit in preparation for the marriage feast. The go-between on our side is Lü Fan, on theirs Sun Qian. Both of them are be-ing entertained in the guesthouse." The news astonished Lady Wu.

When Sun Quan came to see his mother in her private quar-ters, she was beating her breast and weeping. "What is the mat-ter, Mother?" Quan asked. "So this is how you regard me," she sobbed, "as a thing of no consequence. Have you forgotten my elder sister's last injunction?" Startled by this outburst, Sun Quan responded, "Speak plainly, Mother. Why are you so dis-tressed?" She replied, "When a man is grown, he must take a wife; and a woman, when grown, must be married. This is how things have been done since most ancient times. I am your mother. For such an event my approval should have been sought first. How could you invite Liu Xuande to join our family behind my back? She is my daughter!" Sun Quan, taken aback, demanded, "What are you saying?" "As they say, 'If you don't want it known, don't let it happen!' The whole city knows, and you're still trying to fool me!" Lady Wu exclaimed. Then State Elder Qiao spoke: "I myself learned of it many days ago. I came here to congratulate the state mother." "You've got it all wrong!" cried Sun Quan in despair. "It was a scheme of Zhou Yu's to retake Jingzhou. We used the pretext of a marriage to trick Xuande into coming here so that we could detain him and then trade him back for Jingzhou, or kill him if they refused. That was the plan. There was no actual marriage intended."

The state mother, angrier than ever, directed her wrath toward the absent Zhou Yu. "You, chief commander of our six districts and eighty-one townships," she cried, "have no better strategy for recovering Jingzhou than to use my daughter in a 'seduction scheme' that would leave her a widow before she ever was a bride? Who will seek her hand after this? Her life will be ruined. You are all preposterous!" "Even if the scheme succeeded," the state elder Qiao added, "we would be the butt of general ridicule. Such a plot could never work." Sun Quan sat glum and silent.

The state mother continued her denunciation of Zhou Yu, but State Elder Qiao said, "Since things have progressed as far as they have, let us not forget that Imperial Uncle Liu is after all related to the imperial house. I would advise making the invitation to marry your sister genuine before we make utter fools of ourselves." "But they are so far apart in age," Sun Quan objected. "Imperial Uncle Liu is one of the eminent men of our day," replied Elder Qiao. "To have him marry your sister is no disgrace to her." "I have yet to see the imperial uncle," the state mother interjected. "Arrange for us to meet in the Temple of Sweet Dew tomorrow. If he fails to suit me, you are free to do as you like. If he does suit me, I will personally give your sister to him."

Sun Quan, a man of the deepest filial devotion, quickly consented to his mother's demand. On leaving her presence, he instructed Lü Fan to arrange a banquet in the reception hall of the Temple of Sweet Dew so that the state mother could receive

Liu Bei. "We could have Jia Hua hide three hundred men in the flanking corridors," suggested Lü Fan. "At the first sign of Her Grace's displeasure, you would have only to say the word and the soldiers would take Liu Bei and his attendants." On this advice Sun Quan summoned Jia Hua and ordered him to await the state mother's view.

State Elder Qiao, returning home after his visit with Lady Wu, sent word to Xuande: "Tomorrow Lord Sun and the state mother will receive you personally. Do be careful!" Xuande took counsel with Sun Qian and Zhao Zilong. "This meeting tomorrow," Zilong said, "is more ominous than auspicious. I will take our five hundred guards along."

On the following day State Mother Wu and State Elder Qiao arrived first at Sweet Dew Temple and took their seats in the abbot's chamber. Sun Quan arrived next, leading a retinue of counselors, and sent Lü Fan to the guesthouse to escort Xuande. Xuande, dressed in light metal armor under a brocade surcoat, was attended closely by his personal guard, swords slung over their shoulders. The party rode with Lü Fan to the temple. Zhao Zilong was in full battle dress at the head of the five hundred guards. They reached the temple and dismounted. Sun Quan received them first and, noting Xuande's extraordinary bearing and appearance, felt a queasy sensation come over him. The two leaders concluded the formalities and entered the abbot's quarters to present themselves before the state mother.

State Mother Wu was delighted at the sight of Xuande. Turning to State Elder Qiao, she said, "This is the son-in-law for me!" "He has the earmarks of an emperor," he replied. "A man, moreover, to combine anew humanity and virtue and manifest them throughout the world. You are truly to be congratulated on acquiring so excellent a son-in-law." Xuande prostrated himself and voiced his thanks. The feast began; Zilong came in presently, armed with a sword, and stood by Xuande. "Who is this?" the state mother asked. "Zhao Zilong of Changshan," replied Xuande. "Not the man who rescued your son, Ah Dou, at Steepslope in Dangyang?" the state mother went on. "Yes it is," Xuande answered. "A good and worthy general," she said, ordering wine for him.

At this point Zilong said quietly to Xuande, "I was just looking around the hallways and saw armed men hidden in the rooms. They mean us no good. You'd better inform the state mother." Xuande kneeled in front of Lady Wu and tearfully appealed to her: "If you would have me killed, then let it be here." "What are you saying?" she exclaimed. "Armed men are hidden in the corridors," he said, "what other purpose could they have?" The state mother turned wrathfully on Sun Quan and berated him: "Today Xuande has become my son-in-law; that is to say, he is my child. Why have you placed men in ambush in the corridors?" Feigning ignorance, Sun Quan demanded an explanation of Lü Fan, who put the blame on Jia Hua. The state mother summoned Jia Hua, who bore her denunciation in silence. The state mother would have ordered him executed, but Xuande intervened. "To kill a general," he said, "bodes no good to bonds of kinship. I would not be able to serve you as a filial son for long." State Elder Qiao added his own pleas, and Lady Wu relented, dismissing Jia Hua with a sharp rebuke. His armed followers beat a shamefaced retreat.

Xuande walked outside to wash his hands. There, in front of the temple hall he saw a large rock. Borrowing a sword from an attendant, he raised his eyes to Heaven and pledged, "If I am to return to Jingzhou and complete my hegemon's mission, let this sword cleave this stone. If I am to die here, let the stone stay whole." So saying, he struck a blow, and the stone broke apart in a shower of sparks. Sun Quan, who had been observing from behind, asked, "Lord Xuande, what grudge do you bear this stone?" "Though nearly fifty," Xuande replied, "I have failed to purge the dynasty of traitors, a matter of acute distress. Now—honored by the state mother as son-in-law—now is the most fortunate moment of my life. So I put a question to Heaven: if we are to destroy Cao and revive the Han, let the stone crack—and it happened!" Sun Quan mused, "Can Liu Bei be trying to put something over on me?" Gripping his own sword, he said, "I too shall put a question to Heaven!" But to himself he swore, "If I am to regain Jingzhou and if the Southland is to thrive, let the rock split in two." He brought the sword down upon the giant stone, and it broke again. To this day there remains a Rock of Rue bearing this oath. In later times a poet visiting the site composed these lines in admiration:

> The treasured sword, the rock that split in two,
> Engendering sparks where two sharp blades struck true:
> Two houses' fortune Heaven here ordained;
> From this moment, threefold power reigned.

The two men left their weapons and hand in hand reentered the hall. After several more rounds Sun Qian looked meaningfully at Xuande, who announced apologetically, "The wine is too much for me. I beg to retire." Sun Quan escorted Xuande to the front of the temple, where the two men stood side by side contemplating the scenery. "There is no sight to equal it!" Xuande exclaimed. To this day a stele by the temple bears these words, "There is no sight to equal it." A later poet has left these lines of appreciation:

> Rain clearing o'er the scape; winecup firm in hand.
> Our realm is free of care; content prevails.
> Where long ago two heroes fixed their gaze
> Stony cliffs still beat back wind-blown waves.

The two leaders looked on as the wind swept the river. Great waves rolled and foamed, and white breakers snatched at the heavens. Among the breakers a slip of a boat was moving as if on flat land. Sighing, Xuande said, "'Southerners steer boats; northerners ride horses.' How true." Sun Quan thought, "He's trying to make fun of my riding," and had his aides bring over a horse. He leaped on and charged down the slope; then laying on the whip, he raced up again. Smiling, he remarked to Xuande, "Southerners can't ride, you say?" At this, Xuande threw off his cloak and sprang to horseback. He flew down and swept back in a swift career. The two men stayed their mounts on the rise and laughed as they swung their whips. Today the spot is known as Halting Hill. A later poet wrote:

> What spirit in their charging dragon-steeds!
> Mounted side by side, they viewed the hills and vales:
> For Wu and Shu—east, west—two hegemons.
> And the Halting Hill remains, untouched by eons.

The two men returned riding side by side, and the people of Nanxu voiced their approval to a man.

In chapter 55 Zhao Zilong watches anxiously as Liu Xuande succumbs to the charms of his new life. He opens Kongming's second secret message instructing him to tell Xuande to return to Jingzhou to meet a new threat from Cao Cao. On pretext of performing rites for his parents, Xuande persuades his new wife, Lady Sun, to depart with him. When pursuers overtake them, Lady Sun humbles them by denouncing them as rebels against her royal person as instructed by her husband. This display of royal authority was Kongming's third strategem.

In chapter 56 Sun Quan is persuaded that to continue his conflict with Liu Xuande will only open his kingdom to a new threat from Cao Cao. And Cao Cao, though smarting from his defeat at Red Cliffs, is deterred by the combined strength of the Sun and Liu houses. To stir his enemies' mutual antagonism Cao Cao recommends to the throne that Zhou Yu be made governor of Jingzhou. Cao's main plan is to build up his separate sphere (which will become the kingdom of Wei). At a grand banquet his advisers praise him as fit to receive the Mandate of Heaven and rule as emperor.

CHAPTER 56

Cao Cao Feasts at Bronze Bird Tower; Kongming Riles Zhou Yu for the Third Time

Cao Cao read each [poem offered] in turn and smiled. "Gentlemen," he said, "your praise goes beyond the measure. I am but a crude and simple man who began his official career by being cited for filial devotion and integrity. Later on, because of the disorder in the realm, I built a retreat fifty *li* east of the fief at Qiao, where I wished to devote myself to reading in spring and summer and hunting in autumn and winter until tranquility returned to the world and I could enter public life. Beyond all my expectations the court assigned me to serve as commandant for Military Standards, and so I forsook my life as a recluse and dedicated myself to achieving distinction by punishing the rebels in the Emperor's behalf. If after I die my tombstone reads 'Here Lies the Late Lord Cao, Han General Who Conquers the West,' my lifelong ambition will have been fulfilled.

"Let it be remembered that since bringing Dong Zhuo to justice and rooting out the Yellow Scarves, we have eliminated Yuan Shu, defeated Lü Bu, wiped out Yuan Shao, and won over Liu Biao. Thus peace has been restored in the realm. I have become the Emperor's highest servant, the chief steward of his realm. What greater ambition could I have? If not for me, who knows how many would have declared themselves emperor, or prince of a region?

"There are those who have drawn unwarranted conclusions concerning my power, suspecting me of imperial ambitions. This is preposterous. I remain constantly mindful of Confucius' admiration for King Wen's 'ultimate virtue.' His words burn bright in my heart. I long only to relinquish my armies and return to my fief as lord of Wuping. But practically speaking I cannot; for once I relinquish power, I might be murdered—and that would imperil the house of Han. I cannot expose myself to real dangers for the sake of reputation. So it seems, gentlemen, that not one of you understands my thinking." The officials rose as one and made obeisance. "Not even the great prime ministers of old, Yi Yin and the Duke of Zhou," they said, "approach Your Excellency." A poet of later times wrote:

> Once Zhougong feared the slander of the world;
> Once Wang Mang treated scholars with respect.
> What if they had perished then, misjudged,
> Their chronicles forever incorrect?

*   *   *   *

Now governor of Nanjun, Zhou Yu pondered his revenge against Xuande even more intently. His first step was to petition Lord Sun Quan to have Lu Su try again to reclaim Jingzhou. Accordingly, Sun Quan commanded Lu Su: "You served as guarantor when we loaned Jingzhou to Liu Bei. But he's dragging things out. How long must we wait to get it back?" "The document," Lu

Su said, "provides for its return only after they acquire the River-lands." This answer provoked Sun Quan to say, "That's all I hear, but so far they haven't sent one soldier west. I don't intend to wait for it until I've grown old." "Let me go and speak to them," responded Lu Su. And so he sailed to Jingzhou once more.

In Jingzhou, Xuande and Kongming had gathered ample supplies of grain and fodder, upgraded their armed forces, and attracted talented men from far and wide. When Xuande asked the meaning of Lu Su's visit, Kongming replied, "Recently Sun Quan proposed you, my lord, as protector of Jingzhou out of fear of Cao Cao. Cao Cao countered by appointing Zhou Yu governor of Nanjun, intending to set our two houses at odds and to pluck his advantage from between. Coming after Zhou Yu's appointment, Lu Su is here to demand Jingzhou." "How do we handle him?" Xuande asked. "If he refers to the question of Jingzhou," Kongming answered, "just bellow and wail, and at the height of the scene I will step forth and make certain representations." Thus the plan was made.

Lu Su entered Xuande's headquarters. After the formalities, he was offered a seat. "Now that the imperial uncle is a son-in-law of the Southland," he began, "he is my master too. How dare I sit in his presence?" "You are my old friend," Xuande said, smiling. "Such modesty is unnecessary." With that Lu Su seated himself. Tea was served. "I bear today the important mandate of Lord Sun Quan," Lu Su began. "My mission concerns Jingzhou. Imperial Uncle, you have occupied it too long and its return is overdue. Now that Sun and Liu are kinsmen, the territory should be returned as soon as possible in the interests of family harmony." At these words Xuande covered his face and burst into tears.

Startled, Lu Su asked, "What is this?" Xuande continued crying as Kongming stepped out from behind a screen and said, "I have been listening for some time. Do you know why my master cries?" "Indeed I do not," was the reply. "Is it not apparent?" Kongming said. "When my lord first borrowed the province, he promised to return it after taking the Riverlands. I have given this matter careful thought. Yizhou province is ruled by Liu Zhang, my master's younger cousin, who, like himself, belongs to the imperial family. Were Xuande to march on Liu Zhang's capital, the world would lose all respect for him. But if he returns Jingzhou to you, where will he live? And if he doesn't, he offends his brother-in-law. Torn by this dilemma, Lord Liu cries from heartfelt pain."

Kongming's words seemed to strike Xuande deeply, for he smote his breast and stamped his feet, wailing as bitterly as before. Lu Su tried to assuage him. "Imperial Uncle," he said, "do not fret and grieve like this. Perhaps Kongming has some plan." "I would trouble you," Kongming said, "to return to Sun Quan and, sparing no details, sincerely describe to him this most distressing scene that you are witnessing and beg him to allow us a little more time." "And if he will not?" Lu Su asked. "Lord Sun has given his own sister to the imperial uncle," Kongming replied. "How can he refuse? We are counting on you to place the matter before him in the right way." Lu Su, the soul of generosity and benevolence, was moved to act on Xuande's complaint. Xuande and Kongming offered their respectful thanks. The banquet ended, they escorted their guest to his boat.

Lu Su sailed straight to Chaisang and delivered the message. Zhou Yu stamped his foot and said, "He's trapped you once again. Back when Liu Biao ruled Jingzhou, Liu Bei was already dreaming of taking over. Why should he have any scruples about Liu Zhang's land? This last bit of foolery may land you in trouble, old friend. I have a plan, however, that should confound even Zhuge Liang—but it will mean another trip." "Let me hear your esteemed strategy," Lu Su replied. "You will not go to Lord Sun," said Zhou Yu. "Rather, you will go back to Jingzhou and tell Liu Bei this: 'The Suns and the Lius are now one family. If you cannot bear to take the Riverlands, the Southland will raise an army and do so. We will then turn it over to you as a dowry, and you can return Jingzhou to us.'"

To this proposition Lu Su responded: "The Riverlands is too far to be easily conquered. I wonder if your plan is feasible, Chief Commander." "You are too virtuous," said Zhou Yu. "Do you think I really mean to take the Riverlands and give it to them? It is only a pretext. I mean to catch them unprepared and capture Jingzhou. As our army moves west via Jingzhou, we will ask them for coin and grain; and when Liu Bei comes out of the city to receive our men, we will kill him and take control. That will redeem my name and get you out of trouble."

This plan won Lu Su's immediate approval, and he returned to Jingzhou. Xuande took counsel with Kongming. "Lu Su can't have seen Sun Quan in so short a time," Kongming said. "He probably went to Chaisang, and he and Zhou Yu have cooked something up. Whatever he says, watch me. If I nod, give consent." Xuande agreed to act accordingly.

Lu Su entered; the formalities were concluded. "Lord Sun Quan," Su began, "sends his praise of the bounteous virtue of the imperial uncle. Having taken counsel with his command, he has decided to raise an army to capture the Riverlands for the imperial uncle—as a kind of dowry. Once this is done, you may give us Jingzhou. When our army passes through, however, we will expect a little cash and grain from you." At these words Kongming hastened to nod. "Such kindness from Lord Sun!" he said. Xuande, folding his hands in a gesture of respect and gratitude, added, "We owe this entirely to your persuasiveness." "When your heroic legions come," Kongming assured him, "we shall go out of our way to see that they are amply provided for." Inwardly pleased with his reception, Lu Su took his leave after the banquet had ended.

"What are they up to?" Xuande asked Kongming. "Zhou Yu does not have long to live," Kongming said with a loud laugh. "He's making plans that wouldn't fool a child, using the ancient ruse of 'passing through on the pretext of conquering Guo.' Their real objective is Jingzhou, not the Riverlands. They want you to come out of the city so they can nab you, 'attacking the unprepared, doing the unanticipated.'" "But what can we do?" asked Xuande. "It's nothing to despair over," Kongming said reassuringly. "Just keep in mind that 'it takes a hidden bow to catch a fierce tiger, and delicate bait to hook a giant tortoise.' When we get through with him, Zhou Yu will be more dead than alive." Next, Kongming communicated certain instructions to Zhao Zilong. Xuande was delighted with Kongming's scheme. According to the verse of later times,

> Zhou Yu framed a plan to take Jingzhou
> Whose opening move Liang knew from history.
> Yu thinks his bait secure below the tide;
> The hook that's meant for him he does not see!

Lu Su reported back to Zhou Yu his hosts' enthusiasm for the plan and their willingness to come out of the city and provide for the Southland army. Zhou Yu laughed aloud and said, "This time I will have them!" He told Lu Su to inform Sun Quan and to have him send Cheng Pu with reinforcements. Zhou Yu's arrow wound had gradually healed and his condition was good. He placed Gan Ning in the van, while he himself and Xu Sheng and Ding Feng formed the second contingent; Ling Tong and Lü Meng made up the rear. Counting land and naval forces, they had fifty thousand men marching toward Jingzhou.

On his boat Zhou Yu chuckled to himself, confident that Kongming was trapped. When his advance guard reached Xiakou, Zhou Yu asked, "Has Jingzhou sent anyone to greet us?" "Imperial Uncle Liu," he was told, "has sent Mi Zhu to receive the chief commander." Zhou Yu summoned the man and demanded to know how his forces would be provisioned. "Lord Liu," Mi Zhu replied, "has made all the preparations and arrangements." "And where is the imperial uncle?" Zhou Yu asked. "He is outside the gates of Jingzhou awaiting the moment to offer you a toast," Mi Zhu responded.

Zhou Yu said, "For the sake of your house, we have undertaken a long expedition. The provisioning of our forces is not to be taken lightly." Mi Zhu took Zhou Yu's admonition back to the city. The Southland's war-boats advanced in order up the river. Soon they made Gong'an, but not a single soul nor war-boat was there to meet them. Zhou Yu urged his fleet on. Barely ten *li* from Jingzhou, he saw that the river was calm and quiet. Scouts reported back to him: "The city wall flies two white flags, but the city seems deserted."

Perplexed, Zhou Yu went ashore and rode on horseback to the city; Gan Ning, Xu Sheng, and Ding Feng, leading three thousand picked troops, followed him. They reached the foot of the wall but there was no sign of life. Zhou Yu reined in and had his men shout to open the gate. Someone above asked who had come. A Southland soldier answered, "The Southland's chief commander, Zhou Yu himself." At that moment they heard the rap of a stick as a row of soldiers armed with spears and swords appeared on the wall. From the guard tower Zhao Zilong emerged and said,

"Chief Commander, what is your purpose in coming here?" "I have come to capture the Riverlands for your master," he answered. "Don't tell me you know nothing of it!" But Zilong answered back: "Director General Kongming knows full well that the chief commander means to 'borrow passage to destroy Guo.' That's why he left me here. As for my lord, he said that because Governor Liu Zhang of the Riverlands is, like himself, an imperial kinsman, it would be dishonorable to seize his province. If you Southlanders actually mean to seize the Riverlands, he said, he will have to unbind his hair and go off into the hills rather than lose the trust of men forever."

At these words Zhou Yu swung away; just then he saw a man holding the command banner and standing before his horse. "Four field corps," he reported, "are converging on us: Guan from Jiangling, Zhang Fei from Zigui, Huang Zhong from Gong'an, Wei Yan from Chanling. We don't know how many they have in all, but the hills are ringing for a hundred *li* with shouts that they want to capture Zhou Yu!" The chief commander cried out and fell from his horse. Again his wound opened. Indeed:

> A subtle move is hard to counteract;
> Every shift he tried had come to naught.

Would the marriage-sealed alliance break apart?
Read on.

CHAPTER 57

Sleeping Dragon Mourns Zhou Yu at Chaisang; Young Phoenix Takes Office at Leiyang

Zhou Yu, his chest pounding, toppled from the saddle; aides carried him aboard ship. When he recovered, they informed him that Xuande and Kongming had been sighted on a hilltop, drinking and enjoying themselves. Zhou Yu said grimly, "They think I can't take the Riverlands, but I swear I will." At that moment Sun Yu, Sun Quan's younger brother, arrived. Zhou received him and described the battle. "My brother sends me with orders to help you, Chief Commander," Sun Yu said; and so Zhou Yu directed him to advance on Jingzhou. Soon, however, Zhou Yu learned that Sun Yu's troops had been stopped at Baqiu by Xuande's commanders Liu Feng and Guan Ping, who already controlled the upper course of the Great River. The news deepened Zhou Yu's distress. Soon after, a messenger brought him a letter from Kongming:

> Director General for the Han, Imperial Corps Commander Zhuge Liang, addresses the eminent Chief Commander of the Southland, Master Zhou Yu: Since we parted at Chaisang, you have been much in my thoughts. When I heard that you were planning to take the Riverlands, I felt it could not be done. The people are sturdy, the terrain is rough, and Protector Liu Zhang, admittedly a bit foolish and feeble, can still manage to defend it.
>
> Now your army has commenced a long campaign and will face many trials and uncertainties before victory is secure. Even the great strategists of old, Wu Qi and Sun Wu, could not guarantee their calculations nor ensure an outcome. I must remind you that revenge for the defeat at Red Cliffs is not absent from Cao's thoughts for a single moment! If he strikes while your army is far off, the Southland will fall. To prevent such an unbearable loss I have written this note which I hope you will favor with your attention.

Zhou Yu sighed, called for brush and paper, and wrote a statement for Sun Quan. Next, he summoned his commanders and said, "Far be it from me to withhold the service I owe to our land, but my time on earth ends here. No one can help that. I want you all to serve Lord Sun to the best of your ability and bring his great cause to fruition." With those words Zhou Yu lost consciousness, then seemed to revive momentarily. Looking Heavenward, he cried, "After making me, Zhou Yu, did you have to make Zhuge Liang?" He groaned several times and passed away; his age was thirty-six. A later poet wrote of Zhou Yu:

> Glory had crowned this hero since Red Cliffs,
> From earliest years hailed a champion.

In lute-set song he showed his sense of grace;
With cup in hand he bade his friend farewell.
Three thousand bushels from Lu Su he once begged;
Ten legions took the field at his command.
Baqiu, now Zhou Yu's final resting place,
Still draws men who mourn in heartfelt grief.

While Zhou Yu lay in state in Baqiu, his testament was taken to
Sun Quan, who grieved uncontrollably for his chief commander.
Quan then read the document, which recommended Lu Su as
his replacement.

> Despite my commonplace abilities, I was favored with exceptional
> recognition as confidential adviser and supreme military com-
> mander. Could I do otherwise than strain every fiber of my being
> attempting to render due service? Alas, the day of death is never
> known beforehand; life's duration is destined. That my flesh
> should succumb before my humble purpose was achieved over-
> whelms me with remorse.
>
> At present, with Cao Cao to the north, our borders are uneasy.
> With Liu Bei living in our land, we are rearing a tiger. The lead-
> ership of the realm remains in doubt, and it is imperative that all
> vassals of our court remain ever vigilant and that the sovereign
> exercise careful judgment.
>
> Lu Su, distinguished for his loyalty and dedication, serious and
> scrupulous in all affairs, may replace me as chief commander. A
> man's dying words are his best, they say. If this letter receives your
> consideration, I have not died in vain.

Sun Quan finished reading and said tearfully, "Zhou Yu, with the
talent of a king's righthand man, is dead, suddenly and prematurely. Whom else have I to depend on? How can I ignore his
recommendation?" That day he appointed Lu Su chief commander and ordered Zhou Yu's coffin sent home for burial.

*   *   *   *

In Jingzhou, Kongming pondered the constellations. Observing
a falling "general" star, he smiled and said, "Zhou Yu has died."
The next morning he told Xuande, whose spies soon confirmed
it. "What shall we do now?" Xuande asked Kongming. "Lu Su is
bound to be the new chief commander," was the reply. "I have
been watching the 'general' stars clustered in the east. I think I
should take a trip to the Southland, ostensibly to offer condo-

lences, and see if any of their worthy men would be willing to serve you, my lord." "What if they harm you, master?" Xuande asked. "I was not afraid while Zhou Yu lived; what have I to fear now?" was his reply.

And so with Zhao Zilong and five hundred warriors and an assortment of funerary gifts, Kongming sailed to Baqiu. En route he learned that Sun Quan had already made Lu Su chief commander and that Zhou Yu's coffin had been returned to Chaisang, so Kongming headed for Chaisang, where Lu Su received him according to protocol. Zhou Yu's commanders wanted to kill Kongming, but Zilong's armed presence deterred them. Kongming had his funerary gifts placed before the coffin. Then he personally offered a libation, kneeled on the ground, and read his eulogy:

Alas, Gongjin! Woefully fallen in your prime! Heaven numbers our days and leaves man to grieve. Heartbroken, I spill this flask of wine. May your spirit savor my libation.

I pay homage to your youth, remembering your deep friendship with Sun Ce. You stood for honor and disdained wealth, and you offered him your home. I pay homage to your early manhood when you flexed your wings like the storm-embracing roc and constituted a new state in the south. I pay homage to your mature years when in the fullness of your powers you made Baqiu an outpost of the Southland: pressure for Liu Biao, relief for Sun Quan. I pay homage to your style and the dignity you wore when you took the junior Lady Qiao to wife. Son-in-law to a Han minister, you were a man who graced the court. I pay homage to your bold spirit, when you argued against sending Cao Cao tribute. You held your ground and ended up the stronger. I pay homage to your conduct at Poyang, when you resisted Jiang Gan's blandishments, showing self-possession, superb character, lofty ideals. I pay homage to your scope of talents, your capable administration, and worthy strategies, which broke the foe with fire, subduing a stronger enemy.

I think back to that time, your dashing mien and brilliance. I weep for your untimely demise, head bowed, heartsore. Loyal and honorable of mind, noble in spirit! Three twelve-year spans of life, a name for a hundred ages. I mourn, distraught, my insides knotted with grief. While a heart beats here, this sorrow cannot end. Heaven darkens over. The whole army blanches with despair. Your lord mourns; your friends pour out their hearts.

I have no talent, yet you sought my counsel. We aided the

Southland against Cao Cao, supported the Han, and comforted the Liu. Our mutual defense was perfectly coordinated, and we did not fear for our survival. Alas, Gongjin, the living and the dead can never meet. You preserved your integrity with simple devotion, and it will survive the mists of death and time. Perhaps the dead can discern our thoughts, but what man alive truly knows me now? Alas, alas. Partake of this offering.

Kongming finished his eulogy and prostrated himself on the ground. Tears of grief gushed forth. The southern commanders remarked, "Everyone said they were enemies; but after watching him at the ceremony, we don't believe it." Lu Su, also deeply moved, thought, "Kongming is a man of such depth! Zhou Yu was narrow. He brought on his own death." A poet of later times wrote:

> Before Nanyang's Sleeping Dragon woke,
> Another star was born in Shucheng town.
> When fair blue sky brought Gongjin into being,
> Did sullied earth have to make Kongming?

Lu Su feasted Kongming. Then Kongming took his leave. He was about to descend into his boat, when a man in a Taoist robe and bamboo-leaf hat, a black sash of plaited silk and plain sandals accosted him. "You drove Master Zhou to his death," he said, laughing, "and yet have the nerve to come and pay your victim homage—as if to mock the Southland for having no one of stature!" Kongming turned and faced the man. It was Master Young Phoenix, Pang Tong. Kongming laughed in turn, and the two men entered the boat hand in hand, recounting all that had passed during their long separation. Then Kongming handed his old friend a letter and said, "My guess is that Sun Quan won't have much use for you. If so, come to us in Jingzhou and work for Xuande. Here is a note to him. I think you'll find my lord tolerant and humane, a man of ample virtue who will put your vast learning to good use." Pang Tong nodded and left. Kongming returned to Jingzhou.

In chapters 57 to 59, Pang Tong eventually joins Liu Xuande's advisory staff. Meanwhile, in the west Ma Chao wages war, seeking revenge for the murder of his father, Ma Teng (a Han loyalist), at Cao Cao's hands. Ma Chao takes the western city of Chang'an, but in a treacherous final battle, Cao Cao seizes Chang'an himself.

Abandoning his schemes for another southern campaign, Cao Cao turns his attention west where his growing strength threatens Zhang Lu, ruler of the buffer region of Hanzhong. Like Xuande and Cao Cao, Zhang Lu prepares to conquer the great western province of Yizhou, also called the Riverlands (more or less contemporary Sichuan). Yizhou governor Liu Zhang (Liu Xuande's kinsman) sends an envoy, Zhang Song, to the Han capital to urge Cao Cao to attack Hanzhong and relieve the threat to the Riverlands from Zhang Lu.

In chapter 60 the envoy Zhang Song is rebuffed by Cao Cao, though he debates and wins over Cao Cao's assistant, Yang Xiu. Zhang Song changes course and requests Liu Xuande's aid for his lord, Riverlands' governor Liu Zhang.

CHAPTER 60

Zhang Song Confounds Yang Xiu; Pang Tong Proposes the Conquest of Shu

In the main hall of the government buildings ritual greetings were exchanged and a banquet was laid. Throughout the repast Xuande confined himself to commonplace conversation, studiously avoiding any reference to the western Riverlands. Zhang Song probed: "I wonder how many districts the imperial uncle holds in Jingzhou?" "Jingzhou is only on loan to us from the Southland," Kongming replied with a smile, "and they are always sending somebody to reclaim it. However, Lord Liu, as a brother-in-law of Sun Quan, has been granted temporary tenure." "Does that mean," Zhang Song continued, "that the Southlanders are not satisfied, despite their six districts and eighty-one regions, the strength of their people and the wealth of their state?" "Lord Liu,"

Pang Tong said, "though an imperial uncle of the dynasty, has never taken a piece of the realm, unlike those grubbing traitors to the Han who depend on forced seizures. But men of true understanding decry this injustice."

"Refrain from such statements, gentlemen," Xuande said. "What virtue have I to justify ambition?" "Not so," Zhang Song said. "My enlightened lord, you are a royal kinsman whose humanity and sense of honor reach far and wide. Far more than 'a piece of the realm'—it is not beyond expectation that you might one day occupy the imperial throne as a successor in the legitimate line." Xuande joined his hands and made a gesture of disavowal. "Good sir," he said, "you far overestimate whatever I may deserve."

And there the matter lay during three days of feasting. Then, at a parting banquet at the first way station, Xuande toasted Zhang Song: "We are deeply grateful to you for sharing these three days with us. But now the time to take leave of one another has come, and I wonder when I may again have the benefit of your advice." Having spoken, Xuande shed tears freely, while Zhang Song wondered inwardly, "He is magnanimous and humane, a lover of learned men. Can I pass over him? Better to persuade him to take the Riverlands." Song said aloud, "I have long wished to be of service to you but despaired of finding the occasion. From Jingzhou, I see Sun Quan on the east, like a tiger ready to strike, and to the north Cao Cao with a whale's appetite. This place can hardly have enduring appeal for you."

Xuande replied, "I know it all too well. But there is not a place I can put my foot down safely." "The province of Yi, the Riverlands," Zhang Song said, "is protected by formidable barriers. Its fertile territory extends thousands of *li*. The people are thriving and the state prospers. Our wise and capable officials have long held the imperial uncle's virtue in high regard. If you will mobilize your forces to make the long trek west, your hegemony can be established and the house of Han restored." "How could I undertake such a thing?" Xuande said. "The provincial protector, Liu Zhang, is a royal kinsman like myself, and he has long dispensed favor throughout the land of Shu. What third party could upset things?"

"I am not one to sell my sovereign for high position," Zhang

Song answered. "But having met with Your Lordship, I must bare my innermost thoughts. Liu Zhang, though in possession of Yizhou, is endowed with so ignorant and irresolute a nature that he has kept worthy and competent men from office. Now with the threat from Zhang Lu in the north, confidence is shaken, and people's thoughts turn to acquiring an enlightened lord. This excursion of mine was for the sole purpose of making an offer to Cao Cao; but in him, to my surprise, I found a perverse traitor who uses deceit for statecraft, who disdains the worthy, who insults those willing to serve. For these reasons I have made a point of coming to see you. My lord, take the Riverlands and make it your base, plan an attack on the Hanzhong buffer, then go on to incorporate the northern heartland and set the dynasty to rights. Your fame will pass into history and you will outshine all rivals. Should you be inclined to adopt this suggestion, I would be willing to do whatever is necessary to coordinate matters from within. Let me know your esteemed decision."

"Your concern touches me deeply," Xuande responded. "Alas, Liu Zhang and I share the same ancestor. If I attacked him, I would be reviled and repudiated by all." "A man of noble ambition," Zhang Song said, "spares no effort to establish his worth and his estate. Apply the whip and assume the lead! For if you do not take Yizhou, others will—and then it will be too late for regrets." "They say the roads are so hilly and rough," Xuande remarked, "that neither carriage nor horse can ride abreast. Even if I wanted to take it, what strategy would work?"

Producing a map from his sleeve, Zhang Song said, "I am moved by my lord's ample virtue to present this. A single glance will apprise you of the road system of the Riverlands." Casually, Xuande unrolled the map and examined it. The geographic details of the region were fully spelled out: topography and marching stages, dimension and distance of roads, strategic intersections, repositories of coin and grain. "Strike now, my lord," Zhang Song urged. "My two close and trusted friends there, Fa Zheng and Meng Da, can be counted on. Should they come to Jingzhou, you may consult them in complete confidence." Xuande raised his clasped hands in an expression of gratitude. "You will be well rewarded when the plan is realized," he said, "as sure as the hills stay green and the rivers ever run." "I look for no re-

ward," Zhang Song asserted. "Having met a lord who is wise and
enlightened, I could do nothing but make known to him all the
facts of the case." With that, they parted. Kongming ordered Lord
Guan and the others to escort the guest several dozen *li*.

*   *   *   *

Back in Yizhou, Zhang Song went first to see his close friend Fa
Zheng (Xiaozhi), a man from Mei in West Fufeng, son of the worthy officer Fa Zhen. Zhang Song gave Fa Zheng a complete account of his interview. "Cao Cao," he began, "has utter contempt
for learned, honorable men. He turns to them in trouble, and
from them in success. I have promised our province to Imperial
Uncle Liu, and I want to discuss it with you, brother." "In my judgment," replied Fa Zheng, "Liu Zhang is an incapable leader. I
have had my eye on Liu Xuande for some time. Since I share your
view, you need have no doubts."

A while later Meng Da (Ziqing) arrived. He was a fellow townsman of Fa Zheng's. Seeing the two talking together, Meng Da
said, "It looks like you are ready to surrender the province." "Such
is our wish," answered Zhang Song. "What is yours, elder brother?
Who is the best choice?" "Xuande! Who else?" responded Meng
Da. Each of the three clasped his hands and laughed. Then Fa
Zheng said to Zhang Song: "And what will you say to Liu Zhang
tomorrow, brother?" "I am going to recommend that he send
both of you to Jingzhou as his envoys," Zhang Song replied. The
others agreed.

The next day Liu Zhang received Zhang Song and asked, "How
did you fare?" "Cao is a traitor to the Han!" Zhang Song exclaimed. "His lust for power is unspeakable. He is after our land."
"Then what are we to do?" asked Liu Zhang. "I have a plan for
keeping both Cao Cao and Zhang Lu from invading us," Zhang
Song answered. "Yes?" said Liu Zhang. "Imperial Uncle Liu
Xuande of Jingzhou," Zhang Song began, "is a member of the
royal house, my lord, as you yourself are. Benevolent, kind, magnanimous, liberal, he has the aura of a man who is honest and
self-respecting. Since the battle at Red Cliffs, the mere mention
of his name throws Cao Cao into panic, not to speak of Zhang
Lu! I think, my lord, that you would do well with such friendship

and support from the outside in your struggle against Cao Cao and Zhang Lu."

"I have been thinking along these lines for some time," the imperial inspector said. "Whom could we send as envoys to Jingzhou?" "Fa Zheng and Meng Da," Zhang Song replied, "no one else will do." Liu Zhang summoned the two men. He gave Fa Zheng a letter to establish good relations with Xuande, and Meng Da five thousand men to escort Xuande and his supporting force into the province. But while this discussion was under way, a man burst into the room, his face covered with perspiration. "My lord, listen to Zhang Song," he cried, "and your forty-one departments will pass into the hands of another."

Zhang Song stared at him in astonishment. It was Huang Quan (Gongheng) from Xilangzhong in Ba, presently serving Imperial Inspector Liu Zhang as first secretary. "Xuande and I are royal kinsmen," Liu Zhang said. "That is why I enlist his support. How can you make such a statement?" "I am quite familiar with Xuande's magnanimity," was the reply, "how his gentle approach has overcome the hardest resistance the empire's heroes have put up so far. He has won the allegiance of men from afar, and gratified the hopes of those he has ruled. On top of that, he has two wise counselors in Zhuge Liang and Pang Tong; and he has the support of such valiant warriors as Guan, Zhang, Zhao Zilong, Huang Zhong, and Wei Yan. If you call him into Shu and treat him as a subordinate, how long do you think he will be willing to remain compliant? On the other hand, if you accord him the reception of an honored guest—well, one kingdom can't hold two kings. Heed my words and our rule can be secure as Mount Tai. Heed them not and your own position will become as precarious as a pile of eggs. Zhang Song must have arranged something with Xuande when he passed through Jingzhou. Execute Zhang Song, break off with Liu Bei, and the Riverlands will enjoy unlimited good fortune."

"And how am I going to stop Cao Cao and Zhang Lu?" Inspector Liu Zhang asked. "Seal the borders and close the passes," Huang Quan replied. "Improve defenses and wait for the threat to blow over." "With the enemy at our borders, we cannot waste time," Liu Zhang said; he rejected Huang Quan's strategy in favor of Fa Zheng's mission. But another man cried out in opposition. It was Wang Lei, an aide in Liu Zhang's personal service. Touching his head to the ground, Wang Lei said, "My lord, Zhang Song's advice spells disaster." "No!" Liu Zhang shot back. "Alliance with Xuande will block Zhang Lu." "Zhang Lu," Wang Lei continued, "is a superficial problem. Liu Bei represents a threat to our vitals, for he is the most treacherous of villains. Once he served Cao Cao; then he plotted his destruction. Next, he joined Sun Quan and ended up stealing Jingzhou. Can you co-exist with such duplicity? If you summon him, it means the end of the Riverlands!"

Liu Zhang dismissed the speaker sharply: "Stop this nonsense! Would a kinsman steal my estate?" The inspector had attendants escort the protesters from the hall and sent Fa Zheng to Jingzhou.

Fa Zheng went straight to Jingzhou and was granted audience. After presenting himself, Fa Zheng handed Liu Xuande a written proposal. It read:

> Your cousin, Liu Zhang, respectfully commends the following to the attention of General Xuande as an elder of the clan. Long have I esteemed your lofty name, but the difficult roads of Shu have prevented me from sending tribute. For this I feel deepest shame. They say, "Share trouble, bear trouble." This goes for friends, not to speak of kinsmen. Now Zhang Lu's army on our northern front gives me no peace, and so I send this earnest petition for your weighty consideration. If you decide to take cognizance of our common ancestry and preserve honor among brothers, you will raise an army at once to rid us of these violent marauders. In that way we will remain mutual adherents, "lips and teeth," and you will be richly rewarded. No letter can say all that I wish. I expectantly await your arrival.

Xuande exulted on reading the letter. He ordered a banquet for Fa Zheng. As the wine was circulating, he dismissed his attendants and said confidentially, "I have long admired your splendid name, and Zhang Song has spoken much of your ample virtue. This opportunity to benefit by your counsel answers hopes long held."

Disclaiming the compliment, Fa Zheng replied, "A minor official from the Riverlands is hardly worth notice. But they say horses whinnied when they met the master trainer Bo Luo: a man will sacrifice all for one who appreciates him. General, have you

thought further on Lieutenant Inspector Zhang Song's proposal?" "My life as an exile," Xuande replied, "has never been
free of woe and discontent. I often think of the little wren that
keeps a cozy spot for itself and the cunning hare that maintains
three holes in case of escape. Men should do the same. Don't
think I would not have your overabundant land—but I cannot
bring myself to conspire against my clansman." "The Riverlands
is a natural storehouse," Fa Zheng responded. "A sovereign who
cannot keep control cannot last. Liu Zhang has proved unable
to assign good men to office, and his patrimony is doomed to
pass to someone else. It would be unwise, General, not to take
what he offers you so freely. As the saying goes, 'He who gets to
the rabbit first, wins the chase.' I stand prepared to give you my
full support." Xuande folded his hands in a gesture of appreciation and said, "Much yet remains to be discussed."

After the banquet Kongming personally escorted Fa Zheng to
the guesthouse. Xuande was alone, pondering, when Pang Tong
approached him and said, "It is a foolish man who fails to resolve
a matter that demands resolving. You are high-minded and understanding, my lord. Why hesitate?" "What do you think we
should do?" Xuande asked. Pang Tong replied, "Jingzhou's present situation—Cao Cao to the north and Sun Quan to the east—
confounds our ambitions. But the Riverlands, in population, territory, and wealth, offers the wherewithal for our great endeavor.
If Zhang Song and Fa Zheng are going to help us from within,
that is a godsend. Do not hesitate!"

"The man who is my antithesis," Xuande responded, "who
struggles against me as fire against water, is Cao Cao. Where his
means are hasty, mine are temperate; where his are violent, mine
are humane; where his are cunning, mine are truehearted. By
maintaining my opposition to Cao Cao, my cause may succeed.
I can't throw away the world's trust and allegiance for personal
gain." Smiling, Pang Tong said, "My lord, that accords well
enough with sacred universal principles. But in a time of division
and subversion, when men strive for power by waging war, there
is no high road to follow. If you cling to accustomed principle,
you will not be able to proceed at all. Rather, you should be flexible. You know, 'to incorporate the feeble and attack the incompetent,' to 'take power untowardly but hold it virtuously,' was

the way of the great conquerors, kings Tang and Wu. When things are settled, and if you reward Liu Zhang honorably with a big fief, what trust will you have betrayed? Remember that if you do not take power, another will. Give it careful consideration, my lord."

Inspired by these words, Xuande answered, "Your memorable advice shall be inscribed on my heart." Soon after he consulted with Kongming about raising a force to move west. "Jingzhou is too important to leave undefended," Kongming said. "Then," Xuande replied, "I shall go ahead with Pang Tong, Huang Zhong, and Wei Yan. You remain behind with Lord Guan, Zhang Fei, and Zhao Zilong." Kongming agreed and assumed overall responsibility for Jingzhou province, assigning Lord Guan to defend the route into Xiangyang from the pass at Qingni; Zhang Fei to take charge of the four districts along the river; and Zhao Zilong to hold Jiangling and protect Gong'an, the seat of Xuande's administration.

Sun Quan plots to invade Jingzhou in Xuande's absence, beginning with a trick that lures Lady Sun back home. His plans evaporate when Cao Cao assumes the title of Lord Patriarch and threatens the Southland. Nominally loyal to Emperor Xian, Cao Cao lays the foundation for supplanting the Han as the reigning dynasty. Liu Xuande, meanwhile, builds his independent kingdom in the west. His kinsman Governor Liu Zhang ignores his own advisers and welcomes Liu Xuande.

The takeover is not smooth. Pang Tong is killed and Xuande summons Kongming from Jingzhou. With trepidation Kongming entrusts Jingzhou to Lord Guan and gives him eight words of warning: "North—repel Cao Cao; east—conciliate Sun Quan."

Zhang Fei follows Kongming west. The impetuous warrior Ma Chao makes a temporary ally of Zhang Lu, who himself covets the Riverlands. But after fierce single combat with Zhang Fei in which neither wins, Ma Chao is persuaded to join Liu Xuande's cause. Outmaneuvered, Liu Zhang submits, and Liu Xuande triumphantly enters Chengdu, his new city, as Protector of the Riverlands.

CHAPTER 65

Ma Chao Attacks Jiameng Pass; Liu Bei Assumes the Protectorship of the Riverlands

Kongming said to Xuande, "We have the Riverlands. But there is no room for two lords: Liu Zhang should be sent to Jingzhou." "We have hardly taken possession of the capital district of Shu," Xuande answered. "We cannot command Liu Zhang to leave." "Indecision has cost him his estate," Kongming continued. "My lord, if you rule with womanish benevolence, this land will not long be yours." Xuande was persuaded. He held a grand banquet, requested Liu Zhang to gather up his goods, bestowed on him the insignia of General Who Exhibits Might, and had him take his family and household servants to Gong'an in Jingzhou that very day.

Having conquered the Riverlands, Xuande proposed to grant his officials Chengdu's most desirable lands and buildings. Zhao Zilong, however, protested: "The people of this province have been through the flames of war so long that they have deserted their fields and dwellings. These properties should be restored to those who live here, for resettlement and economic revival— not taken away for rewarding our own. In that way, our rule will gain acceptance." Xuande gladly followed this advice.

Next, Xuande instructed Director General Zhuge to revise the legal code, which provided for severe corporal punishment. Fa Zheng said, "When the Supreme Ancestor entered the Qin capital at Xianyang, he reduced the legal code to three provisions, and the common people rejoiced in his benevolence. I would like the director general to satisfy our people's expectations by easing the punitive provisions and curtailing the scope of the laws." "You don't see the whole problem," Kongming replied. "The laws of Qin were punitive and harsh, and the people detested them. That is why the Supreme Ancestor's kindness and leniency won their allegiance. But in this case, Liu Zhang was foolish and weak. His benevolence inspired no dedication, his severity no respect, so relations between lord and vassal have gradually broken down. Vassals he favored with office became cruel as their authority increased; vassals his generosity kept dependable became indifferent as his generosity was exhausted. Herein lies the true cause of Liu Zhang's failure. Our new administration must win respect through legal authority; when the laws are carried out, then the people will appreciate our kindnesses. Moreover, we must use rank to limit ambition so that when rank is granted, the honor will be appreciated. Balanced bestowing of kindness and honor will restore proper relations between lord and vassal, and the principles of good governance will again be manifest." Fa Zheng was persuaded and withdrew his suggestion. Henceforth there was good order in the army and among the population.

The Riverlands' forty-one subdistricts were placed under military control and pacified. Fa Zheng, serving as governor of Shu district, repaid the smallest favor and avenged the slightest grievance. Someone complained to Kongming that Fa Zheng should be rebuked for his overzealous administration. But Kongming replied, "I remember when Lord Liu was a virtual prisoner in Jingzhou, dreading Cao Cao to the north and fearful of Sun Quan to the east. Thanks to Fa Zheng, who lent our lord wings, he soared beyond anyone's reach. How can we restrict Fa Zheng or deny him his way?" Thus, the matter was dropped; but when the complaint came to Fa Zheng's attention, he began to show restraint in his conduct.

One day Xuande and Kongming were chatting, when a message came that Lord Guan had sent his son Ping to thank Xuande for the gold and silk he had been awarded. Xuande summoned the lad. After performing the ritual prostration, Guan Ping delivered Lord Guan's letter. "My father knows that Ma Chao's martial skill surpasses that of other warriors," Ping said. "He wants to come to the Riverlands for a trial of skill and has asked me to petition you, uncle, on this matter." Xuande was shocked. "If Lord Guan comes now to test his strength against Ma Chao," he said, "we will lose one of them." But Kongming said, "I see no harm. Let me send an answer." Xuande, fearing Lord Guan's hasty temper, had Kongming reply; Guan Ping sped the letter to Jingzhou. Lord Guan asked his son, "Did you discuss my trial of strength with Ma Chao?" "Here is the director general's response," Guan Ping replied. Lord Guan unsealed the letter, which read:

> I understand you wish a trial with Ma Chao. In my judgment, although Ma Chao is a fiercer warrior than most, he belongs in the category of Ying Bu and Peng Yue. He might prove the equal of your worthy brother, Yide, but could hardly compare with the unique and incomparable ability of our Long-Bearded Lord. Your present governorship of Jingzhou is no slight responsibility. If you came here and Jingzhou were lost, it would be the gravest offense. Please favor us with your discernment.

After reading the letter, Lord Guan stroked his beard and said with a smile, "How well Kongming knows me." He had the letter shown to his companions, and lost all interest in traveling to the west.

*   *   *   *

In the Southland Sun Quan learned that Xuande had taken possession of the Riverlands and moved the former inspector, Liu Zhang, to Gong'an. Sun Quan summoned Zhang Zhao and Gu Yong. "At the beginning," he told them, "Liu Bei pledged to return Jingzhou province after taking the Riverlands. He already holds the forty-one subdistricts of Ba and Shu and is about to extend his rule to the Hanzhong districts on the River Han. Either he returns the province now, or the time has come for war." Zhang Zhao objected. "Our land is at peace," he said. "We must not start a war. I have a plan to make Liu Bei restore Jingzhou to us with all humility and respect." Indeed:

> As a new day dawns in the Riverlands,
> The Southland seeks to satisfy its longstanding claim.

What was Zhang Zhao thinking?
Read on.

———————

The Southland seeks to have at least part of Jingzhou returned, but Lord

Guan refuses. Separated from his brothers and comrades in the west, Lord Guan seems to be building a base in Jingzhou.

In chapters 67 to 68 Cao Cao extends his reach west by conquering Hanzhong, the buffer region also known as the East Riverlands. In the year 215 he arranges the murder of Emperor Xian's queen, Empress Fu, together with her two sons. Cao Cao then marries his daughter to Emperor Xian. In 216 Cao Cao assumes the title wang or king of Wei, his first heritable title, naming his eldest son Cao Pi heir apparent. Cao Cao is building his dynasty through both territory and lineage.

At this point Kongming relieves the pressure in the west by convincing Sun Quan to attack Cao Cao's eastern flank at Hefei. The fighting ends in a stalemate, and Cao Cao again sends his generals against the west; but counter-attacks by Riverlands forces (chapter 71) and Kongming's capture of Hanzhong (chapter 73) force Cao Cao to retreat. The momentum of these victories allows Liu Xuande to assume a new title, King of Hanzhong, thus extending his western base toward the east and matching Cao Cao's titular status. Liu Xuande will soon establish an heir of his own, Liu Shan, also known as Ah Dou.

CHAPTER 73

Xuande Becomes King of Hanzhong; Lord Guan Storms Xiangyang District

The military leaders wanted to raise Xuande to the imperial dignity; but, reluctant to broach the subject directly, they petitioned Director General Zhuge Liang. "I have already decided on that," he told them and went with Fa Zheng to see Xuande. "Cao Cao has so aggrandized his power, the people have lost their rightful sovereign," Kongming began. "But Your Lordship, celebrated for humanity and justice, now has full control of the Riverlands. It might be well to accept the will of Heaven and follow the mood of the people—to assume the throne. Thus, rightfully and justifiably you could bring the traitor to justice. This brooks no delay; we appeal to you to select an auspicious time."

Xuande was taken aback. "You are quite mistaken, Director General," he said. "I may be of the royal house, but I am a subject nonetheless. If I do this, it will be an act of opposition to the dynasty." "That is not so," Kongming went on. "At present the empire perishes of its divisions. Contenders arise one after the other declaring their dominion over one portion or another, while throughout the realm virtuous and talented men who have faced death in the service of a sovereign long to clamber onto a dragon, to attach themselves to a phoenix, thereby to establish their merit and their fame. If now, merely to deflect criticism, you cling to a narrow sense of honor, you will risk failing the expectations of the people. I beg Your Lordship to reconsider."

To this appeal Xuande replied, "If you mean for me to occupy the imperial dignity unlawfully, I must refuse. Try to come up with a better plan." His commanders said, "If you decline, my lord, the commitment of the people will slacken." Kongming added, "Your Lordship, for whom honor is principle, may be reluctant to proclaim the imperial title outright. But now that you hold Jingzhou and the Riverlands, you might become king of Hanzhong."

To this proposal Xuande replied, "Though you would all honor me as king, without the Emperor's public edict, it would be usurpation." "It would be more appropriate to depart from the norm in this case," Kongming responded. "Do not cling to convention." At this point Zhang Fei shouted, "Other men who bear surnames other than Liu are trying to become sovereign, yet you, brother, are a branch of the lineage of the Han dynasty. Never mind 'king of Hanzhong'—declare yourself August Emperor. There is no reason not to!" "You have said too much," retorted Xuande in a tone of rebuke. Kongming spoke again: "Merely as an expedient, Your Lordship, you might first assume the title of king; then memorialize the Emperor. It will still be in good time."

After declining repeatedly, Xuande finally acceded. In the seventh month of Jian An 24 [A.D. 219], an altar for the ceremony was erected at Mianyang in a space nine *li* around.

Cao Cao is ready to attack the Riverlands, but his first secretary, Sima Yi, urges him to ally first with Sun Quan and capture Jingzhou. Cao Cao sends Man Chong to the Southland to pursue these negotiations.

Sun Quan approved the plan of his counselor Zhang Zhao and arranged for Man Chong to be escorted into the city. The ceremonies concluded, Sun Quan treated Man Chong as an honored guest. Submitting Cao Cao's letter, Man Chong said, "The Southland and Wei have no quarrel; Liu Bei has been the cause of the hostilities between us. The king of Wei has sent me here to work out an agreement whereby you, General, will attack and take over Jingzhou while he brings his army up to Hanzhong so that we can attack Liu Bei on two fronts. Once he is destroyed, we can divide his territories, pledging to respect the boundary between." After reading the letter, Sun Quan held a grand banquet for Man Chong and then had him escorted to the government's guesthouse to rest.

Again Sun Quan turned to his advisers. Gu Yong said, "Although their plan is self-serving, it is reasonable. Let us send the messenger back with our agreement to coordinate against Liu Bei; but send an agent over the river, too, to probe the activities of Lord Guan. That is the way to proceed." Then Zhuge Jin suggested, "I have heard that Liu Bei found Lord Guan a wife when he came to Jingzhou. First she bore him a son, then a daughter. The daughter, still young, has not yet been promised in marriage. I would like to seek her hand for your heir. If Lord Guan consents, we can begin planning joint action against Cao Cao. Otherwise, we help Cao Cao take Jingzhou." Sun Quan adopted the plan; he sent Man Chong back to Xuchang and Zhuge Jin on to Jingzhou.

Zhuge Jin presented himself before Lord Guan. The ceremonies concluded, Lord Guan asked Zhuge Jin's purpose in coming. "I come for one particular purpose," responded Zhuge Jin, "to bind the amity of our two houses. My master has a son, a youth of high intelligence. And, I understand, you have a daughter; it is her hand I come to seek. If our two houses form this union and combine to destroy Cao Cao, it will be truly splendid. I beg you to consider it, my lord." Lord Guan's answer came in a burst of anger: "My tiger-lass married off to a mongrel? I'd have your head if you weren't Kongming's brother! Speak of it no more!" Lord Guan called for his aides, who drove Zhuge Jin scurrying off.

Back in the Southland Zhuge Jin could not conceal what had happened. Hearing the report, Sun Quan exclaimed, "What insolence!" and summoned Zhang Zhao and others to consult on a strategy for taking Jingzhou. Bu Zhi argued, "Cao Cao has been planning to usurp the dynasty for a long time; all he fears is Liu Bei. Now he wants us to attack Liu Bei, deflecting the blow intended for him." But Sun Quan said, "I have waited too long for Jingzhou!" "Cao Ren has troops in Xiangyang and in Fan," Bu Zhi replied. "No river bars his way; he could take Jingzhou by land, yet he wants to get you to do it. Why? This shows his real mind. Your Lordship, send a representative to Xuchang with a proposal that Cao Cao first have Cao Ren move by land against Jingzhou. Lord Guan will surely try to capture Fan. And once Lord Guan takes that step, a single Southland general will suffice to make the province ours, and with little trouble."

Sun Quan approved the suggestion and sent a man across the river to present the proposal to Cao Cao. Cao Cao was delighted and sent his acceptance back by the same messenger. He then ordered Man Chong to Fan to assist Cao Ren in planning the operation. At the same time he sped a call to the south to have marine forces ready to reinforce his land troops in the attack on Jingzhou.

*   *   *   *

Xuande, king of Hanzhong, having made Wei Yan responsible for the defense of the east Riverlands region, brought his court back to Chengdu. There he assigned officials to supervise construction of a palace. In addition he had way stations built for a post road; from Chengdu northeast to Baishui more than four hundred were set up. Grain was widely stored and many weapons manufactured. All these measures envisioned the eventual capture of the northern heartland.

Spies brought word that Cao Cao and Sun Quan had formed an alliance for the purpose of taking Jingzhou; the king of

Hanzhong, Xuande, hastily called Kongming to counsel. "This plan of Cao Cao's is not at all unexpected," the director general said. "And the Southland is well provided with advisers of its own who will make sure Cao Ren takes the field first." The king replied, "And what do we do then?" "Send a messenger to inform Lord Guan of his new office," Kongming advised, "then have him capture Fan. That should scare the enemy and make them scatter." The king, delighted, sent Fei Shi, a captain in the forward unit, to perform the mission.

Lord Guan received Fei Shi personally in front of the city walls and led him to the government buildings. The amenities concluded, Lord Guan asked, "With what rank has the king invested me?" "Chief of the 'Five Tiger Generals,'" was the reply. "What 'Five Tiger Generals'?" Lord Guan wanted to know. "Yourself, Zhang Fei, Zhao Zilong, Ma Chao, and Huang Zhong," Fei Shi answered. Lord Guan said angrily, "Zhang Fei is my younger brother; Ma Chao comes from a family of long-standing eminence. Zilong has followed my elder brother for many years and is as good as my younger brother, too. For them to have a position equivalent to my own is perfectly understandable. But who is Huang Zhong to rank alongside me? No self-respecting warrior would ever league himself with an old common soldier." Thereupon Lord Guan refused the seal and cord that Xuande had sent to confirm his appointment.

Fei Shi smiled and said, "You are making a mistake, General. Remember that prime ministers Xiao He and Cao Shen participated with the Supreme Ancestor in creating the dynasty. No man was closer to the Emperor than those two; yet Han Xin, a general who had defected from the enemy, was honored as a king— a position greater than Xiao He's or Cao Shen's. Neither of the prime ministers, however, is known to have complained. In this case, although the king of Hanzhong has named you as one of the 'Five Tiger Generals,' there is also the bond of brotherhood between you and him. To him, you and he are one. General, you are as good as king of Hanzhong; and the king of Hanzhong, you. How could you be classed with those others? You have the king's generous favor and should share joy and grief with him, blessing and misfortune, without niggling over status and titles. I beg you to consider this, General."

Lord Guan realized his mistake and saluted Fei Shi with clasped hands. "My ignorance, but for your advice, might have ruined the whole endeavor," he acknowledged, and received the seal of office with due reverence.

Now Fei Shi produced the royal writ directing Lord Guan to capture Fan. Lord Guan accepted his assignment and sent Fu Shiren and Mi Fang, forming the vanguard to station their men outside the city wall.

Lord Guan responds vigorously to the crisis by making a bid to drive Cao Cao from north China altogether. He wins battle after battle, but in the siege of the city of Fan, his arm is pierced by a poison arrow.

CHAPTER 75

Hua Tuo Scrapes the Poison from Lord Guan's Bone; Lü Meng Sends Mariners Across the River in Disguise

The moment he saw Lord Guan fall, Cao Ren and his men came charging out of the city for the kill. But Guan Ping fought the northerners off and brought his father safely back to camp. There the arrow was removed from his right arm. The arrowhead, however, had been poisoned; ulceration had reached the bone, and the arm, greenish and swollen, would not move. Guan Ping hastily convened the commanders and said, "If my father loses his arm, he will never fight again. It will be best to go back to Jiangling and take care of it." He then went with the commanders to see their leader. "What have you come for?" Lord Guan asked. "In view of Your Lordship's wound," they replied, "we are afraid the shock of battle could be bad for you. Our consensus is for all to return to Jiangling with you for treatment."

Lord Guan responded angrily, "Fan is within our grasp, and once we have it, we can reach Cao's capital at Xuchang by forced march. Then we can flush out the traitor, destroy him, and secure the house of Han. I cannot ruin this enterprise for the sake of a minor wound. Don't sap the morale of the troops." Guan Ping and the rest retired silently.

Lord Guan would not retreat, and the wound would not heal. His commanders were searching high and low for a good doctor when one arrived unexpectedly by boat from the Southland. A petty officer led him to Guan Ping, who studied the man. He had a square cap and loose-fitting clothes. A black satchel hung from his arm. Volunteering his name, he said, "I am Hua Tuo (styled Yuanhua) from the Qiao district in the fief of Pei. Hearing that General Guan, the world-renowned hero, has been wounded by a poisoned arrow, I have come especially to cure him." "I believe you are the man who once treated Zhou Tai of the Southland," Guan Ping said. "That is true," Tuo replied. Guan Ping was delighted, and in company with the commanders he took Hua Tuo in to Lord Guan.

Lord Guan was in terrible pain and worried about morale in the army. He was playing chess with Ma Liang to divert himself when they arrived. He invited the doctor in and, after the formalities, offered him a seat. Tea was served and drunk. Hua Tuo then asked to examine the wound. Lord Guan bared his arm and stretched it out. "This is from a crossbow," Hua Tuo said. "There is aconite infiltrating the bone. The arm will be useless if not treated soon." "What would you use?" Lord Guan asked. "I can save it," Hua Tuo answered, "but I am afraid Your Lordship would shrink from the treatment." With a smile Lord Guan responded, "To me, death is my homecoming. I will not shrink."

Hua Tuo continued, "In a quiet room we will have to set up a post with a loop nailed to the top. I will ask you to put your arm through the loop and let us tie it. We will cover your head with a blanket. I will cut through to the bone with a razor and scrape the poison off the bone; then after applying some medicine, I will sew up the wound. Nothing will happen to you; I am only afraid you will shrink from the surgery." "Is that all? It won't bother me a bit," Lord Guan replied. "And you can dispense with post and loop." With that he ordered a feast set forth.

After a few cups, Lord Guan resumed his game of chess with Ma Liang as he extended his arm and instructed the doctor to start the operation. An attendant held a basin under the arm to catch the blood. Hua Tuo took up his knife and said, "I am ready. Have no fear, Your Lordship." "Do what is required," said Lord Guan. "Don't think I shrink from pain like any common fellow." Hua Tuo parted the flesh, exposing the bone: it was already coated green. The knife made a thin, grating sound as it scraped the surface, until everyone present blanched and covered his face. But Lord Guan continued eating and drinking, laughing and talking as he played, showing no sign of pain.

In a short time the basin filled with blood. Hua Tuo finished the scraping, applied medicine, and sewed the wound shut. Lord Guan got up, smiled, and said to his commanders, "The arm is as flexible as ever. There is no pain at all. Master, you are a marvelous physician." Hua Tuo replied, "In a lifetime of practice I have never seen anything like this! It is Your Lordship who is more than human!" A poet of later times left these lines:

> Physic and surgery—two branches of one art—
> The rare and subtle science of the mortal world.
> For superhuman might, Lord Guan may take the crown;
> For sacred skill in healing, Hua Tuo wins renown.

When his wound was better, Lord Guan held a banquet to thank Hua Tuo. "Your Lordship's wound is cured," the doctor said, "but it must still be protected from any shock of anger. It will take a hundred days before everything is normal." Lord Guan offered Hua Tuo one hundred taels of gold, but the physician said, "I seek no reward. Your reputation for a high-minded sense of honor brought me here." Firmly refusing payment, Hua Tuo left a prescription for medicine to put on the wound; then he took his leave and departed.

After Lord Guan's stunning victories—the capture of Yu Jin and the execution of Pang De—his name resounded across the northern heartland, impressing one and all. When spies reported Lord Guan's triumph in the capital, Cao Cao summoned his advisers and said in alarm, "I have always known that Lord Guan surpassed all others in wisdom and valor. Now he holds Xiangyang: the tiger has grown wings! Yu Jin has been captured, Pang

De killed, and our own keen mettle blunted. What if they come straight to the capital? I think we should take the precaution of transferring the government."

Sima Yi objected to this proposal: "Yu Jin's men drowned in the flood, not in battle. Jin's defeat does not affect the government's position. Moreover, current discord between the Liu and Sun houses means that if Lord Guan gets what he wants, Sun Quan will be very unhappy. This is the time, Your Highness, to send someone down there who, by judicious argument—and by offering the entire Southland to Sun Quan as his fief once peace is restored—will be able to convince Sun Quan to muster a force and quietly pounce on Lord Guan from behind. That is how to relieve the siege at Fan."

First Secretary Jiang Ji added, "Sima Yi is right. Send a man to the Southland. There's no need to move the capital and disturb the people." Cao Cao assented, and the idea of moving the capital was dropped. In a tone of dismay Cao said to his commanders, "Yu Jin followed me for thirty years. It surprised me that at the moment of truth he didn't measure up even to Pang De. Now I want a man to take the letter to the Southland, and I also want a ranking commander to check Lord Guan's advance." Even as he spoke, a commander standing below volunteered. Cao Cao turned to him. It was Xu Huang. Well pleased, Cao Cao put fifty thousand picked men in Xu Huang's command, with Lü Jian as his deputy. On the appointed day the army advanced to Yangling Slope and camped there, waiting for an answer from the Southland before marching on.

*   *   *   *

On receiving Cao Cao's letter, Sun Quan readily accepted the proposed plan and swiftly dispatched his answer. He then assembled his counselors. Zhang Zhao made the first argument: "The recent news is that the north is so shaken by Lord Guan's victories over Yu Jin and Pang De that Cao Cao wants to move the capital and thus avoid the brunt of Guan's attack. Now that Fan may fall, he sends to us for help. But after the situation is stabilized, he will only go back on his word." Before Sun Quan had time to speak, a report came in: "Commander Lü Meng has arrived by boat from Lukou with important business to present in person."

Sun Quan summoned his commander, who said, "Lord Guan has deployed around Fan. Now is the time to attack Jingzhou, when he is on a far-off campaign." "I was thinking rather of going north and taking Xuzhou," Sun Quan replied. "Cao Cao, too, is far from his base on the north side of the Yellow River," Lü Meng said, "and has no time to look east to Xuzhou, it's true. Moreover, the province is lightly defended and should fall easily. However, the terrain favors the army rather than the navy. Even if we capture it, holding it will be another matter. I would take Jingzhou first; and then with the whole of the Great River secured, we can consider our next move." "Exactly my thought," Sun Quan responded. "I only wanted to sound you out. Quickly devise a plan. I will follow you with my army."

Lü Meng bade Sun Quan good-bye and returned to Lukou. There, mounted scouts informed him: "Up and down the river there are warning-fire beacons, some twenty, some thirty *li* apart." Lü Meng also learned that the Jingzhou forces were magnificently marshaled and fully prepared for attack. Startled, he said, "If that is how things stand, our plans are in trouble. A day ago I was trying to convince Lord Sun to capture Jingzhou. And now—how am I going to put my words into deeds?" Unable to come up with a solution, Lü Meng hid from his lord under cover of illness.

Sun Quan was deeply saddened by the news of Lü Meng's illness. Another commander, Lu Xun, came forward and said, "Lü Meng's illness is not real; it is put on." "If you are sure of that," Sun Quan said, "look into it." As ordered, Lu Xun went to Lukou and saw Lü Meng, whose face, as he had expected, showed no sign of illness. Lu Xun said to him, "I have been instructed by Lord Sun to inquire most respectfully into what has given discomfort to your esteemed self." Lü Meng replied, "Some unforeseen disorder afflicts my humble person—hardly worth troubling yourself to inquire after." "Lord Sun has entrusted a heavy responsibility to you," Lu Xun went on. "But instead of seizing the time to act, you vainly nurse this melancholia. Why?" Lü Meng studied his visitor a long while but said nothing. Lu Xun continued, "I would be so foolish as to proffer a little prescription that should remedy your disorder, General. However, I am not certain it applies." Lü Meng dismissed his attendants and said,

"Vouchsafe the precious remedy, and soon." With a smile Lu Xun said, "Your disorder is due to the magnificent marshaling of the Jingzhou army and its flare warning system along the river. But I have a plan to keep the guardians of the flare stations from raising the signal, a plan that will bring the armies of Jingzhou to surrender tamely. Would that suit you?" Lü Meng blurted out startled thanks, saying, "You speak as if you could see into my vitals. I would learn your worthy plan."

"Lord Guan counts too much on his heroic valor," Lu Xun explained, "and assumes he has no equal. You alone cause him concern. General, take this opportunity to resign your office, pleading ill health. Yield your command here at Lukou to someone else, someone whom we will instruct to acclaim and exalt Lord Guan with self-deprecatory phrases in order to feed his arrogance. Then he will be sure to pull back from Jingzhou and concentrate on Fan. If he leaves Jingzhou unprepared, a surprise attack by one of our contingents will yield control of it with a minimum of effort." Lü Meng was delighted with the ruse. He persisted in claiming he was too sick to appear, and finally submitted a written resignation.

Lu Xun returned and explained the strategy to Sun Quan, who accordingly summoned Lü Meng back to Jianye to convalesce. Coming before Lord Sun, Lü Meng was told, "Originally, Zhou Yu recommended Lu Su as his replacement for the post you hold; Lu Su recommended you. Now you, too, should recommend someone able and well regarded to replace you." "If we appoint an important person," Lü Meng said, "Lord Guan will be on his guard. Lu Xun is a profound strategist and, having no more than a local reputation, is unlikely to cause Lord Guan anxiety. If you appoint him in my place, our plan should carry." Delighted, Sun Quan made Lu Xun subordinate commander and inspector on the Right, replacing Lü Meng as defender of Lukou.

Lu Xun declined the honor, saying, "I am too young and inexperienced to assume so heavy a task." But Sun Quan said, "Lü Meng's recommendation could not be wrong. I will not take no for an answer." And so Lu Xun accepted the seal of office and departed at once for Lukou. After assuming command of all infantry, cavalry, and naval forces, Lu Xun drew up a letter to Lord

Guan and sent it by messenger together with champion horses, rare silk damasks, wine, and other gifts.

While Lord Guan was recuperating from his wound and refraining from military action, the announcement came: "The Southland's chief commander at Lukou, Lü Meng, is dangerously ill. Sun Quan has recalled him for treatment and assigned Lu Xun to replace him. Lu Xun has sent a man with a letter and gifts as a gesture of respect." Lord Guan summoned the messenger and, pointing at him, said, "It seems rather shortsighted of Sun Quan to appoint a mere boy as general." The messenger bowed down to the ground and said, "General Lu presents this letter and these ceremonial gifts not only to honor Your Lordship, but with an earnest desire for accord and amity between the houses of Liu and Sun. I pray your indulgence in accepting them."

Lord Guan unsealed the letter and studied it. The language was the ultimate in self-deprecation and reverence. After perusing it, Lord Guan looked up and laughed, ordered his aides to receive the gifts, and sent the messenger back. The messenger told Lu Xun: "Lord Guan was appreciative and delighted. The Southland should not concern him any further."

Lu Xun could not have been more pleased. He sent spies into Jingzhou who reported that Lord Guan had indeed shifted most of his men to the siege at Fan and was waiting only for his wound to heal before launching the attack. After verifying the details, he dispatched the news to Sun Quan overnight. Sun Quan summoned Lü Meng and told him, "As expected, Lord Guan has pulled troops out of Gong'an and Jiangling in order to attack Fan. We can prepare the tactics to surprise the province. You and my younger cousin, Sun Jiao, shall lead the offensive. What do you say?" Sun Jiao (Shuming) was the second son of Quan's uncle Sun Jing.

Lü Meng responded, "If Your Lordship has confidence in me, use me alone. If you have confidence in Sun Jiao, use him alone. You must remember how much conflict there was when Zhou Yu and Cheng Pu were left and right field marshals; that was because Cheng Pu felt his senior status compromised by Zhou Yu's authority to make decisions. Cheng Pu had to see Zhou Yu's talents at work before he paid him the respect he deserved. My own talents fall far short of Zhou Yu's, and Sun Jiao is closer to you than Cheng Pu was; I'm afraid things wouldn't balance out."

Sun Quan saw the wisdom of Lü Meng's point and made him chief commander with authority over all armed forces. He ordered Sun Jiao to oversee supply and support operations from the rear. Lü Meng prostrated himself in gratitude; then he called up thirty thousand men and eighty swift craft. He selected a group of able sailors, disguised them in the plain clothes that merchants usually wear, and placed them at the oars. Concealed in the hulls were crack troops. Next, he assigned seven ranking commanders—Han Dang, Jiang Qin, Zhu Ran, Pan Zhang, Zhou Tai, Xu Sheng, and Ding Feng—to advance in series. The rest of the commanders were to remain with Sun Quan to provide support and reinforcement. The preparations complete, Lü Meng sent a letter to Cao Cao telling him to attack Lord Guan from the rear; and Lu Xun in Lukou was informed of all steps taken. Finally, the sailors dressed as merchants began their mission. They steered their light craft to the Xunyang River, moving at full speed day and night until they hit the north shore.

When challenged by Lord Guan's soldiers at the signal-flare stations, the Southlanders replied, "We are all merchants from afar. The wind blocked our course on the river, so we have come to take refuge here." They offered gifts to the station guards, who took their word and permitted them to anchor along the shore. Toward the second watch, the troops hidden in the boats emerged as a body, seizing and binding the station guards. At a silent signal the troops in all eighty boats appeared, captured the soldiers at the key signal stations, and hustled them back to the boats. Not one escaped. The Southlanders then struck out for Jiangling in unimpaired secrecy.

As they approached Jiangling in Jingzhou, Lü Meng used fair words to placate the men he had captured by the river; by means of various generous gifts he got them to agree to deceive the gate guards and, once inside, to start signal fires. The captives followed orders. Lü Meng had them lead the way. Late that night when they reached the walls, the gatekeepers recognized their own men and opened at their call. A united shout arose from the crowd of soldiers, and just inside the gate they set the signal fires. The Southlanders rushed in and took the city by surprise.

Lü Meng immediately issued a decree: "If any soldier kills one man or takes one article, he will be dealt with by strict military law." The city's administrators were told to continue in their current duties. Lord Guan's family was moved to different quarters and placed under protective custody. A report was sent to Sun Quan.

Rumors that his southern line of defense has fallen to Southland forces reach Lord Guan as he maintains the siege of Fan. Cao Cao sends General Xu Huang to defend Fan.

CHAPTER 76

Xu Huang Wages War on the River Mian; Lord Guan Flees to Mai in Defeat

At this moment Xu Huang's army arrived. It was reported to Lord Guan, who called for his horse. Guan Ping said, "You cannot engage the enemy, Father, while your strength is still impaired." "I've known Xu Huang many years," Lord Guan replied, "and am fully aware of what he can and cannot do. If he doesn't pull back, I will take the initiative and kill him; that'll give the generals of the north a good scare!"

Lord Guan emerged, vigorous and fearless, appointed with sword and armor. As he rode, he struck fear into the northmen who saw him. He reined in and called out his challenge: "Xu Huang, where are you!" Where banners parted at the entrance to the northerners' camp, Xu Huang rode forth. He bowed deeply. "My lord," he began, "since we parted, many years have fled. Who would have thought your hair and beard would turn so grey! Yet well and fondly do I remember the lusty years of our companionship, when I gained much from your tutelage. Today the effect of your triumphs is felt throughout our land. It makes an old friend sigh in admiration. Here fortune grants us a meeting, and long-endured yearnings are appeased."

To this Lord Guan replied, "The friendship between us is deep indeed—deeper than any other. Why, then, have you time and again driven my son so utterly to the limit?" Xu Huang turned to the commanders behind him and cried out harshly, "A thousand pieces of gold to the man who takes his head!" Lord Guan was astonished. "My friend," he said, "how can you say this?" Xu Huang answered, "Today I serve the government. I am not one to set public duty aside for personal sentiment." With that, he took on Lord Guan in direct combat, his poleaxe whirling. In a fury Lord Guan met him with circling blade. After some eighty bouts Lord Guan finally felt his right arm begin to weaken, though his fighting skill was at its peak. Fearful for his father, Guan Ping hastily sounded the gongs, and Lord Guan rode back to the base.

All of a sudden a deafening clamor surrounded the camp. What had happened was this: the moment Cao Ren had heard that Cao Cao was coming to relieve Fan, he had led his troops out of the city and joined forces with Xu Huang. Together they attacked and routed the Jingzhou troops. Lord Guan took flight, riding pell-mell with his men to the upper reaches of the Xiang River, the troops of Wei in hot pursuit. Lord Guan crossed quickly and headed south for Xiangyang. On the way, an express courier found him and informed him that Jiangling had fallen and that Lü Meng had his family in custody. Lord Guan began to panic. Xiangyang was no longer safe, so he led his men toward Gong'an. But scouts brought a new report: "Fu Shiren has surrendered Gong'an to the south." Lord Guan was furious. Then his quartermaster arrived and announced, "Fu Shiren has gone to Nanjun, killed your messenger, and induced Mi Fang to surrender."

At this latest news, Lord Guan exploded in anger. His wound split open, and he passed out on the ground. When his commanders revived him, he said to Major Wang Fu, "Things would never have turned out so badly had I followed your advice and not trusted Fu Shiren." Lord Guan then asked, "What happened to the beacon flares along the river?" The scout replied, "The guards never got to raise their flares. Lü Meng crossed the river with his mariners dressed like merchants. The boats held crack troops, who overwhelmed the station guards." Lord Guan staggered and groaned. "Trapped by the cunning enemy! How can I face my elder brother again?" Commissariat Chief Zhao Lei said, "The situation is critical. We must send to Chengdu for help. And we must take the land route to try and recapture Jiangling." Lord Guan agreed. He sent Ma Liang and Yi Ji racing west to Chengdu with letters seeking aid. Lord Guan himself set out for Jiangling; he took the van, Guan Ping and Liao Hua the rear.

*   *   *   *

Lord Guan had no base and nowhere to turn. He said to Zhao Lei, "The southern forces are ahead, the northern behind. I am caught in the middle, and no rescue has come. What are we to do?" Zhao Lei answered, "Lü Meng once wrote to Your Lordship from Lukou committing himself to the common effort to punish the traitor Cao. Now, instead, he is helping Cao Cao by attacking us. I advise you to station the army here, Your Lordship, and write to Lü Meng reproving him for betraying the alliance. See what he says." Lord Guan sent a messenger to Jiangling.

In Jiangling in Jingzhou, Lü Meng had issued orders that the families of the warriors accompanying Lord Guan, whatever district they might be in, were to be issued monthly rations, shielded from any harassment, and provided with medical care. The grateful families went on with their lives peacefully. When Lord Guan's representative arrived, Lü Meng met him outside the wall and welcomed him into the city as an honored guest. On delivery of Lord Guan's letter, Lü Meng told the messenger, "In concluding an accord with General Guan, I acted on my own. Today I am under orders. I am not my own master here, and I must trouble you, when you report back to the general, to convey my view as amicably as you can." Lü Meng ordered a banquet for the representative and escorted him to the post station, where the families of Lord Guan's warriors surrounded him for news. Some pressed letters on him and some gave him spoken messages, all to the effect that the families were well and had enough food and clothing. Lü Meng escorted Lord Guan's courier outside the city.

When the messenger brought back Lü Meng's answer and the tidings of Lord Guan's and his commanders' families, Lord Guan was moved to rage. "Treacherous, treasonous tricks!" he cried. "But I will take revenge, for I will kill him while I live, or else after I am dead!" Lord Guan roughly sent the messenger out, and the man was quickly surrounded by commanders seeking news of their families. As they took in hand the letters from home and learned of the security and comfort their loved ones enjoyed and the pains Lü Meng had taken to be considerate, the commanders felt grateful and began to lose their will to fight.

Lord Guan led his army on toward Jiangling, but during breaks in the march many there deserted and fled. Hate and anger rose up in him, and he pressed the army to advance. Suddenly there was a thunderous clamor. A band of soldiers blocked his way, at the head a chief commander—Jiang Qin. Reining in, he raised his spear and shouted, "Guan! Surrender now!" Lord Guan swore back, "I am a Han general and will never surrender to a rebel!" Laying on the whip, his blade dancing, Guan went for Jiang Qin. The clash was brief. Qin fled in defeat. Lord Guan had pursued him some twenty *li*, when more shouting began. On the left Han Dang came charging out of a ravine; on the right Zhou Tai came out of another. Then Jiang Qin reversed direction and gave battle. Caught between three forces, Lord Guan pulled back and fled.

After proceeding several *li* Lord Guan saw groups of men on the ridges of some hills to the south. Near them, a white flag bearing the words "Natives of Jingzhou" caught the breeze. They shouted down a plea: "All native warriors surrender quickly!" Lord Guan wanted to rush the hills and kill them. But he was assaulted by two more units, which had sprung from the shady side of the hills: to the left, Ding Feng; to the right, Xu Sheng. Their men now joined those of Jiang Qin, Han Dang, and Zhou Tai. Amid earth-shaking yells and drums and horns that filled the sky with noise, they closed in. Lord Guan's immediate commanders were slowly being eliminated as the fighting wore on into the sunset. Lord Guan saw Jingzhou troops on the surrounding hills, brothers calling to brothers, sons searching for fathers and fathers for sons. It went on and on; the men were turning against him, quitting in response to the calls, ignoring Lord Guan's commands. Soon he was left with only three hundred followers.

The fighting went on into the third watch. Due east a great cry went up. It was Guan Ping and Liao Hua. They had broken through the encirclement to rescue Lord Guan. Guan Ping said, "The troops are out of control. We have to get to a fortified place and hold it until help comes. The town of Mai, though small, should serve." Lord Guan approved and urged his remnant force toward the town. After entering, they sealed the four gates tight. Then they took counsel. Zhao Lei said, "We are close to Shangyong. Liu Feng and Meng Da are defending it. Send to them for help. Even a small contingent, just to relieve us until a larger force comes from the Riverlands, will restore morale."

At this moment it was reported that Southland troops had surrounded Mai. Lord Guan asked, "Who will break out and go to Shangyong for help?" Liao Hua volunteered, and Guan Ping agreed to escort him through the enemy lines. Lord Guan composed a letter, which Liao Hua concealed on his person. The two volunteers supped well, mounted, and went out the gate. Ding Feng of the Southland confronted them. Guan Ping attacked valiantly and drove him off. Seizing the moment, Liao Hua got through the siege and made for Shangyong. Guan Ping reentered the city and resolutely refused to appear.

Trapped in the town of Mai, Lord Guan's hopes fade.

CHAPTER 77

At Mount Yuquan Lord Guan Manifests a Divine Presence; In Luoyang City Cao Cao Feels the Force of Guan's Soul

Lü Meng offered Sun Quan the following plan: "Guan has few troops and is unlikely to flee by the main road. He'll take the steep path just north of Mai. Have Zhu Ran place five thousand of our best men there in ambush twenty *li* down the way and strike after the enemy passes. They'll be in no mood to fight and will flee toward Linju. Then let Pan Zhang hide another five thousand men in the hills by Linju—we will have Lord Guan! For now, attack Mai on all sides except the north and wait for them to go out through there." Sun Quan agreed and asked Lü Fan to judge the prospects of this plan in the light of the *Book of Changes*. When the hexagram had been formed, Lü Fan announced, "The hexagram signifies an enemy fleeing northwest. Well before midnight Guan is sure to be caught." Satisfied, Sun Quan ordered Zhu Ran and Pan Zhang to carry out Lü Meng's plan.

Inside Mai, Lord Guan counted up his forces. Of infantry and cavalry there remained a mere three hundred all told. His grain and fodder were exhausted. During the night southern soldiers called out the names of their brethren within the walls, many of whom slipped over and fled, for no sign of rescue was to be seen. At his wits' end, Lord Guan said to Wang Fu, "How I regret ignoring your good advice. In the present crisis, what more can be done?" Wang Fu wept as he answered, "Not even the ancient strategist Jiang Ziya could find a way out!" And Zhao Lei said, "We have had no relief from Shangyong because Liu Feng and Meng Da won't act on our appeal. Why not abandon this isolated town and flee for the Riverlands, reorganize an army and plan the reconquest of Jingzhou?" "That's my own inclination," Lord Guan replied. Then he ascended the wall and saw few enemy troops around the north gate.

Lord Guan asked a resident of Mai, "What is the terrain like going north?" "North of here," the reply went, "are paths in the foothills that lead to the Riverlands." "That's the route I want to take," Lord Guan said. But Wang Fu objected: "Small roads are vulnerable to ambush. Take the main road." "Even so," Lord Guan answered, "I'm not afraid." With that, he issued an order for all his soldiers and officers to pack and dress for the evacuation. Again Wang Fu wept as he said, "My lord, take care on the roads. I will remain here with one hundred men and hold Mai to the death. If they take the town, we will not submit but wait for you to rescue us."

Lord Guan and Wang Fu parted tearfully. Then, leaving Mai in the hands of Wang Fu and Zhou Cang, Guan bolted out the north gate accompanied by Guan Ping, Zhao Lei, and two hundred followers. Lord Guan rode with his sword leveled for action. By the end of the first watch, when he had gone about twenty *li*, drums and gongs began sounding from the pockets and hollows in the hills. Voices rang in the air as a band of troops appeared, Zhu Ran at the head. He charged, spear raised, and shouted: "Go no further! Surrender or die!" Lord Guan advanced, whirling his blade. Zhu Ran fled at once; Lord Guan pursued hotly. At the sound of the drum, troops sprang up on all sides. Resistance was unthinkable; Lord Guan fled by a narrow road toward Linju. Zhu Ran harried the rear, reducing Lord Guan's retinue.

After another four or five *li* Lord Guan was confronted with earth-shaking cries and sky-reaching flames as Pan Zhang charged in for the kill. Maddened, Lord Guan met him. After three clashes Pan Zhang fled in defeat; but Lord Guan could not afford to continue fighting, and headed out toward the hills. Guan Ping overtook him and reported that Zhao Lei had fallen in the melee. Sorrow and despair overcame Lord Guan. He ordered Ping to cover the rear while he forged ahead. A dozen followers were all that remained to him.

Lord Guan came to a place called Breach in the Rocks where the hills squeezed the road. Reeds and shriveled grass grew against the hills, crowded by tangles of shrubs and trees. The fifth watch had nearly ended. Suddenly a voice cried out, springing another ambush. Spear-length hooks and loops reached out and yanked Lord Guan from his mount. As he tumbled to the ground, Pan Zhang's commander, Ma Zhong, took him prisoner. Guan Ping rushed to his father's aid. But Pan Zhang and Zhu Ran had surrounded him. Ping fought on, alone, until he was spent; then they took him, too. As the day broke, Sun Quan was informed of the capture of Lord Guan and his son. Immensely pleased, he called his commanders together.

After a short while Ma Zhong hustled Lord Guan into Sun Quan's tent. Sun Quan said, "General, out of long-standing admiration for your splendid virtues, I sought to work out a liaison through marriage. Why did you spurn the offer? You have ever clung to the view that you are without peer in the empire. How has it come about that you are my prisoner today? Do you, General, acknowledge yourself beaten?" Lord Guan damned him harshly: "Green-eyed scamp! Red-whiskered rodent! I gave my allegiance to Imperial Uncle Liu in the peach garden when we swore to uphold the house of Han. What would I be doing in the ranks of traitors in revolt such as you? Now that I have blundered into your treacherous devices, death alone remains. There is no more to say."

Sun Quan turned to his assembled officers. "Lord Guan," he said, "is one of the valiant champions of our time, a man I cherish deeply. I propose that we treat him with the utmost courtesy to encourage him to come over to us. What do you say?" First Secretary Zuo Xian said, "It will not work. That time when Cao Cao had him, he enfeoffed him as a lord, granted him rank, and feasted him—every third day a minor banquet, every fifth day a major one. Whenever he got on his horse, Cao handed him gold. Whenever he got down from his horse, Cao handed him silver. With such kindnesses Cao failed to hold him, and saw Guan leave and kill his pass guards on the way. And today Cao Cao is on the verge of shifting his capital to avoid the thrust of Guan's offensive. My lord, Guan is our captive. If you do not do away with him immediately, I fear the consequences."

Sun Quan pondered for some time until he admitted the truth of the secretary's words and ordered the prisoner removed. And so Lord Guan and his son, Ping, were beheaded in the twelfth month of the twenty-fourth year of Jian An [A.D. 220]. Lord Guan was fifty-eight years of age. A poet of later times has left these lines expressing his sorrow and admiration:

> Unrivaled in the latter years of Han,
> Lord Guan towered high above all men.
> Bold in arms by dint of godlike might,
> He knew his letters in a scholar's right.
> Like glare of day, his heart reflected true,
> His *Spring and Autumn* honor touched the clouds—
> A shining spirit to live through history,
> Not just the crowning glory of a world in three.

Another verse says:

> For the paragon of men, look back to Jieliang;
> There men vie to honor Lord Guan of the Han.
> For the peach grove brother oath he sealed one day,
> A thousand autumns' tribute of royal rites.

His manly soul had power like wind or thunder;
His glowing purpose shone like sun or moon.
And now the realm abounds in statued shrines
With winter-braving crows on olden boughs.

After the passing of Lord Guan, his glorious steed, Red Hare, captured by Ma Zhong, was presented to Sun Quan, who made Ma Zhong a gift of the horse. But Red Hare refused to eat and died after several days.

Inside the town of Mai, meanwhile, Wang Fu, trembling and fearful, asked Zhou Cang, "Last night our lord came to me in a dream. Covered with gore, he stood before me. As I questioned him, I woke with a violent start. What does it signify?" Then came the report: the southerners were at the gate with the heads of Lord Guan and Guan Ping, calling for the surrender of the town. Wang Fu and Zhou Cang quickly climbed the wall and looked down at the heads. The report was all too true. Wang Fu let out a cry and fell to his death. Zhou Cang cut his throat. Thus, the town of Mai, too, came into the possession of the Southland.

The vapor from Lord Guan's soul remained undissolved, floating attenuated until it came to rest on Jade Springs Hill in Dangyang county, Jingmenzhou. On the hill lived an old monk whose Buddhist name was Pujing, or Universal Purity. He was the abbot of Zhenguo Temple at the Si River pass. In his jaunts through the realm, he had come to the mountain and, attracted by its charming scenery, had built himself a thatched shelter there. In this hermitage he would seat himself for meditation each day, searching for the truth of life. Beside him was a single novice; they lived on the food they could beg.

The night Lord Guan died, the moon glowed pale and a breeze blew cool and fresh. Some time after the third watch, as the monk was sitting in meditation, a voice in the sky called out, "Return my head." Pujing scrutinized the air. A man was riding the steed Red Hare and brandishing the sword Green Dragon. Two men were in his train, a general of fair complexion and a swarthy man with curling whiskers. Together the three alighted from a cloud onto the summit of Jade Springs Hill. Pujing realized that it was Lord Guan and struck the door with a deer-tail whisk for protection against the spirit. He said, "Lord Guan, where are you now?" Lord Guan's glowing cloud-soul seemed to comprehend instantly as it dismounted and dropped on the wind before the monk's hut. Palms together, the wraith spoke: "Who are you, master? I would know your name-in-Buddha." "This old monk is known as Pujing," he replied. "We met once before at the Zhenguo Temple, my lord. Can you have forgotten?"

Replied Lord Guan: "My gratitude for the help you once gave me is engraved in my memory. A calamity has befallen me, and I appeal to you now for the redeeming counsel that will point me out of the darkness of my wandering." "Right and wrong, past and present are relevant no more; retribution follows human action with the certainty of fate," the monk answered. "Now you cry out for your head, having met your death at the hands of Lü Meng. From whom shall Yan Liang, Wen Chou, Cao Cao's six pass guards, and the countless others whom you killed seek their heads?" In a flash Lord Guan realized the truth and, bowing his head in submission to Buddha's law of karma, he departed. Thereafter he frequently manifested himself in divine form on Jade Springs Hill to afford protection to the common people. And the local dwellers showed their gratitude by building a temple on the summit, where they made offerings each season. Later someone inscribed the following couplet on the temple wall:

> Behind the ruddy face, a ruby heart—
> Lord Guan astride Red Hare outrode the wind.
> But far as he rode, he served the Fire King.
> By oil lamp light he studied history;
> In war he trusted to his dragon sword.
> His inmost thought would welcome light of day.

Now that Lord Guan was dead, Sun Quan consolidated his hold on all the territories of Jingzhou. After rewarding all units of the army, he held a grand banquet for the commanders in honor of Lü Meng. Turning to the assembly, Sun Quan said, "After long frustration, our easy acquisition of Jingzhou is owing to the meritorious service of Lü Meng." Lü Meng tried repeatedly to decline the testimonial, but Sun Quan continued, "At an earlier time, Zhou Yu, a man of exceptional talent and vision, defeated Cao Cao at Red Cliffs. Alas, he died prematurely and was replaced by Lu Su, who in his very first interview with me broached a grand imperial strategy for the Southland—the first boon. When Cao Cao descended upon us, I was universally counseled to surrender. Lu Su alone urged me to call in Zhou Yu, to oppose and attack Cao Cao—the second boon. The only fault I found in Lu Su is that he talked me into allowing Liu Bei to borrow Jingzhou. But today it is you, Lü Meng—you worked out the strategy for retaking Jingzhou, and thus you excel the other two by far."

Sun Quan personally poured out wine and presented it to Lü Meng. Lü Meng received it and was about to drink, when he dashed the cup to the ground instead and seized Sun Quan with one hand. "Green-eyed scamp!" he screamed. "Red-whiskered rodent! Have you forgotten me? Or not?" The assemblage looked aghast. Everyone moved to rescue Sun Quan, but Meng knocked him to the ground, strode to his throne, and seated himself upon it. Meng's eyebrows arched, his eyes grew round and prominent as he bellowed, "I have crisscrossed the empire for thirty-odd years since defeating the Yellow Scarves, only to have your treacherous trap sprung on me. But if I have failed to taste your flesh in life, Lü Meng, I shall give your soul no peace in death—for I am Guan Yunchang, lord of Hanshou precinct!"

Fear-stricken, Sun Quan led the assemblage in offering obeisance. But lo! Lü Meng collapsed on the ground, blood ran out of his orifices, and he died. There was general terror. Sun Quan had Lü Meng's corpse coffined and buried, and posthumously appointed Meng governor of Nanjun and lord of Chanling; Meng's son, Ba, inherited his rank. Thereafter Sun Quan was tormented with anxiety over the execution of Lord Guan.

Unexpectedly, Zhang Zhao arrived from the southern capital, Jianye; he was summoned by Sun Quan. "My lord," Zhang Zhao said, "when you put Lord Guan and his son to death, you brought the Southland to the verge of disaster, for the man had bound himself to Liu Bei. By the peach garden oath they swore to live and die as one. Today Liu Bei controls the forces of all the Riverlands. Add to that the cunning of Zhuge Liang and the valor of the remaining 'Tiger Generals,' Zhang Fei, Huang Zhong, Ma Chao, and Zhao Zilong—when Liu Bei learns how Lord Guan and Guan Ping died, he will mobilize the whole kingdom and do his utmost for revenge, a threat the Southland is going to find difficult to meet." Badly shaken by Zhang Zhao's words, Sun Quan stamped his feet as he said, "I have miscalculated. What can we do about it?"

"All is not lost, my lord," Zhang Zhao replied. "I have a plan to keep the westerners from attacking and thus keep Jingzhou as secure as a rock." "Tell us," said Sun Quan. Zhang Zhao went on, "Cao Cao has command of a million men. His glance scours the empire like a tiger's. But Liu Bei's urgent wish for revenge will require him to come to terms with Cao Cao. The Southland will hardly survive if those two combine forces and invade, so you would be well advised to make the first move. Have Lord Guan's head sent to Cao Cao in such a way as to make it appear to Liu Bei that it was all at Cao's direction. His animosity will be redirected toward Cao Cao and his armies will turn on the kingdom of Wei while we observe the fortunes of both and from a neutral vantage seize our opportunity."

Sun Quan agreed, and the head was taken in a wooden box to Cao Cao. At the time Cao Cao had just returned to Luoyang from Mopo. Hearing that Sun Quan had sent Lord Guan's head, Cao Cao exclaimed delightedly, "With him dead, I shall spend my nights secure indeed." But a member of the court stepped forward and said, "This is actually a device for transferring disaster away from the Southland." Cao Cao studied the speaker, First Secretary Sima Yi. Cao Cao demanded an explanation, and Sima Yi replied, "At the time when Liu, Guan, and Zhang pledged their honor in the peach garden, they swore to die for one another. Now, having put Lord Guan to death, the Southland fears the brothers' reprisal. That is why Sun Quan presented the head to Your Majesty—to make Liu Bei shift his hatred and attack us instead of them, while they look for ways to exploit the situation."

"What you say is correct," Cao Cao responded to Sima Yi, "but how do we get out of it?" "It is not difficult at all," Sima Yi replied. "Let Your Highness have Lord Guan's head fitted with torso and limbs carved of fragrant wood so that he may be buried whole with the ceremony due a high minister. When Liu Bei learns of it, his hatred for Sun Quan will deepen, and he will concentrate on the southern expedition. Then we can sit back and await developments. If the Riverlands is winning, we attack the Southland;

if the Southland is winning, we attack the Riverlands. Once one falls, the other cannot last."

Delighted with the scheme, Cao Cao called in the messenger from the Southland. The messenger presented the wooden box. Cao Cao opened it and saw Lord Guan's face, just as it had been in life. With a smile, Cao Cao said, "You have been well, I trust, General, since we parted?" Before Cao Cao could finish, the mouth opened, the eyes moved, and the hair and beard stood up like quills. Cao fell in a faint, reviving only after a long spell. He said to the officers who had rushed to his aid, "General Guan is no mortal!" The messenger told Cao Cao how Lord Guan had taken possession of Lü Meng, reviled Sun Quan, and then hounded Meng himself. Cao Cao shivered at the report. Adopting Sima Yi's advice, he held a grand ceremony with sacrificial animals and libations honoring the great man as a prince before burying his head and the wooden corpse outside the southern gate of Luoyang. Cao Cao ordered officials of all ranks to attend the funeral, and he personally made offerings and advanced Lord Guan's rank to prince of Jingzhou. Guards were then dispatched to the tomb, and the Southland messenger was sent home to report.

Ignorant as yet of Lord Guan's fate, Liu Xuande lets himself be persuaded to take a new royal wife, Lady Wu. Soon she bears two sons, Liu Yong and Liu Li. Then Guan's ghost visits Xuande who learns of the tragedy and mourns the loss of his brother, swearing to avenge his death, even if it means his own.

CHAPTER 78

Treating an Affliction, a Famous Practitioner Dies; Delivering the Last Command, the Tyrant Ends His Days

The king of Hanzhong dropped to the ground, grieving for Lord Guan and his son. Military officers and court officials rushed to offer him assistance. Finally the king revived, and they helped him to his rooms. "Try to stay calm," Kongming urged him. "From the beginning of time, death has been ordained. Lord Guan's willful arrogance caused this catastrophe. Your Highness must guard your precious health while we plan revenge step by step." "I took an oath of brotherhood with Lord Guan and Zhang Fei," Xuande answered. "We vowed to die as one. With Lord Guan gone, what meaning do wealth and honor have for me?"

As Xuande was speaking, Guan Xing entered, wailing piteously. At the sight of Lord Guan's son, Xuande cried out and fainted again. Officers rushed to his side. Five times Xuande fell from grief that day. For three days, refusing all food and drink, he howled out his pain until his cries brought flecks of blood to his tear-soaked robes. Kongming and the officers pressed him to desist, but he said, "Neither this sun nor this moon shall I share with the Southland: so I swear." "They say," Kongming responded, "that the Southland has presented Lord Guan's head to Cao Cao, who has interred him with royal ceremony." "What does it mean?" Xuande asked. "It means," Kongming replied, "that the Southland is trying to shift the blame for his death to Cao Cao—who, however, has seen through the scheme and buried Lord Guan with full honors so that your revenge may fall on the Southland." "Then," Xuande answered, "we must bare our weapons now and visit that vengeance on the south."

Kongming objected: "That we must not do, for the south would have us embroiled in the north just as the north would have us in the south, each evolving its own schemes and awaiting the opportunity to strike. Your Highness needs to refrain from action for now and simply initiate the funeral services for Lord Guan. When the accord between north and south breaks down, we can start our punitive expedition." The assembly of officials joined in earnest appeal, and Xuande finally accepted food; then he ordered the armed forces from the generals down to the rank and file to go into mourning. In front of the southern gate of the capital the king personally led the rites for summoning the souls of the dead and performed the sacrifices. His lamentation continued the entire day.

Meanwhile Cao Cao's health is failing, and the ghost of Lord Guan haunts his nights. The physician Hua Tuo is summoned, but when he proposes surgery on Cao Cao's skull, Cao Cao has him put in jail, where he dies. Soon after, early in the year 220, Cao Cao dies. His son Cao Pi succeeds him as king of Wei.

Having fended off challenges to his succession by two of his brothers, Cao Pi prepares to depose Emperor Xian and declare a new dynasty.

CHAPTER 80

Cao Pi Deposes the Emperor, Usurps the Liu Throne; The King of Hanzhong Assumes the Throne, Continues the Han Line

Accompanied by a delegation of civil and military officials, Hua Xin entered the court and addressed Emperor Xian: "Reverently we observe that since the new king of Wei has come to the throne, his virtue has spread throughout the land to the benefit of all. Not even the sage founders of our civilization, Tang and Yu, surpass the king. The assembly of the court, after collective consultation, now deeming that the sacrifices of Han have come to term, beseech Your Majesty to emulate the ancient sage-king Yao by ceremonially relinquishing the mountains, rivers, and dynastic shrines to the new king of Wei. This will fulfill the will of Heaven and satisfy the minds of men and also will enable Your Majesty to secure the blessings of untroubled leisure, a boon to your ancestral clan and the living souls of the realm. Our conclusion having been reached, we come to deliver this formal appeal."

The Emperor listened in fear and shock. After a long silence, he turned his gaze to the court of officials and began to sob. "I think back to the time," he said, "when the Supreme Ancestor, founder of the Han, slew the white serpent with his three-span sword and led the rebellion that quelled Qin and crushed Chu. He thus founded this house whose rule has passed from generation to generation in the Liu clan for four hundred years. Small though my talent be, what offense have I committed, what fault have I that justifies abandoning my ancestral right? Let the court reopen discussion!"

Hua Xin then brought forth two astrologers, Li Fu and Xu Zhi, and continued, "If Your Majesty has doubts, let these two answer them." Li Fu addressed the throne: "Since the accession of the king of Wei, the unicorn has descended, the phoenix has manifested itself, the yellow dragon has appeared, prize grains grow luxuriantly, and sweet dew has dropped from the skies. Thus does Heaven give sign and token that Wei shall replace Han." Xu Zhi added: "We who monitor the divine configurations can see that the allotted time of the fire-signed Han has expired. Your Majesty's imperial star has dimmed, while stellar configurations representing Wei, from the cope of Heaven to the margins of the horizon, outnumber all telling. Furthermore, the occult auguries show first the graphs *gui*, 'ghost,' and *wei*, 'consign,' in association. Thus the supplanting of Han is indisputable. Next the auguries show *yan*, 'word,' and *wu*, 'meridian,' side by side; and finally they show two suns, *ri*, vertically aligned. The conclusion is clear: Your Majesty must abdicate, for the graphs properly joined together read 'Wei Xuchang'—that is, 'Wei to receive the abdication of Han in the capital at Xuchang.' I beg Your Majesty to take heed."

To this Emperor Xian responded, "Your tokens, your graphic riddles—all hollow and preposterous! Would you have me set aside my patrimony on the strength of baseless delusions?" Wang Lang came forward next and addressed the throne: "From time immemorial, what has flourished must decay; what has prospered must decline. Every dynasty ends; every house falls. The house of Han has reigned more than four hundred years; with Your Majesty its line expires. Retire now, do not delay—or who knows what may happen next." Aggrieved, the Emperor retired to his rear chambers. The officials left smirking.

The next day the courtiers reassembled in the great hall and sent a eunuch to request the presence of Emperor Xian. The sovereign, anxious and fearful, refused to appear. Empress Cao said, "How can Your Majesty obstruct an official request to hold court?" The Emperor sobbed as he replied, "Your brother, who intends to usurp my throne, has instructed the officials to coerce me. That is why I will not go." Angrily the Empress said, "How dare my brother commit lese majesty?" As she was speaking, Cao Hong and Cao Xiu, armed, entered and requested the Emperor to appear before the officials in the great hall. The Empress denounced them. "This comes of your sedition and treachery!" she cried. "Angling for wealth and power has led you into treason and conspiracy. Never did my father, whom the world admired above all others for his high and glorious deeds, covet the hallowed instruments of supreme authority. And yet my brother, who has hardly succeeded to the kingship of Wei, boldly yearns to supplant the Han. August and luminous Heaven will never confer its blessing." So saying, the distraught Empress withdrew to her palace, leaving the attendants weeping emotionally.

Cao Hong and Cao Xiu strenuously urged the Emperor to attend the court session. Unable to resist further, he donned his formal attire and proceeded to the front of the hall. Hua Xin addressed the throne: "Let Your Majesty be guided by our discussions of yesterday lest disaster strike." The Emperor cried bitterly, "All of you have long enjoyed rich recompense as servants of the Han. Can the many sons and grandsons of renowned vassals among you bear to commit this act of insubordination?" "If Your Majesty will not comply with the consensus," Hua Xin continued, "I fear disorder in the inner sanctum could erupt at any time. This is not a case of our disloyalty to Your Majesty." "Who would dare to murder me?" the Emperor demanded.

Stridently Hua Xin replied, "All the empire knows that Your Majesty, lacking the 'great blessing' by which Heaven mandates the ruler of men, must take responsibility for the chaotic state of the realm. If not for the late king of Wei, Cao Cao, there would have been more than one who would have put Your Majesty to the sword. But still you refuse to acknowledge his past concern and repay his erstwhile kindness, and seem to want a general assault upon your imperial person." Appalled, the Emperor rose with a sweeping motion of his sleeves. Wang Lang eyed Hua Xin meaningfully. Hua Xin advanced boldly, laid hands on the sacred dragon robe and, his face contorted, said, "Agreed? Or not? Speak. Now."

The trembling Emperor could not respond. Cao Hong and Cao Xiu drew their swords and called for the keeper of the regalia. The keeper, Zu Bi, responded, "Present." Cao Hong demanded the jade seal. Zu Bi protested, "The jade seal is the treasure of the Son of Heaven. How dare you demand it?" Cao Hong called for his guards who removed the keeper and cut off his head. Zu Bi continued to protest until the moment of his death. A poet of later times left these lines of tribute to Zu Bi:

> Treachery reigned; the Han passed from the scene:
> "Thus Yao yielded to Shun," they falsely cried.
> A courtful of courtiers paid homage to the Wei;
> In defense of the seal a single vassal died.

The Emperor shook violently. At the base of the stairs leading to his throne all he could see were hundreds of armed men of Wei. Tearfully, the Emperor addressed the assemblage: "We intend here solemnly to abdicate our rule, transferring all under Heaven to the king of Wei. Kindly spare what breath still remains to me, that I may live out my natural years." Jia Xu said, "The king would never dismay Your Majesty. Quickly issue the edict and give peace to the hearts of all." The Emperor had no choice. He ordered Chen Qun to draft the edict; next, he ordered Hua Xin to receive the document and the imperial seal and then to bring the whole court to the king's palace to make the ritual presentation.

Cao Pi was delighted. He unsealed the edict and read it:

My reign of thirty-two years has seen great trouble in the empire. Fortunately, the spirits of my forefathers have rescued me from peril. But today, searching the configurations of the heavens and examining the hearts of the people, I see that the cycle of the fire element has expired and that a new element corresponding to the Cao clan now prevails. Indeed, that change of period is attested by the late King Cao's martial success and the present King Cao's manifest and glorious virtue. The new succession thus fulfills the expectations of all.

It is said, "When the way of the sages prevails, the empire belongs to all." For not favoring his own son, Yao earned an immortal name. I venture to emulate him. Today, abdicating to the prime minister and king of Wei, I follow in the footsteps recorded in the "Canon of Yao." Let Your Highness not decline.

When the edict had been read, Cao Pi was anxious to accept the decree, but Sima Yi warned him, "That would be wrong. Even though the edict and seal were brought here, let Your Highness decline in due modesty so as to forestall criticism in the outside world." On this advice Cao Pi had Wang Lang prepare a memorial which declared his virtue too meagre to assume the throne and advised searching elsewhere for someone of true worth. The Emperor, perplexed by the memorial, said to his vassals, "The king is modest and self-effacing. What shall I do?" Hua Xin replied, "Previously, when his father, Cao Cao, was offered the kingship of Wei, he declined three times but finally accepted as the edict required. Let Your Majesty send down another edict. The king should accept it."

The Emperor had no recourse. He ordered Huan Jie to draft another edict, and sent Zhang Yin as envoy of the Ancestral Temple to deliver document and seal to the palace of the king of Wei. Cao Pi opened the memorial, which read:

Let the king of Wei be advised with regard to his humble refusal of our throne: we have recognized the slow decline of the Han. How fortunate we were to have the help of King Wu, Cao Cao, whose virtue proved able to cope with all that destiny demanded, eliminating baneful violence, purging and securing our heartland.

The present king, Cao Pi, continues in that great tradition. His splendid virtue shines brilliantly forth. His sagely teachings cover the realm. His humane influence spreads in every direction. In his person the divine succession rests.

In ancient times after Shun had effected twelve accomplishments, Yao resigned the empire into his charge; and after Yu the Great distinguished himself in managing the floodwaters, Shun abdicated in his favor. The Han, in the tradition of Yao, is obliged to transfer its rule to a worthy sage, conforming to the spirits above and below, properly responding to Heaven's clear Mandate. Thus, we have empowered Imperial Censor Zhang Yin to proffer the imperial seal. Let His Majesty now receive it.

Cao Pi accepted the edict with delight. Turning to Jia Xu, he said, "Despite this second edict, I still fear that the world as well as future generations will condemn the usurpation." "There is a simple solution," Jia Xu replied. "Command Zhang Yin to take the edict back once again with instructions for Hua Xin to have the Emperor build an Altar for Acceptance of the Abdication. Then, on a propitious day, convene the senior and junior officials at the foot of the altar and have the Emperor personally tender the seal as he abdicates. That should resolve all doubts and check all criticism."

Delighted with this advice, Cao Pi had Zhang Yin return the regalia and prepare another memorial announcing his humble refusal of the imperial place. When Zhang Yin presented the new memorial, the Emperor asked his courtiers, "What is the king of Wei's purpose in declining a second time?" Hua Xin said to the Emperor, "Your Majesty, build an Altar for Acceptance of the Abdication, then gather the high officials and commoners around it so that the abdication will be plain and public. That way, the future generations of your line will enjoy the grace of the Wei." The Emperor complied. He sent an officer of the Department of Imperial Sacrifices to divine for a favorable site in Fanyang. There an altar of three levels was set up. They designated the predawn hours of *gengwu,* the seventh cyclical day in the tenth month, for the abdication ceremony to take place.

When the appointed time came, Emperor Xian invited Cao Pi, king of Wei, to ascend the altar. Around the base clustered a vast assemblage of four hundred officials, major and minor, as well as some thirty thousand warriors including the Royal Guard, the Imperial Guard, and the Palace Guard. The Emperor held the jade seal in both hands and transferred it respectfully to Cao Pi. Below, the assembly kneeled to hear the declaration of transmission:

Be it known to you, O King of Wei, that anciently Yao solemnly relinquished the mandate to Shun, who in turn passed it to Yu. For the Mandate of Heaven does not abide but finds its home only where virtue is. The way of Han is failing; our generations have lost their proper sequence. When the succession reached my own person in the spreading gloom of great upheaval, a multitude of malefactors ran unchecked and havoc was all within our sphere.

Thanks to the martial genius of King Wu, Cao Cao, who retrieved our empire from rebellions in all quarters, the integrity of our northern region was preserved, and our ancestral sanctum kept safe. Not I alone benefited; the capital and its nine subject domains stand in his debt. You, King, have honorably followed in his footsteps and added glory to his great virtue; you have magnified the great cause of the founders of the Zhou, kings Wen and Wu; and you have given new luster to the boundless fame of your late father.

The spirits of former emperors send down auspicious signs; men and gods affirm the auguries: Cao Pi is the ideal successor to manage the dynasty's affairs. To all I confer my sovereign charge. All concur in enjoining you to model yourself after Shun, so that I may reverently abdicate to you in accordance with the "Canon of Yao." Oh, heed this! "The Heavenly calendar is invested in your person." May you conform to this great ritual with humility before the spirits and thus solemnly receive Heaven's Mandate to preside over the regions and districts of the realm.

After the ceremonial reading, Cao Pi undertook the eight-round inauguration ceremony and ascended the imperial throne. Below the altar Jia Xu led the body of officials in paying homage to the new sovereign. They then changed the reign period from Yan Kang, "Prolonged Prosperity," year 1, to Huang Chu, "Commencement of the Yellow," year 1 of a new dynasty called Great Wei. Next, Cao Pi issued a general amnesty. He gave his father Cao Cao the posthumous title Great Ancestor and August Martial Emperor.

Hua Xin memorialized the new Emperor: "'Two suns do not shine in heaven; two sovereigns cannot rule.' The Han Emperor should now retire to a remote feudatory kingdom. We petition for your sage instruction on the enfeoffment of the leader of the Liu clan." With these words, he helped Emperor Xian kneel below the altar to listen to the imperial word. Cao Pi directed that the Han Emperor be honored as lord of Shanyang and depart forthwith. Hua Xin placed his hand on his sword and, pointing at Emperor Xian, said harshly, "Putting one emperor in power and removing another was routine in the old days. The present sovereign is humane and merciful and wishes you no harm; he honors you as lord of Shanyang. You are to leave at once, never to enter the court again except on official summons."

Holding back tears, Emperor Xian made the ritual gesture of appreciation, bowing low; then he mounted and set off under the grieving gaze of the commoners and soldiers around the altar. Cao Pi said to the assembly, "Now I can appreciate the succession of Shun and Yu." The courtiers shouted, "Long life to the sovereign!" In later times a poet, viewing the Altar for Acceptance of the Abdication, left these lines:

> The two Hans' governance made a heavy task;
> Then all at once they had no "hills and streams."
> The Wei in Yao and Shun had found their model;
> Too soon the Simas learned this lesson well.

The assembly invited Cao Pi to offer Heaven and earth his thanks. But as the new emperor began descending to prostrate himself, a freak storm sprang up, driving sand and stones before it like a sudden downpour. All went dark; the altar lanterns blew out. Cao Pi collapsed in fright and had to be carried down, regaining consciousness only after a long while. Attendants took him into the palace, where he remained for several days, unable to hold court. Then, feeling stronger, he appeared in the main hall to accept the courtiers' congratulations on assuming the sovereignty. He honored Hua Xin as minister of the interior and Wang Lang as minister of works. Other officials were promoted and rewarded.

Cao Pi did not completely recover, however, and he began to suspect that the capital buildings were haunted. He therefore moved from Xuchang to Luoyang and built a palace complex there.

*   *   *   *

Word soon reached Chengdu that Cao Pi had taken the throne as august emperor of the Great Wei and was constructing a new palace in Luoyang. And there were rumors that the Han Emperor had already been killed. The king of Hanzhong grieved the whole day at the news and ordered his court into mourning. He also arranged sacrifices for the distant Han Emperor, honoring him posthumously as August Emperor Min the Filial.

These events made Xuande too ill to administer government affairs, and he turned everything over to Kongming. Kongming consulted Imperial Guardian Xu Jing and Imperial Steward Qiao Zhou; the three decided to establish the king of Hanzhong as emperor on the grounds that the empire may not be without a sovereign even for a single day. Qiao Zhou said, "Recently we have had the good omen of auspicious winds and clouds. In the northwest corner of Chengdu a yellow haze several hundred spans high rose into the evening sky. The imperial star was seen in the area of Stomach, Mane, and Net, shining with an august fire and bright as the moon. These correspondent signs indicate that the king of Hanzhong should assume the imperial throne and continue the great line of Han. Their meaning is unmistakable."

And so Kongming, together with Xu Jing, led a general assembly of officials to petition the king of Hanzhong to take the imperial throne. The king read over the memorial and said in astonishment, "Would you urge on me a course both disloyal and dishonorable?" Kongming addressed the king: "Not at all! Cao Pi has usurped the Han and taken power. As a kinsman of the Han, Your Majesty should by rights succeed in the line so as to maintain the ritual sacrifices." The king of Hanzhong, his countenance altered, said angrily, "Shall I emulate the conduct of renegade traitors?" Flicking his sleeves, he arose and retired to the rear of the palace; the assembly dispersed.

Three days later Kongming returned to court with the body of officials and requested that the king come forth. The courtiers prostrated themselves when he appeared. Xu Jing addressed the king: "Cao Pi has murdered the Emperor of Han. Unless Your Majesty assumes the royal seat and takes the field to suppress the renegades, you will fail in your obligations of loyalty and honor. The whole world desires Your Majesty to reign and redeem the humiliation suffered by the August Emperor Min the Filial, Emperor Xian. You will fail the hopes of the people if you decline." The king replied, "Though a descendant of Emperor Jing, I lack sufficient virtue to extend to all the people. Were I suddenly to establish myself, how would it differ from the crime of usurpation?" Kongming's strenuous appeals could not move the king, so he conceived a plan that he shared with the officials. Then, claiming to be ill, he went home and remained unavailable.

When the king heard that Kongming's illness was serious, he went to Kongming's quarters, walked straight to his bedside, and asked, "What ails you, Director General?" "A burning anguish," Kongming replied, "so sharp, I fear I have little time to live." "The cause?" the king asked. He repeated the question a number of times, but Kongming, intending to look too sick to reply, lowered his lids. The king pressed him until finally, with a long sigh, Kongming said, "Since the day I left my thatched hut to serve Your Majesty down to the present, I have stayed beside you. You have had implicit faith in me and heeded my every counsel. Good fortune has placed the whole of the Riverlands in Your Majesty's hands, exactly as I predicted long ago. Now that Cao Pi has usurped the throne, and terminated the ritual sacrifices of the Han, all our officers and officials, both civil and military, earnestly desire to serve Your Majesty as emperor and to share in the glory of eliminating the Cao clan and reviving the Liu. Your refusal was unthinkable; but now the whole court may soon disperse in dismay, leaving the Riverlands vulnerable if Wei and Wu were to attack. How could your devoted servant not despair?"

The king replied, "I do not decline on pretext. I fear the adverse judgment of the world." Kongming said, "Confucius said that incorrect names make for illogical positions. Now Your Majesty would be entirely justified in taking such an action. There is nothing to criticize. But can you have forgotten the saying, 'What Heaven grants is refused only at peril'?" The king said, "When your illness improves, there will be time enough to act." At these words Kongming sprang up from his couch and knocked the screen aside. A host of civil and military officials strode in and flung themselves to the ground. "With Your Majesty's agreement, we shall select a day for the ceremony." From the crowd before him the king recognized Imperial Guardian Xu Jing; Mi Zhu, General Who Secures the Han; Xiang Ju, lord of Qingyi; Liu Bao, lord of Yangquan; Zhao Zuo, lieutenant governor; Yang Hong, provincial secretary; Du Qiong, a counselor; Zhang Shuang, an aide; Lai Gong, minister of protocol; Huang Quan, the palace director; He Zong, the libationer; Yin Mo, the scholar-official; Qiao Zhou, the imperial steward; Chief Commander Yin Chun; Auxiliary Commander Zhang Yi; Treasurer Wang Mou; Academician Who Sheds Light on Texts, Yi Ji; Assistant Aide Qin Mi; and many others.

With trepidation the king said, "You are forcing me into a dishonorable position." "Since Your Majesty has already granted our request," Kongming said, "we may build the altar and select a propitious day for the reverent performance of the inauguration." He sent the king back to the palace and ordered Imperial Academician Xu Ci and Court Counselor Meng Guang to take charge of the ceremonies and have an altar built south of Mount Wudan.

When all arrangements had been made, the officials had the royal carriage escort the king to the altar, where he performed the sacrifice. Qiao Zhou was on the altar and read out the accompanying text in a loud, clear voice:

It being the day *dingsi*, fifty-fourth of the cycle, twelve days after the beginning of the fourth moon on *bingwu*, the twenty-sixth year of Jian An, I, Bei, the August Emperor, resolve to proclaim to the august shining Heaven and the fruitful earth that the Han hold the empire in unbroken succession. There was one instance of usurpation: Wang Mang seized the throne, but August Emperor Guang Wu made his fury felt, executed the traitor, and restored our sacred shrines.

Now Cao Cao has committed atrocities and cruelly murdered the reigning sovereign, a hideous crime that assails the very skies. His son Pi gives free rein to nefarious treason, unlawfully seizing the sacred instruments of rule. The whole of our civil and military ranks hold that, with the services of the Han lapsed and void, it is proper for me, Bei, to resume them and, as heir to our founders, personally carry out Heaven's retribution.

Fearful lest my virtue prove unequal to the station, I have taken counsel among the common people and the chieftains around our borders. All agree that the Mandate of Heaven must be heeded, that the patrimony must not remain displaced, and that the realm must not be without its ruler. Throughout the land expectation rests on me, Bei.

Yet do I tremble before that clear mandate. Yet do I fear that the estate of the two founders, Han Gao Zu and Emperor Guang Wu, may come to ruin. With deep reverence have we selected an auspicious day to ascend the platform and offer sacrifice, that our acceptance of the royal seal may bring solace throughout the realm. May the gods relish the dynastic offerings and bestow lasting harmony on our domain.

When the reading was done, Kongming led the assembly in tendering the jade seal. The king took it in his hands and placed it reverently on the altar. Again and again he declined the honor, saying "I, Bei, have neither talent nor virtue; you should find someone else who has, and elevate him." But Kongming addressed the throne thus: "In bringing order to the realm, Your Majesty has illumined the empire with merit and virtue. And since you are a member of the royal house, it is fitting that you occupy the proper seat. The gods above have already received the sacrifice and the announcement. To defer is not possible any longer." A chorus of "Long live the Emperor!" went up from the assembly.

At the conclusion of the ceremonies, they changed the reign title to Zhang Wu, Manifest Might. The Emperor's consort, Lady Wu, was made Empress. His eldest son, Shan, was appointed heir apparent; his second son, Yong, was honored as king of Lu; and his third son, Li, was named king of Liang. Zhuge Liang became prime minister; Xu Jing, minister of the interior; and all the other officials, high and low, were advanced. An amnesty was declared throughout the empire, and the people of the Riverlands, soldier and civilian alike, rejoiced.

The next day in full court, before the civil and military in their respective stations, the First Ruler delivered his first edict: "With Lord Guan and Zhang Fei we bound ourselves in honor and allegiance in the peach garden, swearing to live or die as one. Alas! My second brother, Lord Guan, met his doom at the hands of Sun Quan of the Southland. Unless we take revenge on this enemy, the covenant is betrayed. Therefore we intend full mobilization for war against the south to take alive the renegade traitor and to redeem our shame." But before the First Ruler had finished, someone stepped out from the ranks and threw himself at the First Ruler's feet to object: "No!" he cried. It was one of the "Five Tiger Generals," Zhao Zilong. Indeed:

> Before the Emperor could execute the punishment ordained,
> His vassal Zhao Zilong brought forward a complaint.

How did the great warrior remonstrate?
Read on.

There are now two emperors, two claimants to the realm: Cao Pi, head of the house of Wei, and Liu Xuande, ruler of the kingdom of Shu-Han. But Liu Xuande has yet to decide between his two conflicting roles: emperor of a restored house of Han or senior member of the Peach Garden brotherhood.

CHAPTER 81

Eager for Revenge, Zhang Fei
Is Assassinated; To Avenge His Brother,
the Emperor Goes to War

Zhao Zilong spoke against the expedition: "Cao Cao is the traitor, not Sun Quan. Cao Pi has usurped the Han throne, to the common indignation of gods and men. Let Your Majesty first make the land within the passes your target. Station your men along the upper Wei River in order to bring these hateful renegades to justice; and the Han loyalists east of the passes will then bundle their grain and urge on their horses to welcome the royal host. But if, instead of the northern kingdom of Wei, you attack the southern kingdom of Wu, once your forces are engaged, they cannot be quickly recalled. May Your Majesty consider this carefully."

The Emperor replied, "Sun Quan murdered my brother, and others have earned their share of my hatred: Fu Shiren, Mi Fang, Pan Zhang, Ma Zhong. Until I've gnawed their flesh and exterminated their clans, my humiliation will not be effaced. Why would you stand in my way?" Zhao Zilong answered, "War against the traitors to Han is a public responsibility. War for the sake of a brother is a personal matter. I urge Your Majesty to give priority to the empire." To this the Emperor replied, "If I should fail to avenge my brother, the possession of these ten thousand *li* of mountains and rivers would make an unworthy prize." Ignoring Zhao Zilong's opposition, the Emperor ordered mobilization, sending envoys to Wuxi to borrow fifty thousand troops from the Qiang nation. At the same time he promoted Zhang Fei, who was in Langzhong, to General of Chariots and Cavalry and Commander of the Capital Districts, and further honored him as lord of Xixiang and protector of Langzhong. An envoy took the edict to him.

* * * *

The Emperor went regularly to the training field to direct army maneuvers. He set the day for the expedition, which he intended to lead personally. The high officers of the court went to the prime minister's quarters and complained to Kongming: "The Son of Heaven has held the throne for too brief a time to be taking personal command of the army. The sacred shrines will be neglected as a result. Your Excellency, you hold the most influential position. Could you not urge him toward a better course?" Kongming responded, "I have protested—many times—to no avail. Come with me today to the training grounds and I'll try again."

Kongming, at the head of the assembly, addressed the Emperor: "Your Majesty has assumed the throne so recently; if it is your purpose to bring the northern traitors to justice so that the principle of allegiance to legitimate authority may prevail in the empire, then it is altogether right for you to take command of the entire army yourself. But if you simply mean to attack the Southland, ordering one of your superior commanders to lead the campaign should suffice. Why should your own sagely self bear the burden?" In view of Kongming's strenuous objections, the Emperor was experiencing some uncertainty about the invasion when Zhang Fei's arrival was announced. The Emperor summoned him at once. Zhang Fei bent to the ground before the reviewing stand, weeping as he hugged his lord's feet. The Emperor wept too.

"Today Your Majesty reigns," Zhang Fei said, "and already the peach garden oath is forgotten! Can you leave our brother unavenged?" "Many officials oppose taking revenge. I cannot act rashly," was the reply. "What do others know of our covenant? If you will not go, I will avenge him whatever the cost to myself. Should I fail, I shall be content to die and see you no more." "Then I shall go with you," the Emperor said. "You start out from Langzhou with your own troops. I shall meet you with an elite force at Jiangzhou. Our joint campaign against the Southland will redeem our shame." Zhang Fei was about to leave when the Emperor added a warning, "You have often turned violent after wine, beaten your stalwarts, and then reassigned them in your personal guard. That is a good way to destroy yourself. Hereafter change your ways; make an effort to be tolerant and understanding." Zhang Fei bowed low, took leave, and departed.

Rejecting the counsel of Kongming and Zhao Zilong, Liu Xuande decides to attack the Southland, despite two ominous events: first, Zhang Fei is murdered by his bodyguards. Next, Sun Quan, fearing invasion by Xuande, submits to the new Wei dynasty. Cao Pi, emperor of Wei, honors Sun Quan as king of the Southland but offers him no military aid (chapter 82).

In the year 222 Emperor Liu Xuande leads Riverlands forces east against the Southland. He captures the town of Xiaoting. Guan Xing, with the help of his father Lord Guan's ghost, kills those responsible for his father's death. Others who turned traitor at the fall of Jingzhou are executed. Fearful of Liu Xuande's force, Sun Quan tries to bargain. He delivers Zhang Fei's murderers to be ritually killed, offers the restoration of Lady Sun and Jingzhou province, and pledges to break with Cao Pi, but the emperor of the west is neither swayed nor appeased. Desperate, Sun Quan appoints little-known scholar, Lu Xun, to take charge of defending his kingdom against the Riverlands invasion (chapter 83).

Preparing his defense, Lu Xun ordered the commanders to secure the several passes and avoid engaging the enemy. Mocking Lu Xun's caution, the commanders disdained to keep a strict guard. The following day Lu Xun called a meeting in his tent and said to them, "As royally appointed chief commander, I have repeatedly enjoined you to maintain the strictest defense at the various strongpoints. Why have you disregarded my orders?" Han Dang replied, "Since joining General Sun in the conquest of the

Southland, I have been in hundreds of battles. Some commanders have served his elder brother Sun Ce; others have served His Majesty. Every one has seen long years of combat. Now the king commands your service as our chief in order to drive back the western army. A plan needs to be made at once for coordinating our forces in several lines of march so that our purposes can be accomplished. But all you have done is call for a strict defense and no fighting. Do you mean for us to wait until Heaven itself puts the enemy to death? We are not men who covet life and fear death. What is gained by depressing our spirits like this?"

The commanders in the tent responded in unison, "General Han Dang is right! A battle to the death is what we want!" Facing their demand, Lu Xun took Sun Quan's sword and cried harshly, "I may be no more than a pedant. But his lordship has appointed me because I have something to offer him; and I will suffer any humiliation, bear any burden required of me. You have only to defend the access points and take no rash action. Whoever disobeys, dies." The crowd withdrew indignantly.

*   *   *   *

Meanwhile, the Emperor (Liu Bei) had moved out from Xiaotang and reached the eastern border of the Riverlands. His forces stretched over a distance of seven hundred *li*, occupying forty base camps. By day their banners darkened the sun. By night their fires lit up the sky. Suddenly a spy sent in a report: "The Southland has given Lu Xun general command of their forces, and he has ordered his commanders to hold their strongpoints and not come out." The Emperor replied, "What kind of man is Lu Xun?" Ma Liang said, "Though he is a scholar, he has great talent for his youth and lays deep plans. It was he who planned their successful attack on Jingzhou." "By a boy's tricks I lost my second brother! I want him captured!" the Emperor said angrily and ordered a general advance. But Ma Liang remonstrated, "He is no less capable than Zhou Yu was! Do not risk a rash engagement." "I am seasoned in the ways of war," the Emperor replied. "Do you think a milksop of a child too much for me?" So saying, he took personal command of the forward contingent and attacked the various fords and passes.

Han Dang informed Lu Xun of the advance of the western

forces; Lu Xun sped to the front to survey the situation and forestall any rash move on Han Dang's part. Lu Xun arrived when
Han Dang, sitting astride his horse on a hilltop, was viewing the
enemy swarming over the hills and covering the flatlands; dimly
visible in the distance was a yellow silk umbrella. Han Dang received Lu Xun, and they reined in their horses side by side to
observe. Pointing toward the umbrella, Han Dang said, "Liu Bei
must be there. I want to attack." Lu Xun replied, "After more than
ten victories on this eastern expedition, Liu Bei's fighting spirits are at their peak. All we can do now is occupy the highground
and defend our strongpoints. If we go forth against them, we will
suffer defeat. We need to whet the mettle of our officers and men,
to broaden our defensive strategy until the situation changes. At
the moment they enjoy control of the flatlands before us. But by
maintaining a strict defense, we deny them the engagement they
seek, causing them to move into the wooded hills—that is when
we shall take them by surprise."

Han Dang, though he gave verbal assent to this plan, remained
unconvinced. The Emperor sent his vanguard to provoke the
southerners, reviling them in a hundred ways. Lu Xun ordered
everyone to stuff up his ears, however, and would not permit any
engagement of forces. He personally went to each control point
to cheer the men and reaffirm his orders for maintaining the defense. No southern soldiers appeared, and the Emperor seethed
with impatience. Ma Liang said to him, "Lu Xun is a deep planner; and Your Majesty has come a long distance to wage war.
Spring has turned to summer. They are keeping behind their defenses, hoping that something will happen to our troops. Let Your
Majesty look into this." The Emperor answered, "What can their
plan be? They fear us, that's all. After their string of defeats, they
don't dare show themselves." Vanguard Commander Feng Xi addressed the Emperor. "The weather is scorching hot," he said.
"Camped in this burning plain, the army is having trouble getting water." Consequently, the Emperor commanded him to
move into the lush hills, near the mountain streams, and deferred
the attack until autumn. Feng Xi, as ordered, had the commanders shift all camps into the shade of the woods.

Ma Liang addressed the Emperor, saying, "If we make this
move and the southerners come suddenly, what will you do?" "I

have had Wu Ban take ten thousand inferior troops and position them on the plain near the southern defenses. I myself will take eight thousand elite troops and place them in ambush in the ravines. When Lu Xun learns of our move, he will not fail to strike. When he does, I have told Wu Ban to feign defeat. If Lu Xun pursues those inferior troops, I will charge in and seal off his retreat. The little devil will be ours!" All civil and military officials praised his plan, saying, "Your Majesty's ingenious designs and exquisite calculations are beyond us all!"

Ma Liang said, "I heard recently that Prime Minister Zhuge is in the east Riverlands inspecting our defenses in anticipation of incursion by northern troops of Wei. Your Majesty, why not make a map of the positions you intend moving into for the prime minister to look over?" The Emperor replied, "I am versed in warfare well enough to do without his opinion." "There is an old saying, 'Broad consultation makes one wise; one-sided consideration makes one blind.' I hope Your Majesty will not ignore this," was Ma Liang's answer. The Emperor said, "Then chart the area yourself and go to the east Riverlands to show the prime minister your maps. Report to me at once anything unfavorable in them." Ma Liang departed with his orders.

And so the Emperor moved his army into the woods where the shade afforded some relief from summer's heat. Spies quickly informed Han Dang and Zhou Tai of these changes in the western position. And the two commanders were delighted to report to Lu Xun: "They have moved their camps, more than forty in all, into the wooded hills, where their proximity to mountain streams affords them drinking water and cooling relief. Chief Commander, now is the time to strike." Indeed:

> Planning to spring an ambush was the ruler of Shu,
> Sure of catching the bold and hardy troops of Wu.

Would Lu Xun accept the proposal?
Read on.

CHAPTER 84

Lu Xun Burns a Seven-Hundred-Li Line of Camps; Kongming Deploys the Eightfold Ramparts Maze

Southern commanders Han Dang and Zhou Tai hurried to inform Lu Xun that the Emperor had shifted to cooler ground. Delighted, the chief commander came to the front to scan the field. There on the flats before him he found a single campsite with a mere ten thousand men, most of them unfit for service; their banner read, "Vanguard Wu Ban." Zhou Tai said to Lu Xun, "This looks like child's play. Allow General Han Dang and myself to attack with two companies. If we fail, we will welcome whatever punishment martial law imposes." After examining the enemy's position for some time, Lu Xun pointed with his whip and said, "In the distance ahead I detect lethal signs marking ambush points. They have purposely placed these troops on flat ground to lure us out. I absolutely forbid you to show yourselves." All took his caution for cowardice.

The next day Wu Ban led some troops to the pass and challenged the southerners, swaggering and casting scorn on them. Most of Wu Ban's men had slipped out of their battle gear and were lolling about half-naked. Xu Sheng and Ding Feng entered the command tent and petitioned Lu Xun. "The westerners' insults are unbearable," they cried. "Let us go and attack them." Lu Xun smiled as he replied, "You are trusting to sheer physical courage and ignoring the fine points of warfare as taught by the masters. This is a trick to entice the enemy. In three days the deception will be apparent." Xu Sheng answered, "In three days their position will be too consolidated to attack." "I am waiting for them to complete the transfer," Lu Xun said. The commanders smirked as they withdrew.

After the three days had passed, Lu Xun gathered the commanders on the pass to survey the ground below. Wu Ban had already pulled back. Pointing ahead, Lu Xun said, "Those lethal signs are in the air. Liu Bei will be coming out from the gorges." As Lu Xun was speaking, lo and behold, the western army fully uniformed crossed before them, the Emperor in their midst. The sight struck panic in the southern troops. "This is why I could not listen to your advice," Lu Xun said to his commanders. "But now that the ambush is in the open, we will destroy the western army in ten days." "We should have done that to begin with," the commanders said. "Now their network of mutually defended camps stretches over five hundred *li,* and after these seven or eight months all strategic points are well fortified. How can we defeat them?" Lu Xun replied, "Gentlemen, you are unfamiliar with the art of war. Liu Bei is the craftiest owl of our day, the most cunning and ruthless of men. When he first deployed his forces, their order was precise, their discipline tight. Now after their long but fruitless wait, his men are worn down and frustrated in their aims. This is the moment for us to take them." Finally, Lu Xun convinced the commanders. A poet of later times left these lines of admiration for Lu Xun's qualities:

> He'd mastered war's six arts when he spoke before the chiefs;
> Angling for one mighty fish, he set a tasty bait.
> For this divided Kingdom now has paragons enough!
> And shining high above them all—Lu Xun of the south.

Having made his plans, Lu Xun dispatched a letter informing Sun Quan of the expected victory. Sun Quan read it with excitement. "The Southland has another genius like Zhou Yu!" he exclaimed. "My worries are over. The commanders' complaints of his cowardice never persuaded me. And now my confidence is confirmed." So saying, he mustered the southern army to support Lu Xun.

From Xiaoting the Emperor directed his entire naval force to proceed downstream. Pitching camp along the river, the mariners cut deeply into southern territory. Huang Quan raised an objection: "The marine forces are moving downriver easily enough, but retreat will prove difficult. Allow me to advance while you stay back—just in case." "The bastards of Wu have lost their nerve. Nothing can stop our massive onslaught," the Emperor replied, firmly rejecting all further appeals. He divided his forces into two field armies: one north of the river under Huang Quan, defending against Wei; one to the south, which he himself took charge of. Thus, they established separate camps on either shore to deliver the attack.

*   *   *   *

Spies soon told Cao Pi, ruler of Wei, "The army of Shu has gone to war against Wu. Their fortifications stretch in a line over seven hundred *li* long; they have built more than forty bases beside hills and woods. At present Huang Quan commands the forces on the northern shore, and their daily patrols range over one hundred *li*. We do not know what he is up to."

Cao Pi threw back his head and laughed at this report. "Liu Bei is done for!" he said. When his vassals pressed for an explanation, the Wei ruler continued, "Liu Xuande knows nothing of warfare. Camps strung out like that won't deter his enemy. And to pitch on such irregular, densely wooded ground is a classic blunder. Within ten days look for news of his defeat at Lu Xun's hands." The vassals, unconvinced, requested troops for preventive action. The Wei Emperor said, "If Lu Xun prevails, he will move ahead in force to take the Riverlands itself. With troops so far afield, the Southland will be left undefended. And we shall send down three armies, ostensibly as aid, which will make short work of them." The assembly voiced its admiration. The Wei Emperor ordered Cao Ren, Cao Xiu, and Cao Zhen to take command and move out from Ruxu, Dongkou, and Nanjun. The order read: "On the appointed day, coordinate a covert strike on the Southland. I will reinforce from the rear." Thus, Wei completed preparations for another southern campaign.

*   *   *   *

Ma Liang reached the Riverlands and presented Kongming with maps of the Emperor's positions. "At present we have more than forty bases on both sides of the river, covering a stretch of seven hundred *li*. Each is pitched close to a stream or creek near thick woods. His Majesty has sent me to show these sketches to Your Excellency." Kongming finished examining the documents and slammed his hand on the table. "Whoever," he cried in anguish, "whoever advised our lord to pitch camp in this way should be executed." Ma Liang responded, "It was entirely our lord's own doing. No one advised him." Kongming said with a sigh, "Then the vital cycle of the Han draws to a close."

Ma Liang asked the meaning of these words, and Kongming replied, "To pitch the camps like that violates every rule. If they attack by fire, he cannot be saved; nor can such a string of forts hold off the enemy. The end is not far off. Now I see why Lu Xun holds back so strictly and does not show himself. You must rush to the Son of Heaven and have him change the positions. They cannot be left like this." "And if the southerners have already overwhelmed them?" Ma Liang asked. "Lu Xun will not dare pursue. The capital is safe." "Why so?" Ma Liang asked. "Because they have the northern army behind them to worry about," Kongming explained. "If our lord finds himself in trouble, he should find safety in the city of Baidi. When I came into the Riverlands, I left ten legions there at Fishbelly Meadow." Ma Liang was amazed. "I have been through Fishbelly Meadow any number of times and have never seen a single soldier. Why is Your Excellency trying to deceive me?" "You will find out later," Kongming replied. "Don't trouble yourself any further." Ma Liang took Kongming's written petition and sped back to the imperial camp. Kongming returned to Chengdu and prepared to rescue the Emperor.

*   *   *   *

Lu Xun observed that the troops of the Riverlands were beginning to flag and were growing negligent about their defenses. He gathered his commanders before his tent and told them, "Since assuming command, I have refrained from giving battle; but we now know enough about the enemy's movements. I want to capture a single camp on the southern side of the river. Who dares to do the job?" The sound of the chief commander's voice still hung in the air as Han Dang, Zhou Tai, and Ling Tong stepped forward to volunteer. But Lu Xun rejected their offer and instead summoned a subordinate commander from the lower ranks, Chunyu Dan. "I am giving you five thousand men," Lu Xun said to him. "Take the fourth camp on the southern side, the one Fu Tong is guarding. I want a victory this very evening. I will reinforce you." Chunyu Dan left to carry out his mission.

Next, Lu Xun called Xu Sheng and Ding Feng and said to them, "Take three thousand men each and station them five *li* from our camp. If Chunyu Dan returns in defeat, go to his rescue. But whatever you do, do not pursue the enemy." The two commanders departed on their mission.

As dusk fell, Chunyu Dan advanced, reaching the western camp after the third watch. As he penetrated the ambit, his men raised a wild din at his order. Fu Tong came forth, and the battle was joined. Fu Tong went straight for Chunyu Dan, who wheeled his mount round to retire, unable to withstand the charge. Suddenly the air rang with loud cries: a band of soldiers was blocking his retreat, General Zhao Rong at their head. Chunyu Dan now broke away and fled. Half his men were lost. A company of Man warriors blocked his way: their leader, Shamoke, the Qiang chieftain. Fighting for his life, Chunyu Dan struggled free again, the three enemy companies hot on his heels.

Five *li* from the camp, the Southland ambush was sprung. Xu Sheng and Ding Feng forced back the western army and then escorted Chunyu Dan back to the Southland side. Chunyu Dan, with an arrow lodged in him, went before Lu Xun to accept his punishment. "It was not your fault," Lu Xun reassured him. "I had to test the enemy's strength in order to form my plan for destroying Shu." "They are too strong for us to defeat," Xu Sheng and Ding Feng said, "we will lose men and leaders in vain." Lu Xun smiled as he replied, "My plan would never fool Kongming. But by Heavens's favor the man is not here, and this will help me to victory."

Again Lu Xun gathered his officers and men and issued his orders: "Zhu Ran is to advance on the river. Tomorrow after noon the southeast wind will blow strong. Load your boats with straw and proceed according to plan. Han Dang is to attack the north shore, Zhou Tai the south. In addition to spear and sword, each soldier is to carry a bundle of grass with sulphur and saltpeter inside and something to ignite it. Everyone is to advance together; as soon as you reach the enemy camps, use your torches according to the winds. They have forty encampments: fire every other one. Carry dry provisions and pursue them relentlessly day and night until you have taken Liu Bei." The commanders went severally to their ordered tasks.

*   *   *   *

In the main camp the Emperor was pondering his strategy, when the banner in front of his tent overturned even though there was no wind. He turned to Cheng Ji and asked, "What does this signify?" "The southerners will raid tonight," Cheng Ji answered. "We put them to rout last night," the Emperor said. "They would not dare return." "And if it was a probe?" Cheng Ji replied. As they spoke, someone reported that hilltop sentinels had spotted southern troops in the distance moving eastward along the range of hills. "Decoys," the Emperor said and ordered his troops to take no action. Instead, he sent Guan Xing and Zhang Bao with five hundred riders each to reconnoiter. At dusk Guan Xing returned to report that fires had sprung up in the north shore encampments. The Emperor sent Guan Xing to the north shore and Zhang Bao to the south to investigate. "Tell me as soon as the southern troops arrive," the Emperor concluded.

The two commanders set off. At the first watch a southeast wind sprang up sharply. The camp to the left of the Emperor's burst into flame. Before anyone could go to its aid, the camp to the right of the Emperor's also began burning. The wind quickened and the fire sped in its wake. Trees and bushes caught fire; screams rent the air. Soldiers and horses dashed from the burning camps and away from the Emperor's campground, causing countless soldiers to trample one another to death. From behind, a mass of southern soldiers bore down for the kill.

The Emperor sprang into his saddle and raced to Feng Xi, but his camp was already an inferno. North and south of the river the glare was bright as day. Feng Xi dashed to his horse and led away a few score of cavalry, only to meet the murderous advance of Xu Sheng. The Emperor turned west and fled. Xu Sheng passed Feng Xi by and led his troops after the Emperor, around whom everything was in confusion. Ahead of him another troop— led by Ding Feng—blocked his advance. Trapped on either side, the Emperor panicked. Suddenly, amid thunderous shouts a band of soldiers led by Zhang Bao broke through and pulled him to safety; together with the Royal Guard they bolted away. Moments later General Fu Tong joined forces with the Emperor, and they proceeded together.

Pursued by southern troops, the Emperor came to Saddle Hill. Zhang Bao and Fu Tong urged him to the top. A tumult welled up from below as Lu Xun's massive contingents surrounded the base. Zhang Bao and Fu Tong fought to control the pathway up as the Emperor looked out upon the fires raging across the plain and the bodies of the dead choking the river.

The following day the Southlanders set fires around the hill. The Emperor's troops scurried away in disorder, leaving him in extremity. But through the glare of the blaze, a few riders cut their way up the hill; their leader was Guan Xing. Kneeling before the Emperor, he said, "The flames press closer. We must move on. Make haste to Baidi, Your Majesty, where we can regroup." The Emperor said, "Who will hold the rear?" Fu Tong volunteered, and as darkness fell they battled their way down the slopes, Guan Xing in front, Zhang Bao in the middle, Fu Tong in the rear guarding the Emperor. The southern commanders, spotting the fleeing Emperor, vied eagerly for the glory of capturing him, and the hosts they led west across the battle ground darkened the sky and covered the earth.

The Emperor had his men discard their surcoats and armor, and burn them to clog the road and prevent pursuit. They were continuing west, when a hue and cry went up: the southern general Zhu Ran had led a company from the riverbank to block their way. The Emperor cried out, "Here I die!" Guan Xing and Zhang Bao, thrusting and surging, fell back before the flurries of arrows. Seriously wounded, they could not fight their way out. More shouts from behind told them that Lu Xun was bringing up the main army.

General Zhao Zilong rescues Liu Xuande and escorts him to safety, but many die in the battle that rages all around. Lady Sun comes to the river. Believing Liu Xuande dead, she drowns herself.

Lu Xun, triumphant, rode west in swift pursuit. Approaching Kui Pass, he saw a lethal miasma arising from among the looming mountains and the river alongside. Turning, he said to his followers, "There must be an ambush ahead. The army must not

advance." Lu Xun retreated ten *li* and set up defensive formations on open ground. The scouts he sent to investigate came
back with nothing to report. Lu Xun did not believe them. He
climbed a hill on foot and scanned the terrain: the same sensation of danger made itself felt. He ordered a minute investiga-
tion, which turned up neither man nor horse. As the sun began
to set, the mysterious signs seemed stronger. Still undecided, he
sent one of his trusted followers to examine the area. He reported
finding only eighty or ninety chaotic rock piles alongside the
river, but no military forces.

But Lu Xun's doubts remained. He had some local people
brought to him for questioning. "Who made these piles," he
asked them, "and why does an aura of death seem to come from
them?" One man replied, "This is Fishbelly Meadow. When
Zhuge Liang came to the Riverlands he sent troops here to
arrange these rock formations on the sandflats. Since then, a kind
of cloudlike effluvium seems to emanate from their interiors."

Lu Xun led a few score of cavalry to examine the rocks. From
a hillslope he could see openings on all sides. "A device to per-
plex whoever comes," Lu Xun said with a smile. "What use is it?"
He guided his men down from the slope directly into the formation to inspect it. A lieutenant said, "The sun is setting; we
should return, Chief Commander." But when Lu Xun tried to
get out, violent winds came up from nowhere. Instantly, streams
of sand and stone covered the sky and the ground until all Xun
could see were monstrous rocks sawing the air, jagged like sword
blades, and the relentless sand heaping up and rising into mountains. The voice of the river rumbled and rolled like the beating
of war drums.

In terror Lu Xun cried, "Trapped by Zhuge Liang!" He was
searching frantically for a way out, when an old man appeared
in front of Lu Xun's horse and said with a smile, "You desire to
leave, General?" "Would you lead us out, your reverence?" Lu
Xun answered. The old man, supporting himself with a staff,
slowly traversed the formations, escorting them back without the
slightest difficulty to the hillslope they had come from. "Who are
you, your reverence?" Lu Xun asked. "Huang Chengyan," he
replied, "father-in-law of Zhuge Kongming. My son-in-law passed
here on his way west and deployed these rocky ramparts, which

he called the Eightfold Maze. There are eight endlessly shifting openings arranged according to the 'Taboo Days' formula: Desist, Survive, Injure, Confound, Exhibit, Perish, Surprise, and Liberate. During every time period of every day the openings move unpredictably, like ten crack legions in constant motion. As Kongming was leaving, he cautioned me, 'The time will come when a commanding general of the Southland will lose his way in this maze. Do not show him how to get out.' Just now from the cliffs I saw you go in by the gate called Perish and judged that you would be entrapped out of ignorance of the system. But I've always been disposed to do a good turn, and rather than see you get swallowed up in here, I came over to show you out by the gate Survive."

"Good sir," Lu Xun asked, "have you mastered this system of formations?" Huang Chengyan answered, "The transformations never end. They cannot be mastered." Lu Xun hurriedly dismounted, paid his respects to the old man, and returned to his camp. The poet Du Fu has described Kongming's stone ramparts:

> Deeds to vault a thrice-torn realm,
> Fame at peak with the Eightfold Maze,
> Now steadfast stones in the river's run—
> Monument to his rue
> That his king had choked on Wu!

"Kongming's a 'Sleeping Dragon,' indeed—more than a match for me," Lu Xun conceded, and he gave the order to retreat. His advisers protested: "Liu Bei's army is ruined; his power is exhausted. We have him backed into a single walled town. This is our opportunity to attack. Why retire because of some rock formations?" Lu Xun responded, "I am not retreating for fear of the rocks. My guess is that Cao Pi, lord of Wei, is no less cunning than his father was. He knows we are pursuing the army of the Riverlands and will attack our undefended homeland. If we push too far west, it will be very difficult for us to pull back in time to defend it." And so Lu Xun assigned one general to block the rear while he led the main army back to the Southland. Less than two days after the retreat began, scouts urgently reported to Lu Xun the movements of the three northern armies: "Cao Ren has come down from Ruxu, Cao Xiu from Dongkou, and Cao Zhen from

Nanjun. These three armies numbering in the hundreds of thousands have reached our borders by swift night marches, but their intentions are as yet uncertain." Lu Xun smiled and said, "Exactly what I anticipated! I have already sent troops to check them." Indeed:

> Ambition to devour the west yielded to a wiser course:
> Contain the north.

How did Lu Xun retreat?
  Read on.

CHAPTER 85

First Ruler Liu Finds a Guardian for His Heir; Zhuge Liang Calmly Holds Off Five Armies

After defeat in the battle of Xiaoting, Liu Xuande takes refuge in the city of Baidi (which means White Emperor). He dies the following year in 223. With his final words he appoints Kongming guardian of his heir, Liu Shan, and inheritor of his hopes to restore the Han.

In the Palace of Enduring Peace the Emperor was confined to his bed by a worsening illness. In the fourth month of the third year of Zhang Wu [A.D. 223] the Emperor knew the disease had spread into his limbs. Weeping for his brothers had aggravated his symptoms. His vision grew dim. Disgusted with his attendants, he discharged them and lay back on his couch in solitude. A chill, gloomy wind sprang up. His lantern darkened, then flared. Two men stood in the circle of the shadow it cast. The Emperor spoke irritably: "I thought I had dismissed you to give my mind a moment's calm. What brings you again?" They ignored his dismissal.

The Emperor arose to examine them: one was Lord Guan, the other Zhang Fei. "Then you are still alive!" the Emperor exclaimed. "We are ghosts, not men," responded Guan. "The supernal sovereign recognized that in our lifetimes we two never forsook our good faith or our allegiance, and so he made gods of us. Elder brother, the time of our reunion is not far off."

The Emperor reached for them, emitting a cry, then awoke with a spasm. The two were gone. He summoned his attendants to ask the hour. It was the third watch. The Emperor sighed, saying, "My time will be short in the world of men." He sent to Chengdu for Prime Minister Zhuge Liang, Imperial Secretary Li Yan, and other high officials, and they rushed to the Palace of Enduring Peace to receive his final instructions. Kongming and the Emperor's younger sons Liu Yong, king of Lu, and Liu Li, king of Liang, came before the Emperor. The heir apparent, Liu Shan, remained in Chengdu.

Kongming, seeing that the Emperor's condition was critical, prostrated himself at the royal couch with reverent haste. But the Emperor expressed his wish that the prime minister sit at the edge of the couch. Placing his hand gently on Kongming's back, he said, "Through you alone the imperial quest was achieved. How could I have foolishly rejected your advice and thus brought on this defeat? Wracked by remorse, I stand at death's door. My heir is an inconsequential weakling, and so I must entrust you with my cause." Tears covered his face.

Kongming, also in tears, replied, "Your Majesty must preserve his dragon form to fulfill the hopes of the empire." The Emperor glanced around the room and, spotting Ma Liang's younger brother, Ma Su, told him to retire. The Emperor asked Kongming, "What is my prime minister's estimate of Ma Su's talents?" "Among the most splendid of the age," was the reply. "You are wrong," the Emperor said. "In my view he's a braggart. Give him no important assignment. Take careful note of this, Prime Minister." Having issued this warning, the Emperor summoned his officials into his chamber and transcribed his testament before them. Handing it to Kongming, he said with a sigh, "I am no scholar; and my knowledge is crude and superficial. The Sage said, 'Doleful, the notes of a dying bird; precious, the words of a dying man.' Together we have tried to annihilate the traitor Cao and uphold the house of Han. Alas, midway in our undertaking we must part. I would trouble the prime minister to impart my edict to the heir and teach him its importance. I rely on you to guide him in all matters, Prime Minister."

Weeping, Kongming and the others bowed to the ground and said, "We beg Your Majesty to enjoy a measure of repose. Each of us will spare no pains in gratitude for your generous treatment." The Emperor ordered his attendants to raise Kongming up. Brushing his tearful eyes with one hand and taking Kongming's hand in the other, he said, "I am going to die, and I have something more to say." "What sacred instruction?" Kongming asked. The Emperor wept as he responded, "Your ability exceeds Cao Pi's by ten to one, and I know you will be able to secure and preserve the empire and in the end attain our goal. If my heir proves worthy of support, support him. If he proves unfit, take the kingship of the Riverlands yourself." Kongming broke into a sweat; in extreme agitation, he prostrated himself again. "Could I do otherwise," he said tearfully, "than serve him as aide and vassal, persevering in loyalty unto death?" He knocked his forehead to the ground until blood showed.

Again the Emperor called Kongming to sit on his couch. He summoned Liu Yong and Liu Li to approach and charged them: "Mark well my words. After I am gone, I want you and Liu Shan to serve the prime minister with all diligence and respect, as if he were your father." So saying, he ordered the two princes to prostrate themselves before Kongming. "Were I to lay my innards on the ground, I could never requite the kindness Your Grace has shown me," Kongming concluded.

To the larger assembly the Emperor said, "I am entrusting my heir to the prime minister. I have instructed my heir to serve him as his father. Let none of you neglect this charge and betray my hopes." The Emperor turned to Zhao Zilong and said, "We have been through many a trial and ordeal together. Who could have anticipated such a parting? For the sake of our old friendship, will you keep a constant watch over my sons and honor my wishes?" Tearfully, Zhao Zilong prostrated himself and said, "I am bound to exert every fibre of my being in this service." Next, the Emperor said to the assembly, "I cannot give an individual charge to each one of you. But I hope you will all care well for yourselves and keep your self-respect." The Emperor finished speaking; then he was no more. He had reached the age of sixty-three. It was the twenty-fourth day of the fourth month of Zhang Wu 3. Du Fu has left this poem lamenting the fate of Liu Bei:

> His view trained south, Shu's ruler graced Three Gorges
> And two years thence was dead, in Yong'an Palace still.
> Picture regal plumes upon those vacant hills;
> How blank and bare his hall of state in a country shrine!
> Fir and pine by the old fane keep cormorants
> Till solstice feast days stir the old folks out:
> With Kongming's sanctum always right next door,
> In sacred union liege and man share the rites of worship.

Grieving officials, led by Kongming, bore the royal coffin back to Chengdu, where Heir Apparent Liu Shan received them outside the city walls. He had his father's body placed in state in the main hall of the palace. After the rites and mourning the testament was read:

> It began with no more than severe stomach cramps, but complications developed, and recovery became less and less likely. They say, "After fifty, one no longer dies young," so to die after sixty is hardly cause for regret, though you and your brothers still occupy my thoughts. Be vigilant! Be vigilant! If an evil is minor, resist it nonetheless. If a good deed is trifling, perform it all the same. Only wisdom and virtue can truly win men's devotion. My meager virtue was unworthy of your emulation. Serve the prime minister as if he were your father; be neither negligent nor remiss. Seek to make a name for yourself. Such is my final charge.

After the reading of the will, Kongming said, "A dynasty cannot go a single day without a sovereign. Let us enthrone the heir in order to continue the line of Han unbroken." The assembly thus inaugurated Liu Shan emperor and changed the reign title to Jian Xing, "Commence the Revival." Zhuge Liang was made lord of Wuxiang and protector of Yizhou. The late Emperor was interred at Huiling and posthumously titled August Emperor Zhao Lie, or Reflected Glory. The Empress, Lady Wu, was honored as queen mother. Lady Gan, the mother of Liu Shan, was posthumously honored as August Empress Zhao Lie. Lady Mi was posthumously remembered as Empress. The body of officials was promoted and rewarded; amnesty was proclaimed throughout the empire.

———————————

With Liu Shan (Ah Dou) as emperor of Shu-Han, Kongming dominates court affairs and military policy. His determination to finish Liu Xuande's mission—the conquest of the northern heartland (zhong-yuan) and the restoration of Han rule—does not waver. Since Jingzhou is in southern hands, Kongming must invade Wei from the west; but before he can do so, he must secure the regions south of the Riverlands (modern Guizhou, Guangxi, perhaps part of northern Vietnam), which are the regions occupied by the Man peoples, whose leader is Meng Huo.

In a series of campaigns during 225, Kongming awes Meng Huo and wins his cooperation, convincing him to abandon his rebellion against Shu-Han and serve as a regional leader. This arrangement spares Shu-Han the trouble of stationing military forces among the Man (chapters 87 to 91).

After returning from the Man campaigns, Kongming learns of division and dissension in the northern kingdom following upon the death of Cao Pi, who had reigned seven years. The new emperor of Wei, Cao Rui, is a child. Kongming plots to undermine confidence in the leading northern general, Sima Yi, who is relieved of his command. At the same time he petitions Liu Shan, emperor of Shu-Han, to authorize military operations against Wei (chapter 91).

———————————

Spies soon reported these events in the Riverlands, and Kongming received the news with delight. "I have long wanted to wage war against Wei," he said, "but could do nothing with Sima Yi leading the army in Yong and Liang. Now that he has fallen victim to this trap, my worries are over."

The next day the Second Emperor held court early in the day. Kongming stepped forth and in front of the grand assembly submitted a memorial to the sovereign entitled "Petition on Taking the Field." It read:

> Permit your servant, Liang, to observe: the late sovereign was taken from us while his life's work, the restoration of the Han, re-

mained unfinished. Today, in a divided empire, our third, the province of Yizhou, war-worn and under duress, faces a season of crisis that threatens our very survival. Despite this, the officials at court persevere in their tasks, and loyal-minded officers throughout the realm dedicate themselves to you because one and all they cherish the memory of the exceptional treatment they enjoyed from the late sovereign and wish to repay it in service to Your Majesty.

Truly this is a time to widen your sagely audience in order to enhance the late Emperor's glorious virtue and foster the morale of your dedicated officers. It would be unworthy of Your Majesty to demean yourself by resorting to ill-chosen justifications that would block the avenues of loyal remonstrance.

The royal court and the ministerial administration constitute a single government. Both must be judged by one standard. Those who do evil and violate the codes, as well as those who are loyal and good, must receive their due from the proper authorities. This will make manifest Your Majesty's fair and enlightened governance. Let no unseemly bias lead to different rules for the court and the administration.

Privy counselors and imperial attendants like Guo Youzhi, Fei Yi, and Dong Yun are all solid, reliable men, loyal of purpose, pure in motive. The late Emperor selected them for office so that they would serve Your Majesty after his demise. In my own humble opinion, consulting these men on palace affairs great or small before action is taken will prevent errors and shortcomings and maximize advantages. Xiang Chong, a general of fine character and fair-minded conduct, profoundly versed in military matters, proved himself in battle during the previous reign, and the late Emperor pronounced him capable. That is why the assembly has recommended him for overall command. In my humble opinion, General Xiang Chong should be consulted on all military matters large or small to ensure harmony in the ranks and the judicious use of personnel.

The Former Han thrived because its emperors stayed close to worthy vassals and far from conniving courtiers. The opposite policy led the Later Han to ruin. Whenever the late Emperor discussed this problem with me, he decried the failings of Emperors Huan and Ling. Privy Counselors Guo Youzhi and Fei Yi, Secretary Chen Zhen, Senior Adviser Zhang Yi, and Military Counselor Jiang Wan are all men of shining integrity and unshakable devotion. I beg Your Majesty to keep close to them and to trust them, for that will strengthen our hopes for the resurgence of the house of Han.

I began as a common man, toiling in my fields in Nanyang, doing what I could to keep body and soul together in an age of disorder and taking no interest in making a name for myself among the lords of the realm. Though it was beneath the dignity of the late Emperor to do so, he honored my thatched cottage to solicit my counsel on the events of the day. Grateful for his regard, I responded to his appeal and threw myself heart and soul into his service.

Hard times followed for the cause of the late Emperor. I assumed my duties at a critical moment for our defeated army, accepting assignment in a period of direst danger. Now twenty-one years have passed. The late Emperor always appreciated my meticulous caution and, as the end neared, placed his great cause in my hands. Since that moment, I have tormented myself night and day lest I prove unworthy of his trust and thus discredit his judgment.

That is why I crossed the River Lu in the summer heat and penetrated the barren lands of the Man. Now, the south subdued, our arms sufficing, it behooves me to marshal our soldiers to conquer the northern heartland and do my humble best to remove the hateful traitors, restore the house of Han, and return it to the former capital. This is the way I mean to honor my debt to the late Emperor and fulfill my duty to Your Majesty.

As for weighing the advantages of internal policy and making loyal recommendations to Your Majesty, that is the responsibility of Guo Youzhi, Fei Yi, and Dong Yun. My only desire is to obtain and execute your commission to chasten the traitors and restore the Han. Should I prove unfit, punish my offense and report it to the spirit of the late Emperor. If those three vassals fail to sustain. Your Majesty's virtue, then their negligence should be publicized and censured.

Your Majesty, take counsel with yourself and consult widely on the right course. Examine and adopt sound opinions, and never forget the last edict of the late Emperor. Overwhelmed with gratitude for the favor I have received from you, I now depart on a distant campaign. Blinded by my tears falling on this petition, I write I know not what.

After reading the memorial, the Second Emperor said, "Prime minister and second father, your southern campaign was marked by ordeal and hardship, and you have still to settle down after your recent return. A northern campaign will strain you physically and mentally." Kongming replied, "My devotion to the late Emperor's charge to assist his heir remains undiminished. With the south pacified, we are free of internal troubles and must chasten the traitors and win back the north; this opportunity may never come again." Suddenly from the ranks Grand Historian

Qiao Zhou stepped forth and addressed the Emperor, "Last night I was watching the heavenly correspondences: signs to the north suggest the height of vigor; the northern stars are doubly bright. This is no time to plan action there." Turning to Kongming, he went on, "Your Excellency has a deep knowledge of the constellations. Why do you persist?" Kongming answered, "The way of Heaven changes constantly. No one can cling to its patterns. I am going to post our forces in Hanzhong and observe the enemy's movements before advancing." Qiao Zhou's earnest objections were ignored.

The first step in Kongming's offensive is to seize the Qishan mountain region west of Chang'an. From Qishan he plans to invade the north. In the course of battles for Qishan, he wins over a talented young commander, Jiang Wei. It is Jiang Wei who will continue the struggle against the north after Kongming dies. During this last period of his life, Kongming has to fight politically in Chengdu for his military campaigns, because antiwar Riverlands factions are growing stronger (chapters 92 to 94).

CHAPTER 95

Rejecting Advice, Ma Su Loses Jieting; Strumming His Zither, Kongming Drives Off Sima

In 228, restored to his command, Sima Yi leads northern armies west to oppose the forces of Shu-Han. The surprise capture of Xincheng enables Sima Yi to threaten Kongming's gains in Qishan. On Kongming's eastern front is the town of Jieting, defended by Ma Su. Jieting is a salient crucial to the Riverlands' planned attack on Chang'an. Now Lord of Wu, Kongming is called His Excellency.

Ma Su and Wang Ping reached Jieting and studied the lay of the land. With a smile Ma Su said, "What could have made His Excellency so uneasy? The Wei army is unlikely to come to this forsaken spot." Wang Ping said, "All the same, we had better camp at the intersection of these five roads and then have the men fell trees for palings for a strategic defense." But Ma Su replied, "The road is no place for a camp, with an isolated hill so near and all four fronts impossible to link. Also, the broad woods offer a natural strategic advantage. The army should move to the hilltop." "Surely you are mistaken, Military Adviser," Wang Ping replied. "If we station the army along the road and build a wall, not even one hundred thousand rebels will be able to get by us. But if we abandon this key point for the hilltop and the northerners charge in and surround us, nothing will save us." Ma Su laughed out loud and retorted, "That's really a woman's way of seeing things! The laws of warfare state, 'Depend on heights, surveying all below, and the enemy will be like bamboo to a cleaver.' Let them come! I won't let a shield go back!"

Wang Ping persisted, "How many times have I been with His Excellency when he managed formations? At every new site he would give exhaustive directions. If we isolate our men on this hill and the northerners come and sever the water lines, the army will collapse without a battle." "Enough of your stupidity!" Ma Su cried. "Sunzi has said, 'Soldiers always survive when threatened by death.' If they cut the conduits, won't the Riverlanders fight for their very lives, one of ours a match for a hundred of theirs? I know my military texts. Even His Excellency has come to me with questions. Don't make things difficult!"

Wang Ping said, "Would you be willing, Adviser, to form two camps, one on top and one below, giving me a portion of the troops to place at the west foot of the hill so we can create a pincer formation? Then we can deal with the northerners should they come." Ma Su refused.

Suddenly, dwellers from the hills came thronging to report the arrival of the northerners. Wang Ping wanted to take his leave. Ma Su said, "Since you will not obey my orders, take five thousand and pitch camp where you will. But after my victory, you will not get a scrap of credit when we stand before the prime minister." Wang Ping led his men ten *li* from the hill and camped.

Then he prepared maps and had them carried to Kongming along with a description of Ma Su's hilltop position.

*   *   *   *

From the city, Sima Yi sent his second son, Sima Zhao, to explore the road ahead, instructing him not to proceed if he found soldiers defending Jieting. After making his survey, Sima Zhao said to his father, "There are soldiers protecting Jieting." In a tone of resignation Sima Yi said, "Zhuge Liang is marvelous! Far beyond me!" "Don't despair, Father," Sima Zhao said with a smile. "Jieting looks easy enough to capture." "Is this an empty boast?" asked Sima Yi. "When I scouted the road, I saw no fortifications—all their men had been put on the hill—so I am sure we can defeat them." Delighted, Sima Yi said, "If that's true, then Heaven itself ensures our success." He dressed in war gear and, attended by a hundred cavalry, went to inspect the site himself.

It was a clear night; the moon shone bright. Sima Yi and his son rode straight to the foot of the hill, explored all around it, and went back. From the hill Ma Su watched it all, smiling. "They are doomed if they surround this hill," he said, and he issued orders to his commanders: if the enemy comes, swoop down on all sides when you see a red flag waving on the summit.

Sima Yi got back to camp and sent a man to find out who the Riverlands commander at Jieting was. "Ma Su," was the answer, "younger brother of Ma Liang." Sima Yi smiled and said, "A man with an undeserved reputation. If Kongming is using men of such commonplace abilities, he will defeat only himself." Then he asked another question: "Have they any other forces near Jieting?" The scout reported: "Wang Ping is camped ten *li* away." Sima Yi accordingly ordered Zhang He to block Wang Ping's position with a corps of men. He also ordered Shen Dan and Shen Yi to take two contingents to surround the mountain and cut off the water conduits. Sima Yi intended to strike after the Riverlands forces had become disorderly; that night he completed his deployment.

The following dawn Zhang He led his men behind the mountain as Sima Yi advanced in force, cordoning the base with his troops. Ma Su looked down on the swarm of northerners spreading over hill and dale, their flags and ranks in perfect order. His

Riverlands troops lost heart and refused to go down. Ma Su raised the red flag to signal the attack, but none of the commanders or soldiers would take the initiative. Enraged by this show of resistance, Ma Su personally killed two commanders. The soldiers, afraid for their lives, halfheartedly descended and attacked. But the Wei troops held firm, and soon the Riverlanders retreated uphill. Ma Su, seeing his situation worsening, ordered a tight defense of the camp until outside help had arrived.

The fall of Jieting blunts the momentum of Kongming's eastward drive.

Meanwhile, after ordering Ma Su to hold Jieting, Kongming could not decide on a course of action. Suddenly he was told that Wang Ping's sketch of the Jieting defenses had come. Kongming received the sketch from his attendants and unrolled it on his table. Examining it, he struck the table in consternation. He cried, "The fool, Ma Su, has led my army to its doom!" "Why is Your Excellency so excited?" his attendants asked. "I can see from the map that Ma Su has abandoned the main roads and fortified the hilltop," Kongming replied. "If the northerners of Wei come in strength to surround him and cut off his water, our men will go to pieces in two days. And where can we retreat to if Jieting falls?" Senior Adviser Yang Yi advanced a proposal: "Despite my lack of talent, permit me to go and replace Ma Su." Kongming subsequently gave the adviser explicit instructions on preparing the ground for the camp at Jieting.

Yang Yi was about to leave, when Kongming was told of the fall of both Jieting and Willow Rows. He stamped his foot in despair and sighed. "Our cause is lost and it is my doing!" he cried, and he summoned Guan Xing and Zhang Bao. "Take three thousand crack troops each," he ordered them, "and head for the bypaths of the Wugong Hills. If you run into Wei troops, don't launch any major action; just beat the drums and howl to the skies so they'll think you are a decoy force. If they go, do not pursue. When they withdraw, head for Yangping Pass." At the same time Kongming had Zhang Yi ready Saber Gateway for the return of the army to Shu; he issued secret instructions for the main army to prepare quietly for the march home; he had Ma Dai and Jiang Wei secure the rear of his retreat route by placing ambushes in the valleys with orders not to pull back until the main forces had withdrawn. He also sent trusted agents to Tianshui, Nan'an, and Anding to inform the officers and men as well as officials and townsmen that they should move into Hanzhong; and finally, he sent a trusted agent to Jicheng to move Jiang Wei's mother into Hanzhong.

After making these arrangements, Kongming took five thousand men back to Xicheng to move grain and provender. Suddenly a dozen mounted couriers arrived and reported: "Sima Yi is leading a multitude of one hundred and fifty thousand toward Xicheng." At this point Kongming had no commanders of importance beside him—only a group of civil officials—and half the five thousand in his command had been detailed to move food supplies, leaving a mere twenty-five hundred troops in the town. The officials turned pale at the news of Sima Yi's approach. When Kongming mounted the city wall to observe, he saw dust clouds in the distance rising skyward as the two northern field armies advanced for battle.

Kongming ordered all flags and banners put out of sight and instructed the wall sentries to execute anyone who tried to pass in or out without authority or who raised his voice. Next, Kongming ordered the town's four gates opened wide; at each a squad of twenty, disguised as commoners, swept the roadway. The soldiers had been told to make no untoward move when the Wei army arrived, as Kongming was following a plan of his own. After this Kongming put on his crane-feather cloak, wrapped a band around his head, and, followed by two lads bearing his zither, sat down on the wall. He propped himself against the railing in front of a turret and began to strum as incense burned.

Meanwhile, Sima Yi's scouts had reached the wall of Xicheng. Finding the scene as described, they advanced no further but reported at once to their commander. Sima Yi laughed and dismissed the report. He then halted his army and rode forward himself to view the town from a distance. There indeed was Kongming sitting by the turret, smiling as ever and burning incense as he played. To his left, a lad held a fine sword; to his right, another held a yak-tail whisk. By the gate two dozen sweepers plied their brooms with lowered heads, as if no one else were about.

Puzzled, Sima Yi turned his army around and retreated toward the hills to the north. His second son, Sima Zhao, asked, "What makes you sure Kongming isn't putting this on because he has no troops? Why simply retreat, Father?" Sima Yi answered, "Kongming has always been a man of extreme caution, never one to tempt the fates. He opened the gates because he had set an ambush. On entering, we would have been trapped. You are too young to know! Hurry the retreat!" Thus the two Wei armies withdrew.

After the retreating army was well into the distance, Kongming rubbed his palms together and laughed; but his officials were left amazed. One of them asked, "Why did a famous Wei general like Sima Yi with one hundred fifty thousand in his command withdraw after one look at Your Excellency?" "The man," Kongming replied, "assumed I was too cautious to tempt fate. He saw my preparations, suspected ambush, and withdrew. It was not recklessness. What choice had I? Sima Yi is sure to head for the northern hills. I have already told Guan Xing and Zhang Bao to be waiting for him there." The astonished officials acknowledged his genius, saying, "The very gods could not outwit Your Excellency. We would have abandoned the town!" "Could I have gotten far enough with twenty-five hundred men," Kongming asked, "to escape Sima Yi?" A poet of later times has left these lines of admiration:

> A zither three spans long subdued a puissant host
> When Liang dismissed his foe at Xicheng town.
> A hundred fifty thousand turned themselves around—
> And townsmen at the spot still wonder how!

His explanation made, Kongming clapped his hands and laughed aloud. "But were I Sima Yi, I would not have gone back!" he said. Next, he ordered the people of Xicheng to follow the troops into Hanzhong in view of the expected return of Sima Yi. And so Kongming set out for Hanzhong from Xicheng, followed by the officials, officers, soldiers, and people of the three districts Tianshui, Anding, and Nan'an.

Meanwhile, Sima Yi was heading for the Wugong Hills. Suddenly from behind a slope murderous shouts rent the air and drumbeats shook the ground. "Had I stayed, I would have fallen into Zhuge Liang's trap," Sima Yi was saying, when he saw a company of men advancing upon him; their banner read "Winged Tiger General Zhang Bao of the Right Guard." The Wei soldiers flung down their shields and weapons and fled. But they had hardly gone one stage when fresh cries came thundering out of another valley. Drum and horn rent the air and before them a banner held high on a pole bore the words "Prancing Dragon General Guan Xing of the Left Guard." Their clamor echoed in the valley; no one could tell how many Riverlands troops there were. Too confused to take up positions, the Wei army abandoned their wagons and fled. As instructed, the two warriors did not pursue; they took quantities of grain and weapons and withdrew.

Seeing that the valleys were filled with Riverlands soldiers, Sima Yi did not dare come out on the main road but retreated to Jieting. By this time Cao Zhen had learned of Kongming's retreat and gave eager chase. But behind a nearby hill bombards sounded, and Riverlands troops spread over the terrain: their leaders, Jiang Wei and Ma Dai. Cao Zhen, surprised, quickly withdrew; his vanguard commander, Chen Zao, had already been slain by Ma Dai. Cao Zhen led his army in a race for safety; and the Riverlands troops hurried back that night without halt to Hanzhong.

CHAPTER 96

Shedding Tears, Kongming Executes Ma Su; Cutting Hair, Zhou Fang Deceives Cao Xiu

Kongming dismissed Wang Ping and summoned Ma Su, who placed ropes around himself and knelt before the prime minister. Kongming, wearing an angry expression, said, "From your youth you have read your fill of military texts and have been thoroughly versed in battle tactics. Time and again I warned you that Jieting was a vital base when you took the responsibility of defending it, pledging the lives of your family. Had you listened to Wang Ping, you could have avoided this disaster. You must bear the blame for our defeated army, our fallen commanders, our abandoned territory, and our lost towns. If military regulations are not clear and correct, how can I discipline the soldiers? Your violation of the rules was no fault of mine. Your family, however, will be provided with a monthly allowance of cash and grain; therefore set your mind at rest." So saying, Kongming ordered Ma Su removed and executed.

Ma Su wept and said, "You have been a father to me, and I a son to you. My punishment is unavoidable. I ask only that Your Excellency remember the legend of Shun, who employed Yu after executing Gun, and I shall bear you no grudge in the netherworld below." With that, Ma Su wept loudly. Kongming brushed away his tears, saying, "Brothers could not be closer than we two. Your son will be my son. Say no more."

The guards took Ma Su outside the main gate of the camp and were about to perform their duty, when Military Adviser Jiang Wan arrived from Chengdu. Seeing the execution being prepared, he cried out in alarm, "Spare him!" He went before Kongming and said, "In ancient times the leader of Chu killed General Cheng Dechen after a great defeat and gave Duke Wen of Jin, Chu's enemy, great satisfaction thereby. With the empire so unstable, it is surely a shame to put a wise counselor to death." Weeping freely, Kongming replied. "In ancient times Sunzi was able to impose his control over the empire because his application of the laws was clear and unmistakable. Now strife afflicts every part of the empire, and warfare is constantly breaking out. If the law is set aside, how can we continue the campaign against the rebels? It is necessary to execute Ma Su."

Soon after, the guards presented Ma Su's head to the prime minister's attendants. Kongming wept long and loud. Jiang Wan said to him, "The law has punished Ma Su for his crime. Why do you lament, Your Excellency?" "It's not for Ma Su that I weep," he answered. "I am thinking of the late Emperor—at Baidi when the end was near—warning me not to use this man because his deeds would not match his boasts. The late king's words have proved too true, leaving me now to rue my blindness. I weep to recall it." Senior and junior commanders and officers wept with him. Ma Su died at the age of thirty-nine during the summer, in the fifth month of Jian Xing 6 [A.D. 228]. A later poet left these lines:

> Ma Su, for losing Jieting—no small crime—
> Earned only scorn for his claims of skill
> And paid before the camp the law's full due
> As tearful Kongming thought, how much the late king knew!

After the execution Kongming had Ma Su's head displayed in all the camps and then sewn back on his corpse that it might be interred whole. Kongming personally prepared the memorial text and the sacrificial offering; he showed Ma Su's family especial concern and provided them with cash and grain each month.

Kongming then wrote a petition for Jiang Wan to present to the Second Emperor requesting his own demotion from the position of prime minister. Jiang Wan returned to Chengdu and presented the document to his lord. It read:

> Though a man of commonplace ability, I came to hold a position far beyond my scope. I tried my best to inspire the army as bearer of the imperial battle-axe and flag of command; but I failed to enforce the statutes, to clarify the laws, and to act with prudence. The result was the loss of Jieting, when my command was violated, and of Winnow Basket Gorge, when my warnings were ignored. The fault rests with me for delegating authority so wrongly. Clearly, I did not choose well and made grave mistakes in affairs entrusted to me. In the *Spring and Autumn Anals* it is the commander who bears responsibility when things go wrong; it is thus fitting that I be demoted three grades to punish my fault. Overcome with shame, this vassal prostrates himself awaiting your decision.

Having read the petition, the Second Emperor said, "Victory and defeat are commonplace to the master of warfare. Why does His Excellency make this statement to us?" Privy Counselor Fei Yi said to the Emperor, "It is this vassal's understanding that in government nothing outweighs reverence for the law. When the law is not applied, authority is not accepted. For the prime minister to demote himself after a grave defeat is entirely appropriate." The Second Emperor accepted Fei Yi's judgment and issued an edict demoting Kongming to general of the Right and acting prime minister but preserving his overall military authority. The Emperor then sent Fei Yi to Hanzhong to deliver the edict.

———————————

After a period spent in Chengdu, Kongming petitions his emperor to authorize another invasion of the north. The petition granted, Kongming returns to the front in Qishan, the hilly region on Wei's western frontier. From the northerners' point of view, control of Qishan by Wei means securing "the land within the passes" surrounding Chang'an as well as gaining a forward position for attacking Chengdu (chapter 97).

In the summer of 229, about half a year after the loss of Jieting, western forces defeat the Wei armies in Qishan, bringing Chang'an once again within Kongming's reach. Sun Quan declares himself emperor. Renouncing his vassalage to Wei opens the door to repairing relations with the Riverlands. At this time Liu Shan restores Kongming's status as prime minister.

In the second half of 230, Cao Rui, emperor of Wei, and his chief commander, Sima Yi, renew military operations in Qishan. In the fighting Kongming is gaining the upper hand when he is recalled to Chengdu by the Emperor, who has been persuaded that the costs of continuing the war are too high. For the next three years Kongming remains in Chengdu slowly rebuilding his forces (chapters 98 to 101).

Kongming finally returns to Qishan and again engages the forces of Sima Yi, who retreats. At the same time Sun Quan sends a Southland army against the Wei. Wei forces drive the Southland back but are stopped, and the Southland is again shown to be more capable in defense than in offense. In the west Kongming and Sima Yi settle in for a long campaign.

Kongming lures Sima Yi into Gourd Gorge, which he has mined with firebombs. However, as the trap springs on Sima Yi, a heavy rain extinguishes the fires, enabling Sima Yi to escape. Kongming camps at Wuzhangyuan (chapters 102–103).

CHAPTER 103

Sima Yi Is Trapped in Shangfang Gorge;
At Wuzhangyuan Zhuge Prays
to Reverse His Star-told Fate

After stationing himself at Wuzhangyuan, Kongming sent soldiers to challenge the northerners, but none responded. Kongming then placed a maiden's headdress and a mourning garment of white silk in a large box and sent it to the Wei camp with a letter enclosed. The northern commanders could not conceal the matter; they brought the envoy before Sima Yi, who opened the box in front of his commanders. He looked at the clothes and opened the letter, which read:

> Sima Yi, you are a great general and you command the forces of the heartland; but you have no taste for the real combat that would decide which of us shall prevail, content instead to huddle in the nest, careful to stay beyond the reach of spear or arrow, exactly like a woman! Today I send you this dress and chapeau, therefore, which, unless you choose to come out and face me, you may receive with humble thanks. If a spark of self-respect still burns inside you, however, if your breast still holds a manly heart, reply to me at once and face me on the field at a time of your choosing.

Rage welled up inside Sima Yi as he finished the letter. But feigning a smile, he said, "So he takes me for a woman!" He took the gift and rewarded the bearer well; then he said, "Tell me something about Kongming: how he eats and sleeps, how taxing his duties are." The bearer answered, "The prime minister rises early and works late. He personally sees to any infraction punishable by more than twenty strokes. He eats no more than a few pints of grain each day." Sima Yi turned to his commanders and said, "Eating too little and working too hard. How long can he last?"

The envoy returned to Wuzhangyuan and told Kongming, "Sima Yi expressed no anger when he took the clothing and read the letter. He simply asked how you were eating and sleeping and inquired about your workload. He said nothing at all about military matters. When I answered his questions he said, 'He eats too little and works too hard. How long can he last?'" Kongming sighed and said, "He knows me well!"

First Secretary Yang Yong tried to get Kongming to reduce his workload: "I have seen Your Excellency checking over our books and records personally. It seems to me unnecessary. Every governing system has to have a structure whose higher and lower levels function independently, much as the operation of a household requires menials to farm and maids to prepare food. No chores are neglected and all needs are supplied; thus, the master of the house can eat and drink carefree and at ease. But if the master busies himself with every last detail, it leads to physical and mental exhaustion, and in the end nothing gets done. Does that mean his knowledge is inferior to that of a menial or a maid? No. It means he has not found the right way to run the household. Indeed, as the ancients proclaimed, 'To sit and discuss the true way is for the three elder lords of the kingdom; to act on policy is for the imperial officeholders.' In ancient times Bing Ji showed concern only for the panting ox and was indifferent to those who had fallen dead by the roadside. Similarly, Chen Ping had no knowledge of state receipts of grain and money. 'Others are in charge of that,' he said. Now Your Excellency wastes energy attending to the most trivial matters—and for what? What Sima Yi said is all too true." Weeping, Kongming replied, "I am not unaware of this. But I carry the heavy responsibility given to me by the late Emperor, and I fear that others may not be so conscientious." The assembly wept with him. Thereafter, Kongming felt his confidence and peace of mind slipping away, and his commanders became reluctant to advance.

It was soon widely known among the Wei commanders that Kongming had sent mourning garb and a woman's headdress to humiliate Sima Yi and that after receiving them Sima Yi still refused to fight. The outraged commanders protested before Sima Yi: "How can the renowned commanders of a great kingdom bear this insult? We request permission to take on the enemy and show them who the rooster is, who the hen." But Sima Yi responded, "Don't think I am afraid to take the field or content to bear this insult: the edict to defend our position and not give battle ties my hands. A rash move would violate the Emperor's order." Sima Yi's commanders were not satisfied with this answer, so he added, "If you wish me to attack, give me time to petition for the Emperor's approval to take the battle to the enemy. Agreed?" The commanders agreed, and Sima Yi subsequently memorialized Cao Rui, who was at army headquarters in Hefei. Cao Rui opened the document, which said in sum:

> My responsibilities being greater than my abilities, I labor under your all-seeing guidance. Your Majesty has enjoined me to keep to the defensive until the Riverlands army breaks up of its own accord. What am I to do when Zhuge Liang insults me by sending me a woman's headdress? With all due reverence, I must make known to Your Majesty in all your sagely wisdom that I shall soon have to fight the foe to the death, both to requite the court's kindness and to redeem my army's shame. With anguish greater than this vassal can master. . . .

Cao Rui read the appeal and said to his officials, "Sima Yi has been holding firm. Why does he petition again for permission to take the field?" Xin Pi, chief of Palace Security, said, "Sima Yi has no real desire to fight. He seeks reaffirmation of your sagely purpose in order to check his commanders' indignation over Zhuge Liang's insult." Cao Rui agreed, and he authorized Xin Pi to bear his injunction against engaging the enemy back to Sima Yi's camp on the northern bank of the River Wei. Sima Yi received the edict and entered the main tent with Xin Pi, who declared on behalf of the sovereign, "The next man to argue for taking the field shall be considered in violation of the imperial dictate." The commanders had no choice but to accept the edict. Privately, Sima Yi said to Xin Pi, "You know my mind well." Then he informed the army that Xin Pi had come to communicate the ruler's injunction against combat.

    The Riverlands commanders learned of the new edict and reported to Kongming, who remarked with a smile, "It's only Sima Yi's way of keeping his army quiet." Jiang Wei said, "How does Your Excellency know?" "He never meant to fight in the first place," he replied. "He sought permission to fight only to show his men his militant spirit. Have you forgotten? 'No general in the field is bound to obey an edict.' Who ever heard of a general requesting permission to fight from a thousand *li* away! Sima Yi has to use Cao Rui to control his army, because the commanders and officers are seething. And they publicize it to weaken our resolve."

During this conference Fei Yi's return from the Southland was announced. Kongming called for his report. Fei Yi said: "When the Southland invaded with three armies, Cao Rui took the main northern force to Hefei and had Man Chong, Tian Yu, and Liu Shao counter the southern armies. Man Chong burned out the southerners' supplies and weapons; and most of the southern troops contracted disease. Lu Xun therefore petitioned the king of Wu, Sun Quan, to set a time for a combined attack front and rear—on the north. But the bearer of this petition was seized en route by northern troops. The plan was compromised, and the southern army withdrew without a victory."

As Kongming listened, a long sigh escaped him. He lost consciousness and fell down. His commanders rushed to his assistance, but some time passed before he came to himself. "My mind is confused," he said, sighing again. "That old trouble again. The end may be near."

That night the ailing Kongming managed to get himself out of his tent. He gazed at the constellations overhead in astonishment. Reentering, he said to Jiang Wei, "My days are numbered." "Why does Your Excellency say so?" Jiang Wei asked. "The guest stars in Triple Platform are doubly bright, the host stars darkened; the ranged luminaries supporting them are dimmer, too. These heavenly phenomena disclose my fate." "Despite these signs," Jiang Wei said, "does Your Excellency not have a way to pray for a reversal?" "I have," Kongming replied, "but everything depends on what Heaven decrees. I want forty-nine men in armor, each holding a black flag and dressed in black, to form a circle outside my tent. Inside I will pray to the Northern Dipper. If the main lamp stays lit seven more days, my life may last another circuit of the zodiac. If the lamp goes out, I will die. Please keep unauthorized persons out of the area. Anything I need can be brought in by my two young assistants." Jiang Wei left to make the preparations Kongming required.

It was midautumn, halfway through the eighth month [A.D. 234]. That night the Milky Way sparkled brilliantly, and a crystalline dew formed in perfect droplets. The flags hung slack in the windless air; the night gong was stilled. Outside Kongming's tent Jiang Wei commanded the guard of forty-nine. Inside, Kongming laid out fragrant flowers and sacrificial articles. On the ground were seven large lamps surrounded by forty-nine smaller ones; at the center of these rings he placed a single lamp for his own life. He bowed low and chanted: "Born into an age of disorder, I would have gladly spent my years in the countryside. But August Emperor Zhao Lie claimed my love when he came three times seeking my service. Later, he put his young son in my care, and I had to continue humbly serving his cause, having vowed to suppress the rebellion against Han. I did not expect my guiding star would slip and bring my mortal hours to a close. With reverence I address this final text to the blue span above, hoping Heaven will vouchsafe me its sympathetic attention and bend its rule by amending my mortal allotment. That would enable me to fulfill my duties to the Emperor and to rescue the common folk from their peril; to restore the manners, morals, and traditions of the former era, and to perpetuate the holy rites of Han. This is no desperate prayer I offer here but one which springs from heartfelt anguish!" The incantation finished, Kongming remained bent to the floor awaiting the dawn. The next day he forced himself to conduct business, but he spat blood all day. By day he discussed military affairs; by night he paced the Northern Dipper.

Sima Yi meanwhile had been keeping fast to his positions. Then one night he saw something in the heavens that delighted him. "A guiding star has lost its position," he said to Xiahou Ba. "Kongming must be ill. He is not long for this world. Take a thousand men to Wuzhangyuan and find out all you can. If the Riverlanders are disorderly and make no attempt to engage, Kongming is mortally ill—and we must seize our chance to attack!" Xiahou Ba left with his troops.

Kongming remained at his devotions. On the sixth night the main lamp still burned bright and his heart was eased. Jiang Wei entered the tent and saw Kongming, hair loosed, leaning on his sword; he was pacing the Dipper in his mind's eye, hoping to stabilize his guiding star. Suddenly he heard an uproar outside his compound. He was about to have someone investigate, when Wei

Yan came dashing into the tent crying, "The Wei army has come!" Wei Yan was running so fast that he overturned the main lamp, and it went out. Kongming set his sword aside and said with a sigh, "Death is a fate no one can avert." Wei Yan, overcome with confusion, flung himself down pleading for forgiveness. Jiang Wei wrathfully drew his sword. Indeed:

> No man can master the infinity of possibility;
> No heart can match wits with destiny.

Would Jiang Wei kill Wei Yan?
  Read on.

CHAPTER 104

The Guiding Star Falls, and the Han Prime Minister Returns to Heaven; The Wei Field Marshal Is Terrified by the Sight of a Wooden Statue

Jiang Wei drew his sword, but Kongming checked him, saying, "It was not his fault. My time has come." Jiang Wei put up his weapon. Kongming spat several mouthfuls of blood and lay down on his couch. He said, "Sima Yi guessed I was ill and sent soldiers to probe our position. Engage them at once!" Wei Yan left the tent and rode out of the compound to confront the northern force; Xiahou Ba hastily withdrew. Wei Yan pursued for more than twenty *li* before turning back. Kongming then sent Wei Yan back to his camp.

Jiang Wei came to the side of Kongming's couch to attend him. Kongming said, "I have tried my best to return the heartland to Han rule. But Heaven's wishes rule us all. My end is near, very near. The results of a lifetime of study are written in these twenty-four essays in 104,112 characters. They contain esoteric information on the Eight Principal Concerns, the Seven Precautions, the Six Dangers, and the Five Alerts. None of my commanders is fit to receive it; to you alone I transmit it. Treat it with all seriousness." Jiang Wei wept and prostrated himself on receiving the text. Kongming continued, "I have invented a bow that releases arrows simultaneously, but I have never had a chance to test it in combat. It shoots ten eight-inch arrows at a time. The sketches have been collected into a volume. Have the weapon built according to design." Jiang Wei received these papers also. Kongming continued, "The regions of the Riverlands are rather secure, except Yinping, which needs careful watching. Even though the terrain is arduous, we may soon have a problem there."

Next he summoned Ma Dai, to whom he whispered certain instructions and gave a secret plan, saying, "Carry it out after my death." Ma Dai agreed and left. Shortly afterward Kongming received Yang Yi by his bedside, handed him a brocade sack, and secretly instructed him: "After I am dead, Wei Yan will turn against us. When he does, accompany him to the front line and then open this. You will find the right man to execute him." After disposing of all items of business, Kongming blacked out. Later that night, he regained consciousness and prepared a petition to the Second Emperor.

On receiving Kongming's memorial, the Second Emperor was agitated. He hastily ordered Chief Secretary Li Fu to the front to inquire about Kongming's health and to seek his advice about the future. After reaching Wuzhangyuan by rapid stages, Li Fu entered Kongming's presence and transmitted the Emperor's command. Li Fu asked about Kongming's illness; shedding tears, Kongming said, "Ill fate takes me now, my task but half done. I have forsaken the Emperor's cause and I have failed the empire. After my death all of you must guide and support the Emperor with unstinting devotion. The dynasty's institutions must not be altered, nor the men I have brought into service dismissed. My military methods and doctrines have been handed on to Jiang Wei, and he will exert himself for the dynasty in continuing my work. My life hangs in the balance. Let me now give you one final petition to submit to His Majesty." Li Fu noted Kongming's words and departed in haste.

Kongming lifted himself with difficulty, and his attendants put him onto his wagon so he could inspect the campsites outside the fortifications. The autumn wind blew against his face, and a sharp chill took his bones. With a long sigh he said, "Never shall I go to the front and fight the rebels again! Oh, you infinite skies, what could be more sad?" After pondering for some time, Kongming returned to his tent. His condition worsened.

Kongming summoned Yang Yi and instructed him: "Wang Ping, Liao Hua, Zhang Ni, Zhang Yi, Wu Yi, and the others are loyal and honorable men. Having survived arduous trials through long years of war, they will prove worthy of whatever you require of them. After my death I want everything to go on in our accustomed manner. Make a slow and deliberate retreat; show no haste. You are well versed in our strategy and need no further instruction. Jiang Wei has the wit and courage to protect the rear." Yang Yi wept as he received his commands. Kongming called for writing materials and in his bed penned his testament for the Second Emperor:

> Mortality is man's common lot; his years are numbered. Now death approaches, and I wish here to give full expression to my humble loyalty.
>
> I, Liang, endowed with a nature both ordinary and graceless, encountered a time of troubles. After I was granted military authority, major decisions were placed in my hands. I fielded armies for the northern expedition but failed to reach the goal I sought. Now, stricken by unforeseen and incurable illness, I face imminent death, and I despair that my service to Your Majesty remains unfinished.
>
> I humbly beg that Your Majesty keep an honest mind and limit your desires, disciplining yourself and caring tenderly for the people. Serve the late Emperor in a spirit of filial piety; show humane generosity throughout your kingdom. Promote those not in the public eye to advance the cause of true excellence; deny access to the vicious and depraved to strengthen the moral tone of the realm.
>
> My home in Chengdu, with its eight hundred mulberry trees and a meagre fifteen hundred *mu* of land, should provide for my children. On assignment outside the capital I have acquired nothing of value; beyond the food and clothing that Your Majesty's officers supplied, I have had no other income. Hence, after my death no excess silks, no surplus wealth, nor any other violation of Your Majesty's trust will be discovered.

When Kongming had finished writing, he instructed Yang Yi further: "After my death no funeral is to be held. Make a large case to hold my corpse in a sitting position. Place seven grains of rice inside my mouth. Set a lamp at my feet. Keep everything quiet and normal in the army: no mourning cries at all. That will prevent my guiding star from falling to earth, for the darker of my souls will rise to steady it. Sima Yi will be puzzled when he sees the star holding its place. The rear forces should decamp first; next, the various sites, slowly and singly. Should Sima Yi pursue, reform your battle line and turn your banners and drums around to face them. Wait for them to arrive, then take the wooden statue I've had carved, set it in my wagon, and push the wagon to the front flanked by the entire leadership high and low. That should frighten Sima Yi away." Yang Yi noted each command.

That night Kongming's attendants helped him out of his tent. Looking up at the Northern Dipper, he pointed to one of its stars and said, "There—my guiding star." Everyone studied the star, which dimmed and wavered as if it would fall from its place. Kongming pointed his sword to it and read a magical charm. Then he hurried back into the tent and fainted. At this moment of confusion and despair among the commanders, Chief Secretary Li Fu reappeared. Seeing Kongming unconscious, he could hardly speak. Through tears, he said, "I am too late. I have failed my kingdom!"

Moments later Kongming revived, opened his eyes, and looked around. Seeing Li Fu by his bed, Kongming said, "I know why you have come." Excusing himself, Li Fu said, "The Son of Heaven mandated me to inquire of Your Excellency what man, after your mortal term, might be entrusted with this great mission. But in my distress I neglected to consult Your Excellency, and so I have returned." Kongming answered, "Jiang Wan (styled Gongyan) would be the most suitable." "And second to him?" Li Fu then asked. "Fei Yi (styled Wenwei)," Kongming replied. "And then, if not Fei Yi, who should it be?" Li Fu asked again. Kongming gave no answer. The commanders pressed closer to the bed to study him, but he had succumbed. It was the autumn of the twelfth year of Jian Xing, the twenty-third day of the eighth month. Kongming was fifty-four. Du Fu has left this poem:

The star that dropped last night upon his camp
Announced to all: "The master fell this day."
No longer from his tent will orders flow;
The Hall of Fame will honor his success.
Three thousand followers left masterless,
The hosts in his mind's eye denied their day.
Nor, in the green woods, clear and sunlit,
Will Kongming's fine-voiced chants be heard again.

Bai Juyi has also left a poem:

Ensconced in hills, the master hid his tracks.
By twist of fate a sage king sued three times.
Only in Nanyang could "fish" and "water" meet:
"The dragon flies to Heavenly Han—a wholesome rain."
To Liu Bei's heir Kongming gave zealous care.
Serving the state, he poured forth his loyal heart.
And still today his calls to war live on;
How many readers can restrain their tears?

At an earlier point Liao Li, Chang River commandant in Shu,
had considered himself able and renowned enough to become
Kongming's lieutenant. Subsequently, Liao Li had scanted his
official duties, worn the air of a man who had been treated shab-
bily, and complained no end. Kongming had therefore removed
him from office, made him a commoner, and transferred his residence to Minshan. When Liao Li learned of Kongming's death,
he wept freely and said, "Then I am doomed to live apart from
Han for good!"

When Li Yan heard the news of Kongming's death, he took
sick with grief and died. Apparently, Li Yan had hoped that Kongming would restore his position and allow him to amend his previous mistakes; Kongming's death ended Li Yan's hopes of returning to service.

In later times Yuan Weizhi left these lines in praise of Kongming:

To set the times aright he backed Liu Bei;
With earnest zeal he took the orphan king.
His splendid gifts surpassed Guan Zhong's, Yue Yi's;
His unique schemes excelled Sunzi's, Wu Qi's.
How awe-inspiring his two-part call to war!
How proud and grand the Eightfold Ramparts plan!
Such a lord as this—all virtues' height—
Had never been, nor ever was again.

That night Heaven despaired and earth grieved. The moon waned as Kongming's fleeting soul went home to Heaven. Jiang Wei and Yang Yi, as Kongming had advised, forbade public mourning. They dressed the corpse and placed it in a case, as arranged; it was guarded by three hundred trusted captains and soldiers. Then they issued secret orders to Wei Yan to protect the rear while the army withdrew from the various encampments and strongpoints in perfect order, one after another.

*   *   *   *

Sima Yi, watching the night sky, saw a large, ruddy star with a horn rising on its awn. The star began streaming from the northeast toward the southwest and fell to earth within the Riverlands camps; thrice it had lurched and risen again before landing with a faint rumble. Startled but delighted, Sima Yi cried, "Kongming has died!" and ordered the whole army to strike out after the enemy. But on leaving the base, he reconsidered: "Kongming knows well how the Six Ding deities and the Six Jia deities control celestial phenomena. He sees how long we have refrained from battle and now tempts us forth with false news of his death. Pursuit will play into his hands." Thus, Sima Yi returned and kept to his base, only letting Xiahou Ba quietly take a few score of riders to scout the hills by Wuzhangyuan.

Xiahou Ba reached Wuzhangyuan; not a soul was there. He reported at once to Sima Yi: "The Riverlands army has evacuated." Losing composure, Sima Yi said, "So Kongming has died. Pursue at once!" "Not too hastily, Field Marshal," Xiahou Ba advised him. "Let a subordinate commander go before you." "This time I need to go myself," Sima Yi answered.

Sima Yi and his two sons raced for Wuzhangyuan. Shouting and swinging their banners, they charged into the evacuated base: it was deserted. Turning to his sons, Sima Yi said, "Follow up with your troops. I will start after them." With Sima Shi and Sima Zhao bringing up the rear, Sima Yi tracked the Riverlanders to the foot of some hills and, seeing them still within range, pursued vigorously. Suddenly from behind one hill a bombard sounded, and the noise of war cries shook the ground. Sima Yi watched amazed as the Riverlands army reversed banners and drums to face him. Laced by trees' shadows, the grand banner of the central army billowed out, bearing a single line of large characters: "Zhuge Liang, Prime Minister of Han, Lord of Wuxiang."

Stunned, Sima Yi turned pale. Looking intently, he saw several dozen ranking commanders grouped around a four-wheeled wagon; inside sat Kongming with his Taoist headdress, feather fan, crane plumes, and black tunic. "Kongming, alive?" cried the astounded Sima Yi. "I have blundered into their strongpoint and sprung their trap." He wheeled his mount and fled. Behind him Jiang Wei shouted: "Stand your ground, rebel! You're in my prime minister's hands!" The northern soldiers felt their souls take flight, and flinging down armor and helmets, lances and halberds, they trampled one another in the stampede to escape. Those killed were beyond numbering.

Sima Yi had gone some fifty *li*, when two Wei generals overtook him and took hold of his horse's reins. "Do not panic, Field Marshal," they shouted. Sima Yi rubbed his head with his hand and said, "Have I still got it?" "Have no fear. The Riverlands troops are far away," they replied. Sima Yi caught his breath and calmed himself. He looked steadily at the two generals; recognizing Xiahou Ba and Xiahou Hui, he slowly let go of the reins. The three hurried back to their base along a small path and told their commanders to patrol on all sides.

Two days later some local villagers came to tell Sima Yi, "When the Riverlands army entered the gorge, their mourning cries shook the ground and a white banner went up amongst them. Kongming has in fact died. Only Jiang Wei stayed behind with a thousand men to hold the rear. It was a wooden statue in the wagon." Sima Yi sighed and said, "I could gauge him in life, but not in death." After this, a saying gained currency in Shu, "A dead Zhuge puts a live Sima to flight!" A poet of later times has left these lines:

> That night from Heaven's Pole a fireball fell,
> But Sima fled for fear his foe lived still.
> And western mockers still remember how
> He wondered if his head were on or no!

Having verified the news of Kongming's death, Sima Yi resumed pursuit. On reaching Redbank Slope, however, he saw the enemy was beyond overtaking, so he led his force back. He said to his commanders, "With Kongming gone, we can sleep in peace!" Bringing the army home to the capital, he passed the camps and bases that Kongming had set up—each superbly laid out—and he said with a sigh, "A rare genius!" On reaching Chang'an, he sent his commanders to protect the various strongpoints and continued on to Luoyang to see the sovereign.

With Kongming dead, Yang Yi and Jiang Wei lead the Shu-Han armies home to Chengdu.

CHAPTER 105

Kongming Leaves a Plan in the Brocade Bag; Cao Rui Removes the Ambrosia-collecting Bowl

When the Emperor returned to court, Yang Yi presented himself, in bonds, to beg forgiveness. The Emperor had an imperial attendant remove the cords; then he said, "Because you followed the prime minister's final orders, his bier has come home and Wei Yan has been eliminated. Your effort has preserved our government intact." He appointed Yang Yi director general of the Center. Ma Dai, who had distinguished himself by bringing the renegade to justice, was granted Wei Yan's rank.

Yang Yi submitted Kongming's final petition. The Emperor read it and wept; he then commanded the diviners to locate a site for the interment. Fei Yi petitioned the throne: "When near death, the prime minister ordered that he be buried on Dingjun Mountain. He wanted no brick wall around the grave and no funerary articles." The Emperor approved the petition, and an auspicious day was selected in the tenth month of the year [A.D. 234] for the Emperor himself to escort the bier to the burial place. At the Emperor's command the sacrificial ceremonies commenced, and Kongming received the posthumous title Loyal and Martial Lord. The Emperor ordered a shrine built at Mianyang and ceremonies performed there each season. Du Fu has left this poem in memory of the loyal dynastic servant:

> "His Excellency's shrine, where would it be found?"
> "Past Damask Town, where cypresses grow dense."
> Its sunlit court, gem-bright greens—a spring unto themselves.
> Leaf-veiled, the orioles—sweet notes to empty air.
> Thrice to him Liu Bei sued, keen to rule the realm:
> Two reigns Kongming served—steady old heart—
> To die, his host afield, the victory herald yet to come—
> Weep, O heroes! Drench your fronts, now and evermore.

Du Fu left another poem to celebrate Kongming:

> Zhuge's mighty name hangs proudly on the upper sphere;
> Stern and grand, the royal liege man's likeness claims respect.
> In the tri-part world below he spun deep schemes.
> In the age-old realm of cloud, one single plume unites our
>   gaze.
> Who rank his peers? Yi Yin and Jiang Ziya;
> In command he was more sure than Xiao or Cao.
> But the stars had turned; he could not save Han's reign,
> Toiling to the end, body broken, will unbroken.

––––––––––––––

Over the next three decades Jiang Wei tries to carry out Kongming's grand plan for reconquering the north.

Luxury and corruption in the Wei court weaken the ruling Cao clan, and the Sima clan positions itself to usurp the throne. In 251 Sima Yi dies. His sons Sima Shi and Sima Zhao prepare to establish their own dynasty. The Shu-Han general Jiang Wei has mounted several campaigns against the north but has never prevailed. In 249–250, at the battle at Ox Head Mountain, the Wei commander Sima Shi forces Jiang Wei, the Shu-Han commander, to retreat. In 256 Sima Shi dies, leaving sole power to Sima Zhao. Jiang Wei mounts another offensive against the north, but Deng Ai, a talented Wei general, defeats Jiang Wei.

In 252 Sun Quan dies, spurring the Wei leadership's ambition to take the Southland. The southern leadership, aware of conflict in the northern court, also plans to attack the north. In 258 Jiang Wei learns of this developing war and attacks the forces of the Wei general Deng Ai. An agent for Deng Ai exploits Liu Shan's doubts about the war policy, and the Shu-Han emperor recalls Jiang Wei.

In 260 the forces of Deng Ai and Jiang Wei are again engaged. Sima Zhao murders Cao Mao, the penultimate Wei emperor, and puts Cao Huan on the throne. Sima Zhao intends to have Cao Huan abdicate in favor of his son Sima Yan.

In 263, as Jiang Wei mounts his last offensive, pressure to call off the war builds on the Shu-Han home front. Jiang Wei defeats Deng Ai only to be recalled to Chengdu once again. To ease home front concerns Jiang Wei establishes soldier-tiller colonies in Qishan. He returns to the front for the last time.

Deng Ai breaks through the western passes, and his forces seize Chengdu. The Shu-Han dynasty falls. Its last emperor, Liu Shan, is sent to the northern court.

In 265 Sima Yan accepts the abdication of the last Wei emperor, Cao Huan, and establishes a new dynasty, the Jin. As the Liu clan had ruled the Han, and the Cao the Wei, so the Sima will rule the Jin.

In 280 the Jin dynasty, having digested its western conquest, launches an invasion of the Southland. Victory comes swiftly, and the last of the three kingdoms falls. One dynasty rules the realm (tianxia) *again.*

———————

Thereafter, the three kingdoms came under the rule of the Jin Emperor, Sima Yan, who laid the foundation for a unified realm, thereby fulfilling the saying, "The empire, long united, must divide, and long divided, must unite." Liu Shan, the Illustrious Emperor of the Eastern Han, had passed away in the seventh year of the Jin reign period Tai Shi, "Magnificent Inception" [A.D. 271]. Cao Huan, ruler of Wei, passed away in the first year of Tai An, "Magnificent Peace" [A.D. 302]. Sun Hao, ruler of Wu, passed away in the fourth year of Tai Kang, "Magnificent Prosperity" [A.D. 283]. All died natural deaths.

A poet of later times wrote this ballad in the old style marking the highlights of the era:

As Gao Zu entered Xianyang, sword in hand,
Han's fiery sun climbed the Tree of Dawn.
Then dragonlike Guang Wu restored Han's rule,
And the solar crow soared to the noon of sky.
But when this great realm passed on to Xiandi,
The fiery disc set in the Pool of Night.
He Jin's folly sparked the eunuchs' coup,
And Dong Zhuo came and seized the halls of state.
Wang Yun formed a plan and struck the rebel down,
But Li Jue and Gue Si rose up in arms.
Across the land rebellions seethed and swarmed
As vicious warlords swooped down on all sides.
The house of Sun emerged beyond the Jiang.
In the north the clan of Yuan held sway.
To the west Liu Yan and Zhang ascended.
Liu Biao's legions camped in Jing and Xiang.
Zhang Yan and Lu were Hanzhong's overlords;
Defending Xiliang, Ma Teng and Han Sui.
Tao Qian of Xu, Zhang Xiu, and Gongsun Zan
Cut bold figures in their several *zhou.*
Cao Cao took power, Xiandi's minister,
Drawing valiant men with arts of peace and war.
Xiandi in his thrall, Cao ruled the lords
And with his martial hosts controlled the north.
"Twin Mulberry" Xuande, descendant of the throne,
Leagued with Guan and Zhang to save Xiandi.
He scrambled round the realm (he had no home),
His forces scant, a stranger wandering.
Thrice Xuande's ardent quest led to Nanyang,
Where Sleeping Dragon unveiled Han's partition:
"First take Jingzhou, next the Riverlands;
On that rich region, base your own royal stand."
Near death in Baidi, having reigned three years,
Bei sadly placed his son in Kongming's care.
By six offensives from the hills of Qi
Kongming sought to change Han's destiny.
But the time of Han had run—could he not tell?—
That night his master star fell past the hills.
Jiang Wei alone still strove with might and main:
Nine times more he fought the north—in vain.
Zhong Hui and Deng Ai next led armies west:
And to the Cao, Han's hills and streams now passed.
Cao Pi, Cao Rui, Fang, Mao, and briefly, Huan—
The Sima took the empire in their turn.
Cao's abdication changed the face of all;
No mighty battles marked the Southland's fall.

Three kings no more—Chenliu, Guiming, Anle.
The fiefs and posts must now be filled anew.
The world's affairs rush on, an endless stream;
A sky-told fate, infinite in reach, dooms all.
The kingdoms three are now the stuff of dream,
For men to ponder, past all praise or blame.

AFTERWORD
TO THE
UNABRIDGED EDITION

About Three Kingdoms
Moss Roberts

HISTORICAL ORIGINS:
THE PERIOD AND THE NOVEL

If any literary work captures the drama of Chinese history, it is
Three Kingdoms. This historical novel, dating from the early or
mid-Ming period, tells the story of the fall of the Han dynasty
and the division of its empire into three warring states at the
turn of the third century, A.D. The Chinese of the Ming dynasty
(1368–1644), having ended Mongol rule by force, looked back
to the Han, China's longest and mightiest dynasty, as a model
of imperial order. The Han had stability in its ruling house, a
powerful, centralized bureaucracy, and cohesive organization of
its territory. The Ming founder had for these and other reasons
publicly lauded the Han founder. However, the fall of the Han
also held important lessons for the Ming; foremost among them,
perhaps, was that disunity invites conquest.

In China *Three Kingdoms* has given mythic status to the century it chronicles (A.D. 168–280). In a somewhat similar way,
Shakespeare's historical plays chronicling the reigns of Richard
II to Richard III have transformed the century from 1377 to 1485
for Western audiences. During the Ming *Three Kingdoms* must
have attracted many readers. The 1494 preface to the first printed
edition of 1522 says that "when the text was completed, gentle-

men and scholars with a keen interest [in the subject] competed in transcribing copies for the convenience of readers." During the following centuries the novel grew in popularity even though it did not always have official approval. In the twentieth century *Three Kingdoms,* despite its length and chronologically remote subject matter, commands a universal audience in China; thus the novel has become an integral part of Chinese culture. Moreover, *Three Kingdoms* has been widely read in Japan, Korea, and Vietnam. In part, its popularity is due to the fact that in the four nations of Asia directly influenced by Confucianism, history is the main concern of the respective cultures.

Three Kingdoms describes China's traditional political culture and its struggle to define its political form, transporting the reader from the highest councils of dynastic power to the lowest fringes of society, from the capital and key provinces to the edges of the empire and beyond. It is a tale of China itself in its infinite variety, a tale peopled with kings and courtiers, commanders and scholars, magicians and peasant rebels. Women seem to play a small part, but their roles have the utmost significance. The novel offers a startling and unsparing view of how power is wielded, how diplomacy is conducted, and how wars are planned and fought; and the novel has in turn influenced the ways the Chinese think about power, diplomacy, and war. *Three Kingdoms,* like all of China's major novels, offers Western readers an understanding of China from the perspective of the Chinese themselves.

Three Kingdoms tells of one epoch-marking dynastic cycle: the fall of the Han dynasty, the subsequent division of its empire into three kingdoms—Wei, Wu, and Shu—in A.D. 220, and the reunification of the realm in A.D. 280 under a new ruling house, the Jin. The novel covers one hundred and thirteen years, from A.D. 168 to A.D. 280, a time of crisis and dissolution in Western history that spans the end of the Roman era under Marcus Aurelius and the beginning of the Byzantine under Diocletian and then Constantine. But the novel's main concern is the reign of the last Han emperor, Xian (r. A.D. 189–220). To this period the author devotes two-thirds of his work, the first eighty chapters; he describes in rich detail the final crisis of the four-hundred-year Han dynasty culminating in the displacement of its ruling house (*guojia*), the Liu, by the Cao family. The last third of the complete novel, the final forty chapters, deals with the subsequent Three Kingdoms or Three Dynasties (Sanguo) period; the founding of the Jin and the reunification of A.D. 280 is recounted in chapter 120.

This "dynastic cycle," the pattern of many eras in Chinese history, is epitomized in *Three Kingdoms*' opening line: "The empire, long divided, must unite; long united, must divide." One hundred and twenty chapters later the tale ends with the line reversed: "The empire, long united, must divide; long divided, must unite." The history of this period of crisis and resolution is both unique and universal—unique for the heroic figures that dominate it, universal for the questions it must address. How is dynastic rule established and maintained? How and why does it fail? What are the qualities of an ideal emperor (*di* or *tianzi,* Son of Heaven), an ideal minister (*xiang*), an ideal vassal (*chen*)? What is the relation between the ruling house and the empire? If the empire loses its unity, how is it regained?

Some twelve hundred years after the historical events, the novel *Three Kingdoms* was written. In Chinese the title is *Sanguozhi tongsu yanyi.* The significance of this title and its variants will be taken up shortly. Scholarly attempts to date the work have produced various suggestions, ranging from as early as the Northern Song to as late as the mid-Ming. The oldest complete printed edition, published in 1522, has a preface dated 1494 in addition to its own preface. The author of the later preface says that "the text was so voluminous and a good edition of it so hard to find that I had requested that it be put in print and widely made public." This suggests the possible existence of an earlier printed edition but more probably refers to manuscript copies, of which there must have been many. The 1494 preface cited above says, "Gentlemen and scholars . . . competed in transcribing copies for the convenience of readers." Furthermore, interlinear notes accompanying the 1522 edition seem to postdate the text itself; this too suggests an earlier date for the text. The question is, how much earlier?

The dating problem is complicated by the problem of authorship. The novel has been traditionally assigned to the late

Yuan–early Ming (say, 1350–90), and many accept this approximation, if only because the presumed author, Luo Guanzhong, lived at that time. Luo Guanzhong is the author named in the 1522 edition, and his accepted dates are 1330?–1400?—though recent research has convincingly limited his date of birth to the period 1315–18. Thus, there is a gap of about one hundred years between the presumed date of Luo Guanzhong's death and the 1494 preface. And there is no record prior to this preface connecting Luo and *Three Kingdoms*. To establish Luo Guanzhong's authorship therefore requires postulating an earlier text that has been lost. Put another way, those who argue that the 1522 text is the earliest version as well as the earliest printed edition of the novel cannot accept Luo Guanzhong as the real author.

A number of modern and contemporary Chinese scholars who tie the work to the end of the Yuan (Mongol) dynasty or the early Ming see it as a product of the great Han nationalistic movement that drove the Mongols from the northern heartland (*zhongyuan*) and in 1368 established the first Chinese dynasty—the Ming—to occupy the heartland since the fall of the Northern Song in 1127. In this view the novel culminates a tradition, which goes back to the Song, of using the Han dynasty to symbolize Han nationality in periods of conflict with the non-Han nations of the north, such as the Mongols and their predecessors. This important issue, mentioned here only in connection with the dating problem, will be taken up later in this essay.

At the present time, a Ming author and a Ming audience—either "early" or "mid"—seems likeliest. Hence, *Three Kingdoms* may be called a Ming novel whose subject matter is Han. Its Ming aspect is literary; its Han aspect is historical. Everything about the novel may be considered from these two angles. As a literary work, *Three Kingdoms* spans three genres, epic, drama, and novel: it has the scale and mythic atmosphere of the epic; the action and dialogue of the drama; and the texture and design of the novel. If comparison to Western literary works is attempted, it may be said that *Three Kingdoms* bears some resemblance to parts of the *Iliad*, to certain of Shakespeare's historical plays (perhaps the Henry VI trilogy), and to Malory's *Morte d'Arthur* or certain novels by Sir Walter Scott. As a history, however, *Three Kingdoms* has a large body of nonliterary material taken from various historical sources. The twofold nature of the novel prompted the Qing scholar Zhang Xuecheng to remark that if *Journey to the West* (*Xiyou ji*) was purely imaginative and the *Chronicles of the Kingdoms* (*Lieguozhi*) purely factual and historical, then *Three Kingdoms* was "seven parts fact and three parts fiction." The present translator used the subtitle *China's Epic Drama* in an earlier abridged edition, but perhaps "historical novel" is a better description as it combines the Ming and Han aspects of the work; the phrase may also serve as a translation of the term *yanyi*. (In his 1925 translation of the novel, C. H. Brewitt-Taylor interpreted yanyi as "romance." This word has not been used in this translation because it denotes a world removed from reality.)

When we speak of "the novel," another complication arises. There are two different texts: the 1522 version mentioned above and the mid-1660s version—the Mao edition—which eclipsed the earlier version and was exclusively circulated in China for three centuries. The 1522 version had fallen into oblivion and remained undiscovered until early in the twentieth century; a popular edition of it was published in 1975 and again in 1980 by the Guji chubanshe in Shanghai. In the notes and afterword to the present translation the 1522 edition is usually referred to as the *Tongsu* (*TS*); at times "the novel" or *Three Kingdoms* refers to both versions together.

This is a translation of the Mao edition. It was chosen in order to present to the reader the novel as it has been (and presently is) best known in China. Among scholars each version has its advocates. Some prefer the *TS* because it is richer in historical documents and information as well as franker and less moralistic about political power. Others praise the Mao edition as smoother and more effective as literature. Some regard the differences as minor; others hold them to be significant. The reader who wishes to examine some of the differences between the *TS* and the Mao editions may consult the notes and afterword of the unabridged translation.

VIRTUE, LINEAGE, AND LEGITIMACY

In *Three Kingdoms'* vast world nearly one thousand characters cross the stage. The action, moving on several planes at once, encompasses the four corners of the realm. And the novel's themes are varied and complex. In lively discussion during the 1980s, Chinese scholars have attempted to identify a single main theme in *Three Kingdoms*. Some say it is the theme of ideal liege finding ideal minister, their rise to power, and their tragic end. Some consider the struggle of ideal liege and ultimate villain to be the principal theme. Some see in the novel an exposé of the cruelties and injustice of feudal (i.e., dynastic) government itself. Others attach less importance to character and values; they emphasize the larger, impersonal theme of the restoration of national unity after a period of civil wars. Still others see the book primarily as military history, a dramatic record of personal combat, raids, surprises, offensives, sieges, pitched battles, and protracted campaigns, by an author well versed in the art of war. All of these themes or general topics are important in *Three Kingdoms;* yet all of them are engaged by a single conflict that dominates the first two-thirds of the novel, the conflict between Liu Xuande and Cao Cao. Moreover, when Cao Cao and Liu Xuande pass from the scene, their rivalry continues, as the kingdoms they have founded, Wei in the north and Shu-Han in the west (the Riverlands) exhaust themselves in civil war.

Liu Bei (Xuande) and Cao Cao (Mengde) both appear in the opening chapter. Cao Cao's father, a high military minister, provided the backing that enabled his son to rise in the bureaucracy. But however privileged, Cao Cao is a leader of Napoleonic genius, committed to advancing men on the basis of ability rather than family influence. He has a sardonic streak and keeps his own counsel. His characteristic gesture is a laugh or a smile, but without warmth. He seems isolated from even his closest advisers and kinsmen. Liu Xuande has no family backing, though he claims a remote kinship to the imperial house, whose surname he bears. His immediate circumstances are humble, and he is devoted to his mother. His virtues being greater than his talents, he seeks able and honorable men to aid him and is usually in the company of his closest companions; he rarely appears alone. His biography says that "he won the hearts of men." His characteristic gesture is weeping. The twentieth-century writer and literary historian Lu Xun has shrewdly described him as "paternalistic and benevolent, though somewhat dissembling."

In chapter 1 we find Cao Cao and Liu Xuande serving the Han emperor Ling on the battlefield as they conduct operations to suppress peasant uprisings led by the Yellow Scarves. In the following chapters the focus shifts to the Emperor. In A.D. 189 Ling dies, and his successor, Shao, reigns briefly. A warlord named Dong Zhuo deposes Shao and places Shao's younger brother Xian on the throne. Emperor Xian will reign until the dynasty ends in A.D. 220. Cao Cao and Liu Xuande appear intermittently until chapter 20, when Cao Cao presents Liu Xuande to Emperor Xian. At this point Cao Cao has command of the armed forces and holds the Emperor in thrall. But like a shogun careful to preserve the facade of imperial rule, Cao Cao refrains from usurping the throne and founding his own ruling house. The Emperor, in an effort to limit Cao Cao's control, tries to make an ally of Liu Xuande. He confirms Liu Xuande's claim to royal lineage by naming him imperial uncle and in A.D. 199 issues an edict written in his own blood and calling for action against the traitor Cao Cao. Liu Xuande joins a group of court loyalists who, inspired by the edict, vow to rescue the Emperor. This intrigue fails, and Liu Xuande leaves the court and the capital.

Henceforth Liu Xuande as well as Cao Cao—but no one else— can legitimately claim to act under imperial sanction, and so they become rival loyalists. Emperor Xian is always at the center of their calculations, and his survival is therefore assured. Cao Cao remains the dominant figure at court; Liu Xuande goes to seek his fortune in the wide world, the "rivers and hills" of China, by proving his virtue (*de*) or worthiness to rule.

The Cao Cao–Liu Xuande struggle, which begins as a court conflict, becomes an empire-wide crisis in chapter 38; the crisis culminates in chapter 50. These thirteen chapters form the novel's first peak; the narrative runs from the meeting of Liu Xuande and his ideal minister, Zhuge Liang (Kongming), in A.D. 207 to the battle at Red Cliffs in A.D. 208. After this pivotal battle, Cao Cao abandons his effort to unify the empire by conquest and proceeds to develop his position in the north; in A.D. 220, with the establishment of the Wei dynasty of the house of Cao, the formal partitioning of the empire begins.

As their influence grows, Liu Xuande and Cao Cao increasingly appear not merely as supporters of the Han emperor but as potential emperors in their own right, though neither one can afford to take any action that would expose him to the charge of treason by the other. Normally, of course, a son of Emperor Xian or Emperor Ling would stand in the line of succession. But Cao Cao neutralizes all the imperial sons by demoting them to minor princes. (This information comes from historical sources, not the novel.) And he murders the one consort permitted to Emperor Xian, Empress Fu, along with her two sons. Finally, Cao Cao marries his sister to Emperor Xian. The care Cao Cao takes to eliminate possible heirs to Emperor Xian only makes Liu Xuande's place in the royal Liu clan, however remote or dubious, all the more significant. He, like Cao Cao, awaits the next generation. For Cao Cao or for one of his sons to become emperor would constitute a change of the ruling house. What principle could justify a nonfamilial succession? This question raises what is commonly known as the issue of legitimacy (*zhengtong*).

Cao Cao himself never takes the final step of usurpation; he always casts himself in the role of regent to Emperor Xian. Accordingly, he often compares himself to the regent of the first reign of the Zhou dynasty (late eleventh century B.C.), the Duke of Zhou (Zhougong), celebrated for fulfilling his custodial office and then returning power to the child-king in his trust when the ruler came of age. By taking the Duke of Zhou as his model, Cao Cao makes it known that he will not depart from his custodial role and depose the Emperor. Cao Cao claims that his regency preserves civil order by restraining a multitude of contenders who, in pursuit of their ends, would plunge the empire into civil war. There is some truth in Cao Cao's claim: Liu Xuande declares himself emperor in Shu-Han only after Cao Cao has died and his son, Cao Pi, has usurped the throne of Han.

If Cao Cao preserves Emperor Xian's position, he also builds his own kingdom and thus lays the foundation for his heirs to found a new dynasty. His first step is to proclaim himself duke of Wei (Weigong), a title last used by Wang Mang, the usurper of the Former Han dynasty. Cao Cao's second step is to proclaim himself king of Wei (Weiwang) and to name an heir. As king he becomes a dynast. And rivalry between two of his sons, Pi and Zhi, swiftly brings home to the house of Cao the curse of dynastic government. Cao Cao dies in A.D. 220, and Cao Pi succeeds him as king of Wei. Within the year Cao Pi demands and receives the abdication (*shan*) of Emperor Xian and establishes himself on the throne of the Wei dynasty. The Han is no more.

To legitimate his usurpation, Cao Pi resorts to another ancient legend, that of the sagekings Yao and Shun. Yao passed over his son and chose a commoner of virtue, Shun, to succeed him. As an apprentice sovereign, Shun ruled alongside Yao. Then, while still possessed of his power, Yao abdicated to Shun. Cao Pi casts himself in the role of Shun in order to portray his enthronement as a reenactment of the hallowed myth that justifies transferring the throne to a man of virtue rather than waiting for inheritance by a son.

On the interkingdom front, Cao Pi's declaration of a new dynasty frees Liu Xuande to take the Riverlands' throne as Han's true heir. Hence the kingdom is called Shu-Han. These events (chapter 80) mark the official beginning of the era called Three Kingdoms. The third king, Sun Quan, who rules Wu, or the Southland, waits until A.D. 229 before proclaiming his own dynasty. From the novel's point of view neither Cao Pi nor Sun Quan deserves to rule all China.

The novel, since the opening chapter, has been developing Liu Xuande's claim to succeed Emperor Xian. This claim rests on two bases, his lineage and his virtue. Liu Xuande bears the imperial surname, but so do other leaders. To reinforce his claim to legitimacy, Xuande traces his ancestry back to Emperor Jing of the Former Han, the emperor from whom the first Later Han emperor, Liu Xiu (posthumously called Guang Wu), claimed descent. Liu Xuande's link to the royal house opens the way to his advancement, especially after Emperor Xian acknowledges him as imperial uncle. In addition, Xuande has his own leadership qualities: his natural charisma or magnetism, called *de* in Chinese and translated "virtue." The force of his persona attracts and holds the allegiance of his associates, his armies, and the populations he governs. He wins men's hearts. Xuande's virtue is the higher reason why he deserves to rule, a reason transcending lineage or possession of territory. Cao Cao of the novel lacks this quality of virtue.

Virtue, a sine qua non of rule, is ascribed to every emperor, but the word describes his character rather than the manner of his accession. If he comes to power by filial right or by election within the royal family—that is, normally rather than by dynastic change—he will claim that his predecessors' virtue flows on in him. If he comes to power by abdication, usurpation, or conquest, his spokesmen will contend that he possesses his own virtue and is entitled thereby to found a new dynasty because the sovereign he is supplanting has lost his virtue. In such a case the genetic flow of virtue within a single lineage is disrupted, and it becomes necessary to turn to the ultimate source of virtue to legitimate the new house. That ultimate source is Heaven. Virtue is thus tied to another primary concept of ancient Chinese political science, the Mandate of Heaven, which should now be considered in order to bring out the full meaning of "virtue." The mandate uses the authority of Heaven to override the claim of lineage and thus justify a change to a new ruling house.

The Mandate of Heaven "finds" a man of virtue who establishes a new dynasty. To appreciate the revolutionary potential of the concepts of virtue and mandate, one may look to traditional Japan, which despite its deep absorption of Chinese influences, does not accept any limitations on the imperial birthright. Officially, Japan has been ruled throughout its history by a single dynasty; no new dynasty can be recognized. The lineage of the royal house, an uninterrupted continuum, is absolutely sacred. But the Chinese, as early as about 1000 B.C., worked out a means for rationalizing a change of dynasty through the concepts of virtue and mandate. In this way the Chinese made the dynasty relatively, not absolutely, sacred. The canonical authority for the Chinese view, apart from the "Zhou Texts" of the *Book of Documents,* is found in *Mencius* (5A.6.7): "Confucius said, 'For Yao and Shun, abdication; for Xia, Shang, and Zhou, inheritance. In principle there is no difference.' "

The Mandate of Heaven comes to the fore in times of transition. It is a concept less active in times of stability, though it is always a useful reminder to the ruler of the penalty for misgovernment. Changes of dynasty are relatively infrequent; they are the exception, not the rule. Most of Chinese history has to do with regimes continuing in power. During such times of continuity the throne—and the mandate with it—passes from father to son, and occasionally to a brother or to some other imperial kinsman by election. The ruling house does not change, and the mandate-holding emperor is assumed to have the virtue of the dynastic founder flowing on through him. In this way lineage subsumes virtue. It is only in a transition crisis that lineage and virtue may separate into opposed principles.

In the final analysis, virtue can itself be seen as a higher form of lineage, and Heaven as universal ancestral authority. Heaven is the universal progenitor as well as the collective dwelling place of the many royal ancestors of the many different past dynasties; it is a quintessence of the ancestors; it must have descendants. Just as ancestors of one line are thought to confer favor on their living representatives, the Great Ancestors through Heaven mandate the living emperor. This is why Son of Heaven (*tianzi*) is another name for the emperor (a name the Japanese did not favor); the term implies transcending lineage and linking the emperor to the Great Ancestors. But it is not enough *only* to be the Son of Heaven. It is not enough *only* to have virtue. The two—virtue and lineage—must recombine. The Mandate of Heaven continues to be the highest legitimation, even after the transition crisis has passed, because it recombines the sanction of a sovereign's lineal ancestors with the sanction of the Great Ancestors, making him *di* (emperor) as well as *tianzi*.

Regardless of how he comes to power, every Son of Heaven for the past thirty centuries (until modern times) has claimed the mandate. The reason, to restate the point a little differently, is that the mandate proclaims the holder's "sonship" both in the larger sequence of dynasties and in the line of his own house. Every Han emperor after Liu Bang has the word *xiao*, "filial," in front of his posthumous title. Emperor Xian is officially named Xiao Xian Huangdi, Emperor Xian the Filial.

The blessing of sonship is sought as well by dynastic founders when they convert their ancestors into pseudo-emperors. Cao Pi, for example, honors his father Cao Cao as Emperor Wu even though Cao Cao never took the throne. Similarly, the first Jin emperor, Sima Yan, creates a royal "back line" out of his ancestors for several generations, though they were but vassals of the house of Cao. Even the Zhou founder King Wu (Wuwang) had to posthumously recast his father Wenwang—who in fact had remained loyal to the Shang—as a dynastic founder. King Wu strengthened his own claim to rule the empire by anchoring his Mandate from Heaven in his father's purpose. (King Wen's support for the Zhou conquest of Shang is duly glorified in the *Book of Odes* and the *Book of Documents*.) And Cao Pi's purpose in posthumously naming Cao Cao Emperor Wu is to authorize his own usurpation; Cao Pi is posthumously called Emperor Wen. In both cases—Zhou and Wei—the actual military conqueror is called Wu.

The family nature of the dynastic form displays itself in the fact that the ruling house is the dynasty: the Liu are the Han, the Cao are the Wei, and the Sima are the Jin, one and indivisible. If a new clan comes to power, it must establish its own dynasty.

Since *Three Kingdoms* is placed in a time of dynastic transition, "virtue" comes to the fore in the novel as the main qualification of a new ruler. This is made clear by a motif in the 1522 edition: "The empire belongs to no one man but to all in the empire; he who has virtue shall possess it." Mao Zonggang drops this recurring phrase because of its too-explicit slighting of lineage, but in his edition he basically preserves the theme of "virtue qualifies for rule." The following remarks, therefore, apply to both editions of the novel unless otherwise specified.

As a royal kinsman and also a man of virtue, Liu Xuande has a twofold claim to the Han throne. The value of the surname is shown, for example, in chapter 11 when Imperial Inspector Tao Qian of Xuzhou turns the province over to Xuande. This gives Xuande his first chance to exercise major political authority. Explaining his choice, Tao Qian says, "Lord Liu, a scion of the royal house, a man of broad virtue and high ability, is fit to govern." But virtue and lineage do not after all weigh equally. What distinguishes Xuande in the novel is his virtue. For if his virtue can attract men to serve him, it may ultimately attract the Mandate of Heaven itself.

To have virtue is to gain men's confidence, to win their allegiance. In his first appearance in the novel Liu Bei spontaneously forms a brotherhood with two strangers, Guan Yu (Yunchang), a fugitive, called Lord Guan in this translation; and Zhang Fei (Yide), a butcher. The three brothers pledge in faith and honor (*jieyi*) to live and die as one, and they consecrate their oath in a peach garden—the peach is a symbol of fidelity—by sacrificing a horse and a bull. Liu Bei is acknowledged as the elder brother (for his virtue, not his seniority, according to the Yuan drama *Taoyuan jieyi*), and they quickly recruit a *Shuihu* or outlaw type of band. A fraternal tie among the three is mentioned once in the *SGZ* (*Sanguozhi*), but the novelist has added oath and sacrifice and made the bonding of brotherhood the overture to his tale. Accordingly, the second brother, Lord Guan, and the third, Zhang Fei, are transformed from sparsely sketched figures in the *SGZ* into fully developed fictional characters. The brotherhood plays a major role in the novel, and the oath haunts the narrative until the pledge "to die for one another" is invoked by Lord Guan's death. Liu Xuande's fidelity to the oath becomes a trial of his worth as a brother and as a king, and the plot turns on his decision.

For what purpose is the brotherhood formed? To combat peasant uprisings led by the Yellow Scarves. What has caused the uprisings? Corruption at court. The court, too weak and divided to cope with the threat to its power, sends out a general call for militia forces to organize and come to the aid of the throne. The brotherhood is formed in response to this call. The rivalry at court takes the form of a family struggle over the succession to the throne. The brotherhood is a kind of egalitarian fraternity with an "underworld" tinge. In its solidarity, based on the principle of honor (*yi*), the brotherhood contrasts with the divided ruling family and also with the great regional families being torn apart by fraternal strife. As the crisis unfolds, the family itself as the dominant political institution is implicitly questioned through comparison with the brotherhood, anti-dynastic in form because it is hostile to filial right. Liu Xuande as elder brother is not a father figure, but *primus inter pares*. The Qing historian mentioned above, Zhang Xuecheng, expressed his misgivings about celebrating the fraternal bond when he wrote, "The most unedifying thing about the novel *Three Kingdoms* is that in the peach garden the oath-brothers go so far as to forget the lord-vassal [*junchen*] relation and simply proclaim the fraternal relation."

The brotherhood, first formed to aid the ruling house, later becomes a means to further Xuande's ambition. Like Xuande, the younger brothers, Lord Guan and Zhang Fei, are brave and gallant heroes, but their fortunes have been mixed. After the fail-

ure of the coup against Cao Cao, Xuande leaves the imperial
court and in A.D. 200 takes refuge with Yuan Shao. The next year
he takes refuge with Liu Biao, protector of Jingzhou, but he is
not safe. Liu Biao's wife (Lady Cai) and her brother (Cai Mao)
threaten him from within, while Cao Cao, who covets Jingzhou,
remains a threat from without.

In A.D. 207 Cao Cao marches on Jingzhou, hoping to annex
it; Xuande is about to be overwhelmed. Xuande has come to understand that neither he nor his brothers are able to master the
rapid changes in the empire, and that to become a major contender for power he needs diplomatic and military guidance. At
this point Kongming enters the scene, both in history and in the
novel. For many he is the protagonist of the novel, and his decision to serve Xuande as chief adviser confirms Xuande's virtue:
Xuande has won his heart. Kongming appears in chapter 36. He
is a young man of twenty-seven by Chinese count, twenty years
Xuande's junior. He dies in A.D. 234 (chapter 104). These sixty-
nine chapters form the heart of the novel.

Despite his youth Kongming proves to be shrewd and erudite
as both a diplomat and a strategist. In his first interview with
Xuande, Kongming presents his three-part project for restoring
the Han dynasty. His immediate goal is for Xuande to join forces
with the Southland in order to save Xuande from Cao Cao and
to inspire the south to resist him. His intermediate goal is for
Liu Bei to establish an independent kingdom in the west, the
Riverlands, and to maintain the alliance with the south against
the north. His ultimate goal is to reconquer the northern heartland and place Liu Bei on the Han throne. As events unfold,
southern resistance to Cao Cao leads to the division of the Han
empire into three warring kingdoms. Thus, at the outset Kongming's career becomes bound up with the central issue of his
time.

To the forward-looking Kongming, the brotherhood is no
more than a military expedient—something to utilize, not an end
in itself. His larger ambition of dynastic restoration revolves
around the virtuous ruler whom he serves and the orderly succession by the son of that ruler when the time comes. Thus, he
values filial over fraternal love, loyalty to higher authority (*zhong*)
over honor among equals (*yi*), and Xuande the benevolent pa-

triarch over Xuande the sworn elder brother. Kongming acts for these values because he believes that the relation of emperor to crown prince (*taizi*) is at the core of dynastic rule and that an orderly transition depends on the security of this relation. The security of this relation ensures continuity of rule through the ruling house (*guojia*) and control over the forces that lead to division, independent kingdoms, and civil war—the troubles that plagued the empire during Kongming's formative years.

Thus, Kongming countenances no intervention in the father-son relation—not by the brothers, not by himself. The true vassal must never exceed his place by supplanting the son. If the worthiest minister supplants the most unworthy ruler, it will lead to disorder. Kongming's role may seem similar to that of the regent Cao Cao, but the two men stand for opposite principles. Unlike Cao Cao, Kongming never promotes his own family's position and never creates a kingdom-fief as a means for his son to supplant the house of Han. Following the same principle, Kongming does not want the brotherhood to take precedence over the father-son relation. Patriarchal benevolence and filial devotion—the essence of Confucian political philosophy—and not the brotherhood provide the answer to the corruption of the imperial house. But Kongming cannot teach this lesson to Xuande.

In the novel, the tension between Xuande's opposing roles of brother and emperor, between the opposing organizational forms of fraternity and *guojia,* between the values of loyalty and honor, and between Kongming and the brothers charges the narrative with thematic force and drives the tale to its tragic conclusion.

THE NOVEL'S USE OF SOURCES

The novel presents two paths for the Han empire to follow after the Han falls: the abdication of the last emperor to Cao Pi, who founds a new house; or the restoration of the *guojia* through Liu Xuande and his son Shan. In history, the house of Cao prevails. The question is, why does the novel favor the claim of Xuande? Earlier texts favored the claim of the Cao–Wei dynasty, above all the first history, Chen Shou's *SGZ.* Luo Guanzhong took Chen Shou as his model; why then did he not follow him on this crucial matter? The *TS* describes itself as "compiled and arranged [i.e., authored] by Luo Guanzhong, Chen Shou's student-follower of later times." Yet Luo Guanzhong chose not to accept Chen Shou's verdict that the Wei dynasty legitimately succeeded the Han, and then went on to depict Cao Cao as the moral as well as the political opponent of Han's rightful heir, Liu Xuande. Why?

Much as Xuande and Cao Cao take certain mythic and historical heroes as models, Xuande and Cao Cao themselves became models—two of the most important—for the post–Three Kingdoms dynasties. At different points in the twelve hundred years between the events and the novel, various dynastic historians, officials, philosophers, and poets sided with one or the other, with Cao Cao or Liu Xuande. On what basis did they make their choices? How did such interpretations of the Three Kingdoms heroes influence Luo Guanzhong?

These questions call for discussion of the sources on the Three Kingdoms period, and also of the political situation in China during the centuries leading up to the time the novel was written. As a rule, pre-Ming northern dynasty writers tend to treat Wei as the legitimate heir to Han, while southern dynasty writers treat Liu Xuande as the true continuator of Han, and Cao Cao as a usurper.

The basic source for the period is the *Sanguozhi* (*SGZ*), or Records of the Three Kingdoms. The author, Chen Shou (d. A.D. 297), served the Shu-Han kingdom and later the Jin dynasty. In A.D. 274 he collected the writings of Kongming (still extant). Then some time after A.D. 280, the year Jin reunified the empire, Chen Shou wrote the *SGZ* in sixty-five chapters, which consist of single or multiple lives (*zhuan*) of the leading figures of the age. Wei is presented in the first thirty chapters, Shu in the next fifteen, Wu in the final twenty.

The first biography is in the form of imperial annals for Cao Cao titled "Wudi ji," or "Imperial Annals of the Martial Emperor." By using the term *ji* instead of *zhuan* for Cao Cao, Chen Shou indicates, at least formally, that Wei is to be regarded as the legitimate successor. In contrast, Chen Shou calls Liu Xuande "Xianzhu," or First Ruler (of Shu-Han), a posthumous honorific that suggests regional rather than empire-wide authority. In the "Wudi ji" Cao Cao is given his imperial temple name, Tai Zu, but in the "Xianzhu zhuan" Xuande is not called by his temple name, Zhao Lie. Otherwise, as the title *Three Kingdoms* suggests, the historian is basically impartial among the three kingdoms and unwilling to elevate the name of any of them as the name of the period. Chen Shou presents the least material on Shu-Han, though the figure of Kongming is well developed. Wei and Wu are treated more fully; the leader of Wu, Sun Quan, is also called *zhu*.

Chen Shou's approach is bureaucratic. He gives essential facts, always in the context of individual lives. But, unlike the novelist, he does not seek to move the reader by tying the fate of China to any particular character or kingdom, nor does he invest any one character or kingdom with positive or negative moral significance. Luo Guanzhong uses the *SGZ* for its scope and periodization as well as its information, and he acknowledges his debt by incorporating the title of the history, *Sanguozhi*, in the title of his novel. But he does not follow the history's method of organization, the biographical series (*liezhuan*). Luo Guanzhong chooses instead chronological narrative, a form best represented in China's history-writing tradition by such works as the *Zuo zhuan* and *Zizhi tongjian*.

About ninety years after Chen Shou's death, Pei Songzhi (A.D. 372–451), a scholar-official of both the Eastern Jin and Liu-Song dynasties, added a vast quantity, some say an overabundance, of material to Chen Shou's *SGZ* in the form of notes drawn from more than two hundred sources. Pei undertook this project at the behest of the Liu-Song emperor. His memorial to the Liu-Song emperor (included in *SGZ*, p. 1471) called the *SGZ* "a superb history for its organization and its judgments and for furnishing the reader with a glorious gardenlike preserve," but he criticized it for "brevity and occasional omissions." Some of the notes with which Pei supplemented the *SGZ* are of historical value, some are anecdotal and colorful though of uncertain authenticity. It might be said that Pei Songzhi became the first to attach some fictional material to the *SGZ*.

The Liu-Song emperor accepted Pei Songzhi's work with high praise, and in A.D. 429 an integrated text—the *SGZ* combined with the notes (*zhu*)—was established; this became the official history of the Three Kingdoms period. In Chinese the title is *San-*

guozhi zhu. These notes created a text three times longer than the original; and as they cite many works lost after the Tang dynasty, their value is inestimable.

Here is a brief example of Luo Guanzhong's use of the *SGZ* notes. In his *SGZ* biography, Liu Xuande is rewarded for his service against the Yellow Scarves with a post as prefect of Anxi county. Soon after he takes office, a district inspector visits the county seat on unexplained business. The inspector's henchmen bar Xuande from the government building, so he barges in and thrashes the inspector. Afterward, Xuande goes into hiding. The novel (chapter 2) follows this account, except that in the novel Zhang Fei commits the battery. The novel also explains that the inspector came to carry out an edict ordering a purge of all recent appointees. This explanation comes from Pei's notes. Another contribution of the notes is the character of Shan Fu, who plays a small but crucial role in the novel. He is Liu Xuande's first military adviser and the man who arranges for him to meet Kongming. Chen Shou barely mentions Shan Fu in Kongming's biography, but the notes provide the material for Luo Guanzhong's telling cameo portrait.

Turning to the question of legitimacy, we find that one of the notes' key sources, Xi Zuochi's *Han Jin chunqiu* (The Han-Jin spring and autumn), denies the legitimacy of the Wei succession. The very title of this work excludes Wei from the great line of dynasties, deriving Jin directly from Han. Xi Zuochi treats the two emperors of Shu-Han, Liu Bei and Liu Shan, as a bridge between Emperor Xian and Sima Yan, the first Jin emperor: "Jin should bypass the intervening Wei and take its succession from the Han." Xi Zuochi is considered the first historian to treat the Shu-Han kingdom openly as the legitimate heir of Han. In keeping with this purpose, his work dates events by the Shu-Han reign years, which are presented as extensions of the Han up to the first reign of the Jin. Since the emperor functions as a personified calendar, the reign title (*nianhao*) projects his Heavenly authority. This is why each of the three kingdoms historically used its own reign titles.

In addition to using Shu-Han reign titles to affirm Liu Xuande's legitimacy, the *Han Jin chunqiu* provides an important description of Liu Bei that anticipates the Liu Xuande of the novel: "The First Ruler's trustworthiness and sense of honor shine only more brightly as he is tossed from peril to peril, never forsaking—even under the direst pressure—the true path. . . . He had compassion for the army . . . and was content to share defeat with men dedicated to honor." As for Cao Cao, Xi Zuochi did not, so far as we know, paint him particularly black. One negative comment of Xi's preserved in the ZZTJ (*Zizhi tongjian*) concerns Cao Cao's arrogance: "The empire split into three as a result of Cao Cao's displays of arrogance." Another source cited in Pei's notes, the *Cao Man zhuan,* makes Cao Cao more of a villain, with anecdotes testifying to his cruelty and caprice. And the *Shishuo xinyu* of Liu Yiqing also contributed a number of stories villifying Cao Cao. Thus, by the early fifth century the Three Kingdoms tradition had a southern branch divergent from Chen Shou's history, and certain key elements of the novel's characterization of Liu Xuande and Cao Cao reflected that new tradition.

Sympathy for Shu rather than for Wei was a political touchstone for these southern writers. Xi Zuochi is a notable example; he lived during the Eastern Jin, a dynasty that, like Shu-Han, was confined to one southern sector of the realm and threatened with extinction by an enemy dynasty occupying the northern heartland. In fact, every southern dynasty between Han and Sui faced a similar danger, until the Sui unification of the late sixth century and the imperium of Tang restored something of the grandeur and glory that was Han.

In the early reigns of the Tang dynasty the ruling house expressed pro-Cao sentiments. The second emperor, Li Shimin (Tai Zong, r. 627–49), who looked back to the Wei dynasty for certain institutional models, made a formal address to the spirit of Cao Cao, praising him as a "sage" who "faced a difficult destiny with heroic demeanor . . . [and who stood] on a par with the great ministers of antiquity." Emperor Xuan Zong (r. 713–56) referred to himself on one occasion as "Ah Man," one of Cao Cao's names. However, the noted historian Liu Zhiji (661–721) disagreed with the respectful treatment Cao Cao usually received. A sharp critic of Chen Shou, Liu Zhiji did not share the view that the kingdom of Wei was legitimate, and he said that the SGZ did not do justice to Kongming.

In the eighth century, the An Lushan rebellion created a split in the Tang empire that reminded many of the time when the Shu-Han kingdom struggled to recapture the northern heartland (*zhongyuan*) from the Wei dynasty. *Zhongyuan,* a term used by Kongming, refers to the two Han capitals, Chang'an and Luoyang, and the territory around them, which was known in the Han as the *sili,* the capital (or administrative) districts. The "inner" region of the Yellow River Basin is China's traditional political and military center. In A.D.756, rebel forces occupied the heartland. The Tang emperor was driven westward "covered with dust" (i.e., in exile). He occupied briefly what had been in Han times the kingdom of Shu; the heartland, however, remained in turmoil for many years. Du Fu, who later became China's national poet, began to use elements of Han history to symbolize the *guojia*'s plight. When Chang'an and Luoyang fell to the rebels and An Lushan was killed by his own son, Du Fu compared An to Dong Zhuo, who deposed Emperor Shao and was later killed by his adopted son, Lü Bu (see chapters 4 to 9 of the complete novel). Du Fu made his way to Chengdu and in A.D. 759 wrote a ballad called "Chengdu fu," in which he speaks of "the heartland fading away into darkest oblivion." And in another poem of this time he speaks of "gazing northward brokenhearted." In A.D. 760 Du Fu composed one of his most famous pieces, "Shu xiang" (The prime minister of Shu), to commemorate his visit to the abandoned shrine of Kongming. The poem's closing lines,

> To die, his host afield, the victory heralds yet to come—
> Weep, O heroes! Drench your fronts, now and evermore!

proved prophetic and gave heart in future times to Chinese who had been driven south by northern invaders. Historically, the victory heralds never arrived, but Du Fu imagines Kongming dying confident of victory. Thus the poem immortalizes the moment when his spirit of determination to recover the heartland, restore the Han, and reunify the empire ran high.

Luo Guanzhong placed this poem in the 1522 edition (it is in chapter 105 of the Mao edition) to mark Kongming's interment and honor his memory. Du Fu wrote a number of other poems celebrating Liu Xuande and Kongming; a few are added in the Mao edition. Long before the novel in any form, these poems

had contributed much to the development of Liu Xuande, Kongming, and others as defenders of an imperiled royal house; in
later dynasties they were to become nationalistic symbols in the
collective imagination of the Chinese. However, Du Fu did not
portray Cao Cao as a villain; and the Tang did not fall. Indeed,
about 764 Du Fu composed a poem, "Danqing yin," honoring
the painter General Cao Ba and praising him for reflecting the
greatness of his ancestor Cao Cao.

The development of Liu Xuande and Cao Cao as symbolic
figures entered a new stage in the Song dynasty (A.D. 960–1279).
The Song suffered a trauma more severe than the An Lushan rebellion, and comparable to the fall of the Han and rout of the
Jin in A.D. 317. In A.D. 1115 the Jurchen nation, northern rival
of the Song, established a dynasty called Jin ("Golden," hereafter
spelled Gin to distinguish it from the Jin that followed the Wei).
In A.D. 1127 Jurchen armies seized the capital, Kaifeng, and captured the emperor (Hui Zong) and his son, thus extinguishing
the imperial line. Another son of Hui Zong fled to southern
China, covered with the dust of exile. There, under the guidance
of Zong Ze and other advisers, he reestablished a southern Song
capital. The new emperor, Gao Zong, proclaimed the new dynasty
as the Jurchen were assuming control of the northern heartland.
The year 1127 divides the Northern Song from the Southern
Song, two periods of markedly different attitudes toward late
Han–Three Kingdoms history.

During the Northern Song, between the years 1066 and 1084,
the historian Sima Guang produced a continuous history of
China covering 1,362 years (403 B.C. to A.D. 959), the *Zizhi tongjian* (*ZZTJ*), or General History for the Aid of Government. Its
rich and accessibly organized data as well as its accuracy and co-
gent style made the *ZZTJ* quite readable, and it quickly became
a classic. Its narrative is basically chronological in structure but
with an occasional shift backward in time to reveal the origin of
a particular development. The *ZZTJ*'s sections on the late
Han–Three Kingdoms period, while based mainly on the *SGZ*
and the *Hou Han shu* (*HHS*), may be considered ancestor to the
format of the novel, just as the *SGZ* may be considered its ancestral source material.

Sima Guang's view of dynastic legitimacy, like Chen Shou's, is "northern," not "southern," acknowledging the Wei—a view other Northern Song historians such as Su Dongpo and Ouyang Xiu share. To construct an orthodox line of dynasties, Sima Guang adopts two standards: territorial control and lineal descent. The six major dynasties—Zhou, Qin, Han, Jin, Sui, and Tang—are credited with unifying the realm and establishing their lines. Thus, they form the main tradition; that is, they enjoyed unchallenged rule. Conversely, Sima Guang holds that those who were unable to bring the "nine provinces [i.e., the empire] under a single rule were Son of Heaven in name only, not in reality." Sima Guang fills out the spaces between these six major dynasties with another list, a list of dynasties that held less than the whole empire but dominated their time, starting with the Wei and ending with the Later Zhou (the nine-year dynasty— A.D. 951–60—immediately preceding the Song).

Explaining his method, Sima Guang writes: "The purpose is not to honor one and denigrate another, or to distinguish legitimate [*zheng*] from transitional [*run*], but in times of division in the empire we have to have reign titles covering the years, months, and days in order to chronicle the sequence of events." Thus, Sima Guang uses the reign titles of certain emperors and not of others merely to standardize the chronology of a trans-dynastic account and not to suggest a moral judgment; no "Spring and Autumn" inferences should be drawn from what he includes or leaves out. Sima Guang explicitly excludes the claims to legitimacy of Liu Bei: "As for the relation between the Zhao Lie Emperor [Bei's temple title] and [Shu-]Han, despite his alleged descent from Prince Jing of Zhongshan, his clan affiliation is quite remote. . . . Indeed, it would be unthinkable to make him the heir to Han rule as if he were on a par with the founder of the Later Han or the Eastern Jin."

This Northern Song consensus changed dramatically after Jurchen armies drove the dynasty south and forced it into a defensive position similar to that of Shu-Han nine hundred years earlier. Southern Song poets, philosophers, and statesmen drew on the Eastern Jin and mid-Tang traditions of championing the cause of Shu-Han. (The opportunistic Southland was never so appealing a model as the militant Riverlands.) The renowned general Zong Ze, a key figure in establishing the Southern Song,

pleaded with the new emperor not to abandon the fight to recover the lost northern capital. Zong Ze's appeals were met with
hostility and indifference at court, and according to his *Song shi*
biography he expressed his despair with the closing lines of Du
Fu's "Shu xiang" cited above:

> To die, his host afield, the victory heralds yet to come—
> Weep, O heroes! Drench your fronts, now and evermore!

The famed poet Lu You, who grew to manhood in the first
generation of the Southern Song, began his "Jiannan" (South of
Saber Gateway) with the oft-quoted couplet:

> Our kingdom's mandate—restore the Han [i.e., Song];
> Heaven's will—smite Cao Cao [i.e., the Jurchens].

Lu You's contemporary General Yue Fei had been an active opponent of the evacuation to the south. After the move, Yue Fei
distinguished himself on the field by retaking a number of key
cities from the Gin conquerors and added his voice to Zong
Ze's in demanding a counterattack to regain the heartland. (In
A.D. 1142 Yue Fei was accused of treason and murdered.) Like
Zong Ze, Yue Fei invoked Three Kingdoms heroes to symbolize
his ambition to clear the homeland of invaders. He is quoted as
saying, "Why begrudge one's life? I want future generations to
know my name from written history; I want to be glorified like
Lord Guan and Zhang Fei."

Other Southern Song writers, struggling against the weak-
willed court, enlisted Shu-Han heroes to represent their cause.
In A.D. 1165 the poet Wang Shipeng visited the restored temples
of Liu Xuande and Kongming. On his visit to the former, he
wrote:

> In the final phase of the Later Han, bandits fastened their cov-
> etous eyes on the sacred instruments of imperial rule, and the em-
> pire was divided into three as if it were a tripod shared by three
> men. But Liu Xuande was emperor still. He had the stature of the
> Supreme Ancestor, the marks and signs of Guang Wu [i.e., the
> founders of the Former and Later Han, respectively], and he had
> vassals fit to serve a true and virtuous king. But he lacked the
> northern heartland. . . . Had I the wine in my hand, I would make
> no offering to the Cao-Wei dynasty.

On his visit to Kongming's temple he wrote:

> From the surviving fragments of the shrine one can glimpse Kong-
> ming's grand manner. Alongside him stand Guan and Zhang—
> one dragon, two tigers. Oh, where shall we find such men today
> to rid us of humiliation at the hands of outsiders?

Through the writings of Lu You and Wang Shipeng, Liu Xuande, Kongming, Lord Guan, and Zhang Fei were becoming popular symbols of Han nationalism, and Cao Cao was being treated as something more than a villainous vassal; he was being turned into a symbol of the foreign conqueror. At the same time, there is evidence that in the opposing Gin court the Shu-Han kingdom was associated with the fallen house of Song. Yang Weizhen's *Song Liao Jin zhengtong bian* (Debates on legitimacy: Song, Liao, and Gin) refers to a discussion before the Gin emperor in 1202; in the discussion the last Northern Song emperor was called "a homeless, wandering soul like Zhao Lie [i.e., Xuande] in Shu." Moreover, some Gin rulers paid annual homage at Cao Cao's burial site.

The most important Southern Song champion of Liu Xuande's cause was the molder of neo-Confucian philosophy, Zhu Xi, another member of the generation of Lu You. In 1172 Zhu Xi completed an unusual project, one that directly influenced *Three Kingdoms*. He recast the *ZZTJ* in a slightly altered form, placing Sima Guang's text under a series of interpretive headlines which imposed a judgment on the events recounted. The *ZZTJ* was too important to ignore, and so Zhu Xi remade it for his own didactic purposes. He called the work *Zizhi tongjian gangmu,* (General history to aid government with a network of headings) adding the word *gangmu* to Sima Guang's title much as Luo Guanzhong added the word *yanyi* to the title of the *Sanguozhi*. Luo Guanzhong must have read both the *ZZTJ* and the *Gangmu* and must have used the sections on the Han and the Three Kingdoms in organizing his novel.

Zhu Xi treated Liu Xuande as the legitimate successor to Han; he rejected Sima Guang's technical acceptance of Wei as Han's heir. Zhu Xi changed the calendrical entries in his *Gangmu* to accord with those of Shu-Han and devised headings whose wording implied a pro–Liu Xuande, anti–Cao Cao judgment. Here is how Zhu Xi presents the crucial year A.D. 220, when Cao Pi proclaimed the new Wei dynasty. First he changes the initial year of Cao Pi's reign from the first year of Huang Chu back to the twenty-fifth year of Jian An, the reign title of the deposed Emperor Xian. Then in the heading for the tenth month, he writes, "The Wei king, Cao Pi, proclaims himself imperial majesty, deposes the [Han] emperor, and makes him [i.e., demotes him to] lord of Shanyang." The second year of the Wei, Zhu Xi names the first year of Liu Xuande's reign: "The imperial majesty of Han, Zhao Lie [i.e., Liu Bei]; Zhang Wu [Manifest Might], year 1 . . . . In summer, the fourth month, the king of Hanzhong [i.e., Liu Bei] ascended the throne of the imperial majesty." In this way Zhu Xi places himself in the tradition of the *Han Jin chunqiu,* treating the kingdom of Shu-Han as an extension of Han and denying the legitimacy of Wei.

Militant as a youth about reconquering the heartland, by the late 1160s Zhu Xi was becoming more inclined toward a policy of compromise and coexistence. Zhu Xi's purpose in advocating the cause of Shu-Han was not to instigate military action by the south but rather to establish a tradition of dynastic sequence in which his own ruling house would take its rightful place. The Southern Song, much like the Eastern Jin, had to assert its "Chinese" (or Han) identity at a time when non-Han powers held the traditional dynastic base, the *zhongyuan,* and could not be dislodged. Zhu Xi did not accept Sima Guang's criterion for legitimacy, control of a unified territory. He turned instead to other criteria, such as cultural continuity with the Zhou thinkers Confucius, Zisi, and Mencius, and the moral integrity of the ideal ruler and vassal, for defining legitimacy.

In fact, Zhu Xi was not a wholehearted advocate of the Shu-Han cause precisely because of its territorial ambition. His great admiration for Kongming is tempered by criticism of Kongming's capture of the Riverlands. He wrote, "Kongming . . . assisted a true king, but he was not completely identified with the Way. . . . A true king . . . would not commit an act of unrighteousness even if he could acquire an empire by doing so [citing *Mencius,* 2A.2.24]. Kongming was determined to achieve success and to capture Liu Zhang. A sage would rather not succeed [in such an undertaking]. Kongming should not have done it." Because he did not favor aggressive military action to regain the north, Zhu Xi often looked to Mencius as an authority for placing virtue above power. Perhaps Zhu Xi saw the cultural tradition as a compensation for the unrecoverable heartland. Mencius, in the passage cited above, had said that men of virtue ruling even a tiny territory of one hundred *li* could win the homage of the lords of the realm.

In the novel, the relationship between territorial control and legitimacy is as important as the relationship between lineage and legitimacy or virtue and legitimacy. How to judge Liu Xuande's acquisitions of territory, especially Xuzhou, Jingzhou, and the Riverlands, is one of the novel's central questions. A related question is how to judge Xuande's conduct when he has no territory and after he has acquired territory (and a measure of feudal power).

The *ZZTJ* furnished Luo Guanzhong with a comprehensive chronological account of the century he wanted to cover. Perhaps one way to look at the word *yanyi* in the novel's title is to derive the *yan* (continuous development) from the *ZZTJ* and the *yi* (moral significance, message) from Zhu Xi's *Gangmu*.

In summarizing the various Three Kingdoms legitimacy debates, the descriptive notice (*tiyao*) of the *Siku quanshu*, the great bibliographical encyclopedia of the Qing period, takes a matter-of-fact attitude that is a refreshing reminder of the ability of traditional Chinese scholars to see through the categories and artifices of dynastic propaganda:

> From the viewpoint of the author's circumstances, it was only an instance of natural obedience for Xi Zuochi to acknowledge the imperial authority of Shu-Han. For Chen Shou such a position would have led to troublesome confrontations, but when Xi Zuochi wrote, the Jin house had already moved south and its circumstances rather resembled those of Shu. So Xi catered to the consensus of the day by claiming legitimacy for a dynasty that was territorially limited and not in control of the heartland. Chen Shou, by contrast, was in the service of Emperor Wu of the Jin; since Jin had succeeded Wei, to deny the legitimacy of Wei would have been to deny the legitimacy of Jin. How could [his history] have circulated [if he had denied Wei's legitimacy]? It was little

different [for a historian then] than [for a historian] at the time
of Tai Zu [the first Northern Song emperor], whose usurpation
[of the Later Zhou] was much like the usurpation by Wei, while
the Northern Han and Southern Tang courts bore resemblance
to the court of Shu-Han.

Consequently, Northern Song Confucians avoided denying the
legitimacy of Wei. Once the Song was driven south and confined
below the Great River, however, and its own situation became more
like that of Shu-Han, with Gin ruling the heartland as the Wei had
once done, the Confucians of the Southern Song, one after the
other, stepped forward to proclaim the legitimacy of Shu. All these
positions need to be evaluated according to the age and not meas-
ured by a single inflexible standard.

Zhu Xi's contemporary and rival, the Southern Song philoso-
pher and statesman Chen Liang (1143–94), advocated a militant
anti–Jurchen policy, and this must have influenced his view of
Zhuge Liang. Chen Liang's contribution to the evolving persona
of Zhuge Liang is an important link between the historical and
the fictional hero. In a paper on Zhuge Liang, "From Regional
Hero to National Hero," presented at a panel of the 1991 convention of the Association for Asian Studies, Hoyt Cleveland Tillman cites Chen Liang's "Zhuge lun," an essay that emphasizes
Zhuge Liang's political and moral virtues as well as his skill in
warfare. Chen Liang contrasts Zhuge Liang to Sima Yi (rather
than to Cao Cao, presumably because Chen Liang, unlike Zhu
Xi, had little sympathy for Han legitimacy, and thus no animus
toward Cao Cao): Sima Yi was treacherous, Kongming loyal; Sima
Yi was selfish, Kongming public-spirited; Sima Yi was cruel,
Kongming humane. Chen Liang then proceeds to praise Kongming as a military tactician. Tillman translates:

> Kongming's eightfold formation . . . would not advance too quickly
> nor retreat too hurriedly. Shock brigades were unable to break
> through its front, and armies that seemed to come from nowhere
> would not be able to go round to strike its rear. An army in am-
> bush could not isolate its wings, and pursuing troops could not
> surprise its rear. Spies would have no way to reconnoiter, and cun-
> ning tricks would have no facility [against this formation].

As Tillman observes, Chen Liang's claim that Kongming was
good at schemes and surprises "is quite noteworthy given later
portrayals in popular literature."

STORYTELLING AND FICTION IN THE YUAN

Some fifteen years after the death of Zhu Xi in 1200, Chinggis Khan began a series of conquests in Central Asia and China. In 1234 the Mongols accepted the capitulation of the Jurchen's Gin dynasty and occupied all of northern China. In 1260 Khubilai Khan proclaimed Zhong Tong (i.e., Zhong*yuan zheng*Tong, or "Unified/Legitimate Rule from the Heartland") the first reign title of the Yuan, as the Mongols called their dynasty in China. Khubilai went on to prosecute a five-year campaign (1268–72) against the principal forward positions of the Southern Song, Xiangyang and Fancheng. After the victory of 1272 the Mongols eliminated all Southern Song resistance, and in 1279 Khubilai Khan became emperor of a China reunified for the first time since 1127. Never before had all China been brought under non-Han rule. During the Yuan, Han resisters mainly demanded the restoration of the Song dynasty, but they had no substantial base.

Under the Yuan the legends of the Three Kingdoms developed and assumed new form. Popular fiction, dramatic recitation, and plays in particular molded and remolded the heroes into types quite removed from earlier traditions. These plays and narratives created a new, extremely fictionalized tradition—three parts fact, seven parts fiction, one might say. The two main genres—both popular—were storytelling and drama. Many scholars have said that these genres furnished Luo Guanzhong with the popular spirit he infused into his novel and that without this imaginative component the historical academic tradition could never have provided sufficient inspiration for the novelist. We will consider the two genres—story and drama—separately, beginning with the *Sanguozhi pinghua.*

Some traditional Chinese historians have treated the Cao-Wei dynasty as legitimate and the Shu-Han dynasty as a rebellious entity. Some have described the achievements of Cao Cao objectively. There are even plays that treat Cao Cao sympathetically. But no significant popular literary tradition makes Cao Cao the hero and Liu Bei the villain. The popular tradition makes Cao Cao the villain and Liu Bei the hero. The novel culminates this tradition, and the primary fictions of the novel stem from the pro-Liu, anti-Cao view: making the peach garden sacrifice and the brotherhood oath the starting point; giving the brothers a dominant role in the story; and emphasizing Shu over Wu as Wei's antagonist.

The Yuan storytelling tradition, judging from trace remarks in various records, may go back to the Northern Song. In the commercial centers of the Song there were public recitations of Three Kingdoms' themes and ample audiences to support the raconteurs. According to the oft-cited remark of Su Dongpo,

> A group of children from the alleys . . . hearing ancient Sanguo tales . . . knit their brows and weep if Liu Xuande is defeated, but shout with delight when Cao Cao is defeated.

But as for extant texts embodying that performance tradition, there is only one, the *Sanguozhi pinghua (PH)* of 1321–23 and its earlier, almost identical edition, the *Sanfen shilüe*. The *PH* may be described as a storyteller's prompt book, and it is apparent that the author of *Three Kingdoms* was familiar with it. Dramas written on Three Kingdoms' subjects developed particular incidents and characters and had a limited focus, usually a single episode, but the *PH* presents the events of the century (A.D. 184–280) in serial fashion, and its influence on the novel is primarily because of this.

The *PH* is crude and episodic; it numbers about 80,000 words (less than one-tenth the length of the *TS*). It strings together more than eighty sparsely sketched incidents without developing much casual connection in their sequence. For the most part these incidents have some historical basis, but a number are sheer invention. Nevertheless, however crude they may be, the *PH*'s techniques of composition—the serial presentation of events, the multiple-track narrative, the interaction of characters, the interplay of character and incident—foreshadow the novel; thus, the *PH* may be called a primitive blueprint for *Three Kingdoms*. Indeed, in the words of one scholar, "these structural features [of the *PH*] make it the foundation stone of the composition of China's [classic] novels."

The *PH* begins with the peach garden oath and the campaigns against the Yellow Scarves; it ends with the death of Kongming. The succeeding events (A.D. 234–80), which take up the last sixteen chapters of the novel, are passed over, though the reunification of A.D. 280 is touched on at the end. The first half of the *PH* is dominated by Zhang Fei—Lord Guan plays a lesser role— and Kongming dominates the second half. The author is friendly to Liu and hostile to Cao, though he is uninterested in the legitimacy question per se. Finally, the narrative includes such oddities as having Emperor Ling execute the Ten Eunuchs and deliver their heads to Liu Xuande (who has become a bandit) to entice him to serve the court *(zhao an)* by suppressing the Yellow Scarves. Another fanciful segment shows Cao Cao forcing Emperor Xian to abdicate to his son Cao Pi. The *PH*'s interest in history is slight. Accordingly, Kongming's famous analysis of the state of the empire (the "Longzhong dui") is only partly introduced, and Kongming's petitions on taking the field (the first and second "Chushi biao") are not included at all. In general, Kongming is characterized more as a magician than as a strategist. Some of the differences between the *PH* and the novel are pointed out in the notes to the translation.

A striking difference between the *PH* and the novel is that the *PH* has a prologue and an epilogue that fall outside the time frame of the novel. The prologue is a supernatural tale in the *chuanqi* tradition and the epilogue is a quasi-factual account of the fall of the Jin in the early years of the fourth century. Apart from their relevance to the study of popular storytelling, the two sections throw an interesting light on the purposes of Luo Guanzhong precisely because he did not use them.

The prologue and epilogue extend the *PH*'s time frame well beyond the novel's. The *PH* puts the genesis of the division of the empire into three kingdoms back to the first reign of the Former Han dynasty. The author manages this by using the following myth based on Buddhist concepts of reincarnation and retribution. During the first reign of the Later Han, Sima Zhongxiang (later reborn as Sima Yi, who laid the basis for the founding of the Jin) enters the imperial park with a book in hand. Reading in it of the dreadful rule of the Qin dynasty, Zhongxiang curses the first Qin emperor and declares that if he had ruled then the people of the empire would have been happy. Suddenly, a team of ghost-officials rushes him to the underworld, where he is outfitted like a monarch and empowered to judge the rights and wrongs of history. The first (and only) case to come before him concerns the founder of the Han, Liu Bang, and his Empress Lü. Three plaintiffs come forward to accuse them of betrayal.

First Han Xin appears and complains of his demotion and ambush. Han Xin was the single most important figure in Liu Bang's victory over Xiang Yu, his rival for the empire. When Liu Bang and Xiang Yu were at a standoff, Han Xin, newly king of Qi, had the opportunity to exploit the stalemate and declare Qi an independent kingdom. This course, which his adviser Kuai Tong urged on him, would have created three kingdoms: his own, Liu Bang's, and Xiang Yu's. Han Xin rejected Kuai Tong's advice and threw his support to Liu Bang, who went on to defeat Xiang Yu and found the Han dynasty (hence his title Gao Zu, or Supreme Ancestor.) But after becoming Emperor of Han, Liu Bang moved against many of the veterans and comrades-in-arms who had helped him to power. Han Xin was the first victim, and this is why his wronged soul appears before Sima Zhongxiang. Zhongxiang rectifies the injustice by arranging for Han Xin to be reborn as Cao Cao so that he can take revenge on the Han. Zhongxiang arranges other reincarnations: Liu Bang as Emperor Xian, and Empress Lü as Lady Fu (Xian's only consort, whom Cao Cao puts to death), and Kuai Tong as Kongming.

In addition to Han Xin, two other plaintiffs present their grievances to the court of the netherworld, Peng Yue and Ying Bu. They, too, had suffered betrayal at the hands of the first family of the Han. To requite their ghosts, Sima Zhongxiang has them reborn as Liu Bei and Sun Quan, respectively. Thus, the *PH* introduces the fall of the Han and the division of the empire as supernatural retribution for Liu Bang's betrayal of his comrades.

The tendency among scholars has been to dismiss the prologue as superstition and to praise Luo Guanzhong for dropping it and getting down to history with the businesslike opening line of the *TS:* "On the death of Emperor Huan of the Later Han, Emperor Ling assumed the throne at the age of twenty." The prologue would hardly make an ideal introduction to the novel, it is true, but the novel is not entirely free of supernatural elements, of ghosts returning to protect or to warn. And the character of Kongming retains certain magical aspects. So something of the prologue's spirit survives in the novel.

Of greater importance is the survival of the theme of retribution in the novel and its use as an organizing principle. Whether accomplished in a few moments' repartee or in the course of decades, secular retribution or cause and consequence is a question the novel pursues. The usurpation of Han by Wei (chapter 80 in the unabridged) is the long-range consequence of the failure of Han to govern well, just as the rise of the Yellow Scarves is a more immediate consequence. And the usurpation of the Wei by the Sima clan is the long-range consequence of the Wei usurpation of Han, just as Liu Xuande's declaration that Han still reigns in Shu is the immediate consequence. The relentless movement from cause to consequence and the wavelike conversion of consequence to cause describes the dynamic of *Three Kingdoms*. It is likely that this narrative design owes something to the theme of retribution, announced by the prologue, that dominates the *PH*.

One contemporary scholar who treats the prologue as thematically relevant to the *PH* sees the legend of Sima Zhongxiang's restitution of territory to the three wronged vassals of merit as a criticism of autocracy: "To write a tale of a *xiucai* [lowest degree holder] who, though holding no office, rectifies historical injustices . . . is a fiction to delight the hearts of men in an age of sacred and inviolable monarchical power." In the novel Zhang Fei comes closest to representing so radical a view of status and authority (see the quatrain ending chapter 1).

Not only does the *PH* trace the cause for the breakup of the Han empire to a far earlier point than the novel, but it concludes a generation beyond the novel. The novel ends in A.D. 280 with the triumphant reunification of the empire under a new dynasty, the Jin, ruled by the Sima house. The *PH* ends with Liu Yuan's siege of Luoyang in A.D. 304 and the fall of the Jin dynasty in A.D. 316. What difference does the ending date make for the story of the Three Kingdoms?

Historically, the Jin reunification of A.D. 280 was nothing to boast about. The dynasty enjoyed twenty years of relative stability. Then in A.D. 300 a Jin prince tried to overthrow Emperor Hui, touching off a six-year fratricidal war called the Disorder of the Eight Princes. As a result, the Jin could not police its borders, and the fourth century began with a series of attacks by "barbarian" nations. Liu Yuan, a sinicized Xiongnu, became the leader of these invasions. Xiongnu pressure soon led to the evacuation of Luoyang and the capture of the emperor. Forced from the north, the Jin reestablished its dynasty in the Southland region in A.D. 317 under the name of Eastern Jin. The new dynasty asserted its "Han-ness" by its first reign title, Jian Wu, the same title used by the founder of the Later Han. The north, meanwhile, was occupied by a variety of non-Han (Hu) nations. The period, referred to by southern writers as the Disorder of the Five Hu, evolved into a three-century era of disunity known as Northern and Southern Dynasties, which lasted until the Sui reunification of A.D. 581.

Why does the *PH* end with an account of Liu Yuan and the fall of the Jin? Liu Yuan was a descendant of Mo Du (often read Mao Dun), the founder of the Xiongnu nation. Mo Du came to power in 209 B.C., shortly before the founding of the Former Han; his heirs adopted the Liu surname. The point the *PH* makes is that a branch of the Liu clan avenges the Han dynasty by destroying the Jin, thus completing the cycle of retribution. The *PH* says:

> Liu Yuan addressed the army: "Han engaged the people's love during its long years of rule, and I, as a maternal nephew of the ruling house, must avenge my uncle, whom the Jin have captured." Then . . . he founded a kingdom that he called Han and, declaring himself king of Han, established the ancestral precedents. He changed the reign title to Yuan Xi, "Original Glory," and honored the late Liu Shan [second emperor of Shu-Han and son of Liu Bei] as His Glorious Majesty Huai the Filial. . . . The third year he moved the capital to Pingyang and assumed the throne. . . . After Emperor Hui [of Jin, r. A.D. 290–306] died, Emperor Huai [of Jin] came to the throne. The king of Han [Liu Yuan] led an army of several hundred thousand against Luoyang, the Jin capital. The Jin emperor [Huai] met the enemy in the field but was defeated. [Liu Yuan's] Han soldiers seized his person and offered him in sacrifice at the temple of Liu Shan.
>
> Next, Emperor Min [of Jin] assumed the throne in Chang'an [capital of the Former Han]. The king of Han [Liu Yuan] sent Liu Yao to conquer the city. Liu Yao captured Emperor Min and took Min's empress, Lady Yang, as his own wife. Liu Yao then escorted the Jin Emperor to Pingyang and extinguished the Jin dynasty. Liu Yao paid homage at the ancestral temple of the Supreme Ancestor [Liu Bang] and at the temple of Emperor Guang Wu

[Liu Xiu, founder of the Later Han], Emperor Zhao Lie [Liu Bei], and Emperor Huai [Liu Shan]. Liu Yao made offerings and declared an empire-wide amnesty.

If we take Liu Yuan's claim of kinship to the royal family figuratively, this account is basically historical. The Xiongnu groups that Liu Yuan led, settlers "inside the [Han] border," had a history of ethnic integration (if not assimilation) with the Chinese, and Liu Yuan himself was versed in Chinese language and culture. So there is nothing absurd about his bid to restore the Han dynasty through his own line. Such a claim might have overawed internal opposition and neighboring Hu nations and thus served Liu Yuan well. Certain of his Xiongnu rivals wanted him to establish an independent Xiongnu nation, however, and not take the road to sinicization. Would he choose to be khan or emperor? His paternal grandfather, Liu Xuan, declared:

> Long ago our forefathers bound themselves to the Han as brother to brother. After the fall of the Han, Wei rose [and fell] and was followed by Jin. Our khans have had empty titles but nary an inch of our land has been returned. Our people's status is as low as the registered [common farmers]. Now the Sima house is destroying itself from within, and the realm is a seething cauldron. The time to revive our nation's heritage has come.

Thereupon Liu Xuan and the various Xiongnu branches secretly made Liu Yuan khan. In A.D. 304 Liu Yuan began to organize a mighty host from his own, the Bingzhou Xiongnu, and associated Xiongnu nations. The eager response of these nations to Liu Yuan's leadership suggests their strong antagonism to the Jin, Wei, and Latter Han dynasties for the suffering caused by generations of civil war. The Disorder of the Five Hu dates from this moment.

Jin's end was swift and ignominious. In A.D. 309 Liu Yuan began an attack on Luoyang. In A.D. 311 he died, and his son Zong continued the siege until Luoyang fell that same year. Xiongnu troops sacked the capital and took Emperor Huai of the Jin captive. The Jin then moved the court to Chang'an under a new emperor, Min. After five more years of fighting, Liu Zong had reduced Chang'an and Emperor Min had surrendered. Jin power then vanished from northern China. Emperor Min was taken and killed together with Emperor Huai.

Liu Yuan accomplished these things as Han emperor, not as Xiongnu khan. In A.D. 309, the year he began the attack on Luoyang, he declared himself emperor of Han, reminding his followers how successful Liu Bei had been in waging war from an isolated province in order to regain the empire.

> Liu Yuan said, "I am a maternal nephew of Han; we are bound as brother to brother. If the elder dies, should not the younger succeed him? Let us proclaim ourselves Han." Then he honored the memory of the Second Emperor [Liu Shan].

Liu Yuan's son, Zong, continued to claim the title emperor of Han until A.D. 318, the second year of Eastern Jin. Shortly thereafter Liu Yuan's house was extinguished.

Extending the story of *Three Kingdoms* to conclude with these events, the *PH* fulfills its theme of retribution (perhaps the dominant theme of Yuan drama as well). In the course of this final generation (A.D. 280–317), other symmetries emerge. For one, the sack of Luoyang aptly closes an era that began with Dong Zhuo's forced evacuation of Luoyang in A.D. 189. (Like Liu Yuan, Dong Zhuo had close non-Han ties.) Second, the return of Emperor Min to Chang'an reverses the shift of capitals from Former to Later Han. Third, the troubled ethnic and economic relationships between the Han and their northern neighbors reaches a kind of conclusion when Chinese dynastic power vacates the north, as if history had refuted Cao Cao's stunning victory over the Wuhuan people and Kongming's astonishing triumph over the Southern Man.

Compared to the *PH,* the novel appears as a work that seeks to restore something of Han's greatness in Jin's reunification, and concluding its narrative in A.D. 280 contributes to that effect. The novel begins with an end and ends with a beginning, leaving the reader with a sense of optimism (or at least renewal) about Chinese history: "The empire, long divided, must unite." But the *PH* begins with an end and ends with an end, and the implications are ominous. The Han—and a unified China—is lost. When will it return? The *PH* expresses a Southern Song or Yuan mood; the novel, a Ming mood. The Ming founder, Zhu Yuanzhang, had publicly and purposefully portrayed himself as another Supreme Ancestor, another founder of the Han, and had succeeded in

1368 in projecting Han power into the north for the first time since 1127. Thus, in reunifying China Zhu Yuanzhang fulfilled a long-frustrated ambition of Han nationalism. *Three Kingdoms* reflects something of Zhu's achievement.

We turn from the *PH* to consider some of the Yuan period Three Kingdoms plays. Drama as an art form thrived in Yuan China, and Three Kingdoms plays were a vital component. Traces of Three Kingdoms drama can be found as early as the Sui and Tang, but no texts survive. For the Gin and Song periods only a handful of titles remain out of hundreds (including non-Three Kingdoms plays) that are listed in early sources. Notices of Three Kingdoms shadow plays in the Northern Song have been found, but again no texts and only a few titles. For the Yuan period, however, the flourishing of Three Kingdoms drama is a striking fact, and the Riverlands heroes are the prominent figures. If whole and partial texts as well as titles (without texts) are counted, the number of Yuan and early Ming Three Kingdoms plays comes to between fifty and sixty, nearly 10 percent of the more than seven hundred (on all subjects) that we know of.

Ten dramatizations of Three Kingdoms tales (half by unknown authors), fragments of another six, and the titles of another eleven survive from the Yuan period. The remaining plays are Ming or fall into the vaguer category of Yuan-Ming because no date can be established. Given the uncertainties about the novel's dating, it is not always possible to say whether a play influenced the novel or the other way around. But taking the sixty plays as a whole, it is striking how thoroughly they cover the novel's century from Dong Zhuo's sedition to the founding of the Jin. Ye Weisi and Mao Xin have drawn up lists showing the corresponding events in the plays, the *PH*, and the novel. These lists show the time span the plays cover and also how popular the legends and characters of the Three Kingdoms had become by the Yuan dynasty. In Yuan times so much fictional material was added to the existing historical base that Luo Guanzhong might well have called himself, as Confucius once did, "a transmitter, not a maker."

By and large, the plays continue the Southern Song tradition of taking the part of Liu Xuande against Cao Cao. Most of the extant plays feature Liu Bei or heroes devoted to him—Kongming,

Lord Guan, Zhang Fei, Zhao Zilong, Ma Chao, and so on; the others deal with Cao Cao, Dong Zhuo, and Lü Bu. Among the plays there is a surprising tendency to treat not only the Wei but also the Southland leadership as enemies of Liu Bei. For example, in Guan Hanqing's *Lone Swordsman Attends the Feast (Dan dao hui)* Lu Su is the villain, with his plot to kidnap Lord Guan and retake Jingzhou. The same plot is found in chapter 66 of the novel, but it is set in a context that makes Lu Su more sympathetic by showing his deep commitment to the Shu-Wu alliance (even if he has to work against it in chapter 66). The novel with its fuller background explores the contradictions between the two kingdoms within the necessity of the alliance.

The novel corrects many other fictional excesses in the dramatic texts, almost always working to bring its narrative into closer alignment with the historical texts, the *SGZ* and the *ZZTJ*. For example, the Southland founder Sun Jian is shown running from the field with a stomachache in *Three Heroes Battle Lü Bu at Tiger Trap Pass (San zhan Lü Bu)*, while the novel restores much of his courage and determination. (Still, the novel does Sun Jian the injustice of crediting his defeat of Hua Xiong to Lord Guan.)

At one crucial point in the story, however, the Southland general Lu Xuan emerges as a hero in his own right, almost on a par with Kongming. When Liu Xuande defies Kongming and invades the Southland, Lu Xun executes a brilliant counterattack and wins the battle at Xiaoting (or Yiling). So humiliated militarily and politically that he cannot return to Shu, Xuande soon dies; the cause of Han restoration from a base in Shu is doomed. Though the *PH* and the Yuan drama virtually ignore Lu Xun, the *SGZ* treats him as a general of the utmost importance. And *Three Kingdoms,* guided here by the *SGZ,* depicts Lu Xun with unqualified admiration and never uses him as a foil to show a Riverlands figure to advantage. The novel treats no other Southland figure in this manner. If the novel has been unfair to other Southland heroes, its treatment of Lu Xun rebalances the scales and gives the Southland a share of its rightful historical glory.

The salient feature of the Yuan plays is that they are either entirely fictional or else fictional elaborations on traces of historical data. Working with a small cast of characters and within a time frame restricted to a few episodes, the plays develop their chosen subjects imaginatively. This was an inspiration to the novelist, who incorporated dramatic dialogue liberally into the narrative. In fact, if Luo Guanzhong is the author of the several plays attributed to him, he might have worked closely with Yuan and Ming dramatists and been familiar with the techniques of staging.

The most striking creation of the dramatists is the character of Lord Guan. From a minor character in history—the *SGZ* devotes less than a thousand words to him—he became a dominant figure of Yuan dynasty Three Kingdoms drama, a pivot around which other parts of the tale were organized. This may be, as Liu Zhijian speculates, because there was a close connection between the cult of Lord Guan in the Yuan period and Three Kingdoms drama, performances of which may have been staged in temples dedicated to "King Guan." The *PH* was dominated by Zhang Fei and Kongming, but the drama made the figure of Lord Guan paramount and in this respect decisively influenced the novel. The single play *The Lone Swordsman,* dealing with Lord Guan's solo visit to the Southland, makes reference to a surprising number of incidents, persons, and details found in the novel: the breakup of the Han empire; the relations between Emperor Xian and Dong Zhuo, as well as between Dong Zhuo and Lü Bu; the peach garden sacrifice and oath of brotherhood; the physiognomy of Lord Guan (phoenix eyes, red face, long beard); the battle at Tiger Trap Pass; the escape from Xuzhou (with Liu Xuande) to join Yuan Shao; the battle at Bowang; the killing of Che Zhou, Wen Chou, and Yan Liang; the killing of Cai Yang (by which Lord Guan proves his loyalty to his brothers); the Xiangyang banquet; holding off Cao Cao at Dangyang slope; the three trips to Sleeping Dragon Hill to find Kongming; the prelude to the battle at Red Cliffs (the beating of Huang Gai); Kongming's strategic ingenuity; Lord Guan's becoming governor of Jingzhou; Liu Bei's becoming king of Shu; Liu Bei's establishing his rule in Hanzhong; the conflict between Liu Bang and Xiang Yu that led to the founding of the Han dynasty. Another play, Gao Wenxiu's *The Meeting at Xiangyang (Xiangyang hui),* develops the circumstances around Xuande's meeting with Shan Fu—a crucial fictional portion of the novel. So full a list of events from Yuan plays would suggest that early in the Yuan, audiences were familiar with a wide range of Three Kingdoms legends and saw Lord Guan as a central figure in those legends.

Lord Guan is also the principal fictional creation of the novel. The plot turns on him more than on any other character. The reader cannot lose the line of narrative so long as he knows what Lord Guan is doing at any given point. And Lord Guan's death, which triggers Liu Xuande's invasion of the Southland, is what drives the tale to its conclusion. After his death, Lord Guan's fictional essence is underscored by his return as a ghost. This shift to a supernatural mode could not have been effected with any other character such as Liu Bei, Kongming, Cao Cao, or Sun Quan because they are historical figures of real substance. Lord Guan can be brought back to life to affect events in the novel because he is made mostly of imaginary materials to begin with. Unlimited by historical reality, he is the novelist's to shape as he will.

The return of Lord Guan as a ghost is based on Guan Hanqing's other surviving Three Kingdoms play, *The Double Dream (Guan Zhang shuangfu xi Shu meng)*. In the play, Liu Xuande, now ruler of Shu, pines for his brothers, who are stationed far away. After they appear to him in a vision, he sends an envoy to Jingzhou for news. The envoy learns of Lord Guan's death. Zhang Fei has died at the same time (the historical Zhang Fei died two years after Lord Guan). Meanwhile, in Shu, Kongming withholds the news of Lord Guan's death, lest Xuande retaliate against the Southland. The soul of Lord Guan then meets the soul of Zhang Fei, and after decrying their unjust deaths to each other, they travel west together to urge Xuande to avenge them. The two ghosts are reunited with their living brother, who executes Mi Fang, Mi Zhu, Liu Feng, and Zhang Da, ending the last act.

In the novel, Lord Guan's soul returns to the world of the living (chapter 77) by undergoing a conversion at the hands of a Buddhist monk, Pujing (Universal Equilibrium). Pujing reproachfully reminds Lord Guan's new ghost of the many heads he took before losing his own. Lord Guan concedes the truth in Pujing's words, that is, that he has been justly repaid for his own acts. Through this recognition of Buddha's Law, Lord Guan transcends historical (and biographical) time and becomes a benign deity, his soul freed from the effects of his lifetime acts. From the mountaintop, Lord Guan can now recognize the unreality *(kong)* of the river of human events, the fearful symmetry of karma, and the chain of cause and consequence (or retribution), in which all other characters remain entrapped. Once transcendent, he can render aid to those he deems wronged, like Sima Zhongxiang in the *PH* prologue.

Luo Guanzhong's novel culminated and synthesized many traditions, both historical and literary. It also eclipsed a number of its predecessors—as far as the literary public is concerned—in particular, the *PH* and Yuan Three Kingdoms drama. Most of the Three Kingdoms plays performed today are Ming or Qing works inspired by the novel.

LUO GUANZHONG AND HAN NATIONALISM IN THE YUAN-MING TRANSITION

In the Yuan period the Liu-Cao rivalry continued to have the kind of symbolic force—Han versus non-Han—that it did in the Southern Song-Gin period. But there were also variations on the theme.

Those Chinese (Southern Song loyalists above all) who saw the Yuan dynasty as a continuation of foreign rule—Mongols replacing the Jurchen rulers of the Gin dynasty—may well have maintained the preference for the Liu Xuande group. But the Mongols were first enemies and then conquerors of the Gin, and they may have shunned the connection with Cao Cao that the Gin had been proud to make. The Mongols may have wished to associate themselves with the Han side of this issue. Thus, the above-mentioned plays were not underground literature covertly directed against Yuan rule. To the contrary, plays sympathetic to the Liu Xuande group were welcomed by Mongol officials and performed at court. In the latter part of the dynasty the government paid homage to the Three Kingdoms' heroes. In 1322, 1328, and 1340, the spirits of Kongming, Lord Guan, and Zhang Fei were honored as kings. These measures came at a time of increasing Han militance against Mongol rule, and the government sought to fortify its legitimacy by appropriating these nationalistic symbols.

The Three Kingdoms played a special role toward the end of

the dynasty when the question of legitimating Yuan rule in relation to the three previous dynasties—Gin, Liao, and Song—was debated in Mongol ruling circles. The Mongol leader Toghto was in charge of a project to prepare a history of these three dynasties, and the solution he accepted was to treat none of them as legitimate, comparing them to the three kingdoms Wei, Wu, and Shu, which had been absorbed into the Jin. Those opposed to this treatment of the three pre-Yuan dynasties, however, most notably Yang Weizhen, sought to preserve the legitimacy of the Song as the basis of Yuan rule and relegated the Liao and Gin to the status of alien houses, treating them like the Xiongnu intruders led by Liu Yuan at the turn of the fourth century. Yang was punished for his theory, but his position was closer to the popular tradition of Liu legitimacy through the kingdom of Shu.

In the final years of the dynasty, anti-Mongol rebel leaders also used Three Kingdoms figures in their propaganda. The future first emperor of the Ming, Zhu Yuanzhang, when leading a Red Scarves peasant revolt in 1363, described the Mongol commander Wang Baobao in a letter: "With armored cavalry and crack troops, he holds the northern heartland in his thrall, his ambition no less bold than Cao Cao's."

When Zhu Yuanzhang founded the Ming dynasty in 1368, Han rule was restored over all China for the first time since 1127. Having overthrown the Yuan by force of arms, and therefore having no interest in depicting itself as a "successor," the Ming denied the legitimacy of Yuan rule. This denial led to a broader effort to restrict acknowledged legitimacy to the "Han" (or Chinese) dynasties of the past. "Hu Han . . . insisted on a distinction between Han and non-Han rule in adjudging legitimacy, thus repudiating the claim of the Mongol rulers. . . . Fang Hsiao-ju [Fang Xiaoru] espoused his theory on legitimate succession . . . and included . . . racial and cultural superiority in addition to moral right and unified political control as bases of dynastic legitimacy." That Zhu Yuanzhang turned to the Han and not the Song as his model dynasty may be explained by the fact that he broke with the group of anti-Mongol rebels who had rallied around the slogan of Song restoration, and sought to erase every trace of his connection with them. He may have been responsible for the death of one rebel leader, "Song Emperor" Han Lin'er in 1367.

The presumed author of *Three Kingdoms,* Luo Guanzhong, lived through these events of the Yuan-Ming transition. It would be satisfying if there were enough biographical information for a consensus about his life and its connection to the dramatic fall of the Yuan dynasty and the rise of the Ming. The information that exists, however, is so sparse and contradictory that there is no thesis, much less a consensus, on Luo's life, his political outlook, and their connection to the novel.

The earliest notice about Luo Guanzhong occurs in a Ming text called *Luguibu xubian* (Supplementary jottings on those who have died). In a brief text of some fifty or sixty words the writer says that in his youth he was a friend of Luo Guanzhong much his senior (perhaps in his fifties), had last seen him in 1364, and now, more than sixty years later (i.e., after 1424), has no information concerning Luo's life or death. The account says that Luo rarely sought human society and was skilled in writing poems (*yuefu,* a genre typically used for social criticism) with implied significance. It mentions Luo's sobriquet, Huhai Sanren ("Wanderer by Lake and Sea"), but no given name (Ben, in some editions of the novel). The sobriquet, which suggests taking refuge in a time of adversity, may also explain the large number of places which he is associated. Nothing is said of a novel called *Three Kingdoms* nor of any other prose or drama he might have authored; nothing is said of Luo Guanzhong's youth or middle age or of his political ambition.

Some scholars argue that Luo Guanzhong was deeply involved with the anti-Mongol leaders in south China and may have entered the service of one of them, Zhang Shicheng (fl. 1353–67), who controlled a considerable empire in the south. When Zhang transferred his allegiance to the Mongols, Luo Guanzhong (who may have tried to dissuade him) then turned to historical writing to express his political aspirations. This interpretation is based on a brief notice in the *Baishi huibian* (Collection of minor romances) by the Ming scholar Wang Qi: "Luo Guanzhong and Ge Kejiu were engaged in a quest for an ideal king to govern the empire; and they did encounter a true ruler. Subsequently . . . [Ge] gave himself to medicine and [Luo] to writing unofficial history." The *zhenzhu* or "true ruler" was Zhang Shicheng, presumably. It is also possible that it was not Zhang Shicheng whose service Luo entered and left, but that of another rebel leader or even Zhu Yuanzhang himself.

Scholars who depict Luo as active in the anti-Mongol movement acknowledge that Luo Guanzhong shows little sympathy for peasant rebels in his novel, but they point out that the novel attributes the rebellion to corruption at court. As chapter 1 explains, Emperors Huan and Ling persecuted able and decent officials while they honored and trusted the eunuchs, who sold office and rank, employing only their relatives and punishing only their political foes. As a result, court administration worsened, the people murmured in discontent, and throughout the empire men's minds turned to thoughts of rebellion. The entire novel could then be seen as a study of the kind of leadership necessary to lead the people through a time of troubles to a reformed court and a reunified empire.

Another group, however, doubts that Luo Guanzhong was a partisan of the rebels. One such scholar explores the significance of Luo's connection with Ge Kejiu (alleged by Wang Qi) and also his probable discipleship to the neo-Confucian scholar Zhao Baofeng. Both Ge and Zhao had participated in organized military action against the Red Scarves rebellion. Presumably, Luo Guanzhong would have been on the same side, the Mongol side; his novel, then, with its clear opposition to rebels, becomes a natural extension of his political position.

If Luo Guanzhong was in fact sympathetic to the pre-Ming rebel movements against the Yuan, or to one of those movements in particular, then the Song dynasty of 1355 should be considered. One Red Scarves leader in north China, Liu Futong, made Han Lin'er emperor of a new Song dynasty. The reign title declared was Long Feng; 1355 was the first year. But the movement was short-lived. In 1359 Mongol armies overwhelmed the new dynasty's forces and bases, driving Liu Futong and Han Lin'er into the arms of Zhu Yuanzhang; the Red Scarves movement in the north then declined, while in the south it developed new strength. There is nothing to connect Luo Guanzhong with this part of the Red Scarves movement, except that the reign title Long Feng, "Dragon and Phoenix," has an extraordinary prominence in the novel through symbolic association with Kongming (Sleeping Dragon) and his alter-ego Pang Tong (Young Phoenix, a minor but key figure). Also, from the standpoint of legitimism, it may be that Luo looked favorably on Song legitimacy even if he did not advocate restoration.

Perhaps one final speculation may be indulged in before we leave the unsolvable problem of the author and turn to the text of the novel itself, about which there is a good deal more information. If the "true ruler" that Luo Guanzhong encountered was Zhu Yuanzhang, then it is possible that Liu Ji, one of Zhu's most important advisers, is the contemporary figure to which the portrait of Kongming refers.

> According to his biography in the *Mingshi*, he had a broad and thorough knowledge of the philosophers and was almost supernatural in anticipating events. In discussing the shape of the empire, righteous honor was written on his face. Moreover, he was a master of astronomy and meteorology. "Zhao Tianze of Shu, in judging the men of the region below the Great River, named Liu Ji first, regarding him as a kind of Zhuge Kongming." Zhu Yuanzhang solicited his service many times before he finally emerged from the hills [to serve him]. Liu Ji participated in the great battle at the Poyang Lakes, which resembles the battle at Red Cliffs. Zhu Yuanzhang called Liu Ji "My own Zifang."

If Luo Guanzhong's "true ruler" was Zhu Yuanzhang, then the connection to the novel might lie in Zhu Yuanzhang's attempt to portray himself as an emperor after the model of Liu Bang, to whom he proudly compared himself. *Three Kingdoms* could be seen as celebrating the restoration of Han-like rule in China, as if perhaps Zhu Yuanzhang had fulfilled the mission that Liu Xuande and Kongming had left unfinished. Thus, the novel naturally builds upon the contradiction between Liu Bei and Cao Cao. As Qiu Zhensheng concludes his essay cited above,

> An anti-Yuan position naturally drove Luo Guanzhong to accept all the more firmly the legitimism of a pro-Liu, anti-Cao view which had been taking shape since the Song and Yuan. For Luo to have affirmed Cao Cao would have been tantamount to affirming the legitimacy of the Yuan dynasty which occupied the northern heartland and extinguished the Song dynasty. Luo Guanzhong, who "strove for kingly government," could never have accepted this . . . and he poured his unrealized ideals into the figures of Liu Bei and Kongming, the sagely sovereign and the able minister.

Perhaps at some future time this theory will be borne out. Even if it is finally determined that the novel (as many have argued) is not a product of the Yuan-Ming transition, but a product of the mid-to late fifteenth century (that is, a generation or two before the first, 1522, edition), then Qiu's view may still have some relevance. Zhu Yuanzhang's victory over the Mongols in 1368 was decisive but not complete. From beyond the Wall, the Mongols continued to pose a serious military threat. In 1449 they inflicted a massive and humiliating defeat on the Ming armies in the battle of Tumu, capturing the Chinese emperor Ying Zong (who had led the offensive) and detaining him in Mongolia—covered with the dust of exile—for more than one year. (1449 was the last year of Ying Zong's reign period Zheng Tong, "Legitimate Rule.") This shocking event led to a resurgence of Han-nationalist hostility toward the Mongols and toward their non-Han predecessors.

In addition, the last half of the fifteenth century saw an upsurge of local peasant rebellion and a concentration of eunuch influence at court under Emperors Xiao Zong (r. 1488–1505) and Wu Zong (r. 1506–21). Such a climate might well have encouraged the composition of *Three Kingdoms*—it is after all a novel about the end of the Han—as a way to remind the Ming Chinese that the Han dynasty so admired by their founder fell and that the Ming might too if it did not maintain the policies of its founder. If such be the case, then the author of the novel chose to remain anonymous and used the name Luo Guanzhong for purposes unknown—perhaps to give the work an air of historical authority, perhaps because Luo had some minor fame as a writer of historical fiction and dramas and was a plausible choice, even if no other work attributed to Luo Guanzhong has anything like the scale, style, and structure of *Three Kingdoms*.

Once the tie between Luo Guanzhong and the novel is severed, many problems are eliminated, and arguments using internal criteria to establish dating can be put forward with greater assurance. A number of scholars have argued for a mid-Ming date (the latter half of the fifteenth century, say) on the grounds that at least a century would have had to pass to allow for the development of the *PH* and the drama to so magnificent a form. The most extensive and comprehensive presentation of a mid-

Ming theory has been made by Andrew Plaks in the *Three King-doms* section of his *Four Masterworks of the Ming Novel.* He argues that the affinities between *Three Kingdoms* and other mid-Ming novels like *Journey to the West* and *Shuihu zhuan* (Outlaws of the marsh) are sufficiently close to justify its being grouped with them. He points to the grand design of the novel, its subtle, finished style, and its self-consciously wrought texture as evidence that *Three Kingdoms* belongs to the literary tradition of the sixteenth century (or perhaps that it was one of the creators of that tradition.)

The preceding discussion is intended as a general introduction for the Western reader to the historical and literary significance of *Three Kingdoms: A Historical Novel.* If he has not already done so, the reader may wish to get into the novel itself at this point. The following, more specialized discussion of the text used for this translation, the Mao text of the mid 1660s, explores the political situation when the editors worked, the nature of the commentary, and the relationship of their text to the *TS* text.

THREE KINGDOMS IN THE MING-QING TRANSITION

We turn now from the Yuan-Ming transition of the mid-fourteenth century to the Ming-Qing transition of the mid-seventeenth century—that is, from the time when the author is alleged to have lived to the mid-1660s when the novel was put in its final form, the form which has eclipsed all other editions and become the universal edition, not only for the Chinese text but for all translations including the present one. Mao Lun and his son Zonggang were the editors of this universal edition. Mao Lun was probably the architect of the project, but as a convention, Mao Zonggang is often spoken of as the editor, though he may have been more an amanuensis.

Mao worked on an edition of the 1522 novel annotated by Li Zhi (Zhuowu); most scholars, however, believe that Ye Zhou, not Li Zhi, was the real annotater. Mao claimed to be revising the "Li" text on the authority of ancient source materials or *guben,* such as the *SGZ,* the *Hou Han shu,* and the *Shishuo xinyu.* But he had far more than textual accuracy on his agenda. Mao took issue with many of Li Zhi's annotations, and his edition is as much a repudiation of Li Zhi's views as it is a revision of the novel itself.

Mao's work was twofold: he revised the actual text; and he added his own commentary to it. The revision entailed reducing the length of the novel by about one-sixth, from some 900 thousand characters to 750 thousand, mostly by removing original Han or Three Kingdoms documents and by smoothing out the narrative at various points. Mao changed, added, and deleted sometimes whole scenes, sometimes only a few words or phrases; he rewrote the chapter headings; and he reduced the number of poems highlighting the text from about four hundred to some two hundred, substituting in the process a number of Tang and Song masterpieces for the more conventional verse in the *TS*. Many significant passages that Mao altered are restored in the notes to this translation, but his stylistic improvements of unclear or wordy passages are not noted, nor in most cases are the deletions and substitutions of verse. However, Mao's tendency to remove lines in praise of Cao Cao's advisers and commanders—in particular his praise of Xun Yu (Wenruo) on the occasion of the latter's death—should be mentioned. According to one scholar, the *TS*'s thirty-four verses in praise of Cao's advisers and commanders were reduced to six by Mao Zonggang.

Aside from revisions of the novel's text, Mao provided a three-part system of commentary: first, the *dufa* (reading method), a lengthy essay on how to appreciate the novelist's narrative method, plus a *fanli* or list of major editorial changes; second, a one-page commentary introducing each chapter; third, the notes interspersed throughout the text of each chapter. This exhaustive system is an invaluable service to the reader and a fascinating example in its own right of literary criticism and aesthetic theory. The Mao edition seems to shift the history-fiction balance toward the "purely literary" end of the scale—literature as enjoyment rather than as lessons. Mao's notes often speak of the novel's literary devices as a means to enhance appreciation. For instance, in chapter 34 Mao writes: "The pleasure of reading: without panic, there is no pleasure; without anxiety, no relief; without tension, no relaxation." Mao also illuminates many subtle patterns of incident and characterization which serve to organize the voluminous and complex material in the novel and to create pleasing designs.

By contrast, didactic concerns dominate the 1494 and the 1522 prefaces that are omitted from the Mao edition. The 1494 preface by Jiang Daqi places the novel in the tradition of the *Spring and Autumn Annals* (attributed to Confucius) and Zhu Xi's *Gangmu,* histories which mark the "rise and fall of kingdoms" in a grand sweep of time while "preserving a moral judgment" in every turn of phrase. Not only is the novel a worthy successor to these works, Jiang Daqi says, it has the added virtue of reaching the broadest possible public *(tongsu)* with its message, which challenges the reader to reflect on how his own conduct measures up to the standards of loyalty and filial piety as they are fulfilled (or betrayed) in the novel. "Merely to read [*duguo*] it but not apply [its lessons] vigorously in one's own life," the preface says, "is inferior to [real] study [*dushu*]."

The author of the 1522 preface, Xiuran Zi, has a comparable lesson to offer: "[The reader] needs no laborious thought to realize that legitimate authority must be supported and usurpers removed; that the loyal, the filial, the self-disciplined, and the honorable are teachers of men, and that treacherous profit-seekers and craven flatterers must be eliminated. [The novel] does wonders for the moral atmosphere by establishing right and wrong clearly and completely before the [reader's] eyes."

In addition to his aesthetic interests, Mao Zonggang also had a powerful concern with moral and historical issues, particularly with the legitimacy of the Shu-Han dynasty and the superior claim of its founder, Liu Bei. Though most of the *dufa* explores the novel's literary technique, the essay begins with a statement on history and morality, a comparison of the three forms of succession: legitimate, transitional, and usurped. Mao then proceeds to distinguish lineage and territory as grounds for legitimacy. "Why deny legitimacy to the house of Wei? In terms of territory, [holding] the northern heartland is the main thing; but in terms of principle, Liu lineage is the main thing. Principle takes precedence over territory . . . and so Zhu Xi's *Gangmu* correctly legitimates Shu." Accordingly, as editor, Mao fortifies Liu Bei's claim to the Han mandate by sharpening the opposition between Liu

Bei and Cao Cao and deleting lines that describe Cao Cao's better and Liu Bei's worse qualities.

If Mao Zonggang, too, was using the Liu Bei-Cao Cao contrast
to serve certain political ends, a review of certain facts concerning the period when the Maos, father and son, prepared the *Three
Kingdoms* text may be in order. Since little is known about the editors' lives or their views, any conclusions on this matter must remain in the realm of supposition and inference.

The Maos lived through the Ming-Qing transition—the decline of the Ming dynasty, and its fall in 1644 to the non-Han
Manchu invaders. They witnessed the establishment of the Qing
dynasty (the form of Manchu rule over China, as the Yuan was
the form of Mongol rule), to which the Han Chinese continued
to offer resistance. There were mass suicides, and there were mas-
sacres. One of the most notorious was a Manchu military action
carried out in 1645 in Jiading, a city close to the Maos' home-
town of Suzhou. At the same time, a Ming dynasty took shape
around a survivor of the Ming imperial house. This dynasty never
mounted a major challenge to Qing power, but it managed to
survive in one form and place or another until 1683, when it
ended its forty-year struggle against the foreign conquerors' rule.

There was much in the fall of the Ming to remind the Maos
of the fall of the Han and the subsequent forty-year struggle of
the Shu-Han kingdom. The Ming court had had a powerful eunuch faction (led by Wei Zhongxian) guiding the emperor and
opposed by a body of scholar-bureaucrats (the Donglin group),
a contest that undermined military solidarity and may well have
recalled the *dang gu* proscriptions and persecutions of the late
Han with which the novel opens. The last Ming reigns, like the
last Han reigns, were plagued by a persisting pattern of peasant
rebellion that, like the Yellow Scarves uprising, forced the dynastic government to divert resources sorely needed for northern border defense to internal control. From the north, where
once the Xiongnu, Wuhuan, and Xianbi made war and peace
with their Han neighbors to the south, the Ming faced a military
threat from the Manchus, a non-Han nation that in 1616 had created the Later Gin dynasty. The name Later Gin was used partly

because many of the leaders traced their descent to the Jurchen and partly to remind the Chinese (the Gin used the particularly intimidating reign title Tian Ming, "Mandate of Heaven") that the Ming might suffer the same fate as the Northern Song after it fell to the Gin in 1127. The picture is completed by the formation after 1644 of the loyalist resistance movement (including Donglin scholars) around remnants of the Ming imperial line, later called the Southern Ming.

Thus, the issues and factors that brought about the Han-Three Kingdoms transition and also went into the making of the Three Kingdoms literary tradition and finally the novel itself, were again evident and interacting powerfully during the period of the Ming-Qing transition.

Scholars differ on how this affected Mao Zonggang. Some argue that his *Three Kingdoms* has a covert pro-Ming side. Others hold the contrary view, that the edition is designed to serve the purposes of the Manchu court. (A translation of the novel into Manchu was made in 1650 at the behest of the Qing court.) It is equally likely (and more in keeping with the overall mood of the novel) that the editor maintained an attitude of resigned but critical detachment rather than passionate advocacy with respect to the change of dynasty.

Far from making statements directly in support of the Southern Ming resistance, the editor seems to have taken steps to avoid offending the Manchus. For instance, Sun Jian, the founder of the Southland, is never called by his Han title (as he is in the *TS*), General Who Destroys the Barbarian *(polu)*. The Manchus, who were trying to present themselves to the conquered Han as a legitimate *Chinese* dynasty, objected to the word *lu* in any context as a xenophobic reference to themselves. Rather than offend the court, Mao eliminated the word from Sun Jian's and all other Southland titles. But Mao's superficial deference to Manchu dignity may have been required for the survival of his book, or himself. Any serious criticism of Qing rule would have to be indirect and ambiguous.

Ye Weisi and Mao Xin claim Mao Zonggang for the anti-Qing camp. They point to his comments in chapter 119 concerning Jiang Wei's false surrender to a Wei general as a ruse for saving the Shu-Han emperor. Mao Zonggang writes: "If Jiang Wei was overdoing it, does that mean Lu Xiufu was overdoing it, or Zhang Shijie, or Wen Tianxiang?" Why, Ye Weisi and Mao Xin argue, would Mao Zonggang bring up this famous trio of Southern Song resisters to the Mongols unless he meant to suggest his own support for Ming opponents of the Manchus, opponents such as Shi Kefa and Coxinga? If Mao Zonggang had such a hidden agenda, his comments in chapter 96 are also relevant: "You ask, why are southerners so deceitful? Don't you realize this is loyalty, not deceit? To fool an enemy is no deceit. To repay the king's love is loyalty. Say rather that the men of the south are full of loyalty, not deceit." Since northerners in the novel (Cao Cao for one) also practice deceit, it is difficult to account for this passage except as a cryptic reference to the ongoing struggle of the Southern Ming loyalists against the Manchu court.

Sharing this view of Mao Zonggang is Du Guichen. In a recent article he argues that Mao Zonggang's pro-Liu, anti-Cao stand was for pro-Ming, anti-Qing purposes and also that Mao Zonggang's formula "principle takes precedence over territory" obliquely drew resistance to the Manchu conquest into a context of resistance to foreign invasion from the Southern Song on. Du suggests a connection between the three mini-dynasties of the Southern Ming (1644–62) and the heroic Shu-Han kingdom, adducing a reply by Shi Kefa to a letter from the Manchu court. The Manchu regent Dorgon had demanded that the first Southern Ming emperor renounce his reign title and declare himself a vassal of the Qing. Shi Kefa, a leading Southern Ming general, replied by placing that reign title, Hong Guang, in a line of imperial titles maintained defensively by Chinese emperors of the past, including Liu Xuande.

Another detail suggestive of Mao Zonggang's pro-Ming views is his use of lines by the poet Yang Shen (1488–1559) to set the stage for the novel. Yang Shen was the son of Yang Tinghe, a prime minister under Emperor Wu Zong (r. 1506–22). Yang Tinghe was famous for his efforts to block the eunuchs at court, but he fell afoul of Wu Zong's successor, Emperor Shi Zong (whose Jia Jing reign began in 1522), and lost his struggle against the eunuchs. In 1524 Yang Shen was exiled to Sichuan and spent the last thirty-five years of his life there. Looking back in the light of the Manchu conquest, Mao Zonggang may have seen the Yangs

as prototypes of the high Ming period, genuine loyalists standing for the integrity of the court, men whose fall marked the dynasty's turn toward its doom. (Yang Shen's better-known contemporary Hai Rui was released from prison in 1567, only days
after Emperor Shi Zong died.) Did Mao Zonggang have a political as well as literary purpose in placing Yang Shen's poem
(without attribution) at the front of his text?

Another figure relevant to the Mao edition is Jin Shengtan
(1610?–61), a widely known literary critic who had succeeded in
giving new life and importance to a number of popular works (and
also to a selection of Du Fu's poems) by providing them with extensive commentary. His method of annotation for *Shuihu zhuan*
influenced the Mao commentary to *Three Kingdoms.* Jin Shengtan
also had a political identity, and it eventually cost him his life. He
participated in the Kumiao or Temple Protest incident of 1661, a
demonstration in opposition to the Qing court's newly appointed
magistrate of Suzhou and his program of punitive taxation. The
Temple Protest came one year after Coxinga, on orders from the
Southern Ming court, led a naval attack against Manchu forces.
Even though the attack posed no serious threat, the government
linked the Temple Protest to it as another instance of sedition.
Like many involved in the protest, Jin Shengtan was executed. The
larger purpose of the Manchu authorities' harshness was to impose social and economic discipline on the province of Jiangsu.

We do not know how Mao Zonggang felt about the death of
his fellow townsman and literary inspiration. But his edition of
Three Kingdoms bears a preface dated 1644 that is attributed to
him. Most modern scholars doubt the date and the authenticity
of this preface, arguing that Mao was trying to enhance the value
of his book (and the prestige of his critical method) with the authority of the critic famed for his annotations to *Shuihu zhuan*. It
seems difficult, however, to believe that Mao Zonggang could
have honored a writer so recently executed by Manchu authorities in this way, and so the more likely possibility is that a later
promoter added the name of Jin Shengtan. There remains a
significant minority of scholars who continue to accept the Jin
Shengtan preface; its presence in any edition has a political un-
dertone that is anti-Manchu, whatever the literary or commercial purposes of its inclusion.

It may never be known what these tantalizing hints add up to. Perhaps the largest clue is the story of *Three Kingdoms* itself with its reputation as a tale of heroes long associated with Han resistance to foreign occupation. That Mao Lun and Mao Zonggang chose to prepare and present this work twenty years into a foreign dynasty seems to support those scholars' arguing that the editors held pro-Ming, anti-Qing attitudes. Certainly the formula quoted above, "principle takes precedence over territory," which opens the *dufa*, could have given comfort to the Ming resisters: Manchu forces had squeezed them off the mainland by 1662 (the first year of the Kang Xi reign), leaving Taiwan province as the sole refuge for the redoubtable Coxinga.

If the Maos had pro-Ming attitudes, one might ask whether they were active sympathizers with the southern Ming loyalist dynasties or simply felt a passive nostalgia for the fallen regime. In an article published in 1989, Chen Xianghua has reprinted a short essay by Mao Zonggang that sheds a little light on this problem. The document is a colophon that Mao Zonggang wrote in 1709 for a volume containing the *juren* examination answer and handwritten testament of the Ming scholar-official Jiang Can. (Jiang Can died in 1661, the year that Jin Shengtan was executed.) Jiang Can was a principled Confucian and a sincere Ming loyalist. Mao Lun had been engaged by Jiang Can as a tutor for his eldest son's grandson, and so Mao Zonggang became friendly with some of the younger members of the Jiang family, especially Jiang Can's grandson Ming, another staunch loyalist. From the Maos' intimate association with the Jiang family, we may infer that at least the Maos were not enthusiastic supporters of the Qing dynasty.

The other side of the issue—that the Mao edition supports the Qing court—is also fortified with strong arguments. In the words of He Lei, who introduces the 1973 edition of the novel published by Renmin wenxue chubanshe:

Mao Lun and Mao Zonggang's revisions catered to the governors of the Manchu dynasty. The Manchu court regarded *Three Kingdoms* as an important book and had even had someone translate it into the Manchu language together with the Four Books [*Analects, Great Learning, Doctrine of the Mean,* and *Mencius*]. In addition, the court lavished praise on Lord Guan as loyalty and honor incarnate . . . and propagandized for the theory of legitimate succession. The Manchu court tried to sell its slogan "Avenge the Ming," positioning itself as the legitimate successor to the Ming dynasty. It denied the legitimacy of the Wei dynasty, treating the Cao house as usurpers.

He Lei's view, which many share, leads us to look into the ideological and psychological tactics of the Manchus in the decades before they assumed governmental power in China. In 1616 Nurhaci, later honored by the Manchus as the dynastic founder, established the Later Gin. In that political form he consolidated his nation's position, winning important battles against the other northern nations and also against Ming outposts. In 1626 Abahai succeeded Nurhaci. Beginning in 1629, Abahai campaigned successfully in the territory of China proper, and many Ming commanders and soldiers went over to the Manchus. By 1635 the Later Gin, ruled by the khan Abahai, had achieved a commanding superiority, having acquired the great seal of the Mongols in a victory over the Chahar branch.

Concomitantly, Abahai began preparing for the conquest of China by refashioning Manchu state organization along Chinese lines, copying certain aspects of Ming administration and assimilating certain elements of Chinese culture. This explains Manchu interest in *Three Kingdoms* and the four Confucian classics. In 1636, a turning point in China's history, Abahai changed his designation from khan to emperor (as Liu Yuan once had done at the beginning of the fourth century, before conquering the Jin); he changed his dynasty's name from Later Gin to Qing; and he changed his reign title to Honoring Virtue (implying "Things Chinese will be preserved").

The new reign title, Honoring Virtue (Chong De), served a symbolic purpose. Virtue refers not only to the rightness of Abahai's claim to rule China as emperor, but also to Five Agents theory, which explains the succession of dynasties in terms of a sequence of symbolic elements. The Manchus used the element water in their dynasty name, Qing, and also in their national name, Manzhou (i.e., Manchu). This element suggests that they would "overcome" the Ming, which like the Han, ruled under the element fire.

The Manchus took these institutional and symbolic steps to deny their previous formal subordination to the Ming and to temper Chinese anxiety at the echo of the "foreign conquest of the Northern Song." The Manchus were also positioning themselves as the rightful successors to the Ming, bringers of a new order that would rescue China from corruption and rebellion, an order that would be fully recognizable and acceptable to the Chinese. And many Chinese did indeed accept Manchu rule, if only out of despair at the prospect of continued Ming rule. (Anti-Qing nationalism built upon a Ming restoration is a concept more of the nineteenth than the seventeenth century.) The small Southern Ming courts never became a serious force or a popular nationalist movement. In this perspective, He Lei's argument for the Maos' pro-Qing sympathy gains strength, and any analogy between the Southern Ming courts and the Shu-Han kingdom is weakened.

Another fact lending support to He Lei's position is the importance of Liu Bei to the Manchus as a symbol of their elder-brother relationship to the Mongols. According to an anonymous late Qing source:

> The Manchus used *Three Kingdoms* as a means of exercising control over the Mongols. Even before the conquest, when [Abahai] first subjugated the various tribes of the inner Mongols he formed fraternal alliances with their khans. Using the oath in the peach garden of *Three Kingdoms* as a model, the Manchus identified themselves with Liu Bei and the Mongols with Lord Guan. After becoming emperor of China's heartland, [Abahai], fearing Mongol disaffection, enfeoffed Lord Guan [with many titles, including] sage and great emperor, in order to demonstrate his respect for the Mongols. At that time the Mongols revered no one more than Lord Guan, except their spiritual leaders, the lamas. And it is solely thanks to [the Manchu policy of honoring Lord Guan] that the Mongol vassals defending the northern marches have remained submissive for more than two hundred years, emulating Lord Guan's scrupulous devotion to Liu Bei.

According to this record, the novel had considerable importance to the Manchus before as well as after the conquest. The Maos therefore may well have been catering to their rulers' interests in preparing their edition. In 1650 the Manchus had *Three Kingdoms* translated into Manchu and required the elite youth to study it. The novel's political, military, and diplomatic information was useful for governing the Chinese; and the novel celebrated the fraternal ties that served as a model for Manchu relations with the Mongols. Or perhaps Liu Xuande stood for the quintessential Han Chinese leader in the Manchus' eyes (after their decision to become more "Chinese"), to whom non-Han nations could and would pay heartfelt homage. Considering how Xuande had represented Han resistance to non-Han conquerors, one might say that the Manchus had successfully appropriated an important symbol of the conquered.

At this point a simple question presents itself. If the novel really represented a pro-Ming position in the eyes of the Manchus, would they not have acted to censor it (as they censored *Shuihu zhuan* for advocating rebellion) instead of seizing on it as a useful instrument? It is not likely that the debate over whether the Maos were pro- or anti-Qing, or neither, can be resolved, but it is a tribute to the thematic complexity of the novel that it can be used to support all three positions.

THREE KINGDOMS AS LITERATURE: THE MAO COMMENTARY

Mao Zonggang's comprehensive commentary on *Three Kingdoms* focuses on structure and character. He subdivides structure into larger and smaller, characters into major and minor. The *dufa*, Mao's analytical introduction, identifies six large narrative segments on which the novel is constructed. These "six beginnings" and "six endings" are:

> [1] The reign of Emperor Xian begins when Dong Zhuo deposes his elder brother [Liu Bian, or Emperor Shao] and places him [Liu Xie] on the throne; it ends when Cao Pi usurps the [Han] throne. [2] The history of Shu begins when Liu Bei declares himself emperor in Chengdu; it ends with Liu Shan [Bei's son, Houzhu or Second Emperor] quitting the town of Mianzhu to surrender [to Wei]. [3] The story of the three brothers begins with the oath in the peach garden; it ends in Baidi with Liu Bei's last act, entrusting his son to the care of Zhuge Liang. [4] The story of Zhuge Liang begins with Liu Bei's three calls to his thatched hut; it ends with the six offensives he led against Wei from the Qishan hills. [5] The story of the kingdom Wei begins with its first imperial reign period, Huang Chu, "Commencement of the Yellow"; it ends with Sima Yan receiving the abdication of the last Wei emperor. [6] The story of the Southland begins when Sun

Jian conceals the imperial seal; it ends when Sun Hao tenders the imperial seal to the Jin emperor [ending the novel].

These six narratives form the novel's framework.

As for the dominant characters, Mao Zonggang chooses three whom he calls incomparable (*jue*): Kongming, Lord Guan, and Cao Cao—the prime minister, the general, and the Machiavellian (or amoral, *jian*) hero. Mao does not need to mention Liu Xuande, since he is the pivotal figure around whom Kongming, Lord Guan, and Cao Cao orbit; the three incomparables define themselves in relation to Liu Bei. Thus, four biographies dominate the novel. Once these larger frameworks are understood, the reader can appreciate the novel's smaller-scale techniques of composition, the sequential plotting and the parallel and contrastive patterning that create its texture.

Causal sequences are of great interest to Mao Zonggang. In one passage of the *dufa* he discusses the author's practice of "probing the origins to find the source":

> The partition into three kingdoms stems from the rivalries among the various lords; these rivalries arose from Dong Zhuo's disruption of the dynastic succession; this disruption arose from He Jin's summoning outside troops into the capital; the troops were summoned because of the tyranny of the Ten Eunuchs; the Ten Eunuchs, then, are the starting point. However, Liu Xuande's career does not start among the various lords, but rather among the marshland [i.e., outlaw] heroes who joined forces to fight for right and justice when the Yellow Scarves created turmoil in the land.
>
> The narrative of *Three Kingdoms* thus has a second point of departure in the Yellow Scarves. But before they started their rebellion, Heaven sent down omens and portents as a warning; loyal counselors and wise planners gave blunt advice and unrestrained remonstrance because of what they foresaw. If only the sovereign had embodied that benevolent love that is the mind of Heaven, accepted the sound judgment of elite vassals, and decisively thrust from him the Ten Eunuchs, then the Yellow Scarves would never have come into being, the heroes of the marshland would never have risen up, the various lords would never have resorted to arms, and the realm would not have been partitioned.

This search for causality is more than a literary device; it is a truism of Confucian political morality. On the authority of Confucius (*Analects*, 12.11), the responsibility for disorder rests on those above: "If the king is not kingly, the vassals will not serve as [as vassals should]; if the father is not fatherly, the sons will not be filial." *Shuihu zhuan* similarly blames rebellion on misgovernment.

Another important technique that Mao Zonggang describes in the *dufa* is foreshadowing and aftereffect. Foreshadowing is "sleet seen before snow, thunder heard before rain. Something to be related formally and directly will be preceded by something informal or indirect. . . . The great fire that burned out Cao Cao in Puyang is preceded by the fire in Mi Zhu's house." Conversely, there are "ripples after the wave, showers after the storm. . . . Every extraordinary passage produces an after-pattern. . . . Liu Bei's three visits to Kongming are followed by Liu Qi's three visits to Kongming." Sometimes the most inconspicuous clue is inserted long before some great event,

> a seed is planted many years in advance. The expert horticulturalist sows in anticipation of future growth. The chess master's casual play anticipates dozens of moves to come. The novel tells its story in much the same way. Liu Zhang, inspector of the Riverlands, is the son of Liu Yan. In the first chapter Liu Yan is mentioned before Liu Bei, planting long in advance the hint of Liu Bei's conquest of the Riverlands. Again, when Liu Bei campaigns against the Yellow Scarves, Cao Cao and Dong Zhuo make their entrances, preparing the way for Zhuo's overthrow of the legitimate emperor and Cao's monopoly of power.

The more one studies the patterns of the novel, the more it seems like a grand cathedral designed by an intelligence purposefully placing even the smallest, most innocent details, not only to create satisfying patterns but also to make a point or suggest a judgment.

Another technique Mao describes is contrast within categories:

> The same tree has different branches, the same branch different leaves, the same leaf different blossoms, the same blossom different fruit. . . . Brothers in conflict include Yuan Tan and Yuan Shang, Liu Qi and Liu Zong, Cao Pi and Cao Zhi. The first pair died; of the second pair one died, one survived; of the third pair both survived. . . . Zhao Zilong saved Ah Dou [Liu Bei's son] twice: the first time on land, the second time on water; the first time receiving him from his natural mother's hands, the second time snatching him from his stepmother's grasp.

Mao Zonggang sees the novel patterned by repetitive incidents; he denies that this creates redundancy and speaks of the patterns as artfully contrived themes and variations.

Another aspect of the patterning is contrastive parallelism or "using the guest [i.e., the secondary figure] to enhance the host."

> The brotherhood in the peach garden is preceded by the story of the three Yellow Scarves brothers. The former is the host, the latter the guest. . . . The story of He Jin is preceded by the story of Chen Fan and Dou Wu [the novel's opening scene describes their efforts to free the court of eunuch influence]. Alongside the brilliance of Liu Bei, Lord Guan, Zhang Fei, Cao Cao, and Sun Jian [the kingdom-founders] one finds the mediocre lords of the various garrison towns. When Liu Bei is about to meet Kongming, he first encounters Sima Hui, Cui Zhouping, and others, who serve to set the stage for Kongming. Xu Shu [i.e., Shan Fu] and Pang Tong also serve as foils for Kongming, who advised two emperors [Liu Bei and his son Liu Shan]; Xu Shu comes early and departs swiftly, and Pang Tong comes late but predeceases Kongming. Zhao Zilong first served Gongsun Zan, . . . Ma Chao first served Zhang Lu, Fan Zheng and Yan Yan first served Liu Zhang. All eventually transferred their allegiance to Liu Bei, [lending him luster]. . . . Regarding the theory of succession by abdication—Li Su used it to deceive Dong Zhuo, but Cao Pi made it real, and so did Sima Yan; Dong Zhuo was the guest, Cao Pi and Sima Yan the hosts. Places as well as persons can serve as host and guest. When Emperor Xian moved from Luoyang to Chang'an, then back to Luoyang and finally to Xuchang, Xuchang was the host, Chang'an and Luoyang the guests. When Liu Bei lost Xuzhou and then gained Jingzhou, Xuzhou was the guest, Jingzhou the host; then when he gained the Riverlands and lost Jingzhou, the Riverlands became the host, Jingzhou the guest.

The host-and-guest technique and the similar technique of contrast within categories are basically spatial. Mao also mentions a temporal or dynamic technique called *bian* (surprise or reversal):

> As the poet Du Shaoling [Du Fu] says, "Clouds—one moment like white clothes in mid-heaven, the next a gray dog." This line speaks of the unfathomable events of this world. . . . He Jin started out plotting to execute the eunuchs, but in the end they killed him. . . . Liu Bei began by following Yuan Shao to chastise Dong Zhuo and ended up helping Gongsun Zan against Yuan Shao. At first Liu Bei wanted to aid Xuzhou, but finally he took over the province himself.

Mao Zonggang enumerates dozens of such reversals and, judging by the length of the list, looked on reversal as the main dynamic of the novel's narratives.

In addition to metaphors of gardening, weather, etiquette, and chess, Mao Zonggang draws on landscape painting to describe the novel's manner of composition:

> Horizontal clouds transect mountains, bridges enclose streams. Certain segments are suited for continuous, others for discontinuous narration. Lord Guan's killing five of Cao Cao's pass guards, Liu Bei's three calls to Kongming's thatched hut, Kongming's seven captures of Meng Huo—all show the author's genius for continuous narration. Kongming's angering Zhou Yu three times, his six offensives from the Qishan hills, and the nine expeditions against the north—all show the author's genius for discontinuous narration. Shorter segments require continuous treatment for coherence; longer segments would fatigue the reader unless broken up with other material.

Another painting technique bears mention here: "Close hills are done with heavier strokes, distant trees with lighter ones." This describes the author's use of different emphases for foreground and background detail.

These are the principal aspects of *Three Kingdoms* composition as analyzed in the *dufa* of Mao Zonggang. To show in fuller detail Mao's method of analysis in practice, the annotations to this translation draw on many of Mao's chapter introductions and interlinear commentary. A number of Chinese scholars (and some Western readers, too) have found the novel's techniques of patterning obvious or burdensome. Some may feel the novel is redundantly structured. The author had to bring order to historical material of great volume and complexity, however, and this may explain his reliance on a variety of transparent organizing devices. In much the same way, Shakespeare resorted to rather transparent parallelisms and contrasts in writing the three Henry VI plays. If Luo Guanzhong's penchant for organization was his way of grappling with a wealth—if not a surplus—of material, the authors of *Shuihu zhuan* and *Journey to the West* were not so burdened, and therefore could give freer rein to their imaginations, unleashing their powers of invention to the full. The resulting spontaneity, many have found, makes these novels more appealing and sets them apart from *Three Kingdoms*. Mao Zonggang, however, contests this view, closing his *dufa* with the claim that *Three Kingdoms* surpasses *Shuihu* and *Journey to the West* because of its fidelity to the historical record. Mao is thinking along the same lines as Han Feizi when he remarked that it is easier to draw a demon than a man because demons do not exist and no one knows what they look like, while everyone knows what men look like. Perhaps this was the test—transforming a stretch of all too familiar history into literary art—that the author faced and passed.

We proceed now to consider how some of the major characters have been recast in the Mao edition, bearing in mind that we are dealing with shifts of emphasis within generally similar portraits.

KONGMING IN MAO ZONGGANG'S EDITION

The *dufa* says, "*Three Kingdoms* has three superlative portraits: Zhuge Kongming's, Lord Guan's, and Cao Cao's." Before comparing the Kongming of the Mao edition with the Kongming of the *TS*, certain thematic differences between the two editions of the novel should be noted. Both editions uphold the cause of Liu Xuande's legitimacy and treat Cao Cao as a tyrant and usurper, though the Mao edition, as noted elsewhere, consistently tries to sharpen the contrast, even at the expense of historical fidelity to the *SGZ* and *ZZTJ*. However, the two editions do not justify Liu Xuande's legitimacy in quite the same way. The *TS* gives priority to virtue (*de*) over Liu lineage; the Mao edition does not. Six times, and in six different contexts, the *TS* states, "The empire belongs to no one man but to all in the empire." The import of this motif, whether expressed or implied, is that "he who has virtue should rule." Mencius expressed similar reservations about making the rights of the blood heir absolute when he said, "Any man can be a [sage-king like] Yao or Shun."

Mao Zonggang cannot accept a formula that advocates non-lineage legitimacy. Therefore, he removes from his edition each of the six occurrences of the phrase "The empire belongs to no one man." For Mao, virtue can never displace lineage, and the figure of Liu Xuande does not require him to confront the possibility of a contradiction between virtue and lineage. Mao's opening statement in the *dufa* that lineage, not territory, determines legitimacy has already been cited. True to that principle, Mao says in his introduction to chapter 80: "In judging Liu Bei's accession to the imperial throne, having a Liu succeed a Liu meant simply that the throne was properly [*shun* as opposed to *ni*] won and properly held." Despite their differences on the basis of legitimacy, both editions of the novel uphold Liu Xuande's Shu-Han kingdom, not the Cao-Wei dynasty, as the rightful heir of the Han dynasty. Accordingly, both editions (and the *PH* as well) protect Xuande's humane image by not including the protest of one Shu-Han official, Fei Shi, to his enthronement as emperor in Shu-Han, though the historical texts, the *SGZ* and the *ZZTJ*, record the protest.

Between the *TS* and the Mao edition the portrait of Kongming varies more significantly than does the portrait of Liu Xuande. Broadly put, the *TS* moves Kongming away from the magic-working immortal of the *PH* and the Yuan plays and back toward the historical figure of the *SGZ*, who, though virtuous, resembles at moments Machiavelli or Clausewitz (and has a touch of da Vinci's engineering genius). The Mao edition portrays Kongming the worthy and able minister (*xianxiang*) by accenting his humane values (*ren* and *yi*), values most closely associated with Xuande. Mao removes from Kongming's portrait most traces of the amoral calculation usually associated with Cao Cao.

Kongming's life is the heart of both editions. Of the *TS*'s twenty-four sections covering one hundred and thirteen years, fourteen are devoted to the last twenty-seven years of Kongming's life (A.D. 207–34); the other eighty-five years flanking this period take up the remaining ten sections of the *TS*. The novel's portrait of Kongming is well-founded in the sources, above all in Chen Shou's *SGZ* and Pei Songzhi's accompanying notes. Among the highlights in the early records are the intellectual powers of the young Kongming; his political aspirations and models; his life in seclusion before Liu Xuande's visit; his analysis of the state of the empire for Xuande; his arranging an alliance with the Southland to defeat Cao Cao; his role in guiding Xuande to the occupation of Jingzhou, the conquest of Shu, and the creation there of the kingdom of Shu-Han (the Riverlands); his regency over Liu Shan after Xuande's death; and his campaigns against the Southern Man and the northern kingdom of Wei. These historical and biographical essentials are preserved in the novel. Kongming's domination of the novel reflects his importance in the *SGZ.*

The virtues the novel ascribes to Kongming also have ample historical basis: his loyalty to his lieges; his untiring dedication to the cause of the Han; his ability in civil and military administration; his strategic insight; his receptivity to the views of subordinates; his personal humility and willingness to accept responsibility for failure; his fairness in applying the law and assigning reward and punishment; his skill as an inventor; and his honorable refusal to use his position to enrich himself. Chen Shou had the highest regard for Kongming the statesman and prime minister of Shu-Han, though he mentions that field tactics were not his forte. And Chen Shou records the high esteem in which the populace of Shu-Han held the prime minister after his death. Kongming consummated the classical Confucian ideal of the conjunction of great virtue (*de*) and talent (*cai*).

Evaluations of Kongming have usually transcended the vicissitudes of the Wei-Shu legitimacy debates. In his own time, key advisers to Cao Cao, Jia Xu, and Liu Ye praised Kongming for his skill in administering Shu. In later times, Kongming was honored even by those who did not advocate the cause of Shu-Han against Wei. Li Shimin, the second Tang emperor, spoke of Kongming's excellence as a prime minister despite having to serve under a weak ruler. And the Northern Song reformer, Wang Anshi, dedicated a poem of praise to him. Nevertheless, the historical Kongming was not without his faults and limits, as we shall see.

When we leave the realm of history to turn to the *PH*, we find a superhuman Kongming, a "godlike immortal" (*shen xian*) with magic powers. At the time of his first meeting with Liu Xuande, he is introduced as a controller of winds and rain, a conjurer of illusions, and a transformer of phenomena, a man who can change beans into soldiers and create a river with a wave of his sword. Perhaps these fictions served to offset the suspicion that he was somewhat wanting as a military tactician. The *PH* as well as Yuan drama develop the image of a leader no less capable in military tactics than in political and diplomatic strategy. Luo

Guanzhong drew mainly on the historical record for his portrait of Kongming; but he also drew on the *PH*, carrying enough of the *PH* magician over into the *TS* to justify the twentieth-century writer Lu Xun's remark that Luo Guanzhong's Kongming is a man of "much wisdom though verging on wizardry." The trait that the Mao edition accents is "much virtue." In the *dufa*, Mao Zonggang says, "In the long annals of our history, worthy and able ministers stand thick as trees, but the name Kongming towers over all throughout the ages."

Mao Zonggang had a special problem with the character of Kongming. The edition of the *TS* that he worked on had been annotated by an editor explicitly hostile to Kongming. As Mao says in the sixth of his *fanli* or explanations: "The *su* edition, erroneously attributed to Li Zhuowu but actually from hands unknown, contains many insults against Zhao Lie [i.e., Liu Bei] and condemns the Martial Lord Kongming. We have removed all such remarks and replaced them with new, corrected commentary." What negative aspects of Kongming's portrait did Mao revise?

The "Li" edition's gravest charge against Kongming is that he plotted to usurp the Shu-Han kingdom and thus acted the part of a traitor, like Cao Cao, rather than that of a loyal minister to Liu Bei. The "Li" edition's commentary in chapter 80 says, "Underneath, Cao Cao and Kongming are one of a kind if different in style, with Kongming, it seems, always a move ahead." The cause of this harsh comment is Kongming's active role in the killing of Liu Feng, the only potential rival to Liu Shan as Liu Bei's heir. "Liu Feng was a loyal servant and a filial son," the "Li" edition argues in its annotation to chapter 79. "Liu Bei had him killed unwittingly, so his crime may be forgiven. But Kongming acted knowingly, so no punishment is harsh enough for him."

The story of Liu Feng's downfall reveals differences in the way Kongming appears in different texts. Shortly before his first meeting with Kongming, Liu Bei arrived in Jingzhou and adopted Feng from the Kou family (Feng's natural father was the lord of Luo; see chapter 36). According to the *SGZ*, Liu Bei has no children at the time of the adoption. Nevertheless, the *TS* and the Mao edition both place the adoption of Liu Feng *after* the birth of Ah Dou (Liu Shan) to Lady Gan. The importance of which brother is elder will shortly be evident.

Eclipsed by Ah Dou, Liu Feng plays little part in the novel until Liu Bei establishes Shu-Han. By that time Feng is in his twenties or thirties and distinguishing himself as a field commander. The succession question remains unsettled until near the end of Liu Bei's life.

The story of Liu Feng's downfall (chapter 79) begins when Liu Bei becomes king of Hanzhong and, as a king must, names his heir apparent: Liu Shan (chapter 73). Kongming's anxieties about a challenge to this decision are recorded in Liu Feng's biography. "Kongming feared that Liu Feng would prove stubborn and assertive [*gang meng*] and difficult to control in the next reign, so he convinced Liu Bei to get rid of him." This information about Kongming, a consistent supporter of Liu Shan, is not to be found in either edition of the novel, which connects Liu Feng's downfall to Lord Guan's plight in Jingzhou and Liu Feng's doom to Lord Guan's death (chapter 77).

Here is the novel's version of the circumstances: during the time when Lord Guan is hunted down, captured, and finally executed by Sun Quan, Liu Feng and Meng Da are the only ones in a position to send a rescue mission to try and save Lord Guan. Liu Feng and Meng Da have been posted as commanders to the eastern reaches of the Shu-Han kingdom and thus are close to Jingzhou, Lord Guan's sphere. But Liu Feng is either unwilling or unable to send help. Perhaps he refuses because he knows Lord Guan spoke for Liu Shan as Liu Bei's heir. Whatever Liu Feng's motives, when Liu Bei receives a report blaming Liu Feng and Meng Da for the death of Lord Guan, he and Kongming are too angry to forgive, and they have Liu Feng executed when he returns to Chengdu; Meng Da defects to Wei soon after Lord Guan is killed.

When he defects, Meng Da writes a letter to Liu Bei explaining his change of masters. The letter is preserved in both editions of the novel. Meng Da also writes to Liu Feng urging him to defect, but Liu Feng hotly rejects the proposal, exclaiming, "This villain would break the bond between nephew and uncle and sunder the love of father and son, making me disloyal and unfilial." So saying, Liu Feng destroys the letter, executes the courier, and goes forth to challenge Meng Da to battle. His stand, however honorable, fails to save him when he returns to Chengdu.

Both editions of the novel have the basic story, but only the *TS* has Meng Da's letter urging Liu Feng to follow him and defect. The contents of the letter suggest Mao Zonggang's motive for not including it. Meng Da appeals to Liu Feng by criticizing Liu Bei's choice of successor: "The selection of Ah Dou [Liu Shan] as heir apparent bitterly disappointed men of discernment. . . . Turmoil and ruin have ever sprung from the changing of the heir apparent." The letter moves on from the Shu-Han succession question to argue the superiority of natural to adopted parenthood: "Now, for one to abandon his [natural] parents to become another's heir violates tradition. . . . If someone of your ability were to give up his status and come east to resume the place of heir to the lord of Luo [Feng's natural father], it could not be a betrayal of a parent."

Even allowing for Meng Da's special pleading, this letter's argument fits the official record: Liu Bei and Kongming decided to get rid of Liu Feng in order to clear the way for the chosen heir, Liu Shan, to succeed Liu Bei as emperor of Shu-Han without a challenge from the only credible rival. And the result of Liu Shan's accession as Second Emperor was that "every governmental matter in Shu-Han, great or small, was decided by Kongming." Thus, the question of Liu Bei's succession, which the Mao edition suppresses, is openly handled in the *TS*, even if some relevant material in the *SGZ* is omitted. Once again the 1522 *TS* proves to be closer to the original record, while the Mao edition tends to develop its own moralizing fictions on certain points.

Mao Zonggang wanted to keep the focus off Liu Feng's status as Liu Bei's son and on his conflicts with Meng Da (whose defection was partly Feng's fault) as well as on his failure to rescue Lord Guan. Mao omitted any material about Liu Bei and Kongming that might have compromised their portraits as embodiments of traditional Confucian values such as virtue (*de*) and humanity (*ren*), the factors of legitimacy. It may be remembered at this point how often the novel makes an issue of the consequences of tampering with succession by the eldest son. Thus, Mao Zonggang's handling of the Liu Feng incident is in keeping with his advocacy of Liu-lineage legitimacy.

Nevertheless, if there is measurable distance between the 1522 *TS* and the Mao edition on certain key questions, their common distance from the *SGZ* is greater. The *SGZ* treats the Cao-Wei dynasty as legitimate, while the two editions of the novel take the pro-Liu, anti-Cao position. Accordingly, both editions omit the express objections of Fei Shi, a leading Shu-Han courtier, to Liu Bei's assumption of the throne, a step Kongming had strenuously advocated.

Mao Zonggang exercised great care in reworking the image of Kongming into an ideal; indeed, this transformation of Kongming may be considered the heart of the difference between the Mao edition and the *TS*. Their divergence is revealed again in the way they treat the case of the Shu commander Wei Yan. Although submerged in the novel, Wei Yan (see chapters 41 and 53) contributed as much to the cause of the historical Shu-Han as Lord Guan, Zhang Fei, or Zhao Zilong.

When Kongming leaves Jingzhou to join Xuande in Shu-Han, he places Lord Guan in charge of the province. When Xuande declares himself king of Hanzhong and departs for Chengdu, he places Wei Yan in charge of the region. The Hanzhong region, a buffer between Shu-Han and the north (or more specifically the Chang'an region) is no less important to Xuande than Jingzhou is. Zhang Fei has privately been expecting to assume control over Hanzhong when Liu Bei leaves, but Bei appoints Wei Yan instead, to the army's amazement. This is noted in the *SGZ* but not in the novel.

Wei Yan is a member of Kongming's inner circle and plays a prominent role in the last series of campaigns against the north. His proposal before one of these campaigns is famous. Wei Yan urges Kongming to strike Chang'an directly, but Kongming chooses instead to maneuver around from Longyou in the west. Later, many think that Kongming might have taken Chang'an had he heeded Wei Yan's advice. Wei Yan comes to prominence after the old guard—Lord Guan, Zhang Fei, and Zhao Zilong—die. Most important, Wei Yan supports Kongming's war policy, which the emperor has some doubts about.

Still and all, Kongming does not trust Wei Yan. "He has treason in his bones," is Kongming's judgment. (The only basis for this in the *SGZ* is a remark by Sun Quan that Wei Yan may prove unreliable after Kongming dies.) And so Kongming attempts to get rid of Wei Yan in the course of his surprise attack on Sima

Yi in the Shangfang Gorge. Kongming uses Wei Yan to draw Sima Yi into the gorge, where a fiery ambush has been set, but a sudden downpour quenches the flames and enables Sima Yi to escape. Wei Yan would have perished too but for the rains. Afterward, Wei Yan protests that Kongming tried to kill him, an accusation found in the *TS* but not in the Mao edition. Kongming then arranges to have Wei Yan executed after his death.

At the time of Kongming's death, Wei Yan has the vanguard. He wants to send Kongming's body home and continue the campaign. He is ordered to turn the van into the rearguard, however, and protect a general retreat. Wei Yan refuses this order, and a leadership crisis erupts on the field. It may be that Kongming thought the army should rest after his death. It may be that Kongming feared his van leader might simply go over to the enemy. It may be that it suited the novelist's purpose to emphasize a crisis over Kongming's successor.

Whatever the problem, the editor of the "Li" edition of the *TS* uses the incident to attack Kongming: "Kongming is no follower of the kingly way, if only because he contrived to murder Wei Yan. . . . If Wei Yan had committed a crime, why did he not make it public, why did he treat Wei Yan like a Sima?" Mao Zonggang drops the paragraph in which Wei Yan accuses Kongming of trying to kill him. Moreover, Mao assumes that Wei Yan is a potential traitor: "Kongming anticipated Wei Yan's rebellion and got rid of him before he could act; this shows wisdom. . . . Once Wei Yan as rebelled, Shu-Han would have a foe in Wei Yan as great as Sima Yi. When Wei Yan burned the cliffside walkway, when he attacked Nanjun, had the northerners found out and turned back, the fate of Shu-Han would have been sealed."

Readers of historical conscience may feel that Wei Yan has been wronged when they turn to the biography that follows Wei Yan's in the *SGZ*, that of Yang Yi, Wei Yan's rival. Yang Yi had expected to succeed Kongming as the prime minister of Shu-Han, but Jiang Wan was chosen instead. Indignantly, Yang Yi said he should have defected to Wei when Kongming died. Since Yang Yi is the source of the accusation of treason against Wei Yan, the charge becomes suspect.

To clarify the difference between the portrayal of Kongming in the *TS* and in the Mao edition has required taking up some of the minor figures of the last sixteen chapters, the chapters after Kongming's death. The temptation to ignore these chapters as anticlimactic should be resisted. The fate of the epigones of the brilliant circle of leaders around Liu Xuande—the sons of Lord Guan and Zhang Fei, Wei Yan, Jiang Wan, and so on—is a part of the novel's aesthetic effect. After Kongming dies, the landscape flattens out: glorious heroes are replaced by lesser figures, and the epic drama subsides into a largely historical account, though military heroics are still part of the story. But in the last chapter, chapter 120, we find the final twist on heroic militarism: the Jin conquest of the Southland is carried out by commanders who have little interest in their campaign and continually think up excuses to defer it, while the southern forces are so weak that the feeblest push by the northern army suffices to consummate the conquest.

There is a third variation worth noting in the two editions of the novel. The Shu-Han campaigns against the Wei dynasty—Kongming's "six offensives from the Qishan hills," followed by Jiang Wei's "nine offensives against the heartland"—are treated a little more critically in the *TS* than in the Mao edition. The *SGZ* records no full-scale debate in the Riverlands on the pros and cons of waging war against the Wei dynasty, only traces of discontent with the policy. The *TS* retains more of these traces, whereas the Mao edition removes almost all of them. The notes to the translation indicate some of the differing passages. By contrast, the novel does contain the full-scale debate on the pros and cons of war that raged in the Southland when Cao Cao's grand army stood at the Yangzi some two decades earlier; for this debate, the novelist was able to draw on the more ample account in the *SGZ*.

In conclusion, the consensus of scholars (with which the translator agrees) is that the *TS* is more comprehensive and perhaps franker in presenting political facts and historical material than the Mao edition, but the Mao edition is the superior literary work, even if an occasional scene in the *TS* is more effective. Undoubtedly, it is mainly for reasons of artistic excellence that the Mao edition eclipsed the older *TS* and remains today the unquestioned favorite, even after the *TS* was republished in a popular edition in 1975. The Mao edition, with most of the Mao notes, was republished in paperback in 1981 by the Inner Mongolia People's Press (Nei Menggu renmin chubanshe). Thus there is continuing contemporary interest in Mao's critical commentary. Some readers, of course, will prefer the *TS* for its more contradictory portraits, its rougher narrative style, and its abundance of documentary material. Most seem to prefer the more streamlined writing and more smoothly drawn characters of the Mao edition.

PRINCIPAL CHARACTERS
IN THREE KINGDOMS

CAI MAO, brother of Lady Cai, enemy of Liu Bei in Liu Biao's court

CAO CAO (MENGDE), commander of Han forces and regent to Emperor Xian, founder of the kingdom of Wei, posthumously Emperor Wu of the Wei dynasty

CAO HONG, brother to Cao Cao, commander of forces

CAO PI, son of Cao Cao and first emperor of the Wei dynasty, Emperor Wen (r. A.D. 220–26)

CAO RUI, eldest son of Cao Pi, Emperor Ming of the Wei dynasty (r. A.D. 227–39), served by co-regents Cao Zhen and Sima Yi

CAO ZHI, son of Cao Cao, passed over as heir in favor of Cao Pi

CHEN LIN, adviser to Yuan Shao, author of tract denouncing Cao Cao

CHENG PU, senior Southland commander, shares authority with Zhou Yu at first

DIAN WEI, bodyguard to Cao Cao

DIAOCHAN, singing girl who undoes Dong Zhuo for Wang Yun

DING FENG, Southland commander

DONG CHENG, relative of Empress Dong, bearer of Emperor Xian's secret decree

DONG ZHUO, warrior from the west who places Emperor Xian on the Han throne after removing Liu Bian (Emperor Shao)

EMPEROR SHAO (LIU BIAN), son of Emperor Ling, elder brother of Emperor Xian; reigns from May to September 189; deposed by Dong Zhuo

EMPEROR XIAN (LIU XIE) replaces his older brother, Bian, as Han emperor in A.D. 189 and reigns until 220

EMPRESS DONG, foster mother of Emperor Xian

EMPRESS HE, mother of Emperor Shao

FA ZHENG, official at Liu Zhang's court who facilitates Liu Bei's conquest of the Riverlands

FEI YI, adviser to the Shu-Han court

GAN NING, Southland expert on naval warfare, defects from Liu Biao's camp

GONGSUN ZAN, friend of Liu Bei, military leader based in Liaoxi

GUAN XING, son of Lord Guan

GUAN YU (YUNCHANG), see Lord Guan

HAN DANG, Southland commander

HUA TUO, physician who cures Lord Guan's wounded arm

HUA XIN, official at Cao Pi's court, instrumental in Emperor Xian's abdication

HUANG GAI, false defector from the Southland to Cao Cao's camp

HUANG ZHONG, veteran warrior and commander for Liu Bei

JI PING, Han court physician, killed by Cao Cao

JIA XU, military counselor to Cao Cao

JIAN YONG, aide to Liu Bei

JIANG WEI, Shu-Han commander, pursues Kongming's policies after Kongming's death in 234

KAN ZE, Southland scholar, aids Huang Gai's false defection to Cao Cao's camp

KONGMING, see Zhuge Liang

KONG RONG, Han scholar, opponent of Cao Cao at the Han court; later, as governor of Beihai, rescued by Liu Bei

LADY CAI, Liu Biao's second wife, sister of Cai Mao, mother of Liu Zong

LADY GAN, wife of Liu Bei, mother of Liu Shan

LADY MI, sister of Mi Zhu, wife of Liu Bei; commits suicide

LADY SUN, sister of Sun Quan, wife of Liu Bei

LADY WU, sister of Sun Ce's late wife, counselor to Sun Quan

LIAO HUA, a commander in Liu Bei's army

LIU BEI (XUANDE), leader of the three oath brothers and founder of the kingdom of Shu (the Riverlands), posthumously First Ruler of the Shu-Han dynasty (r. A.D. 221–22)

LIU BIAN, see Emperor Shao

LIU BIAO, protector of Jingzhou, gives Liu Bei refuge; father of Qi and Zong; husband of Lady Cai

LIU FENG, adopted son of Liu Bei

LIU QI, first son of Liu Biao, first heir to Jingzhou

LIU SHAN (AH DOU), son of Liu Bei, Second Emperor of Shu-Han (r. A.D. 223–63)

LIU ZHANG, protector of the Riverlands before Liu Bei's arrival

LIU ZONG, actual heir to Jingzhou, son of Lady Cai and Liu Biao, killed by Cao Cao

LORD GUAN (YUNCHANG), the second oath brother

LU SU, Southland adviser sympathetic to Liu Bei and Kongming

LU XUN, Southland commander who foils Liu Bei's invasion

LU ZHI, Imperial Corps commander serving Emperor Ling

LÜ BU, companion to Dong Zhuo, suitor to Diaochan

LÜ MENG, Southland commander who captures Lord Guan

MA CHAO, son of Ma Teng, warrior of the northwest

MA TENG, one of the original oath-takers against Cao Cao, warrior of the northwest

MI ZHU, patron and father-in-law of Liu Bei

PANG TONG, adviser to Liu Bei, peer of Kongming

SHAN FU, Taoist name of Xu Shu, military adviser to Liu Bei

SIMA YI, general serving the house of Cao, prepares the way for the Sima clan to usurp the sovereignty of Wei, held by the house of Cao

SUN CE, southern warrior, son of Sun Jian, brother of Sun Quan

SUN JIAN, southern warrior, founder of the Southland

SUN QIAN, high assistant to Liu Bei

SUN QUAN, king, then emperor, of the Southland (r. A.D. 222–52)

TAISHI CI, rival, then friend, of Sun Ce

TAO QIAN, inspector of Xuzhou, abdicates to Liu Bei

WANG YUN, senior counselor of the Han court, uses Diaochan in a plot against Dong Zhuo

XIAHOU DUN, warrior and close companion of Cao Cao

XIAHOU YUAN, cousin of Xiahou Dun

XU HUANG, commander under Cao Cao

Xu Jing, official in Liu Zhang's court

Xun You, relative and ally of Xun Wenruo

Xun Yu (Wenruo), adviser to Cao Cao, opposes his steps
toward usurpation

Yang Yi, Kongming's successor as director general
of the Riverlands

Yi Ji, aide to Liu Bei

Yu Jin, general in Cao Cao's army

Yuan Shao, leader of the confederation against Cao Cao,
controls the northeast until defeated by Cao Cao in the battle
of Guandu, A.D. 200

Yuan Shu, early pretender to the throne, brother of Yuan
Shao

Yue Jin, general in Cao Cao's army

Zhang Bao, son of Zhang Fei

Zhang Fei (Yide), the third oath brother

Zhang He, general in Cao Cao's army

Zhang Song, Riverlands emissary spurned by Cao Cao,
invites Liu Bei to enter his kingdom

Zhang Zhao, adviser to Sun Quan, leader of peace faction

Zhao Yun (Zilong), companion of Liu Bei and leading
commander

Zhou Yu, Southland chief commander, companion
to Sun Quan, leader of war faction

Zhuge Jin, brother of Zhuge Liang, vassal to Sun Quan

Zhuge Liang (Kongming), chief adviser to Liu Bei,
director general of the Riverlands

CHRONOLOGY OF MAIN EVENTS IN THREE KINGDOMS

Years are A.D. Chapter numbers are given in brackets.

168   Death of Emperor Huan; accession of Emperor Ling [1]

184   Uprising of the Yellow Scarves [1]

188   Shift of court appointments from imperial inspector to provincial protector; conflict between Empress He and Empress Dong over the succession to Emperor Ling [2]

189   Death of Emperor Ling (May 13); the reign of Liu Bian (Emperor Shao) begins (May 15); Yuan Wei, uncle of Yuan Shao, made imperial guardian; He Jin and Yuan Shao defend the new sovereign against the eunuchs; Dong Zhuo summoned to the capital [2]; Dong Zhuo deposes Emperor Shao and enthrones Emperor Xian (Liu Xie) on September 28; Yuan Shao and Cao Cao oppose Dong Zhuo [3, 4]

190   Yuan Shao rallies the lords against Dong Zhuo [5]; Dong Zhuo moves the capital from Luoyang to Chang'an (April); Luoyang burned and sacked; Sun Jian holds the royal seal [6]

191   Yuan Shao battles Gongsun Zan and takes control of the provinces northeast of the Yellow River; Sun Jian and Liu Biao wage war [7]

192   Lü Bu kills Dong Zhuo [8, 9]; Cao Cao becomes protector of Yanzhou and receives the surrender of the Yellow Scarves of Qingzhou [10]

194   Liu Xuande defends Kong Rong; Xuande assumes control of Xuzhou [12]

dies; Lu Su of the Southland travels to Xiakou to see Kongming [41, 42]; Kongming goes to the Southland to meet General Zhou Yu and arrange an alliance against Cao Cao; the Battle at Red Cliffs [43–50]

209–10   Xuande occupies Jiangling and Gong'an; Liu Qi dies [51]; Xuande occupies the southern districts of Jingzhou [53]; Xuande marries Sun Quan's sister, Lady Sun; Lu Su demands the return of Jingzhou to the Southland [54]; Xuande leaves the Southland with Lady Sun [55]

211   Zhou Yu dies; Cao Cao kills Ma Teng; Cao Cao threatens Hanzhong; Hanzhong's ruler, Zhang Lu, threatens the Riverlands; Riverlands leader Liu Zhang sends Zhang Song to Cao Cao for help; Zhang Song visits Liu Xuande [57–60]

212   Xuande marches to the Riverlands; Kongming governs Jingzhou [60]

212–13   Cao Cao attacks the Southland; Cao Cao assumes the Nine Dignities of a patriarchal lord; Xuande enters the Riverlands [61–62]

214   Kongming goes to the Riverlands; Lord Guan governs Jingzhou; Xuande takes control of the Riverlands [63–65]

215   The Southland demands Jingzhou; Cao Cao conquers Hanzhong [66–67]

216   Cao Cao becomes king of Wei [68]

217   Cao Cao attacks Southland positions [69]

218   Revolt against Cao Cao crushed in Xuchang; Huang Zhong kills Xiahou Yuan, endangering Cao Cao's hold on Hanzhong [69–72]

219   Cao Cao withdraws from Hanzhong to Chang'an; Xuande becomes king of Hanzhong; Lord Guan takes Xiangyang and Fan; the Southland takes Jingzhou; Lord Guan defeated [73–76]

220   Sun Quan puts Lord Guan to death; Cao Cao dies;

Emperor Xian abdicates (November 24) to Cao Pi, who establishes a new dynasty, the Wei [77–80]

221   Xuande proclaims himself emperor (May) and marches against the Southland (August); Sun Quan accepts the suzerainty of the Wei dynasty; the Southland resists the Riverlands invasion [80–82]

222   Southland forces under General Lu Xun drive back Liu Xuande's invading army; Wei attacks the Southland [83–85]

223   Liu Xuande dies; Liu Shan succeeds him as Riverlands ruler; Sima Yi attacks the Riverlands; Kongming revives the Riverlands-Southlands alliance against Wei [85–86]

224   Cao Pi invades the Southland [86]

225   Kongming subdues the Southern Man people [86–91]

226   Cao Pi dies; Cao Rui becomes the new ruler of Wei; Kongming persuades Liu Shan to wage war against Wei; Sima Yi leads the Wei forces [91–92]

228   Meng Da killed; Kongming launches the war against Wei [94–95]

229   Sun Quan proclaims himself emperor [98]

230   Wei commander Cao Zhen's campaign thwarted by heavy rain [99]

231   Cao Zhen dies; Kongming recalled from the field [100]; Kongming resumes the war [101]

234   Kongming dies on the field; Riverlands armies return to Chengdu; Wei Yan dies [104–5]

239   Cao Fang succeeds Cao Rui as ruler of Wei; Cao Zhen's son, Cao Shuang, becomes co-regent with Sima Yi; decade of conflict between Cao Shuang and Sima Yi begins [106]

249   Cao Shuang killed; Sima Yi seizes control of the Wei kingdom; Jiang Wei, aided by Xiahou Ba, leads a new Riverlands campaign against Wei [106–7]

251–52   Sima Yi dies; Sun Quan dies; war between Wei and the Southland [108]

254   Sima Yi's son Sima Shi deposes Cao Fang and enthrones Cao Mao [109]

255   Commanders Wen Qin and Guanqiu Jian revolt against the coup in Wei; Sima Shi dies and his brother Sima Zhao leads the Sima clan [110]

257   Sima Zhao defeats his opponents; the Riverlands abandons its war against Wei [112]

258   Sun Chen deposes Sun Liang, ruler of the Southland; Sun Xiu assumes power and executes Sun Chen; Wei commander Deng Ai leads the campaign against the Riverlands [113]

260   Cao Mao killed; Cao Huan assumes the Wei throne; Sima Zhao becomes prime minister [114]

263   Wei's campaign against the Riverlands threatens Chengdu [115–117]

264   Liu Shan, Second Emperor of the Riverlands, surrenders to Deng Ai; Sima Zhao marches to Chang'an; Zhao names Sima Yan his heir and dies [118–19]

265–80   The Sima clan establishes a new dynasty, the Jin, and then conquers the Southland; the empire is again united [120]

Designer:	Barbara Jellow
Compositor:	Integrated Composition Systems
Text:	Baskerville
Display:	Trajan
Printer and Binder:	Maple-Vail Book Manufacturing Group